MOON

W9-BYJ-480

# AZORES

CARRIE-MARIE BRATLEY

# Contents

# THE AZORES

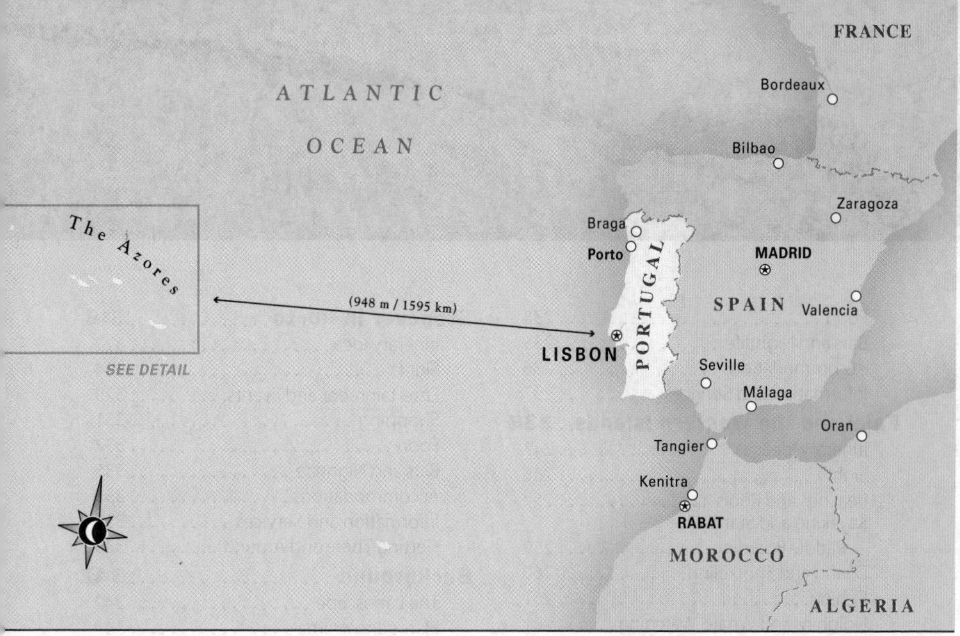

ATLANTIC

OCEAN

*The Azores*

SEE DETAIL

*(948 m / 1595 km)*

FRANCE

PARIS

Bordeaux

Bilbao

Zaragoza

Braga

Porto

PORTUGAL

MADRID

SPAIN

Valencia

LISBON

Seville

Málaga

Oran

Tangier

Kenitra

RABAT

MOROCCO

ALGERIA

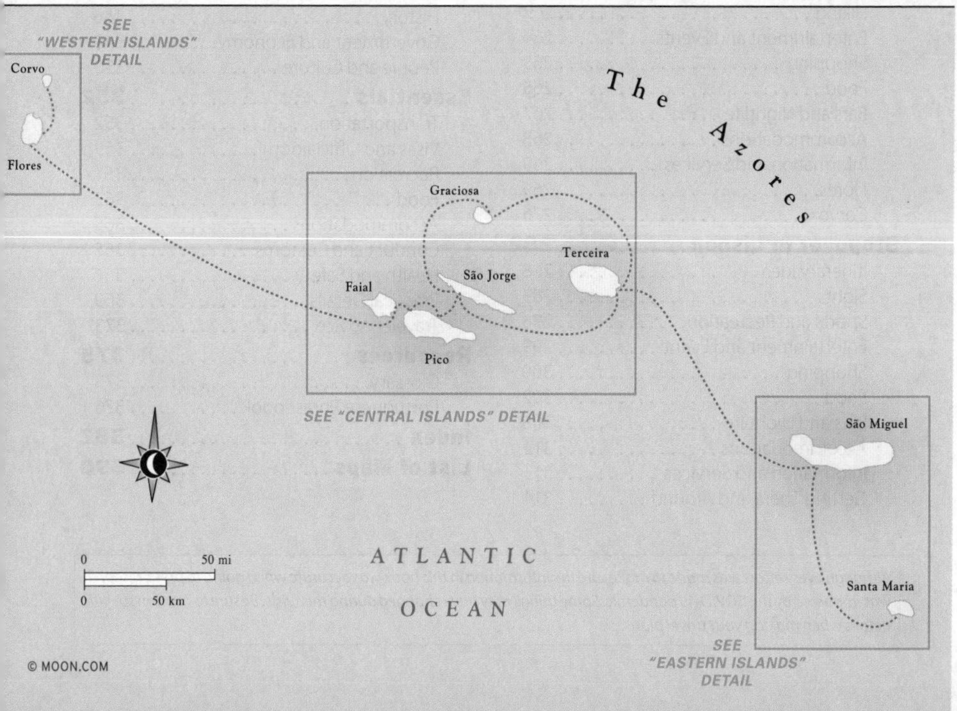

SEE
"WESTERN ISLANDS"
DETAIL

*The Azores*

Corvo

Flores

Graciosa

Terceira

Faial

São Jorge

Pico

SEE "CENTRAL ISLANDS" DETAIL

São Miguel

Santa Maria

SEE
"EASTERN ISLANDS"
DETAIL

0        50 mi

0        50 km

ATLANTIC

OCEAN

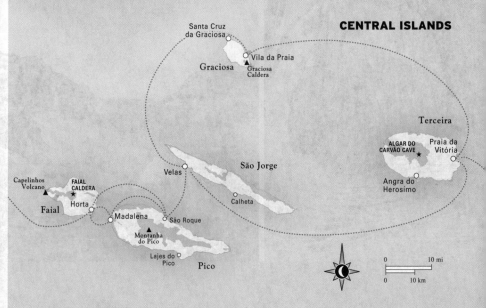

# CENTRAL ISLANDS

Santa Cruz
da Graciosa

Vila da Praia

Graciosa

Graciosa
Caldera

Terceira

ALGAR DO
CARVÃO CAVE

Praia da
Vitória

Velas

São Jorge

Angra do
Herosimo

Capelinhos
Volcano

FAIAL
CALDERA

Horta

Faial

Madalena

Calheta

São Roque

Montanha
do Pico

Lajes do
Pico

Pico

0        10 mi

0        10 km

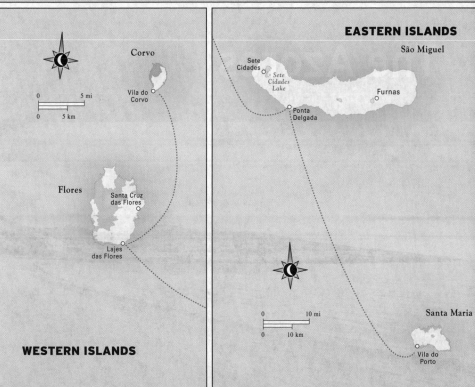

Corvo

# EASTERN ISLANDS

São Miguel

Vila do
Corvo

Sete
Cidades

Sete
Cidades
Lake

Furnas

0     5 mi

Ponta
Delgada

0     5 km

Flores

Santa Cruz
das Flores

Lajes
das Flores

0        10 mi

0        10 km

Santa Maria

Vila do
Porto

# WESTERN ISLANDS

# The Azores

There's something quite thrilling about going to a destination relatively few people have heard of, like being part of an intrepid club or exploring uncharted territory. The Azores, European but isolated in the middle of the Atlantic, have been known to explorers since at least the 15th century but are a relatively recent discovery to tourists.

Landing on a small island in the middle of a vast ocean is sobering; the remoteness doesn't quite hit home until you look around and see endless sea from all sides. The heady fragrance of moist, fertile earth, sea salt, and hot basalt rock perfectly enhances the exoticness of the Azores, with their luxuriant, pristine landscapes, staggering volcanic features, and four-seasons-in-one-day weather. On this archipelago of nine islands—some of which have more cows than people—you can soak in steaming hot spring water even if it's rainy, and cool off in craggy tidal pools when it's hot. If you're a surfer, diver, or snorkeler, the Azorean coasts are a paradise, with good surfing conditions year-round and some of the most breathtaking dives in Europe. If water sports aren't your thing, just enjoying the view is exhilarating. Trek through jungle-like forests, rolling green massifs, and lava plains, and enjoy a slow and simple pace of life among friendly and welcoming people.

**Clockwise from top left:** Congro Lake path; Capelinhos Volcano; Porto Pim Bay; Ajuda Hill; Caldeira Velha thermal pool; Porto Pim Beach.

The influence of Portugal is evident throughout the islands, in genteel, colonial cities like Ponta Delgada on São Miguel and Angra do Heroísmo on Terceira, and in the food, which often riffs on mainland classics like *bacalhau* and hearty stews. But floating more than 1,500 kilometers (1,000 mi) from the nearest landmass means everything has a twist. In Azorean cuisine, the surprise is the ingredients: fresh cheese, unique volcanic wines, pineapples, and even island-grown tea and coffee. In the culture, there's the influence of sailors and whalers who have frequented these Atlantic outposts, visible in famous port cities like Horta on Faial and in relics of the whaling industry like *vigia* watchtowers, now used to spot cetaceans for visitors enjoying some of the best whale-watching on the planet.

It's not hard to romanticize the Azores; they're remote little islands of tranquility, belied by their huge character and overwhelmingly beautiful scenery. But it's even harder to not want to go back once you been.

**Clockwise from top left:** Topo Lighthouse; the landscape of São Jorge; Terra Nostra Park; Furnas Lake church.

# 9 TOP EXPERIENCES

**1** Soaking in a **hot spring in Furnas** on São Miguel, where geothermal activity is part of daily life, from public taps to cooking (page 80).

**2** Experiencing São Miguel island's famous **Sete Cidades Lake** from every angle, climbing to gorgeous viewpoints and kayaking on the calm, greenish water (page 66).

**3** Sampling the best **Azorean products,** from cheese made from the islands' "happy cows," to tea, coffee, wine, and even pineapples (page 35).

**4** Lingering in the picture-perfect historic center of **Angra do Heroísmo** on Terceira, the oldest town in the Azores and a UNESCO World Heritage Site (page 133).

**5** Exploring some of the more than 70 *fajãs* **on São Jorge:** These unique, lush geological formations left over from lava flows are one-stop destinations for hikes, surfing, and stunning views (page 191).

>>>

**6** Summiting **Mount Pico:** This dormant volcano, the highest point in Portugal, towers over its eponymous island and calls to hikers around the world (page 228).

>>>

**7** Sunning on **Santa Maria's beaches,** famed for their soft golden sand (page 107).

**8** Taking in the salty, gritty atmosphere of the **Horta Marina,** checking out murals left by passing mariners and having a drink at the famous sailors' bar Peter Café Sport (page 248).

**9** Getting a sense of the Azores' isolation in the blue vastness of the Atlantic from one of the islands' **best viewpoints** (page 29).

# Planning Your Trip

## Where to Go

The Azores might be part of Portugal, but the archipelago is sharply different from the mainland. Lush, verdant gems with pristine landscapes and nature-infused activities, each of the Azores' nine islands boasts its own distinct character and appeal.

### The Eastern Group
#### SÃO MIGUEL
The archipelago's biggest island, São Miguel is the main gateway and best introductory point to the Azores. A fantastic all-around vacation destination, it is the one to visit if you only have time to explore one island. So verdant it's nicknamed the **Green Island,** São Miguel is blessed with awe-inspiring scenery including the famous **Sete Cidades Lake,** fantastic **hikes,**

and ideal conditions for **whale-watching.** Its steaming **hot springs,** great places to take a dip or even have a meal cooked by geothermal heat, are unique among the islands. (The only other visitable hot springs in the Azores are the Termas do Carapacho on the island of Graciosa.) The vibrant little city of **Ponta Delgada,** the archipelago's economic capital, hosts a healthy **nightlife** scene.

#### SANTA MARIA
If you want to spend a day or two sunning on the beach, head to São Miguel's closest neighbor, Santa Maria, a first-class—if somewhat offbeat and rustic—beach resort. Warmer and drier than the other islands, it's not called the **Sunshine Island** for nothing. The island is famed for its

Sete Cidades Lake

fine blond sands, a rarity in the volcanic archipelago where most of the **beaches** are black and rocky, which means it has some of the best **swimming** conditions in the archipelago. Its sheltered shores and bays are also excellent places for **snorkeling** and **scuba diving.**

## The Central Group
### TERCEIRA

Architectural heritage, ancient **winemaking** techniques, and cavernous underground **lava tubes** await visitors to Terceira island. It's dubbed the **Lilac Island** for the purple hydrangeas that cover almost every surface in the spring. Despite being the archipelago's second-biggest island in terms of inhabitants, it's notably less touristy than São Miguel. It's home to the archipelago's oldest city, charming **Angra do Heroísmo,** a UNESCO World Heritage Site, and the island's unique architecture extends beyond the bounds of the city in the more than 70 tiny **Divino Espírito Santo chapels** scattered around the island.

### GRACIOSA

Graceful Graciosa is an undiscovered gem. The archipelago's second-smallest island lacks the

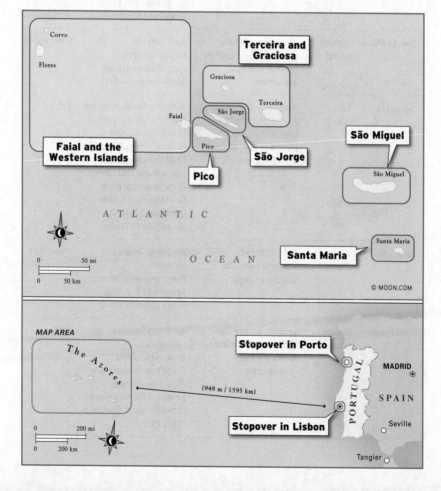

# The Islands at a Glance

| Island | Nickname | Why Go | How to Get There | How Long to Stay |
|--------|----------|--------|------------------|------------------|
| São Miguel | Green Island | verdant woodlands and meadows, hot springs, and scenic Sete Cidades Lake; main gateway to other islands | *Air:* From North America (5-7 hrs), UK and Europe (3 hrs). From Lisbon, Porto (2.5 hrs). Flights to all islands except Graciosa and Corvo. *Ferry:* Seasonal from Santa Maria (3-4 hrs), Terceira (4.5 hrs). | 3 days |
| Santa Maria | Sunshine Island | warm, dry climate; golden-sand beaches; unique volcanic attractions | *Air:* From São Miguel (30 mins). *Ferry:* Seasonal from São Miguel (3-4 hrs). | Overnight |
| Terceira | Lilac Island | purple hydrangeas, Angra do Heroísmo UNESCO World Heritage Site, Algar do Carvão cave system | *Air:* From North America (5-7 hrs), UK and Europe (3 hrs). From Lisbon, Porto (2-3 hrs). Flights to all islands except Santa Maria and Flores. *Ferry:* Seasonal from São Miguel (3-4 hrs), Graciosa (3 hrs), São Jorge (5 hrs 45 mins). | 3 days |
| Graciosa | White Island | light-colored volcanic rock, the Graciosa Caldera | *Air:* From Terceira (30 mins) *Ferry:* Seasonal from Terceira (3 hrs), São Jorge (2 hrs 15 mins) | Overnight |
| São Jorge | Brown Island | unique, earthy *fajã* landscapes; cheese factory; locally grown coffee | *Air:* From Terceira (30 mins), São Miguel (50 mins). *Ferry:* Year-round from Pico (1 hr 40 mins). Seasonal from Terceira (5 hrs 45 mins), Graciosa (2 hrs 15 mins). | 2 days |

| Island | Nickname | Why Go | How to Get There | How Long to Stay |
|--------|----------|--------|------------------|------------------|
| Pico | Gray Island | gray volcanic landscape, wines and vineyards, hiking Mount Pico | *Air:* From Lisbon (2-3 hrs). Flights to Terceira (35 mins), São Miguel (50 mins). *Ferry:* Year-round from São Jorge (1 hr 40 mins), Faial (30 mins) | 2-3 days |
| Faial | Blue Island | blue hydrangeas, the sailors' town of Horta, the Faial Caldera | *Air:* From Lisbon (2 hrs 45 mins). Flights to São Miguel (50 mins), Terceira (35 mins), Flores (45 mins), Corvo (45 mins). *Ferry:* Year-round from Pico (30 mins). Seasonal to Corvo (9 hrs). | 2 days |
| Flores | Pink Island | azaleas, untouched waterfalls and lagoons | *Air:* From São Miguel (1.5 hrs), Faial (45 mins), Graciosa (50 mins) Corvo (15 mins). *Ferry:* Year-round to Flores (40 mins). Seasonal to Faial (9 hrs). | Overnight |
| Corvo | Black Island | dark volcanic soil, the massive Caldeirão Caldera | *Air:* From Flores (15 mins), Faial (45 mins). *Ferry:* Year-round to Flores (40 mins). | Day trip from Flores |

dramatic peaks and volcanic cragginess of its peers, offering visitors a softer, undulating landscape that is easy on the eye and on the legs. It's called the **White Island** for the unique white volcanic rocks, known as trachytes, that make up its terrain. Steeped in tradition, Graciosa's most eye-popping attraction is its gargantuan **Caldera**; hike its 4-kilometer (2-mi) circumference for excellent views of the coast to one side and the massive crater below on the other.

### SÃO JORGE

If São Jorge had to be summed up in one word, that word just might be **cheese.** São Jorge will delight foodies, as it produces one of the Azores' most famous dairy products, São Jorge cheese, as well as other **unique food products** including the time-honored Santa Catarina tinned tuna, and locally grown coffee and clams. São Jorge is known as the **Brown Island** because of the fertile, flat plateaus that jut off its coast on all sides, called *fajãs.* These remnants of cooled lava flows create unique hamlets and scenic bathing spots as well as great conditions for **surfing.**

### PICO

If you enjoy **wines** and bucket-list **hikes,** then make Pico, called the **Gray Island** because of all its exposed volcanic rocks, your destination. Some of the Azores' most famous wines come from Pico, whose landscape, webbed with basalt-rock-built vine pens called *currais,* is a designated UNESCO World Heritage Site. Pico is also home the eponymous **Mount Pico**, Portugal's highest mountain and one of Europe's most epic hikes, and it's also one of the Azores' best islands for **whale-watching.**

### FAIAL

Fair Faial is pretty as a picture, nicknamed the **Blue Island** for its characteristic blue hydrangeas. A key port of call for transatlantic sailors, it is a vibrant, characterful island home to legendary mid-Atlantic hangouts in its picturesque main town of **Horta,** with its colorful **marina.** These serve as the doorway to staggering

sights like the almost lunar **Capelo Volcanic Complex** and its huge **Capelinhos Volcano,** and unique bathing opportunities including lava-black **beaches** and gorgeous **tidal pools.**

## The Western Group
### FLORES AND CORVO

Moody, magnetic, and miniscule, Flores and Corvo make up the Azores' western group of islands. Flores, the **Pink Island,** is so named for its abundant rosy-hued flora; it's an island of **waterfalls** and magical scenery. Nearby Corvo is the Azores' tiniest, most authentic, and untouched island, called the **Black Island** for its dark volcanic soil. It's generally visited as a day trip from Flores: Hike the 6 kilometers (4 mi) up to Corvo's gigantic **Caldeirão Caldera** on the island's only paved road, then head back to town for a snack before getting back on the **ferry.**

## Mainland Portugal

You can get to the Azores from mainland Portugal either via **Lisbon** or **Porto,** two cities that offer very different experiences.

### STOPOVER IN LISBON

Lisbon provides travelers with a genteel introduction to a modern Portugal. The city retains its original character and portrays a true picture of the country's soul and history: Traditional buildings sit alongside chic international fashion boutiques, contemporary **museums** complement ancient **castles** and **convents,** and riverside **cable cars** give the famous **historic trams** a run for their money. Busy and bustling, the traffic and throngs of tourists in Lisbon leave no room for doubt that it is indeed a thriving and popular capital city.

From **Lisbon Airport,** it's possible to fly direct to **São Miguel, Terceira, Pico,** or **Faial.**

### STOPOVER IN PORTO

Loud and without airs and graces, salt-of-the-earth Porto makes no apologies for its lack of polish. For many, this unpretentious authenticity is where the city's charm lies. Visiting industrious

# If You Have...

### ONE WEEK
Divide your time equally between **São Miguel** and **Terceira.**

### TEN DAYS
To your three days in **São Miguel,** add the **Azores "triangle"** islands, with two days each on São Jorge, Pico, and Faial.

### TWO WEEKS
If you're going to devote two full weeks to really get to know the Azores, the best time to visit is the **summer,** when you can island-hop on the seasonal May-September **interisland ferry.** Start with three full days on **São Miguel,** then fly or sail to **Terceira** and spend at least two days there. From Terceira, make your way by plane to spend a full week ferrying between **Faial, Pico,** and **São Jorge.** End your trip with a full day each on **Flores** and **Corvo.**

wine-tasting on Pico

Porto is an immersive experience that stimulates all of the senses. Its gastronomy—think **port wine** and decadent *francesinha* sandwiches—is bold and rich, and the cityscape is haphazard and colorful. Porto's unique attractions, from its bustling historic **waterfront** to its Belle Époque **train station,** tell fascinating stories. And its people are among the friendliest in the country.

From **Porto Airport** it's possible to fly direct to **São Miguel** and **Terceira.**

# When to Go

The best time to visit the Azores really depends on the purpose of your visit. Those interested in outdoor activities will probably get the most from the drier, warmer **summer** months (May-Sept.), while those who want to enjoy the hot springs and culture could visit at any time. That's not to say that you can't also enjoy the outdoors in **winter;** temperatures vary by only 10 degrees Celsius or so throughout the year. However, the weather is so changeable that you could have a fine morning and a wet afternoon—or vice versa—in any season.

Tourism-wise, the archipelago follows the same pattern as the mainland, with **low season** being roughly November-February and **high season** July-August, when hotel prices and car rentals are most expensive and attractions and beaches busiest.

## Spring

Spring is a wonderful time to visit the Azores. The flowers are starting to bloom and the weather is starting to warm up, but hotel and rental vehicle prices will still be cheaper than in the summer season. Though temperatures are pleasant in the Azores year-round, spring is the perfect time for **hiking,** as the region has yet to feel the force of summer's heat. During spring, temperatures hover between 17-20°C (63-68°F) degrees Celsius. **Showers** can occur at any time and with little warning, but spring rainfall tends to be short-lived. **Whale-watching** can also be enjoyed pretty much all year round, but April-September are the best months, with April-May widely regarded as the peak. Spring is also when the archipelago stages its time-honored Holy Spirit or **Holy Ghost festivities,** an authentic slice of Azorean culture, which take place on all islands between Easter and Pentecost Sunday.

## Summer

May-September are the best months to visit the Azores for those who like their weather sunny and warm to enjoy the volcanic **tidal pools** and **beaches.** The weather out in the Atlantic archipelago is unpredictable at best, so showers can occur at any given time, but generally, summer is warmest and driest, with July being the driest month and August the hottest, when thermometers can climb to 25°C (77°F) or higher. The lovely beaches of Santa Maria are the sunniest of the islands. June on the westernmost islands—Flores

and Corvo—is also misty month, when thick fog tends to enshroud the island and can affect travel.

Summer is also when the islands' trademark **hydrangeas** are in full bloom, especially on Terceira (the Lilac Island) and Faial (the Blue Island). It is also when accommodation prices go up, particularly in **peak tourist season,** July and August.

## Fall

In October, the Azores start to gradually cool and become rainier, with average temperatures around 20°C (68°F), although some days can be quite a bit warmer, and hotel prices start to drop. This is also when the islands are most prone to the **changeable weather.** That said, fall is lovely in the Azores; the **foliage** starts to change color, the weather is still pleasant and warm, albeit wetter than summer, and the islands are quiet, with **fewer crowds.**

## Winter

Winter (November-February/March) sees the coldest and wettest weather of the year, and thermometers waver around 17°C (63°F), which can be less than ideal for hiking and other outdoor activities. However, the Azores' **thermal natural attractions** are very enjoyable to visit during the winter months. Just make sure you pack accordingly, with layers of **warm clothes.** It's also wise to remember that **stormy weather** can affect interisland travel, making flight and ferry departures less reliable.

# Know Before You Go

## Getting There

With the exception of a few transatlantic and southern European cruises that might include stops at the archipelago, the only way to get to the Azores is by **plane,** but never before have so many airlines and flights served the archipelago. There are direct domestic flights from **Lisbon** and **Porto,** and direct flights from many other

cities in **Europe,** as well as a few in the **United States** and **Canada.**

Of potential interest to international travelers, the Azores' main airline **SATA Azores Airlines** (tel. 707 227 282; www.sata.pt) offers a **stopover program,** whereby international travelers flying to mainland Portugal (Lisbon, Porto) or to the island of Madeira can include a stop in the

# Coronavirus and Traveling to the Azores

The global coronavirus pandemic is a rapidly changing situation, and one that no travel guidebook can fully capture. Many changes may have happened since this callout was written in early June 2020; at that point, the European Union was barring nonessential travelers from the United States. Please consult the websites below and research current travel restrictions and requirements before planning a trip to the Azores.

## THE NUMBERS

Portugal responded rapidly to the coronavirus outbreak, implementing a national lockdown and shutting its borders. It detected its first cases in early March 2020 and declared a state of emergency in mid-March. Portugal and its autonomous regions had some of the lowest infection and death rates in Europe.

As of early June 2020, the archipelago registered 146 confirmed cases since the outbreak of the pandemic; 129 recoveries, 1 active case, and 15 deaths. The majority of the cases (108) were ascribed to São Miguel, the most populous island. Santa Maria, Flores and Corvo had no cases. At the end of May 2020, eight of the Azores' nine islands were reported to be virus-free.

## MITIGATION MEASURES

While lockdown measures in the Azores started easing in May 2020, a series of blanket rules and regulations were in place as of early June 2020 and will possibly remain in place until more progress is made against the virus:

- **Face masks** are compulsory in all public spaces, indoor venues (shopping centers, supermarkets, etc.) and transport.

- **Social distancing** rules—maintaining a 2-meter (6-ft) distance—indoors.

- When dining out, members of the same household are allowed to sit at the same table, with a minimum of 2 meters (6 ft) between other tables. Indoor and outdoor dining is allowed. Masks are compulsory when circulating in and around restaurants (e.g. walking to the bathroom).

- Establishments such as banks and post offices are exercising a **one-client-in, one-client-out** rule.

- Beaches have maximum attendance capacities

and social-distancing requirements. A minimum distance of 1.5 meters (5 ft) must be kept between people (except those in the same group) and 3 meters (10 ft) between parasols.

In addition, **festivals** and other large-scale events were canceled or postponed.

## REQUIREMENTS FOR TRAVELERS

As of June 2020, there were three options for travelers arriving in the Azores at the islands' two main international airports, Ponta Delgada (São Miguel) and Lajes (Terceira). Upon disembarking, passengers must sign a health form agreeing to one of the options in order to gain entry to the islands.

- **Option 1:** Take a screening test for COVID-19 within 72 hours before the flight departed for the Azores with a negative result; in that case, signed documental proof issued by an accredited laboratory would be required. If the stay is to last for seven or more days, passengers are required to contact the Health Authority about a new screening test five and, if applicable, 13 days from the date of the original test.

- **Option 2:** Take a second screening test at the time of landing followed by a 48-hour confinement period in the planned accommodation.

- **Option 3:** Return to the place of origin of the flight or travel to any airport outside the Autonomous Region of the Azores, remaining until that moment in prophylactic isolation in a hotel indicated for the purpose.

After agreeing to one of the options and completing its requirements, passengers are free to travel between the islands. Refusing to agree to one of the options or failure to comply could result in a 14-day mandatory quarantine at the traveler's expense. If your test is positive, the local health authority will determine what procedures to follow.

## MORE RESOURCES

For more travel information, see the **Azores Regional Government** website (https://covid19.azores.gov.pt). For the latest health recommendations see the **World Health Organization** website (www.who.int) or the **General Directorate of Health of the Government of Portugal** website (www.dgs.pt).

Azores (the islands of Terceira or São Miguel) of a few hours up to seven days, at no extra cost to the direct flight price. Go to https://stopover.azoresairlines.pt for more information.

### FROM MAINLAND PORTUGAL

From mainland Portugal, the Azores is a short and cheap flight, usually around 2 hours 30 minutes. Round-trip flights between the mainland, namely **Lisbon** and **Porto,** and the Azores can be found for less than €100 most of the year. It's possible to fly to **São Miguel, Terceira, Pico,** and **Faial** directly from mainland Portugal; the other islands will require a connecting interisland flight or ferry.

### FROM ELSEWHERE IN EUROPE

Chartered seasonal flights from the **United Kingdom** and other European countries such as **Belgium, Denmark, Germany,** the **Netherlands,** and **Spain** are also available. These flights are generally short (around 4 hours), and fairly cheap (€100-200 round-trip), mostly to **São Miguel,** though flights to **Terceira** can be found as well.

### FROM NORTH AMERICA

**SATA Azores Airlines** currently operates direct flights to the Azores from **Boston** in the United States, with a flight time of just 4 hours and round-trip tickets starting from around €500. There are also flights from **Oakland** (California) in summer. There are also flights from cities in Canada (5-7 hours), including **Toronto** year-round and **Montreal** in the summer months. If you're unable to depart from any of these North American cities, you can connect via Lisbon or Porto.

## Getting Around

There are two ways to get between the Azores islands once there: **plane** or **ferry.** The islands are divided into three groups: the **eastern group** (São Miguel and Santa Maria), the **central group** (Terceira, Graciosa, São Jorge, Pico, and Faial) and the **western group** (Flores and Corvo). In general, it's best to fly between island groups, and take the ferry within groups, though there are some exceptions to this rule.

Ferries are especially useful in the **Azores "triangle"** of Pico, Faial, and São Jorge; most ferries can also carry vehicles, meaning you can rent a car on one island and take it to another.

On the islands themselves, it's easiest to **rent a car,** or even a **scooter,** as public transport is patchy.

## Passports and Visas

**U.S., Australian,** and **Canadian,** travelers require a valid passport, but do not need a visa for stays of up to 90 days within any six-month period. While it is not obligatory to have a return ticket, it is advisable to have one.

The same rules apply to the Azores as to mainland Portugal: **EU nationals** traveling within EU or Schengen states do not require a visa for traveling to the Azores for any length of stay. They do, however, require a valid passport or official ID card (national citizen's card, driver's license, or residency permit, for example).

Citizens of the **UK** and **Ireland** require a passport to travel to the Azores, valid for the duration of the proposed stay, and can remain on national territory for up to three months. After that, they must register with local authorities. It is not yet known exactly how the UK's departure from the EU, commonly referred to as Brexit, will affect travel policies.

**South African** nationals do need to apply for a Portugal/Schengen visa. This should be done at least three months before travel.

## What to Pack

The Azores, having a maritime, subtropical climate, notoriously experiences "four seasons in one day." So when it comes to packing, the best advice is to **layer** up. Feel free to throw in a nice dress or smart-casual wear for going out in the evenings or to a fancier restaurant, but most restaurants are happy to accommodate laid-back shorts and T-shirt looks. A **swimsuit** is a must, for hot springs any time of a year, and for tidal pools and beaches in summer. Old swimsuits are best, as the rusty orange hot spring water can stain clothing. Whether you're an avid hiker or not, don't forget sturdy **walking shoes,** as some of the Azores' finest features are best seen on foot. A **backpack** for water and snacks is also a good idea. A roll-up light **rain jacket** with a hood is a great thing to have in the Azores, to pack in your bag and pull out when necessary.

Travelers from outside Europe should bring a plug adapter. And last but not least, with so many incredible landscapes and photo ops, a **camera** should be at the top of your list.

If coronavirus restrictions are still in place, bring enough **masks** so that you have at least one fresh (or freshly washed) mask for each day.

# The Best of the Azores

This weeklong trip is a great introduction to the archipelago, taking in its easiest-to-access islands, **São Miguel** and **Terceira,** with their quintessentially Azorean main towns, and some of the Azores' most iconic sights. A day on less-visited **Graciosa** at the week's end gives you a taste of the islands at their most remote and authentic.

This itinerary involves some **interisland flights,** which you'll want to book well ahead. **Renting a car** to pick up at each island's airport for that leg of the trip will offer you the most convenience and flexibility. Notwithstanding hire rental bookings, you'll find even the most touristy parts of the Azores relatively uncrowded, with little advance planning or reservations needed; the one exception is **Restaurante Miroma** in Furnas, famous for geothermally cooked São Miguel specialty *cozido das Furnas.*

## São Miguel

**DAY 1**

Put on some comfy walking shoes to spend your first day exploring wonderfully historic **Ponta Delgada,** São Miguel's biggest town and the gateway to the Azores. Ponta Delgada hosts the islands' busiest **airport,** with frequent flights from mainland Portugal and even from North America and elsewhere in Europe.

In the town's historic center, meander the **waterfront,** lined with grand buildings trimmed in distinctive gray basalt stone; the 16th-century **Fort of São Brás;** the **Convent and Chapel of Our Lady of Hope;** and the striking old **City Gates,** guarding the entrance to the ornamental, cobblestoned **Gonçalo Velho Cabral Square.** Have lunch at the **Mercado da Graça** before more sightseeing at the **Carlos Machado Museum** and the **Sant'Ana Garden and Palace.**

Furnas village

You may not realize just how small and remote the Azorean islands are in the vast expanse of blue Atlantic until you fly here; the experience of landing on a tiny green speck after a few hours in a plane over nothing but water is humbling. Once safely arrived, you're constantly reminded of the archipelago's isolation, for example, when you're able to circumnavigate an island in just a few hours by car, with the ocean on all sides. Still, there are some viewpoints throughout the Azores that are particularly humbling. These are some of the islands' best coastal views.

- **Ponta do Sossego, São Miguel:** This stunning viewpoint on São Miguel's eastern coast is only enhanced by terraced gardens, dropping steeply into the sea (page 86).

- **Gonçalo Velho Lighthouse, Santa Maria:** This dramatic lighthouse perches on a thin peninsula, Ponta do Castelo, that protrudes into the sea on southeastern Santa Maria (page 105).

- **Mount Brasil, Terceira:** This landmass formed by a volcano sprouts off the coast of Angra do Heroísmo and offers views of the picturesque town of Angra do Heroísmo, bays, or the ocean depending on the direction (page 137).

- **Rosais Point, São Jorge:** The entire island of São Jorge is a skinny, mountainous strip, and

Rosais Point

this is its northwesternmost tip, where almost-vertical cliffs form a sharp point over the Atlantic (page 188).

- **Monte da Guia, Faial:** A volcanic cone forms a uniquely shaped peninsula south of the town of Horta on Faial, with privileged views of the ocean and surrounding islands (page 250).

## DAY 2

Today you'll be visiting some of São Miguel's most iconic spots, starting with **Sete Cidades Lake,** one of the Azores' most-photographed vistas, on the northwestern tip of the island. After enjoying the awesome view of the crater-lake from the **Vista do Rei viewpoint,** continue west toward the coast to the **Ponta da Ferraria natural pool,** where geothermically heated water from the land mixes with refreshing seawater. From here, keep driving along the island's scenic northern coast clockwise, stopping in a charming village like **Ribeira Grande** or **Rabo de Peixe** en route for some lunch, until you reach the **Gorreana Tea Plantation.** After sampling tea from the only tea plantation in Europe, head back to Ponta Delgada.

## DAY 3

Your third day on São Miguel will be spent in **Furnas,** a charming village renowned as a geothermal hotspot—its signature stew, *cozido das Furnas,* is cooked in the hot sands of the shores of **Furnas Lake.** Make the lake your first stop: You can walk around its shore, admiring the spooky **Chapel of Nossa Senhora das Vitórias,** and, if you're there around noon, see huge pots of *cozido* being lifted out of steaming holes in the sand and ferried to nearby restaurants. The most famous of these is **Restaurante Miroma,** where you'll try the dish yourself for lunch (reserve in advance). Walk it off in the stunning **Terra Nostra Park.** Wrap up a great day with a soak in the park's **thermal pools,** or in the nearby **Poça da Dona Beija hot springs.**

## Terceira

### DAY 4

Fly from São Miguel to Terceira (just under an hour's flight) and head to its main town, **Angra do Heroísmo,** which will be your base for the next two nights. Spend the day exploring the Azores' oldest, history-rich town, designated a UNESCO World Heritage Site, and its plethora of sights and attractions, including the **Church of the Holy Savior's Cathedral,** the central **Old Square,** the **Angra do Heroísmo Museum,** and the magnificent **Duke of Terceira Garden.** Set aside an hour or two to trek around voluptuous **Mount Brasil,** on a peninsula that juts out south of the town, with the 17th-century **Fortress of São João Baptista** and incredible **viewpoints.**

### DAY 5

Terceira island has some amazing volcanic features, and today's itinerary will take in the main ones, conveniently located within walking distance of each other in the middle of the island. The dark, damp, and mysterious **Algar do Carvão Cave**—the cavernous inside of an extinct volcano—is Terceira's most famous attraction. A 5-minute drive away, the **Natal Cave** is a long underground tube formed by lava that beckons to be explored. In the middle of the two is the **Furnas do Enxofre** fumarole field, where a wooden walkway takes visitors through rolling hills pitted with steaming vents.

## Graciosa

### DAY 6

From Terceira, make the short 30-minute hop by plane to petite Graciosa, the Azores' second-smallest island and one of its less-visited. Classified a UNESCO World Biosphere Reserve, Graciosa has one big attraction, a supersized **Caldera:** Hike around its verdant rim, taking in panoramic views, before taking a relaxing dip in the stunning **Carapacho Natural Pools,** cement tanks nestled in a breathtaking sheltered bay south of the Caldera. Head back to the tiny main town, **Santa Cruz,** stopping in its **Main Church** and **Ethnographic Museum,** before an authentic dinner and a good night's sleep.

## Return Home

### DAY 7

Pack your bags and prepare to bid a fond farewell to the Azores after a full trip.

# Wild Encounters

When it comes to getting up close and personal with nature, the Azores are places of superlatives: Some of the best whale-watching, snorkeling, and scuba diving in the world can be enjoyed just off all of the Azores islands, and their isolation in the middle of the Atlantic means they are home to some unique bird species. You can inquire at almost any of the islands' **information centers** or with your accommodation about what type of aquatic and avian species can be seen, but here's where these activities can be experienced at the best of the best.

## DOLPHIN- AND WHALE-WATCHING

Though whales can be seen around the Azores year-round, the best season is generally thought to be **April-September.** Along with many species of dolphins, it's possible to see whale species including sei whales, pilot whales, sperm whales, fin whales, humpback whales, and even blue whales, depending on your luck.

dolphin-watching

**Ponta Delgada** (page 56), the Azorean capital on São Miguel, is a great base for a whale-watching trip, but **Lajes do Pico** (page 227) on Pico island could be considered the archipelago's whale-watching capital.

## DIVING AND SNORKELING

It's difficult to say which of the Azores could be considered the best for snorkeling and diving; each island has its own superlatives, from the high probability of seeing a whale shark off **Santa Maria** (page 110) to the *Edwin L. Drake* shipwreck off **São Miguel** (page 55).

## BIRD-WATCHING

A number of migratory birds visit the Azores throughout the year, and they're also home to a few rare endemic species. Bird-watching is at its best April-October. **São Miguel** (page 57) is home

to the extremely rare Azores bullfinch. **Terceira** (page 141) is a particularly good place to spot seabirds and migrating species, such as Nearctic ducks and a variety of gulls. And the Fajã dos Cubres on the northern coast of **São Jorge** (page 202) is known as one of the best places in the Azores to bird-watch.

## "HAPPY COWS"

Over your time in the Azores, you will inevitably have at least one encounter with their notably contented and well-fed cows, whether you catch one by surprise on a hike, or a herd blocks your car on a rural road. If you want to get to know these wonderful island residents, which sometimes outnumber the humans, try the **Happy Local Experience** (page 164) on **Terceira,** a 2-hour farm tour that includes a cheese-tasting and a chance to milk the cows.

# The Azores Triangle

The islands of **Faial, Pico,** and **São Jorge,** in the Azores' **central group,** are nicknamed the Azores "triangle" for their close proximity, and are conveniently connected by frequent, short **ferries.** Each of these islands is distinct and unique, making this a surprising, dynamic, and rewarding part of the Azores. Once on one of the "triangle" islands, you can **rent a car** for the duration of your stay, as the ferries carry vehicles between the islands.

If it's on your bucket list to summit **Mount Pico,** the highest point in Portugal, be sure to reserve in advance at the **Mountain House** (tel. 967 303 519; http://parquesnaturais.azores.gov.pt/pt/pico/o-que-visitar/centros-de-interpretacao/casa-da-montanha), as the number of people allowed on the mountain at any one time is limited.

## Faial

### DAY 1

Despite being the smallest island of the trio, Faial is generally the starting point of the Azores' "triangle." You can fly to fabulous Faial either via São Miguel or Terceira; less frequent flights from mainland Portugal are also available.

Stay in the main town of **Horta.** Spend your first day getting up close and personal with this quirky sailors' town. Enjoy a pleasant 45-minute walk to **Monte da Guia** hill, south of Horta; stroll along **Porto Pim Bay;** enjoy the colorful **Jetty Murals** decorating the **Marina;** and make sure to have a gin or cold beer in the legendary **Peter Café Sport bar.**

### DAY 2

Today, venture farther afield to see Faial's famed

---

town of Horta

The Azores are a hiker's paradise. With incredible scenery—rolling massifs, jagged volcanoes, gargantuan calderas, pretty hamlets, and endless ocean views—around every corner, walking in the Azores can be as leisurely or as challenging as you like. From climbing the highest mountain in Portugal to circling the ring of a volcanic crater, hikes in the Azores are magnificent and memorable.

- **Mount Pico, Pico:** The Azores' ultimate hiking challenge, this epic daylong trek reaches the highest point in Portugal, at over 2 kilometers (1 mi) high (page 228).

- **Vila do Porto to Formosa Beach, Santa Maria:** This 7-kilometer (4-mi) scenic coastal route from the Fort of São Brás in the island's main town of Vila do Porto ends at Formosa Beach, perhaps the most beautiful strand in the Azores (page 113).

- **Monte Brasil Route, Terceira:** Jutting out from the town of Angra do Heroísmo, Mount Brasil is guarded by the strapping 16th-century **Fortress of São João Baptista.** The luxuriant mount beyond can be explored via a 7-kilometer (4-mi) circular route (page 141).

- **Serra do Topo-Caldeira de Santo Cristo-Fajã dos Cubres, São Jorge:** This 10-kilometer (6-mi) hike is the only way to get to the Fajã da Caldeira de Santo Cristo, a dramatic, flat green peninsula at the foot of São Jorge's mountainous spine (page 201).

Faial Caldera

- **Caldeira Hike, Faial:** Circumnavigate the rim of a volcano on this unusual hike. It takes around 3 hours to walk around the crest of this 2-kilometer-wide (1-mi-wide) crater, with sea views on one side and the gaping caldera on the other (page 262).

landmark, the gargantuan 2-kilometer-wide (1-mi-wide), 400-meter-deep (1,300-ft-deep) crater known as the **Caldera.** Enjoy the bird's-eye island views as you trek around the rim and stop at the **Caldera viewpoint** for the best vantage point of the cauldron, a giant bowl covered in a kaleidoscope of greens that change as the sun flits across. Aim to catch a ferry to make the short crossing between Horta and the town of **Madalena** on **Pico** in the late afternoon. Tuck in early tonight, to rise bright and early to conquer the iconic **Mount Pico** the next day.

## Pico
### DAY 3

Pack a backpack with essentials like a windbreaker, snacks, and water, and head off bright and early to **Mount Pico.** The starting point is the **Mountain House,** where you can get information about the route as well as learn about the history and geology of the mountain; make sure to register there in advance, and hiring an experienced **guide** for the trek is recommended. This hike is a daylong job, taking 7 or 8 hours to complete. After scaling

Fajã da Caldeira de Santo Cristo

Pico, head back to **Madalena** to celebrate with a well-earned dinner and drinks at the stunning **Cella Bar.**

### DAY 4

On your second day on Pico, take in sights like the famed **Landscape of the Pico Island Vineyard Culture,** a UNESCO World Heritage Site, where lattice-like webs of low basalt stone walls protect the vines. Sample wine at the **Pico Wine Museum** and explore the **Torres Cave,** the longest lava tube in Portugal. Prepare to sail to **São Jorge** early the next morning.

## São Jorge

### DAY 5

There are regular crossings between **Madalena** and **Velas,** São Jorge's main town, which will be your base for the next two nights. Spend your first day on the island indulging in the unique food products produced there, from famous São Jorge cheese made at the **São Jorge Union of Agricultural and Dairy Cooperatives,** to coffee grown at **Café Nunes,** to, quirkily, tuna ethically fished and canned at the **Santa Catarina Tuna Factory.** In the late afternoon, visit **Rosais Point** in the **Sete Fontes Natural Reserve,** the dramatic northwesternmost tip of this thin, dagger-shaped island.

### DAY 6

Today, set out to explore São Jorge's *fajãs,* flat, coastal lava plateaus from which São Jorge earns its nickname, Island of the Fajãs. The magical **Fajã da Caldeira de Santo Cristo** is accessible only by a lovely **hike** from another lava plateau, the **Fajã dos Cubres.** When you arrive at the Fajã da Caldeira de Santo Cristo, consider a surfing lesson from **Caldeira Surf Camp,** and definitely stop by the restaurant **O Borges** to sample island clams, a specialty found only in the *fajã's* lagoon—nowhere else on São Jorge.

## Return Home

### DAY 7

After spending your last night in the Azores

# Made in the Azores

The Azores' unique position in the middle of the Atlantic means they have their own microclimate, making it possible for many crops that wouldn't have much of a chance on the Portuguese mainland to flourish here. On their way between the Old and New Worlds, explorers, settlers, traders, and sailors brought and left exotic fruits like pineapples; luxury beverages not grown elsewhere in Europe like tea and coffee; and even cows, who roamed the lush green hills and now produce dairy products considered among the world's best.

## CHEESE

Arguably the most famous Azorean product, cheese from the islands is justifiably famous, produced by the so-called "happy cows" that roam the archipelago. You'll find it in almost every restaurant and market, and it's possible to visit factories where the cheese is made on many islands, including **Queijo Vaquinha** (page 164) on Terceira and the **São Jorge Union of Agricultural and Dairy Cooperatives** (page 186).

## WINE

Though mainland Portugal has a formidable winemaking tradition, wine from the Azores holds up, if only for its uniqueness. Grown in basalt stone pens to protect it from the sea air and battered by changeable weather, Azorean wine is known for its salty, minerally notes. The majority of wine from the archipelago comes from the celebrated **Landscape of the Pico Island Vineyard Culture** (page 214), but you can also try wines near the town of **Biscoitos** (page 151) on Terceira.

## TEA

On São Miguel's northern coast, the **Gorreana Tea Plantation** (page 83) specializes in green and black teas, a perfect souvenir to take home from your trip. The tea is available across the islands, but why not visit the tea fields yourself for a friendly tour and tasting?

Gorreana Tea Plantation

## PINEAPPLES

This South American transplant grows smaller and sweeter in the Azores. São Miguel is the largest producer; you can see for yourself where these tropical fruits grow at the **Augusto Arruda Pineapple Plantation** (page 52), just outside Ponta Delgada.

## COFFEE

Another Azorean oddity is the coffee produced at tiny **Café Nunes** (page 192) on São Jorge, a mini coffee plantation said to have been initially seeded with Arabica from the coffee plantations of Brazil.

## TUNA

Among the quirkier food products to come out of the archipelago is tinned tuna from the **Santa Catarina Tuna Factory** (page 192) on São Jorge; of course, the fish has its own island twist, harvested via sustainable pole-and-line methods and canned by local women using traditional techniques.

a hydrangea on São Miguel

"triangle" on São Jorge, it's time to head back to **Faial** and catch your flight home, either via **Terceira, São Miguel,** or the Portuguese mainland.

## With More Time

If you have more than a week to dedicate to the Azores, you can extend your trip to the western islands, **Flores** and **Corvo.** Flores is easily accessible from **Faial,** a 45-minute plane ride, and Corvo is a 40-minute ferry trip north of Flores. Each island needs about a day, with Corvo best experienced as a day trip from Flores.

# São Miguel

## Dubbed the Green Island, the Azores' biggest

island, São Miguel is fun and stimulating. With pools of rusty-red hot spring water and wild flora interspersed with pretty towns and fishing villages, the volcanic island's landscape is vastly diverse. An emerald tapestry of verdant woodland and meadows—hence its nickname—is hemmed in by dramatic coastal scenery and peppered with postcard-perfect seaside hamlets around a busy main city. While the island currently welcomes a growing number of visitors, São Miguel remains authentic and vibrant, showing few signs of pandering to mainstream tourism.

The unofficial main gateway to the Azores, São Miguel is home to the archipelago's administrative capital and biggest municipality,

# Highlights

Look for ★ to find recommended sights, activities, dining, and lodging.

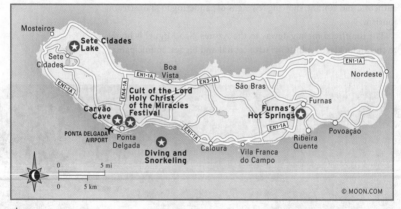

Mosteiros

★ Sete Cidades Lake

Sete Cidades

Boa Vista

EN1-1A

Nordeste

EN1-1A

EN4-1A

EN3-1A

São Bras

★ Cult of the Lord Holy Christ of the Miracles Festival

Furnas

★ Carvão Cave

★ Furnas's Hot Springs

PONTA DELGADA AIRPORT

EN1-1A

Ponta Delgada

Povoação

Ribeira Quente

★ Diving and Snorkeling

Caloura

Vila Franca do Campo

0        5 mi

0        5 km

© MOON.COM

★ **Carvão Cave:** Delve into this deep open-air cave and explore a rare and ancient lava tube, the longest on the island at over 1,900 meters (6,200 ft) (page 52).

★ **Diving and Snorkeling:** With the *Edwin L. Drake* shipwreck just a few hundred meters offshore and some of the islands' most impressive underwater flora, São Miguel is one of the best places in the Azores to dive (page 55).

★ **Cult of the Lord Holy Christ of the Miracles Festival:** The streets are covered in flowers, and pilgrims from around the globe return home for this springtime festival, which celebrates a statue of Christ that made its way to São Miguel 300 years ago (page 58).

★ **Sete Cidades Lake:** Stand and gaze in awe at this stunning blue lake in the crater of a dormant volcano (page 66).

★ **Furnas's Hot Springs:** Stroll through the tropical Eden that is Terra Nostra Park before taking a dip in its steaming red spring pool, or hop from tank to tank at the Poça da Dona Beija hot springs in this geothermal village (page 80).

Ponta Delgada, and its main international airport. Ponta Delgada is also the archipelago's economic pillar, with a high concentration of banks and businesses as well as local commerce, and its higher education nucleus, which injects a shot of youth into the island.

Elsewhere, life moves at an unhurried pace on São Miguel. Outside Ponta Delgada, traffic is sparse, the countryside vast and open, with views of the endless ocean from almost anywhere on the island. Farmers leisurely tend to their land, deep green fields inhabited by the famously "happy cows" that graze carefree on the lush vegetation and provide the delicious island meat and cheeses that are must-tries when visiting. This picturesque tranquility adds to the island's general laidback feel. São Miguel is also where many of the Azores' most famous sights can be found, such as Sete Cidades Lake and Terra Nostra Park, with evocative landscapes and excellent gastronomy far off the beaten track.

## GETTING THERE

Though it's possible to fly to Terceira, Pico, and Faial from mainland Portugal, and some international flights fly in and out of Terceira's airport as well, the majority of travelers will likely start their trip on São Miguel, which boasts the Azores' largest airport. It's also possible to travel by ferry to São Miguel from Terceira and Santa Maria during the summer months (May-Sept.), but it's not recommended as it tends to be slow and unreliable.

A growing number of transatlantic and European **cruises** now also stop in Ponta Delgada, including cruises operated by companies MSC Cruises, Royal Caribbean, P&O Cruises, AIDA Cruises, and Holland America Line.

### Air
**PONTA DELGADA AIRPORT**
**(Aeroporto de Ponta Delgada)**

*Ponta Delgada; tel. 296 205 400; www. aeroportopontadelgada.pt*
Ponta Delgada Airport (PDL), on São Miguel, is the Azores' main airport, also called João Paulo II Airport for Pope John Paul II. It's just a 10-minute drive from the center of Ponta Delgada, the island's main city. It receives the vast majority of international flights to the islands; most travelers to the Azores will start here.

From **mainland Portugal,** TAP, SATA, and Ryanair have regular direct flights from Lisbon and Porto that are short and cheap—around 2 hours—and often available for less than €100 round-trip. SATA also operates direct flights between the Azores and the **US** and **Canada,** notably from Boston (which takes just 4 hours), Toronto, and Montreal (only in the summer months). There are regular and seasonal direct flights from **Europe,** including from the UK, Germany, Brussels, Finland, Denmark, and the Netherlands.

There are **interisland flights** to Ponta Delgada Airport from every island in the Azores except Corvo and Graciosa. Interisland flights are typically short: The longest possible flight, from São Miguel to Flores in the west, clocks in at 1 hour 15 minutes, and most flights between islands can be found for €100-150.

### Ferry
**PONTA DELGADA FERRY TERMINAL**
*Portas do Mar; tel. 296 629 424; open 24/7*
São Miguel can be reached by ferry, operated by **Atlanticoline** (tel. 707 201 572; www.atlanticoline.pt), from Praia da Vitória harbor (Cabo da Praia; tel. 295 540 000) on **Terceira** and Vila do Porto harbor on **Santa Maria** (Cais de Ilha de Santa Maria; tel. 296 882 782), but only from **mid-May to late September,** when the seasonal summer ferry operates. There are at least two weekly departures from these islands to São Miguel during this period, all arriving in Ponta Delgada

---

**Previous:** Furnas village; snorkeling in São Miguel; Poça da Dona Beija hot springs.

# São Miguel

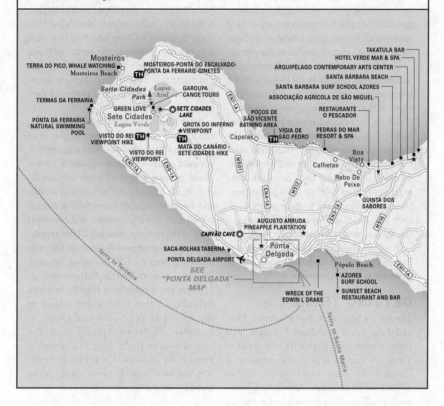

Ferry Terminal, on varying days and times—check the Atlanticoline website for details. Due to the rough Atlantic waters, ferry service is slow and often unreliable. The journey from Santa Maria takes 2.5-3 hours and costs around €50 one-way. From Terceira, the journey takes roughly 6 hours and costs about €70 one-way.

## GETTING AROUND

São Miguel has a **public bus network** that covers most coastal areas and main sights, but not rural inland areas. Buses are cheap but patchy, infrequent on weekends, and can be slow. A **rental car** is the best way to explore São Miguel. Guided excursions and taxis for longer trips can be costly; renting

a car generally proves to be cheaper and provides more flexibility for exploring the island.

### Rental Car

A rental car is your best option for getting around São Miguel. Fuel is cheaper than in mainland Portugal, good highways cover the island, and navigating the quiet, winding roads is easy: Keep the sea on the left, and eventually you'll come full circle (driving around the island in its entirety without stopping would take 4-5 hours). A half-dozen **rental companies** operate at Ponta Delgada Airport (www.aeroportopontadelgada.pt). The desks can get crowded, particularly early in the morning when cars are being returned,

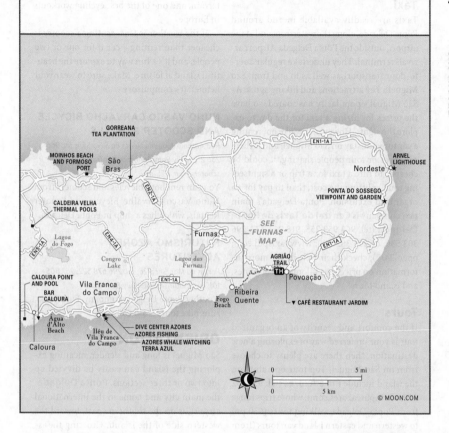

GORREANA
TEA PLANTATION

MOINHOS BEACH
AND FORMOSO
PORT

São
Bras

ARNEL
LIGHTHOUSE

Nordeste

PONTA DO SOSSEGO
VIEWPOINT AND GARDEN

EN1-1A

CALDEIRA VELHA
THERMAL POOLS

EN2-1A

Lagoa
do Fogo

EN5-1A

EN4-1A

Furnas

SEE
"FURNAS"
MAP

EN1-1A

Congro
Lake

Lagoa das
Furnas

AGRIÃO
TRAIL

TH

Povoação

CALOURA POINT
AND POOL

BAR
CALOURA

Vila Franca
do Campo

EN1-1A

Ribeira
Quente

Fogo
Beach

CAFÉ RESTAURANT JARDIM

Água
d'Alto
Beach

Caloura

Iléu de
Vila Franca
do Campo

DIVE CENTER AZORES
AZORES FISHING
AZORES WHALE WATCHING
TERRA AZUL

0          5 mi

0          5 km

© MOON.COM

so allow more time than usual to drop off the car. Local companies such as **Autatlantis** (tel. 296 205 340; www.autatlantis.com) and **Micauto** (tel. 296 284 382; www.micauto. com) have offices in Ponta Delgada's city center and offer competitive rates. Reserve a car well in advance, as they sell out in peak seasons, especially summer.

## Bus

Three bus companies service the island: **Auto Viação Micaelense** (tel. 296 301 358), **Caetano Raposo & Pereiras (CRP)** (tel. 296 304 260), and **Varela & Ca.** (tel. 296 301 800). You can find the timetables here: http://horarios.visitazores.de/smiAVM.pdf. Each operates different routes, but most buses depart from outside the **Ponta Delgada tourist office,** where you should head for fares and timetables. The bus services most frequently used by tourists include a circular and frequent service between Ponta Delgada Airport and Ponta Delagda town center, operated by **MiniBus** (tel. 967 995 536; €4.50 one-way) hourly, every day of the week, 5am-midnight. Tourists may also want to take the bus between Ponta Delgada and Furnas: Two services—the **110** and **318** (http://horarios.visitazores.de/smiAVM.pdf)—depart from various locations in Ponta Delgada, including along the main waterfront avenue, arriving in Furnas in roughly 1.5 hours (€5 one-way).

## Taxi

Taxis are readily available in and around Ponta Delgada, along the waterfront and at the airport, outside the Ponta Delgada Airport arrivals terminal. They undertake regular door-to-door transport as well as to and from São Miguel's key attractions and hiking spots. As São Miguel's popularity has soared, so have the prices for hiring a taxi for the day to explore the sights. However, if you're not renting a car for your stay on São Miguel, and if there are three or four people sharing, it could be cheaper to hire a taxi for a trip or a sightseeing tour, splitting the cost, than to pay for an organized excursion. Ponta Delgada's main taxi company is **Central de Taxis de Ponta Delgada** (tel. 962 959 255, 918 252 777, 296 302 530, or 296 382 000; www.taxispdl.com; open 24/7); check their website for more information on prices per kilometer, set routes, and island tours.

## Tours

If the comfort and security of an organized tour is your preferred way of exploring a new destination, then there are plenty to choose from on São Miguel. Top tour operators on the island include **Pure Azores** (tel. 932 532 200; www.pureazores.com), whose trips range from Ponta Delgada walking tours (€30 pp) to western and eastern island van tours (from €59 pp), and **Greenzone Azores** (tel. 962 770 410; https://greenzoneazores.com), whose fun jeep tours (from €35) are a great way to get off the beaten track.

## Bike and Scooter

Exploring São Miguel by bicycle is an option, but given the size of the island, distance between main towns and attractions, hilly terrain, and busy, narrow roads (often poorly surfaced inland), it's not really the ideal place for a leisurely cycle. Even mountain-bikers and experienced cyclists may find this island a challenge. But those tough enough to try the island out by pedal-power are rewarded with unspoiled mountainous views, exciting

terrain, and one of the best cycling workouts in Europe.

If the weather is fine, renting a scooter is cheaper than renting a car if for one or two people, and it's a fun way to explore the beautiful island at leisure. Make sure to wear your helmet; it's compulsory.

### NUNO VASCO CARVALHO BICYCLE AND SCOOTER RENTALS

*Rua António Joaquim Nunes da Silva 55A; tel. 966 256 212; daily 9am-6pm; bicycles from €10/day, scooters from €25/day*

You can rent both bicycles and scooters from Nuno Vasco Carvalho Bicycle and Scooter Rentals, which has a shop in Ponta Delgada.

### FUTURISMO AZORES ADVENTURES

*Portas do Mar, Shop 26; tel. 296 628 522, 967 805 101; www.futurismo.pt; daily 8am-6pm*

Another Ponta Delgada company, Futurismo, runs bike tours from €30.

# ORIENTATION

São Miguel is long and slender, meaning exploring the island can easily be divvied up into two or three sections. **Ponta Delgada,** the main city and home to the international airport, is on the southern coast, toward the western side of the island. Crossing the island from south to north, across its skinniest point in the middle (from Ponta Delgada to the town of **Rabo de Peixe,** directly north of Ponta Delgada), takes just 20 minutes, whereas traversing from west to east (or vice versa) would take around 1.5 hours, as there is no road directly across its 64-kilometer (40-mi) longitude. The main **EN1-1A** road runs around the rim of the island. Follow this road and eventually (4-5 hours for the full loop) you will come full circle.

Many of the island's main attractions, such as the **Fogo Lake, Congro Lake,** the village of **Furnas** and its hot springs and the **Caldeira Velha thermal pools,** are located inland, to the eastern part of the island; the stunning **Sete Cidades Lake** is located on its western tip, while some of the most **picturesque villages** are on the eastern fringe, along with **laurel forests** famous for **bird-watching** opportunities.

In this guidebook, **eastern São Miguel** is defined as everything east of Ribeira Grande in the north, east to the village of Nordeste (the northeasternmost point on the island) heading south and back around to Ponta Delgada, not including the central area of Furnas. Fogo Lake, Congro Lake, and the Caldeira Velha thermal pools are located in eastern São Miguel.

## PLANNING YOUR TIME

In a rush, the island could be visited in a day, but it's better to dedicate one day or more each to the east and west ends. São Miguel's western half is packed with must-see attractions, such as the **Sete Cidades Lake** and **Ponta da Ferraria** natural pool, as well as Ponta Delgada city, making for one great day. Popular spots including **Furnas village, Furnas Lake,** and **Fogo Lake** occupy the island's center, and some of the prettiest little **coastal towns** and wild **laurel forests** are on the eastern half; both could easily fill another day each. **Renting a car** is the best way to make your way around at leisure.

If possible, set aside another whole day to explore **Ponta Delgada** city center and to enjoy a **dolphin- and whale-watching trip.** Book these trips in advance to avoid disappointment.

Some of the Azores' most resplendent sights are a short drive from Ponta Delgada, making it a good place to base yourself during your time on the islands. In the western and eastern parts of the island, accommodations are fewer and more remote, with fewer amenities.

Outside of Ponta Delgada, **Furnas** village is another popular place to spend a night due to the wealth of interesting attractions on its doorstep, such as the **Terra Nostra Park, Dona Beija hot springs,** and the village itself, with its restaurants selling the traditional *cozido das Furnas* earth-cooked stew.

On São Miguel, make sure you always have a **swimsuit** and a **towel** with you, as jumping into steaming hot springs is a tempting treat, whatever the weather—but make sure it's an old swimsuit, as the iron-rich waters can turn clothes orange. São Miguel has a number of sandy beaches, albeit black volcanic sand, and lots of lovely natural tidal pools, but if it's shimmering golden sands you enjoy, then Santa Maria island is the place to go.

Thanks to its year-round mild weather, São Miguel is less of a seasonal destination than some mainland destinations, but there are a few things to bear in mind when planning a trip: the **ferries** to other islands from São Miguel only run seasonally (May-Sept.); **winter** (Nov.-Feb.) is rainiest and coolest; the **whale-watching** season runs roughly from April to September, and the **busiest months** are July and August, reflecting the summer holidays on the mainland. It's wise to book **hotels** well in advance for the busier months, and reservations for the most popular **restaurants,** particularly those selling the typical *cozido das Furnas* in Furnas village and A Tasca in Ponta Delgada, are also highly recommended year-round.

# Itinerary Ideas

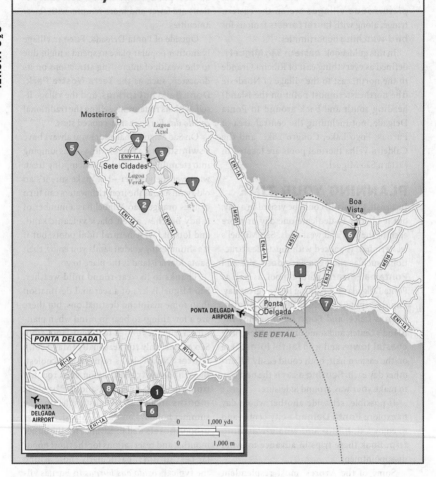

# Itinerary Ideas

## DAY 1: WESTERN SÃO MIGUEL

Be sure to wear comfortable clothes and shoes, and pack a swimsuit and towel, for this is an active day of exploring western São Miguel.

**1** From Ponta Delgada, after breakfast, head straight to the Sete Cidades Lake, following the EN1-1A and then the EN9-1A. Stop first at the **Grota do Inferno viewpoint** for breathtaking views of the largest freshwater lake in the Azores.

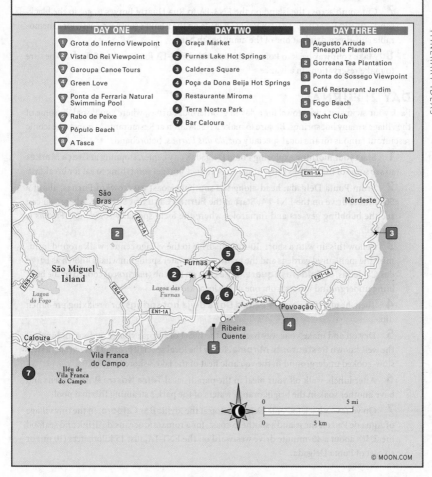

| DAY ONE | DAY TWO | DAY THREE |
|---------|---------|-----------|
| 1 Grota do Inferno Viewpoint | 1 Graça Market | 1 Augusto Arruda Pineapple Plantation |
| 2 Vista Do Rei Viewpoint | 2 Furnas Lake Hot Springs | 2 Gorreana Tea Plantation |
| 3 Garoupa Canoe Tours | 3 Calderas Square | 3 Ponta do Sossego Viewpoint |
| 4 Green Love | 4 Poça da Dona Beija Hot Springs | 4 Café Restaurant Jardim |
| 5 Ponta da Ferraria Natural Swimming Pool | 5 Restaurante Miroma | 5 Fogo Beach |
| 6 Rabo de Peixe | 6 Terra Nostra Park | 6 Yacht Club |
| 7 Pópulo Beach | 7 Bar Caloura | |
| 8 A Tasca | | |

© MOON.COM

**2** From this viewpoint, make the short drive west to the **Vista do Rei viewpoint,** which offers the most iconic views of the lake.

**3** Jump back in the car and drive to the Sete Cidades village, where you can rent a kayak from **Garoupa Canoe Tours** in order to see the lake up close and personal.

**4** After working up an appetite, grab lunch at lakeside **Green Love.**

**5** Back in your car, drive westward toward **Ponta da Ferraria natural swimming pool** on the coast for a quick dip in the ocean, where volcanic hot water and refreshing seawater merge in a natural rock pool.

**6** Continue the scenic drive around the western tip of the island, following the EN1-1A through traditional little coastal villages like Mosteiros and Capelas, ending up at **Rabo**

**de Peixe,** a typical fishing village. Spend an hour exploring the streets of colorful houses and the port.

**7** Cut south across the island on the EN3-1A to Rua Duarte Borges to get to the black-sand **Pópulo Beach,** just east of Ponta Delgada on the island's southern coast, for a memorable sun-down drink at one of the many beach bars.

**8** Make your way back to Ponta Delgada on the EN1-1A for dinner at **A Tasca**—be sure to make reservations in advance.

## DAY 2: FURNAS

Pack your swimsuit and a towel for a day in geothermal Furnas, where you'll soak in some of the village's many hot springs. Be sure to make a reservation at Restaurante Miroma, the iconic restaurant famous for the local specialty *cozido das Furnas,* beforehand.

**1** Start your morning exploring Ponta Delgada's city center, stopping at **Graça Market** to see some of the island's intriguing local produce and get something to eat for breakfast.

**2** From Ponta Delgada, head along the southern coast east toward Furnas, about a 50-minute drive on the EN1-1A. Start at the **Furnas Lake hot springs,** where you can see the bubbling geysers and fumaroles where the local specialty *cozido das Furnas* is cooked.

**3** Follow this up with a short, 10-minute drive to the village center; walk around to admire the manicured gardens and the many natural water springs in what's known as Largo das Caldeiras, or **Calderas Square.** Try a corn on the cob (*maçaroca*) cooked in the bubbling underground waters from one of the local kiosks.

**4** Then, head to the nearby **Poça da Dona Beija hot springs** for a relaxing pre-lunch dip.

**5** Dry off and make your way back into the heart of Furnas village on foot for lunch at the well-known **Restaurante Miroma.** Enjoy the local specialty *cozido das Furnas,* a stew slow-cooked underground in the volcanic heat of the lake's shores.

**6** After lunch, walk off your meal in the paradisiacal **Terra Nostra Park** gardens and have another soak in the bright orange waters of the park's steaming thermal pool.

**7** On your way back to Ponta Delgada, stop at the idyllic **Bar Caloura,** in the tiny village of Água de Pau on the island's southern coast, for a romantic oceanside drink and seafood meal. It's about a 45-minute drive westward on the EN1-1A, just 15 kilometers (10 mi) or so east of Ponta Delgada.

## DAY 3: EASTERN SÃO MIGUEL

Again, wear comfortable clothing and shoes, and pack a bathing suit and towel just in case for this active day, which involves visits to a few plantations and an afternoon hike.

**1** Start your morning at the **Augusto Arruda Pineapple Plantation** on the outskirts of Ponta Delgada, where you can get a free tour and tasting of the plantation's sweet pineapple. It's about a 15-minute drive from Ponta Delgada city center.

**2** From here, head to the island's northern coast on the EN3-1A to the ER3-1 and eventually the EN1-1A, for a scenic coastal drive toward the **Gorreana Tea Plantation** in Maia, where you'll be able to get another tasting, this time of tea made in the only tea plantation in Europe.

**3**   Continue east on the EN1-1A to the **Ponta do Sossego viewpoint** on the island's eastern coast, where terraced gardens angle downward into the ocean.

**4**   Continue on the EN1-1A, turning back westward to Povoação for a light lunch at **Café Restaurant Jardim,** and a local specialty, *fofa*, for dessert.

**5**   Continue west to **Fogo Beach,** a black sand beach whose sands and waters are at times warm, heated by submarine hydrothermal vents.

**6**   Head back toward Ponta Delgada for dinner at the **Yacht Club;** afterward, enjoy a night out on the marina.

# Ponta Delgada

The gateway to the Azores, Ponta Delgada is toward the western end of the island's south coast. Developed from a humble fishing port into a cosmopolitan city, it is quaint yet polished and retains its small-town feel. Its architecture is distinctively two-toned, with whitewashed walls and black basalt trim. Grand monuments, such as the 16th-century Church of São Sebastião, the Portas da Cidade old City Gates, the Convent and Chapel of Our Lady of Hope, and the imposing Fort of São Brás are scattered around, evoking Ponta Delgada's days as a trading port. Most of the vessels that sail into its harbor today are privately owned yachts on transatlantic voyages, the odd transatlantic cruise ship, and ferries to other Azores islands. A must while in Ponta Delgada is whale-watching, with trips departing from the marina at the far eastern end of the harbor promenade.

Ponta Delgada is a busy and bustling city oozing local charm. Elegant gardens give it a genteel feel, tourists mingle with locals, and while the city largely escapes the trappings of tourism, it does cater well to visitors, with plenty of hotels and restaurants, a large, well-equipped hospital (the archipelago's main hospital), good roads, a modern shopping center, and clean streets. The streets throughout Ponta Delgada are an attraction in themselves, boasting fancy black-and-white cobblestone designs in stripes, stars, chains, and other eye-catching symmetrical patterns; make sure you have the camera

ready to capture the fanciful cobblestone creations on every sidewalk,

## ORIENTATION

Devoid of high-rises but densely built, the city is easy to navigate on foot, with most of the restaurants, cafés, shops, and bars located along several streets in the old part of town that frames the harbor. Here visitors will find aristocratic black-and-white buildings, pretty cobbled squares, and manicured gardens. **Avenida Infante Dom Henrique,** a beautiful harborside promenade, is a pleasant stroll from the formidable 16th-century **Fort of São Brás** on the western tip of a cosmopolitan marina, with chic restaurants and trendy bars.

Opposite the fort is another of Ponta Delgada's main squares, the pretty **5 de Outubro Square** (Praça 5 de Outubro), with its charming little central bandstand, flanked by handsome buildings. The **Convent and Chapel of Nossa Senhora da Esperança** is also just across the road from the fort. A little farther down are the imposing old **City Gates** to the city, historic stone archways with the decorative **Gonçalo Velho Square** stretching before them. From the harbor and old town center it's also walking distance to the **Graça Market** and **Carlos Machado Museum,** and if you want to indulge in a little retail therapy, have a wander around the maze of streets in the downtown and explore the quirky little shops.

# Ponta Delgada

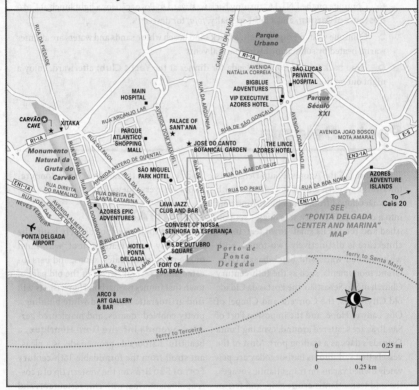

RUA DA PIEDADE

Parque
Urbano

CAMINHO DAL LEVADA

R1-1A

AVENIDA
NATÁLIA CORREIA

SÃO LUCAS
PRIVATE
HOSPITAL

BIGBLUE
ADVENTURES

MAIN
HOSPITAL

RUA ARCANJO LAR

RUA DA ARGUINHA

PALACE OF
SANT'ANA

VIP EXECUTIVE
AZORES HOTEL

Parque
Século
XXI

CARVÃO
CAVE

XITAKA

PARQUE
ATLÂNTICO
SHOPPING
MALL

AVENIDA DOM MANUEL

★ JOSÉ DO CANTO
BOTANICAL GARDEN

RUA DE SÃO GONÇALO

AVENIDA JOAO BOSCO
MOTA AMARAL

E-5

R1-1A

RUA DO PAIM

AVENIDA ANTERO DE QUENTAL

SÃO MIGUEL
PARK HOTEL

THE LINCE
AZORES HOTEL

AVENIDA DOM JOAO III

EN3-1A

Monumento
Natural da
Gruta do
Carvão

EN1-1A

RUA DIREITA
DO RAMALHO

RUA DIREITA DE
SANTA CATARINA

RUA DA VITORIA

RUA DE SANT'ANA

RUA DA MAE DE DEUS

RUA DO PERU

RUA DA BDA NOVA

EN1-1A

AZORES
ADVENTURE
ISLANDS

To
Cais 20

RUA JOSE DAS
NEVES FERREIRA

AVENIDA ALBERTO
PRINCIPE DE MONACO

RUA DE LISBOA

AZORES EPIC
ADVENTURES

LAVA JAZZ
CLUB AND BAR

CONVENT OF NOSSA
SENHORA DA ESPERANÇA

Porto de
Ponta
Delgada

SEE
"PONTA DELGADA
CENTER AND MARINA"
MAP

ferry to Santa Maria

PONTA DELGADA
AIRPORT

RUA PINTOR DOMINGOS REBELO

HOTEL
PONTA
DELGADA

5 DE OUTUBRO
SQUARE

1 RUA DE SANTA CLARA

FORT OF
SÃO BRÁS

ARCO 8
ART GALLERY
& BAR

ferry to Terceira

0          0.25 mi

0          0.25 km

Most of the city's restaurants and hotels are also centered around the waterfront, or scattered among the streets just set back from it. Finding a spot to park in Ponta Delgada can be a chore, even though there is plenty of **parking** along the waterfront (meter fees apply). At busier times there are plenty of parking lots (main city parking lots require payment, while parking on streets on the outskirts is often free) within the city and a large underground parking lot on the marina. Park up and explore the city **on foot.**

# SIGHTS
## City Center and Marina
### CITY GATES AND GONÇALO VELHO SQUARE
### (Portas da Cidade, Praça de Gonçalo Velho)

The imposing old gates to the city, a trio of large freestanding arches with a royal coat of arms on top, were built in the 18th century and are symbols of Ponta Delgada. This iconic gateway was formerly next to the old quay but was painstakingly deconstructed, relocated,

# Ponta Delgada Center and Marina

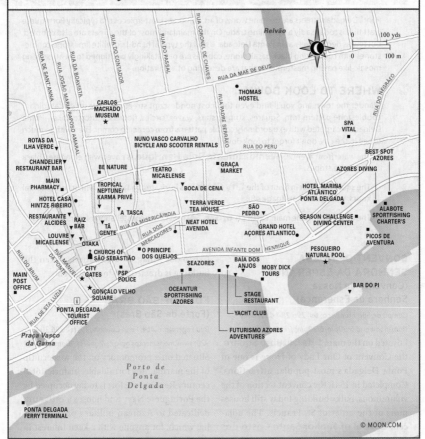

0  100 yds
0  100 m

© MOON.COM

and rebuilt in the decorative Gonçalo Velho Square at the same time as the main waterfront avenue was being built. An age-old local saying goes that those who walk through the gates twice will return to São Miguel, while those who walk through three times will return to the island to stay.

## CHURCH OF SÃO SEBASTIÃO
### (Igreja de São Sebastião)

*Largo da Matriz 62; tel. 296 285 321; Mon.-Sat. 7:30am-7pm, Sun. 7:30am-1pm and 4pm-6pm; free*
Rising from its starry cobblestone base like

the centerpiece on a fancy cake, the magnificent São Sebastião church, also referred to as the city's Mother Church (or main church), is a wonderful example of 16th-century Manueline architecture, with the Azores' trademark white with black trim. It was built on the site of a small chapel and expanded following extensions in the 18th century. The inside of the church is lavish, with intricate carvings, paintings from the 17th and 18th centuries, and swathes of opulent gilding. It also has the distinction of hosting the only tall clock tower in the city.

# The Streets of Ponta Delgada

Ponta Delgada's streets are genuine works of art, elaborate masterpieces of a typically Portuguese craft that is today sadly a dwindling trade: On the mainland most of the streets are also cobbled, but few as decoratively as in Ponta Delgada. Using the typical hand-laid white limestone cobblestones with contrasting black basalt stone, cobbles are painstakingly positioned to create striking mosaic-like paving masterpieces that are deserving of admiration.

## WHERE TO LOOK DOWN

Wander the town and you'll find even the most nondescript street can have an extraordinary cobblestone pattern trim. Squares, stripes, stars, waves, circles, flowers, intricate links—Ponta Delgada is carpeted with extraordinary cobble patterns from corner to corner. Even with so much to see in the city, don't forget to look down!

- The waterfront avenue, **Avenida Infante Dom Henrique,** is paved with elongated black and white stripes.

- The square laid out in front of the **City Gates** is as intricate as a tapestry, with its ornamental knots, twists, and stars (page 48).

- The area flanking the main **Church of São Sebastião** is constellation of stars (page 49).

## CONVENT OF NOSSA SENHORA DA ESPERANÇA (Convento de Nossa Senhora da Esperança)

*Campo de São Francisco; tel. 296 284 453; daily 11am-noon and 5:30pm-6:30pm; free*

Located on the main **5 de Outubro Square,** the Convent of Our Lady of Hope is one of Ponta Delgada's most popular attractions. Completed in 1541, the convent section of the voluminous, bulky building today still houses nuns of the order of St. Francis. The adjacent **Chapel of Senhor Santo Cristo dos Milagres** (Santuário do Senhor Santo Cristo dos Milagres) is closely linked to the worship of the Christ of the Miracles, a revered, spectacularly embellished statue in the image of Ecce Homo said to have been brought to the island in the 16th century. This statue is often hidden away in a sanctuary for safekeeping and can only be viewed at specific times (usually 5:30pm-6:30pm daily in winter, and 11am-noon and 5:30pm-6:30pm daily in summer), when the nuns allow visitors in.

The Convent and Chapel of Our Lady of Hope is one of the main pillars of the extravagant **Cult of the Lord Holy Christ of the Miracles Festival** (Festa do Senhor Santo Cristo dos Milagres) celebrations, when the building is dressed top-to-toe in lights.

## FORT OF SÃO BRÁS (Forte de São Brás)

*Rua Engenheiro Abel Ferin Coutinho 10; tel. 296 304 920; www.monumentos.gov.pt; Mon.-Fri. 10am-6pm; €3*

Situated on a promontory on the western tip of the marina, this formidable, historic 16th-century Renaissance fort is today occupied by the Portuguese Navy and houses a **museum** dedicated to Azorean military paraphernalia, which, for anyone with a keen interest in this field, is a treat. The exhibition halls of this once-active military post house a range of intriguing and characteristically Portuguese equipment and artifacts, ranging from army vehicles to weapons, and an exhibition dedicated to the Overseas War in the 1960s and early 1970s. A pleasant surprise for a rainy day.

Considered the most important example of 16th-century military architecture and the most powerful fortification on the island, the squat, bulky quadrangular fort was built to defend the city against pirate attacks that were

1: Ponta Delgada 2: Fort of São Brás

once a regular occurrence in this part of the Atlantic Ocean. Building of the fort started in 1552, and it underwent several changes and additions in the 19th century.

## CARLOS MACHADO MUSEUM
### (Museu Carlos Machado)

*Rua do Dr. Guilherme Poças 65; tel. 296 202 930; www.museucarlosmachado.azores.gov.pt; Tues.-Sun. 10am-5:30pm; €5*

Located inside the former site of the impressive 16th-century Santo André Monastery (Convento de Santo André), this museum explores natural history and local farming and fishing. Divided between the monastery and two additional sites within walking distance, the museum collection also includes local sacred art. It's a great option for a rainy day.

## JOSÉ DO CANTO
## BOTANICAL GARDEN
### (Jardim Botânico José do Canto)

*Rua José do Canto; tel. 296 650 310; www. josedocanto.com; daily 9am-5pm Oct.-Mar., daily 9am-7pm Apr.-Sept.; free*

North of the city center, the José do Canto Botanical Garden is a peaceful floral oasis in the heart of busy Ponta Delgada. Comprising colorful flowerbeds, exotic trees, a large lake, this area is also home to the **Palace of Sant'Ana** (Palácio de Sant'Ana; Rua José Jácome Correia; tel. 296 301 000, www.azores.gov.pt, Tues.-Sun. 10am-5pm; €2), an impressive salmon-colored palace. Also known as the Palácios da Presidência, today it's the seat of the office of the Presidency of the Regional Government. Built in the second half of the 19th century, it remained a family home until 1977, when it was purchased by the government. It's a lovely little refuge providing peace and tranquility and cooling shade on hotter days.

## Outskirts of Ponta Delgada
## ★ CARVÃO CAVE
### (Gruta do Carvão)

*Rua do Paim - 2ª Circular; tel. 961 397 080 or 296 284 155; http://grutadocarvao.amigosdosacores.pt; daily 10am-12:30pm and 2pm-6pm; €5*

On the northern outskirts of Ponta Delgada, the Carvão (coal) Cave is actually an ancient lava tube, believed to date back some 5,000-12,000 years, and is classified as a Natural Monument. Of great geological importance, the volcanically formed cave's walls are covered in spectacular speleological structures such as lava stalactites and stalagmites, balconies, benches, bridges, and ribbed walls. It is the biggest such formation on the island at nearly 2 kilometers (1 mi) in length. One of São Miguel's top attractions, it attracts some 15,000 visitors annually.

The experience starts at the little **visitor center,** which from the outside is rather underwhelming but inside is packed with information on the attraction. Pay at the ticket counter, then follow a long, narrow passage to a flight of stairs that leads to the belly of the pit. The walls drip with humidity as your eyes take a little while to adjust to the dark; overhead, an opening to the surface unexpectedly lets light in, relieving the claustrophobia of being underground. That being said, this is not an experience for the claustrophobic or less able-bodied.

Two **tours** are available: a shorter €5 tour, taking around half an hour; and an expanded guided tour for 2-4 people (€20, approx. 3 hours), which goes deeper into the cave's various stretches and should be booked in advance to avoid disappointment. Visitors are also free to look around the smaller main cavity by themselves as opposed to taking part in one of the tours. Inside the cave is damp and uneven underfoot, so good walking boots or sneakers are recommended with thick, non-slip soles.

## AUGUSTO ARRUDA
## PINEAPPLE PLANTATION
### (Plantação de Ananases Augusto Arruda)

*Rua Doutor Augusto Arruda; tel. 296 384 438; www. ananasesarruda.com; daily 9am-6pm; free*

Delve into the sticky-sweet joy of the famous

1: Carvão Cave 2: Pesqueiro Natural Pool

Azores pineapples with a trip to this historic plantation, which has a history spanning over 100 years and is open and free for the public to visit. Learn how pineapples are grown and harvested, understand their importance to the local economy, explore the greenhouses, and, of course, sample the delicious fruit. An on-site **gift shop** sells all kinds of pineapple souvenirs, from jams and liqueurs to actual pineapples.

## BEACHES AND POOLS

There are no beaches in Ponta Delgada itself, as the town is fronted by the marina and harbor. However, a short drive to the east of Ponta Delgada you'll find a string of sandy beaches, like **Pópulo Beach,** and a 45-minute drive northwest brings you to one of the best sandy beaches on the island, the surfing hotspot of **Mosteiros Beach.** The coast to the west of Ponta Delgada is peppered with tidal pools. The harbor does have a swimming pool of sorts, the Pesqueiro Natural Pool, fashioned from the sea, which is enjoyed by locals for daily exercise after work and on weekends.

### PESQUEIRO NATURAL POOL
### (Piscinas do Pesqueiro)

*Ponta Delgada Marina; open 24/7; free*
Located at the far end of Ponta Delgada's marina is this natural sea pool, where locals come daily for their exercise. Stairs provide access to the water, and a large cement deck offers space to stretch out and dry off afterward. Public bathrooms and showers are also on hand.

## KAYAKING AND STAND-UP PADDLE BOARDING

Dotted with mirror-like lakes surrounded by magical scenery and boasting a jaw-dropping coastline, São Miguel is a natural kayaker's playground. Kayaking and stand-up paddle boarding (SUP) are some of the best ways to really become immersed in the island's stunning beauty, and there are plenty of reputable companies based out of Ponta Delgada now operating such activities.

Though kayaking and SUP are possible around the marina and open ocean just off Ponta Delgada (kayakers and SUP-ers should avoid the port due to its activity), one of the best places to get out on the water is the **Sete Cidades Lake** in western São Miguel. The tour providers listed here all provide kayaking and SUP tours to this part of the island.

### FUTURISMO AZORES ADVENTURES

*Portas do Mar, Shop 26; tel. 296 628 522 or 967 805 101; www.futurismo.pt; daily 8am-6pm; hourly SUP rentals from €10*
With almost 30 years' experience, Futurismo Azores Adventures aims to showcase the incredible natural diversity of São Miguel on land and sea. Glide on the peaceful waters amid the amazing landscape of the Sete Cidades Lake on a kayak or stand-up paddle board, one of Futurismo's top-selling experiences.

### AZORES EPIC ADVENTURES

*Bairro da Misericórdia 32; tel. 964 874 556 or 913 354 197; www.azoresepicadventures.com; open 24/7; from €40 half day of kayaking*
Epic by name, epic by nature, this company's activities are designed for small groups to provide personalized experiences, built from extensive experience in nature tourism on the island. Though they also offer other types of outdoor activities, particularly canyoning and rock climbing, one of their more popular activities is a kayaking and SUP tour on Sete Cidades Lake.

### AZORES ADVENTURE ISLANDS

*Rua da Praia dos Santos 2; tel. 296 385 620 or 925 80 350; www.azoresadventureislands.com; daily 9am-5pm; from €55*
Canoe, kayak, or stand-up paddle in the tranquility of São Miguel's iconic lakes or open ocean. A personalized service by experienced guides promises fun and unforgettable experiences.

# ★ DIVING AND SNORKELING

The underwater scenery off the shores of São Miguel is exciting and varied. With shipwrecks and submerged volcanoes, seamounts and sharks, the most beautiful underwater flora in the archipelago, and interesting marine life, the waters around the island are justifiably among the Azores' top dive spots.

São Miguel also has some great spots for snorkelers. The best snorkeling in São Miguel is found away from the shoreline, such as at the famous **wreck of the *Edwin L. Drake,*** or the **hydrothermal vents** off the **Vila Franca do Campo Islet.** Various companies, such as those listed below, run snorkeling and dive excursions to these spots from Ponta Delgada. Joining one of these tours is the easiest and safest way to explore São Miguel's best dive spots, some of which are quite remote.

## Dive Spots
### WRECK OF THE *EDWIN L. DRAKE* (SS DORI)
*off Ponta Delgada*

Explore this unique dive site, a designated Subaquatic Archeological Park, located about 800 meters (2,600 ft) off the parish of São Roque, just east of Ponta Delgada, one of the most popular wreck dives in the Azores. This Liberty Ship, a cargo ship mass-produced in the United States, was built during World War II and sank off Ponta Delgada in 1964, en route from Europe to New Orleans, and has since attracted divers in droves. It's an awesome and eerie underwater landscape. The artificial reef it created over the decades teems with marine life, flora, colorful reef fish and grouper, octopus, and moray eels. Its well-preserved stern is particularly impressive, sitting at a depth of 9 meters (30 ft). Dive specialists, including Ponta Delgada-based **AzoresDiving,** organize dives to the *SS Dori* wreck.

## Diving Centers
### SEASON CHALLENGE DIVING CENTER
*Booking Center: Av. Dr. João Bosco Mota Amaral; tel. 914 464 511; www.seasonchallenge.pt; daily 8am-8pm; from €40*

This local Ponta Delgada-based company provides professional and personalized services for all levels of divers and trips to the best dive spots around the island.

### AZORESDIVING/AÇORDIVING SSI/MARES DIVE CENTER
*Marina Pêro de Teive, Kiosk A; tel. 296 285 900 or 927 382 023; www.azoresdiving.com; Mon.-Fri. 8am-8pm, Sat.-Sun. 8am-3pm; from €75*

A highly qualified and experienced team with modern equipment promises safe and unforgettable diving experiences in some of the many fascinating dive spots around the São Miguel coastline. Scuba diving (from €32 pp) and dive courses are also available.

### BEST SPOT AZORES DIVE CENTER
*Marina Pero de Teive, Kiosk B; tel. 963 469 932 or 912 108 658; www.bestspotazores.com; daily 8am-7pm; from €50*

Specializing in water activities and diving, Best Spot Azores runs dives and courses for everyone from beginners to the experienced, with customer satisfaction, safety, and sustainability underpinning the company's mission.

# FISHING

From deep sea fishing to a leisurely few hours casting off around the lakes, São Miguel island and its local companies cater to all genres of fishing. On land, **Fogo Lake** is a renowned spot for trout fishing, while the **Sete Cidades Lake** is popular among fly-fishers for carp, pike, perch, bass, and trout, among others.

However, fishing in lakes independently could require a **license;** double-check on the **Citizens Advice Portal** (https://riac.azores. gov.pt) before you venture off. **Befriending a** local with a little boat (most recreational fishermen will have one) is another way to reach the secret spots just offshore that locals fish in; otherwise, it may be easiest to join a **tour** organized by any of the companies below. For the best and biggest São Miguel fishing, join an organized fishing trip and be rewarded with lots of different—and large—species that thrive in the Azores' warm azure waters, like the famous tuna and marlin.

### OCEANTUR SPORTFISHING AZORES

*Av. Infante Dom Henrique; tel. 915 744 048; www. azores-sportfishing.com; daily 8am-5pm; half day of big-game fishing from €600 per group (max. 4 people)*

All aboard one of Oceantur's two boats for a few hours of exciting big-game fishing on the Azores' deep blue waters. An experienced captain and team are on hand to assist with all activities, from deep sea fishing to shark and big-game fishing, family fishing, and sunset and sea tours. Tours can be enjoyed even by those with little or no experience.

### SEAZORES

*Marina de Ponta Delgada Portas do Mar; tel. 962 812 678 or 962 642 737; www.seazores.net; daily 7:30am-7:30pm; from €490 half day*

Family-activity-oriented Seazores operates three types of fishing trips—Big-Game Fishing, Coastal Fishing, and Family Fun Fishing—and has the know-how to suggest the best techniques and spots to get the most from all options.

### ALABOTE SPORTFISHING CHARTERS

*Alabote Sportfishing Charters; tel. 917 405 792 or 912 271 414; https://sportfishingazores.com; daily 7am-11:30pm; from €600 half day*

This experienced local crew specializing in sportfishing and trolling for big-game species has been operating from Ponta Delgada since 1998. Fully equipped with all safety equipment, insured, and licensed, the spacious Alabote boat and its team—all lifelong fishermen, among them a marine biologist—is the go-to for a rewarding fishing experience.

# DOLPHIN- AND WHALE-WATCHING

The Azores' deep waters are home to one of the largest whale populations on the planet, with both resident and migrating species roaming the royal blue depths. Dolphin- and whale-watching trips run year-round, although generally the best time to see the graceful giants is spring, in **April and May,** when the seas are busiest with migrating species. Numerous companies operating on São Miguel specialize in these tours; a sighting is almost guaranteed on every trip. Dolphin- and whale-watching trips can be booked via hotel receptions or directly at the marina and normally run twice a day, morning and afternoon, starting from around €40.

### AZORES WHALE WATCHING TERRA AZUL

*tel. 296 581 361, www.azoreswhalewatch.com; daily 8:30am and 12:30pm; €55-60 for 2.5 hours*

This is one of Ponta Delgada's foremost whale-watching companies. Based at the Ponta Delgada marina and with over 15 years' experience in whale-watching, it provides a thrilling and educational experience. Trips depart from the marina and are guided by experienced marine biologists and naturalists.

### MOBY DICK TOURS

*Av. Infante Dom Henrique; tel. 919 942 831; www. mobydick-tours.com; 9am and 2pm; €40*

Jump onboard this restored former ferry to spend a few hours sailing the deep blue waters of the Atlantic in search of majestic whales. Be mesmerized as playful dolphins jump out of the water to play in the boat's wake. You might even spot a turtle gliding gracefully alongside the boat. An insightful experience is provided by the family-run company, who knows the Azores' waters like the backs of their hands.

## TERRA DO PICO

*Rua do Porto; tel. 910 330 029 or 296 915 264;*
*https://terradopico.com; 9am and 2:30pm; from €50*

Get up close and personal with some of the biggest mammals in the oceans on one of Terra do Pico's whale-watching excursions. Two tours are available—half day (2.5 hours) and full day (5 hours). Head out to some of the best spots to see the amazing wild animals in their natural habitat with this knowledgeable and experienced crew.

### BIGBLUE ADVENTURES

*tel. 914 372 990 or 966 078 829; www.bigblue-*
*adventures.com*

Explore São Miguel by sea or on foot with Big Blue Adventures, who specialize in island hikes and whale-watching tours. Embark on memorable adventures across the island, see its iconic sights, and learn everything there is to know from Big Blue Adventures's insightful guides.

## BIRD-WATCHING

The best time to visit the Azores for bird-watching is between **April and October,** but there's always something exciting happening on the islands for ornithologists. São Miguel houses a wide variety of habitats, from craggy coastal areas to boggy marshes, woodlands, lagoons, and misty mountains. One of the primary attractions for bird-watchers on São Miguel is the chance to spot the rare and elusive **Azores bullfinch,** found only in a small area of in the northeast part of the island. It's one of Europe's rarest birds. **Cory's shearwater** and **roseate terns** can also be seen on São Miguel, as can a wealth of migrant birds from the United States, ranging from shorebirds and wild-fowl to wood-warblers and vireos, which pass through the islands circa October. The **Vista do Rei viewpoint hike** in western São Miguel is a particularly popular trail among bird-watchers.

## PICOS DE AVENTURA

*Marina Pêro de Teive, Av. João Bosco Mota Amaral;*
*tel. 296 283 288; https://picosdeaventura.com; €75*
*full day*

Get ready for a full day of bird-watching with Picos de Aventura, whose guides take participants from the famous laurel forests of the northeast of the island to the island's coasts and lakes to see some of the more than 30 species of birds that can be found on the island. A picnic lunch is included. Binoculars and comfortable walking boots are a must!

## SPAS AND RELAXATION
### SPA VITAL

*Hotel Antillia, Rua do Peru n 105; tel. 296 098 889;*
*www.spavital.pt; Mon.-Fri. 10am-7pm, Sat. 9am-6pm;*
*treatments from €30*

Professionalism and impeccable attention to detail have made this little privately owned spa hugely popular among visitors and locals. A wide range of pampering treatments—some incorporating island produce such as Gorreana tea—at reasonable prices provide a relaxing and restorative experience for mind and body.

## ENTERTAINMENT AND EVENTS
### The Arts
### TEATRO MICAELENSE

*Rua de São João s/n; tel. 296 308 340; www.*
*teatromicaelense.pt; Mon.-Fri. 9am-6pm, Sat.*
*2pm-7pm; prices vary per event*

Once visited by legendary actor John Wayne, among other illustrious guests, the Teatro Micaelense cultural center was designed to promote local and regional culture as well as engage locals in the performing arts. Evocative of the grand theater of the 1950s, it shows an ever-changing program of cinema, plays, musical concerts, and dance productions. Inaugurated in 1951, the center occupies a historic building—a former convent—in the heart of Ponta Delgada.

## Festivals and Events
### ★ CULT OF THE LORD HOLY CHRIST OF THE MIRACLES FESTIVAL
### (Festa do Senhor Santo Cristo dos Milagres)

*Convent of Nossa Senhora da Esperança; starting fifth Saturday after Easter*

Held every year on the fifth Sunday after Easter, the time-honored, weeklong Cult of the Lord Holy Christ of the Miracles Festival dates back to the 17th century and is the most popular festival in the Azores and one of the most ancient in Portugal. It is intrinsically linked to local religious belief, and it attracts thousands of people every year to take part in and witness the processions and merriment.

The celebration venerates an ancient and ornate wooden statue of Christ in the Renaissance style, which is believed to date back as early as the 16th century. This cult image is usually tightly guarded in the Sanctuary of the Lord Holy Christ at the **Convent of Nossa Senhora da Esperança.** It is believed that the sacred statue was gifted in the 16th century by Pope Paul III to a group of nuns who went to Rome to request establishing their convent, which would become the first on the island, near Ponta Delgada. Devotion to the statue gained pace in the 17th and 18th centuries. History has it the roots of the festival are embedded in the year 1700 (although some historians would argue the late 1600s), when a series of earthquakes rattled São Miguel. Ponta Delgada's devout noble folk believed if they paraded the revered image along the streets it might clam God's wrath and stop the tremors. And so it became an annual tradition. The exact date of the very first procession is a point of controversy, with April 1700 and the year 1698 both being put forward.

Once a year the statue is brought out of the confines of the sanctuary and gleefully paraded through the main streets of Ponta Delgada, feted and festooned in bejeweled flowers and colorful garlands. It seems that the island's entire population pours into the streets of Ponta Delgada, along with pilgrims from all over the globe, to take part.

The festivities start on Saturday, marked by the Blessing of the Bread and Meat, and end on Ascension Thursday. The highlight is the huge three-hour procession on Sunday, with hundreds of brightly dressed participants singing and hoisting the revered statue. The entire city is decked out for the occasion, with flower rugs carpeting the main streets. In addition to what seems like São Miguel's whole population, many thousands of Azores emigrants also returning home at least once in their lives for the time-honored event.

Find yourself a nice spot along one of the main avenues, if possible on the waterfront or near the Convent Sanctuary, to really be amid the action as the caravan of the faithful files through. During the week of festivities, the town's main streets are carpeted with flowers and lit up with illuminations, carousels, and food stalls, and play host to a series of concerts.

### WALK & TALK FESTIVAL

*Streets of Ponta Delgada; https://walktalkazores.org; two weeks in mid-July*

Held every year in July (roughly around the two middle weeks of the month) the Walk & Talk Festival is a street art festival created to promote the island's cultural offerings in the realm of urban art. Every year scores of street artists descend on the city to create works of art, decorating the city's streets with colorful murals, sculptures, and performing arts shows. Designated routes are crated to take participants on a tour of these works of art. In 2016, the program expanded to Terceira Island.

### GREAT FESTIVAL OF FOLKLORE OF RELVA

*Relva parish; https://pt-pt.facebook.com/ festivalfolclorerelva; late July/early August*

A showcase for authentic island folk tradition, originally started to celebrate the local patron saint, this quirky one-day festival in the parish of Relva (just northwest of the city, near the Ponta Delgada Airport) sees people dress up in traditional costumes and dance the night away to the sound of island folk music. During the highlight of the event, local folk-dance groups show off their fancy footwork to live music. It also features folk-dancing groups from other guest countries and is usually held in Relva parish's 5 de Agosto garden.

## SHOPPING
### Souvenirs
#### BE NATURE

*Rua de São João 19 21; tel. 914 218 297; www. facebook.com/benatureportugal; Mon.-Fri. 10am-7:30pm, Sat. 9am-1pm*

At Be Nature, natural local materials are used to make beautiful souvenirs, from wooden handcrafted objects to handmade jewelry, soaps, and crockery. Pop into this amazing store for a unique gift.

### Malls
#### PARQUE ATLANTICO SHOPPING MALL

*Rua da Juventude; tel. 296 307 550; www. parqueatlanticoshopping.pt; Sun.-Thurs. 8:30am-10pm, Fri.-Sat. 8am-11pm*

This good size, modern shopping mall houses a range of European clothing chain stores, a large supermarket, a cinema, and food courts. With free underground parking, it's a good place to bear in mind if it's raining. It's also across the road from (or more precisely wedged between) two wonderful gardens, the historic **Jardim António Borges Garden** (Rua de São Joaquim 22; daily 9am-8pm; free), which has caves and exotic plants, and the well-groomed **José do Canto Bontanical Garden** (Rua José do Canto; tel. 296 650 310; daily 9am-7pm Apr.-Sept., daily 9am-5pm Oct.-Mar.; €4), sister garden of the Furnas Lake Forest Garden.

## FOOD
### Markets and Local Produce
#### GRAÇA MARKET
(Mercado Da Graça)

*Rua do Mercado; tel. 296 282 663; Mon.-Wed. 7:30am-6:30pm, Thurs. 7:30am-7pm, Fri.-Sat. 7am-2pm*

The local market, Mercado da Graça, is an opportunity to get up close with the island's intriguing local produce. Products to take home include cheeses and honey, hand-rolled cigars, and, of course, the island's famous Gorreana tea.

#### ★ O PRÍNCIPE DOS QUEIJOS

*Rua dos Mercadores 50; tel. 916 531 433; www. oprincipedosqueijos.pt; Mon.-Sat. 8am-8pm*

The ultimate cheese deli, O Príncipe dos Queijos (Prince of Cheese in Portuguese) is practically a temple of cheese. Packed with local cheeses in rounds of all sizes, a vast range of wines, and other local products to complement the cheeses, this little shop is a brilliant place to pop into for a souvenir or trappings for a picnic.

#### LOUVRE MICHAELENSE

*Rua António José D'Almeida 8; tel. 938 346 886; www.facebook.com/louvremichaelense; daily 9am-11pm*

Wall-to-wall wooden shelves are stocked with local artisanal produce at Louvre Michaelense, a former boutique that sold hats and fabrics from Paris. Today the shop is also a deli-café with a small menu and just a handful of tables, where patrons can sample local treats before they buy.

### Azorean
#### ★ A TASCA

*Rua do Alijube 16, tel. 296 288 880, Mon.-Sat. 11am-2am, Sun. 5pm-1am, €12*

Big portions of traditional Azorean food are served up at A Tasca, an unassuming back-street tavern with rustic wooden tables that are usually full due to its reputation as the island's best place to eat. Local fare is given a creative twist without being pretentious, and it's cheap. Due to demand, reservations are necessary.

# Pineapples, Tea, and Cheese

Gorreana Tea Plantation

Rustic, rich, and hearty, Azorean cuisine is bolstered by **homegrown cheeses,** of which many islands have their own varieties. On São Miguel, typical Azorean fare is accompanied by fresh **pineapples** and local **tea.**

- **Pineapples:** Dinky little sweet pineapples are grown widely in greenhouses and are unique to the archipelago, often eaten as a snack or as jam or a liqueur. To see where the pineapples are grown, pay a visit to the **Augusto Arruda Pineapple Plantation,** just outside Ponta Delgada, where you can take a free tour (page 52).

- **Tea:** A box of Gorreana tea from the island of São Miguel makes a fantastic gift. Distinctive to the Azores, it is lightweight and compact and can be enjoyed for months. Close your eyes and you'll be back in the Azores with every sip. Boxes of Gorreana tea (€4-8) can be purchased from any supermarket on the island; better yet, visit the **Gorreana Tea Plantation,** on the island's northeastern coast, to try some from the source (page 83).

- **Cheese:** You can almost taste the joy in cheeses produced by Azorean cows, which are jokingly widely referred to as "happy cows" thanks to their privileged lifestyle of tranquilly grazing lush green pastures with sea views from almost every field. They say on some islands there are more cows than people, and the archipelago is indeed a trove for quality dairy products. Most islands produce their own local cheeses; among the most popular on São Miguel are the **São Miguel Island Cheese,** a mature, hard cheese, and **Queijo do Vale,** which is produced in the spring town of Furnas. One of the best cheese shops on the island is **O Príncipe dos Queijos** (page 59).

## ★ CAIS 20

*Rua do Terreiro 41, São Roque; tel. 296 384 811, www. restaurantecais20.pt, daily noon-5am, €12*

Simple, understated Cais 20 is a restaurant with amazing sea views and amazing flavors, a 30-minute walk or a 4-minute drive east from Ponta Delgada's marina. Among the array of intriguing dishes and tapas, including the freshest island-caught shellfish, are barnacles and limpets, tuna kebabs, and whelk salad. Meat options to try are the local snack *pica-pau* (woodpecker) and small cubes of succulent beef in tasty beer gravy, as well as *pregos* (beef sandwiches). The restaurant is open late in the parish of São Roque, 2 kilometers (1 mi) east of Ponta Delgada.

## SACA-ROLHAS TABERNA

*Rua Nova 50, Relva; tel. 296 716 747; www. sacarolhas.pt; Mon.-Sat. noon-3pm and 7pm-11pm; €18*

Another of Ponta Delgada's most popular little taverns, Saca Rolhas Taberna, which translates as "corkscrew," is a cozy eatery where the menu showcases a wide range of typical local fish and meat, along with cold meats, cheeses, homemade soups, and desserts.

## RESTAURANTE SÃO PEDRO

*Largo Almirante Dunn 23A; tel. 296 281 600; www. restaurantesaopedro.com; Mon.-Fri. noon-3pm and 6pm-11pm, Sat.-Sun. 6pm-11pm, €18*

The island-inspired interior design of Restaurante São Pedro reflects its vast traditional menu of Azorean classics. Dishes include codfish tenderloin, forkbeard (a deep-sea fish) fillets, and Azorean beefsteaks.

## RESTAURANTE ALCIDES

*Rua Hintze Ribeiro 61-77; tel. 296 282 677; https:// alcides.pt; Mon.-Sat. noon-3pm and 7pm-10pm; €20*

Renowned for its steaks, Alcides pays homage to the local happy cows. Azorean cheeses and wines and local desserts like island-grown pineapple also feature on the regional menu, along with a rainbow of traditional Azorean recipes, although it is the steaks that give Alcides its reputation. A lovely little restaurant with stone arches in a bright red townhouse, Alcides leaves an impression.

## XITAKA

*R. do Paim 149B; www.facebook.com/ xitakapontadelgada; noon-midnight daily; €30*

Renowned for having some of the best fresh fish and seafood on the island, elegant Xitaka showcases regional Azores gastronomy in huge, heaped portions. The restaurant is also large and decorated with a clean, modern style. An added bonus is that Xitaka provides a free shuttle service to nearby hotels.

## International
## ★ YACHT CLUB

*Av. Infante Dom Henrique 111; tel. 296 284 231; www. grupoanjos.pt; daily 11am-midnight, €20*

On the main marina at the newer end of the waterfront, the Yacht Club restaurant overlooks the pretty docks. Its waterfront location is the perfect place to enjoy fresh seafood and quality meats in a polished cosmopolitan environment.

## STAGE RESTAURANT

*Portas do Mar, Loja 23; tel. 296 284 231; www. grupoanjos.pt; Sun.-Thurs. 11:30am-11pm, Fri.- Sat. 11:30am-midnight; €20*

Located on the waterfront, near the marina, Stage restaurant is a perfect option for inexpensive, laid-back dining with a spot of people-watching. It has an indoor and outdoor seating area, and serves cuisine spanning an international spectrum that will be familiar to many Europeans, from fish and chips to burgers, pasta dishes, and fruity panna cottas for dessert, washed down with a great selection of beers and wines.

## BOCA DE CENA

*Rua de São João 4; tel. 965 055 455; daily 7pm-10pm; €30*

Delicious local cuisine, from starters to desserts, graces the tables of Boca de Cena. The chef here is the main man—welcomer, waiter, and chef—and he takes great pleasure in sharing his hosting and cookery skills with patrons. Local beef and tuna steaks take pride of place on the menu, in a dimly lit theatrical setting.

## OTAKA

*Rua Hintze Ribeiro 5; https://otaka-restaurant. negocio.site; Tues.-Sat. 7pm-10:30pm; €30*

Asian meets Azores at this fabulous fusion restaurant. Beautifully presented dishes created from a fusion of Japanese and South American cuisine flavors (nikkei cuisine), in a modern, intimate, and welcoming atmosphere. Desserts made from island fruits add a local twist to this high-end, pancontinental experience.

## Vegetarian
### ROTAS DA ILHA VERDE

*Rua de Pedro Homem 49; tel. 296 628 560; www. rotasilha.blogspot.pt; Mon.-Fri. lunch, Mon.-Sat. dinner 7pm and 9pm; €12*

As its name, "Routes of the Green Island," suggests, highly regarded Rotas da Ilha Verde takes diners on a vegetarian gastronomic journey through the island's cuisine. This small, charming restaurant has a wide and creative range of delicious vegetarian and gluten-free meals made from fresh local produce. Reservations are advised.

## Fine Dining
### CHANDELIER RESTAURANT BAR

*Rua de Pedro Homem N43, ground floor; tel. 968 474 569; Wed.-Sun. noon-2:30pm and 6:30pm-midnight; €30*

Chandelier is one of the island's swankiest restaurants, where gastronomy is a glamorous experience. The top choice for fine dining, it's one of those places where words like "deconstructed" are found on the menu, and presentation is as important as flavor and creativity. Super-cool, classy design with sleek wooden applications meets even sleeker food for an amazing dining experience.

## Cafés and Light Bites
### TERRA VERDE TEA HOUSE

*Rua de São João 16; tel. 296 628 264; https:// terra-verde-tea-house.negocio.site; Mon.-Sat. 9:30am-8pm; tea from €5*

This pretty little teahouse is in a traditional town building, where delicious Portuguese pastries and freshly baked local sweet treats are served with a large selection of teas.

# BARS AND NIGHTLIFE

There are a number of trendy bars toward the end of the marina. In addition, many little cafés and taverns that stay open late—some even hosting open-air karaoke—are scattered throughout the waterfront area.

## Bars
### BAR DO PI

*Av. Infante Dom Henrique, Portas do Mar; tel. 916 467 946; www.facebook.com/bardopi; Mon.-Thurs. 6pm-2am, Fri.-Sun. 4pm-4am*

This simple, busy bar on the waterfront has friendly service and fantastic views of the marina.

### TÃ GENTE

*Rua Manuel Inácio Correia 38; tel. 966 919 410; https://pt-pt.facebook.com/tagente; Mon.-Thurs. 5pm-1am, Fri.-Sat. 5pm-3am, Sun. 5pm-midnight*

Occupying the ground floor of a typical town building, the outside of Tã Gente bar gives no indication of how cool it is on the inside. Part historic part industrial, it's an architecturally intriguing place for a drink in the heart of Ponta Delgada.

### TROPICAL NEPTUNE

*Rua Manuel Inácio Correia 50; tel. 296 283 141; https://tropicalneptune.com; Mon.-Thurs. 8:30am-9:30pm, Fri. 8:30am-2:30am, Sat. 8:30am-3:30pm and 7:30pm-2:30am*

Tropical by name tropical by nature, Tropical Neptune bar is an oasis of thirst-quenching natural juices, smoothies, and cool cocktails. Accommodating staff, chill-out music, and relaxed vibes make this lively haunt popular with the cool crowd.

## Nightclubs
### ARCO 8 ART GALLERY & BAR

*Rua Azores Park 191; tel. 296 284 103; www.arco8. blogspot.pt; Tues.-Sat. 9pm-2am*

Ponta Delgada's top cultural venue, Arco 8 Art Gallery & Bar is on the western fringes of town, a 10-minute walk west of the Fort of São Brás but worth the trip, as the unique warehouse-like building has an alternative art gallery, cocktails, and frequent events.

### KARMA PRIVÉ

*Rua Manuel Inácio Correia 66; www.facebook.com/ karmaprive; Fri.-Sat. 11pm-8am; entry cover on some events: €3 women, €7.50 men*

Located in the heart of Ponta Delgada, Karma

Privé opens late; the DJ keeps the party going until dawn. Sponsored events and themed parties make it one of São Miguel's most popular late-night dance venues.

## Live Music
### LAVA JAZZ CLUB AND BAR
*Av. Roberto Ivens; tel. 917 350 418; Tues. and Sat. 9pm-midnight, Wed.-Fri. 5pm-late*

One of the island's most popular haunts, the Lava Jazz Club and Bar casts the spotlight on a foot-tapping live music scene, as well as providing a popular and cozy place for a drink.

### RAIZ BAR
*Rua Antonio Jose D'Almeida; tel. 966 919 410; www. facebook.com/raizbar; Tues.-Thurs. 10pm-3pm, Fri.-Sat. 10pm-6am*

Dark and funky, with an antique bathtub counting as part of the décor, alternative Raiz Bar is the place to go for an interesting drink and a dance. Located on the first floor of a historic 19th-century building in the heart of Ponta Delgada, overlooking the Portas da Cidade City Gates, Raiz puts on live entertainment and DJs on weekends.

### ★ BAÍA DOS ANJOS
*Portas do Mar, Loja 22; tel. 296 284 231; www. grupoanjos.pt; daily 9am-4am*

One of the biggest and busiest restaurant-bars on the waterfront, Baía dos Anjos enjoys a lovely location overlooking the harbor. Service is a well-oiled machine, and you can stop for a drink or dinner, with a menu comprising a number of traditional Azorean dishes. For a pre-dinner cocktail, try the unusual and refreshing pineapple gin and tonic. There is also live music some nights.

## ACCOMMODATIONS
### Under €100
### ★ THOMAS HOSTEL
*Rua da Mãe de Deus 20; tel. 296 653 921; https:// thomas-place.business.site; €80*

Located near Ponta Delgada's university—walking distance to the town center—small and friendly Thomas Hostel is a bright and clean budget-friendly accommodation in a great location. Basic but spacious rooms, from basic doubles to family rooms, some with sea views, are serviced daily.

### VIP EXECUTIVE AZORES HOTEL
*Rua de São Gonçalo; tel. 296 000 100; www. hotelazoresvipexecutive.com; €99 d*

The handsome VIP Executive Azores Hotel is a 1-kilometer (0.6-mi) stroll inland from the marina and has sleek yet simple rooms, two restaurants, and an indoor pool.

### €100-200
### NEAT HOTEL AVENIDA
*Rua Dr. José Bruno Tavares Carreiro; tel. 296 209 660; www.neathotelavenida.com; €100 d*

With 120 bedrooms, a cafeteria, lounge, gym, and meeting room, Neat Hotel Avenida is simple, smart, and conveniently located in the heart of Ponta Delgada. Accents of mossy green and dark basalt stone give this young and fresh unit a local vibe.

### THE LINCE AZORES HOTEL
*Av. Dom João III 29; tel. 296 630 000; www. thelince-azores.com; €120 d*

Contemporary and clean-lined with a modern glass facade, The Lince Azores Hotel, just a few hundred meters' walk up from the main waterfront, offers casual rooms with full amenities, a posh bar, and an indoor and outdoor pool.

### HOTEL MARINA ATLÂNTICO PONTA DELGADA
*Av. João Bosco Mota Amaral 1, 767; tel. 296 307 900; www.bensaude.pt; €120 d*

Hotel Marina Atlântico Ponta Delgada overlooks the marina and harbor in the heart of Ponta Delgada. An upscale choice, it has classically elegant rooms, a trendy bar, and an indoor lap pool.

### HOTEL PONTA DELGADA
*Rua João Francisco Cabral 49; tel. 296 209 480; www.hotelpdl.com; €136 d*

Excellently located in the heart of Ponta

Delgada, three-star Hotel Ponta Delgada offers reasonably priced clean and simple rooms, a heated indoor pool, a sauna, and a Turkish bath.

### ★ SÃO MIGUEL PARK HOTEL

*Rua Manuel Augusto Amaral s/n; tel. 296 306 000; www.bensaude.pt; €144 d*

Back from the western end of the main waterfront promenade, São Miguel Park Hotel is an easy stroll down into a quiet part of town near a large supermarket. Modern, welcoming, and well-presented, it has an outdoor pool, a heated indoor pool, a jetted tub, and very friendly, helpful staff.

### HOTEL CASA HINTZE RIBEIRO

*Rua Hintze Ribeiro 62; tel. 296 304 340; www.casahintzeribeiro.com; €150 d*

Ensconced on one of the main streets leading to the town center, family-friendly Hotel Casa Hintze Ribeiro is packed with charming details that nod to local heritage; *azulejo* tiles and overtones of deep blue and white give this little hotel a personalized feel. It also has a nice rooftop pool.

## Over €200

### ★ GRAND HOTEL AÇORES ATLANTICO

*Av. Infante Dom Henrique 113; tel. 296 302 200; www.grandhotelacoresatlantico.com; €250 d*

The grand dame of São Miguel hotels, the Grand Hotel Açores Atlantico is as impressive as it is imposing. Right on the waterfront with superb sea views, this classic hotel is a short walk to the town center. Immaculate rooms, impeccable service, and stylishly elegant modern-retro décor make staying at this hotel a special and enjoyable experience.

## INFORMATION AND SERVICES

Ponta Delgada, the largest town on the archipelago's main island, is well equipped with basic amenities, such as pharmacies and post offices, and to deal with medical emergencies. Only extreme cases of ill health are evacuated to the mainland. **ATMs** are easily found; there are several along Ponta Delgada's waterfront, throughout the main town, in all banks and most gas stations and large supermarkets, and also in the Parque Atlantico shopping mall.

- **Tourist office:** Av. Infante Dom Henrique; tel. 296 308 625; www.visitazores.com; daily 9am-6pm fall-spring, daily 9am-7pm summer
- **National emergency number:** 112
- **PSP police:** Rua da Alfândega 1; tel. 296 205 500; www.psp.pt
- **Main hospital:** Hospital do Divino Espírito Santo, Matriz, Av. D. Manuel I; tel. 296 203 000; www.hdes.pt
- **Private hospital:** São Lucas Private Hospital, Rua Bento José Morais 23, 1st Norte Direito; tel. 296 650 740; www.hpsl.pt
- **Main pharmacy:** Farmácia Popular, Rua Machado dos Santos 34; tel. 296 205 530
- **Main post office:** Rua Conselheiro Doutor Luís de Bettencourt Câmara; tel. 296 304 071; Mon.-Fri. 8:30am-6:30pm

## GETTING THERE
### From the Airport

The Ponta Delgada Airport's small single terminal is on the immediate outskirts of the city, 3 kilometers (2 mi) west of Ponta Delgada center, a 5-minute drive. A shuttle bus operated by **MiniBus** (tel. 967 995 536) runs hourly, every day of the week, 5am-midnight, between the airport and Ponta Delgada. Tickets are available from the airport kiosk on weekdays (7am-midnight), as well as on board from the driver. Tickets cost €4.50 one-way and the trip takes about 20 minutes.

There are plenty of **taxis** outside the airport's arrivals area (€10 into the city); **Associação Taxis Ponta Delgada** (tel. 296 302 530, 296 382 000, or 938 346 759, www.taxispdl.com) offers 24-hour service. Taxis are also found widely throughout the city. Fares vary depending on the time of day and whether you have luggage.

There is one main route—the **EN1-1A**

road—for the short, 5-kilometer (3-mi) drive between Ponta Delgada and the airport, and plenty of **parking,** paid and free, can be found throughout the city, although the waterfront area can get full, especially on weekends. Most roadside parking is free at night; the farther from the city center, the easier parking becomes to find.

## Bus

Collective transport on São Miguel is operated by three major companies: **Auto Viação Micaelense** (tel. 296 301 358), **Caetano Raposo & Pereiras (CRP)** (tel. 296 304 260), and **Varela & Ca.** (tel. 296 301 800). You can find the timetables here: http://horarios. visitazores.de/smiAVM.pdf. There are several major bus routes in and out of Ponta Delgada, connecting the city to the other main urban areas around the island and to its key locations including **Furnas, Nordeste Fogo Lake,** and **Sete Cidades.** Public transport to smaller, more rural areas can be patchy, however.

Useful routes for tourists include the Ponta Delgada-Furnas service (**110** and **318;** http:// horarios.visitazores.de/smiAVM.pdf; €5 oneway), which departs from various locations in Ponta Delgada including along the main waterfront avenue. Both routes take around 1.5 hours to Furnas and depart roughly every two hours between 7am-6pm. The bus from Ponta Delgada to Sete Cidades town (line **205**) takes around an hour and costs €3 oneway. It runs twice a day: once in the morning around 8:30am and once in the late afternoon around 6:50pm.

## GETTING AROUND

Getting around Ponta Delgada city can be done easily **on foot,** especially its historic center and waterfront area, as most of the main town attractions are found here. For attractions on the fringes of Ponta Delgada, a city-hall-run **mini-bus service** (www.cm-pontadelgada.pt/pages/16) is an option. It zips around the city center on four lines: Yellow, Green, Blue, and Orange. Single-trip tickets bought from the driver cost €0.50. On a rainy day, this is a great (and inexpensive way) to tour the less touristy parts of the city and get your bearings. A **rental car** comes in handy, however, to explore farther afield.

Using **taxis** for short hops in and around Ponta Delgada is affordable. The main company in Ponta Delgada is the **Central de Táxis de Ponta Delgada** (tel. 296 302 530; 24/7 service).

# Western São Miguel

Home to vastly diverse flora and staggering scenery, and prone to the four-seasons-in-one-day phenomenon, everything about western São Miguel is breathtaking and fleeting. The ever-changing landscapes and weather only add to this portion of the island's rugged and unpredictable allure. From sun-soaked coastal springs to misty mountains and mirror-like lakes surrounded by deep green vegetation, this side of the island boasts some of its most iconic landmarks and popular tourist spots, like the Sete Cidades Lake—São Miguel's ultimate calling card—and the Vista do Rei viewpoint. The western side of the island is also home to the Ponta da Ferraria natural pool, where hot spring water mixes with refreshing seawater, and the village of Mosteiros and its popular beach.

## ORIENTATION

From Ponta Delgada heading west, it is about a 40-minute drive, mostly on the **EN1-1A** road to the **Sete Cidades Lake,** arguably one of the island's most popular attractions. The Sete Cidades Lake lies inland, at the end of the **EN9-1A,** a windy road that forks off from the EN1-1A, but keep heading along the coast, and, close to its westernmost tip, you'll come to **Ponta da Ferraria,** a popular spa and coastal spot. Keep following the main EN1-1A and eventually you'll arrive at the town of **Rabo de Peixe,** where a modern freeway, the **EN3-1A,** cuts down the middle of the island, back to Ponta Delgada, opposite it on the south coast.

# SIGHTS

## ★ Sete Cidades Lake
### (Lagoa das Sete Cidades)

*EN9-1A; tel. 296 249 016; open 24/7; free*

The Azores' most famous vista is postcard-perfect and luxuriant Sete Cidades (Seven Cities) Lake. Five kilometers (3 mi) long and 12 kilometers (7 mi) around, the largest freshwater lake in the Azores is on the western tip of the island. Technically two large twin lakes in the crater of a giant dormant volcano surrounded by vibrant vegetation, the lakes are connected by a narrow, bridged strait and are locally called "Green Lake" and "Blue Lake," differing in how they reflect the sun. Folklore has it that the lakes were formed by the tears of a young princess and a local shepherd who fell in love but were forbidden from seeing each other by the king. The strikingly vivid colors of the lake are said to represent the princess's green eyes and the shepherd boy's blue eyes.

The natural area surrounding the lake is **Sete Cidades Park;** helpful information on sights and recreation in the area can be found at the park's **visitor center** (Arruamento da Lago das Sete Cidades; tel. 296 249 016; http://parquesnaturais.azores.gov.pt; Tues.-Fri. 10am-1pm and 1:30pm-5pm, Sat.-Sun. 2pm-5:30pm).

Down by the shores of Sete Cidades Lake is the **Vila das Sete Cidades,** or Sete Cidades village, a pretty little town of less than 1,000 inhabitants that comes to life in summer. The focal point in the village is the ever so cute and dainty **São Nicolau church,** built in 1857, with its scenic walkway, typical whitewash with basalt trim, and stairs that climb to the bell tower. The village hems the lake; you could spend a couple of hours down here on this green, lush shoreline. Enjoy lunch in one of the modern, wooden-box-like **restaurants** or rent a **kayak** or **SUP** board to take to the waters of the mirror-like lake.

**Trails** surround the lake, allowing hikers to appreciate the beauty from various angles. A popular trail for hikers in this area is from the cool and fragrant **Mata do Canário** pine woods, southeast of the lake, to Sete Cidades village. Another popular hike starts from the **Vista do Rei** viewpoint and also ends in the village, following a dirt path along the crater rim, with wide open sweeping views on both sides.

## VISTA DO REI VIEWPOINT
### (Miradouro da Vista do Rei)

*Road 9-1 142; tel. 917 189 250; open 24/7; free*

Perhaps São Miguel's most famous viewpoint, the Vista do Rei is the ultimate photo-op. Overlooking the stunning Sete Cidades Lake, with its twin lakes of different colors, one jade the other blue, this is also where'll you find an eerie abandoned old hotel that is being slowly reclaimed by nature. Located at the southern end of Sete Cidades Lake, the Vista do Rei viewpoint also has parking spaces, snack vans, toilets, and benches. It's possible to hike between Sete Cidades village and the viewpoint on the **Visto do Rei viewpoint hike (PR3SMI).**

Expect it to become pretty crowded, especially if the weather is lovely and sunny or if a tour bus pulls up—visit later in the day to avoid congestion and early-morning clouds. Make sure you check your weather app; the viewpoint is at its best with good, clear weather.

## GROTA DO INFERNO VIEWPOINT
### (Miradouro da Grota do Inferno)

*Rua Ribeira do Ferreiro 117, Candelaria; http://parquesnaturais.azores.gov.pt; open 24/7; free*

East from the Vista do Rei viewpoint is another famous belvedere, the Grota do Inferno viewpoint. Offering a fabulous side view over the lagoon-filled craters, the vistas from here are breathtaking. Slightly higher than the Vista do Rei, this viewpoint involves a few minutes' hike up to it from the parking lot, but the views more than reward the trek.

## Ribeira Grande
### ARQUIPÉLAGO CONTEMPORARY ARTS CENTER
### (Arquipélago Centro de Artes Contemporâneas)
*Rua Adolfo Coutinho de Medeiros s/n; tel. 296 470 130; http://arquipelagocentrodeartes.azores.gov.pt; Tues.-Sun. 10am-6pm; €3*

The rather severe-looking Arquipélago Arts Center, in the town of **Ribeira Grande,** was conceived as a home to the contemporary arts. Created from black basalt rock in a traditional-contemporary hybrid architectural design, it aims to promote and divulge the visual, audiovisual/multimedia, and performing arts. Housed in a converted alcohol factory, it comprises exhibits, shows, performing arts, and workshops on its program.

# BEACHES AND POOLS

Bathing sites along São Miguel's west coast on the south side of the island are predominantly natural tidal pools rather than sandy beaches. One of the island's—indeed the archipelago's—most famous tidal pools, Ponta da Ferraria, where hot spring water mixes with cool seawater, is on this stretch. The western side of São Miguel does have some outstanding sandy beaches, such as Mosteiros and Santa Bárbara Beach, on the north coast.

## Mosteiros
### PONTA DA FERRARIA NATURAL SWIMMING POOL
### (Piscina Natural da Ponta da Ferraria)
*Rua Padre Fernando Vieira Gomes; open 24/7; free*

The Ponta da Ferraria natural pool, a 35-minute (26 km/16 mi) drive west from Ponta Delgada along the EN1-1A road, is a unique attraction located on rocky volcanic cliffs at the end of a rather steep, hairpin road. The pool is formed by the island's far southwesternmost edge sitting in the sea, which on the one hand receives hot spring water from São Miguel's innards, and on the other is mixed with bursts of cool seawater that come and go with waves from the ocean, making the water consistently lukewarm, more pleasant than the pure waters of the nearby Atlantic.

Small ladders lead down to the pool, which is unsupervised but crisscrossed with rope for swimmers to hang onto as they bob about in the surf, which at times can get pretty rough. Take care if it is choppy, as the rocks are jagged and quite sharp. If you want to dry off afterward, spread your towel out on the black basalt rock and soak up some rays. A little thermal spa nearby, **Termas da Ferraria** (Rua Ilha Sabrina; tel. 296 295 669; http://termasdaferraria.com; Tues.-Sun. 11am-7pm; massages from €35), harnesses hot water from another local spring for its spa and treatments, and it has restrooms and a café.

### MOSTEIROS BEACH
### (Praia dos Mosteiros)
*Rua da Areia, Mosteiros; open 24/7; free*

A 45-minute drive northwest of Ponta Delgada, Mosteiros Beach is one of São Miguel's most popular black sand beaches. It's shaped like a bay, with basalt stacks poking out of the sea just offshore, and when the weather is fine the waters here are tranquil and calm. A rocky outcrop at the top end of the beach provides some protection on choppier sea days, though the sea can at times get rough, making this beach also popular with surfers. The sunsets on this gorgeous stretch of shoreline are famed, and plenty of parking and little cafés can be found within the vicinity of the beach.

## Capelas
### POÇOS DE SÃO VICENTE BATHING AREA
*São Vicente Ferreira parish; 24/7; free*

Close to the parish of São Vicente Ferreira, this dramatic tidal pool is moody and untamed. Fronted by dramatic, spiky volcanic

rocks and with a smooth cement deck and stairs, it's a remarkable blend of man-made and mother nature at her best. It's one of the area's most popular natural bathing spots, and there is plenty of **parking** along a waterfront road that hems the coast and connects to the site, which also has **showers** to rinse off the salt water and a **bar** nearby.

## Ribeira Grande
### SANTA BÁRBARA BEACH
### (Praia de Santa Bárbara)
*Ribeira Grande; open 24/7; free*

Wedged between two large grass-covered cliffs on the north side of São Miguel island, a 20-minute drive from Ponta Delgada, this long, black sand beach near the town of Ribeira Grande is spacious and scenic. Manned by lifeguards for most of the year, this beach also offers great surfing, with **Santa Barbara Beach Surf School** (www.santabarbarasurfschoolazores.com) on site. There's also a **café, changing rooms, showers** and a free **parking lot** on its doorstep.

## São Roque
### PÓPULO BEACH
### (Praia do Pópulo)
*Estrada Regional do Pópulo, São Roque; 24/7; free*

A 10-minute (4-km/2-mi) drive east along the coast from Ponta Delgada lies the large Pópulo Beach, one of the best beaches on the island for a swim and a sundowner, thanks to its awesome sunsets. It has plenty of free parking in the immediate surroundings and a fantastic beach bar, the **Sunset Beach Restaurant & Bar,** for a snack and a drink with a view.

# KAYAKING AND STAND-UP PADDLE BOARDING

The mirror-like waters of Sete Cidades Lake are also perfect for kayaking and stand-up paddle boarding, available from

1: Sete Cidades Lake 2: Ponta da Ferraria natural swimming pool 3: town of Ribeira Grande 4: Mosteiros Beach

rental outfitters on the shore in the parish of Sete Cidades. Many outfitters based in Ponta Delgada, such as **Futurismo Azores Adventures** (www.futurismo.pt) also operate tours to the Sete Cidades area.

## Sete Cidades Lake
### GAROUPA CANOE TOURS
*Lagoa das Sete Cidades, Sete Cidades; tel. 917 158 701; www.garoupa.pt; open 24/7; from €10*

Specializing in kayaking and SUP, Garoupa organizes canoe tours across the island. The company is based near Sete Cidades Lake.

# SURFING

São Miguel's north coast, toward the western end of the island, is one of Europe's best secret surf spots. **Mosteiros Beach** and **Santa Bárbara Beach** are both considered the best places to surf on the island—Santa Bárbara thanks to its long beach breaks and great waves, and Mosteiros due to its fun swells and awesome backdrop. Closer to Ponta Delgada, on the south coast, **Pópulo Beach** is also a popular, albeit tamer, surf spot, great for beginners, where local surfers often hang out.

## Ribeira Grande
### SANTA BARBARA SURF SCHOOL
*Estrada Regional, No.1, 1 Morro de Baixo (Ribeira Grande - north coast); tel. 963 428 849 or 927 319 437; www.santabarbarasurfschoolazores.com; daily 9am-7pm; lessons from €30, board rentals from €20/day*

With over 20 years' experience surfing the Azores, the Santa Barbara Surf School, on the west side of Santa Bárbara Beach, was created with the aim of unlocking the door to the delights of São Miguel's little-known surf scene. Experienced instructors, quality equipment, and local insight make for unforgettable moments on the waves. Lessons, board and equipment rentals (surfboards, SUP boards, boogie boards, duck feet, goggles, winter and summer wet suits, and even snorkels), and guided trips are all available from this certified company.

# Island Charm: Western São Miguel's Seaside Villages

Heading northeast from **Ponta da Ferraria** on the **EN1-1A**, you'll encounter **Mosteiros Beach** and the village of Mosteiros, the first in a series of picturesque villages as you round the island's northwestern coast. Driving the coast and making stops in these villages makes for a wonderful afternoon.

**Parking** in all of these villages is free and relatively easy, though in the peak of summer the island can be a little more crowded.

## MOSTEIROS

Occupying the westernmost tip of São Miguel, Mosteiros (8.6 km/5.3 mi, 15 minutes north of the Ponta da Ferraria natural pool along the EN1-1A) is a charming seaside village surrounded by deep green pastures smattered with little whitewashed cottages. Sought after for the long black-sand **Mosteiros Beach,** it is a quiet village and a popular holiday home destination.

## CAPELAS

A quaint parish on the north coast of São Miguel, Capelas (24 km/15 mi, 35 minutes east from Mosteiros along the EN1-1A) seems to be untouched by the hands of time. Its pretty whitewashed town **church** with dark basalt trim is unmistakably Azorean. The landscape surrounding it varies from farmlands to mountains, river valleys, and ancient volcanic cones. It has two small **ports,** one of which played a vital role during the centuries when Capelas was a key whaling center.

## CALHETAS

The smallest parish in the Ribeira Grande region of São Miguel's north coast, Calhetas (7.7 km/4.8 mi, 12 minutes east along the EN1-1A from Capelas) takes its name from its jagged, rocky terrain. Despite its small size, this pint-sized parish contains a number of historically interesting buildings, such as the monastery of **Nossa Senhora das Mercês,** a working monastery, and the parish **church,** which dates to 1830.

## RABO DE PEIXE

Northeast of Ponta Delgada and neighboring Calhetas to the west, Rabo de Peixe (whose name means "Fish Tail") is a traditional, down-to-earth town. One of the most populated towns on the north coast, it is an area deeply influenced by local heritage and culture and whose modern **harbor** is the community's lifeblood. It's fishing history—Rabo de Peixe is famed for being the largest fishing community and port in the Azores—and strong links to the sea are also accentuated in the local architecture.

## São Roque
### AZORES SURF SCHOOL

*Canada do Borralho 26; tel. 914 012 978; http://azoressurfschool.com; Tues.-Sat. 8:30am-10:30pm, Sun.-Mon. 8am-10:30pm; lessons from €30, board rentals from €20/day*

Located next to popular surf spot Pópulo Beach on São Miguel's south coast, just outside Ponta Delgada, the Azores Surf School was founded in 2004 by national big rider and coach José Seabra. It provides everything traveling surfers need to enjoy the Azores waves. Lesson, equipment rentals, workshops, guided trips, and even surf yoga are some of the services provided by this busy and fully certified school.

## HIKING

Western São Miguel is home to some of the most iconic hikes in the entire Azores. Both hikes alongside the Sete Cidades Lake, from the Mata do Canário woods or Vista do Rei viewpoint, are stunningly scenic and easy. Enjoy verdant volcanic landscapes on one side and endless glinting ocean on the other, and make sure to bring a camera and some water.

## MOSTEIROS-PONTA DO ESCALVADO-PONTA DA FERRARIA-GINETES

**Hiking Distance:** 9.9 (6.2 mi) round-trip
**Hiking Time:** 2 hours round trip
**Trailhead:** Varzea parish
**Information and Maps:** www.alltrails.com/ trail/portugal/azores/varzea-and-mosteiros?u=i

Breathe in the bracing air on this popular, easy circular hike that follows scenic coastline between two pretty villages and skirts the ridge of the Sete Cidades caldera. Starting in the northwestern parish of Varzea, you then follow the route inland through the countryside toward the ridge of Sete Cidades. The landscape vistas from the ridge, of deep green on one side and bright blue on the other, are glorious. From here begins a gradual downward trek toward the coastal village of Mosteiros, from where you'll head south along the coastline, with its scenic vistas of offshore volcanic rock formations, back to the starting point in Varzea. Once back in Varzea, if you fancy a relaxing soak to soothe your legs, it's an extra 40-minute walk—or 7-minute drive—south to Ponta da Ferraria. You can catch the bus to Varzea and back to Ponta Delgada (**Line 206;** http://horarios. visitazores.de/smiAVM.pdf; runs every couple of hours; 40 minutes; €3).

## VISTO DO REI VIEWPOINT HIKE (PR3SMI)

**Hiking Distance:** 15.4 kilometers (9.6 mi) round-trip
**Hiking Time:** 4-5 hours round-trip
**Trailhead:** Visto do Rei viewpoint
**Information and Maps:** http://trails. visitazores.com; maps also available from tourist offices

An easy, though lengthy, linear hike exploring the verdant slopes of the southwest Sete Cidades ridges, this hike takes in the interior of the volcano's crater and incredible twin lakes and views of Mosteiros village, and ends in **Sete Cidades village.** It goes through scenic protected landscape and is also a popular bird-watching trail.

## MATA DO CANÁRIO-SETE CIDADES (PRC4SMI)

**Hiking Distance:** 11.8 kilometers (7.3 mi) one way
**Hiking Time:** 3.5-4 hours one way
**Trailhead:** Mata do Canário woods (eastern ridge of Sete Cidades Lake)
**Information and Maps:** http://trails. visitazores.com; maps also available from tourist offices

This stunning hike follows the crest of the volcanic caldera, from the Mata do Canário woods to the **Pico da Cruz viewpoint,** and runs around the rim of the lake to end in **Sete Cidades village.** Amazing views can be enjoyed at every twist and turn of the trek, from rolling meadows on one side to the sea on the other—make sure to bring a camera. The trail is mostly easy but can be steep and slippery in parts if the weather is inclement. It ends near the **São Nicolau church** in Sete Cidades village, where you can catch the bus (**318** or **110;** http://horarios.visitazores.de/ smiAVM.pdf; at least twice daily; €3-5 one way) back to Ponta Delgada.

## VIGIA DE SÃO PEDRO (SÃO VICENTE FERREIRAS-CALHETAS) (PR1SMI)

**Hiking Distance:** 6.5 kilometers (4 mi) one way
**Hiking Time:** 2 hours one way
**Trailhead:** Poços de São Vicente bathing area
**Information and Maps:** http://trails. visitazores.com/en/trails-azores/sao-miguel/vigia- de-sao-pedro

Starting in the parish of São Vicente Ferreira (13 km/8 mi, 15 minutes straight north of Ponta Delgada) at a bathing area near the local fishing port, this easy, linear route is an enjoyable leg-stretch along the north coast between the Poços de São Vicente bathing area and the town of Calhetas. See the remnants of an old whaling factory, traditional 17th- and 18th-century houses, churches, and chapels, and wonderful views over the north coast. From Calhetas, you can catch the bus back to São Roque, just east of Ponta Delgada (line **102;** http://horarios.visitazores.de/ smiAVM.pdf; departs hourly; 18 minutes; €2), and walk the 45 minutes back to Ponta Delgada (3.5 km/2.2 mi).

# SPAS AND RELAXATION

There are, generally, two types of spas on São Miguel island: sumptuous hotel spas, found in the island's more up-market hotels, and natural spring spas, called termas, whose hot waters are channeled into well-equipped indoor facilities where bathing pools are complemented by massage treatment rooms. Termas will require a small payment for access (treatment options cost extra) and will often also ask visitors to wear a swimming cap and flip-flops.

## Mosteiros
### TERMAS DA FERRARIA

*Rua Ilha Sabrina; tel. 296 295 669; http://termasdaferraria.com; Tues.-Sun. 11am-7pm; massages from €35*

Situated on the black volcanic outcrop of Ponta da Ferraria, overlooking the Atlantic at the southwesternmost point on the island, this small spa retreat harnesses the local hot volcanic spring water to provide soothing dips in its indoor pool to ease your aches and pains. It also offers a range of massages and treatments, including the Azorean Stone Massage, and has an outdoor pool and a restaurant/bar.

## Calhetas
### PEDRAS DO MAR RESORT & SPA

*Rua das Terças 3; tel. 296 249 300; http://pedrasdomar.com; daily 9am-7pm; massages from €45*

Indulge in a little relaxation and restoration at the elegant Pedras do Mar Resort's beautiful spa. From a signature Volcanic Stones massage to anti-stress and therapeutic back massages, the Pedras do Mar spa also has beauty treatments and facials on its extensive menu.

## Ribeira Grande
### HOTEL VERDE MAR & SPA

*EN1-1A, Ribeira Grande; tel. 296 247 710; https://verdemarhotel.com; daily 9am-9pm; massages from €45*

Located a short walk from Monte Verde Beach with stunning views of the island's north coast, the Hotel Verde Mar & Spa's wellness center offers all treatments to soothe and pamper body and soul. From medical therapies to indulgent signature rituals, beauty treatments, and massages, this refined spa is a haven of well-being.

# FOOD AND BARS

Small cafés and eateries dot the little settlements along São Miguel's northwest coast. Many of western São Miguel's best eateries can be found in **Rabo de Peixe** and **Ribeira Grande,** just a 20-minute drive or so north from Ponta Delgada.

## Sete Cidades Lake
### GREEN LOVE

*9-1 23, Sete Cidades; tel. 296 915 214 or 914 229 699; Mon.-Thurs. 9:30am-6pm, Fri.-Sun. 9:30am-9:30pm; €15*

Located on the grassy edge of Sete Cidades Lake, this café is a lovely spot to sit and enjoy a coffee and a cake, or a light lunch while the kids run free on the embankment. Sandwiches, burgers, fries, and more substantial meals like grilled chicken make up the reasonably priced menu at this cafeteria-like eatery.

## Rabo de Peixe
### QUINTA DOS SABORES

*Rua Caminho Da Selada, n10; tel. 917 003 020; www.facebook.com/QuintadosSabores.Oficial; Tues.-Sat. 7:30pm-9pm; €40*

With its homely setting, dining at Quinta dos Sabores provides an authentic island dining experience, like enjoying a meal with a local family. All dishes are typically regional and use the freshest locally grown ingredients. The menu is spread over a set multicourse experience, with each course providing the real flavors of São Miguel, from cheese and dips to trigger fish and braised steak on local bread. Originality and flair shines through what is a subtle fine-dining experience.

## Ribeira Grande

### ASSOCIAÇÃO AGRICOLA DE SÃO MIGUEL

*São Miguel Farming Association, Campo do Santana, Recinto da Feira exhibition venue, Rabo de Peixe; tel. 296 490 001 or 926 385 995; www.restauranteaasm. com; daily noon-11pm; €20*

The Associação Agricola de São Miguel, despite its countrified name, is actually a refined restaurant in a contemporary exhibition building. The star of the show is local beefsteak, although plenty of other Azorean specialties, like black pudding with pineapple, are on the menu. The restaurant is in the parish of Rabo de Peixe, 15 kilometers (9 mi) northeast of Ponta Delgada.

### RESTAURANTE O PESCADOR

*EN1, Rua do Biscoito, n.1/3; tel. 925 105 405; Wed.-Mon. noon-10pm; €25*

O Pescador (which appropriately translates to "The Fisherman") does seafood—really well. It's a bit of an institution for all foods from the sea, though from the outside the restaurant looks deceivingly simple and basic. Inside, its sea-inspired color scheme and fishing paraphernalia décor is pleasant, but the menu, full of delicious recipes like seafood stew, fish soup, fresh grilled fish, and shellfish starters, is fantastic.

### TUKÁ TULÁ BAR

*Rua Areal Santa Bárbara, Ribeira Grande; tel. 296 477 647; www.facebook.com/tukatula.bar; Tues.-Sun. 10am-8pm; €15*

Like a burst of sunshine on Santa Bárbara beach in Ribeira Grande, this tropical beach bar is popular for its amazing sunset and beach views. It's a lovely spot for a drink and snacks; try the wraps, tuna steak burger, and pineapple gin sundowners.

## São Roque

### SUNSET BEACH RESTAURANT & BAR

*Canada do Borralho, Pópulo Beach; tel. 911 050 309; Thurs.-Fri. 8am-2am, Sat.-Wed. 8am-1am; €15*

Overlooking the lovely Pópulo Beach, this pleasant beach bar offers some of the best sunset views on the island. Drinks are reasonably priced, and the menu is uncomplicated and solid with good fresh produce. It's a great place for a family meal after a few hours at the beach or a relaxed sundowner.

# INFORMATION AND SERVICES

There are fewer amenities like banks and big supermarkets at this end of the island despite it being home to one of the island's most famous landmarks. That said, most little towns and parishes will have an ATM, and the bigger ones perhaps a pharmacy and post office.

# GETTING THERE AND AROUND

**Sete Cidades Lake** is 25 kilometers (16 mi) northwest from Ponta Delgada, a 30-minute drive on the **EN1-1A** and **9-1** roads. It is possible to get to Sete Cidades village by local **bus;** the **205** line runs between Ponta Delgada's **Bairro do Ramalho stop** and drops off near the São Nicolau church in Sete Cidades. This takes around an hour, but costs just €3. Be aware, though, there are only a couple of direct services every day, one at around 8:30am and the other just before 7pm. Alternatively, a **taxi** will cost between €30 and €40, one-way, and takes 30 minutes.

There is a regular bus service along the coast between Ponta Delgada and **Ponta da Ferraria** (line **206**), which stops in the nearby village of Ginetes, and from there it's about a 2-kilometer (1-mi) walk to Ponta da Ferraria. The same line also runs on to the village of Mosteiros. It takes roughly 45 minutes to **Ginetes** and 55 minutes to **Mosteiros** (€3). That said, as with the rest of the island, the best way to get around this part of São Miguel is either by guided **tour,** for example a kayak excursion out of Ponta Delgada with **Futurismo Azores Adventures,** or by **renting a car.**

# Furnas

The unique valley of Furnas and its eponymous village and nearby lake are under an hour's drive from Ponta Delgada, almost in the island's center. This inland hamlet is a spa resort, a busy tourist attraction, and a kooky gastronomic outpost, all fueled by simmering geothermal activity. Geysers and fumaroles hiss and splutter with boiling water; steaming springs form popular, privately managed communal thermal pools, and the island's signature dish, *cozido das Furnas,* is cooked underground on the shores of Furnas Lake and served in restaurants around the village. Visitors flock to Terra Nostra Park, a luxuriant oasis of tranquility in the heart of the busy little hamlet. The nearby Poça da Dona Beija hot springs are another of the island's top attractions. A whole day or two can be spent in this exhilarating community. It's a beautiful place for a romantic break for two.

## SIGHTS
### Furnas Lake
#### (Lagoa das Furnas)

A 10-minute drive southwest of Furnas village, Furnas Lake is the second-largest lake on São Miguel. It lacks the breathtaking beauty of Sete Cidades but is still compelling; its intense heat and sulfurous smell make for a humbling hike if you choose to walk some of the **trails** surrounding the lake. It's impressive to experience the trembling power of the earth rumbling underfoot. The town's famed culinary curiosity—stew cooked in the underground heat of the lake's shore—takes place in the fumaroles *(fumerolas)* at the northern tip of the lake, in an area known as the Caldeiras.

### FURNAS LAKE HOT SPRINGS
#### (Caldeiras da Lagoa das Furnas)

*Furnas Lake shore; tel. 296 588 019; open 24/7; €2*
The northern swathe of the Furnas Lake shore is occupied by bubbling fumaroles where the local specialty, *cozido das Furnas,* is cooked.

Here visitors can follow a wooden walkway that snakes safely through the hissing, spitting geysers and bubbling mud pools. Be prepared to be enveloped by hot, eggy-smelling sulfurous steam as you wander around. The steaming holes offer an indication of just how hot the earth's core is. In the early morning, huge steel pots are lowered into the ground and covered, then left for several hours to cook the local stew before being removed around midday, loaded into waiting vans, and zipped off to nearby restaurants. This culinary curiosity has taken place for decades, having started as a local delicacy before rocketing into a massive tourist pull. Some of the fumaroles are allocated to designated local restaurants while others belong to locals, who bring their own pots and pans and ingredients to cook their own *cozido.* To appreciate this unique geothermal gastronomy, visit around noon, when the large metal pots are lifted out.

The Caldeiras have ample **parking** on-site, included in the €2 entry fee.

### FURNAS MONITORING AND RESEARCH CENTRE

*Rua da Lagoa das Furnas 1489; tel. 296 584 436; http://parquesnaturais.azores.gov.pt/pt/ smiguel/o-que-visitar/centros-ambientais/centro- de-monitorizacao-e-investigacao-das-furnas; daily 10am-6pm; €3*
The Furnas Monitoring and Research Centre (CMIF) is part of a wider and unique project, the Furnas Lake Land Development and Watershed Plan, created with the purpose of promoting and protecting the history and evolution of the Furnas Volcano and surrounding protected landscape. Located on the Furnas Lake south bank, the futuristic-looking angular slate building, which has won architectural awards, houses a number of interesting exhibitions, including interactive and multimedia exhibits, on the region's singular volcanic geodiversity, biodiversity,

# Furnas

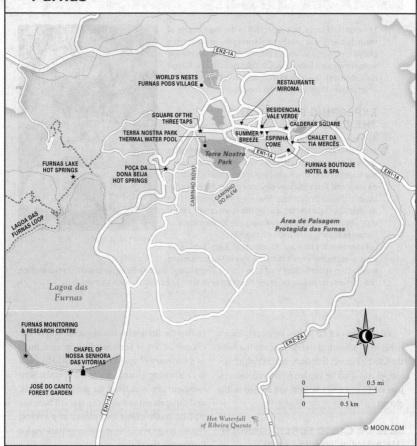

hydrology, and culture. It's worth the small admission fee for the in-depth understanding of the area. Outside there are also pleasant grassy areas with swings, overlooking the lake.

## CHAPEL OF NOSSA SENHORA DAS VITÓRIAS
### (Ermida Nossa Senhora das Vitórias)

*Furnas Lake, south bank; tel. 918 779 700; https:// matajosedocanto.com; daily 10am-6pm; €3*

As far as spooky-looking buildings go, this is perhaps one of the spookiest you'll come across. On the south bank of Furnas Lake, near the Monitoring and Research Centre, the Chapel of Nossa Senhora das Vitórias takes gothic to a whole new level. Set against a backdrop of lush foliage with the vast Furnas Lake spread out in front of it, this creepy chapel leaps out, lending a shot of the sinister to the lake's serenity. Built in the 19th century, it was originally intended to be a mausoleum. A little unkempt and abandoned, its age is starting to show, but from the outside, the stained glass windows, spiky spire, and unpolished bell tower are still majestic.

# Public Taps

Throughout Furnas, but especially in the main center of town, hot and cold geothermal spring water flows from public taps, also known as *caldeiras*. See and sample the water in an area known as **Calderas Square** (Largo das Caldeiras). The high iron content in the water gives it a bitter taste that fizzes on the tongue.

Furnas public taps

## EXPLORING FURNAS AND THE *CALDEIRAS*

Just next to Calderas Square is a large free parking lot and little stalls selling another local specialty, **corncobs** cooked in the steaming geysers. Wander around Furnas's town center and you'll also see more hissing, spitting geysers and thick plumes of vapor rising from the fissures in the earth's surface. These are incorporated into **manicured gardens,** giving the town center a tranquil, almost surreal feel, revealing the fervent force of nature bubbling away beneath one's feet.

From here it's about a 20-minute (1.5-km/1-mi) walk southwest to the **Terra Nostra Park.** En route, make sure to stop at the **Square of the Three Taps** (Largo das Três Bicas), on the ER1-1 road and see the century-old public fountain, **Fontanário das Três Bicas,** with its three taps.

The chapel can be visited by purchasing a ticket from a booth at the entrance to the **José do Canto Forest Garden,** against which the chapel stands. The garden's original owners, José do Canto and his wife, are buried in the chapel.

### JOSÉ DO CANTO FOREST GARDEN (Mata Jardim José do Canto)

*Furnas Lake, east bank; tel. 918 779 700; https://matajosedocanto.com; daily 10am-6pm; €3*

Covering around 10 hectares (25 acres) of the east bank of Furnas Lake with swathes of leafy green trees, this garden hides delightful surprises like a massive California sequoia tree, pretty flower gardens, and a magical waterfall. It was founded by José do Canto, a distinguished 19th-century Azorean landowner and intellectual with a keen interest in agricultural technologies and plants. This small park on the banks of Furnas Lake is believed to have been created by do Canto to acclimatize new plants he imported from overseas. He

is also credited with the construction of the Chapel of Nossa Senhora das Vitórias, built as a funerary chapel for his family. His park is a surprising gem of a garden to spend one or two hours in; watch out for goblins, wizards, and animals carved into the trees. There are **public bathrooms** and plenty of **parking** (€0.40/hour) available in the large parking lot just before the chapel.

## Calderas Square (Largo das Caldeiras)

*open 24/7; free*

For a real taste of Furnas, head to the town's calderas, active fissures incorporated into the villagescape, the best example of which can be seen in Calderas Square on the northeast outskirts of town, a 20-minute walk from the Terra Nostra Park. In the square, you'll find incredible bubbling geysers right in the middle

---

**1:** Furnas Monitoring and Research Centre **2:** Terra Nostra Park

of the pretty little hamlet, with steam rising in columns from the pavement and manicured gardens. Stroll among them; protection has been put up around the openings to prevent people falling in, but there are some gruesome stories that locals tell to this end. The square is surrounded by little stalls selling corn on the cob cooked in the boiling underground water, another local specialty. Water also flows from public drinking taps, which, thanks to its high iron content, has a bitter taste that fizzes on the tongue. Various types of water can be sampled from the fountains, some more palatable than others. There's a large, free **parking lot** just next to Calderas Square.

### Terra Nostra Park
### (Parque Terra Nostra)

*Rua Padre Jose Jacinto Botelho; tel. 296 549 090; www.parqueterranostra.com; daily 10am-6pm; adults €8, children 3-10 €4*

If there were a paradise on earth, it might look like the Terra Nostra Park, a captivating Eden of sprawling gardens, secret grottoes, shady tree-covered walkways, babbling streams, lily-covered ponds, and a big pool of hot, rusty-red spring water that soothes aching muscles and joints. The park is decorated with exotic plant life from around the world, including more than 2,000 different types of trees.

More than 200 years old, this sublime botanical park was the brainchild of wealthy American consul Thomas Hickling, who had a summer house on the site nicknamed **Yankee Hall** and started shaping the gardens in 1775. Yankee Hall today dominates the hill overlooking the gardens' famous **thermal pool.**

### TERRA NOSTRA PARK
### THERMAL WATER POOL

*Rua Padre Jose Jacinto Botelho; tel. 296 549 090; www.parqueterranostra.com; daily 10am-6pm; adults €8, children 3-10 €4*

This thermal pool, part of Terra Nostra Park, was built in 1780 and extended in later years. The volcanic water that feeds the pool ranges 35-40°C (95-104°F) and is an uninviting,

murky dark-orange color due to its iron content, but it is perfect for a dip after walking around the glorious gardens (so long as you don't mind the rust-colored water staining your bathing suit!). Admission to the gardens also grants you access to the pool. Good **changing facilities,** with hot showers, are found on site.

### Poça da Dona Beija Hot Springs

*Lomba das Barracas; tel. 296 584 256; www. pocadadonabeija.com; daily 7am-11pm; €4*

Take a soothing, invigorating soak in the Poça da Dona Beija hot springs, one of São Miguel's best-known attractions. Deep tanks filled with steaming crystalline water transform this former wild spring into an indulgent open-air spa. The first construction was in 1988 following an influx of visitors to the site after news of its restorative properties spread, but public access was only regulated in 2007 due to the growing number of visitors. Nowadays the spot is well managed and equipped with a small parking lot (though finding parking can still be a challenge due to the spa's popularity), a ticket office, and changing rooms. The several large tanks were redesigned by a group of architects in 2015 to blend in with the surrounding landscape of lush greenery, stone walls, and stone-block houses. At nighttime, when it's all lit up, is particularly lovely. Or, enter the steaming water when it's rainy and cold—a pleasant novelty.

### Hot Waterfall of Ribeira Quente
### (Cascata da Ribeira Quente)

*EN2-2A road; open 24/7; free*

Blink and you'll miss it: Keep an eye out for this unusual single-drop waterfall in the weirdest of locations—in between two road tunnels. This hot waterfall (it's not actually steaming hot, but it is warm) is one of the island's best-kept secrets. To find it, you have to pass through the tunnels on the EN2-2A road from Furnas to Ribeira Quente, park at a little unmarked dirt area on the left after the last tunnel, and make the precarious walk back through the tunnel to the waterfall. Note how the iron in the water has changed the color of the rocks behind it to a shimmery shade of copper.

# HIKING
## LAGOA DAS FURNAS LOOP (PRC6SMI)

**Hiking Distance:** *9.5 kilometer (5.9 mi) round-trip*

**Hiking Time:** *3.5-4 hours round-trip*

**Trailhead:** *Três Bicas, Furnas village*

**Information and Maps:** *http://trails. visitazores.com; maps also available from tourist offices*

Beginning and ending in the town of Furnas, near Square of the Three Taps (Largo das Três Bicas), this trail follows the rises and falls of the terrain surrounding Furnas Lake. Flat, easy, and beautiful, the peaceful route takes hikers past some of Furnas's iconic sights, including the spooky, abandoned, gothic **Chapel of Nossa Senhora das Vitórias,** the **Furnas Monitoring and Research Centre,** and the fumaroles.

# FOOD
## Azorean
### CHALET DA TIA MERCÊS

*Rua das Caldeiras s/n; tel. 914 295 470; https:// azores-essentials-lda.business.site; Fri. 2pm-10pm, Sat.-Sun. 10am-10pm; €10*

Excellent Azorean foods and drinks are served at this homely, emblematic restaurant. With a large selection of delicious foods from across the archipelago, all made from quality regional ingredients, this charming chalet-like teahouse (originally a 19th-century public bath) overlooks bubbling calderas and offers some of the best views of Furnas. It's a great choice for tea and a light lunch—tuck into delicacies like local pastries, cheeses and pâtés, seaweed patties, and fresh bruschetta.

### ★ RESTAURANTE MIROMA

*Rua Dr. Frederico Moniz Pereira 15; tel. 296 584 422; daily 9:30am-9:30pm daily; €15*

This simple and traditional, yet large and lofty restaurant, which feels a bit like a fancy barn, seats 200. It's one of the top places to go in town for the traditional *cozido das Furnas* and is usually always buzzing with tourists and local families. Diligent waiters place heaped servings of the famed stew on the table, along with bread and rice and other staple trimmings. Other dishes like fried ribs, grilled chicken, and tuna steak are available if you don't fancy the flavorful stew. Because it's rather large you should be able to walk in and enjoy *cozido* most days, even without a reservation, but book ahead to make sure. You wouldn't want to miss this must-do experience.

## Cafés and Light Bites
### ESPINHA.COME

*Av. Pereira Atayde no. 11; tel. 296 588 204; www. facebook.com/espinha.come; Fri.-Wed. noon-4pm and 6pm-10pm; €10*

A simple and quirky little restaurant, Espinha. Come is tapas and snacks galore. Sticky chicken wings, deep-fried prawns, sandwiches on the local *lêvedo* bread, salads, burgers, and more substantial meals like meat and tuna steaks can be enjoyed in this laid-back, casual eatery.

### SUMMER BREEZE

*Rua das Caldeiras 18; tel. 296 588 363; Tues.-Fri. noon-4pm and 6:30pm-9:30pm, Sat.-Sun. noon-9:30pm; €10*

Friendly service and casual fresh food keep Summer Breeze highly regarded among locals and visitors. Huge helpings made from quality local ingredients elevate the simplest snacks and meals, like burgers and grilled meats, to gourmet feasts.

# ACCOMMODATIONS
## Under €100
### HOTEL RESIDENCIAL VALE VERDE

*Rua Das Caldeiras 3; tel. 296 549 010; http:// hotelvaleverde.com; €80 d*

A good little hotel in a great location, Hotel Residencial Vale Verde makes a solid base

# ☆ Visiting Furnas's Hot Springs

Pitted with hundreds of hot springs and fumaroles, Furnas is perhaps the most blatantly volcanic and beautiful little spa town in the entire archipelago. Home to a lake whose steaming shores are used to braise the island's flagship stew underground, two of the most famous hot springs in the Azores, and a town center dotted with hissing geysers and around 20 ornate public fountains, Furnas has enjoyed growing popularity since the 18th century, when people began to travel purposely to the town to soothe their ailments in the highly mineralized spring water.

Today, there are two main springs to enjoy, which have become huge tourist attractions: the **Poça da Dona Beija hot springs,** a series of small tanks filled with volcanic water that varies between 28-38°C (82-100°F); and the luxuriant **Terra Nostra Park,** with its huge, rusty-red communal bath. Both springs are privately run and require entry fees, but have good facilities like showers, storage lockers, and toilets. In the busier summer months, they have, however, fallen victims of their own success, as the **parking lots,** especially the Poça da Dona Beija parking lot, can become packed and the usually tranquil springs rather crowded.

Furnas is a magical and romantic place to visit; to make the most of it, enjoy a night at the exceptional **Terra Nostra Garden Hotel** or the charming **Furnas Boutique Hotel & Spa.**

## TIPS

- If you want to enjoy a soak, take an **old swimsuit** or one that you're not too attached to, as the bright orange water can stain lighter materials.

- Avoid soaking for too long **when the weather is hot,** as the steaming hot water coupled with hot sunshine can sometimes make bathers feel unwell.

- A lovely time to enjoy the steaming hot baths is at night, **under the stars,** or when the weather is **overcast and cool.** Even a little rain can't dampen the joy of the experience.

- Make sure you have **footwear** that's appropriate for the wet areas surrounding the baths, and an old **towel** on hand for after.

---

for staying in Furnas at a reasonable price. Comfortable and very clean, it is within walking distance of all of Furnas's main attractions. Fantastic value for a no-frills hotel.

## €100-200
### WORLD'S NESTS FURNAS PODS VILLAGE

*Rua da Pedra, EN1-1A 9; tel. 918 253 029; http:// worlds-nests-furnas-pods-village.visit-azores.info/ en; €100 d*

Surrounded by nature, in the thick of Furnas's stunning countryside, these extraordinary concrete-looking bungalow pods provide comfortable accommodation. Equipped with small kitchenettes, they

overlook forest-like scenery while still being within walking distance of all of the local sights. The buffet breakfast is a celebration of local produce.

### TERRA NOSTRA GARDEN HOTEL

*Rua Padre José Jacinto Botelho 5; tel. 296 549 090; www.bensaudehotels.com; €160 d*

One of the Azores most iconic hotels and the Bensaude group's flagship unit, the Terra Nostra Garden Hotel is ensconced in the leafy grounds of the incredible Terra Nostra Gardens. It's refined, exotic, and has an art-deco style that sits in harmony with its luxuriant surroundings. Guests enjoy privileged access to the 18th-century Terra Nostra Park.

communal bath in Terra Nostra Park

## IF YOU WANT...

- **History:** People have been enjoying the iron-rich, warm waters of **Terra Nostra Park's thermal pool,** surrounded by lush gardens, since the late 18th century (page 78).

- **Gorgeous Scenery:** The **Poça da Dona Beija hot springs** were designed by a group of architects to blend into the lush greenery surrounding it, making it a beautiful place for a soak (page 78).

- **Luxury:** For the ultimate in comfort, visit the **Furnas Boutique Hotel & Spa,** where luxurious massages and other treatments accompany the geothermal water (page 81).

## Over €200
### ★ FURNAS BOUTIQUE HOTEL & SPA

*Av. Dr. Manuel de Arriaga; tel. 296 249 200; www. furnasboutiquehotel; €306 d*

The Furnas Boutique Hotel embodies the serenity and beauty of Furnas with a hip bar, an outdoor hot-spring pool, and minimalist-modern rooms with distant mountain views. It is just a 10-minute walk to the gorgeous Terra Nostra Park.

This hotel's large **spa** (daily 9am-6pm, pools and gym open 24/7; treatments from €45) is the ultimate retreat; it has 10 treatment rooms and promises a unique sensorial experience based on the properties of famous local hot spring waters, as well as a range of indulgent massages and treatments by experienced therapists.

## GETTING THERE AND AROUND

Furnas is 46 kilometers (29 mi) east of Ponta Delgada, a 40-minute drive on the **EN1-1A** road. A **bus** (lines **318** or **110;** www. smigueltransportes.com) from Ponta Delgada to Furnas village (1.5 hours; €3-5) depart roughly every two hours from Ponta Delgada's main waterfront avenue 7am-6pm. Ask at the **Ponta Delgada Tourist Office** for bus timetables and fares.

There's plenty of **parking** throughout the

# Geothermal Cooking

*cozido das Furnas* at Restaurante Miroma

Furnas's most famous dish, *cozido das Furnas,* is a one-pot wonder slow-cooked in the volcanic heat of the earth and made exclusively in the village of Furnas. It is São Miguel's take on the traditional *cozido à portuguesa,* a stew made from several types of meat (often chicken, pork, and beef), chouriço and blood sausage, offal, and an array of vegetables, including potatoes, carrots, and cabbage, cooked together and served with rice. The raw ingredients are taken to the Furnas Lake site at dawn in huge sealed pans, placed into deep fumaroles, and then covered with soil and left to cook in the volcanic heat for several hours before being unearthed and hoisted out before lunchtime. Each pan is identified by a nameplate next to its hole, then sped off to the many local restaurants that serve the specialty.

In this area, known as the **Furnas Lake Hot Springs** (Caldeiras da Lagoa das Furnas), the banks of the vast lake are pitted with boiling fumaroles and bubbling geysers. Walkways have been created around the site so visitors can wander safely. Most local restaurants in the small town serve the specialty and are so in demand that it's a good idea to reserve in the morning. Head off to the fumaroles and, around midday, watch as the pots are lifted out of the ground before heading back to your restaurant to taste the *cozido*. Some say they can taste sulfur from the volcanic heat in the dish.

## WHERE TO TRY IT

- Most people make a beeline for **Restaurante Miroma,** which has a reputation as the best local restaurant for *cozido das Furnas* (page 79).

- Another local specialty, *maçarocas de milho* (corn on the cob), is cooked in the steaming volcanic water and somewhat easier to get, as it's sold from the little stalls in the center of Furnas village, near the *caldeiras* (page 76).

town, most of it roadside, but there are also a number of large parking lots in the main spots, like near the Terra Nostra Park and the town springs. The Poça da Dona Beija parking lot is small and can often be full, so finding parking nearby may be necessary, and given the town's popularity, finding parking on Furnas's narrow streets can be a challenge.

Furnas is an easily **walkable** town. It takes roughly 15 minutes to cross the town from the main springs to the Terra Nostra Park. In parts, walkways can be narrow and the roads busy, but the streets are well signposted and the locals are used to helping out lost tourists.

# Eastern São Miguel

Awash with spectacular scenery at every twist and turn and packed with family-friendly facilities, like parks, picnic spots, and stunning viewpoints, eastern São Miguel is wilder and more remote than the west coast, with a dramatic coastline, historic monuments, waterfalls, and lesser-known attractions. The beautiful Fogo Lake, Congro Lake, and Gorreana Tea Plantation can be found on this side of the island, along with one of the prettiest belvederes on São Miguel—Ponta do Sossego—and some of its quirkiest attractions, like the Ribeira Quente hot waterfall and Arnel Lighthouse, the oldest lighthouse in the Azores. Rugged, untamed, and unharnessed, this is São Miguel at its purest.

## ORIENTATION

Main towns and villages along the eastern coast include (counterclockwise from Ponta Delgada) **Povoação,** home of the famed *fofas da Povoação* biscuit, **Vila Franca do Campo** and its famous offshore islet, and **Nordeste.** Nordeste is almost a 60-kilometer (40-mi), 50-minute drive northeast from Ponta Delgada, along the **EN1-1A** road. Accommodations are sparser here than on the rest of the island, and the relative lack of amenities means that the east is better for a day trip from Ponta Delgada than a base for your stay.

## SIGHTS
### Fogo Lake
(Lagoa do Fogo)
Though not quite as famous as the Sete

Cidades Lake, Lagoa do Fogo is also a crater lake that almost meets the Atlantic Ocean. An arresting natural attraction of unquestionable beauty, the sprawling blue lake fills a dormant volcano crater, spanning two municipalities. A dip in the rim makes it look like the lake could spill out into the sea behind it at any given time. Fogo Lake is another popular destination for hikers, thanks to its fascinating landscapes. Endemic Azorean plant species carpet the rim of the lake, which also provides a home to different types of birds. Halfway up the crater are the mystical, jungle-like Caldeira Velha thermal pools.

### CALDEIRA VELHA THERMAL POOLS
*EN5 2A, Ribeira Grande; tel. 296 206 700; www. parquesnaturais.azores.gov.pt; daily 9:30am-5:30pm; €8*
Visiting the Caldeira Velha thermal pools is a bit like finding steaming hot baths in the middle of a tropical jungle. Not quite as organized and tidy as the Poça da Dona Beija hot spring pools in Furnas, Caldeira Velha has a wilder, more natural feel, with lush overgrown vegetation swaddling the hot dip pools fashioned from rock boulders. A **gift shop, changing rooms,** and **restrooms** are on hand, and you can also visit an **environmental interpretation center** created at the spot to promote the area's natural heritage.

### Gorreana Tea Plantation
(Plantações de Chá Gorreana)

# Day Trip to Vila Franca do Campo Islet

Located less than 1 kilometer (0.6 mi) off São Miguel's shore, opposite the town of **Vila Franca do Campo,** unique little Vila Franca do Campo Islet (Ilheu de Vila Franca) makes for a fascinating day trip. A classified nature reserve, shaped by over 4,000 years of tides, it has become one of São Miguel's top attractions. It is the crater of an ancient underwater volcano, and its sea-filled innards, known as "the ring of the princess," make a perfectly round lagoon that offers wonderful snorkeling conditions. Accessed via a narrow channel and fringed by a tiny sandy beach, the inner basin also has a little dock, where the boat from nearby Vila Franca do Campo lets off and picks up passengers. Services once on the islet are limited; there are **washrooms** with a small changing area and lifeguards, but nowhere to buy food or drinks, so bring them with you.

Vila do Campo has also gained worldwide fame as the host of the jaw-dropping **Red Bull Cliff Diving Festival** (https://cliffdiving.redbull.com/en_PT/video/red-bull-cliff-diving-3). The islet has welcomed the breathtaking, world-class competition for elite cliff divers more times than any other location around the world, providing a phenomenal setting for a truly gripping sport.

## DIVING AND SNORKELING

Some of the best diving spots around São Miguel are off Vila Franca, including the **Fontes Hidrotermais** ("hydrothermal vents"), whose crystalline, shallow warm waters are home to a fun variety of sealife, like cucumber fish and jellyfish. A relatively shallow dive at just 8 meters (26 ft) deep, the Fontes Hidrotermais is unique because it is one of few diving spots in the world with underwater volcanic activity. Diving at this spot will require an organized excursion with a company such as **Dive Center Azores** (Marina da Vila, Vila Franca do Campo; tel. 918 755 853; http://azoressub.com; daily 9am-6pm; diving trips from €53 pp, offshore diving from €175 pp). If you would like to snorkel in the islet lagoon, you can buy a snorkel set from most sport or tourist shops on the island, or rent one from companies such as Dive Center Azores or the Azores Surf School, or directly from the little booth on the marina that sells the boat tickets to the islet (€5).

## GETTING THERE

The boat to the islet leaves from the **Vila Franca do Campo marina** (tel. 296 582 333; www.cnvfc.net/ilheu-da-vila; daily hourly 10am-6pm; €5 boat round-trip). Make sure you also take towels, snorkeling gear (which you can rent from the marina ticket booth for €5), and a camera. The number of people allowed to visit the islet at any one time is capped at around 40, or a maximum of 200 in a day, so either turn up early to purchase tickets in advance at the marina, or try to purchase online. It is a very popular place in summer, when the weather is at its best. Free **parking** is available next to the marina.

---

*just off EN1-1A road, Maia; tel. 296 442 349; www. gorreana.pt; Mon.-Fri. 8am-7pm, Sat.-Sun. 9am-7pm; free*

The only tea plantation in Europe, the family-run Gorreana Tea Plantation has been producing world-class organic green and black teas since 1883. In the parish of Maia, 33 kilometers (21 mi) northeast of Ponta Delgada, a 30-minute drive along the EN1-1A road, the 32 hectares (79 acres) of vivid green fields blend perfectly with the rest of the island's emerald tapestry and contrast with the sea. A **boutique, café, and museum** are on the site, along with the factory, to offer insight on how the tea came to the island, how it is produced, and its evolution. Gorreana currently produces 33 metric tons (36 tons) of tea per year. A small portion stays in the Azores market, with the rest exported to mainland Portugal and other countries. Visitors can stroll at

---

1: Fogo Lake 2: Congro Lake 3: Caloura Point and Pool 4: Ponta do Sossego Viewpoint and Garden

leisure among the fields along the Atlantic, a sight to behold and the perfect place to enjoy a cup of fresh tea. A visit to the plantation and museum, whether self-guided or on a guided **tour** (which run roughly every 30 minutes until 5pm), is free, as is a tea-tasting offered at the end. A box of Gorreana tea makes a great souvenir.

## Arnel Lighthouse
### (Farol do Arnel)

*EN4-2A, Vila Franca do Campo; Wed. only 2pm-4:30pm; free*

The oldest lighthouse in the Azores, Arnel is situated on a remote outcrop, the north-easternmost tip of the island, on the rugged and wild east coast. Inaugurated in 1876, the main building houses an exhibition on the Azores' lighthouses. Access down to the lighthouse is by foot only and is long and steep, but if you happen to be visiting on a Wednesday, **free guided tours** make it worth the effort to learn more about the archipelago's heritage and history.

## Ponta do Sossego Viewpoint and Garden
### (Miradouro da Ponta do Sossego)

*EN1-1A, Nordeste; open 24/7; free*

Ponta do Sossego is a bit of an unexpected attraction, worth stopping at for the landscaped gardens and incredible views. Carefully tended gardens envelop the viewpoints, which also have a number of benches and barbecue facilities on hand. Covering some 13,000 square meters (3 acres) over stepped terraces, these lovely gardens and compelling vistas are a memorable stop when exploring the coast of Nordeste.

## Congro Lake
### (Lagoa do Congro)

*EN4-2A, Vila Franca do Campo; open 24/7; free*

Another of the island's lesser-known attractions, Congro Lake is moody and mysterious. To get there, you have to park on a country road and walk about 1 kilometer (0.6 mi), 10-15 minutes, through dense, enchanting woodland, until you reach this turquoise green lake flanked by dark green forest. Signposted from the main road, where there is parking at the start of the trail, the hike down to the lake is short and relatively easy. There's little else to do once down there except make the most of the photo op, but the unspoiled natural beauty of this hidden gem is worth the stop.

Ribeira Quente

# BEACHES AND POOLS

Eastern São Miguel's beaches are mostly spacious, bay-like, and generally have soft black sand. Some of the island's most beautiful and popular beaches are found this end of the island, and they have family-friendly facilities like concessioned parasols and sun beds (in summer), ample parking lots, and beach bars.

## Moinhos Beach and Porto Formoso
### (Praia dos Moinhos e Porto Formoso)

*M518, Porto Formoso; open 24/7; free*

A little sheltered bay, Moinhos Beach, in the hamlet of Porto Formoso, is a slice of heaven. A sandy cove with crystal, clean water, protected by high cliffs and with a little stream running through the middle of it, it is a natural amphitheater. A gem of a beach with beige and black sand and usually uncrowded, it has changing facilities including **showers** and **toilets,** a **snack bar** overlooking the beach, and beachside **parking.** It's supervised by a lifeguard during the main beach season, and the rockier end of the beach is perfect for snorkeling—bring your equipment since there are no rental outlets nearby. Moinhos Beach is just around the corner from the picturesque Porto Formoso fishing port, which is located in the parish of Ribeira Grande, on São Miguel's north coast, not far from the Gorreana Tea Plantation on the eastern side of the island.

## Ribeira Quente
### FOGO BEACH
### (Praia do Fogo)

*EN2-2A 24, Ribeira Quente; open 24/7; free*

Shaped like a beak, Fogo Beach, in the village of Povoação, Ribeira Quente, boasts an unusual natural beauty, with turquoise waters and black sands contrasting the lush deep-green-topped mountains that back it.

One of the main attractions to this beach is that, due to underwater hydrothermal springs, the sea water is always warm. Food vans sell snacks nearby on the local docks. The beach is pristine and spacious, and there is plenty of parking available at the nearby docks.

## Vila Franca do Campo
### ÁGUA D'ALTO BEACH
### (Praia de Água d'Alto)

*Estrada Regional 1-1, Água de Alto, Vila Franca do Campo; 24/7; free*

A spacious bay, Água D'Alto Beach is widely regarded as one of the best beaches on the island. Clean sand and water, coupled with plenty of space, make it a favorite for islanders and holidaymakers alike. Showers, a beach bar, and plenty of nearby parking make this one of the island's busiest beaches.

## Caloura
### CALOURA POINT AND POOL

*Água de Pau - Lagoa; open 24/7; free*

A stunningly pretty little fishermen's port, Caloura Point is home to the famed **Caloura Bar.** Taking a dip in the little jetty with a human-made sea-filled pool plonked in the middle of the sea is a unique and picturesque experience all-round.

# FISHING
## Vila Franca do Campo
### AZORES FISHING

*Marina de Vila Franca de Campo, Rua Eng. Manuel António Martins Mota, s/n; tel. 915 136 364 or 918 459 657; www.azoresfishing.pt; daily 9am-6:30pm; big-game fishing from €500*

Jump on one of the best big-game fishing charters on São Miguel and experience the ultimate fishing thrill out on the deep blue waters of the Azores archipelago. If catching tuna or marlin is your dream, Azores Fishing can make it happen.

## Fofas da Povoação, a Povoação Specialty

*fofas da Povoação*

*Fofas* are one of the most revered sweets on the island. It's like an éclair, filled with a vanilla cream and topped with chocolate-flavored buttercream, and people travel from far and wide across the island to enjoy a *fofa* from Povoação. It's the town's claim to fame and a closely guarded recipe, said to have originated from one talented baker, a local woman Dona Angelina, now deceased.

### WHERE TO TRY IT
Dona Angelina's legacy is widely available in most local cafés and pastry shops, such as **Café Restaurant Jardim** (Largo D. João 1, Povoação; tel. 296 585 413; daily 7am-11pm; €15), which overlooks the village's main square.

## DOLPHIN- AND WHALE-WATCHING
### Vila Franca do Campo
#### AZORES WHALE WATCHING TERRA AZUL
*Rua da Marina 4, Vila Franca do Campo; www. azoreswhalewatch.com; 8am-10pm; from €55*
Set sail for the high seas with whale-watching experts Terra Azul, who provide unique and interactive experiences showcasing São Miguel's amazing marine life as well as a focus on sustainability.

## HIKING
### Povoação
#### AGRIÃO TRAIL (PR12SMI)
**Hiking Distance:** *7.6 kilometers (4.7 mi) one way*
**Hiking Time:** *3.5-4 hours one way*
**Trailhead:** *Fogo Beach, Povoação*
**Information and Maps:** *http://trails. visitazores.com; maps also available from tourist offices*

This coastal trail was once widely used by farmers and is also a crossing point for religious pilgrimages throughout the island. Starting on Fogo Beach, it crosses an ancient bridge and streams, and follows the coast to a viewpoint from where Santa Maria island can be seen on a good day. The route ends near **Ribeira Quente port.** There is a taxi rank in Ribeira Quente (Rua Doutor Frederico Moniz Pereira, near the post office in the middle of town) from where a taxi back to Povoação will cost around €20, or back to Ponta Delgada will cost €45-55.

# FOOD
## Caloura
### ★ BAR CALOURA

*Rua da Caloura 20, Água de Pau, Lagoa; tel. 296 913 283; daily noon-9:30pm; €15*

A short drive east of Ponta Delgada in the small parish of Água de Pau is Bar Caloura, a hidden gem in a stunning scenic seaside setting, where excellent fresh seafood and great cocktails make the journey worthwhile. This is the spot to head to for a great meal in a memorable setting. Água de Pau is 15 kilometers (9 mi) east of Ponta Delgada, not far off the EN1-1A.

# GETTING THERE AND AROUND

Getting around eastern São Miguel is pretty straightforward. As with most of the Azores, **renting a car** is the best and most affordable way to explore independently. If traveling by car, just follow the main **EN1-1A** road that circumnavigates the edge of the island, and you'll pass by most main villages and attractions.

The island's northeasternmost point, **Nordeste,** is a 50-minute drive (about 60 km/40 mi) from Ponta Delgada, whereas **Vila Franca do Campo** (and its famous islet) and **Ribeira Quente** are a 25-minute and 55-minute drive east, respectively. **Bus lines 315** and **318** run to the villages of Vila Franca do Campo, Ribeira Quente, and Povoação, while line **105** goes all the way to Nordeste (but takes over 2 hours to get there). Buses cost €3-7 for a one-way ticket (http://horarios.visitazores.de/smiAVM.pdf).

# Santa Maria

**With its golden beaches and general sunny dis-**
position, combined with stunning turquoise waters and distinctive
architecture, Santa Maria is a paradisiacal—if somewhat alternative—
beach getaway destination. An island of many firsts—the first to be
formed geologically, the first to be encountered by Portuguese explorers in 1427, and the first to be settled by Portuguese from the mainland, circa 1439 (giving Santa Maria its other nickname, the Mother
Island)—its lighter, brighter landscape distinguishes Santa Maria from
the other islands.

Often referred to as the Sunshine Island, its warmer, drier climate
gives the landscape a palette of sunny hues, ranging from dark ocher
to golden yellow to bright red and arid beige. It is the only island in

# Highlights

Look for ★ to find recommended sights, activities, dining, and lodging.

Barreiro
da Faneca
Protected
Landscape

Angels' Bay

Anjos

Pico Alto
Mountain

*Baia do
São Lourenço*

Santa
Barbara

Sao
Pedro

SANTA
MARIA
AIRPORT
EN1-2A

Almagreira
EN1-2A

Santo
Espirito

Vila do
Porto

Formosa
Beach

Diving and
Snorkeling

Regional
Natural Monument
of Pedreira do Campo

0        2 mi

0      2 km

© MOON.COM

★ **Regional Natural Monument of Pedreira do Campo:** Just east of Vila do Porto, this precious landscape is strewn with millions of years' worth of oceanic fossils, a basalt flow to climb, and a cave to explore (page 99).

★ **Barreiro da Faneca Protected Landscape:** Locally referred to as the "Red Desert," the arid-looking, rusty-colored, clayish landscape of Barreiro da Faneca has an almost Martian feel (page 103).

★ **Angels' Bay:** Located toward the western tip of the northern coast, this bay has heavenly connotations thanks to its charming little fishing dock and natural swimming pool, a picture-perfect inlet that attracts summer sunbathers in droves (page 105).

★ **Formosa Beach:** This beach's soft golden sand makes it one of the most famous in the Azores (page 107).

★ **Diving and Snorkeling:** There are a number of excellent and exciting dive sites in the pristine, bountiful waters off Santa Maria, including Pedrinha Reef, just 10 minutes from Vila do Porto marina (page 110).

the archipelago to be fringed entirely by blond sand beaches, as opposed to the black volcanic sand found on its peers, and it's is also home to the largest walking trail in the Azores, the famed Great Route of Santa Maria, one of the Azores' most enjoyable hiking challenges.

Pretty Santa Maria is the Azores' southeasternmost island and the third smallest of the archipelago. It and São Miguel, 81 kilometers (50 mi) to the northwest, make up the eastern group of islands. The main town, Vila do Porto, is believed to be the oldest settlement in the Azores, with a current population of around 5,500 inhabitants. Compact and whitewashed, with the typical Azorean black basalt rock trimmings, the island's main town of Vila do Porto sits in the southwest corner of Santa Maria Island; its pretty marina, with the town climbing the hillside rising up behind it, is one of the main entry points to the island. And while the island might be modestly sized, with a surface area of just under 97 square kilometers (37 sq mi), Santa Maria is home to a surprising array of compelling and unique attractions, such as the Ribeira de Maloás lava rock formation, the Pedreira do Campo basalt flow, and the Martian-like Barreiro da Faneca "Red Desert," which make spending a few days here worth it.

## GETTING THERE

Depending on the time of year, Santa Maria is accessible both by **air** and **ferry** from São Miguel—there are no direct flights from outside the archipelago. With regular daily (30-minute) flights throughout the year between the two islands, flying is the more dependable option. The seasonal (May-Sept.) ferry crossing takes 3-4 hours each way, depending on the seas. If you're pushed for time, jump on the short flight from São Miguel, though fares may be slightly more expensive. Ferry crossings may make sense for those visiting in summer with a sense of adventure, who are spending a night or two on Santa Maria island.

## Air
### SANTA MARIA AIRPORT
*tel. 296 820 020; www.ana.pt/pt/sma/home*

**SATA** (tel. 707 227 282; www.sata.pt) runs daily flights between bigger island São Miguel's **Ponta Delgada Airport** (also known as João Paulo II Airport; tel. 296 205 400; www.aeroportopontadelgada.pt) and Santa Maria Airport. Flights take approximately 30 minutes and start from around €70 one way.

Santa Maria airport is located approximately 3 kilometers (2 mi) northwest of **Vila do Porto** town center, an 8-minute drive. You can **rent a car,** which is generally the best way to get around the island, and collect it at the airport; reputable companies including **Avis** (tel. 296 886 528; www.avis.com.pt), **Europcar** (tel. 296 886 528; www.europcar. pt), **Ilha Verde Rent a Car** (tel. 296 886 528; www.ilhaverde.com), and **Autatlantis** (tel. 296 886 530; https://autatlantis.com) all have desks at the airport, open from early morning (6am-7am) till 9pm or later.

**Buses** (tel. 296 882 115; www.transportesdesantamaria.com) run roughly every hour (less frequently on weekends and low season); there are two lines: **4** and **4A.** The journey by bus takes around 15 minutes, and tickets, which can be bought from the driver, cost just a few euros.

You will also find **taxis** outside the airport; a ride from the airport to Vila do Porto will cost about €10 one-way. There's also a **tourism counter** (tel. 296 886 355) at the airport where you can ask for information on transport or any other queries regarding your stay.

**Previous:** landscape of Santa Maria; Barreiro da Faneca Protected Landscape; sunrise at Formosa Beach.

## Ferry

### VILA DO PORTO
### PASSENGER TERMINAL

*Cais de Ilha de Santa Maria; tel. 296 882 586; www.*

*portosdosacores.pt; open 24/7*

The passenger ferry operated by Azorean ferry group **Atlanticoline** (tel. 707 201 572; www.atlanticoline.pt) runs between **Ponta Delgada** on São Miguel and Santa Maria's **Vila do Porto** from **May-Sept.** (exact start and end dates differ yearly—check the website for exact information). The trip takes 3-4 hours one-way (round-trip fares from €50). The Vila do Porto passenger terminal is located 2 kilometers (1 mi) south of Vila do Porto town center and about 4 kilometers (2 mi) from the airport. **Bus lines 4** or **4A** run hourly between all three, with tickets costing just a few euros. A **taxi** from the harbor to the town center costs around €5 and takes just a couple of minutes.

## GETTING AROUND

As with most Azorean islands, public transport—buses and taxis—are available, but **renting a car** is the best way to explore the island at leisure. Car rentals are generally affordable, and fuel is somewhat cheaper than on the mainland. The roads are mostly good and easy to navigate. With a surface spanning just under 97 square kilometers (37 sq mi), Santa Maria island is compact, and traveling from one end to the other (east to west) by car takes less than 30 minutes. The island is generally well signed and the main landmarks are easy to find. If in doubt, just ask a local, and they'll be happy to point you in the right direction. The roads are also pretty quiet, busier in summer, but hilly, so take care when it's raining. The **EN1-2A** road is the main road crossing Santa Maria, from the airport in the west to the southeastern tip, about 24 kilometers (15 mi).

Once you arrive, Santa Maria's main town, **Vila do Porto,** and its main attractions can all be covered **on foot.**

## Rental Car

Car rentals in the Azores are reasonably priced, from around €50/day in high season, and fuel is on average 10-20 cents cheaper than on the mainland. Several reputable international and car rental agencies including **Avis** (tel. 296 886 528; www.avis.com.pt), **Europcar** (tel. 296 886 528; www.europcar.pt), **Ilha Verde Rent a Car** (tel. 296 886 528; www.ilhaverde.com), and **Autatlantis** (tel. 296 886 530; https://autatlantis.com) operate from **Santa Maria Airport** and can be booked in advance online.

Road conditions on the island are generally good and straightforward, and parking is fairly easy and usually free. Unlike many of the other islands, Santa Maria doesn't have one main ring road skirting the coast, but it does have a main thoroughfare, the **EN1-2A,** which snakes from the airport in the west past Vila do Porto to the island's southeasternmost tip, the Aveiro Cascade, stretching roughly 24 kilometers (15 mi).

## Bus

Public bus transport on Santa Maria is decent and cheap, operated by **Transportes de Santa Maria** (TSM; tel. 296 882 115; www.transportesdesantamaria.com), running from the main town **Vila do Porto** to other bigger parishes and villages around the island, and to the **airport.** As on most islands, Santa Maria's bus service is geared toward working islanders as opposed to tourists. Public transport on weekends and holidays, and inland to more rural areas, can be limited.

Buses run regularly (about hourly) from main points in Vila do Porto, such as the marina, main church, and the airport to other major parishes on the island, such as **Anjos** and **Santo Espírito,** as well as **Formosa Beach.** Average fares will seldom cost more than a few euros one-way, but traveling by bus will take significantly longer than by car due to the many stops en route. Some routes may operate only during school periods and summer; check online for exact timetables

# Santa Maria

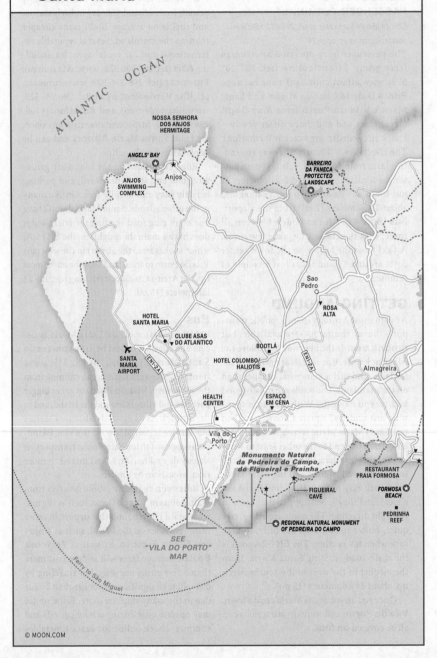

ATLANTIC OCEAN

NOSSA SENHORA
DOS ANJOS
HERMITAGE

BARREIRO
DA FANECA
PROTECTED
LANDSCAPE

ANGELS' BAY
Anjos

ANJOS
SWIMMING
COMPLEX

Sao
Pedro

ROSA
ALTA

HOTEL
SANTA MARIA

CLUBE ASAS
DO ATLANTICO

BOOTLÁ

HOTEL COLOMBO/
HALIOTIS

Almagreira

SANTA
MARIA
AIRPORT

EN1-2A

EN1-2A

HEALTH
CENTER

ESPAÇO
EM CENA

Vila do
Porto

Monumento Natural
da Pedreira do Campo,
do Figueiral e Prainha

RESTAURANT
PRAIA FORMOSA

FIGUEIRAL
CAVE

FORMOSA
BEACH

PEDRINHA
REEF

REGIONAL NATURAL MONUMENT
OF PEDREIRA DO CAMPO

SEE
"VILA DO PORTO"
MAP

Ferry to São Miguel

© MOON.COM

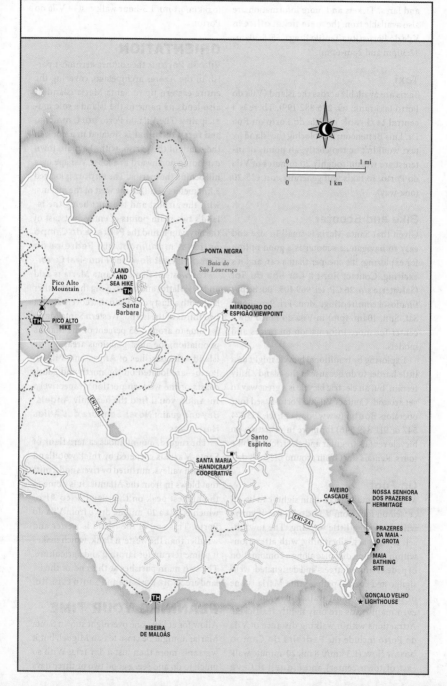

PONTA NEGRA

*Baia do
São Lourenço*

LAND
AND
SEA HIKE
**TH**

Pico Alto
Mountain

**TH** PICO ALTO
HIKE

Santa
Barbara

MIRADOURO DO
ESPIGÃO VIEWPOINT

0 ——— 1 mi
0 ——— 1 km

○ Santo
Espirito

SANTA MARIA
HANDICRAFT
COOPERATIVE

AVEIRO
CASCADE
★

NOSSA SENHORA
DOS PRAZERES HERMITAGE

EN1-2A

PRAZERES
DA MAIA -
O GROTA
★

MAIA
BATHING
SITE

**TH**

RIBEIRA
DE MALOÁS

GONÇALO VELHO
★ LIGHTHOUSE

and fares. Tickets and more information are also available from the **main ticket office** in Vila do Porto (Rua Teófilo Braga, 55; 8:30am-12:30pm and 2pm-6pm).

## Taxi

Taxis are available across the island (Vila do Porto taxi rank; tel. 296 882 199). There is a central **taxi rank** in Vila do Porto on Rua Dr. Luís Bettencourt; exploring the island by taxi wouldn't be too costly; all points of interest are within roughly 20 minutes of Vila do Porto, so taxis will generally cost €15-20 (one-way).

## Bike and Scooter

Given that Santa Maria is small in size and easy to navigate, a scooter is a good option for exploring: It's cheaper than a car, and it's exciting. Contact **Rent a Car Ilha do Sol** (Salvaterra s/n, 26 CP; tel. 969 405 700; http://ilhadosol.com/renting; Mon.-Fri. 9am-5pm, Sat.-Sun. 10am-4pm) in Vila do Porto town center for more information on prices and models.

Exploring by traditional bicycle might be a little harder to do because of the island's hilly terrain, but an electric bicycle is a great way to get around. Contact Vila do Porto-based tour operators **Bootlá** (www.bootla.pt; tel. 963 874 547 or 911 849 546) for more information on bicycle rentals (regular and electric) and bike tours. Rentals start from around €15/half day.

## On Foot

Many of Santa Maria's main sights can be accessed on foot from **Vila do Porto,** if you're willing to do a little walking. The town itself is compact, albeit hilly, with attractions within walking distance along a combination of pedestrianized streets and designated, well-signposted coastal paths. Santa Maria is one of the Azores' most walkable islands, and even main roads are only lightly trafficked. Attractions within walking distance of Vila do Porto include the **Pedreira do Campo basalt flow** (1.3 km/0.8 mi, 20-minute walk east of town center) and **Figueiral Cave**

(6.6 km/4.1 mi, 1.5-hour walk east of Vila do Porto).

## ORIENTATION

**Vila do Porto** is the southeasternmost parish in the Azores archipelago, covering the entire eastern tip of Santa Maria island. It also lends its name to the island's sole municipality. The Vila do Porto **port, marina,** and **ferry terminal** is situated in a nook in the south of the parish, with the main town extending northward in a loose V shape up a hill behind the marina. The **airport** is located 3 kilometers (2 mi) to the west of the marina, with the airport and the port being the island's two main points of entry. Just east of the city, you'll find the **Pedreira do Campo national monument,** the **Pedreira do Campo basalt flow,** and **Figueiral Cave.**

The western flank of Santa Maria is arid and dry, flatter and lower-lying than its other half, with a dusty clay plain that covers almost two thirds of the island. Western Santa Maria is home to around 65 percent of the island's population; the most populous areas on the island—the parishes of **Anjos** and Vila do Porto—are located on the north and south coasts of the western portion, respectively. In Anjos, you'll find the heavenly **Angels' Bay** and quaint **Nossa Senhora dos Anjos Hermitage.**

The rugged, mountainous eastern flank of Santa Maria is carpeted by thick woodland and lush valleys, nurtured by rivers and a mist that blows in from the Atlantic. It is home to the highest peak on the island, **Pico Alto,** which is just a 10-minute drive from Vila do Porto. This end of the island is wetter and windier than the western flank, which makes it prime terrain for farming and agriculture. The two main parishes at this end of the island are **Santa Bárbara** and **Santo Espírito.**

## PLANNING YOUR TIME

Allow for at least one overnight stay in Santa Maria; it might be close to São Miguel, but it warrants more than just a day trip. With so much to do and see, a good two or three days are advisable. Stay in the main town, **Vila do Porto,** and work your way around the island's main attractions.

Access to the island is best from **May to September,** when the seasonal ferry crossing from neighboring São Miguel island is operational, and (as with most Portuguese holiday destinations), when the weather is at its best. That being said, temperatures vary very little throughout the year, with average highs from 16-26°C (61-79°F). The warmest times to visit are August and September; the wettest months are December, February, and March, although there is a good chance of rain for at least half of the year (Nov.-Apr.). August can see the island's hotels fill up, due to the popular **August Tide (Maré de Agosto)** music festival and local religious celebrations that take place throughout the month.

**Health centers** and **pharmacies** are available on Santa Maria, but make sure you take a full supply of essential medication with you for the duration of your trip. The nearest hospital is on neighboring São Miguel island.

# Itinerary Ideas

## TWO DAYS ON SANTA MARIA

### Day 1: In Town
Spend a day in Santa Maria's main town to see all the attractions and historic sights. Be sure to wear comfortable walking shoes.

**1** Pop into one of Santa Maria's little *pastelaria* bakeries, **A Cagarrita,** for a fresh-baked breakfast. Don't forget to try the local *biscoito de orelha* biscuit.

**2** Visit the **Nossa Senhora da Assunção Church,** located on the main road near the marina, possibly the oldest building on the Azores archipelago.

**3** From here, make the short 10-minute walk to **Fort of São Brás** on the Cimo da Rocha hilltop, with a dominant view of the town.

**4** Head back inland to enjoy lunch at **A Garrouchada,** where you can choose between hearty portions of meat and fish or lighter sausage and cheese platters.

**5** Fueled up, walk just over 1 kilometer (0.6 mi) east, along the South Coast coastal route that starts near the Fort of São Brás, to the **Regional Natural Monument of Pedreira do Campo,** where you can hike among oceanic fossils.

**6** Return to Vila do Porto to freshen up at the hotel and head out to dinner at the swanky **Mesa d'Oito** restaurant.

**7** Finish the night off with a drink at one of the local bars, like **Docas Bar,** which is named for its location right on the docks.

### Day 2: On the Coast
Pack hiking shoes, a bathing suit, and a towel for this active day crisscrossing the island.

**1** Start your day at Vila do Porto's **Municipal Market** to pick up some breakfast and local produce to pack for a picnic.

**2** Picnic packed, head north to the **Barreiro da Faneca Protected Landscape,** or "Red Desert," a 10-minute drive in your rental car from Vila do Porto starting on the

# Itinerary Ideas

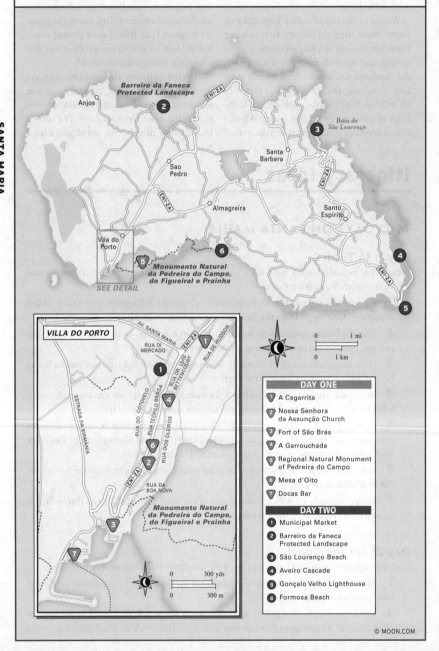

Barreiro da Faneca
Protected Landscape

Anjos

**2**

Baía do
São Lourenço

**3**

Santa
Barbara

Sao
Pedro

Almagreira

Santo
Espírito

**4**

Vila do
Porto

**5**

Monumento Natural
da Pedreira do Campo,
do Figueiral e Prainha

**6**

**5**

SEE DETAIL

**VILLA DO PORTO**

AV. SANTA MARIA

RUA DO
MERCADO

RUA DO HUDSON

RUA DR. LUÍS
BETTENCOURT

ENT-2A

**1**

**1**

**4**

RUA DO COTOVELO

RUA TEÓFILO BRAGA

ESTRADA DA BIRMANIA

**6**

**2**

RUA DOS OLEIROS

ENT-2A1

RUA DA
BOA NOVA

Monumento Natural
da Pedreira do Campo,
do Figueiral e Prainha

**3**

**7**

0        300 yds

0        300 m

0        1 mi

0        1 km

| **DAY ONE** | |
|---|---|
| **1** | A Cagarrita |
| **2** | Nossa Senhora da Assunção Church |
| **3** | Fort of São Brás |
| **4** | A Garrouchada |
| **5** | Regional Natural Monument of Pedreira do Campo |
| **6** | Mesa d'Oito |
| **7** | Docas Bar |

| **DAY TWO** | |
|---|---|
| **1** | Municipal Market |
| **2** | Barreiro da Faneca Protected Landscape |
| **3** | São Lourenço Beach |
| **4** | Aveiro Cascade |
| **5** | Gonçalo Velho Lighthouse |
| **6** | Formosa Beach |

© MOON.COM

EN1-2A before continuing on to the EN2-2. Spend an hour or so exploring this unique natural area.

**3** From here, head east to **São Lourenço Beach,** a 30-minute drive on the EN2-2 and EN1-2A roads. Once you arrive in this perfect, secluded inlet, enjoy your picnic al-fresco. Linger here to take a dip in the water and sunbathe.

**4** Head south on side roads hugging the coast that will eventually bring you back to the EN1-2A. After driving for about 20 minutes, the road ends at the **Aveiro Cascade,** where a waterfall splashes into an idyllic lagoon.

**5** Get back in your car and backtrack 7 minutes down the EN1-2A to the island's most southeastern point, Ponta do Castelo, where **Gonçalo Velho Lighthouse** perches dramatically over the Atlantic.

**6** En route back to Vila do Porto, stop after a 20-minute drive hugging the island's southern coast at **Formosa Beach** for a sundowner and dinner at one of the local beach bars.

# Sights

## VILA DO PORTO

Vila do Porto is a small town covering a hilly ridge that stretches northward from a marina, having developed around two or three main through roads. The town itself is a long fork of red roofs and whitewashed buildings with the ubiquitous Azorean black basalt trims. The town's core comprises old townhouses, a traditional commerce street **(Rua Teófilo Braga),** and historic monuments such as the **Nossa Senhora da Assunção Church.** The **Fort of São Brás** peers over the marina.

### Nossa Senhora da Assunção Church
**(Igreja de Nossa Senhora da Assunção)**

*Largo da Igreja; tel. 296 882 254; open 24/7; free*

Widely noted as one of (if not the) oldest religious buildings in the Azores archipelago, the Nossa Senhora da Assunção church dates back to the late 15th or early 16th century. With a simple whitewashed facade and gray stone trim, the pretty church underwent a series of alterations during the 18th century but still retains some preserved original features, such as a Gothic side door and Manueline chapel ceiling. Located on the town's main through road, the church is a short 450-meter (1,500-ft) walk

north from the Fort of São Brás, just above the marina.

### Fort of São Brás
**(Forte de São Brás)**

*EN1-2A; tel. 296 886 355; open 24/7; €3*

Also known as the Castle of São Brás, this whitewashed fortress occupies a dominant position high on the hilltop known as Cimo da Rocha, overlooking Vila do Porto. It sits at the town's southernmost tip, about 750 meters (a half mile) from the marina, or a 12-minute walk. Built in the 17th century, its original purpose was to protect the island from pirates and sea raiders on their way back from Brazil. The oldest fort in the Atlantic, at over 500 years old, the fort's original ramparts and cannons harken back to its defensive history. Inside are the commander's house and troop barracks, as well as the chapel of Nossa Senhora da Conceição and an obelisk in honor of Commander Carvalho Araújo. The fort offers wonderful views over the marina and ocean and is a great spot for photos.

### ★ Regional Natural Monument of Pedreira do Campo
**(Monumento Natural da Pedreira do Campo)**

# Vila do Porto

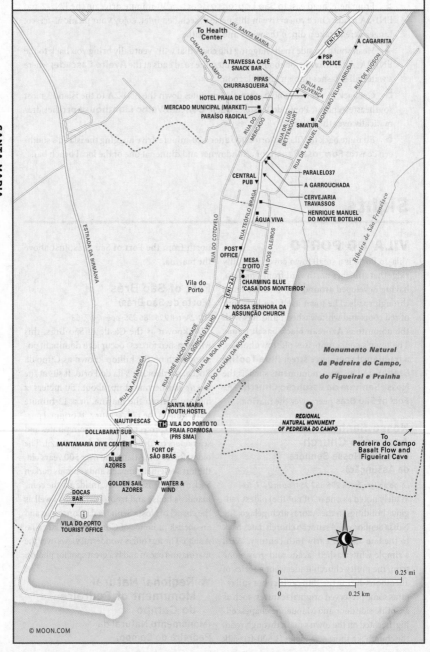

To Health Center

AV. SANTA MARIA

CANADA DO CAMPO

EN1-2A

A CAGARRITA

PSP POLICE

RUA DE OLIVENÇA

RUA DE HUDSON

A TRAVESSA CAFÉ SNACK BAR

PIPAS CHURRASQUEIRA

HOTEL PRAIA DE LOBOS

MERCADO MUNICIPAL (MARKET)

PARAÍSO RADICAL

RUA DO MERCADO

RUA DR. LUÍS BETTENCOURT

RUA DR. MANUEL MONTEIRO VELHO ARRUDA

SMATUR

CENTRAL PUB

RUA TEÓFILO BRAGA

RUA DO COTOVELO

PARALELO37

A GARROUCHADA

CERVEJARIA TRAVASSOS

HENRIQUE MANUEL DO MONTE BOTELHO

ÁGUA VIVA

RUA DOS OLEIROS

Ribeira de São Francisco

POST OFFICE

MESA D'OITO

CHARMING BLUE 'CASA DOS MONTEIROS'

EN1-2A

Vila do Porto

NOSSA SENHORA DA ASSUNÇÃO CHURCH

ESTRADA DA BIRMÂNIA

RUA JOSÉ INÁCIO ANDRADE

RUA GONÇALO VELHO

RUA DA BOA NOVA

RUA DO CALHAU DA ROUPA

*Monumento Natural da Pedreira do Campo, do Figueiral e Prainha*

RUA DA ALFÂNDEGA

SANTA MARIA YOUTH HOSTEL

VILA DO PORTO TO PRAIA FORMOSA (PR5 SMA)

NAUTIPESCAS

DOLLABARAT SUB

MANTAMARIA DIVE CENTER

BLUE AZORES

FORT OF SÃO BRÁS

WATER & WIND

GOLDEN SAIL AZORES

DOCAS BAR

VILA DO PORTO TOURIST OFFICE

REGIONAL NATURAL MONUMENT OF PEDREIRA DO CAMPO

To Pedreira do Campo Basalt Flow and Figueiral Cave

0          0.25 mi

0          0.25 km

© MOON.COM

*Almagreira Village, Pedreira do Campo Natural Monument; open 24/7; free*

Located just east of Vila do Porto town, this 2-square-kilometer (500-acre) swathe of land is rich in excellently preserved examples of oceanic fossils, which has allowed for a specific assessment of the island's make-up and age. Once an area used for rock quarrying, Pedreira do Campo has, since 2004, been classified a protected area due to its unique rock sediments, some of which date back over 5 million years. The rock sediments map the island's geological past and reveal its secrets, proving that Santa Maria was underwater until a few thousand years ago.

The site contains volcanic rocks, marine sediments, and fossils that are unique in the Azores. Within this site is **Figueiral Cave,** a human-made grotto from which clay was extracted to use in the construction of typical Santa Maria houses, and the **Pedreira do Campo basalt flow,** a towering wall of volcanic rock. This area, favored by hikers looking to spot the exceptional fossils, is untouched by urban development. Showcasing the traditional Santa Maria landscape of small walled fields for grazing and farming, it was classified as a protected Natural Monument due to its scientific, educational, and touristic importance.

It's a pleasant 1.3-kilometer (0.8-mi) walk east from Vila do Porto town center, through town and along the coast, to the Pedreira do Campo basalt flow. A designated 160-meter (520-ft) **walkway** takes you through the area, with informative signage posted along the path. To get there, on foot, you can take the South Coast coastal path, which is signposted and starts from the Fort of São Brás. If driving, take the Estrada Municipal de Valverde and turn right along a road called Facho, toward Lugar do Brasil. There's a little area at the start of the walkway for **parking.** One of the best ways to explore Pedreira do Campo is to follow the **PR5 SMA Trilho da Costa Sul hiking trail** (http://trails.visitazores.com/en/node/42), which starts in Vila do Porto

and extends through Pedreira do Campo to Formosa Beach.

## PEDREIRA DO CAMPO BASALT FLOW

*EN1-2A, Almagreira Village; tel. 292 293525, 961638466, or 924126964; www.azoresgeopark.com; open 24/7; free*

Located just east of Vila do Porto, the Pedreira do Campo field is mostly occupied by a show-stopping 200-meter-long (700-ft-long) basalt flow, a fascinating natural attraction classified a Natural Monument due to its geological importance. Standing at over 100 meters (300 ft) high, the basalt flow, formed from a mound of lava that cooled after coming into contact with the sea, towers over visitors. It features unique rock formations, lava pillars that look like a wall of pencils, and a wealth of oceanic fossils embedded in its face, proving that this part of the island was once submerged. A contemporary 160-meter (520-ft) wooden walkway snakes through the site from where visitors can enjoy the best angles of the volcanic masterpiece.

## FIGUEIRAL CAVE (Gruta do Figueiral)

*Almagreira Village; open 24/7; free*

Also located along the South Coast trail (Trilho da Costa Sul), a short walk from the Pedreira do Campo basalt flow, the Figueiral Cave is not a natural cave: It was created for the extraction of limestone and clay for tiles and traditional house construction in the late 1800s-early 1900s. Nearby is an old masonry oven in which the clay was baked. Bring a flashlight to see stalactites and marine fossils in the sedimentary rocks.

## Pico Alto

*Almagreira; open 24/7; free*

A short drive east of Vila do Porto, Pico Alto is the highest point on Santa Maria, at 586 meters (1,920 ft) above sea level. A number of well-posted **hiking trails** and mountain bike routes make it possible to scale Pico Alto, which takes around two hours on foot.

The summit is also accessible by car, with a **parking lot** near a flight of stairs supported by a handrail to ascend to the summit's viewing platform. This is ideal for those not up for a strenuous hike, as some of the climbs are quite steep. On a clear day, the views of the island and its two clearly distinct halves—one green and scenic the other flat and plain—are astounding.

# WESTERN SANTA MARIA

The most populous settlement in western Santa Maria outside of Vila do Porto is the village of **Anjos,** a quaint, peaceful hamlet comprising a handful of whitewashed houses that are mostly rented out as holiday homes today. Its first inhabitants were, history has it, from the Algarve and Alentejo regions on mainland Portugal, and this is to some extent reflected in Anjos's characteristic architecture, with its rectangular houses and cylindrical chimneys. Today, Anjos maintains a quiet, predominantly agricultural way of life.

## Nossa Senhora dos Anjos Hermitage

*EN2-2, São Pedro parish; free*
Located in the village of Anjos, a 10-minute drive or 1.5 hour walk directly north of Vila do Porto, is this beautiful little 15th-century hermitage. Originally built circa 1439, entirely from wood and covered in hay, this tiny whitewashed chapel is said to be the first temple erected on the island of Santa Maria and, consequently, the first in the Azores. In front of the hermitage is a bronze sculpture of Christopher Columbus, who, according to local legend, worshipped at the chapel on his return from the Americas. A freestanding rock window frame is the only remnant of the original hermitage and still stands on the site of the more recent chapel.

Inside, the hermitage has a unique nave and altarpiece, with the altar boasting a polychrome *azulejo*-tiled frontispiece, featuring exotic creatures and birds. The hermitage does not have fixed opening hours and is usually locked, but a lady who lives in a little side-house holds the key. She's happy to open the hermitage to visitors if you knock on the door and catch her at home.

You can **walk** from Vila do Porto to the hermitage (7.9 km/4.9 mi, 1 hour 40 minutes one-way), through the middle of the western flank of the island; from the marina, head north following the Av. da Terceira, the Caminho de Santana de Baixo, and Caminho da Escola. If you're driving, head north on the **EN1-2A** out of Vila do Porto, taking the Estudante de Santana route (9 km/6 mi, 15 minutes).

## ★ Barreiro da Faneca Protected Landscape

*São Pedro parish; open 24/7; free*
Also known as the "Red Desert," the protected landscape of Barreiro da Faneca, located in the parish of São Pedro (on the northern coast of the island, northeast of Vila do Porto), is a remarkable sight. Spanning 8.35 square kilometers (3.22 sq mi), the protected landscape also includes a number of picturesque bays on the coast. Barreiro da Faneca is arid, clay-colored, and sparse; the desert-like landscape is almost Martian, a wrinkly bald patch in the middle of dense woodland. Barreiro da Faneca's distinctness comes from the volcanic pyroclastic minerals contained in this little spot of the island, which became reddish and clay-like in the island's warm and humid weather. Everything seems to stand still here in this surreal red-hued scenery, a clay pan that's gradually being reclaimed by nature. It seems astounding that anything can grow here, but fringing the Red Desert are endemic species of flora, such as St. John's wort and Azorean laurel. It's also home to birds, including the endemic island subspecies the Santa Maria star goldcrest.

A half hour should be enough time to walk around the well-trodden paths left by visitors,

---

**1:** Nossa Senhora da Assunção Church **2:** forest on the slopes of Pico Alto **3:** Barreiro da Faneca Protected Landscape **4:** architecture in Vila do Porto

but beyond the eerie landscape, there's little else of note in this area.

This extraordinary mini-desert can be a little tricky to find despite being signposted. It is a 12-minute drive north from Vila do Porto, along the **EN1-2A** road to the **EN2-2**. Head toward the parish of São Pedro, then toward the north coast to Lugar da Faneca. From here, keep an eye out for the signposts—there are dirt roads and surfaced roads that both lead to the Red Desert. If you want to cover more ground, the site can be crossed with your rental car on dirt roads when the weather is warm and dry, but this is not advisable at rainy times when the terrain is muddy. If you have more time and want to slow down and explore **on foot,** park on the outskirts in a little designated **parking lot** just before the footpath through the site, on its eastern edge.

# EASTERN SANTA MARIA
## São Lourenço Bay
### (Baía de São Lourenço)
*Santa Bárbara parish; open 24/7; free*
Shaped like an open-air amphitheater, the dramatic high cliffs encasing the sparse scattering of whitewashed cottages that line São Lourenço Bay seem to dwarf the tiny houses at their feet. Covering some 113 hectares (279 acres), the São Lourenço Bay Nature Reserve is formed from a volcanic crater that became bay-shaped after a section of it disintegrated. The bay is located in parish of Santa Bárbara, on the northeast coast of Santa Maria. São Lourenço Bay is bookended by **Matos Point** to the north and **Black Point** (Ponta Negra) to the south, an interesting rock formation with prime examples of pillow lava and fossil deposits. The lovely brownish-sand **São Lourenço Beach** stretches in between.

### ESPIGÃO VIEWPOINT
### (Miradouro do Espigão)
*São Lourenço Bay, Vila do Porto; open 24/7; free*
Locally referred to as the Espigão viewpoint, the São Lourenço Bay viewpoint is perched high above the bay. It provides panoramic views over the dramatic sloped cultivated hillside and the stunning bay and ocean below.

## Nossa Senhora dos Prazeres Hermitage
*EN1-2A, Maia, Santo Espírito; open 24/7; free*
Dating from the 17th century, the pretty Nossa Senhora dos Prazeres Hermitage is a prime example of the typical whitewashed and black basalt trim architecture characteristic of the Azores. It was first erected circa 1685 and restored centuries later in 1997, with funds from emigrants in the United States and Canada. Strongly linked to local folklore, it is the village of Maia's main church.

The hermitage is intrinsically entwined with the local legend of a man, a local vintner, who was kidnapped after the little chapel was plundered by pirates. They stole all items of value, including a statue of Nossa Senhora dos Prazeres (Our Lady of Pleasures). The vintner, whose family believed he had been killed, was held captive by the pirates for refusing to join their group. The vitner made a promise to Nossa Senhora to acquire a new statue if he ever returned to Santa Maria alive, but he fell ill in the meantime. Taking pity on the ailing Azoreans, the pirates eventually returned him to the island, and he did indeed fulfill his promise, though he died a few years later from a disease he contracted during his time held captive.

## Aveiro Cascade
*EN1-2A, Santo Espírito; open 24/7; free*
Toward the end of the small village of Maia on Santa Maria's east coast is the Aveiro Cascade, an idyllic spot with a stunning, towering waterfall that pours into a small lagoon at the bottom, much to the delight of the resident ducks. It is a short 700-meter (0.4-mi), 8-minute hike from the nearby Nossa Senhora dos Prazeres Hermitage. A few rocks and a wooden bridge are involved to reach the beautiful spot, but the magical scenery is well worth the effort. Park near the Nossa Senhora dos Prazeres Hermitage and follow the EN1-2A road to the spot. To reach

the waterfall, take the **EN1-2A** from Vila do Porto, heading southeast toward the parishes of Fornos and Valverde and the island's southeasternmost tip. Then follow the coast north (3 km/2 mi, 5 minutes by car) till you arrive at the waterfall.

## Gonçalo Velho Lighthouse
### (Farol do Gonçalo Velho)

*Ponta do Castelo; tel. 296 884 252; open Wed. 2pm-5pm, other days by appointment; free*

A seemingly infinite narrow stairway unfurls along a hilltop crest from the end of the road toward the truly beautiful Gonçalo Velho Lighthouse, also known as the Maia Lighthouse, named after the nearby local village. It's located a 30-minute drive east of Vila do Porto town.

Set on a dramatic pointy outcrop in the pretty hamlet of Maia, which splays at the foot of Santa Maria's soaring coastline, the lighthouse opened in 1927, with a square stone tower 14 meters (46 ft) high. Its red flashlight is visible up to 54 kilometers (34 mi). A nearby old **whaling station,** or *vigia*, a small white-washed house on the hillside from where whalers used to scour the ocean for signs of whales, can be also be seen on the way to the lighthouse by taking a right turn off the main pathway. The views along the route are stunning.

# Beaches and Pools

Santa Maria is the Azores' ultimate beach destination, famous for its soft, golden beaches (a rarity in the archipelago), translucent waters, and laid-back island way of life. Formosa—meaning Formidable—Beach is the island's most popular stretch of sand and one of the best-known beaches in the Azores.

## WESTERN SANTA MARIA
### ★ Angels' Bay
### (Baía dos Anjos)

*Anjos; open 24/7; free*

On the northern coast of Vila do Porto is Baía dos Anjos, or Angels' Bay, which is indeed a heavenly sight. The rocky bay takes its name from nearby Anjos village. It's a natural amphitheater of volcanic rock and ocean pools with a small fishing port, and it's a classified Natural Reserve. It is also of historic importance as it is said to be the spot where Christopher Columbus landed on his return from his voyage to the Americas. The explorer reputedly worshipped at a nearby chapel, the **Nossa Senhora dos Anjos Hermitage.**

The scenic bay is hugely popular among locals and tourists in summer for its fabulous natural pool, and it's also a popular spot for migrating birds. Given its role as one of the most popular seaside resorts in the archipelago, charming Anjos can become rather busy in peak summer months, but it generally offers enough space to not feel overcrowded. Anjos is a place to wind down and soak up the sun around the lovely natural pool.

## ANJOS SWIMMING COMPLEX

*Lugar dos Anjos; open 24/7; free*

Located in the Anjos Bay, a classified Natural Reserve, the quaint and peaceful Anjos swimming complex is great spot for the whole family on a warm day. Backed by volcanic cliffs that keep the wind at bay, the pool complex comprises a vast, segmented pool that fills with refreshing seawater, complemented by chunky steps on which visitors can lay out their towels and soak up the sun. Above the pool complex is a barbecue area. The water temperature is generally pleasant year-round, reaching an average 21°C (70°F) through summer. The site is also accessible for visitors with disabilities.

Stick around until sunset for a sun-down drink with a stunning sea view at the local **Bar dos Anjos** (Rua Francisco Lopes Anjo; tel. 296 886 734; Thurs.-Tues. 9am-10pm), which overlooks the pool. Parasols can be

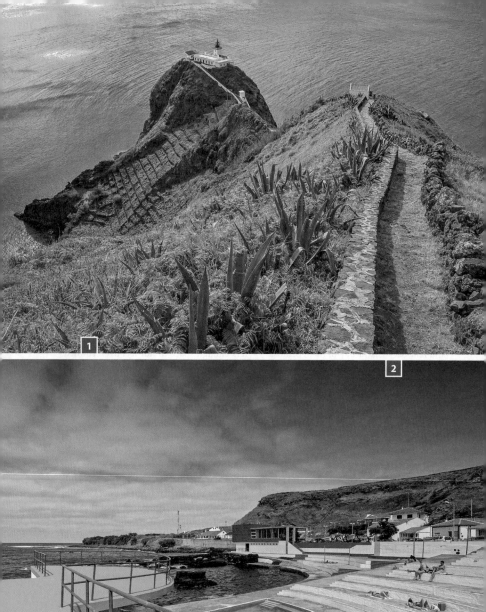

# Santa Maria's Golden Sand Beaches

Santa Maria is the oldest, driest, and warmest island in the archipelago, plus it spent various periods of time submerged under the sea. All these factors created a unique geological formation and natural sediment that make Santa Maria different from the other islands. It has a distinctly Mediterranean feel, and its beaches—due to the island's high limestone composition—have fine, pale sands, rather than the gruff black volcanic sands of its peers.

## IF YOU WANT...

- **Spectacular views:** The coast of **Angels' Bay** is shaped like an amphitheater, with a natural pool the star of the show (page 105).

- **Picture-perfect golden sand:** With its golden strand and clear blue waters, **Formosa Beach** is the perfect alternative beach destination (page 107).

- **To get close to nature:** The protected area of **São Lourenço Bay** offers the chance to see endemic flora and fauna while you're taking a dip (page 109).

beach on São Lourenço Bay

rented on-site, and there are also showers to rinse off after a dip in the salty seawater. During peak months a lifeguard is on duty, and there is plenty of parking in a nearby lot.

## EASTERN SANTA MARIA
### ★ Formosa Beach
### (Praia Formosa)

*Almagreira; open 24/7; free*

Formosa Beach is one of the finest beaches in the entire Azores archipelago. Found in the parish of Almagreira, a short 10-minute drive east of Vila do Porto, it is a long slither of fine blond sand bathed by crystal-clear warm waters. One of only two golden sand beaches on the island (the other is in São Lourenço Bay) and a rarity in the Azores, Formosa Beach offers plenty of space for visitors. It is equipped with public parking, restrooms, showers, and a snack bar. The beach is set against a

---

**1:** Gonçalo Velho Lighthouse **2:** Anjos Swimming Complex

stunning backdrop of lush green hillsides and cliffs. The ruins of an old 16th-century fort, the **Fort of São João Baptista,** can be found on the western edge of the beach, while at the eastern end is a **campsite** (tel. 296 883 959; www.cm-viladoporto.pt/SITE/servicos/pcampismo.php; tents from €5/night, bungalows from €50), open only during summer.

Every year over a weekend in late August, the beach hosts the hugely popular **August Tide** (Maré de Agosto) music festival (www.maredeagosto.com), one of the best-known festivals in the Azores, which is when the village really reaches a fever pitch. Despite its popularity, this beach rarely feels too crowded, even in summer, but it does become significantly smaller in size at high tide.

## Maia Bathing Site
### (Piscina da Maia)

*ER 1-2, Vila do Porto; open 24/7; free*

The Maia bathing site is the ultimate infinity pool: a circular, natural pool filled with

crystalline water that reaches 22°C (72°F) in summer. It's flanked by distinctive volcanic rock formations and green walled hillside terraces. The bathing site is set among a protected Nature Reserve, and its peaceful, natural setting overlooking the Atlantic is much appreciated by visitors and locals. In peak summer months, a bar opens to provide refreshments, but make sure you bring your own towels, which can be laid out on the cement steps surrounding the pool. Access is unregulated, but the pool is rarely too crowded to enjoy.

## São Lourenço Bay
(Baía de São Lourenço)
### SÃO LOURENÇO BEACH
(Praia de São Lourenço)
*ER 1-2, Vila do Porto; open 24/7; free*
Located on the northeast flank of Santa Maria, a 20-minute drive east from Vila do Porto along the main **EN1-2A road,** the shell-like São Lourenço Bay is breathtakingly beautiful. A unique, almost tropical landscape—a classified protected area—awaits visitors. Tiered, dry stone vine corrals slope down in a semi-cone toward a pure white bay lapped by crystalline water, with the azure sea and blond sand separated from the green hill backdrop and its web-like corrals by a string of whitewashed seafront houses.

The bay itself is home to a number of endemic plant species, such as green heather, *pau-branco*, Azorean euphorbia, local laurel, and the fire tree, and it's also considered a very important habitat for the nesting of various protected marine birds. Park along the São Lourenço village beachfront and explore this magical area on foot, or by kayak or stand-up paddle board; inquire at **Paraíso Radical** in Vila do Porto for information about renting a kayak or paddle board.

# Kayaking and Stand-Up Paddle Boarding

Another bonus of Santa Maria's clear, calm waters is that they lend themselves perfectly to kayaking and stand-up paddle boarding, so non-divers need not miss out on the island's underwater beauty. The rocky coast around **São Lourenço Bay** is a popular spot for kayaking and SUP.

## VILA DO PORTO
### PARAÍSO RADICAL
*Rua Frei Gonçalo Velho, 74; tel. 962 587 537 or 962 588 940; www.paraisoradical.pt; Mon.-Fri. 9:30am-noon and 2pm-6pm, Sat. 9:30am-1pm; from €43*
Paraíso Radical operates an array of fun water sports and on-land activities, including kayak excursions and jet-ski tours. You can also rent equipment (for example, kayaks for three adults and one child from €27.50/day) as well as enjoy the organized activities.

**1:** Maia Bathing Site **2:** view of São Lourenço Bay

# ★ Diving and Snorkeling

With crystalline waters that offer excellent year-round visibility, Santa Maria is one of the Azores' top islands for snorkeling and diving. One of its main attractions is that in summer, the island's waters are visited by the largest fish in the world, the majestic **whale shark.** The **Formigas Islets** and **Dollabarat Reef** seamount, some of Europe's best dive spots, are on Santa Maria's doorstep, approximately 45 kilometers (28 mi) northeast of the island, with a wealth of sea life in the waters surrounding it. In addition, the island has at least another 50 well-known spots, including underwater caves, passages, walls, and plains, most of which are accessible only by boat. Organized dive groups are generally limited to small numbers, which is intended to help preserve the region's natural heritage. A number of island-based companies run guided tours and equipment rentals for visitors to safely and comfortably enjoy the island's stunning underwater attractions.

## DIVE SPOTS

Most dive centers operating on Santa Maria have tours to the top diving spots, like the ones listed below.

### PEDRINHA REEF

At less than one mile (a 10-minute boat trip) from Vila do Porto marina, Pedrinha Reef is a popular spot for diving and snorkeling. Gentle currents and a relatively shallow depth make it a good spot for all levels of divers, from beginners through to the more experienced, and it's also an excellent site for night dives and underwater photography. Easily accessed, it is one of the best-known spots on Santa Maria. Underwater, there is a large platform covered with schools of fish, ranging from colorful swallowtail seaperches to large dusky groupers, throngs of pelagic species, and even devil rays at the deepest points of the reef, which drops to a depth of 20 meters (66 ft)

in the north flank and over 40 meters (130 ft) on the south slope. Caves and cracks are other features to explore at the Pedrinha Reef. The **Haliotis** tour to Pedrinha is particularly recommended.

### AMBRÓSIO REEF

One of the most popular protected areas for diving is the unmissable Ambrósio Reef. Shallow in parts and deep in others, and at times prone to strong currents, this spot is great for divers of all levels of experience, from the less experienced to those who enjoy an adventure. It's also a great spot for snorkelers, due to the sheer abundance of marine life that can be found relatively close to the surface. Just 5 kilometers (3 mi) from the northwest tip of the island, it offers the experience of a remote seamount without having to travel long distances by boat. Curious devil rays as well as schools of large pelagic fish make regular appearances, as does the graceful whale shark, on occasion, in summer when the waters are warmest. Contact **Mantamaria Dive Center** for information on tours to this reef.

### FORMIGAS ISLETS NATURE RESERVE AND DOLLABARAT REEF

The Formigas Islets, also sometimes called the Formigas Bank, are a group of rocky outcrops designated a Natural Reserve off the eastern group of the Azores archipelago, located some 43 kilometers (27 mi) or a 70-minute sail northeast of Santa Maria island. Documented by explorers Diogo de Silves and Gonçalo Velho Cabral in 1431, the bank extends over 13 kilometers (8 mi), comprising 4-million-year-old basalt flows and calcareous fossiliferous sediments dating back 4-6 million years. Essentially a submarine volcano, inhabited by deep-dwelling marine species, coral, and sponge, it is home to many popular dive spots, namely the *Olympia* shipwreck—at a depth of 30-50 meters (100-160ft)—and a number of shallow reefs. Given its remote location and strong currents, the Formigas Islets are only recommended for experienced divers, but for divers who do have advanced skills, this is one of the finest dive sites in the Azores.

Located 5 kilometers (3 mi) south-southeast of the Formigas Islets, the Dollabarat Reef offers a unique dive experience, but, like the Formigas, due to its remoteness and strong currents, it is only recommended for experienced divers. The reef is part of the Formigas Islets Nature Reserve, which covers 35 square kilometers (14 sq mi). Both spots are classified marine reserves and teem with fascinating sea life, from turtles to tunas, barracudas, rays, and even the reclusive giant mantas, if you're lucky enough to spot one, as well as the Galapagos shark. Many dive operators combine the two spots in one trip. **Mantamaria Dive Center** and **Dollabarat Sub** both offer tours to these diving spots.

# DIVE CENTERS AND SCHOOLS
## Vila do Porto
### MANTAMARIA DIVE CENTER
*Vila do Porto marina; tel. 296 882 166; https:// divecenter.mantamaria.com; Mon.-Fri. 8:30am-noon and 2pm-5:30pm; snorkeling from €40*
Mantamaria's team of experienced and professional diving instructors and divemasters, skippers, and support personnel strive to provide a safe and relaxing subaquatic experience to Santa Maria visitors. The center operates three vessels, specially equipped for diving and dive tours around the island. Minimum group numbers (eight people) apply.

### HALIOTIS
*Rua Cruz Teixeira, Hotel Colombo; tel. 913 123 828; www.haliotis.pt; daily 9am-6pm; dives from €75*
With dive centers in half a dozen locations in the Azores and mainland Portugal, dive specialists at Haliotis run dive courses and excursions. Trips include dives in underwater spots around Santa Maria island, exploring caves, canyons, and lava formations.

### DOLLABARAT SUB
*tel. 916 497 176; www.dollabaratsub.com; daily 9am-8pm; dives from €45 plus equipment rental (€25)*
Maritime tourism company Dollabarat Sub offers a host of seasonal leisure activities (June-Oct.) designed to provide visitors will unforgettable moments. It operates boat trips around Santa Maria island as well as to the Formigas Islets and São Miguel island, and dive trips to Santa Maria's top spots. Snorkeling trips to the Ambrósio and Pedrinha reefs are also available from €30.

# Fishing

Santa Maria's coastline is rich in fish: Among the species are sea bream, porgy, grouper, wrasse, mackerel, bluefish, barracuda, and sawfish, as well as huge blue and white marlins, Atlantic bluefin tuna, and other species of tuna. Two particularly good spots to cast off from shore are the **São Lourenço Bay,** historically a popular fishing port, and the **Maia** coastline on the southeastern tip of the island. A number of companies operate open-sea tours for sports and recreational fishing, both from Santa Maria and from Ponta Delgada on nearby São Miguel. There's a well-stocked fishing shop, **Nautipescas,** in Vila do Porto, or contact the **Vila do Porto Harbor Village Marina** (tel. 296 882 782; https://portosdosacores.pt) for more specific information on fishing in Santa Maria.

## VILA DO PORTO

### HENRIQUE MANUEL DO MONTE BOTELHO

*Rua Teófilo Braga, 127; tel. 919 289 945*

For all your big-game fishing needs and manned or unmanned boat rentals, get in touch with local expert Henrique Manuel do Monte Botelho.

### NAUTIPESCAS

*EN1-2A; tel. 296 883 381; www.nautipescas.pt/online; Mon.-Fri. 10am-noon and 1pm-6pm, Sat. 10am-noon*

Fishing store Nautipescas is packed with everything you could need for a spot of fishing on Santa Maria—all sorts of fishing, including spear-fishing. From rods to reels, lures, nets, and bait, this shop is a must for fishing enthusiasts.

# Whale-Watching and Boat Tours

Sightings of whales, including sei whales, pilot whales, sperm whales, and even the massive whale shark, can be seen year round from most of the Azores' islands, Santa Maria included, but the best time to enjoy a boat trip is **May to October,** when the sea is calmest.

With its excellent sailing conditions for most of the year—especially April through October—and abundant stunning bays, steep green terraced hills, and crystal-clear waters that make for unique approaches by boat, Santa Maria is an exceptional and riveting spot for sailing. Most trips leave from Vila do Porto marina.

## VILA DO PORTO

### PARALELO37

*Rua Dr. Luís Bettencourt; tel. 296 883 455; www. paralelo37.pt; daily 9am-6pm; prices on request*

Head out for the high seas aboard one of Paralelo37's vessels for a spot of whale- and dolphin-watching. Seize the opportunity to swim with the beautiful marine creatures. Other boat trips and sea safaris are also available.

### GOLDEN SAIL AZORES

*Vila do Porto marina; tel. 966 302 056 or 296 884 277; www.goldensailazores.com; trips from €35 pp, charters from €1,300/weekend in high season*

Explore Santa Maria and the Azores' other islands with a yacht charter. Golden Sail provides sailboat rentals with or without a skipper, as well as sailboat tours, day and half-day trips along Santa Maria's coast, weekends in São Miguel (from €180 pp), and experiences like romantic sunset sails and group events.

### WATER & WIND

*Vila do Porto Marina; tel. 912 533 509; www. waterandwind.eu; one-week diving-live-aboard from €2,250*

Head out to some of the Azores' top diving spots aboard a sumptuous catamaran. Water & Wind offers a range of experiences and activities, from sunset trips (from €40 pp), to overnight snorkeling excursions, all-inclusive tailored diving vacations, diving expeditions, charters, and general sailing experiences.

## EASTERN SANTA MARIA

### BLUE AZORES

*Calheta, Santo Espírito; tel. 916 039 582; www. blueazores.com, from €3,290/week high season (Apr.-Oct.)*

See Santa Maria's stunning coastline from the comfort of a chartered sailboat. Blue Azores's luxurious catamaran with its traditional handcrafted interior, complete with an experienced skipper, provides plenty of space and is perfect for families with children. Island-hop to your heart's content, explore Santa Maria's coastline, spend a day at sea whale-watching, or enjoy a day trip to nearby São Miguel island.

# Hiking

## WESTERN SANTA MARIA
### VILA DO PORTO (SÃO BRÁS FORT) TO FORMOSA BEACH (PR5 SMA)

**Hiking Distance:** 7 kilometers (4 mi) one-way
**Hiking Time:** 3 hours
**Trailhead:** São Brás Fort
**Information and Maps:** http://trails.visitazores.com/pt-pt/trilhos-dos-acores/santa-maria/costa-sul

Santa Maria has many popular, well-mapped hiking routes, but perhaps the best-known trek is the São Brás Fort to Formosa Beach trail. The signposted trailhead starts at the São Brás Fort and takes hikers on a scenic 7-kilometer (4-mi) route heading east along the island's southern coast. The medium-intensity route, also known as the South Coast Trail, runs through the Regional Natural Monument of Pedreira do Campo, Figueiral Cave, and Prainha seaside village, and it ends at the Formosa Beach parking lot. In Pedreira do Campo, underwater volcanic formations and fossil deposits from two different formation periods can be observed. Once at Formosa Beach, catch the **Line 2 bus** (www.transportesdesantamaria.com/Horarios/SantoAntónioViladoPorto.aspx; at least four times daily 10am-6pm; around €5) back to Vila do Porto, or call a **taxi** (tel. 296 882 199), which will take around 6 minutes back to town and cost about €10.

### PICO ALTO HIKE (PRC2SMA)

**Hiking Distance:** 6.2 kilometers (3.9 mi) round-trip
**Hiking Time:** 2 hours round-trip
**Trailhead:** Pico Alto parking lot
**Information and Maps:** http://trails.visitazores.com/en/trails-azores/santa-maria/pico-alto

This two-hour round-trip trek around Pico Alto mountain rewards hikers with stunning 360-degree vistas of the island and its two distinct sides: the southern side, which is flat and plain, and the northern side, lush and scenic. Hikers pass through several natural viewpoints en route and climb to the Pico Alto peak. The final section of the trail passes a monument erected in memory of the victims of the biggest plane crash in Portugal (Independent Air Flight 1851), which occurred in 1989 when a Boeing 707 charter flight from Bergamo, Italy, to Punta Cana, Dominican Republic, struck Pico Alto while on approach to Santa Maria Airport for a scheduled stopover.

Take a bottle of water and a snack with you, as there are no facilities en route or at the top.

### LAND AND SEA HIKE (PRC3SMA)

**Hiking Distance:** 9.7 kilometers (6 mi) round-trip
**Hiking Time:** 2.5 hours round-trip
**Trailhead:** Next to Santa Bárbara church, parish of Santa Bárbara
**Information and Maps:** http://trails.visitazores.com/en/trails-azores/santa-maria/entre-serra-e-o-mar

This 2.5-hour round-trip hike takes trekkers from the parish of Santa Bárbara, located on the northeast of the island, on a gentle climb past ancient windmills to **Poço da Pedreira** pond, a tropical-looking, rain-filled former quarry. It also passes along the panoramic São Lourenço Bay and back to the parish of Santa Bárbara, showcasing Santa Maria's finest countryside and coastal views.

## EASTERN SANTA MARIA
### RIBEIRA DE MALOÁS

**Hiking Distance:** 1 kilometer (0.6 mi) one-way
**Hiking Time:** 20 minutes one-way
**Trailhead:** Caminho do Gigante road, off the EN1-2A in Santo Espírito parish; park at the end, near the site
**Information and Maps:** Vila do Porto Tourist Office (www.visitazores.com)

# The Great Route of Santa Maria

The hike of all hikes in the Azores, the ultimate island trail, the Great Route of Santa Maria (GR01SMA; http://trails.visitazores.com/en/grand-routes/great-route-santa-maria) takes hikers around the entire island on a 78-kilometer (48-mi) counterclockwise circular journey through heritage and culture, past all the island's major sights and most beautiful, unspoiled island scenery. Starting at the historic Fort of São Brás, this fascinating walk showcases Santa Maria's rich and unique geomorphology, paleontology, and culture, passing highlights such as Praia Formosa Beach, São Lourenço Bay, the oldest chapel in the Azores in Anjos parish, and the highest point of the island, Pico Alto. It strings together sections of five existing smaller trails, weaving through all the island's important geosites and protected natural parks.

The Great Route of Santa Maria was conceived by a group of friends with a shared passion for walking and showing their island off to visitors. It was formalized and made official in 2015. While not necessarily strenuous, there are stretches that are steep and testing on legs and lungs, and, in some parts, on the nerves. Given its length, this is a hike for avid walkers.

## EATING AND SLEEPING ALONG THE WAY

For provisions, you can stock up at local **mini-markets** or **grocery stores** in the parishes along the way or have a meal in a **local café.** Another option is to pay a little extra and book with **Ilha a Pé** (tel. 964 474 768; https://ilhape.com), which provides accommodation specifically for the Great Route in the form of clean and simple eco-cottages (renovated barns) along the way. The cottages sleep up to six in bunks, and they ferry ahead luggage and meals. Packages start from €225 for four nights of accommodation with dinner and breakfast.

## THE FOUR STAGES

The Great Route is broken down into four stages of roughly 20 kilometers (12 mi) each, usually spread over four days, starting at the Fort of São Brás in Vila do Porto. Each stage can be enjoyed independently. If you're pushed for time and can only do one leg, **Stage 1** is a good choice due to its proximity to Vila do Porto, and you'll take in many island highlights.

### Stage 1: Vila do Porto to Cardal Parish

**Trailhead:** *Fort of São Brás*

The Great Route of Santa Maria starts with a 16.5-kilometer (10.3-mi) trek along the scenic coast west of main town Vila do Porto, running past some of the island's iconic geological sites. This first stage, which will likely take around 6.5 hours to complete if you keep a steady pace, sets off from the **Fort of São Brás.** It hems the island's south coast heading east to the volcanically rich **Pedreira do Campo** site, passing the **Figueiral Cave** and its old clay ovens and relics of fortresses. Keep an eye out for **fossils** in the rocks that can also be spotted in this area. The route then leads on to the fabulous **Formosa Beach,** following an old beach road to the parish of Santo Espírito. A string of farming paths and rural roads give way through this area, to the **Ribeira de Maloás** site, a geological formation unique in the

A 20-meter-high cascade of water pours over a towering curtain of magmatic pillars, reminiscent of a smaller version of the Giant's Causeway in Northern Ireland. This huge rock wall, an important geological site, is one of Santa Maria's most distinctive and unique attractions. However, the waterfall is only active in the wetter months, November-March. Located a 25-minute drive east of Vila do Porto, the Ribeira de

archipelago, then following more country lanes and dirt tracks to the end of this stretch: the rural hamlet of **Cardal.**

## Stage 2: Cardal to Norte Parish

**Trailhead:** *Cardal parish*

The second leg of the Great Route covers the entire extension of the east coast, a 21.5-kilometer (13.4 mi), 7.5-hour trek between the rural parish of Cardal and Norte parish. This walk encompasses the island's most southeastern point, Ponta do Castelo, where the **Gonçalo Velho Lighthouse** perches dramatically on an outcrop jutting into the Atlantic, connected to the mainland by an endless stairway running along the crest. This area is scattered with endemic flora and interesting geological formations. Another incredible sight along this section of the Great Route is the staggering **São Lourenço Bay** backed by its delicate vineyards. Keep trekking north toward Norte parish, more specifically **Lugar do Norte,** where this leg ends, with glorious views over the entire north coast and little islets out at sea.

## Stage 3: Norte to Bananeiras

**Trailhead:** *Lugar do Norte*

Stage 3 of this island-size walk is a 16.5-kilometer (10.3-mi), 6.5-hour hike through the rural inland, between the parishes of Norte and Bananeiras. This stretch is peppered with ponds and peaks, waterfalls, old windmills, and fountains. It first traverses the parish of **Santa Bárbara,** through the hamlets of Lagos, Poço Grande, and Boavista. A highlight is the **Poço da Pedreira pond,** with its sheer, soaring back wall and singing pond life—a spot that looks almost prehistoric. From here, the route goes along country lanes and hikers' pathways towards Cruz dos Picos, where **Pico Alto,** the island's highest point at 587 meters (1,926 ft), can be found. From here it's all downhill toward **Bananeiras,** and you'll enjoy privileged open views along the way.

## Stage 4: Bananeiras back to Vila do Porto

**Trailhead:** *Bananeiras parish*

Bananeiras to Vila do Porto is the last and longest leg of the Great Route, at 23.5 kilometers (37.8 mi), taking 8 eight hours to complete. It unfurls along the entire west coast, skirting beautiful bays, old watermills, and intriguing geosites. It takes in the Martian-red, weirdly barren **Barreiro da Faneca** geosite, where the island's last eruptive phase occurred. A number of marked side roads lead off on detours from this spot to lovely viewpoints with sprawling vistas over the north coast. From here it's onward toward the charming parish of **Anjos,** with its distinctive square houses, famed for being home to the oldest chapel in the Azores, which was once visited by Christopher Columbus in 1493. In Anjos, you'll also find the heavenly **Angels' Bay** and the popular **Anjos swimming complex.** Once you've circumvented this highly scenic spot, the airport should begin to come into sight, and from here it's the homeward stretch, back toward the starting point: the historic center of **Vila do Porto.**

Maloás site is accessed via a short hike from the main EN1-2A road, most of which hugs the cliffs along the coast. The turn-off is signposted, but some caution is advised as the hike can be tricky and slippery in places. Tourist offices supply maps and more information on how to reach the site.

# Adventure Sports

In addition to its compelling underwater attractions, Santa Maria on land is an adventurer's playground, boasting conditions for thrilling activities like canyoning, jeep safaris, coasteering, biking, and rappel.

## VILA DO PORTO

### BOOTLÁ

*Lugar da Cruz Teixeira; tel. 911 849 546; www.bootla. pt; open 24/7; bike rentals €25 for full day (8 hours)*

Sustainable tourism company Bootlá provides various services, including organized adventure activities such as island jeep safaris, canyoning and coasteering, trekking and rappel, and bus tours with English-speaking guides, to showcase Santa Maria's unique attributes. Bike rentals are also available.

### SMATUR

*Rua Dr. Manuel Monteiro Velho Arruda, 115; tel. 969 213 532 or 918579524; www.smatur.pt; daily 8am-midnight; activities from €25 pp*

With deep understanding of Santa Maria's history and heritage, eco tour agency Smatur runs a number of nature-inspired activities, namely guided hikes, mountain biking, customized tours, and bird-watching.

# Festivals and Events

Santa Maria plays host to a number of colorful and thrilling festivities through the year, but things really reach fever pitch in August, with the **Our Lady of the Assumption Festival** to celebrate the island's patron saint. This is followed swiftly by the **August Tide** (Maré de Agosto) music festival, one of the largest and most popular in the archipelago. This means accommodations will usually be pretty full throughout summer, especially during August, so make sure to book well in advance if visiting Santa Maria at that time of year.

## SPRING

### LORD HOLY CHRIST OF THE MIRACLES FESTIVAL
### (Festas de Senhor Santo Cristo dos Milagres)

*Vila do Porto; end of May*

Vila do Porto's contribution to the Holy Ghost Festivals that take place throughout the Azores between April and September happens at the end of May. The festival of Senhor Santo Cristo dos Milagres (Lord Holy Christ of the Miracles) is a popular annual religious celebration on Santa Maria, involving mass and a procession. Across the islands, these festivities harken back to the original settlements, having been introduced by the Order of Christ and the Franciscan monks in the 14th century. Hotels fill up for these festivals, so book well in advance during this period.

## SUMMER

### OUR LADY OF THE ASSUMPTION FESTIVAL
### (Festas de Nossa Senhora da Assunção)

*Vila do Porto; mid-Aug.*

Every year in mid-August, Santa Maria commemorates its patron saint, Our Lady of the Assumption, with varied celebrations that make up the island's biggest festival. August 15th is the high point of celebrations, which include a plethora of activities that are staged in and around Vila do Porto. Festivities include religious events intertwined with dancing, concerts, handicraft stalls, and gastronomic fairs.

## AUGUST TIDE MUSIC FESTIVAL
### (Maré de Agosto)

*Formosa Beach; tel. 296 883 151; www.maredeagosto.com; last week in August*

Perhaps the coolest festival on Santa Maria, and one of the most famous in the Azores, is the Maré de Agosto (August Tide) music festival: a weekend-long party on the beach with concerts, held one of the latter weekends in August. Staged on Formosa Beach, it features national and international world music acts, attracting droves of locals and tourists. There is a **campsite** to one end of Formosa Beach for those who enjoy camping festivals. Plenty more accommodation is available in the form of local rentals and B&Bs, but book well in advance for this weekend.

## FALL
### SÃO PEDRO GONÇALVES FESTIVITIES

*Vila do Porto docks; beginning of Sept.*

Locally known as the "Fishermen's Festivities," the São Pedro Gonçalves celebrations are held over the first few days in September to commemorate the patron saint of seafarers, São Pedro Gonçalves Telmo, who is honored with a religious program of masses and processions, music events, dance performances, and street entertainment, in thanks for the year's catches. The festivities also serve as a kind of farewell to summer.

# Shopping

## VILA DO PORTO
### ÁGUA-VIVA

*Rua Teófilo Braga 13; tel. 915 088 719; www.facebook.com/aguaviva.pt; Mon.-Fri. 10am-6:30pm, Sat. 10am-1pm*

For the best typical souvenirs, handcrafted jewelry, and personalized, hand-dyed cotton goods, head to Água-Viva in Vila do Porto, a gem of a shop whose custom T-shirts have amassed quite a following.

## EASTERN SANTA MARIA
### SANTA MARIA HANDICRAFT COOPERATIVE
### (Cooperativa de Artesanato de Santa Maria)

*Termo da Igreja de Santo Espírito; tel. 296 884 888; Mon.-Fri. 8am-12:30pm and 1:30pm-4pm, Sat. 8am-2pm*

A working handicraft cooperative-cum-museum, this is the place to head for genuine local artifacts and to see them being made according to tradition. Located in the Santo Espírito parish, Santa Maria Handicraft Cooperative is a great place to find artisanal linen clothes, typical farmers wool caps, locally made products such as colorful quilts and tablecloths, and baked goods, including local specialty biscuit *biscoito de orelha*.

# Food

## VILA DO PORTO

Most of Vila do Porto's restaurants are located along the main **EN1-2A** road through the town.

### Markets
#### MUNICIPAL MARKET
#### (Mercado Municipal)

*Rua do Cotovelo; tel. 296 882 247; www.*
*cm-viladoporto.pt/SITE/sdmsa/mercado.php;*
*Mon.-Fri. 8am-6m, Sat. 8am-1pm*
If you're off exploring the island for the day, pop into Vila do Porto's municipal market to see, sample, and stock up on fresh local produce, perfect for a picnic.

### Azorean
#### PIPAS CHURRASQUEIRA

*EN1-2A; tel. 296 882 000; https://pt-pt.facebook.*
*com/Churrasqueirapipas; Mon.-Sat. noon-3pm and*
*6pm-1pm; €15*
Pleasing on the eye, with modern stone walls and sleek tables, Pipas serves typical Azorean fare, including grilled tuna steaks, fried octopus, and a regional sausage platter.

#### A GARROUCHADA

*Rua Dr. Luís Bettencourt 25; tel. 296 883 038; daily*
*9am-midnight; €20*
Hearty portions of meat and fish make up the local-cuisine-inspired mains at small and rustic Garrouchada, a warm, welcoming restaurant with a cozy wooden interior. Lighter dishes, like sausage and cheese platters and tasty soups, are perfect options for a quick lunch.

#### MESA D'OITO

*Rua Teófilo de Braga No. 1; tel. 296 882 083; www.*
*facebook.com/mesadoito; daily noon-10:30pm; €30*
Modern Mesa d'Oito takes regional cuisine to another level, with specialties such as squid

risotto and grilled tuna, homemade soups and pastas. Elegant and calm, with contrasting glass and rock walls, it is a relaxing place for a quiet meal.

### Contemporary
#### A TRAVESSA CAFÉ SNACK BAR

*Rua Dr. Luis Bettencourt 97; tel. 964 960 191; www.*
*facebook.com/ATRAVESSAsantamaria; Mon.-Fri.*
*7:30am-10pm, Sat. 6pm-11pm; €10*
This is a cute and casual eatery known for its amazing veggie burgers, light crepes and salads, and wholesome, unfussy Portuguese food. One of the newest arrivals on the Santa Maria restaurant scene, this spotless, modestly sized eatery is immaculate with an exposed white brick wall and wooden booths.

#### ESPAÇO EM CENA

*EN1-2A; tel. 961 809 446; facebook/Espaço-em-cena;*
*Tues.-Sat. 4pm-late; €20*
A funky little restaurant with an arty feel thanks to its ample wood finishings, open staircase, mish-mash of wall hangings, and rainbow of different chairs. The menu of simple, tasty food takes Azorean classics and gives them a fresh and creative new twist. The menu changes daily, featuring unusual local ingredients like triggerfish.

### Pub Grub
#### ★ CENTRAL PUB

*Rua Dr. Luís Bettencourt, 20; tel. 296 882 513; www.*
*facebook.com/Central-Pub-171231092904180; daily*
*5pm-2am; €15*
This is a large and airy buzzing local pub, clad in gleaming wood, that serves typical pub food like spicy chicken wings, thin-crust pizza, and banana splits—with a huge helping of island hospitality. Located in the heart of Vila do Porto, meals are served until late.

# Biscoito de Orelha:
# Santa Maria's Local Cookie

This intricate little biscuit is Santa Maria's *pièce de résistance*. Of huge cultural importance, this trademark sweet is distinct to the island and one of the Azores' best-loved and most-recognizable cookies. Made honoring a traditional recipe of primarily popular products like flour, eggs, sugar, butter, and lard, the *biscoito de orelha* ("ear biscuit," so-called due to its shape) is dexterously handmade, twisted and shaped like a triangular Celtic knot, with three distinct "ears."

## HISTORY

In the olden days it was known as a ceremonial biscuit, made for all formal and celebratory occasions, like weddings and christenings, and for welcoming guests and visitors. It was made by the hands of the island's confectioner women, using an original and creative technique that has been passed down through generations.

## WHERE TO TRY IT

Today, the *biscoito de orelha* can be found on tables in all Santa Maria homes, especially for special occasions and celebrations. It is a long-held Christmas tradition for godparents to gift godchildren a supersized *biscoito de orelha* over the festive season. The best places to try—and buy—this prized local delicacy are **A Cagarrita** bakery in Vila do Porto town (page 119) and from the **Santa Maria Handicraft Cooperative** (page 117).

## Cafés and Light Bites
### ★ A CAGARRITA

*Rua Dr. Manuel Monteiro Velho Arruda, no. 85A; tel. 296 883 406, https://a-cagarrita-padaria-docaria-tradicional.negocio.site; Mon.-Sat. 8am-5pm; €5*

Here you'll find a nice little cake shop in Vila do Porto town where freshly baked cakes, bread, and traditional sweets like the *biscoito de orelha* are made every day. The shop sells bags of other quirky cookies to-go, inspired by the island's heritage, like bags of biscuits shaped like shells, fossils, and sharks teeth. It's a great place to stock up on unusual and delicious souvenirs.

# WESTERN SANTA MARIA
## Seafood
### PRAZERES DA MAIA - O GROTA

*Rua do Divino Espirito Santo; tel. 927 296 708 or 296 884 184; https://m.facebook.com/prazeresdamaia; daily 11am-11pm; €15*

With a blue exterior as bright as the sea behind it, this little oceanside tavern, a rustic whitewashed cottage located in the hamlet of Santo Espírito, serves up delicious local dishes like octopus and fish stew. Family-run and homey, its good old-fashioned regional recipes are revered by the local community.

### RESTAURANT PRAIA FORMOSA

*Lugar da Praia; tel. 296 884 154; daily noon-3pm and 6:30pm-10pm; €15*

Set just back from the famous Formosa Beach, this spacious villa-type restaurant specializes in light, fresh flavors, like wonderful salads, grilled fish, marinated shrimps, and breaded scallops. A friendly and efficient service keeps patrons coming back.

### PONTA NEGRA

*Road s/n São Lourenço; tel. 296 098 148; www.facebook.com/PontaNegraRestauranteBarDePraia; Tues.-Sun. 11am-11pm; €15*

Charming beach restaurant Ponta Negra, with its vast seaside deck esplanade and open wood-clad interior, has amazing coastal views and a tasty menu largely showcasing fresh fish, seafood, and other tasty local produce.

## EASTERN SANTA MARIA
### Azorean
### ROSA ALTA

*Termo da Igreja São Pedro; tel. 296 884 990 or 961 637 078; www.facebook.com/RosaAltaRestaurante; Wed.-Mon. 7pm-11pm; €15*

A warm and modern wooden interior awaits diners at large, bright, and airy Rosa Alta, where the gastronomic experience is rooted in fresh, local seasonal ingredients, with a particular emphasis on excellent meat.

# Bars and Nightlife

## VILA DO PORTO
### DOCAS BAR

*Cais da Ribeira; tel. 296 884 800; www.facebook.com/oseupontodeencontro; daily 8am-8pm*

On the Vila do Porto docks, Docas Bar is a popular meeting point for locals, with refreshing drinks and tapas for sharing in a stunning waterfront location.

### CERVEJARIA TRAVASSOS

*EN1-2A; Mon.-Sat. 6am-9pm*

A busy watering hole with a down-to-earth feel, Cervejaria Travassos is the place to go for a cool beer and a chat with the locals.

### ★ CLUBE ASAS DO ATLANTICO

*Rua da Horta; www.asasdoatlantico.pt; daily 9am-midnight*

Half club, half radio station, Asas do Atlantico is a local cultural association with a bar that puts on events and showcases the island's radio broadcasting history. Founded in October 1946, this cultural-association-working-broadcaster crossover welcomes all visitors to its headquarters, where—as well as keeping the local community informed on upcoming events—it also has snooker, ping-pong, and a beautiful carved-wood library containing some 6,000 regional and international books and historic publications. It hosts dances and concerts, too.

# Accommodations

Santa Maria is home to a handful of medium-size hotels, most of which are centered on the main town, Vila do Porto, and just a short drive from the airport. However, there are plenty of private local lodgings available for rental scattered across the island, particularly in Vila do Porto and along the island's popular beachy east coast. **Airbnb** (www.airbnb.com) is a great place to look for private lodgings and might come in handy for accommodations of the beaten track or in rural spots, especially if you're thinking of attempting the Great Route.

## VILA DO PORTO
### Under €100
### SANTA MARIA YOUTH HOSTEL

*Rua Frei Gonçalo Velho; tel. 296 883 592; www.pousadasjuvacores.com/?page=santa-maria; €35-55*

If it's accommodation on a budget you're looking for, then look no further than the Santa Maria Youth Hostel. Despite the name, there are no age restrictions. The hostel is bright and airy, with basic, clean rooms, a pool, sea views, and an excellent location near the port. Bathrooms are shared, rooms can be communal or private, and a standard breakfast is included in the price.

## €100-200
### HOTEL SANTA MARIA
*Rua da Horta; tel. 296 820 660; www.*
*hotel-santamaria.pt; €50-150 d*

A pretty, expansive, farmhouse-style hotel, elegant Hotel Santa Maria is located midway between the airport and Vila do Porto. Surrounded by nature, the hotel provides regular paid transportation to the town and beaches, as well as clean and bright rooms with garden views.

### ★ CHARMING BLUE "CASA DOS MONTEIROS"
*Rua Teófilo Braga 31; tel. 296 883 560; www.*
*charmingblue.com; €85-150 d*

Located in the heart of Vila do Porto, Charming Blue is a petite hotel, born from a renovated typical Azorean farmhouse, with bundles of character. Arty, clean-line rooms and leisure areas complement a modern style hotel with a sparkling pool and a well-reputed restaurant, **Mesa d'Oito** (daily noon-10:30pm; €30).

### HOTEL PRAIA DE LOBOS
*Travessa do Mercado; tel. 296 249 660; www.hotel-praiadelobos.pt; €100-150 d*

In the very heart of Vila do Porto, housed in a handsome whitewashed town building, Hotel Praia de Lobos is a welcoming, homey hotel

with 34 comfortable rooms, a very convenient town center location, and a free airport transportation service.

## Over €200
### HOTEL COLOMBO
*Rua Cruz Teixeira; tel. 296 820 200; www.*
*colombo-hotel.com; €150-250 d*

Well located—a 5-minute drive from the airport and a 20-minute walk to the town center—Hotel Colombo is large and spacious, with good size rooms, which are well-equipped but could use a little updating. Aged but very clean, Hotel Colombo also has a pool, dive centers, Turkish bath, and a bar with a sea-view deck. It boasts amazing sea views and is highly recommended for its convenient location.

## EASTERN SANTA MARIA
### Under €100
### PRAIA FORMOSA CAMPSITE
*Formosa Beach; tel. 296 883 959; www.*
*cm-viladoporto.pt/SITE/servicos/pcampismo.php;*
*reception daily 9am-1pm and 2:30pm-8:30pm; €5-50*

Open in summer (June 15-Sept. 30), the Praia Formosa campsite is located right on Formosa Beach. It is intended mostly for tent camping, but it does have six bungalows for visitors who don't have their own tent. Silence is required between midnight and 8am.

# Information and Services

While small, Santa Maria is well equipped with amenities and services. There are two pharmacies in Vila do Porto town, a large health center (the USI Santa Maria), and a post office, and emergency services such as police and fire brigade cover the entire island. **ATMs** are also widely available on the island.

- **Vila do Porto tourist office:** Vila do Porto docks (Cais de Ilha de Santa Maria); tel. 296 886 355; www.visitazores.com

- **PSP police:** Rua Dr. Luís Bettencourt 107; tel. 296 882 324 or 296 820 110; www.psp.pt

- **USI Santa Maria (Unidade de Saude da Ilha de Santa Maria) Health Center:** Avenida Santa Maria, Vila do Porto; tel. 296 820 100; open 24/7

- **Post office:** Rua Teófilo Braga, 38; tel. 296 682 366; Mon.-Fri. 9am-12:30pm and 2pm-5:30pm

# Terceira and Graciosa

**Packed with fascinating volcanic attractions,** from basalt-walled vine pens to underground lava tubes, Terceira island is approximately 220 kilometers (140 mi) northwest of São Miguel. Terceira is the Azores archipelago's second largest island in terms of population (after São Miguel) and third largest in size (after São Miguel and Pico).

It is part of the central group of islands, along with São Jorge, Graciosa, Pico, and Faial. Quieter and less touristy than the archipelago's main island of São Miguel, but modern enough to cater for travelers who appreciate creature comforts, it is one of the Azores' top stops, and it's the only other island besides São Miguel to have an airport that receives international flights. Terceira (which translates as

# Highlights

Look for ★ to find recommended sights, activities, dining, and lodging.

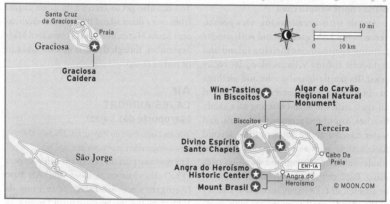

★ **Angra do Heroísmo Historic Center:** The center of Angra do Heroísmo, the Azores' oldest town, is a designated UNESCO World Heritage Site, a lovely place for a stroll and to base your stay in Terceira (page 133).

★ **Mount Brasil:** Hiking around this extinct volcano tip, with privileged views over Angra do Heroísmo, is like exploring a magical forest (page 137).

★ **Algar do Carvão Regional Natural Monument:** The Carvão Cave, Natal Cave, and Furnas do Enxofre fumaroles are all within walking distance of each other in this unique natural area (page 147).

★ **Wine-Tasting in Biscoitos:** Try the distinctive wine produced from Verdelho grapes after learning about winemaking history on Terceira in the Biscoitos Wine Museum (page 151).

★ **Divino Espírito Santo Chapels:** Choose your favorite little chapel from among the 70 that dot Terceira island (page 158).

★ **Graciosa Caldera:** A highlight of any visit to Graciosa, the island's caldera is a must-see, a huge pockmark on the landscape home to impressive volcanic formations (page 170).

third) takes its name from the fact it was the third Azores island to be inhabited. Known as the Lilac Island, due to the number of purple hydrangeas that blanket it in spring, it is home to the Azores' oldest city, Angra do Heroísmo, a UNESCO World Heritage Site, and is also famous for being home to a strategic international air base, Lajes.

The island has a cheery, colorful vibe, as the houses that make up its towns and villages are painted in varying hues of pastel pinks, yellows, blues, and purples, as opposed to the usual whitewash and black basalt trim seen on most other islands. Also unique to Terceira are its colorful Divino Espírito Santo chapels, or *impérios;* at least 70 of these quirky little chapels dedicated to the Holy Spirit (or Holy Ghost) dot the island. Finally, there's the island's distinctive Verdelho wine, produced near the charming village of Biscoitos on the island's northwestern coast.

Awash with breathtaking viewpoints, Terceira is a lush, green island with unique farming communities thriving inland and tight-knit fishing villages along its rocky coast. Its family-friendly vibe and plethora of outdoor activities caters for travelers of all ages, with the island offering nice sandy beaches, lots of picturesque tidal pools, and water-based activity opportunities around its coastline such as sailing, dolphin- and whale-watching, diving, and stand-up paddling. Explore the scenic roads by car, bike, or scooter, or take in the incredible scenery of the island's coast from the sea with a sea-kayaking excursion in the protected bays off Angra or the island's other main town, Praia da Vitória—or even the Cabras Islets, off eastern Terceira.

Graciosa, meaning Graceful, is one of the most remote of the Azores' islands, 140 kilometer (87 mi) northwest of Terceira island and three hours by ferry or a half hour by plane. Flatter and drier than its peers, Graciosa is a UNESCO World Biosphere Reserve and home to some of the archipelago's most unusual volcanic attractions. With undulating hills that roll gently to the sea, it's an unusual little island, famous for its white trachytes (distinctive, light-colored volcanic rocks), gaping caldera, and obsession with Carnival. Often referred to as the White Island, Graciosa is mainly accessible by plane via Terceira or São Miguel year-round, or by ferry in the summer.

## GETTING THERE

Traveling to Terceira island is almost as easy as getting to São Miguel, the Azores' main island. **By air** is easiest and quickest, both from the mainland and other islands. Terceira is the only other island in the archipelago to receive direct flights from mainland Portugal, as well as some international flights (though these are mostly seasonal charter flights). You can also get to Terceira on direct flights from every other island in the archipelago except Santa Maria, or by **ferry,** operated May-September, though flying is quicker and can be just as cheap.

### Air
#### LAJES AIRPORT
#### (Aeroporto das Lajes)
*Vila das Lajes, Praia da Vitória; tel. 295 545 454; www.aerogarelajes.azores.gov.pt*
The main airport on Terceira is Lajes Airport (TER), also known as Lajes Civil Air Base (Aerogare Civil das Lajes), is in Praia da Vitória, on the northeastern tip of Terceira, 24 kilometers (15 mi) from Angra do Heroísmo, the island's main city. There are direct flights to Lajes almost daily from Lisbon, and at least three times a week from Porto. Flight time from both Lisbon and Porto is around 2.5 hours, and round-trip flights can often be found for less than €100, depending on the season. Internationally, direct seasonal flights are operated from Amsterdam in the Netherlands (TUI fly), London (Ryanair),

---

**Previous:** view from Pico das Cruzinhas; Algar do Carvão; Mount Brasil.

and Oakland, California, in the United States (Azores Airlines), among others.

Interisland flights on smaller propeller planes are operated exclusively by **SATA** (www.azoresairlines.pt/en); you can fly to and from Terceira via every island in the archipelago except Santa Maria. These also generally cost under €100 round-trip, and most flights between the islands take less than an hour.

A number of local and international car rental desks, such as **Ilha Verde Rent a Car** (www.ilhaverde.com) and **Europcar** (www.europcar.pt), operate at the airport. The drive from Angra to Lajes Airport takes 20 minutes on the **VR** freeway.

There is a limited, roughly hourly bus service between Angra and Lajes operated by **Empresa de Viação Terceirense** (tel. 295 217 001; www.evt.pt;1 hour; €5). **Taxis** (about €25-30 to Angra) are available outside the terminal.

## Ferry
### PRAIA DA VITÓRIA PORT

*Cabo da Praia Industrial Area, Praia da Vitória; tel. 295 105 134; www.amn.pt*

Praia da Vitória Port, on Terceira's east coast, receives the seasonal **interisland ferry** (www.atlanticoline.pt/en); from May-September, you can take the ferry from Terceira to Ponta Delgada on São Miguel (4 hours 30 minutes; 4 ferries/week), Vila da Praia on Graciosa (3 hours; 3 ferries/week), or Sao Roque on Pico (6 hours 45 minutes; 10 ferries/week), or Horta on Faial (8 hours 15 minutes; 4 ferries/week). Check the website for fares.

Praia da Vitória Port is a 10-minute drive or taxi ride (€10) from Lajes Airport. A public bus service operated by **Empresa de Viação Terceirense** (tel. 295 217 001; www.evt.pt; lines 151 and 3; 10 minutes; €2) runs hourly between the two. It's a 20-minute drive or taxi (€25) northeast of Angra do Heroísmo on the **VR** freeway.

The **Angra do Heroísmo Port** (Porto das Pipas; tel. 295 204 570; www.amn.pt) on Terceira's south coast hems the town center, but as the interisland ferry does not leave from this port, it is unlikely to be of use to tourists.

# GETTING AROUND

As with other Azores islands, the best and most cost-effective way to explore Terceira is **renting a car.** The roads are decent and the driving leisurely. A new-ish freeway, the **VR**, connects the island's two main towns, **Angra do Heroísmo** and **Praia da Vitória,** making the 23-kilometer (14-mi) drive between them quick and easy (20 minutes). A ring road, the **EN1-1A,** skirts the entire hem of the island; well-signposted secondary roads take drivers to inland attractions. It takes just under 2 hours to drive around the entire island.

**Public bus services** can be limited, more so to inland locales, but there are plenty of **tour operators** running excursions to the island's main attractions, on and offshore (these are obviously more expensive than public transport). Given the compact size of the island and manageable road system, another affordable option is renting a **motorbike.**

## Rental Car

Renting a car is undoubtedly the best way to travel around Terceira. Car rentals in the Azores tend to be well-priced, and fuel is usually cheaper than on the mainland. (Although rental prices can go up significantly during peak summer season and also other major holidays, such as New Year's). There are half a dozen or so vehicle rental desks at Terceira Airport, such as **Ilha Verde Rent a Car** (www.ilhaverde.com) or **Europcar** (www.europcar.pt), or ask at your hotel to arrange one. Book as far ahead as possible for the best prices, and collect the vehicle at the airport for extra convenience.

A word of warning: Cows roam freely in many parts of Terceira, and accidents involving cows and rental cars have been known to happen quite regularly, so full insurance coverage is worth considering.

## Bus

The island public bus service head office,

# Terceira

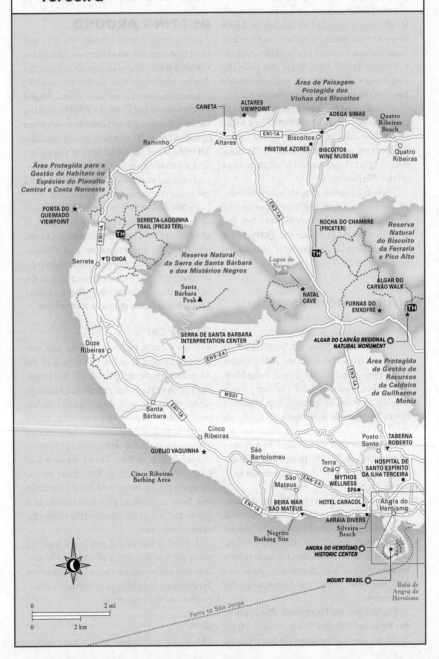

Área de Paisagem
Protegida das
Vinhas dos Biscoitos

CANETA

ALTARES
VIEWPOINT

ADEGA SIMAS

Quatro
Ribeiras
Beach

Raminho

Altares

EN1-1A

Biscoitos

PRISTINE AZORES

BISCOITOS
WINE MUSEUM

Quatro
Ribeiras

Área Protegida para a
Gestão de Habitats ou
Espécies do Planalto
Central e Costa Noroeste

EN3-1A

PONTA DO
QUEIMADO
VIEWPOINT

SERRETA-LAGOINHA
TRAIL (PRC03 TER)

ROCHA DO CHAMBRE
(PRC6TER)

Reserva
do Biscoito
da Ferraria
e Pico Alto

TH

EN1-1A

TH

Serreta

TI CHOA

Reserva Natural
da Serra de Santa Bárbara
e dos Mistérios Negros

Lagoa do
Negro
Lake

ALGAR DO
CARVÃO WALK

Santa
Bárbara
Peak ▲

NATAL
CAVE

FURNAS DO
ENXOFRE ★

TH

SERRA DE SANTA BARBARA
INTERPRETATION CENTER

Doze
Ribeiras

EN5-2A

ALGAR DO CARVÃO REGIONAL
NATURAL MONUMENT

Área Protegida
de Gestão de
Recursos
da Caldeira
de Guilherme
Moniz

EN3-1A

M501

EN1-1A

Santa
Bárbara

Cinco
Ribeiras

QUEIJO VAQUINHA ★

São
Bartolomeu

Posto
Santo

TABERNA
ROBERTO

Cinco Ribeiras
Bathing Area

São
Mateus

EN6-2A

Terra
Chã

HOSPITAL DE
SANTO ESPÍRITO
DA ILHA TERCEIRA

MYTHOS
WELLNESS
SPA

HOTEL CARACOL

Angra
do
Heroísmo

EN1-1A

BEIRA MAR
SÃO MATEUS

ARRAIA DIVERS

Silveira
Beach

Negrito
Bathing Site

ANGRA DO HEROÍSMO
HISTORIC CENTER

MOUNT BRASIL

Baía de
Angra do
Heroísmo

0        2 mi

0        2 km

Ferry to São Jorge

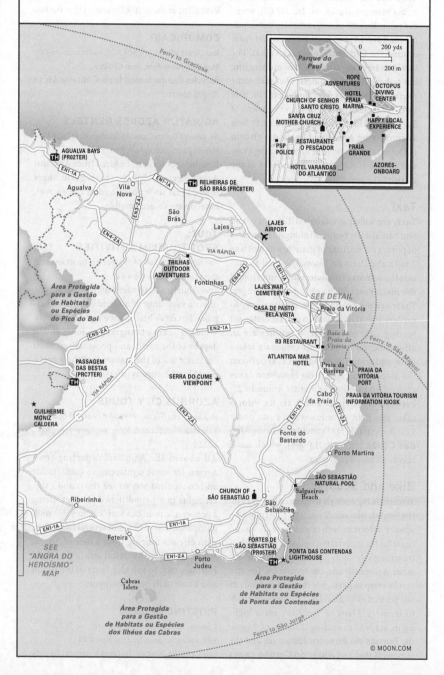

© MOON.COM

**Empresa de Viação Terceirense** (Rua Dr. Sousa Meneses, no. 15; tel. 295 217 001; www. evt.pt), is located in Angra do Heroísmo, just off the EN1-1A, but most buses depart from around the **Old Square** (Praça Velha). The local bus service is not geared toward tourism, but rather caters to islanders. That said, some routes that tourists may find useful include **line 1,** connecting Angra with the towns of **Serreta** and **Biscoitos** (15 minutes; €4); **line 2,** connecting Angra and **Praia da Vitória** (45 minutes; €3), and **line 3,** connecting Praia and Biscoitos, also stopping in front of the **airport** (1 hour; €5).

## Taxi

Taxis are widely available on Terceira island and can usually be found alongside the likes of ports and marinas in main towns (such as Angra and Praia da Vitória), as well as outside the airport arrivals terminal and around the main Praça Velha old square in Angra. Taxis are not really a cost-effective way to explore the island—you would be better off renting a car or a scooter—but they are an affordable way to travel between main towns or to and from the airport. A taxi between the airport and Angra do Heroísmo takes around 20 minutes and costs around €25; between the airport and Praia da Vitória takes less than 10 minutes and costs under €10. A reputable taxi provider is **Táxis Alto das Covas** (tel. 295 213 088), which has a taxi rank based in Angra.

## Bike and Scooter

Terceira is big enough to spend a few days on the island, but small enough to explore by scooter or bicycle, both of which are cheap and cheerful transportation options, especially if travelling solo or as a pair. Like many of the other Azores islands, the terrain on Terceira can be steep in parts, but the scenery lends itself perfectly to bike rides, and the quiet roads to scooters. Many of Terceira's main highlights are within cycling distance of Angra: the **Furnas do Enxofre** fumaroles and the famous **Natal** and **Algar do Carvão caves**

are 18 kilometers (11 mi) away; the village of **Biscoitos** is about 20 kilometers (12 mi) away.

### COMUNICAIR
*Rua Direita 69; tel. 910 503 800; www.comunicair.pt; Mon.-Sat. 10am-6pm; from €20/day*

Bicycles can be rented from ComunicAir in Angra town.

### AGUIATUR AZORES RENTALS
*Av. Tenente Coronel José Agostinho; tel. 917 553 111; http://aguiaturazores.com; from €30/day*

Reliable scooters can be hired from Aguiatur Azores Rentals, which has branches in Angra town, Praia da Vitória, and at the airport; hotel drop-offs are possible.

## Tours
### SPOT TOURISM ACTIVITIES
*Rua Nova 19; tel. 964 242 969; https://spottours.pt; Mon.-Sat. 9am-6am; from €37*

Spot Tourism Activities, based out of Angra, offers a vast range of on-land activities to explore Terceira's best-known and secret spots. Walking tours of Angra, geo tours to the depths of the earth, and personalized tours are just a few of the options that this experienced local company offers.

### AZORBUS CITY TOURS
*Rua da Sé, no. 190; tel. 969 668 829 or 969 668 839; http://azorbus.com; Mon.-Sat. 10am-6pm; from €22.50*

All aboard the AzorBus, departing from Angra, for some sightseeing: a comfortable and convenient way to see the island's finest sights in air-conditioned comfort. Using a panoramic mini bus with a removable roof, guided tours are offered in several languages, with circuits ranging from a tour of Angra, around the entire historical area of the World Heritage city, to full-day tours of the island and a tour of its best viewpoints.

### PRISTINE AZORES
*Caminho do Outeiro no. 12, Biscoitos; tel. 963 289 993; www.pristineazores.com; from €40*

Soak up the best of Terceira's natural beauty

with this experienced nature tour company based in Biscoitos. Choose from walking tours, photography trips, 4x4 excursions, and themed routes, such as wine tours and whaling heritage tours.

## ORIENTATION

Terceira is the roundest of all the Azores islands, albeit slightly squashed, as if the top and bottom have been pressed together. **Lajes Airport** and beachy **Praia da Vitória,** one of the island's two main towns and the location of the interisland **ferry terminal,** are on the island's northeast coast, while the capital, **Angra do Heroísmo,** is 23 kilometers (14 mi) southwest on the south coast, connected by the free and easy **VR** freeway, a 20-minute drive. Landmarks like **Mount Brasil** and **São Sebastião Fortress** are located along Angra's coast; the **EN1-1A** runs through the middle of town, and most of Angra's historic center is between the road and the waterfront.

Three of the island's main sights, the **Natal Cave, Algar do Carvão,** and the **Furnas do Enxofre** fields, are located inland, in central Teceira. They are conveniently close together, almost slap-bang in the middle of the island. To the west, you'll find **Santa Bárbara Peak,** the highest point on Terceira, as well as the charming winemaking village of **Biscoitos** and the **Cinco Ribeiras** bathing site and caves, a great place for snorkeling. Finally, on the east coast, just south of the beach resort of **Praia da Vitória,** is the village of **São Sebastião,** and the scenic snorkeling and kayaking hotspot of the **Cabras Islets.**

**Graciosa** is about 80 kilometers (50 mi) to the northwest of Terceira, accessible via 30-minute flight from **Lajes** or a 3-hour ferry ride from **Praia da Vitória** in the summer months. On a clear day, it's visible from the **Ponta do Queimado viewpoint.**

## PLANNING YOUR TIME

Plan to spend at least three full days on Terceira. One day alone can be filled exploring its main city, **Angra do Heroísmo,** and the beautiful **Mount Brasil.** Even though **Praia da Vitória,** Terceira's other main town, is closer to Lajes Airport, Angra is a better base as it is livelier year-round; Praia has a quieter, summer seaside resort feel. You could opt to spend two nights in Angra, exploring the city and its attractions on day one, and the west coast on day two. On the way to Praia from Angra, stop at the island's main inland attractions: **Natal Cave, Algar do Carvão,** the **Furnas do Enxofre** fields, and **Serra do Cume viewpoint.** Though most of the attractions are concentrated in the island's center, this is also the island at its least developed; the restaurants, accommodations, and amenities for the most part line Terceira's coast.

There is a wide selection of accommodation to suit all budgets across Terceira island. Angra and Praia da Vitória are home to larger hotels; Angra has some very elegant coastal hotels, while Praia da Vitória's hotels have a bijou beachfront vibe. Elsewhere there are plenty of smaller, privately run B&Bs and rural-style lodgings to enjoy.

Graciosa's main attractions could possibly be seen in a day trip from Terceira—travel arrival and departure times allowing. It's a 30-minute flight from Lajes Airport (from €50 round-trip), or a 3-hour ferry if you're traveling May-September. If you'd like to stay the night, of Graciosa's main towns, you should stay in **Santa Cruz da Graciosa** if you enjoy architecture, or **Praia da Graciosa** if you prefer the beach.

Santa Cruz da Graciosa, which most visitors make their base, is a charming and compact village, home to around one third of the island's population, and easily walkable. It has elegant whitewashed buildings, a main square lined with mansions, a number of quaint, centuries-old churches, a handsome town hall, and pretty town-center ponds once used a reservoirs, creating an overall genteel look that harks back to the island's more prosperous times. Attractions such as the **Monte da Ajuda** and **ethnographic museum** are within walking distance. The rest of the island is best explored by car or scooter.

# Itinerary Ideas

## TWO DAYS ON TERCEIRA

### Day 1: Angra and Mount Brasil

Wear comfortable walking attire for a day spent hiking Mount Brasil and exploring Angra city center.

**1** Enjoy breakfast at your hotel before taking a short stroll to Mount Brasil, a 10-minute walk from the historic city center. Start at the 16th-century **Fortress of São João Baptista** at the foot of the mountain.

**2** Next, hike the 7.4-kilometer (4.6-mi) **Monte Brasil route (PRC4TER)** around the extinct volcano, which should take about 2.5 hours to complete, starting and ending in Relvão Municipal Park.

**3** After a morning full of walking, stop for lunch at **Birou Bar** back in the city center, a contemporary little tavern serving tapas.

**4** After lunch, pop into the **Church of the Holy Savior's Cathedral**, the largest church on the island.

**5** Next, wander along the marina, toward the former **São Sebastião Fortress**, on the eastern side of Angra Marina, now converted into a boutique hotel, the Pousada de Angra do Heroísmo. It boasts lovely views over Angra and Mount Brasil.

**6** Finish your day with a delicious dinner of typical Azorean fare at **Taberna Roberto** before heading back to the hotel for a good night's sleep.

### Day 2: Central and Eastern Terciera

Once again, make sure to wear suitable hiking attire for today's adventure.

**1** After breakfast, make the 15-minute drive north from Angra do Heroísmo inland along the VR freeway to the cavernous, dripping **Algar do Carvão Cave.** Allow about 30 minutes to visit the cave.

**2** After exploring the cave, make the 15-minute walk to the **Furnas do Enxofre** fumarole fields; follow the wooden boardwalk through rolling hills amid plumes of sulfurous steam.

**3** From here, follow the VR east to the town of Praia da Vitória, a 30-minute drive, where you can enjoy a seafood lunch at the famed **Restaurante O Pescador.**

**4** Walk lunch off with a wander around Praia da Vitória and some fresh sea air along **Grande Beach.**

**5** In the afternoon, join the fun **Happy Local Experience,** a cow-farm excursion based out of Praia da Vitória.

**6** Start making your way back to Angra, taking a coastal detour southwest on the EN1-2A. After about 20 minutes, you'll reach the pretty little village of São Sebastião. Stop to visit the austere, medieval **Church of São Sebastião,** which dates back to the 15th century.

# Two Days on Terceira

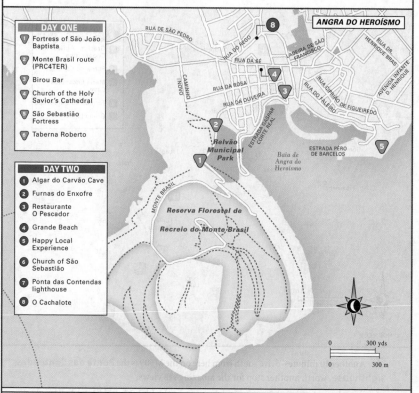

### DAY ONE

1. Fortress of São João Baptista
2. Monte Brasil route (PRC4TER)
3. Birou Bar
4. Church of the Holy Savior's Cathedral
5. São Sebastião Fortress
6. Taberna Roberto

### DAY TWO

1. Algar do Carvão Cave
2. Furnas do Enxofre
3. Restaurante O Pescador
4. Grande Beach
5. Happy Local Experience
6. Church of São Sebastião
7. Ponta das Contendas lighthouse
8. O Cachalote

**TERCEIRA AND GRACIOSA**
ITINERARY IDEAS

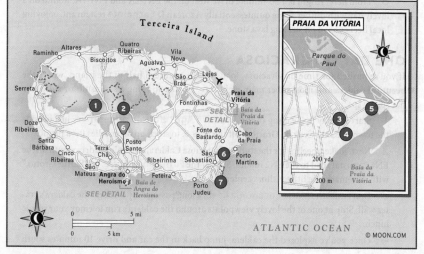

© MOON.COM

# One Day on Graciosa

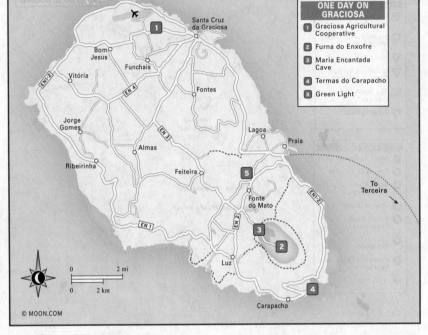

**ONE DAY ON GRACIOSA**

1 Graciosa Agricultural Cooperative
2 Furna do Enxofre
3 Maria Encantada Cave
4 Termas do Carapacho
5 Green Light

© MOON.COM

**7**  Another 10 minutes' drive south from here on the M509 is the **Ponta das Contendas lighthouse,** worth another stop for the amazing sea views.

**8**  From here, Angra is a 20-minute drive west on the EN1-2A and EN1-1A. Round off a lovely day with dinner at the quintessentially Azorean **O Cachalote** restaurant, enjoying local beef cooked on sizzling lava stone.

## ONE DAY ON GRACIOSA

If you're pushed for time on Graciosa, focus on the southern half of the island, where the beautiful caldera and most other main sights are. Be sure to bring a swimsuit for a dip in a hot spring spa.

**1**  Start the day by heading to the **Graciosa Agricultural Cooperative,** just outside the town of Santa Cruz da Graciosa off the EN5-5, to stock up on goodies for a picnic.

**2**  Next, make a beeline for the stunning Graciosa Caldera, a 15-minute drive south on the EN1-2 coastal road to the EN2 inland. Start at the **Furna do Enxofre,** or "Sulfur Grotto," with its remarkable little visitors center.

**3**  Don't miss the **Maria Encantada Cave,** a long passageway through the caldera's crater wall. Stop at one of the lovely viewpoints around the caldera's rim to enjoy your picnic lunch.

**4**  Once you've explored the caldera, jump back in the car and drive 10 minutes south along the EN2 to the **Termas do Carapacho** spa. Spend an hour or so soothing your muscles in the steaming waters.

**133**

**5** Dry off and head toward the town of Praia, another 10-minute drive along the EN1-2, this time north. Have dinner at the **Green Light** restaurant, which offers fantastic food made from local produce and stunning views.

# Angra do Heroísmo

Angra do Heroísmo, or simply Angra, is an exquisite little city with a palpable charm, its historical center classified a UNESCO World Heritage Site in 1983. Angra was founded in the 15th century as a main mid-Atlantic port of trade and navigation, and an exotic coexistence of imperial Portuguese and Spanish architecture characterizes the town, with well-maintained, colorful houses and streets contrasting with the modern waterfront. Around 70 percent of Angra's houses were destroyed in a violent earthquake in January 1980, which caused severe damage across much of the island. With government help, the island was faithfully rebuilt to its unique original 15th-century heritage, which landed it the UNESCO title. The heart of the town is the Praça Velha, or Old Square, a few streets back from the marina, from where most of the buses run and locals enjoy their daily coffee—a sign that customs and habits in Angra shifted little with tourism.

Angra is packed with interesting attractions, from museums, fabulous public gardens, and monuments such as the São Sebastião Fortress (converted into a posh boutique hotel), to the glorious Mount Brasil, an ancient, extinct volcano that juts out from the bottom of Angra city, a true hikers' playground.

## ORIENTATION

Most of Angra city is wedged between **Mount Brasil** to the west and the **São Sebastião Fortress** to the east. The town center, which revolves around the bustling **Old Square** (Praça Velha), pools back from the **Angra Bay** waterfront, which links Mount Brasil in the west, the **Angra Marina**, also known as Porto das Pipas, and the fortress to the east. Near the marina, with its row of modern shops housing bars, restaurants, and maritime businesses, is **Prainha Beach**, protected by a breakwater. A 1.3-kilometer (0.8-mi) **waterfront walkway** stretches from the foot of Mount Brasil, past the beach, all the way to the São Sebastião Fortress.

Angra is best explored on foot, so comfy footwear is a must. The town's two main commercial arteries are the **Rua Direita** main street and **Rua das Salinas**, which runs parallel to it; these link the Old Square to the waterfront. The area between the marina to the south and the **EN1-1A** ring road, which cuts through Angra, is a grid, making it easy to navigate.

## SIGHTS

**TOP** EXPERIENCE

### ★ Angra Historic Center

You could spend a whole day soaking up the colorful streets and sounds of cheery, culture-packed Angra city center. If you want more of the history behind Angra, or to boil it down into a shorter time, **Angra Travel Tours** (Rua Direita 155; tel. 295 206 900; www.angratravel.net; Mon.-Fri. 9am-6pm; from €35) offers half- and full-day historic city walking tours.

### OLD SQUARE
**(Praça Velha)**
*Open 24/7; free*

Flanked by the grandiose Town Hall, the

# Angra do Heroísmo

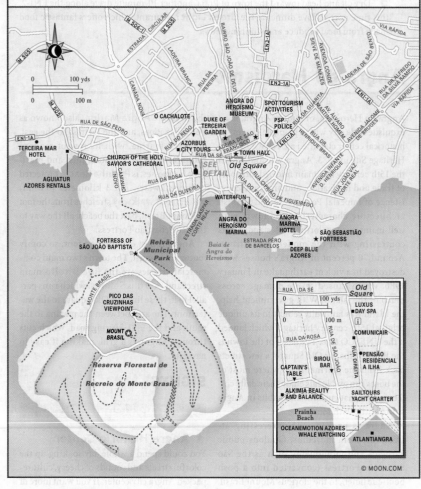

elegant Azoris Garden Hotel, and cafés, and restaurants, the Praça Velha is Angra's beating heart. The city's central square is where main streets and public transports converge, with its expansive black-and-white patterned cobblestone paving forming a monochrome carpet. Locals enjoy coffee, buses and taxis all pass through, and special events like concerts are put on here. Rooted in the age-old tradition of the main square as a social

meeting point, the **Town Hall** of Angra do Heroísmo (Paços do Concelho de Angra do Heroísmo; Ladeira de São Francisco 2; tel. 295 401 700; https://angradoheroismo.pt; daily 8am-6pm; free) a grand 19th-century building with a palatial look about it, takes center stage. Inside the Town Hall is every bit as regal as outside; it houses some interesting artifacts linked to Angra, and it's free to wander around.

## DUKE OF TERCEIRA GARDEN
### (Jardim Duque da Terceira)

*Rua Direita 130; tel. 295 401 700; daily 8am-6pm; free*

The impressively manicured Duke of Terceira Garden, dating from the late 19th century, is a shining example of a municipal garden. Located in Angra's historic center, just off the main square and down the road from the cathedral, the garden features a pretty central bandstand in the heart of the green oasis, flanked by an intricate design of landscaped lawns, ponds, and a compelling diversity of towering trees and indigenous and international flora. Water features, a soundtrack of frog and birdsong, and a little **café** make this a lovely spot to whittle away an hour. The highest point is the **Outeiro da Memória,** or Memorial Hill, a gentle climb up to a bright yellow obelisk in memory of King Pedro IV; it's worth the effort for the sweeping views of Angra do Heroísmo.

## ANGRA DO HEROÍSMO MUSEUM
### (Museu de Angra do Heroísmo)

*Ladeira de Sao Francisco; tel. 295 240 800, http:// museu-angra.azores.gov.pt; Tues.-Sun. 10am-5:30pm; €2*

Just across from the Duke of Terceira Garden, the Angra Museum pays testament to the Azores' and the island's heritage, covering a vast range of topics relating to the archipelago, from military to modern art, religion to farming and geology. It's a celebration of the archipelago's autonomy, and you could spend a good hour or two in this surprisingly informative and interesting museum, housed in a 17th-century Franciscan monastery updated with an eye-catching pink trim. The displays document 500 years of the Azores' history, with fascinating artifacts including ancient armor, embroidery, artwork, traditional clothing, an exhibit on the 1980 earthquake, and an amazing hall of carriages and metal horses. The museum also houses a stunning medieval church. Most of the exhibits have information provided in English.

## CHURCH OF THE HOLY SAVIOR'S CATHEDRAL
### (Igreja do Santíssimo Salvador da Sé)

*Rua Carreira dos Cavalos 53; tel. 295 216 670; www. igrejaacores.pt; Mon.-Fri. 10am-6pm, mass Sat.-Sun.; €2 (free to attend mass)*

Built by the Cardinal-King Henry in 1568, the handsome Church of the Holy Savior's Cathedral is the biggest church on the island and one of its main monuments. Peering over Angra, overshadowed only by Mount Brasil, the cathedral has an imposing Gothic exterior and twin bell towers, topped by distinctive black-and-white-striped pyramid spires. The church is located right in the historic heart of the city, a few streets back from the waterfront. The inside is smart but understated, with stone arches and a famously large pipe organ. The three naves inside have undergone a series of reconstructions following the devastating earthquake of 1980 and a large fire in 1983.

## SÃO SEBASTIÃO FORTRESS
### (Forte de São Sebastião)

*Estr. Pero de Barcelos 1; tel. 295 403 560; www. pousadas.pt; open 24/7; free to visit for a look around*

Fronting the city of Angra to the east is the former São Sebastião Fortress, now a boutique hotel, the **Pousada de Angra do Heroísmo.** This was the first fortification to be built to protect Angra and is one of the most imposing fortresses in the Azores. Also known as the São Sebastião Castle or Castelinho, it's a little walk up from the marina. It's a working hotel, but still it's worth a visit to take in the views and admire how the historic fortress has been merged with the hotel's contemporary architecture. Built in 1580 by order of King D. Sebastião, the fortress towers over Porto dad Pipas and bay, overlooking Angra town and facing Mount Brasil. In its heyday, the São Sebastião Fortress worked together with the Fortress of São João Baptista on Mount Brasil to shield Angra from attacks and invasions from both sides. Remnants of its role as an important defensive structure can still be seen in

the ramparts and watchtowers that were part of the original building.

## ★ Mount Brasil
### (Monte Brasil)

*Sé parish; open 24/7; free*

For the best views of Angra and its sandy bay, climb this attraction-packed mountain, a remnant of a mostly submerged crater. A 15-minute stroll west of Angra's waterfront and marina, covered in shrubbery, Mount Brasil juts out between Angra Bay to the east and the Fanal Bay to the west. Named after Brazil, a former Portuguese colony, this forested peninsula was formed by an extinct volcano and extends into the Atlantic, a naturally protective positioning that made it a point of defense for Terceira and Angra's port.

Most of Mount Brasil is a government-managed **nature reserve** (Terceiraís Forestry Service; tel. 295 206 310; daily sunrise-sunset; free). It is scattered with picnic spots, well-maintained hiking routes, whaling lookouts, and viewpoints on each of the mountain's four main peaks: **Pico das Cruzinhas, Pico do Facho, Pico da Vigia,** and **Pico do Zimbreiro.** Asphalt roads allow visitors to explore on foot or by car. Entry, in a **guardhouse** at the foot of the mountain, is controlled by the military. Most of the mapped hiking trails start at **Relvão Municipal Park** (Parque Municipal do Relvão), at the foot of the mountain, just before the Fortress of São João Baptista and guardhouse. The ruins of the 17th-century Quebrada Fortress and the cute Santo António da Grota hermitage, part of the Diocese of Angra do Heroísmo, are other historic monuments that litter this fascinating volcanic peninsula.

### FORTRESS OF SÃO JOÃO BAPTISTA
### (Fortaleza de São João Baptista do Monte Brasil)

*Mount Brasil; tel. 295 214 011; daily 10am-11am and*

*2pm-6pm June-Sept., daily 10am-11am and 2pm-5pm Oct.-May; free escorted tours*

A number of forts in the island's defensive network were built around Mount Brasil, including the elaborate 16th-century Fortress of São João Baptista, which looks over Angra. Construction began in 1593 during Spanish occupancy and finished circa 1640. The fortress was used to house troops and protect the trading port from pirate attacks. In the 20th century, it served as a political prison, and is currently used as a military base. Five bastions reinforce the sprawling monument's 4-kilometer-long (2-mi-long) fortified wall, within which visitors will find **São João Baptista Church, Santa Catarina Chapel, catacombs,** and the **Governor's Palace.** In recent times the imposing fortress's edges have begun to soften and merge into the landscape as its chunky stone blocks are covered in fine moss, but its former sober splendor is still evident.

Escorted **tours** around the fortress are free, but visit times need to be negotiated at the guardhouse.

### PICO DAS CRUZINHAS VIEWPOINT
### (Miradouro de Pico das Cruzinhas)

*Mount Brasil; tel. 295 401 700; daily 8:30am-8:30pm; free*

One of Mount Brasil's best vantage points is the Pico das Cruzinhas viewpoint, a short walk from the fortress. It's the closest of the mountain's viewpoints to reach on foot, and it offers sweeping vistas of Angra's terra-cotta roofs; visitors will find a pair of binoculars up there to zoom in on the town. So high you feel like you could almost reach up and touch the planes overhead on their transatlantic journeys, the spot is marked with an evocative monument to Portugal's Age of Discoveries, a large stone pillar crowned by the Order of Christ cross.

## BEACHES
### PRAINHA BEACH
### (Zona Balnear da Prainha)

*Next to Angra Marina; open 24/7; free*

1: Duke of Terceira Garden 2: Mount Brasil walkway 3: Church of the Holy Savior's Cathedral 4: São Sebastião Fortress

# The Lilac Island

Claims as to why Terceira is nicknamed the Lilac Island range from the color of the hydrangeas that blanket the island, to the abundance of lilac bushes, to the stunning palette of its incredible sunsets.

When they're in full bloom in summer, it's hard to miss the **hydrangeas** on Terceira as they explode like elegant fireworks along pretty much every road on the island. The same can be said for its **lilac bushes,** which seem to burst out at every given opportunity, along town streets and in gardens throughout the island. Lilac hues are also incorporated into the rainbow of pastel colors that the **house facades** in historic Angra town center are painted.

But if you want to try out the sunset theory, head to the **eastern flank of Mount Brasil,** as the unobstructed ocean views from the ancient volcanic outcrop provide a the perfect opportunity to enjoy a magical moment as the sun goes down.

A thick crescent-moon-shaped beach, Prainha Beach, also known as Angra do Heroísmo Beach, is the town's main strand, stretching between Mount Brasil and the marina. It is a smallish beach with limited parking. There are plenty of little restaurants nearby in the main part of town, and it is easy to reach on foot from almost anywhere in Angra. Protected by the marina breakwater, it is usually calm and wave-free. The sand, unusually, is soft, and is a lighter blend of dark and blond than the Azores' normally black volcanic sand.

### SILVEIRA BEACH
### (Zona Balnear da Silveira)
*Largo da Silveira; open 24/7; free*
Silveira Beach is a short drive west from Angra and is very popular, despite the fact that it doesn't have any sand; it's more of a bathing spot, with a series of big cement sun decks and handrails that provide access into the sea. It has its own parking lot, toilets and showers, and access for those with limited mobility.

## KAYAKING AND STAND-UP PADDLE BOARDING

The sheltered waters of **Angra Bay** are a wonderful place for a kayak; otherwise, the kayak rental provider **ComunicAir** also offers excursions to **Praia da Vitória Bay,** or the **Cabras Islets** off Terceira's eastern coast.

### COMUNICAIR
*Rua Direita 69; tel. 910 503 800; www.comunicair.pt; Mon.-Sat. 10am-6pm; from €60 pp*
In addition to renting kayaks and offering kayak excursions, ComunicAir also gives walking and cycling tours.

## DIVING AND SNORKELING

The waters surrounding Terceira island house some of the Azores' most intriguing and iconic dive sites, with exciting dives for all levels of experience. These spots offer plenty to see, be it down in the depths of the Atlantic Ocean, from the surface, or around the coast, so snorkelers are also spoiled for choice.

### Dive Spots
### UNDERWATER ARCHAEOLOGICAL PARK OF THE BAY OF ANGRA DO HEROÍSMO
*Angra Bay; http://dive.visitazores.com/en/divespots/cemiterio-das-ancoras*
Dive into an underwater world of history at this unique submarine spot, the only underwater archaeological park in Portugal. Located just a few minutes from Angra, the

---

1: Pico das Cruzinhas viewpoint and monument
2: Prainha Beach with Mount Brasil in background

historically important park comprises various spots of archeological interest to divers, mapped out with underwater signposts and markers, the **Cemetery of Anchors** being its most popular and famous. One of the Azores' most iconic dive sites, marked by buoys, this spot is a watery graveyard for dozens of anchors of varying ages and sizes that have been deposited over several centuries. Some 100 meters (300 ft) from this spot is the resting place of the **Lidador steamer wreck,** which sank on its way to Brazil in 1878. It is said that over 70 shipwrecks littler the Bay of Angra, but most remained unlocàted. Companies including **Arraia Divers** organize dives to this spot. Most of the spots in the park can be visited by all levels of divers, but the deepest spots are only recommended for the more experienced.

### DOM JOÃO DE CASTRO BANK SUBMARINE VOLCANO (Banco Dom João de Castro)

*midway between São Miguel island and Terceira island (2 hours 20 minutes from Angra do Heroísmo Marina); http://dive.visitazores.com/en/divespots/banco-d-joao-de-castro*

Located halfway between São Miguel island and Terceira, the Dom João de Castro Bank is a vast underwater volcano and a popular Azores dive spot. The volcano last erupted in 1720, but the bank is still a seismically active zone, with gassy fumaroles and thermal springs making the crystalline water warm and bubbly. This, along with the rich fauna covering the seamount, attracts an unusual variety of marine life, like yellowmouth barracudas, Atlantic bonitos, Bermuda chubs, and wahoos, as well as rarer species such as sea turtles and devil rays. Located just over a 2-hour boat ride from Angra Marina, and at 13 meters (43 ft) depth, this bank provides a spectacular dive site, mainly centering around the volcano's old caldera. Due to its remoteness and tendency for strong currents, it is recommended for experienced divers only. Dive companies including Angra-based Deep

Blue Azores organize dive trips to this spectacular spot.

## Dive Centers and Schools
### ARRAIA DIVERS

*Estrada Regional no. 1, Silveira; tel. 914 241 939 or 295 705 164; www.arraiadivers.com; Mon.-Sat. 10am-5pm, Sun. 10am-2pm; dives from €55*

Arraia Divers specialize in dive spots around Terceira's coastline, including **Cinco Ribeiras,** west of Angra, home to one of the most famous underwater caves in Terceira; the stingray-inhabited **Cabras Islets,** off Angra's eastern coast, and the famed Cemetery of Anchors in the Bay of Angra's **Underwater Archaeological Park.**

### DEEP BLUE AZORES

*Porto das Pipas; tel. 962 772 199; www. deepblueazores.com; daily 8:30am-6pm; scuba diving from €55*

Created by two local dive enthusiasts, Deep Blue provides memorable dive experiences in and out of the water, to some of the Azores' best dive spots. Trips are purpose-designed to showcase the best of the Azores' underwater heritage with traditional dives, snorkeling, and free-diving expeditions.

## DOLPHIN- AND WHALE-WATCHING

Terceira island is one of the Azores' top islands for whale- and dolphin-watching, with plenty of companies running tours daily. The odds of spotting one of these majestic mammals from Terceira are high, particularly along the south coast. Tours usually depart from Angra do Heroísmo and Praia da Vitória, and between spring and autumn you might also be lucky enough to spot the majestic blue whale from land, as it swims between Terceira and São Jorge.

### OCEANEMOTION AZORES WHALE WATCHING

*Angra Marina; tel. 295 098 119 or 967 806 964; www. oceanemotion.pt; daily 9am-6pm; from €50*

Specializing in whale- and dolphin-watching

trips, as well as offering excursions to the Cabras Islets, snorkeling trips, and sunset cruises, Oceanemotion is all about amazing moments at sea. With a focus on responsible and sustainable tourism, trips are professional, educational, and fun with high-quality customer service.

## ATLANTIANGRA

*Angra Marina; tel. 911 855 090; www.atlantiangra.pt; daily 8:30am-8pm; from €50*

Explore the beautiful Azores waters with Atlantiangra. Located in Angra Marina, the company is driven by its passion for the sea and sea life, and is proud to share its passion and knowledge with visitors. Dolphin- and whale-watching trips are among its most popular tours.

## WATER4FUN

*Angra Marina, kiosk 5; tel. 969 296 485 or 295 212 017; www.water4fun.pt; daily 9am-noon and 1:30pm-6pm; from €50*

Jump on Water4Fun's glass-bottom boat and see the sea from a different perspective. This is a great option for the Azores' crystal-clear ocean, coupled with a comfortable, friendly, and insightful service. Whale- and dolphin-watching, swimming with dolphins, and night trips are available.

# SAILING AND BOAT TOURS

## SAILTOURS YACHT CHARTER

*Angra Marina; tel. 961 132 213; www.pt.sailtours.pt; daily 9am-8pm; from €100 pp for 4 hours*

Sail away on the Azores' beautiful seas on a yacht cruise. Hire a fully equipped and manned yacht and explore the archipelago from the comfort of a modern sailboat, or enjoy it for a social occasion or sunset cruise. For all your sailing and yachting needs, contact Sailtours Yacht Charter.

# BIRD-WATCHING

If spotting seabirds and migrating species is your thing, then Terceira is your island. Terceira is known for being one of the best places in the Azores to spot gulls and tern colonies migrating from the Arctic, particularly around **Praia da Vitória** and **Ponta das Contendas,** while the island's many little lagoons attract waders and ducks in droves. Regular visitors include Nearctic ducks, waders, and gulls like the Mediterranean gull, laughing gull, and glaucous gull. Rarer sightings of bufflehead, double-crested cormorant, yellow-crowned night heron, red-footed falcon, and belted kingfisher are also reported on Terceira. The main species of resident birds include common buzzard, wood pigeon, grey wagtail, blackbird, blackcap, European robin, and island canary. Like on most of the other islands, the best time to visit is **spring** or **fall,** when the birds are migrating or nesting, even though they can be spotted in all seasons.

## COMUNICAIR

*Rua Direita 69; tel. 910 503 800; www.comunicair.pt; Mon.-Sat. 10am-6pm; €55 pp*

ComunicAir, based out of Angra, provides expert bird-watching tours along with a series of other land and sea activities. The half-day bird-watching trip takes advantage of the Azores' central position in the North Atlantic to observe seabirds and several migratory species from the American and Eurasian continents. Wear comfortable clothes and shoes, and bring binoculars and a raincoat.

# PARKS

## RELVÃO MUNICIPAL PARK

*Mount Brasil (next to Fortress of São João Baptista); tel. 295 401 700; open 24/7; free*

Wrapped around the foot of the eastern side of Mount Brasil, on the doorstep of the Fortress of São João Baptista, this well-kept grassy park is a great spot for kids or a picnic. With Mount Brasil on one side and scenic views of Prainha Beach on the other, it also has sports fields and a children's playground.

# HIKING

## MONTE BRASIL ROUTE (PRC4TER)

**Hiking Distance:** *7.4 kilometers (4.6 mi) round-trip*

**Hiking Time:** *2.5 hours round-trip*
**Trailhead:** *Relvão Municipal Park*
**Information and Maps:** *http://trails.*
*visitazores.com/en/trails-azores/terceira/monte-brasil*

This is an easy, circular hike that will take about 2.5 hours to complete, starting and ending in Relvão Municipal Park at the foot of Mount Brasil. It takes trekkers on a tour of the imposing mountain, through its shady woodland and past its main features, such as the 16th-century **Fortress of São João Baptista,** a whale lookout, an old World War II station, and a particularly nice stretch around the old volcano's caldera. This route can be divided into sections with certain stretches done individually if you want to explore Mount Brasil a bit at a time. All pathways and routes are well signposted, though some are steep climbs up dirt tracks. Keep your eyes peeled and you might see wildlife like deer while you're hiking. You could spend a good few hours exploring Mount Brasil and its intriguing attractions; pack some snacks and water as there are no little cafés or pit stops. There are toilets at the Pico das Cruzinhas viewpoint.

# CYCLING

Cycling in Angra city center itself might not be the best way to get around, but along the waterfront and coastline west of Angra there are some great scenic routes.

## Routes
### AROUND THE ISLAND CYCLING ROUTE
**Cycling Distance:** *80 kilometers (50 mi) round-trip*
**Cycling Time:** *4-5 hours round-trip*
**Trailhead:** *Angra do Heroísmo's Old Square*
**Information and Maps:** *http://biking.*
*visitazores.com/en/route/volta-a-ilha-terceira*

Enjoy this scenic route around Terceira island, starting and ending at Angra's main square, the Praça Velha. Start following the main EN1-1A road along the southwest coast, passing through pretty seaside parishes and the stunning **Ponta do Queimado viewpoint.** En route, stop off at the **Cinco Ribeiras bathing site** if you need to cool down after working up a sweat. From Ponta do Queimado, continue on to **Biscoitos,** where you can hop off and pay a visit to the town's brilliant little wine museum and tidal bathing area. After leaving Biscoitos, continue along the north coast to Lajes, past the airport, to Praia da Vitória, where you can stop to enjoy the sandy beach and pristine waters. From here, head south, passing Ponta das Contendas back to Angra's historic center.

## DOZE RIBEIRAS CYCLING ROUTE
**Cycling Distance:** *43 kilometers (27 mi) round-trip*
**Cycling Time:** *3.5 hours round-trip*
**Trailhead:** *Angra do Heroísmo*
**Information and Maps:** *www.viamichelin. com/web/Maps/Map-Ilha_Terceira-_-Ilha_de_ Terceira-Portugal*

A circular ride from Angra, west to Doze Ribeiras parish, then inland heading east, along the EN5-2, to the **Natal Cave, Furnas do Enxofre,** and **Algar do Carvão** attractions. After spending some time exploring these volcanic sights, head back down to Angra along the EN5-2A and M1018 roads.

## Cycling Rentals
### COMUNICAIR
*Rua Direita 69; tel. 910 503 800; www.comunicair.pt; Mon.-Sat. 10am-6pm; from €20/day*

Bicycles and other leisure equipment like kayaks can be rented from ComunicAir. The price includes helmet, air pump, tools, and a locker; ID and a €200 deposit are required.

### AGUIATUR AZORES RENTALS
*Av. Tenente Coronel José Agostinho; tel. 917 553 111; http://aguiaturazores.com; from €30/day*

Rent a reliable scooter to nip around the island from Aguiatur Azores. Hotel drop-offs possible.

---

1: Angra Marina 2: Relvão Municipal Park

## ADVENTURE SPORTS

### PRO ISLAND TOUR

*CND Do Moinho, 10, Biscoitos; tel. 920 581 523; https://proislandtour.pt/index.php/en; Mon.-Sat. 9am-6pm; from €50*

Experience the thrill of adventure sports on Terceira island with one of Pro Island Tour's exhilarating excursions. Specializing in all-terrain Jeep tours, all tours include a guide, meals, and insurance. Visit the island's caves, tour the island, or enjoy a food tour; take advantage of Pro Island Tour's personalized, adrenalin-packed excursions.

## SPAS AND RELAXATION

### MYTHOS WELLNESS SPA
### AZORES - HOTEL DO CARACOL

*Estrada Regional no. 1; tel. 910 449 945; www. mythos.pt; Tues.-Sat. 10am-7pm, Mon. 1pm-5pm; from €58*

Located in the Caracol Hotel just outside Angra town center, Mythos Spa combines state-of-the-art technology with traditional massage and relaxation techniques to provide a truly deep, restful, and sensorial experience.

### LUXUS DAY SPA

*Rua Direita 82; tel. 295 628 204; www.facebook. com/luxusdayspa; Mon.-Sat. 9am-8pm; from €110*

An elegantly decorated private day spa in Angra city center, Luxus uses local ingredients to provide sumptuous and relaxing treatments, such as the Azorean Bio Massage. Other treatments like manicures and pedicures are also available.

### ALKIMIA BEAUTY AND BALANCE

*Rua Direita 52, 1st floor; tel. 295 216 294; www. mythos.pt; Mon.-Fri. 8am-8pm, Sat. 9am-8pm; from €30*

Located near Angra beachfront, Alkimia Beauty and Balance provides treatments that aim to rest and restore mind, body, and soul. An eclectic and exotic mix of beauty and spa treatments is available, from acupuncture and Ayurveda massage to mud and algae wraps with an exfoliating of Himalayan salt or rice powder. A shop selling essences, essential oils, crystals, and precious stones is on the premises.

## FOOD

Angra do Heroísmo's food scene is somewhat limited in terms of choice and variety, in comparison to other Azorean cities such as the much more international Ponta Delgada. But what it does have is quality over quantity. The same can be said for the entire island. There is a decent selection of European and upscale eateries, particularly in hotels and down by Angra Marina, as well as a good selection of down-to-earth local restaurants, and great seafood restaurants in coastal villages.

### Azorean
### BIROU BAR

*Rua de São João, 25; tel. 295 702 180; https://m. facebook.com/Birou-Bar-1744384252445367; Mon.-Thurs. 10am-noon, Fri.-Sat. 10am-2am; €10*

This cool little bar-tapas tavern serves tasty, authentic island food and drink, as well as typical Romanian specialties. Trademark dishes include stuffed peppers with a side of mashed potatoes, delicious shrimp pasta, and swordfish and meat stew, all washed down with fruity sangria or a cocktail. The funky interior is reminiscent of a contemporary art gallery.

### TABERNA ROBERTO

*EN3-1A 3; tel. 966 431 126; www.facebook.com/ tabernadoroberto; Tues.-Sat. 11:30am-3:30pm and 6:30pm-10:30pm, Sun. 10am-3pm; €15*

This exceptional, lively little restaurant looks a bit like a wine shop when you walk in, with a huge shelving unit loaded with hundreds of types of wines. The menu includes local fish and meats all cooked in a traditional wood oven, complemented by an extensive wine list. Taberna Roberto is renowned for specialties such as its wood-oven-baked ribs, roast octopus, and homemade cinnamon ice cream.

### ★ O CACHALOTE

*Rua do Rego 14; tel. 914 237 459, Mon.-Sat. noon-11pm; €20*

How much more quintessentially Azorean can you get than excellent beef cooked on a sizzling lava rock? That's what O Cachalote specializes in. Ignore the sterile interior and garish red-and-green color scheme and enjoy the best steak for miles.

## Seafood
### BEIRA MAR SÃO MATEUS

*Canada do Porto; tel. 295 642 392; www.facebook. com/pages/category/Seafood-Restaurant/Beira-Mar-S%C3%A3o-Mateus-465356256869367; Tues.-Sun. noon-3pm and 6:30pm-10pm; €15*

Bright and clean with ocean-inspired colors, Beira Mar São Mateus, a 5-minute drive west of Angra, brings the delights of the sea to the table. Here you can enjoy a kaleidoscope of excellent seafood concoctions, from traditional *lapas* (limpets) and grilled octopus, to a fresh seafood soup in a bread bowl. This is a busy place, popular among the locals, so make sure to make a reservation, especially for Fridays and weekends.

## International
### ★ CAPTAIN'S TABLE

*Rua da Rocha 14; tel. 295 216 358; https:// captainstabledangra.negocio.site; Mon.-Fri. noon-10pm, Sat. 6pm-10pm; €10*

A small, bright restaurant with colorful checkered tablecloths, Captain's Table excels in fresh Mediterranean cuisine. Offering the freshest farm-to-table ingredients, the menu is a fusion of Portuguese, Turkish, and Italian cuisine using local Azorean ingredients. Popular specials include slow-cooked dishes, grilled tuna steaks, seafood pasta, and a family secret crunchy pumpkin dessert with a delicious passion fruit ice cream. It's fancy but with a laid-back atmosphere.

## ACCOMMODATIONS
### Under €100
#### PENSÃO RESIDENCIAL A ILHA

*Rua Direita 24; tel. 295 628 180; €55 d*

Budget 12-room inn Pensão Residencial A Ilha is in a great city-center location 100 meters (300 feet) from the marina and the beach. Rooms are clean and simple and breakfast is included, but there's no elevator.

### €100-200
#### HOTEL CARACOL

*Estrada Regional 1; tel. 295 402 600; www. hoteldocaracol.com; €100 d*

Offering good value for money, the tasteful four-star seaside Hotel Caracol is across the road from a handy grocery store and is a 15-minute walk west from Angra city center. It has bright, pleasant rooms, all with garden or sea views, a beautiful pool hanging over the ocean, and a cement sundeck jetty.

#### TERCEIRA MAR HOTEL

*Portões de São Pedro 1; tel. 295 402 280; www. bensaude.pt; €109 d*

Stately Terceira Mar Hotel is on the waterfront of Fanal Bay, in an exceptional location at the foot of Mount Brasil. Floor-to-ceiling windows throughout this resort-style hotel make the most of its stunning setting.

#### ★ ANGRA MARINA HOTEL

*Estrada Pero de Barcelos, Porto de Pipas; tel. 295 204 700; www.angramarinahotel.com; €154 d*

Large and imposing, modern five-star Angra Marina Hotel is cut right into the cliff face that hems Angra do Heroísmo. All 157 gleaming rooms have sea views and aquamarine accents. There is a panoramic rooftop restaurant, a spa, and an outdoor pool. It is on the marina side, a 10-minute walk east from the city center.

## INFORMATION AND SERVICES

As Terceira is one of the Azores' main and most populous islands, Angra's services can generally cater for all eventualities and emergencies. For specific or critical health concerns, patients could be transferred to the archipelago's largest hospital, on São Miguel, or to the mainland.

- **Tourist Office:** Rua Direita 70-74; tel. 295

404 810; www.visitazores.com; Mon.-Sat. 9am-7pm

- **PSP Police:** Praça Doutor Sousa Júnior 1; tel. 295 212 022; www.psp.pt

- **Main hospital:** Hospital de Santo Espírito da Ilha Terceira, Canada do Briado; tel. 295 403 200; www.hseit.pt

# GETTING THERE AND AROUND

The best way to get around Angra is **on foot.** Compact and clean, it's a great place to walk, but make sure you have comfortable footwear on because there's a load to see and a quite few hills and steps involved.

## Bus

The local bus service is not really geared towards tourism, catering instead to islanders. Most routes depart from around the **Old Square** (Praça Velha) and go around the coast; there are regular services between Angra and **Lajes Airport** (Line 5; 1 hour 20 minutes; €5), as well as Angra and **Praia da Vitória** (Line 2; 1 hour; €3), but routes inland are less frequent. Visit the main office, **Empresa de Viação Terceirense** (Rua Dr. Sousa Meneses no. 15; tel. 295 217 001; www.

evt.pt), or the website for more information on routes.

**AzorBus City Tours** (Rua da Sé no. 190; tel. 969 668 829 or 969 668 839; http://azorbus. com; Mon.-Sat. 10am-6pm; from €22.50) runs routes around the city and the island that are more suited to tourists.

## Bike and Scooter

Another good way to explore the city is on a **scooter. Cycling** could be an option for the waterfront, but a lack of cycle paths in the city itself and the narrow, busy roads, which are steep in parts, make leisurely cycling in Angra a little tricky.

### COMUNICAIR

*Rua Direita 69; tel. 910 503 800; www.comunicair.pt; Mon.-Sat. 10am-6pm; from €20/day*

Bicycles, in addition to kayaks and other equipment, can be rented from ComunicAir.

### AGUIATUR AZORES RENTALS

*Av. Tenente Coronel José Agostinho; tel. 917 553 111; http://aguiaturazores.com; from €30/day*

Rent a reliable scooter from Aguiatur Azores Rentals; hotel drop-offs are possible.

Terceira Mar Hotel

# Central Terceira

Several of Terceira's main attractions can be found in the heart of the island. Volcanic sights abound in the Algar do Carvão Regional Natural Monument, including the Algar do Carvão Cave, the Natal Cave, and the Furnas do Enxofre fumarole fields.

Just south of all this is a region dominated by the Guilherme Moniz Caldera (Caldeira de Guilherme Moniz), the largest volcanic crater in the Azores, a gaping, shallow dish 15 kilometers (9 mi) in diameter. Despite its size, it is rather underwhelming on sight, as much of its once-towering, jagged walls have eroded and collapsed. The caldera, belonging to the now-extinct Mourião Volcano, is today covered with trees and green shrubbery, its flat bottom having given way to pastures for cows where luminous molten lava once bubbled. This is also prime hiking territory, wild, lush, and green, with herds of cows sashaying down country lanes and expansive views of rolling green fields.

There are few towns of note in this geologically fascinating area, but the amenity-rich areas around Angra and Praia are just 15 minutes (10 km/6 mi) and 25 minutes (25 km/16 mi) to the south and east, respectively. Stock up on food before heading inland if you plan to spend the better part of the day here.

## SIGHTS
### ★ Algar do Carvão Regional Natural Monument

Due to its environmental importance and wealth of volcanic attractions and peculiarities, the area flanking the Algar do Carvão Cave has been declared a Regional Natural Monument. Covering 40 hectares (100 acres), it's an area of fascinating landscapes, showcasing the variety of landscapes made possible by geology. It is a fabulous place for compelling hikes and seemingly infinite volcanic vistas.

### ALGAR DO CARVÃO CAVE

*EN5-2A, Algar do Carvão Regional Natural Monument; tel. 295 212 992; www.montanheiros. com/algarCarvao; daily 2:30pm-5:15pm Mar. 25-May 31, daily 2pm-6pm June 1-Oct. 15, Tues.-Wed. and Fri.-Sat. 2:30pm-5:15pm Oct. 17-Mar. 23; €6, €9 combined ticket with Natal Cave*

Vast and dripping with water, the mesmerizing Algar do Carvão Cave takes its name ("coal pit") from its black volcanic walls. This is a unique opportunity to descend into the depths of an extinct volcano with formidable features that include a huge chimney and spectacular chambers, created in an eruption some 2,000 years ago. Beautiful milky-white stalactites and stalagmites cover the cavern; the walls change color as you descend through the layers of earth. A mysterious world is revealed on a series of staircases (at least 250 steps, some quite steep) and tunnels to a place once filled with lava. This eerie landscape has an ethereal touch, with dim, modern spotlights that enhance the natural light from the chimney. The cavernous volcano innards, with a mouth open to the heavens, is unique, and is one of the most popular and memorable attractions on the island.

You'll find a guide or two at the bottom of stairs on a landing; they offer information on the caves upon request. The local conservation association, **Os Montanheiros** (tel. 295 212 992 or 961 362 215; www.montanheiros.com), manages the caves.

The caves are 11 kilometers (7 mi) north of Angra do Heroísmo, a 15-minute drive on the EN3-1A road. There's plenty of parking in a designated lot for visitors right next to the reception office. A combined €9 ticket provides access to a smaller lava tube, the Natal Cave, 6 kilometers (4 mi) away.

### NATAL CAVE
### (Gruta do Natal)

*tel. 295 212 992; www.montanheiros.com; Tues.-Wed.*

*and Fri.-Sat. 2:30pm-5pm; €6, €9 combined ticket with Algar do Carvão Cave*

Amateur geologists will be delighted by the riveting array of craggy rock formations that line the Natal Cave. A 700-meter-long (2,000-ft-long) lava tube, it is a dark, damp underground system, formed by naturally cooled lava in the earth's belly. Hard hats are supplied at the entry, as the cave is quite low in parts and visitors have to stoop to pass through certain parts. Another novel island experience of unique natural beauty, the Gruta do Natal (Christmas Cave) takes its name from the fact that Christmas mass and other special ceremonies, such as christenings and weddings, are celebrated in the grotto. Entry to the cave is via a traditional stone house, unassuming from the outside, but with an interpretive center proving plenty of information on the Natal Cave inside.

### LAGOA DO NEGRO LAKE
*opposite Natal Cave; open 24/7; free*

Small and tranquil, the Lagoa do Negro lagoon is located directly opposite the entrance to the Natal Cave, the result of the accumulation of rainwater and run-off from the slopes of nearby hills and fields. This peaceful little lake is not suitable for bathing or water sports, but it is a perfect spot for picnics and relaxation. It has a unique beauty, peppered with Japanese cedar and interesting aquatic vegetation, and it's a popular spot for meditation.

### FURNAS DO ENXOFRE
*off the EN5-2A road, follow signs between the Algar do Carvão and Gruta do Natal; http://parquesnaturais.azores.gov.pt/pt/terceira/o-que-visitar/areas-protegidas/monumento-natural/furnas-do-enxofre; open 24/7; free*

Another unique (and free) attraction, the Furnas de Enxofre sulfur field, located between the Algar do Carvão Cave and the Natal Cave, is extraordinary. A raised wooden walkway allows visitors to walk around an area pitted with underground fumaroles. Sulfurous vapor rises in steamy plumes from perforations in the ground, giving the area a steamy, almost ethereal feel. Take 15-20 minutes to wander around in the smelly steam.

# HIKING
## MISTÉRIOS NEGROS (PRC1TER)
**Hiking Distance:** *4.9 kilometers (3 mi) round-trip*
**Hiking Time:** *2.5 hours round-trip*
**Trailhead:** *Lagoa do Negro lagoon*
**Information and Maps:** *http://trails.visitazores.com/en/trails-azores/terceira/misterios-negros*

Starting at the tranquil Lagoa do Negro lagoon, this demanding, circular hike will satisfy seasoned hikers. The Mistérios Negros trail takes trekkers through rich pastures hemmed by large trees, blankets of endemic vegetation and beautiful flora, a trio of small lagoons that are a popular spot for migrating birds, and shady forests, to Pico Gordo Peak, one of the island's highest points on its swollen central massif. It ends back at the Lagoa do Negro lagoon, where hikers can round off the trek with a visit to the Natal Cave.

### ALGAR DO CARVÃO WALK
**Hiking Distance:** *6.1 kilometers (3.8 mi) one-way*
**Hiking Time:** *1 hour 20 minutes one-way*
**Trailhead:** *Algar do Carvão Cave*
**Information and Maps:** *Follow signs, or ask for directions at Algar do Carvão Cave or Gruta do Natal Cave visitor centers*

Instead of making the short drive, it's possible to walk between the Algar do Carvão Cave and Natal Cave, a 1 hour 20 minute walk east to west, following the **EN5-2A** and **EN3-1A** roads across the very heart of the island. Starting at the **Algar do Carvão Cave,** head west to the **Natal Cave.** En route, take a right turn following the road sign toward the **Furnas do Enxofre** fields. Spend 15-20 minutes here following the wooden walkway through the steamy, smelly landscape, before continuing to the Natal Cave. The scenery is

---

**1:** Natal Cave interpretive center **2:** Furnas do Enxofre

lush and green, vast and volcanic. You'll either have to walk back again or call for a taxi.

### ROCHA DO CHAMBRE (PRC6TER)

**Hiking Distance:** *8.8 kilometers (5.5 mi) round-trip*

**Hiking Time:** *2.5 hours round-trip*

**Trailhead:** *Macadam dirt road, at the intersection with Estrada Regional 3-1*

**Information and Maps:** *http://trails. visitazores.com/en/trails-azores/terceira/rocha-do-chambre*

This circular route takes trekkers through the heart of the island's rural interior. It climbs to an altitude of 700 meters (2,000 ft) and is therefore advisable only on fair-weather days with good visibility. It starts on a dirt road that carves through fields of endemic flowers, later following a stream, toward open pastures. Viewpoints over open valleys and sheer escarpments can be enjoyed during the most demanding stretch of the hike, a climb to the highest point, known as Rocha do Chambre. At the top, you'll take in panoramic views.

### PASSAGEM DAS BESTAS (PRC7TER)

**Hiking Distance:** *4 kilometers (2 mi) round-trip*

**Hiking Time:** *2.5 hours round-trip*

**Trailhead:** *Caldeira de Guilherme Moniz parking lot*

**Information and Maps:** *http://trails.*
*visitazores.com/pt-pt/trilhos-dos-acores/terceira/passagem-das-bestas*

This short, enjoyable circular route explores the area's woods and peatlands. A highlight of this route is the old oxcart tracks deeply engraved in the rocky ground, and from which the trail takes its name, Passagem das Bestas (Beasts' Passage). These tracks run alongside a stream that leads to a wood of Japanese cedars, across pastures wedged between hills, and up to its highest point, Morião Hill. Descend following ravines back to the old oxcart tracks, returning to the parking lot.

## GETTING THERE AND AROUND

A **car** or **scooter** is ideal for exploring central Terceira. The distance between the attractions is a short drive, or a considerable (but manageable and enjoyable) walk.

Getting to this area is also tricky by public transport (except by **taxi**), as local buses run infrequently to inland areas. You could opt for an organized excursion to the main sights, such as the Algar do Carvão Caves; companies such as **Angra Travel Tours** (Rua Direita 155; tel. 295 206 900; www.angratravel.net; Mon.-Fri. 9am-6pm; from €45) and **AzorBus City Tours** (Rua da Sé, no. 190; tel. 969 668 829 or 969 668 839; http://azorbus.com; Mon.-Sat. 10am-6pm; from €46) run excursions to the island's central attractions.

# Western Terceira

The western Terceira coastline is dramatic and vertiginous. This portion of the island is more heavily forested than the other side, due to strong westerly winds that bring rain to the area. A large swathe of this part of the island is occupied by the Serra de Santa Bárbara and Mistérios Negros Nature Reserve; the Mistérios Negros Massif is formed by four small volcanic peaks, created by a huge volcanic eruption in 1761, which explains the baldness of some spots. This also resulted in a string of natural swimming pools, formed by seawater that fills the rocky coast's crevices, such as those near the village of Biscoitos on the island's craggy north coast, almost due north of Angra. It was in Biscoitos that the island's famous Verdelho wine originated, thanks to its unique terroir of mineral-rich, fertile, volcanic soil.

# SIGHTS
## Santa Bárbara Peak

*Serra de Santa Bárbara and Mistérios Negros Nature Reserve*

Santa Bárbara Peak, the highest point on Terceira island, is a dormant volcano whose summit stands at 1,021 meters (3,350 ft). The views from this peak are magnificent. A long, steep road climbs to the peak, meaning those less inclined to hike to the summit can enjoy a very scenic drive to the top, taking in landscape covered with Japanese cedars and colorful hydrangea bushes along the way. Up at the top there is a viewpoint—the **Miradouro da Serra da Santa Bárbara**—which offers sweeping views over the surrounding area and out to sea, though they are slightly obstructed by the various satellite dishes and radio antennae that litter the peak. You can also see neighboring islands from up here.

Also up on the peak is an old whaling station, from where whales were spotted, and the small **Serra de Santa Bárbara Interpretation Center** (Estrada Regional ER5, 2nd ["Estrada das Doze"]; tel. 924 403 957; http://parquesnaturais.azores.gov.pt/pt/terceira/o-que-visitar/centros-ambientais/centro-de-interpretacao-ambiental-de-santa-barbara; Tues.-Sat. 10am-1pm and 1:30pm-5pm; €3), which explains the history and geology of the volcano and the rest of the island. Like with many of the archipelago's main viewpoints, it pays to check the weather in advance and visit on a clear day—although the Azores' weather is notoriously unpredictable.

## Ponta do Queimado Viewpoint
### (Miradouro da Ponta do Queimado)

*EN1-1A 20; open 24/7; free*

The Ponta do Queimado Viewpoint is a soaring headland marking the westernmost point of the island, from where, on a clear day, you can see the neighboring island of Graciosa. This scenic spot was formed by the eruption of Santa Bárbara Peak in 1761. A steep flight of chalky white stairs climbs to a raised landing on the jagged rocks, an old whale lookout, from where views of the imposing, sheer coastline get even better.

On the way down the curvaceous road that branches off the main EN1-1A road to the coast and viewpoint, you'll pass the **Serreta Lighthouse,** inaugurated in November 1908. This historic lighthouse no longer has the size and grandeur it once boasted, as it was badly damaged by a violent earthquake in 1980 and was reduced to the size you see today. Originally powered by gasoline and clockwork, it was electrified in 1958, boosting its beam to a visibility of 30 miles.

## Altares Viewpoint
### (Pico Matias Simão)

*Canada do Pico Matias Simão Peak, Altares village, off EN1-1A road; open 24/7; free*

Located on the northwestern flank of the island, the Pico Matias Simão viewpoint, also known as the Altares viewpoint, protrudes from the coastal stretch that fronts the village of Altares. A long dirt road makes the gradual slope up to the top of the tufty peak, from where endless ocean views can be enjoyed on one side, and undulating patchwork fields on the other. Cars can be left in a little parking lot while you climb the 135 steps to the peak.

# ★ WINERIES AND WINE-TASTING

The peaceful and character-packed village of **Biscoitos** is one of Terceira's best-loved villages, known for its winemaking heritage, wine museum, traditional architecture, and colorful *império* chapels. Here visitors can see typical basalt stonewall vineyards, sample the locally produced wine, and enjoy a dip in the glorious tidal pools that attract bathers in droves when the weather is hot. It is said that the village took its name from the heaps of black basalt rocks that cover the local landscape, endearingly nicknamed *biscoitos* (biscuits) as they allegedly resembled the dry, bready biscuits used to sustain sailors on the long maritime journeys back in the Age of Discoveries.

The local wine from the Biscoitos parish is

an island specialty. Vine fields here are still hemmed in by distinctive basalt-rock stone walls, shaping little squares called *curraletas*, built centuries ago to protect the vines from the Atlantic's strong, salty winds. Thanks to this unique convergence of natural attributes, Biscoitos's wines have a unique composition and flavor, with a deep golden straw color and a taste that is dry, crisp, and, some say, with a distinct hint of saltiness from the volcanic island terrain and Atlantic sea breeze.

The wine is made from grapes of the **Verdelho** variety. It's a specific type of wine protected and promoted since 1993 by the Vinho Verdelho dos Biscoitos Fraternity. This local wine can be tried at the Biscoitos Wine Museum, where the unique Chico Maria liqueur, a fortified wine liqueur with different flavors like cherry, blackberry, and passion fruit, can also be sampled.

### BISCOITOS WINE MUSEUM
### (Museu do Vinho dos Biscoitos)
*Canada do Caldeiro 3; tel. 965 667 324; https://pt.azoresguide.net/servicos/museu-do-vinho-dos-biscoitos; Tues.-Sat. 10:30am-5:30pm; free*

For a small space, this charming, atmospheric wine museum packs a lot of information on the history of local wines, in addition to tastings. A family-run estate since 1890, now in its fifth generation, the Biscoitos winery was one of the first producers of local wines, using Terceira's Biscoitos Verdelho variety. Belonging to the Brum family, the estate carries that legacy to this day, and centuries of hard work are encapsulated in a fascinating little museum—complemented by a beautiful flower garden, a bijou vineyard, and a little museum displaying tools used over the years, plus an old cask storehouse where tastings are held and products sold. The dedicated staff take pride in sharing the estate's history and products with visitors. A small garden at the back of the museum gives a sense of how the vines were planted and cultivated and provides information on the varieties planted in the region.

### ADEGA SIMAS
*Canada Tenente Coronel 5; tel. 961 329 139; https://adega-simas.webnode.pt; Mon.-Sat. 2pm-5pm, call two days ahead to book; €5 pp*

For a taste of locally produced wines, jams, and preserves, head to the family-run Adega Simas winery, also in the village of Biscoitos. Enjoy a unique wine-tasting of the famous island Verdelho, accompanied by homemade jams and tapas, or stay for a home-cooked regional-inspired lunch or dinner in their on-site **restaurant,** which features the famous island-reared beef rump (*alcatra*). This pretty little boutique winery and vineyard is a great place to see how vines are grown and wines are made, while enjoying sea views with your tipple.

# BEACHES AND POOLS
## NEGRITO BATHING SITE
## (Zona Balnear Negrito)
*São Mateus da Calheta parish, near Negrito Fort; tel. 295 401 700; open 24/7; free*

In the parish of São Mateus da Calheta, between the Cinco Ribeiras bathing site and Angra, the Negrito bathing site is located near the remains of a quirky old 16th-century maritime fort named the **Negrito Fort,** which is made entirely of black basalt rock and wood. The coastline hemming this area is fairly low and made up largely of chunky basalt slabs and a flat-bottom bay. With a pier, a natural pool, and wide cement decks, there is plenty of space for stretching out towels and soaking up the sun.

## CINCO RIBEIRAS BATHING SITE
## (Zona Balnear das Cinco Ribeiras)
*Canada do Pilar, Conceição; tel. 295 401 700; open 24/7; free*

A short drive west of Angra on the island's south coast, the Cinco Ribeiras bathing site comprises a string of natural pools fed by sea water. Encased by stunning scenery, it has a good-size parking lot and a small bar serving

**1:** Biscoitos Wine Museum **2:** Negrito bathing site **3:** Cinco Ribeiras bathing site **4:** Biscoitos bathing site

it. Nearby is an old military fort built during the Spanish occupancy period (1583-1640) and the quaint Nossa Senhora de Lurdes Chapel. This spot is also one of the island's top diving sites. The tidal pool is the starting point to a series of underground caves, chambers, and galleries, and it is also a great spot for snorkeling.

### BISCOITOS BATHING SITE
### (Piscinas Naturais Biscoitos)

*Zona Balnear dos Biscoitos; open 24/7; free*

On Terceira's rugged north coast, the Biscoitos bathing site is an area of outstanding beauty. Natural cooled lava crevices that fill with seawater have been given a little man-made hand to make them more comfortable and accessible for bathers, with a lining of cement and some steps. This is a very popular seaside spot in summer, as the extraordinary jagged pockets fill with refreshing, translucent water. The natural landscape offers a remarkable contrast of turquoise seawater and black volcanic rock, against a deep blue ocean. There's plenty of parking, and in summer a couple of huts open to provide refreshments.

### QUATRO RIBEIRAS BEACH
### (Piscinas Naturais das
### Quatro Ribeiras)

*Zona Balnear das Quatro Ribeiras; open 24/7; free*

Another popular bathing site, located almost directly opposite Angra on the north coast, the Quatro Ribeiras bathing site consists of rocky tidal pools and a human-made cement pool, both filled with fresh seawater. This spot has a large parking lot and clean restrooms serving it, but nowhere to buy food or drink, so make sure to bring snacks if you want to spend a few hours enjoying the sun. There's also a flight of stairs down to the pools from the parking lot to negotiate. From the main EN1-1A road, follow the brown signs with binoculars on them to find Quatro Ribeiras.

# DIVING AND SNORKELING

## CINCO RIBEIRAS CAVES

*accessed from Cinco Ribeiras bathing site*

Widely reputed to be one of Terceira's best diving and snorkeling spots, the Cinco Ribeiras site is 15 minutes by car from Angra do Heroísmo, where you can rent gear. With gentle currents and good visibility, it is suitable for divers of all levels of experience. This exciting string of coastal grottoes and underwater caves can be accessed from the Cinco Ribeiras bathing site, following the rocky coastline. Sting rays are commonly sighted here, along with moray eels and nudibranchs inside the caves. At the start of the dive, you will also see the huge boiler of a ship, the Union, which sank here in 1911.

# HIKING

The compelling landscape of western Terceira ranges from dramatic coastline to the bumpy interior of the Serra de Santa Bárbara and Mistérios Negros Nature Reserve, covering over 1,800 hectares (4,400 acres) in a zillion different shades of green. This verdant landscape, with soaring valleys and tranquil lakes, looks more Hawaiian than European, a testament to its natural richness and diversity. These mountains are home to important species of fauna and flora born from this type of natural phenomena, and whose importance and need of preservation resulted in the area being classified a Nature Reserve. This area is prime hiking territory, although some parts of the Nature Reserve may have limited access.

### SERRETA-LAGOINHA
### TRAIL (PRC03 TER)

**Hiking Distance:** *6.8 kilometers (4.2 mi) round-trip*
**Hiking Time:** *2.5 hours round-trip*
**Trailhead:** *M1044, Canada do Fonte crossroad (Serreta parish)*
**Information and Maps:** *http://trails. visitazores.com/en/trails-azores/terceira/ rocha-do-chambre*

# Terceira and Trás-os-Montes: A Culinary Connection

It is said that the first settlers on Terceira were from the Trás-os-Montes region, in northeastern mainland Portugal, and some of its dishes originate from recipes brought to the island by its earliest settlers.

Terceira's quintessential local dish is *alcatra,* a typical beef or fish dish slow-cooked in an unglazed earthenware pot until it is fall-off-the-bone and melt-in-the-mouth delicious. The sauce, a rich, aromatic combination of bacon, onion, garlic, bay leaf, pepper, and wine, among other ingredients, is reduced until thick and usually accompanied by bread or kneaded dough. History has it *alcatra* derives from the Transmontano specialty *chanfana,* which is typically made with goat meat.

Here are the best places on Terceira to get *alcatra:*

- **Adega Simas:** The restaurant of this winery in the village of Biscoitos serves up a mean version of this aromatic beef dish (page 152).

- **Ti Choa:** This restaurant in western Terceira, not far from Biscoitos, the Serreta Lighthouse, and the Ponta do Queimado viewpoint, is another great place to sample *alcatra* (page 156).

- **Caneta:** Sample the delectable specialty in this rustic farmhouse-style restaurant in the village of Altares, known for its authentic food and ambience (page 155).

This circular trail starts near Canada do Fonte in Serreta village, around Lagoinha, a small lagoon surrounded by cedars. It's a somewhat demanding hike, taking trekkers from scenic elevations to the folds of a deep valley. Dirt roads pass through endemic vegetation, dense woodland trails flanked by cedar wood forests, pastures, and a stream running through a deep valley.

### SERRA DE SANTA BÁRBARA VIEWPOINT

**Hiking Distance:** *5.7 kilometers (3.5 mi) one-way*

**Hiking Time:** *1 hour 40 minutes one-way*

**Trailhead:** *Serra de Santa Bárbara Interpretation Center*

**Information and Maps:** *Serra de Santa Bárbara Interpretation Center*

Climb through the clouds to the highest point on Terceira island, to the windy Serra de Santa Bárbara viewpoint, a long, challenging, and exciting hike. Not the easiest hike on the island but very rewarding, it entails a strenuous, almost continuous ascension through eerie forest canopies to the Santa Bárbara Peak, which stands at 1,021 meters (3,350 ft). The

last stretch of the route is particularly steep. On a clear day, the vistas from the viewing platform at the peak are breathtaking, considered by many to be the best on the island, and go on for miles around, over an ancient volcanic crater and out to sea.

Signs reading *"trilho turístico"* (tourist trail) in Santa Bárbara village direct hikers to the starting point of the route and to the Serra de Santa Bárbara Interpretation Center. The interpretation center aims to be the starting point for understanding the natural heritage of the Terceira Natural Park and provides information on the formation process and geomorphological evolution of the island.

## FOOD

### CANETA

*Rua As Presas 13, Altares; tel. 295 989 162; www.restaurantecaneta.com; Tues.-Sun. noon-3pm and 6pm-10pm; €20*

This rustic farmhouse-style restaurant serves local favorites like great beefsteaks, barnacles, *alcatra,* smoked island sausages, and a prawn and squid kebab. Restaurant A Caneta is a short, 3-minute drive from the Altares viewpoint, in the village of Altares, on Terceira's rocky north coast. It's worth a visit for the authentic food and ambience.

### ★ TI CHOA

*Grota do Margaride 1, Serreta; tel. 295 906 673; Mon.-Sat. noon-3pm and 6:30pm-10pm; €12*

A hub of the finest Terceira cuisine, cozy, family-run Ti Choa occupies an unassuming old rural farmhouse with rustic décor and ambience. It serves hearty homemade stews including *alcatra* in typical terra-cotta pots, a mixed meat platter with pulled pork and sweet potatoes, and great homespun desserts. The restaurant is on the island's western fringe, a 7-minute drive south from the Ponta do Queimado viewpoint, in the village of Serreta.

## GETTING THERE AND AROUND

Like elsewhere on Terceira, a form of personal motorized transport such as a **car** or **scooter** is ideal for exploring the western end of the island, given the flexibility it allows to stop and visit the many numerous sights at leisure. This mode of transport is also best to reach places father inland such as the Serra de Santa Bárbara and Mistérios Negros Nature Reserve.

### Bus

Local **EVT buses** (tel. 295 217 001; www. evt.pt/percursos) run a few times a day from **Angra** to main villages along the west coast of Terceira island. **Line 1,** from Angra's Duke of Terceira Garden to **Biscoitos** (24 minutes; €4 one-way), runs every four hours and stops at villages such as **Cinco Ribeiras, Santa Bárbara, Serreta,** and **Altares** en route.

# Eastern Terceira

Dominated by lush green pastures and farmland peppered by the Azores' trademark black-and-white "happy cows," eastern Terceira is a patchwork of agricultural bliss. Less densely forested than the western flank of Terceira, as it sees less rainfall and humidity, this end of the island is where Lajes Airport, the beach resort of Praia da Vitória, and the famed Serra do Cume viewpoint are found. This side of the island also has a string of sandy beaches hemming its coast, which makes it popular with surfers. One of the prettiest little hamlets along this stretch of coast is São Sebastião, home to a gorgeous little *império* and the Ponta das Contendas lighthouse.

Located just above the middle of the island's east coast, around 2 kilometers (1 mi) from Lajes Airport, is Praia da Vitória, Terceira's second city. Praia da Vitória is also home to the island's most important seaport and main fishing fleet. Praia boasts a generous sandy beach and pleasant beachfront, a modern marina, a colorful historic center and pedestrianized shopping street, and an enjoyable seaside feel—although it can feel rather empty outside peak season.

## SIGHTS
### Praia da Vitória

Compact in size for the island's second most important town, Praia da Vitória is a pleasant place to take a stroll and enjoy a coffee on the way to or from the airport. With a couple of very striking churches, a long main street paved like a carpet with fancy patterned cobblestones, an eye-catching historic center, a smart beachfront, and a nice long boardwalk, it has a seaside holiday feel to it. Its neat little marina and tidy seafront are attractive, but the rolling green pastures that envelop the town really steal the show.

### SANTA CRUZ MOTHER CHURCH (Igreja Matriz de Santa Cruz)

*Praça Francisco Ornelas da Câmara 1761; tel. 295 542 100; open 24/7*

The pretty Santa Cruz Mother Church is a large whitewashed church with yolk-yellow trim, which, dating from the 15th century, is one of the oldest in the archipelago.

## CHURCH OF SENHOR SANTO CRISTO
## (Igreja do Senhor Santo Cristo)

*Rua da Misericórdia; tel. 295 512 127, Mon.-Fri. 9am-5pm and Sat.-Sun. 2pm-5pm; free*

Just around the corner from Santa Cruz Mother Church, somewhat hidden on a discreet backstreet, is the fancy and flamboyant Church of Senhor Santo Cristo, also locally called the Igreja da Misericórdia (Mercy Church). White with a dark blue, highly decorative trim, the church's exterior immediately draws visitors in, although the inside, whose main feature is a baroque carved-wood altarpiece, pales in comparison to the uniqueness of the exterior. This resilient little church, whose fussy bell towers can be seen from afar, was almost completely destroyed by a violent fire in 1921 and rebuilt in 1924, and suffered more extensive damage during the 1980 earthquake.

## LAJES WAR CEMETERY

*Bairro Joaquim Alves; open 24/7; free*

Also known as the British Cemetery, the Lajes War Cemetery was established during the World War II when Commonwealth forces were stationed on the island and the aerodrome was used by both Commonwealth and US air forces. It is a sobering, well-tended little military cemetery that is the final resting place for 47 Commonwealth casualties of World War II. It originally contained both Commonwealth and US war graves, but the remains of the American servicemen were later sent home. The cemetery is kept open around the clock, though as its register box has sadly been the target of vandalism on occasions, the cemetery register is now kept at a local contractors' office (Angraflor, Canada das Almas 49, São Pedro; tel. 351 295

331 440, Mon.-Fri. 9am-noon and 1pm-5pm, Sat. 9am-1pm).

## SERRA DO CUME VIEWPOINT
## (Miradouro da Serra do Cume)

*Rua Nossa Senhora da Saude 23; open 24/4; free*

This wooden platform that soars over the fields below is perhaps one of the most stunning viewpoints on Terceira. If your knees don't turn to jelly, walk to the end and peer out over Praia da Vitória, noting how the seemingly endless plains and little squares of pastures change color as the light ripples across: a patchwork of green that becomes a lively kaleidoscope of vibrant, verdant hues. Even the drive up is scenic, with curious cows popping their heads over the dry stone walls as the cars cruise past.

## São Sebastião

*on the road from Praia da Vitória to Angra do Heroísmo (EN1-1A)*

If you want to experience authentic Terceiran village life, make a pit stop in São Sebastião, located almost halfway between Praia da Vitória and Angra. Snuggled in a southeastern nook of Terceira, a 15-minute (10-km/6-mi) drive south of Praia da Vitória, the charming village of São Sebastião was one of the earliest settlements on the island, and it remains a genuine hamlet unspoiled by the hands of time. In this authentic gem, life revolves around the leafy village square.

## CHURCH OF SÃO SEBASTIÃO
## (Igreja do São Sebastião)

*Rua Direita; tel. 295 904 554; Mon.-Sat. 8:30am-6:30pm, Sun. 8:30am-noon*

The sober-looking, gothic Church of São Sebastião—an architectural style uncommon on the island—was reputedly built by the first settlers on Terceira circa 1455. Over the centuries it underwent a series of repairs following catastrophes such as a major fire in 1789. Noteworthy points of interest are the trio of naves, Manueline portals, arches and ribbed vaults, and late- medieval frescoes, unique in the Azores. This church is widely regarded as

# Terceira's Divino Espírito Santo Chapels

Locally referred to as *impérios*, these intriguing little chapels immediately catch the eye. All islands have these chapels, but none quite as many or as grand and flamboyant as those found on Terceira. It is thought there are more than 70 of these small, quirky temples on the island, each individual and unique, some embellished with vibrant block designs, others with frilly frescoes. Richly decorated with bright colors and busy patterns, they can be found in almost all towns and villages on Terceira, run by local fellowships, most taking center stage in the heart of each hamlet.

## RELIGIOUS SIGNIFICANCE

The *impérios* are integral to the Azores' famed religious Espírito Santo—Holy Spirit (also called Holy Ghost)—festivities, held over the 50 days between Easter Sunday and Pentecost Sunday.

The *impérios* are shrines to the Holy Spirit festivities and are central to their staging, as they are used as space for storing paraphernalia for the events, cooking or distributing offerings, and performing some of the religious services associated with the popular festivities.

## HISTORY

The origins of the eye-catching little *impérios* are believed to date back to the 15th century, when food, clothes, and money were distributed to the poor from the chapel of a hospital in Angra. By the 18th century, this was replicated across the islands. On Terceira island, the oldest surviving *império* is believed to be the Outeiro chapel in Nossa Senhora da Conceição parish.

## STANDOUT *IMPÉRIOS*

Below is a list of some of the finest examples of *impérios* on Terceira:

- **Império do Espírito Santo de São Sebastião** (Império da Santa Isabel, rua da Igreja, opposite main church, São Sebastião parish): With its elaborate mural of flowers and a feast of bread and wine, and its fancy banister, the São Sebastião Império is vivid and almost cartoon-like.

- **Império da Cariedade** (Largo das Figueiras do Paim, Praia da Vitória): Decorated with a rainbow trim of bright colors, the Caridade Império is bold and exotic.

- **Império do Espírito Santo dos Biscoitos** (Império do Caminho do Concelho, Largo Francisco Maria Brum, Biscoitos parish): Like a little wedding cake, the famous Biscoitos Império, with its frilly cream hat and salmon columns, takes pride of place in the heart of the village.

- **Império do Terreiro do Porto Judeu de Baixo** (EN1-2A 29, Porto Judeu): Distinctively extravagant, the Terreiro do Porto Judeu de Baixo Império is busy with its kaleidoscope base, tricolor trim, flags, and curtained windows.

- **Imperio do Divino Espírito Santo da Rua Nova** (Rua Nova 21, Angra do Heroísmo): A vision in lilac, this sweet little chapel gives a burst of color to an Angra backstreet.

- **Império do Divino Espírito Santo da Rua de Baixo de São Pedro** (Rua de Baixo de São Pedro, Angra do Heroísmo): This *império* is, in comparison to the others, one of the more understated and simple chapels, with a plain forest-green trim and splaying staircase.

- **Império do Outeiro da Conceição** (Ruas das Maravilhas, Nossa Senhora da Conceição parish): Dated to the year 1670, this *império* is believed to be the oldest on Terceira island, if not in the Azores.

---

**1:** Santa Cruz Mother Church **2:** Lajes War Cemetery **3:** Serra do Cume viewpoint **4:** Church of São Sebastião

one of the most beautiful and important in the Azores.

### PONTA DAS CONTENDAS LIGHTHOUSE (Farol das Contendas)

*3 km (2 mi) from São Sebastião village*

Just down the road from São Sebastião village is the Ponta das Contendas lighthouse, situated proudly on the Contendas Promontory. Construction of the handsome lighthouse began in 1930.

## BEACHES AND POOLS
### Praia da Vitória
### GRANDE BEACH (Praia Grande)

*Praia da Vitória; open 24/7; free*

Praia Grande is Praia da Vitória's main beach. Stretching along the entire town front, it takes its name ("Grande," meaning big) from its size. Of generous proportions, this large beach has soft sand and is the biggest sandy beach on the island. In summer, local concessions bring out parasols and awnings that can be rented for shade. A long beachfront walkway runs along the spine of the beach, dividing it from the town center, and there are showers, bars, and restaurants in the vicinity.

### RIVIERA BEACH (Praia da Riviera)

*Cabo da Praia; open 24/7; free*

Situated toward the southern end of Praia da Vitória, this untamed, soft sandy beach is a great spot for families. Clean and with shallow, calm waters, it is within walking distance of a couple of bars and the amazing R3 Restaurant. It's quiet and safe, and it is sheltered by a lighthouse pier on one side and Praia da Vitória Bay on the other. The reedy dunes forming a backdrop are home to a wealth of migratory birds.

### São Sebastião
### SALGUEIROS BEACH/SÃO SEBASTIÃO NATURAL POOL (Zona Balnear e de lazer dos Salguieros/Piscina Natural de São Sebastião)

*Ribeira da Seca Baixa parish; open 24/7; free*

A short drive east of Angra near the village of São Sebastião, Salgueiros Beach is a rocky bay with no sand, but it does have a cement deck and a picnic spot, plus a small seawater swimming pool. Nearby there is a parking lot, toilets, and showers.

## KAYAKING AND STAND-UP PADDLE BOARDING
### ROPE ADVENTURES

*Avenida Beira Mar, Praia da Vitória; tel. 961 804 496; www.ropeadventures.pt; Mon.-Sat. 9am-8pm; sea kayaking €40*

Unleash your adventurous spirit and explore Terceira's most thrilling spots, canyoning, coasteering, and zip-lining with Rope Adventures. A wide range of exciting land and sea tours have been created, including Mega SUP (giant stand-up paddle boarding) and kayaking at sea, as well as special expeditions to neighboring islands and private adventure tours. Sea-kayaking and SUP-ing on giant SUP boards in Praia da Vitória's beautiful bay are among Rope Adventures's top activities.

## DIVING AND SNORKELING
### Dive Spots
### CABRAS ISLETS (Ilheu das Cabras)

*off Porto Judeu coast, 10 km (6 mi) east of Angra*

This dual islet off the east coast of Terceira was formed by the remains of an underwater eruption. The islets were originally used by shepherds to keep their goats, although local folklore tells the tale of a young man being banished to the islets for several years by the

---

**1:** Ponta das Contendas lighthouse **2:** Grande Beach

father of his fair maiden love interest. History also claims a German submarine was hidden in the waters around the islet during World War II. The islet is also home to the Azorean bat, a mammal endemic to the Azores and the smallest European bat species.

The Ilhéu Grande (Large Islet) on the left, and the Ilhéu Pequeno (Small Islet) to the right, are well-known among divers for being a hotbed of marine activity, especially abundant in rays and one of few spots where eagle rays reproduce. Rocky and hard to access unless by boat, the islet has numerous grottoes, caves, and niches formed by its volcanic history for divers to explore. Its cavern can be accessed by boat, but the main attraction, an underwater cave, is at a depth of 15 meters (49 ft). This is also an excellent spot for snorkeling.

If you're not a snorkeler, for the best views of the Cabras Islets, stop at the **Cruz do Canário viewpoint** in Porto Judeu parish, on Terceira's south coast, just east of Angra (13 km/8 mi south of Praia da Vitória, along the EN1-1A and EN1-2A roads).

### Dive Centers and Schools
#### OCTOPUS DIVING CENTER
*Avenida Beira Mar, Praia da Vitória; tel. 912 513 906; www.octopusportugal.com; Tues.-Wed. and Fri.-Sat. 9am-5:30pm; from €40*

Located on Praia da Vitória's main seafront, the Octopus Diving Center has over a decade of experience conducting dives in Terceira's best spots. Excursions include special dives, such as shark dives, boat trips, and snorkeling trips, and the company knows and can recommend the best coastal and offshore dive sites for all levels of experience.

## SAILING AND YACHTING
### AZORESONBOARD
*Praia da Vitória Marina; tel. 938 509 683; www.azoresonboard.com; daily 9am-7pm; from €960 pp/week*

Enjoy a private cruise around the Azores on a luxury yacht with this young and dynamic charter company. Based on Terceira, this wonderful vessel and the experienced crew are ready to take guests on a tailor-made voyage to the archipelago's most beautiful locations. Up to 10 people (including 2 crew members) can be accommodated on this sumptuous and spacious sailboat.

## HIKING
### FORTES DE SÃO SEBASTIÃO (PR05TER)
**Hiking Distance:** *5.7 kilometers (3.5 mi) one-way*
**Hiking Time:** *2.5 hours one-way*
**Trailhead:** *Main road near Ponta das Contendas, Contendas Promontory, just south of São Sebastião village*
**Information and Maps:** *http://trails.visitazores.com/en/trails-azores/terceira/fortes-de-sao-sebastiao*

This is an easy linear hike that runs along the southeast coast of the island, through the Cinco Picos (Five Peaks) volcanic massif and past the remains of a number of ancient 16th- and 17th-century maritime defensive forts. The trailhead starts on the main road near the Ponta das Contendas Promontory, and the hike ends in the charming village of São Sebastião, passing historic ruins of fortresses, the Ponta das Contendas lighthouse, and views over the Cabras Islets along the way. Ask at any of the little cafés in São Sebastião to call for a cab to take you back to the start point.

### RELHEIRAS DE SÃO BRÁS (PRC8TER)
**Hiking Distance:** *5 kilometers (3 mi) round-trip*
**Hiking Time:** *2 hours round-trip*
**Trailhead:** *Parking lot in São Brás parish, north of Praia da Vitória*
**Information and Maps:** *http://trails.visitazores.com/en/trails-azores/terceira/relheiras-de-sao-bras*

A very pleasant, interesting, and easy loop around the landlocked parish of São Brás, this hike starts and ends next to the São Brás picnic area and parking lot. The impact of old oxcarts on the island features heavily on this route, which takes hikers past a monument honoring the oxcarts, and *relheiras* wheel tracks carved in stone by the ancient oxcarts are visible throughout the hike. It also passes by an old watering hole, the Fonte do Cão, and through countryside where the common buzzard, a bird endemic to the Azores, can often be spotted.

### AGUALVA BAYS (PR02TER)
**Hiking Distance:** *3.8 kilometers (2.4 mi) one-way*
**Hiking Time:** *2 hours one-way*
**Trailhead:** *Dirt road to Lagoon Grotto, Agualva parish, on Terceira's north coast*
**Information and Maps:** *http://trails. visitazores.com/en/trails-azores/terceira/ baias-da-agualva*
This is an easy linear route along the island's rugged north coast. The trail is partially integrated in the Alagoa da Fajãzinha Natural Reserve. The route connects the village of Agualva to Quatro Ribeiras, beginning on a dirt road through agricultural fields to the Lagoon Grotto (Grota da Lagoa), a waterway that winds its way from Pico Alto to the Atlantic Ocean. The trail ends on the main road to Ponta das Quatro Ribeiras. From here, you can either walk back to the start point, or ask for a taxi to drop you off and pick you up at the agreed end point and time.

## ADVENTURE SPORTS
### TRILHAS OUTDOOR ADVENTURES
*Largo São João no. 13, Fontinhas parish; tel. 963 218 833; https://trilhas.pt; daily 7am-11pm; prices vary according to size of group*
Enjoy Terceira's invigorating fresh air and its stunning outdoors with Trilhas Outdoors Adventures. Uncovering the best trails on Terceira, all excursions are kept small and personalized, ranging from underground hiking and archeology tours, to photographic tours and best views tours.

## FOOD
### Azorean
### CASA DE PASTO BELA VISTA
*Vale Farto 30, Praia da Vitória; tel. 295 513 424; www.facebook.com/CasaDePastoBelaVista; Tues.-Thurs. noon-3pm and 6pm-10pm; €10*
A down-to-earth, authentic local restaurant with genuine island fare, this unpretentious, family-owned spot is welcoming and homely. They serve local specialties such as braised goat, fried quail, and traditional pork sausage and rib dishes.

### Seafood
### RESTAURANTE O PESCADOR
*Rua Constantino José Cardoso, 11, Praia da Vitória; tel. 295 513 495; www.facebook.com/O.Pescador.PV; Mon.-Sat. noon-2:30pm and 6pm-10pm; €20*
General consensus is O Pescador is one of the best restaurants on the island. Specializing in fish bought fresh from local fishermen, the restaurant combines great seafood with a vast selection of wines.

### Contemporary
### R3 RESTAURANT
*Boa Vista 40, EN1-1A 34, Praia da Vitória; tel. 295 513 878 or 912 310 990; www.facebook.com/pages/ category/Portuguese-Restaurant/R3-Restaurante-295159497250555; Wed.-Mon. noon-3pm and 6:30pm-10:30pm; €20*
An amazing feat of architecture, a contemporary-looking cocoon of wood, glass, and cement, this extraordinary restaurant takes typical island fare and elevates it to a memorable fine-dining experience. Fried blue jack mackerel with herb sauce and sweet potato gratin, rump steak with mustard and honey sauce, and seafood rice are just a few of the delicious dishes on the menu.

## ACCOMMODATIONS
### Under €100
### HOTEL VARANDAS DO ATLANTICO
*Rua da Alfândega 19, Praia da Vitória; tel. 295 540 050; www.hotelvarandas.com; €90 d*

# The Azores' Happy Cows

Terceira's happy cows

Left to freely roam the lush rolling hills, the Azores cows—which on some islands are famously said to outnumber the resident population—have every reason to be among the happiest animals on the planet: They graze carefree year-round with sea views from every angle, on an island that is largely free of traffic, pollution, and noise. The Azores cows are relaxed and well-fed, and this is reflected in the quality of the dairy and meat products they produce.

For decades, dairy farming has been fundamental to the Azores' economy, and Terceira island accounts for just over a quarter of the Azores' total dairy farms. You can hardly turn any bend on Terceira without coming into close contact with one of the docile animals, which are so used to curious tourists whipping out their cameras that they almost seem to pose.

## TRY AZORES CHEESE

Terceira produces one of the Azores' best-known dairy products—handmade Queijo Vaquinha cheese—at a small, family-run factory in the parish of Nossa Senhora do Pilar, a short drive west of Angra, just before Cinco Ribeiras. The **Queijo Vaquinha factory** (Canada do Pilar, 5; tel. 295 907 138; https://queijovaquinha.pt; daily 10am-10pm; free) can be visited for a cheese-tasting. See the busy factory in full swing, get up close and personal with the cows and calves, and pop into the gift shop and coffee shop for snacks and souvenirs.

## SEE THE COWS UP CLOSE

Another way to experience Terceira's dairy heritage and cattle raising is with a quirky farming and milking excursion. Totally unique, authentic, and fun, the **Happy Local Experience** (Circular Interna; tel. 916 592 283; https://happylocalexperience.pt; tours daily at 9am and 4pm; €32 pp) involves a 2-hour tour to the Terceira countryside to visit a typical Terceira farm and find out exactly why Azores' cows are known as happy cows. The experience includes milking cows, meeting locals, and tasting cheese.

This low-rise beachfront hotel, snuggled between two other buildings, has a Miami vibe about it. Its sunny yellow exterior, with monochrome checkered paving and balconies with white railings, tends toward a diluted art deco feel. Offering a great value for quality-to-convenience ratio, the quiet and clean rooms have extra-long beds. All of Praia da Vitória's shops, bars, and restaurants are on the doorstep, making this small, modest hotel a good base.

## €100-200
### ATLANTIDA MAR HOTEL
*Boavista 9, Praia da Vitória; tel. 295 545 800; www. atlantidamarhotel.com; €100 d*

This is an attractive, modern, bright, and airy hotel located on Praia da Vitória seafront, with an outdoor sea-view pool and hot tub. Rooms are comfortable and fully equipped with free Wi-Fi, flat-screen TVs, mini fridges, and tea- and coffee makers, not to mention balconies, some with ocean views. A lobby bar, a sauna, a gym, and a playground also make up the spotless facilities.

### HOTEL PRAIA MARINA
*Avenida Álvaro Martins Homem, Praia da Vitória; tel. 295 540 055; www.hotelpraiamarina.com; €100 d*

Hotel Praia Marina is a small, classic town hotel located in the center of Praia da Vitória, on the beachfront. A stone's throw from the main square and shopping street, this non-smoking hotel has rooms with balconies overlooking Praia da Vitória Marina. Smartly and tastefully decorated, it boasts spacious, clean rooms, a fresh local produce breakfast, sound service, and a great location.

# INFORMATION AND SERVICES

Most services in this area are located in Praia da Vitória.

- **Praia da Vitória Marina (Marina da Praia da Vitória):** tel. 295 512 082 or 295 514 121; http://marina.praiadavitoria.net
- **Tourism Information Kiosk:** Praia da Vitória Marina; tel. 295 543 251; www. visitazores.com
- **PSP Police:** Largo Conde da Victória 1; tel. 295 545 480; www.psp.pt

# GETTING THERE AND AROUND

Driving from **Angra** to Praia is quick and easy; it's 20 minutes (22 km/14 mi) along the inland **VR** freeway, or 30 minutes (24 km/25 mi) along the **EN1-1A** coastal road heading east.

Praia da Vitória town center and waterfront are easily covered **on foot;** however a **car, scooter,** or **taxi** will be required to get to nearby attractions such as São Sebastião village, Serra do Cume viewpoint, and the Ponta das Contendas lighthouse.

## Bus

There are regular **EVT bus** services (tel. 295 217 001; www.evt.pt/percursos) between Angra do Heroísmo and Praia da Vitória, and Praia da Vitória and Lajes Airport. The service between **Angra** and Praia is **Line 2,** from Praça Almeida Garrett square in Angra (50 minutes; €3 one-way). There are two hourly services between Praia and **Lajes Airport,** lines **151** and **3** (10 minutes; €2 one way).

# Graciosa

Dubbed the White Island due to the dry, light-colored terrain composed largely of white trachytes, which are light-colored volcanic rocks, Graciosa means "graceful," and easy on the eye it is. This bijou beauty is the second-smallest island in the archipelago after Corvo, and is relatively flat in comparison to the other islands, with gently undulating hills that softly meet the sea, as opposed to the sheer, rugged cliffs shown off by its neighbors. Classified a World Biosphere Reserve by UNESCO, Graciosa is the northernmost of the five islands that make up the Azores archipelago's central group. One of Graciosa's main distinguishing features is its distinctive architectural heritage, notable particularly in its intriguing ancient "water course" architecture, century-old tanks that provide fresh water to island, and Flemish-influence windmills with their characteristic red dome hats. Life unfurls slowly on Graciosa, and everything is petite, from the tiny hamlets scattered across the island, to the size of the hills and mountains.

## GETTING THERE

Getting to Graciosa requires flying via Ponta Delgada on São Miguel or Lajes Airport on Terceira, as there are no direct flights from the mainland, or taking the seasonal (May-Sept.) ferry from Terceira or São Jorge.

### Air
#### GRACIOSA AIRPORT
*2 km/1.2 mi west northwest of Santa Cruz da Graciosa; tel. 295 730 170; www.sata.pt/pt-pt/sata/ graciosa-handling*
There is at least one direct flight from Terceira island to Graciosa a day. Most flights from São Miguel will fly via Terceira island, although there has been a seasonal direct flight from São Miguel in summer. One-way prices from Terceira island are generally around €50, and the flight takes 30 minutes. There are two

main options for getting from the airport to the final destination on Graciosa: either by taxi or by collecting a rental car from the airport.

### Ferry
#### VILA DA PRAIA PORT
*Porto da Praia da Graciosa, Vila da Praia, tel. 295 712 269; https://portosdosacores.pt/portos/porto-da-praia-da-graciosa*
Graciosa can be reached on the seasonal (May-Sept.) interisland ferry (www.atlanticoline.pt/en), from **Terceira** (3 hours; 3 ferries/week; €30-40 one-way) or **São Jorge** (2 hours 15 minutes; 1 ferry/week; €30). The main port on Graciosa island is in the town of Praia (which also goes by its official name, São Mateus) on the north coast. There are taxis dockside.

## GETTING AROUND

Graciosa's main towns, **Santa Cruz** and **Praia,** are easily explored on foot, but if you want to venture farther afield, renting a car, scooter, or bicycle are the best and cheapest ways to get around.

### Rental Car
The best way to get around Graciosa is by renting a car. The island's roads are winding and scenic; another stunning view hides around every bend. Car rental bureaus can be found at the small airport and in the main towns. Contact a local company such as **Rent-a-Car Graciosa** (tel. 295 712 274, 918 449 954, or 967 869 218; www.rentacargraciosa.com), who will drop off and pick up vehicles anywhere across the island.

### Bus
The Santa Cruz da Graciosa-based **Empresa de Transportes Colectivos da Ilha Graciosa** (Rua da Boa Vista; tel. 295 732 363 or 916 456 470; https://en.azoresguide .net/servicos/empresa-de-transportes-colectivos-da-ilha-graciosa) operates daily

# Graciosa

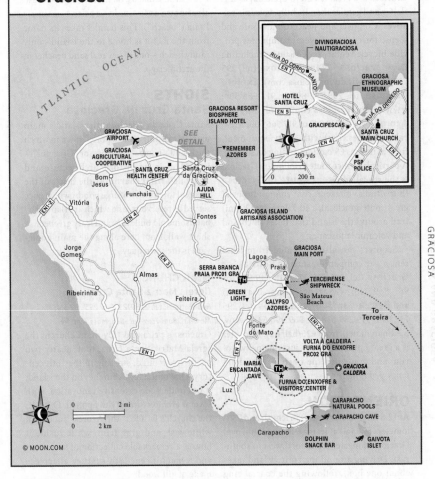

© MOON.COM

bus routes around the island connecting main towns and points of interest, as well as sightseeing tours. The services are organized in three circuits; the one visitors to the island might find most useful is **Circuit 2,** which passes by the airport.

**Circuit 1** is a daily service between Santa Cruz and Praia. Times vary on these services depending on the number of stops, but are generally under 20 minutes, and tickets cost a few euros. Hotel receptions and tourist bureaus should be able to provide printed timetables and more information on exact times and prices.

## Taxi

Taxis are available on Graciosa and could be a good—albeit pricier—option to travel around. For more information or quotes on trips, transfers, and excursions, contact **Taxi Quadros** (tel. 967 677 445 or 916 518 924; www.facebook.com/TaxisIlhaGraciosa).

## Bike and Scooter

Graciosa is a great island to cycle on, as it is flatter and gentler than its hilly, volcanic relatives. Compact and peaceful, it is safe and scenic for cyclists. Several companies provide bicycle rentals on Graciosa, including **Divingraciosa - Nautigraciosa** (tel. 295 732 877; www.divingraciosa.com), **Explore Graciosa** (tel. 295 732 892 or 917 566 500; www.exploregraciosa.com), and **Calypso Azores** (tel. 295 732 892 or 917 566 500; www.calypsoazores.com) with safety equipment, from as little as €5/day (depending on season). A particularly nice route to follow on Graciosa is the so-called **Great Route of Graciosa** (http://trails.visitazores.com/en/grand-routes/great-route-graciosa), a 40-kilometer (25-mi) trail around the island that takes in coastal and volcanic landscapes.

Scooters can also be rented from local rent-a-car companies, such as **Rent-a-Car Graciosa** (tel. 295 712 274, 918 449 954, or 967 869 218; www.rentacargraciosa.com) and **Rent-a-Car Medina & Filhos** (tel. 295 712 094, 919 289 538, or 969 996 644; www.medinarent.net), from €25/half day. A scooter is a great option if there's just one or two of you, and you enjoy the open air but don't fancy pedaling.

## ORIENTATION

At 12.5 kilometers (7.8 mi) in length and 7 kilometers (4.3 mi) at its maximum width, oval Graciosa elongates from northwest to southeast. Driving around the entire island takes about one hour, following the coastal ring road, the **EN1-2.**

The island's main town, **Santa Cruz da Graciosa,** often referred to simply as Santa Cruz, covers the northeastern flank of the island and is its most populous location. Santa Cruz is a whitewashed, cobbled-street hamlet that spread from a large water tank situated in the heart of town, flanked by elegant buildings with wrought-iron balconies. **Graciosa Airport** sits in Santa Cruz on the island's northernmost tip.

The main **ferry port** is located 9 kilometers (6 mi/15minutes) south of Santa Cruz, in São Mateus, on the island's east coast, also known as **Praia da Graciosa** or simply Praia ("beach"). This hamlet takes its name from the fact it is home to the island's only sandy beach—one of few real sand beaches in the archipelago.

# SIGHTS
## Santa Cruz da Graciosa

Santa Cruz da Graciosa, the island's main town, is a distinguished, poised town in which the island's name—Graciosa, or "Graceful"—is evident in its historic architecture and unspoiled rural charm. At the heart of the classical town are two large ponds, which once served as reservoirs, and which are flanked by handsome old buildings and leafy greenery. A short walk from here along the main boulevard is the town quay.

### MAIN CHURCH
### (Igreja Matriz Santa Cruz)

*Rua Matriz 8; tel. 295 712 120 or 295 732 514; Mon.-Fri. 8am-7pm, Sat.-Sun. mass 7am; free*

Graciosa's prim and tidy main church, the Igreja Matriz Santa Cruz, took nearly two centuries to build, starting in the 16th century. One of the first churches on the island, it has undergone extensive renovation, with several architectural styles applied. Outside, the church's facade is the Azores' trademark whitewash and gray trim, while inside it houses a remarkable collection of sacred art and a magnificent 18th-century altarpiece made of gilt wood.

### GRACIOSA ETHNOGRAPHIC MUSEUM

*Rua das Flores de Santa Cruz, 2; tel. 295 712 429; www.azores.gov.pt/Portal/pt/entidades/pgra-drcultura-mg; Mon.-Fri. 9am-12:30pm and 1pm-5:30pm, Sat.-Sun. 2pm-5pm June-Aug.); €1*

Plain and simple on the outside, the Graciosa Ethnographic Museum, in Santa Cruz town

---

**1:** Santa Cruz Main Church **2:** Furna do Enxofre
**3:** Graciosa Caldera

center, houses a fascinating ethnographic collection that aims to portray daily life on the island, depicting winemaking, farming, and a reproduction of a typical island home. Established in 1982, this delightful little museum comprises over 2,000 exhibits, many of which are traditional household objects still used to this day, said to have been left behind by islanders who emigrated to the United States and Canada. On show outside in the garden are cannons from historic fortifications that defended the island. Two smaller museums away from the main museum building complete the ethnographic nucleus, one in a windmill in the parish of Fontes, and the second in an old whaling canoe storehouse, which displays whale-hunting paraphernalia.

### AJUDA HILL
### (Monte da Ajuda)

*south of Santa Cruz da Graciosa; open 24/7; free*

The Monte da Senhora da Ajuda, or simply Monte da Ajuda, as it is more often referred to, offers a fantastic viewpoint with excellent vistas over Santa Cruz town and the island's inland area. It's also dotted with three cute chapels, each one different to the next, around its semicircular crater rim. A half hour walk from Santa Cruz, it is a 130-meter (430-ft) climb to the mount's highest point. Given its volcanic origins, the flattened inner crater creates a natural amphitheater, which has been used to install a small bullring. This forested hill is part of an area classified as protected, where construction is forbidden—a rule that extends to the entire volcanic cone of Monte da Ajuda above 30 meters (100 ft) altitude.

### ★ Graciosa Caldera
### (Caldeira da Graciosa)

*southeastern Graciosa island; open 24/7; free*

The Graciosa Caldera is home to one of the Azores' most unique volcanic formations and the island's biggest draw, the Furna do Enxofre sulfur grotto. The caldera is a super-sized oval crater with a circumference of almost 4 kilometers (2 mi), occupying a large

## The White Island

Flatter and drier than the other eight islands, Graciosa also has the particularity of being abundant in a volcanic rock called *traquito*, or **trachytes,** which, with age, take on a whitish coloring that gives the island its moniker. One of the best places to see trachytes on Terceira island is in the **Serra Branca** (White Mountain range massif), which, at its highest point stands at 375 meters (1,230 ft).

swathe of the southeastern flank of the island. A must-see natural monument, the gargantuan cauldron is lined with dense forest, leafy vegetation, and pastures. A decently paved **walkway** runs around the rim of the crater, making for an enjoyable hour-long hike with amazing views of Graciosa and neighboring islands. Straight down from the tunnel is the entry to the Furna do Enxofre, via the contemporary **visitor center.**

This feat of nature is best reached via the road from Canada Longa parish; from **Santa Cruz,** take the EN1-2 and then the EN2, 10.5 kilometers (6.5 mi/12 minutes) south, toward Canada Longa. From **Praia,** follow the EN2 to Canada Longa, for 4 kilometers (2 mi/7minutes). It's a 2-kilometer (1-mi), 4-minute drive southeast from the parish of Canada Longa to the caldera. Access to the caldera is via a tunnel that passes through the crater wall. To the left, there's a pleasant picnic area with barbeque facilities.

### FURNA DO ENXOFRE

*Graciosa Caldera; http://parquesnaturais.azores. gov.pt/pt/graciosa/o-que-visitar/centros-ambientais; daily 10am-1pm and 2pm-6pm; €5*

The menacingly named "Sulfur Grotto" is surprising and impressive. This volcanic vent, surrounded by forest, is Graciosa's prime attraction and a real highlight of any visit to the island. Access to the site is via the remarkably modern **Furna do Enxofre Visitor Center** (Graciosa Caldera; tel. 295 714 009), which provides plenty of information on the unusual natural wonder. A damp stone staircase, in part cut into a towering volcanic chimney, descends some 100 meters (300 ft) down to a secret world in the depths of the earth, where the smell of sulfur is omnipresent. Below the surface, there's a cavernous dome some 130 meters (430 ft) in diameter and 80 meters (260 ft) high, which experts argue could be the largest volcanic cave on the planet. Inside, a misty sulfur lake and bubbling fumaroles show the effects of the earth's white-hot heat in full glory.

### MARIA ENCANTADA CAVE

*Fonte do Mato; open 24/7; free*

Located on the rim of the Graciosa Caldera, close to the Furna do Enxofre, the Maria Encantada Cave was formed from a long lava tube nearly. Entwined with local legend, this long volcanic passage takes visitors through the Graciosa Caldera's crater wall. The views at the other side of the 15-meter-long (50-ft-long) tunnel, of the gaping inside of the crater, are fabulous, and little benches have been set out for explorers to sit and enjoy the vistas.

# BEACHES AND POOLS

## Graciosa Caldera

### CARAPACHO NATURAL POOLS

### (Piscina Natural do Carapacho)

*south of the caldera; open 24/7; free*

Located on the island's south coast, the Carapacho Natural Pools are possibly Graciosa's most famous tidal pools. A three-sided cement tank and sun-bed apron built into the rocky volcanic coastline, open to the ocean, fills with refreshing seawater while the rippling waves keep things exciting for swimmers. This spot is also a popular area for spear-fishers due to the abundance of fish species that inhabit the craggy coastline. The pools have toilets and showers on site, and a lifeguard (in summer months), and they are also accessible for people with disabilities. Just above the tidal pools is the **Carapacho Thermal Spa,** with its steaming hot therapeutic volcanic spring waters.

## Vila da Praia

### SÃO MATEUS BEACH

### (Praia de São Mateus)

*Vila da Praia; open 24/7; free*

The locals call it simply Praia; Praia de São Mateus is Graciosa's only sandy beach. Centrally located on the lovely east coast in the second-largest town on the island—São Mateus—it has good facilities, such as nearby parking, toilets and showers, a bar, and a lifeguard (in summer months), and is accessible for people with disabilities.

# KAYAKING AND STAND-UP PADDLE BOARDING

See Graciosa's graceful shoreline from a different perspective with a kayak or SUP board. Most kayak and SUP outfitters are based around the beach resort of Praia, whose coast is a popular place for water sports.

### CALYPSO AZORES

*Rua Rodrigues Sampaio 10; tel. 295 732 892 or 917 566 500; www.calypsoazores.com; Mon.-Sat. 9am-5pm; from €10*

Among its vast range of land- and sea-based activities, Calypso Azores provides SUP board rentals to enjoy on the island's gentle shoreline. Rentals include paddles and life jackets.

# DIVING AND SNORKELING

The pristine, unspoiled waters around Graciosa are an enjoyable playground for diving enthusiasts, with shipwrecks, underwater caves, and islets off the south and east coasts and fish-laden reefs around the north of the island, offering interesting underwater experiences for divers of all expertise.

## Dive Spots

### TERCEIRENSE SHIPWRECK

Located approximately 15 minutes from Santa Cruz da Graciosa harbor and just a few minutes from Praia, the Terceirense Shipwreck is one of Graciosa's top dive sites. At a relatively shallow depth of around 21 meters (69

ft) below the surface and close to shore, this sunken ship is a great dive spot for divers of all levels. The Terceirense cargo vessel went down in 1968 in an attempt to enter Praia Harbor and, languishing in this watery resting place, has become an amazing artificial reef, attracting a wealth of fish species. The stern remains most intact, with its impressive propeller a sobering and somewhat eerie underwater sight. Elsewhere the ship's remains have become home to reclusive species like congers and moray eels.

## GAIVOTA ISLET

Also off Graciosa's south coast, the Gaivota (Seagull) Islet is a shallow, protected dive spot some 1.4 nautical miles offshore from the Carapacho tidal pools. This spot tends to have calm waters even when other sites are affected by strong currents, making it perfect for beginners and less confident divers, as well as night dives. Dives here center on the submerged walls of the islet, which feature intriguing rock formations whose cracks and crevices provide shelter to a rainbow of common and unusual fish species. Depths range from 4 to 14 meters (13-46 ft), although thanks to the pristine clarity of the waters, on a good day visibility can reach up to 20 meters (66 ft). It also has an underwater arcade through which it is possible to cross the islet from one side to the other.

## CARAPACHO CAVE
### (Gruta do Carapacho)

In close proximity to the Gaivota Islet is the Carapacho Cave, a vast underwater grotto, which, despite being called a cave, is more of a cavern. It's largely open to the surface and therefore suitable for divers of all levels. The scenery in this magnificent cave is surprisingly breathtaking as the light plays. It was formed from a colossal crack in one of the Carapacho Islets, which are scattered off

the coast of Carapacho and visible from the Carapacho tidal pools and spa complex.

## Dive Centers and Schools
### DIVINGRACIOSA - NAUTIGRACIOSA
*Santa Cruz port and São Mateus port; tel. 295 732 877; www.divingraciosa.com; daily 8:30am-9:30pm; dives from around €100*

Explore all of Graciosa's best dive spots with Nautigraciosa's experienced and well-equipped team. Fully certified dive instructors provide safe and insightful guided tours of the island's dive sites. The company has facilities on the harbors of both Santa Cruz da Graciosa and São Mateus Beach.

# FISHING

Graciosa island provides excellent fishing conditions in all seasons and for all types of fishing, from big-game fishing to spearfishing, or just a leisurely few hours bobbing on a boat, rod in hand, admiring the scenery.

### DIVINGRACIOSA - NAUTIGRACIOSA
*Santa Cruz port and São Mateus port; tel. 295 732 877; www.divingraciosa.com; daily 8:30am-9:30pm; price on consultation*

Count on Nautigraciosa's experienced and knowledgeable professionals to find the best spots for all seasons and types of fishing. With a well-equipped boat and full equipment, all you have to do is turn up and cast off.

# DOLPHIN- AND WHALE-WATCHING

There are also dolphin- and whale-watching trips from Graciosa island, albeit not as many companies as on some of the other islands. Nonetheless, being in the central group still affords an excellent chance at spotting one of these enchanting sea creatures.

### GRACIPESCAS
*Casa das Faias, Rua Serpa Pinto, 5; tel. 295 712 001 or 916 053 023; www.gracipescas.com.pt; normal working hours; from €35*

Founded in 2001, local company Gracipescas has a solid reputation in sea- and land-based

---

**1:** Maria Encantada Cave **2:** Carapacho Natural Pools **3:** São Mateus Beach **4:** hiking on Graciosa

tourism activities. They offer a vast list of trips and excursions, and one of the most popular is the boat rides out to sea to spot dolphins and whales. See Graciosa from a different angle and enjoy a magical few hours in the company of the Azorean sea's famous inhabitants.

## HIKING

From the heights of the Graciosa Caldera to the gently descending shoreline, Graciosa's softly undulating terrain means it is a pleasant island for walking, with few challenging or strenuous routes, making it enjoyable for walkers of all levels of fitness.

### SERRA BRANCA-PRAIA (PRC01 GRA)

**Hiking Distance:** 8.7 kilometers (5.4 mi) one-way

**Hiking Time:** 2.5 hours one-way

**Trailhead:** Pico da Caldeirinha, near Eolic Park

**Information and Maps:** http://trails. visitazores.com/en/trails-azores/graciosa/serra-branca-praia

This easy, linear hike crosses the island diagonally northeast to southwest, from Pico da Caldeirinha to Porto da Praia. It takes hikers through the island's rural hinterland, showcasing Graciosa's famed volcanic structures made from sturdy white trachytes, and past orchards, pastures, and woods of eucalyptus and Australian cheesewood trees. Other points of interest en route include ponds, ancient water reservoirs, and typical windmills. There are plenty of little cafés and snack bars along Porto da Praia from where you can ask to call a cab to get back to the starting point.

### VOLTA À CALDEIRA-FURNA DO ENXOFRE (PRC02 GRA)

**Hiking Distance:** 10.8 kilometers (6.7 mi) round-trip

**Hiking Time:** 3 hours round-trip

**Trailhead:** Canada Longa

**Information and Maps:** http://trails. visitazores.com/en/trails-azores/graciosa/volta-caldeira-furna-do-enxofre

This is another easy and enjoyable circular

hike around the island's most famous feature, the Graciosa Caldera, and its various attractions. The hike starts and finishes in the parish of Canada Longa. Along this walk, trekkers will be able to visit the awesome Furna do Enxofre lava cave, see an underground water reservoir, take in the Maria Encantada Cave, and soak up the stunning bird's-eye island views from the crater's rim.

## SPAS AND RELAXATION
### TERMAS DO CARAPACHO

Rua Dr. Manuel de Menezes; tel. 295 714 212; www. visitazores.com/en/companies/termas-do-carapacho; Tues.-Fri. noon-7pm Tues-Fri, Sat.-Sun. 10am-5pm; €3 entry to pool, massages extra

Located on the tip of the south coast, peering over the Carapacho tidal pools, are the Termas do Carapacho. This simple, basic spa houses a pool of hot volcanic spring water, discovered in 1750, whose sulfurous properties are widely sought after to soothe aches and pains. A swimming cap is obligatory and can be bought at the spa.

## FESTIVALS AND EVENTS
### CARNAVAL BALLS

across Graciosa island; Carnival week: late Feb. or early Mar.

Graciosa's most famous celebration is Carnival—the island goes all-out to enjoy it. With balls to rival Venice's famous masquerades, locals stage parties across the island, dress up, and dance the night away. Over three days, Graciosa celebrates Carnival in an intense and singular way, with cheery processions along the main streets of Praia and Santa Cruz, and much dancing, singing, drinking, and general merriment. The highlight of the day is usually a colorful procession along the town's main street, showcasing decorative floats and energetic dancers, as children throw confetti and streamers. This carries on long into the night at smaller Carnival Balls held indoors, to typical carnival music. Most people will get into the spirit by getting dressed in costumes, or at least donning a mask.

To really experience the merriment of Graciosa's Carnival Balls, take to the streets (main streets, especially in the larger towns, will host parades) or head to the local Casa do Povo community center or other cultural institutions such as theaters, which will no doubt be hosting masked balls and satirical plays. One of the top venues in Santa Cruz for Carnival Balls is the **Cultural, Sport and Recreational Center** in Santa Cruz (Caminho de Cima, no. 97). Or, in Praia, pop into the **Casa do Povo da Praia** (Rua Fontes Pereira Melo, no. 30).

### LORD CHRIST OF MIRACLES (Senhor Santo Cristo dos Milagres)

*across island; www.facebook.com/ FestasDoMunicipio; Aug.*

Enjoy a colorful celebration of faith and religion when the Lord Christ of Miracles festivities explode in early August. Featuring boat races and bullfights, religious services, processions, concerts, and other events, the Lord Christ of Miracles celebrations are believed to have originated in Ponta Delgada on São Miguel island, but rapidly spread to the other islands of the Azores. Graciosa is renowned for having one of the largest celebrations in honor of the event after São Miguel. Festivities, including concerts, parades, and street performers, take place along the main streets and squares of Santa Cruz da Graciosa.

## SHOPPING

### GRACIOSA ISLAND ARTISANS ASSOCIATION

*Rua D. Henrique, 50, Santa Cruz da Graciosa; tel. 295 712 837; www.facebook.com/pages/category/ Regional-Website/Associa%C3%A7%C3%A3o-de-Artes%C3%A3os-da-Ilha-Graciosa-A%C3%A7ores-1490856391179078; Mon.-Fri. 9am-5pm*

Bag a beautiful handmade souvenir straight from the artisans at the Graciosa Island Artisans Association, on the southeastern fringes of Santa Cruz da Graciosa. This artisans' association shop was created with the main mission of promoting the island's traditional Graciosense embroidery. Make sure to admire the delicate traditional handmade Richelieu embroidery, and watch as the local women weave their magic.

## FOOD

### Santa Cruz da Graciosa

### GRACIOSA AGRICULTURAL COOPERATIVE

*Charco da Cruz no. 12; tel. 295 712 169; https://pt-pt. facebook.com/adegacooperativagricola; Mon.-Fri. 8:30am-5:30pm*

Fill up your backpack with wonderful fresh produce for a picnic while out exploring the island by popping into the Graciosa Agricultural Cooperative, located on the northern fringe of Santa Cruz. A trove of locally grown fresh fruit and vegetables, the cooperative also stocks the island's Pedras Brancas wine, produced exclusively on Graciosa.

### REMEMBER AZORES

*Graciosa Resort - Biosphere Island Hotel; tel. 295 730 500; https://graciosaresort.com/en/estilo-de-vida/ restaurante; Sun., Tues.-Wed. and Fri. noon-3pm and 7:30pm-10pm, Mon. noon-3pm and 7:30pm-midnight; Sat. 12:30pm-8pm; €20*

A polished fine-dining experience in an elegant setting, this restaurant is located in one of the island's top-ranking hotels on the little outcrop that hems Santa Cruz. Remember Azores aims to provide an experience to be savored, with the onus on fresh seafood and local wines, and adds a little lux to the island's dining scene.

### Graciosa Caldera

### DOLPHIN SNACK BAR

*Caminho do Carapacho; tel. 295 712 014; Tues.-Sun. noon-2:30pm and 6pm-9:30pm; €10*

A little snack bar just outside the Carapacho Thermal Spa, on Graciosa's southeastern tip, Dolphin is a great spot to grab a quick bite or a tasty dish of the day. All food is made from local island produce. It's bright blue on the inside, but otherwise basic, and it has an outdoor terrace with great sea views to go with the no-frills food. Lunchtime buffet and Azorean specialty *lapas* are also available.

### Vila da Praia
#### GREEN LIGHT

*Canada Dos Ramos, Fonte Do Mato; tel. 915 766 724; daily 11am-11pm; €12*

Simple and serving traditional Portuguese foods, Green Light, near the town of Praia, looks a little underwhelming from the outside. But its homey menu, featuring local meats and recipes, and gorgeous island views make it worth a visit.

## ACCOMMODATIONS
### Santa Cruz da Graciosa
#### HOTEL SANTA CRUZ

*Largo Barão, Rua Nossa Sra. de Guadalupe 9; tel. 295 712 345; www.santacruzhotel.pt; €80 d*

Located in the heart of Santa Cruz, with 18 nicely appointed and well-sized rooms with private bathrooms, this homey little hotel is within walking distance of all of the town's main features and attractions.

#### GRACIOSA RESORT - BIOSPHERE ISLAND HOTEL

*Porto da Barra; tel. 295 730 500; www. graciosaresort.com; €100 d*

Architecturally acclaimed Graciosa Resort embodies the island's natural soul, reflected in the building and décor materials used and its contemporary-rustic style. Located just out Santa Cruz, overlooking a lovely bay, it has 44 standard rooms, 2 suites, and 6 villas, plus a pool and on-site restaurant.

## INFORMATION AND SERVICES

Despite its small size, there are decent amenities on Graciosa, including a largish health unit for ailments, equipped to deal with emergencies, although more patients with more serious health problem will likely be transferred to larger island hospitals, such as those on Terceira or São Miguel. Graciosa also has an ambulance service, pharmacies, and supermarkets or minimarkets in larger towns and villages, ATMs, and a tourism office in Santa Cruz.

- **Santa Cruz Tourist Office:** Rua Dom João IV; tel. 295 712 430; www.visitazores.com/pt; Mon. 8am-6pm, Tues.-Fri. 9am-6pm

- **PSP Police:** EN3 road; tel. 295 730 200; www.psp.pt; open 24/7

- **Santa Cruz Health Center:** Avenida Mouzinho de Albuquerque; tel. 295 730 070, 295 730 077, or 295 730 076; open 24/7 for emergencies

# São Jorge

**Long and slender and shaped like a knife, pristine** São Jorge is a geological masterpiece sculpted by Mother Nature herself. Arguably one of the Azores' most beautiful islands, noble São Jorge is famous for its dramatic landscapes of gaping ravines and soaring cliffs. Rising strikingly from the sea, São Jorge's ragged coastline sits in the Atlantic like the back of a sleeping dragon. Its terrain offers some of the Azores' most fabulous hikes, and its shores are the archipelago's surfing Mecca.

A compelling combination of sculpted nature and well-preserved heritage, the island oozes tradition. The famous Queijo da Ilha cheese is still produced to time-honored recipes, the trucks that ferry the milk from the dairy farms to the factories darting around the island

# Highlights

Look for ★ to find recommended sights, activities, dining, and lodging.

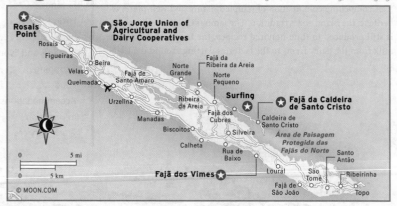

★ **São Jorge Union of Agricultural and Dairy Cooperatives:** See how the famous local cheese is made and sample it for yourself at this popular working factory (page 186).

★ **Rosais Point:** The dramatic northwestern tip of São Jorge provides one of the island's most spectacular views of the ocean and other islands (page 188).

★ **Fajã dos Vimes:** In addition to stunning scenery, a visit to this unique coastal plain boasts two quirky attractions: a traditional textile workshop and the only coffee plantation in Europe (page 191).

★ **Fajã da Caldeira de Santo Cristo:** This unique, flat toe at the foot of the Santo Cristo Caldera, left over from a long-ago lava flow, is one of the prettiest places on the island (page 194).

★ **Surfing:** Great year-round conditions and the legendary Caldeira Surf Camp on Fajã da Caldeira de Santo Cristo arguably make São Jorge the best island in the archipelago to catch a wave (page 197).

like busy little ants. The island is home to the Azores' most famous fish-canning factory, Santa Catarina, whose legendary tuna is world-renowned, and it also boasts the only coffee plantations in Europe.

São Jorge is hemmed by unique coastal formations known as *fajãs,* flat tongues of terrain formed by lava flows that pooled and cooled by the sea, creating unique geological plains that are usually rich and fertile. These lava plateaus are what give São Jorge its nicknames, the Brown Island or the Island of the Fajãs. The most famous *fajã,* Fajã da Caldeira de Santo Cristo, is a surfers' haven, and it's also a unique beauty spot popular with hikers, with an underwater cave and a lovely lagoon where local clams are harvested. Though São Jorge has no sandy beaches, unique tidal pools line the shores of the island.

São Jorge makes up one third of the so-called Azores "triangle," along with neighbors Pico and Faial—which, in addition to Terceira island and Graciosa, comprise the Azores' central group. São Jorge's main town, Velas, is approximately 22 kilometers (14 mi) from Faial's main town of Horta, and 48 kilometers (30 mi) from Lajes do Pico, on Pico island. Due to their proximity, there are ferry links between São Jorge, Faial, and Pico year-round. Founded in 1460, Velas is quaint and welcoming, with an authentic old-world vibe, almost too pretty to be real.

Rural and tranquil, São Jorge's modest population lived in relative isolation until the island's airport was built in 1982, prompting local commerce and tourism to blossom. However, the island still remains one of the archipelago's lesser-visited islands, with an authentic, preserved way of life.

# GETTING THERE

Arriving on São Jorge requires some planning; you will likely need to **fly** there via São Miguel or Terceira island, or hop over on a **ferry** from one of the neighboring "triangle" islands, Pico

or Faial. It's possible to take a ferry from São Miguel in the summer (May-Sept.), but the route is long and circuitous, stopping at most of the other central islands en route.

## Air
### SÃO JORGE AIRPORT
*Queimada; tel. 295 430 360; www.sata.pt/pt-pt/ sata/sata-aerodromos*

The small São Jorge Airport (SJZ) is located about 6 kilometers (4 mi), or a 10-minute drive, southeast of São Jorge's main town **Velas,** along the main **EN1** road, which runs around the edge of the island. It is served exclusively by regional airline **SATA** (tel. 707 227 282 or 296 209 720; www.sata.pt) inter-island flights, receiving a handful of flights mainly from **Terceira** and **São Miguel,** more frequently during summer. The average flight time from Ponta Delgada on São Miguel to Velas, São Jorge, is around an hour, and around 30 minutes from Terceira island. Flights from either island can be found for around €100 round-trip.

**Car rental** companies such as **Ilha Verde Rent a Car** (www.ilhaverde.com), **Sixt Rent a Car** (www.sixt.pt), **Autatlantis** (https:// autatlantis.com), and **AzoreanWay Rent a Car** (https://azoreanwayrentacar.com) are available at the airport. There are usually taxis awaiting flights outside the airport; a taxi from the airport to main town Velas would cost in the region of €10.

## Ferry
### VELAS FERRY TERMINAL (Terminal Porto das Velas)
*tel. 295 432 225; http://marinas.visitazores.com/ marinas/velas*

São Jorge's main port is also in the town of Velas. **Atlanticoline Ferries** (tel. 707 201 572 or 965 995 002; www.atlanticoline.pt) link São Jorge to all other islands between May and September, and sail year-round between São Jorge and nearby **Faial** and **Pico.**

---

**Previous:** the landscape of São Jorge; view of the sea stack at Rosais Point; Fajã da Caldeira de Santo Cristo.

# São Jorge

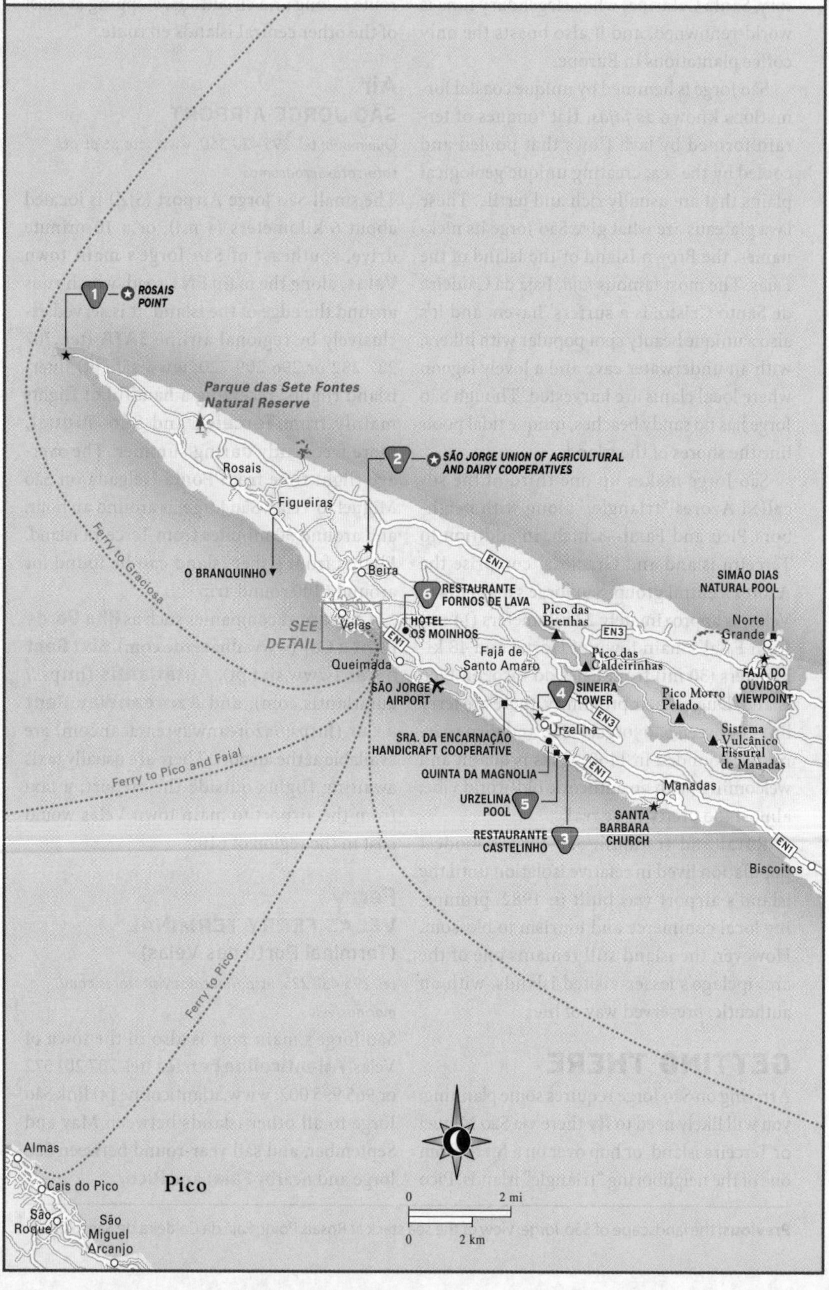

**Map legend / labels:**

- ★ ROSAIS POINT ①
- Parque das Sete Fontes Natural Reserve
- Rosais
- Figueiras
- ▼ O BRANQUINHO
- Beira
- ★ SÃO JORGE UNION OF AGRICULTURAL AND DAIRY COOPERATIVES ②
- Velas
- Queimada
- SÃO JORGE AIRPORT
- RESTAURANTE FORNOS DE LAVA ⑥
- HOTEL OS MOINHOS
- Fajã de Santo Amaro
- Pico das Brenhas
- Pico das Caldeirinhas
- SRA. DA ENCARNAÇÃO HANDICRAFT COOPERATIVE
- QUINTA DA MAGNOLIA
- SINEIRA TOWER ④
- Urzelina
- Pico Morro Pelado
- URZELINA POOL ⑤
- RESTAURANTE CASTELINHO ③
- SANTA BARBARA CHURCH
- Manadas
- Sistema Vulcânico Fissural de Manadas
- SIMÃO DIAS NATURAL POOL
- Norte Grande
- FAJÃ DO OUVIDOR VIEWPOINT
- Biscoitos
- SEE DETAIL

- Ferry to Graciosa
- Ferry to Pico and Faial
- Ferry to Pico

- Almas
- Cais do Pico
- São Roque
- São Miguel Arcanjo
- Pico

0 — 2 mi
0 — 2 km

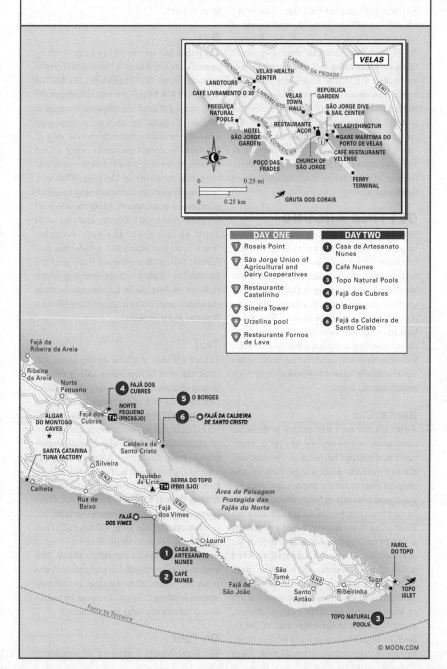

**VELAS**

- VELAS HEALTH CENTER
- LANDTOURS
- CAFÉ LIVRAMENTO O 30
- PREGUIÇA NATURAL POOLS
- HOTEL SÃO JORGE GARDEN
- POÇO DAS FRADES
- CAMINHO DA PIEDADE
- AVENIDA DO LIVRAMENTO
- AVENIDA DA CONCEIÇÃO
- VELAS TOWN HALL
- REPÚBLICA GARDEN
- RESTAURANTE AÇOR
- SÃO JORGE DIVE & SAIL CENTER
- VELASFISHINGTUR
- GARE MARÍTIMA DO PORTO DE VELAS
- CAFÉ RESTAURANTE VELENSE
- CHURCH OF SÃO JORGE
- FERRY TERMINAL
- GRUTA DOS CORAIS
- EN1

0       0.25 mi
0       0.25 km

**DAY ONE**

1. Rosais Point
2. São Jorge Union of Agricultural and Dairy Cooperatives
3. Restaurante Castelinho
4. Sineira Tower
5. Urzelina pool
6. Restaurante Fornos de Lava

**DAY TWO**

1. Casa de Artesanato Nunes
2. Café Nunes
3. Topo Natural Pools
4. Fajã dos Cubres
5. O Borges
6. Fajã da Caldeira de Santo Cristo

**SÃO JORGE**

- Fajã da Ribeira da Areia
- Ribeira da Areia
- Norte Pequeno
- ALGAR DO MONTOSO CAVES
- Fajã dos Cubres
- SANTA CATARINA TUNA FACTORY
- Silveira
- Calheta
- Rua de Baixo
- FAJÃ DOS CUBRES **4**
- NORTE PEQUENO (PRC6SJO) **TH**
- O BORGES **5**
- FAJÃ DA CALDEIRA DE SANTO CRISTO **6**
- Caldeira de Santo Cristo
- Piquinho da Urze
- SERRA DO TOPO (PR01 SJO) **TH**
- EN2
- Área de Paisagem Protegida das Fajãs do Norte
- FAJÃ DOS VIMES
- Fajã dos Vimes
- Loural
- CASA DE ARTESANATO NUNES **1**
- CAFÉ NUNES **2**
- Fajã de São João
- São Tomé
- Santo Antão
- EN2
- Ribeirinha
- Topo
- FAROL DO TOPO
- TOPO ISLET
- TOPO NATURAL POOLS **3**
- Ferry to Terceira

© MOON.COM

There is currently only one route between São Jorge and Faial, between Velas (Cais Velas; tel. 295 412 047) and **Horta,** which runs at least twice a day, and stops at **São Roque do Pico** on Pico island en route. Departure times vary according to day and season; one-way tickets are around €20. There are crossings at least once a day between Velas and **São Roque,** which take around 30 minutes and cost €10. There are also three or four weekly crossings between **Madalena,** on Pico, and Velas, which take around 1 hour 30minutes and cost around €15 one-way. All of these ferry routes are operated on Atlanticoline's **Green Line.**

# GETTING AROUND

Renting a car is not strictly necessary for São Jorge, especially if you are visiting as a day trip from Pico island. As hiking is often the main purpose for visiting, São Jorge's **taxis** have fixed fares for dropping off and picking up at the most popular trailheads. However, if you want to explore the island at leisure and have the time to spend a full day or two on the island, **renting a car** is the way to go. Public transport is patchy, and like on many other Azores islands, geared toward locals, serving mostly coastal areas.

## Rental Car

Renting a car for a day or two is the most convenient way to explore São Jorge, especially as the island has some of the most scenic drives in the archipelago. Pick up and drop off your car at the airport or from a vehicle rental branch in Velas town, or on the harbor from companies such as **Ilha Verde Rent a Car** (www.ilhaverde.com), **Sixt Rent a Car** (www.sixt.pt), **Autatlantis** (https://autatlantis.com), and **AzoreanWay Rent a Car** (https://azoreanwayrentacar.com). There are a few key roads on São Jorge: The **EN1** and **EN3** roads form a ring north of **Velas,** while the **EN2** runs southeast, along the coast to the other end of the island, to **Topo.** When driving on São Jorge, beware of steep terrain, unpredictable foggy weather, bendy roads, and the odd errant farm animal.

## Bus

The public bus service on São Jorge is run by private company **Rumo à Natureza** (Estrada Transversal no. 32, Urzelina; tel. 295 414 260 or 295 414 474; http://horarios.visitazores.de/SaoJorge_1.pdf) and offers limited coverage of the island; coastal parishes are covered with a handful of daily services, but less so inland. Information about times and pricing is hard to come by, making it hard to recommend taking public transport on São Jorge. That said, twice-daily services (early morning and mid-afternoon; 1 hour; approx. €3.50 one-way) run between **Velas** and **Calheta,** carrying on to **Topo.** There is also a twice-daily service between Velas and **Manadas,** which runs past **Rosais Point.** Buses depart from near the **Eurovelas - Compre Bem** shopping center in Velas on Avenida do Livramento, or from the main square in town, **Largo Conselheiro Doutor João Pereira.**

## Taxi

Taxis are widely available on São Jorge, and some can even be hired for a half or full day to take visitors on guided tours of the island. **Simão Silva 007 - São Jorge Taxi** (tel. 962 930 604 or 917 763 280; http://saojorgetaxi.pt), for example, has set routes and prices for tourist excursions, and they also operate airport transfers and single trips. A short 2-hour trip around the northwest half of the island costs €43; this, plus visits to two of the island's most famous *fajãs,* is €110, and a tour of the whole island—approximately 7 hours—is €130.

Most taxis on São Jorge will offer a flat rate for specific **hikes** to drop off and pick up as well as for excursions around the island. This works out as an affordable and practical way to see the island if there are three or four passengers splitting the costs. Taxis can be readily found outside the Velas ferry terminal.

## On Foot

São Jorge boasts a network of wonderful

mapped and signposted walking routes. Pop into a tourist office, in Velas or at the airport, arm yourself with official trail maps, and set off on your journey. While the island is too big to walk in its entirety, local taxi drivers have set fares to drop tourists off and pick them up from popular hikes and attractions.

## ORIENTATION

The island is 55 kilometers (34 mi) in length, from **Rosais Point,** its northwestern extremity, to **Topo,** its southeasternmost point. At just under 7 kilometers (4 mi) in width at its fattest, São Jorge is a craggy slither of a ridge. It stretches diagonally between its nearest neighbors Pico and Faial to the south—separated by the 15-kilometer (9-mi) Pico-São Jorge channel—and Terceira and Graciosa to the north.

São Jorge's main town, **Velas,** is on the southern coast, toward the western end of the island. São Jorge, like many of the Azores, is an island of two halves: a more densely populated and farmed southern coast, and an untamed, jungle-like north coast. Most of the larger towns and parishes (from west to east: **Velas, Urzelina, Manadas,** and **Calheta)** are on the south coast. Calheta is the closest town to the island's most famous *fajãs,* **Fajã dos Vimes** on the south coast, and **Fajã dos Cubres** on the north coast, the latter being a stone's throw from another of São Jorge's top attractions, the **Fajã da Caldeira de Santo Cristo.**

## PLANNING YOUR TIME

Ideally, you should plan to spend at least one night on São Jorge; two days is ideal, one to see its main sights, and the other to enjoy a leisurely **hike.** However, the best of São Jorge can be seen as a day trip from Pico; take the ferry over and **hire a cab** for a half or full day of sightseeing (or asked to be dropped off or collected from a specific hike, if that's the main plan).

If staying on the island, plan to make **Velas** your base, due to its proximity to the ferry terminal and airport. It's also the island's liveliest town. Prioritize the rugged and eerie **Rosais Point** and the **Fajã da Caldeira de Santo Cristo,** on the north of the island. There'll be no crowds on São Jorge, so no need to worry about traffic or congestion, but **car rentals** might sell out fast in the summer months, so book as far in advance as possible if visiting July through September.

# Itinerary Ideas

## DAY 1

If you're not visiting on a Tuesday or Thursday, call ahead to schedule a tour and tasting at the **São Jorge Union of Agricultural and Dairy Cooperatives,** where you can see Azorean cheese being made up close.

**1** From your base in the main town of Velas, drive 25 minutes west along an unnamed coastal road to **Rosais Point.** Jump out here for some fresh air, to admire the views, and to explore the old abandoned lighthouse.

**2** Hit the road again and head back to Velas, turning inland when you reach the EN1, to the **São Jorge Union of Agricultural and Dairy Cooperatives.** The drive should take you another 25 minutes or so. Stop in for a tour and cheese-tasting; scheduled in advance if you're not visiting on a Tuesday or Thursday.

**3** From here, drive 14 minutes southeast along the EN1 toward the parish of Urzelina, where you can enjoy lunch at the cheap and cheerful local **Restaurante Castelinho.**

**4** After lunch, have a walk around Urzelina, visiting the lone **Sineira Tower,** all that remains of a church destroyed by a 19th-century volcanic eruption.

**5** Finish off the afternoon with a dip in the **Urzelina pool** before heading back along the EN1 to Velas.

**6** End the day with stunning views and a lovely dinner at the fancy **Restaurante Fornos de Lava.**

## DAY 2

**1** From Velas, make the short 30-minute drive east on the EN1 to the EN2 to the Fajã dos Vimes lava plateau. Here, first pop into the **Casa de Artesanato Nunes** to admire traditional island textiles still being handmade by local artisans.

**2** Afterward, take a short walk southeast to the famous **Café Nunes,** a miniature coffee plantation. Try some samples and buy a bag of beans to take home.

**3** Get back in the car and a drive along the EN2 road to Topo, the island's southernmost point. Weather permitting, enjoy a dip in the **Topo Natural Pools** while gazing at neighboring Pico.

**4** From Topo, make your way back inland, along the north coast, to **Fajã dos Cubres.** Park here and take the amazing Serra do Topo-Caldeira de Santo Cristo-Fajã dos Cubres hike, which will take you about 2.5 hours to complete.

**5** En route, stop at restaurant **O Borges** to sample the local specialty, clams from the lagoon in the Fajã da Caldeira de Santo Cristo.

**6** Your hike will end at the **Fajã da Caldeira de Santo Cristo** itself, where you can while away the rest of the afternoon lounging on the beach. Call a taxi to take you back to your car, before heading back to Velas for the evening.

# Sights

## VELAS

Velas is São Jorge's main town. Located on the island's south coast, about 14 kilometers (9 mi) down from the northwesternmost tip of Rosais Point, Velas is characterized by its highly decorative cobblestone paving, its pretty main square, **Largo Conselheiro Doutor João Pereira,** straight off the harborside, and the lovely **República Garden** (Jardim da Republica) with its frilly bandstand set amid wonderful island architecture, a short walk north from the ferry terminal. One of the best places to see Velas's cobblestone artwork is along the main **Rua Manuel de Arriaga** high street, which connects the harbor to the garden. In Largo Conselheiro Doutor João Pereira, look for an homage to São Jorge (Saint George), a sculpture of a

dragon made from volcanic rock. Though severely damaged by an earthquake in 1964, a number of beautiful historic buildings in Velas survived, among them the late-15th-century **Church of São Jorge** and the **town hall,** a fabulous example of 18th-century Baroque architecture.

### Church of São Jorge
### (Igreja Matriz de Velas)

*Largo Conselheiro Doutor João Pereira; tel. 295 412 440; Mon.-Sat. 10am-12:30pm and 2pm-4pm, Sun. mass 9am-noon; free*

Built on the spot of the original São Jorge Church in 1460, the Church of São Jorge is the main church, or Mother Church (Igreja

---

**1:** Velas **2:** Church of São Jorge

Matriz), in Velas. Today it has the typically Azorean colors: whitewashed with gray basalt trim. Inside are three naves and a remarkable 16th-century table, gifted by Dom Sebastião, the king at the time. Historic statues from an old Franciscan convent are stored and the **Velas Sacred Art Museum** (tel. 295 412 214; by appointment; free), housed in an annex off the church. It's packed with religious paraphernalia like paintings, statues, and silverware, a collection of sacred art from the 16th-20th centuries. It's an interesting little museum worth popping into for its vast collection. Call ahead to schedule a visit.

### Velas Town Hall
#### (Câmara Municipal de Velas)

*Rua de São João; tel. 295 412 214; Mon.-Fri. 9am-5pm; free*

A fantastic example of the typical 18th-century Azorean Baroque style, the town hall has a number of remarkable features to admire, among them a solid basalt stone portico engraved with Portugal's Royal Coat of Arms and the assembly room with its carved cedar and mahogany ceiling. It houses an important collection of 16th- and 17th-century historic documents.

### República Garden
#### (Jardim da República)

*Rua Dr. Manuel de Arriaga; open 24/7; free*

Enjoy a rest in the small but perfectly formed central República Garden. Positioned around a decorative central bandstand with frilly white banisters and a bold red hat, the shrubbery is teased and groomed into interesting shapes and patterns, adding an extra dimension to the pretty garden, along with colorful flowerbeds and benches in dappled shade.

### ★ São Jorge Union of Agricultural and Dairy Cooperatives
#### (União de Cooperativas Agrícolas de Lacticínios de São Jorge)

*Canadinha Nova, Beira (4 km/2 mi north of Velas); tel. 295 438 274 or 295 438 275; www.lactacores.pt; Mon.-Fri. 9am-5:30pm; €1.50*

São Jorge cheese has become a flagship of Azorean gastronomy. A semi-hard, tangy cheese made from unpasteurized cow's milk, the authentic São Jorge cheese is a classified, controlled island product. This agricultural and dairy cooperative produces the distinctive cheese, staying faithful to its historic roots, which date back to the 16th century when it is believed the famous cheese was developed by the Flemish who settled in the Topo area. In the parish of Beira, just a 10-minute drive north of Velas, you can sample the famous Queijo da Ilha de São Jorge in its birthplace. The São Jorge Union of Agricultural and Dairy Cooperatives is the center for curing, classifying, and certifying the cheese produced on the island to ensure it sticks to the traditional recipes and processes.

Guided **tours** around the industrial, pungent-smelling factory can be taken on Tuesdays and Thursdays, or by appointment (call a day ahead). Tours include a tasting and wind up in the **gift shop** and **café,** which also sells the cheese to take away. Or just pop in on any day to sample the cheese and buy some straight from the source. The cooperative is a 5-minute (3.6-km/2.2-mi) drive north of Velas, mostly on the EN1.

## SETE FONTES NATURAL RESERVE
### (Parque Florestal das Sete Fontes)

*Rosais parish; open 24/7; free*

Founded in 1962 and inaugurated in 1976, the vast Sete Fontes Natural Reserve is one of the most important natural reserves on São Jorge. Spanning some 50 hectares (120 acres), it occupies a portion of the island's westernmost point, Rosais, with gently rolling hills blanketed with dense, lush vegetation. Fairytale-like and often shrouded with mist, there are plenty of frog-inhabited ponds and lakes

**1:** São Jorge is known for its cheese. **2:** cows grazing on São Jorge

where water plants thrive, trails, and a pleasant picnic spot and barbecue area.

## ★ Rosais Point
### (Ponta dos Rosais)

*Northwesterly tip of island; open 24/7; free*

Dramatic Rosais Point marks São Jorge island's most northwesterly tip. This steep promontory pointing sharply northward has an isolated, rugged feel, with vertiginous 200-meter-high (700-ft-high) cliffs plunging into the Atlantic. Along with an eerie old abandoned **lighthouse complex** made up of a 27-meter-high (8-ft-high) tower, living quarters, and auxiliary buildings, Rosais Point provides incredible views of the neighboring islands of Pico, Faial, and, on a good, clear day, Graciosa, and even Flores.

Having been damaged by a series of seismic events in 1964, the lighthouse was briefly abandoned by the keeper, his family, and staff while it was repaired. Another earthquake in 1980, followed by a violent storm, saw the lighthouse once again deserted by its occupants, this time for good. The lighthouse was deactivated, but its beacon was automated and currently runs on solar power; the rest of the vast complex lies in a state of disrepair. There is a breathtaking viewpoint behind the old lighthouse where the headland trails off into the never-ending ocean. Rosais Point and the Sete Fontes Natural Reserve are classified a Natural Monument for their unique beauty.

## URZELINA

The charming little hamlet of Urzelina is about 10 kilometers (6 mi; 15 minutes) south of Velas along the EN1 road. Pretty whitewashed houses are scattered around a string of picturesque bays, which make Urzelina the island's foremost bathing spot in summer.

### Sineira Tower
### (Torre Sineira)

*Urzelina parish; open 24/7; free*

A somber reminder of Mother Nature's unpredictability, the Sineira Tower is a stoic symbol of resilience and resistance. Flanked by a well-tended exotic garden of hibiscus, aloes, rosebushes, and banana trees, this lone bell tower is all that remains of a church that once stood on the spot before it was engulfed by lava following a massive eruption in 1808. Enter through a gate saying "Public Access" next to a sign that says "Private Property."

## MANADAS

A short drive on from Urzelina is Manadas, another pretty parish. This peaceful hamlet has a rural farming vibe, its quaint streets lined with traditional stone-built or whitewashed manor houses. Manadas was put on the map for being home to one of the most extraordinary churches in the entire Azores archipelago, the Santa Bárbara Church, an exquisite example of religious Baroque architecture.

### Santa Bárbara Church
### (Igreja da Santa Bárbara)

*Caminho da Igreja; Tues.-Sat. 10:30am-12:30pm and 2pm-6pm, Sun. 1pm-6pm; free, donations welcome*

For lovers of religious history and heritage, this dainty church is one of São Jorge's highlights. Set in a small bay in the parish of Manadas, a short drive south of Velas, the church's interior is typically Baroque—surprisingly lavish and in sharp contrast with its plain and simple exterior. Elaborate paintings adorn the walls, which, along with the ceiling, are covered in golden gilt work. It's probably not worth making a special trip just to see this church, but a visit should definitely be factored into a tour of the island. An English-speaking guide is usually stationed at the church, and they are happy to give visitors a tour.

## FAJÃ DO OUVIDOR

*Norte Grande parish; open 24/7; free*

Directly opposite Manadas parish on the north coast is one of São Jorge's larger and more populous *fajãs*, with around two dozen houses, some of which are centuries old, many

---

1: Urzelina 2: Manadas

of them nowadays used as holiday homes and occupied only in summer. The community is nonetheless large enough to have amenities including a nightclub, café, restaurant, and lighthouse. The Fajã do Ouvidor is pitted with alluring tidal pools, among them the **Simão Dias natural pool,** one of the island's preferred swimming spots. Tidal erosion has caused the coastline around the *fajã* to erode, creating a hem of caves and grottoes that attract divers and boat trips. Easy road access makes the Fajã do Ouvidor one of the most-visited on the island.

### Fajã do Ouvidor Viewpoint (Miradouro da Fajã do Ouvidor)

*Fajã do Ouvidor, Norte Grande parish; open 24/7; free*

Don't miss one of the best photo ops on São Jorge island: Make sure you stop at this *miradouro* as you make your way to the Fajã do Ouvidor. The views from here, of the *fajã* below and the gorgeous coastline, are spectacular, and it's a 25-minute hike down to the *fajã*. To find this viewpoint, follow the signs from Norte Grande to Fajã do Ouvidor. You'll arrive at a crossroad, about 100 meters (300 ft) after which is a large parking lot that serves the *miradouro.*

## ALGAR DO MONTOSO CAVES

*Pico do Montoso, Alcaçarias parish, Calheta; open 24/7; free*

The cavernous, 140-meter-deep (460-ft-deep) cave system of Algar do Montoso is the deepest in the Azores—and one of the deepest in Portugal. This complex cave system of deep caverns and lava tubes is yet to be explored in full. A string of complex geological formations and volcanic structures—caves, grottoes, and funnels—created by lava tubes and flows, this spot is an absolute playground for mountain- and cave-loving adventurers, but it's not a place for tourists to venture by themselves. As the system is not fully chartered, these caves should only be visited accompanied by an experienced guide. Local adventure company **AvenTour** (Calheta Docks; tel. 912 042 470; www.aventour.pt; open 24/7; from €50/person) does half- and full-day exploration programs of the caves. Algar do Montoso is also known on the island as **Algar do Morro Pelado.**

The caves are located in the parish of Alcaçarias, heading inland (north) from the villages of Urzelina or Manadas; from Velas head east along the ER1-2A for about 9 kilometers (6 mi), until you find a sign indicating "Nortes," following that direction. Climb for about 9 kilometers (6 mi), until you see a dirt road on the right, with a sign to "Pico da Esperança." Follow this path and you'll come to a trail. You can reach Algar do Montoso walking from there.

## FAJÃ DOS CUBRES

*Ribeira Seca parish; open 24/7; free*

One of the most beautiful, exotic, and interesting *fajãs* on the island, Fajã dos Cubres is located in the parish of Ribeira Seca, just after the town of Calheta. It is an important waterfowl habitat, the only place in the world where the extremely rare Monteiro's storm petrel (*Oceanodroma monteiroi*), believed to be endemic to the Azores, can be spotted, making it one of the best and most exciting places in the whole archipelago for bird-watching. The Fajã dos Cubres is also home to a large, crystalline lagoon that the local fishermen flock to, to catch shrimp to use as grouper bait.

There are only a handful of houses on this *fajã*, which were rebuilt after the original community was razed by an earthquake in July 1757. It suffered extensive damage again following an earthquake in 1980, but, tenaciously, the owners returned and again rebuilt their homes. Also on this *fajã* is a little chapel, the **Chapel of Nossa Senhora de Lourdes,** opened on October 18, 1908. Behind this chapel hides an intriguing attraction, a low-water well whose water is considered miraculous. A long-standing tradition, pilgrims walk from across the island to wash with and drink the water to cure their ailments.

# The *Fajãs* of São Jorge

Fajã do Ouvidor

While not exclusive to the island of São Jorge, *fajãs*—sizeable flat platforms formed at the foot of the islands' cliffs by pools of volcanic lava flow and landslides—are found in greatest concentration on this island, giving it its nicknames, Island of the Fajãs and Brown Island. These *fajãs* are generally big enough for communities to set up on them, which in many cases they have, taking advantage of the flat, low-lying fertile land to build farms and homes.

Locals love to talk about their *fajãs* and debate over which *fajã* is the best—São Jorge is said to have over 70. There are *fajãs* of varying sizes on both sides of the island, many of which have carved out their own distinctive trait. In this chapter, a few of the most prominent and unique *fajãs* are covered; here's how to choose which to visit if you have limited time.

- **For Aquaphiles:** Whether you want to soak in a beautiful tidal pool or dive under the surface with a snorkel, **Fajã do Ouvidor** has some of the best opportunities for water sports on the island (page 188).

- **For Nature Lovers:** The protected greenery and lagoon of **Fajã dos Cubres** make it perfect for bird-watchers (page 190).

- **For Souvenir Hunters:** You can stock up on island-grown coffee beans or unique Azorean textiles from the artisans based on **Fajã dos Vimes** (page 191).

- **For Hikers and Surfers:** The famed beauty of **Fajã da Caldeira de Santo Cristo** is accessible via a gorgeous hike, and it's home to the Caldeira Surf Camp (page 194).

## ★ FAJÃ DOS VIMES

*Ribeira Seca parish; open 24/7; free*

Located in the parish of Ribeira Seca, the Fajã dos Vimes has been put on the map by its coffee plantation. This *fajã's* original settlement was wiped out by a strong earthquake in 1757, though it was rebuilt and currently has a resident population of about 70. It's sustained mainly by fishing and farming corn, rye, grapes, potatoes, beans, and taro, as well as by a small, privately owned coffee plantation, **Café Nunes,** that has become

# A Fishy Detour: Island-Canned Tuna

A tour of a tuna canning factory might not sound like a holiday highlight, but the **Santa Catarina Tuna Factory** (Santa Catarina Indústria Conserveira, Rua do Roque, 9, Calheta; tel. 295 416 220; www.atumsantacatarina.com; Mon.-Fri. 8:30am-5pm; €3.90) produces one of the archipelago's most revered and renowned products: canned Azores tuna.

## WHAT MAKES SÃO JORGE TUNA SPECIAL

Embodying the flavor of the sea and the heritage of the region, the factory perpetuates an island tradition: canning locally caught tuna according to artisanal methods used by the old cannery masters. The fish is caught using the **pole-and-line method**, the only fishing method to be considered dolphin-safe and environmentally sustainable. It is then manually processed by the scores of **local women** employed at the factory. The **tins** themselves are lovely little mementos of the island, thanks to their retro, vintage look.

## THE FACTORY

Overlooking the Atlantic, this busy factory welcomes visitors to show them how 10 tons of tuna is still cleaned, cut, and packaged by hand in this factory, according to time-honored methods, every day. Products can also be bought here at the factory shop to take home.

one of the island's quirkiest tourist attractions. This particular *fajã* is also renowned for its locally made quilts and artisanal textiles, produced using traditional techniques and old-fashioned wooden looms at **Casa de Artesanato Nunes.**

## Casa de Artesanato Nunes

*Fajã dos Vimes, Ribeira Seca parish; tel. 295 416 717 or 963 048 929; https://pt-pt.facebook.com/ CasaDeArtesanatoNunes; open 24/7; free*

Watch as local artisans, most of them family members, hand-make the island's traditional textiles as they have done for centuries. Weavers niftily work their magic with their wooden looms to transform fabrics and wools into stunning patterned quilts, carpets, towels, and other unique São Jorge textiles. Artisanal textiles have long been a calling card of the Fajã dos Vimes, especially traditional wool and cotton quilts, made using pedal looms, typical of the locality, for over a century. All of these textiles can be seen and bought at the Casa de Artesanato Nunes.

## Café Nunes

*M 1-2a, Fajã dos Vimes, Ribeira Seca parish; tel. 295 416 717; daily 7am-11:30pm; free*

Café Nunes's claim to fame is being Europe's only coffee plantation. Legend has it that at the end of the 18th century, a man—possibly the great-grandfather of the current owner of Café Nunes, Manuel Nunes—emigrated to Brazil to work on a coffee plantation. He returned to São Jorge at the beginning of the 19th century, reputedly bringing some Arabica coffee seeds with him, from which the famous coffee plantation of Fajã dos Vimes was born.

This mini-plantation, located behind the café owner's home on the Fajã dos Vimes, is visited by scores of tourists. The unique, organic coffee can be sampled and bought at the quirky and simple Café Nunes, along with homemade local pastries. At the small plantation, which produces around 800 kilograms (1,800 lbs) of coffee in a good harvest, you'll be able to see the handpicked beans drying in the sun, and how they're roasted. After visiting the plantation, you can try the coffee, which is robust and flavorful but not bitter.

A signpost to both Café Nunes and Casa de Artesanato Nunes can be found at the entry to the Fajã dos Vimes. Descend a windy coastal

**1:** Topo Lighthouse **2:** a building in Topo **3:** a little church on the Fajã da Caldeira de Santo Cristo

road down to the *fajã*, and the café and handicraft shop are at the bottom.

## ★ FAJÃ DA CALDEIRA DE SANTO CRISTO

*Ribeira Seca parish; open 24/7; free*

Possibly the most famous and scenic *fajã* on São Jorge—and in the Azores—the remote Fajã da Caldeira de Santo Cristo sits at the foot of the Santo Cristo Caldera and is a truly magical spot. Lapped by the Atlantic Ocean, this fertile volcanic plain is accessible only on foot. Hugged by sweeping green cliffs, this popular hiking spot is an intriguing geological formation and one of São Jorge's must-see attractions.

This *fajã* is famed for the waves that close in around it, attracting surfers from across the archipelago and beyond to its **Caldeira Surf Camp** (https://caldeirasurfcamp.com/en). It's also home to a small village, where only a handful of people live year-round, and to a natural **lagoon,** declared a Natural Reserve and Ecological Area, where local fishermen harvest clams, an island specialty, from the glassy water. Like the coffee from Café Nunes, island folklore tells that the clams were brought to the island by an immigrant, and it remains a puzzle as to why they thrive specifically in this lagoon.

The most popular **walking route** to Fajã da Caldeira de Santo Cristo starts at the Serra do Topo parking lot, off the EN2 not far from Fajã dos Vimes. From here, it's just over 5 kilometers (3 mi) to the Fajã da Caldeira de Santo Cristo, taking around 1 hour 45 minutes. The route continues along to coast another 4 kilometers (2 mi) or so to Fajã dos Cubres; the tiny

hamlet has a little café/bar, the **Snack-Bar "Costa Norte,"** and the **Chapel of Nossa Senhora de Lourdes.** You can also begin the hike here.

## TOPO

Topo is São Jorge's easternmost point. A tranquil little village dominated by a lighthouse, the Topo Lighthouse (Farol do Topo), this tip of the island is covered in rolling green pastures and grazing cows. It's peaceful and largely unoccupied. It is believed the first people to arrive on São Jorge, Flemish settlers, disembarked in Topo. Topo was once the most economically important town on the island; the 17th-century grand manor houses are testaments to its historic importance. Just opposite the headland is **Topo Islet,** a dinky islet where, bizarrely, cows graze in the summer.

### Topo Lighthouse (Farol do Topo)

*Pontinha headland; tel. 295 415 157; open 24/7; free*

Topo Lighthouse is the only lighthouse on São Jorge island that still employs keepers to manage it. It is manned by a team of three keepers and their families who live on-site year-round, one of whom is said to have worked at the lighthouse for over three decades. Standing at 58 meters (180 ft) above sea level and with a 16-meter-high (52-ft-high) circular tower, the lighthouse dates from 1927. Its beam, which comes on automatically after nightfall, reaches some 20 miles out to sea. The views from around the lighthouse, over Topo Islet and the neighboring islands of Graciosa and Terceira, are stunning.

# Beaches and Pools

São Jorge's popular bathing spots are mostly volcanic tidal pools dotting the edge of the island. There are no sandy beaches.

## VELAS
### POÇO DAS FRADES
*Avenida da Conceição; open 24/7; free*

A 3-minute walk from Velas center, the Poço das Frades tidal pool is a veritable fish tank, teeming with fish that wash in with the ebbing and flowing of the tides. Geologically formed from volcanic rock, this family-friendly spot is one of the best-known natural pools in the Azores and one of the most popular bathing sites on the island.

### PREGUIÇA NATURAL POOLS
### (Piscina Naturais da Preguiça)
*Rua do Mar; open 24/7; free*

These amazing natural pools are a popular bathing site that lure people from across the island, located on the western outskirts of Velas town. Surrounded by a stunning natural landscape on one side and the Atlantic on the other, this is widely considered one of the best natural pools on the island. With good infrastructure, such as umbrella rentals in summer and a little **bar** nearby, this bathing area's crystal-clear waters are also great for diving and snorkeling.

## URZELINA
### URZELINA POOL
*Urzelina parish (10 km/6 mi south of Velas); open 24/7; free*

Located in the quaint village by the same name on São Jorge's south coast, the Urzelina pool is a pleasant spot for a cooling dip. Family-friendly, the little human-made seaside pool overlooks the Atlantic, and it's just a few steps away from a rocky bay with **natural tidal pools** where visitors can also enjoy a dip in the sea. It's an easy walk to this pool from the village center and **Urzelina camping park** (Canada de Africa; tel. 295 414 401; June 1-Sept. 30).

## FAJÃ DO OUVIDOR
### SIMÃO DIAS NATURAL POOL
### (Piscina Natural Simão Dias)
*Fajã do Ouvidor, Norte Grande parish; open 24/7; free*

Halfway along São Jorge's north coast on the Fajã do Ouvidor is the Simão Dias natural pool, an area of outstanding natural beauty that looks half Hawaiian, half prehistoric. Completely unspoiled by time or tourism, this stunning beauty spot is one of the island's best-kept secrets and one of the most incredible natural pools in the Azores. Impressive soaring black volcanic cliffs some 400 meters (1,300 ft) high set off the crystal-clear turquoise water to perfection. It's also a great place for snorkeling. Located in the central section of the north coast, wedged between mountains and the ocean, this pool is definitely worth making a special trip for. From Velas, it's a 22-minute (18-km/11-mi) drive heading north and then east along the EN1 road to Fajã do Ouvidor.

## TOPO
### TOPO NATURAL POOLS
### (Piscina Natural da Pontinha do Topo)
*Ponto do Topo, Calheta de São Jorge parish (island's southeasternmost tip); open 24/7; free*

Another popular bathing spot, this lovely little tidal pool carved from volcanic rock and filled with refreshing seawater looks like a little spa hugged by cliffs. At high tide, seawater spills over into the depression, refreshing the swimming water. The setting is stunning, with views over Pico island, and is served by a **bar** and a large parking lot nearby.

# Kayaking and Stand-Up Paddle Boarding

São Jorge's unique coastline provides astonishing vistas from the sea, and ocean kayaking or SUP are among the best ways to enjoy them. Particularly attractive coastal stretches are around the *fajãs*, especially off the coasts of the Fajã dos Vimes and Fajã do Ouvidor. If you're feeling particularly energetic and are in the area at the time, take part in the annual São Jorge 2 Pico (www.saojorge2pico.com) channel crossing in early July and paddle the 19-kilometer (12-mi) strait between the two islands.

## VELAS

### SÃO JORGE DIVE & SAIL CENTER

*Velas commercial port; tel. 915 106 268; www.sjzdiveandsail.com; daily 9am-5:30pm; rentals from €30/day, guided tours from €35*

Stand-up paddle boading is an excellent way to really get into the secret nooks and crannies of the São Jorge coastline. Test your balance as you duck and dive through arcs and caves on a guided SUP tour, or rent a board for one, three, or five days and try out some of the famous natural pools and *fajã* lagoons.

## FAJÃ DOS VIMES

### DISCOVER EXPERIENCE AZORES

*Fajã dos Vimes; tel. 968 481 448, 926 360 041, or 967 552 354; www.discoverexperienceazores.com; from €50*

If you want to enjoy the sights and sounds of the São Jorge coast without getting too wet or tired, then a leisurely cruise along the coast in a kayak might be just the thing. Ranging from short routes for the less-experienced kayaker or families with young children, to longer coastal trips, 7-kilometer (4-mi), 9-kilometer (6-mi), and 15-kilometer (9-mi) activities are available. You'll see São Jorge's finest features, like its towering cliffs, magnificent bays, unique *fajãs,* and magical waterfalls.

## ★ Surfing

São Jorge offers up some of the most interesting surf in the Azores. It's known for being one of the best islands for surfing in the Azores—and one of Europe's best-kept surfing secrets—with decent year-round conditions, though November through June are the best months. Fajã da Caldeira de Santo Cristo is one of the best spots on São Jorge, but that's not to say it's the only one. These are mainly found over a 3-kilometer (2-mi) stretch along the north coast between the Fajã da Caldeira de Santo Cristo and the Fajã dos Cubres.

For more information, the website Magic Seaweed (https://magicseaweed.com/

Sao-Jorge-Surfing/288) provides detailed information on São Jorge surf.

### SURF SPOTS

#### FAJÃ DA CALDEIRA DE SANTO CRISTO

*Ribeira Seca parish*

You'll have to park at the Fajã dos Cubres and walk the 4 kilometers (2 mi; 50 minutes) east with your board to get there, or contact the Caldeira Surf Camp (https://caldeirasurfcamp.com/en) to rent a board and arrange a quad-bike transfer, but once you're there, you'll be rewarded with an excellent surf experience. The Fajã da Caldeira de Santo Cristo is washed by world-class waves

1: Simão Dias natural pool 2: Topo Natural Pools

SÃO JORGE
SURFING

that break around its large, glassy lagoon from different angles, making it one of the most reliable and popular spots on the island for steady surfing for all levels.

## FAJÃ DOS CUBRES

*Ribeira Seca parish*

Easier to reach than the Fajã da Caldeira de Santo Cristo, with a **parking lot** on its doorstep, the Fajã dos Cubres is a lesser-known and underrated surf spot. However, with some of the longest waves and most powerful barrels in Portugal, it is trickier to get in and out of the water here, due to strong currents and whitewash that whirl over jagged rock. Surfing here can be world-class, but requires experience and skill.

## SURF CAMPS AND SCHOOLS

### Fajã da Caldeira de Santo Cristo

#### CALDEIRA SURF CAMP & GUESTHOUSE

*Fajã da Caldeira de Santo Cristo; tel. 912 517 001; https://caldeirasurfcamp.com/en; open 24/7; board rentals from €20*

Enjoy the best surfing São Jorge has to offer with the Caldeira Surf Camp. Located on the Fajã da Caldeira de Santo Cristo, this surf camp and guesthouse provides everything from board rentals (body boards, surf boards, and SUP boards) to lessons and accommodation, as well as transfers on quad bikes from the Fajã do Ouvidor.

# Diving and Snorkeling

São Jorge, rich in marine life, is home to a number of natural snorkeling and diving spots that will delight participants. In addition to the spots below, the **Poço das Frades** pool near Velas is a great place to snorkel.

## DIVE SPOTS

### Velas

#### GRUTA DOS CORAIS

*100 meters (300 ft) off Velas shore; open 24/7; free*

You can't dive in São Jorge and not visit the Grutas dos Corais (Coral Cave). Close to the coast, this easygoing dive starts at a reef platform 5-10 meters (16-33 ft) deep, and less than 100 meters (300 ft) from the shore of Velas. The reef is pitted with hollows that house a multitude of fish, among them damselfish, moray and fangtooth moray eels, octopus, and wrasses. From here, the more experienced divers can descend to 24 meters (79 ft), where there is access to the cave itself, vast swathes of which is covered with varying shades of black

coral and teems with colorful sea life, providing a colorful contrast to the dark walls.

### Urzelina

#### PORTINHOS DA URZELINA

*20 minutes from Velas harbor*

Portinhos da Urzelina, straight off São Jorge's craggy coast, is one of the island's most popular dives, a tame spot accessible for divers of all skills. Access to the spot is via the coast of Urzelina parish, from the local natural tidal pools. It's a relatively easy and shallow dive, between 8 and 14 meters (26-46 ft) in a protected area with weak currents. The site comprises interesting features like grottoes and caverns, and you can spot sea life including sting rays and parrotfish. This is a superb spot for underwater photographers, night divers, and snorkelers. That said, it's always advisable to explore new spots with experienced local experts; local provider **São Jorge Dive & Sail Center** runs dive trips from Urzelina.

**1:** Fajã da Caldeira de Santo Cristo is a popular surf spot. **2:** view from the trail to Fajã dos Cubres

## Topo
### TOPO ISLET
*off the southeastern tip of island*

Located just 100 meters (300 ft) off the coast of Topo, this small, 20-hectare (50-acre) islet is a magnet for a plethora of pelagic fish and a treat for experienced divers. Even though it is close to the coast, this spot is hard to reach and is accessible only by boat from Velas harbor; strong currents mean it is recommended for experienced divers only. Once there, divers are rewarded with not one, but two unique dives. The north and south coasts of the island are distinctly different. Dives reach up to a maximum depth of 22 meters (72 ft). Contact the **São Jorge Dive & Sail Center** for more information on dives to Topo Islet.

# DIVING CENTERS AND SCHOOLS
## Velas
### LANDTOURS
*Velas; tel. 919 821 513; https://landtours.pt; prices vary by activity*

LandTours offers snorkeling activities for all levels of comfort and expertise. They can help you explore from the crystalline waters off the tranquil Simão Dias natural pool, to the deep Atlantic, amid the abundance of colorful and interesting fish for which the Azores are famous. Or, to enjoy the best of both worlds, opt for a complete tour of both, plus a meal at a local restaurant to round off the experience.

### SÃO JORGE DIVE & SAIL CENTER
*Velas commercial port; tel. 915 106 268; www. sjzdiveandsail.com; daily 9am-5:30pm; dives from €40*

Enjoy São Jorge's finest underwater attributes with the São Jorge Dive & Sail Center, a local company specializing in dives and sailing on the island. Activities range from diving, scuba diving, and sea expeditions to boat trips see the Azores' renowned marine life. With its own **dive center and school** (Mon.-Sat. 9am-6pm, Sun. 9am-12:30pm) located on Velas Port, this experienced team fulfils all requirements to head up excellent dives.

# Fishing

The crystal-clear waters surrounding São Jorge island are a trove for fishing enthusiasts, home to a true panoply of fish, from tiny sardines to giant species like sharks, tunas, and the prized Atlantic blue marlins.

## Velas
### VELASFISHINGTUR
*Velas Port; tel. 919 821 513; https://landtours.pt; open 24/7; from €50 pp*

Join local fishing expert Jaime Pereira to enjoy a few hours casting off at some of the best fishing sports on the island. Enquire about the best spots at the Velasfishingtur kiosk on Velas docks. Head out to sea by boat for the best big-game fishing or to the top fishing spots along the coast, with half-day or full-day fishing excursions.

# Hiking

Boasting breathtaking scenery around every bend and the singular *fajãs*, São Jorge offers some of the most gripping and visually awesome hikes in the Azores. The mother of them all is the Serra do Topo-Caldeira de Santo Cristo-Fajã dos Cubres hike; it's a long one, but persevere and you'll be in for an unforgettable experience.

## SERRA DO TOPO-CALDEIRA DE SANTO CRISTO-FAJÃ DOS CUBRES (PRO1 SJO)

**Hiking Distance:** *10 kilometers (6 mi) one-way*
**Hiking Time:** *2.5 hours one-way*
**Trailhead:** *Serra do Topo car park, off the EN2, 30 kilometers (19 mi) east of Velas*
**Information and Maps:** *http://trails. visitazores.com*

If São Jorge were a sleeping dragon, this hike along a mountainous ridge in the middle of the island would trace the ups and downs of the dragon's back. A breathtaking medium-difficulty trek of immense natural beauty, it takes hikers from the scenic Serra do Topo mountain range, along the green rim of the Santo Cristo Caldera, to the coastal Fajã dos Cubres.

The hike starts at the Serra do Topo car park, off the EN2, a 30-kilometer (19-mi; 30-minute) drive east of Velas. It then winds north through pretty countryside of infinite green valleys peppered with endemic flora and fauna. There are markers along the way, and much of this trek is downhill. The trail gently slopes past small waterfalls and springs, until you can finally see the Santo Cristo Caldera and the *fajã* at its foot, about 4 kilometers (2 mi) into the hike. From here, you can wander the small **Santo Cristo village,** perhaps taking swim in one of the natural pools en route.

After exploring this area, the route continues northwest along the coast for about 5 kilometers (3 mi), to **Fajã dos Cubres,** where it ends next to the **Chapel of Nossa Senhora de Lourdes.** Here, pop into the local café, the Snack-Bar "Costa Norte" (tel. 917 795 238) to use their phone, or use your cell to call **Simão Silva 007 - São Jorge Taxi** (tel. 962 930 604 or 917 763 280; http://saojorgetaxi.pt) to get back to base. Alternatively, a great way to get to and from this hike is to get a taxi to drop you off at the starting point and pick you up from the finish point—but make sure you agree this in advance, as there will be no taxis readily waiting in Fajã dos Cubres. Make sure to factor in enough time for a refreshing dip or two—and don't forget to pack snacks, water, and a swimsuit!

## NORTE PEQUENO (PRC6SJO)

**Hiking Distance:** *10 kilometers (6 mi) round-trip*
**Hiking Time:** *3 hours round-trip*
**Trailhead:** *Outskirts of Norte Pequeno, near the old Norte Pequeno Dairy Factory, on the ER regional road*
**Information and Maps:** *http://trails. visitazores.com/pt-pt/trilhos-dos-acores/sao-jorge/ norte-pequeno*

This is a medium-difficulty hike, starting and ending in the parish of Norte Pequeno. Passing through several *fajãs*, the trail heads through the village of Norte Pequeno toward the coast. Looping along the cliffs, the route then passes by a small harbor and back up toward Norte Pequeno and the start of the trail.

# Bird-Watching

São Jorge is a relatively undiscovered destination among bird-watchers, yet those who do visit it consider it one of the best islands in the Azores for birdlife. Word is, São Jorge is possibly the island where the **common snipe** is easiest to spot during the breeding period. With dramatic jagged landscapes and costal *fajãs* in lieu of inland lagoons, the island makes for a unique backdrop for the activity. The eastern and western extremities (Topo and Ponta dos Rosais, respectively) and their islets provide fantastic conditions for seabirds, while inland one of the best places for resident birdlife is the **São Jorge Island Natural Park.** The *fajãs* along the northern coast, especially Fajã dos Cubres, are home to a wealth of waterfowl, like songbirds, ducks, herons, and waders.

## AZORES ISLANDS TRAVEL
*tel. 292 679 505; www.bookingsaojorge.com/ birdwatching; open 24/7; from €80 pp/2-4 person*
Book your personalized São Jorge bird-watching excursion via Azores Islands Travel; enjoy an easy, 3-hour trip taking in excellent birding spots such as Rosais Point, Fajã da Caldeira de Santo Cristo, the Planalto Central, Topo Islet and coast, and Fajã dos Cubres, observing local and migratory marine birds. Includes guide, transfers, and binoculars.

# Festivals and Events

### FESTIVITIES OF SÃO JORGE
### (Festas de São Jorge)
*Velas; late April*
The Festas (Festivities) of São Jorge are island-wide festivities and events, staged mainly in Velas, designed to celebrate and promote the island's traditions and ancestral culture, and its patron saint, St. George. They are held over three days in late April, and every year the Festas follow a different theme, such as Emigration in 2019, and Cheese and its History in 2018. Book recitals, fado events, cheese-tastings, and exhibitions are among the events organized to celebrate São Jorge.

### VELAS CULTURAL WEEK
### (Semana Cultural das Velas)
*throughout Velas town; first week in July*
The Velas Cultural Week is staged over the first week in July and comprises a series of events and entertainment throughout the city that bring the area to life. Created to celebrate the island's traditions, music, and folklore, and appeal to its younger generations, the week sees open-air concerts in Velas's main public areas, processions along its main streets, water sports and competitions, and talks and exhibitions on a variety of topics in venues around Velas.

### FESTIVAL DE JULHO
*throughout Calheta de São Jorge; second week in July*
The Festival de Julho follows on from the Velas Cultural Week, taking place in Calheta de São Jorge over the second week in July. Featuring one of the island's best-loved parades, the Festival de Julho (July Festival) involves lots of daily and nightly entertainment, with a merry lineup of ethnographic parades, popular music concerts, sports events, and exhibitions.

### SÃO JORGE 2 PICO SUP
### CHANNEL CROSSING
*www.saojorge2pico.com; July*
If it's a challenge you like, then sign up for

the São Jorge 2 Pico SUP Channel Crossing, a yearly event held in July that sees SUP aficionados from across the Azores and beyond race across the channel. The first event of its kind in the Azores, it starts in Velas and sees participants paddling the 20 kilometers (12 mi) across the channel to finish in São Roque do Pico.

# Shopping

You can find some real treats to take home as souvenirs on São Jorge, especially the São Jorge cheese, which you can buy directly from the **São Jorge Union of Agricultural and Dairy Cooperatives** (or from any grocery store or delicatessen on the island), the colorful tins of canned tuna from the **Santa Catarina Tuna Factory,** and coffee from **Café Nunes** on Fajã dos Vimes.

## URZELINA
### SENHORA DA ENCARNAÇÃO HANDICRAFT COOPERATIVE
*Ribeira do Nabo parish; tel. 295 414 296*

For the ultimate São Jorge souvenir-shopping experience visit the Senhora da Encarnação Handicraft Cooperative in the parish of Ribeira do Nabo, just before Urzelina village, where you will find various types of handiwork by local artisans all under one roof. Beautiful embroidery, wool clothing garments handmade on traditional wooden looms, upcycled textiles, and relief stitch bedspreads dating to the 16th century are among the beautiful items on sale, and you can watch as they're being made in the workshop, perpetuating an increasingly dying art form.

# Food

Most of São Jorge's restaurants are found in the main town Velas, which has an interesting and varied gastronomic scene for a small island town. But there are restaurants in most towns and parishes, as well as on the *fajãs,* and the food is generally fresh and wholesome, made from locally sourced produce. A must-try on the island are steaks—beef and tuna—clams from the Fajã da Caldeira de Santo Cristo, and, of course, the island's famous São Jorge cheese.

## VELAS
### Azorean
### RESTAURANTE AÇOR
*Largo da Fajã de Santo Amaro 93; tel. 295 432 590 or 918 846 362; Tues.-Sun. noon-2pm and 7pm-10pm; €12*
A typical Portuguese restaurant with authentic Azorean fare, this eatery is located in a lovely setting just outside of Velas near the airport. Housed in a traditional stone-built manor house, there is seating inside and outside in a pleasant little courtyard. The menu honors genuine island fare: fresh salads, fresh seafood, and locally reared meat washed down with island wine.

### RESTAURANTE FORNOS DE LAVA
*Hotel Os Moinhos, Travessa de S. Tiago, Santo Amaro; tel. 917 394 977; www.osmoinhos.com; daily noon-3pm and 6pm-11pm; €20*
This lovely round-fronted restaurant has big bay windows that let lots of light in, boasting stunning views over the neighboring islands of Pico and Faial. An intriguing fusion of Azorean and Galician cuisine, among the specialties are fish Cataplana, local delicacy clams from the Santo Cristo Caldera, and avocado mousse for dessert.

# São Jorge Specialties

On an island famed for its homemade products—from cheese to coffee to tuna to textiles—here are some of the specialties you can't leave without trying.

## CLAMS

If you want to sample a real São Jorge delicacy, then head to the Fajã da Caldeira de Santo Cristo to try the local clams. This *fajã's* pristine lagoon is the only place on the island where they are cultivated and picked. Local legend has it that the clams were introduced to the lagoon by a Canadian immigrant, though why it is the only spot on the island where they breed is still a mystery. Many of the island's restaurants, from the swish Restaurante Fornos de Lava (page 203) to the down-to-earth O Borges (page 205), serve this specialty.

## QUEIJO DA ILHA

Produced exclusively on the island of São Jorge—an island where the saying goes there are more cows than inhabitants—the Queijo da Iha cheese is a tangy, semi-soft cheese that has been given a "Protected Designation of Origin" certification to ensure its ingredients and methods follow to the traditional way of making it. The cheese is so important to the island that in 1991 a confraternity was created, the Confraria do Queijo de São Jorge, to ensure and uphold the cheese's taste and traditional production processes. Its origins are believed to date back around five centuries, and have maintained its current format for over 200 years. Sold in rounds, halves, or quarters, made from unpasteurized cow's milk, the rounds typically weigh 7-12 kilograms (15-26 lbs). Queijo da Ilha cheese is one of São Jorge's most recognizable and exported products and can be enjoyed at pretty much every restaurant table as a tasty starter, or you can go to the Union of Agricultural and Dairy Cooperatives (page 186) and try it where it's made.

## COFFEE

The coffee grown at Café Nunes (page 192) is famously the only coffee grown in Europe. Grab a bag of beans and taste some coffee by visiting the tiny plantation. There is at least one other smaller coffee plantation on São Jorge island, but Café Nunes is the only one that grows for production.

## TUNA

The old-school tins from the Santa Catarina Tuna Factory (page 192) have become symbols of São Jorge island. You can taste the care that was put into producing this tuna, from the pole-and-line technique used to catch the fish, to the traditional canning techniques used by the local women employed at the factory. Tins of Santa Catarina tuna can also be found in most supermarkets and delicatessens.

## Seafood
### ★ CAFÉ RESTAURANTE VELENSE

*Rua Conselheiro Doutor José Pereira; tel. 295 412 160; daily 8am-1am; €10*

Located next to Velas quay, Café Restaurante Velense is a friendly eatery whose menu centers mainly on fresh fish and seafood. The dining room is at the back of a dark, tavern-like bar area, which you'll have to walk through—it's a bit like a modern-day sailors' speakeasy. All foods are local, from the cheese and wine to the fresh prawns, *lapas* (limpets), and fish. No airs and graces about this place, it's all about tasty food and down-to-earth island hospitality.

## Cafés and Light Bites
### ★ CAFÉ LIVRAMENTO O 30

*Avenida do Livramento no. 44; tel. 916 673 531; www.facebook.com/cafelivramento44; Mon.-Fri 8am-11pm, Sun. 10am-11pm; €8*

Don't be misled by the fact this plain and

simple little restaurant looks a bit like a run-of-the-mill café from the outside. It is, in fact, one of the highest-regarded eateries on the island and offers a smorgasbord of delectable bites. Home-cooked food is kept simple but full of flavor, with dishes ranging from scrambled eggs and bacon for breakfast, or handmade curry rolls for a snack, cheese and crackers, and daily lunch specials, or a set dinner menu featuring a variety of fish and meat dishes.

## ROSAIS POINT
### Azorean
### O BRANQUINHO

*Ribeira do Belo 48; tel. 919 184 024; www.facebook. com/Restaurante-O-Branquinho-234015517385800; Tues.-Sun. noon-2pm and 6:30pm-10pm; €15*

A few minutes' drive from Velas, O Branquinho offers home-cooked dishes of the day that vary daily—one meat, one fish—and traditional Portuguese and regional fare. The décor may be plain and simple, but that only highlights the quality and flavors of the cuisine and outstanding service.

## URZELINA
### Azorean
### RESTAURANTE CASTELINHO

*Largo Doutor Duarte Sa Urzelina; tel. 295 414 184; Wed.-Mon. 9am-3pm and 6pm-10pm; €13*

Simple and tasty, Castelinho is a no-frills eatery with filling portions of unpretentious food. Traditional Portuguese recipes like roast octopus, fried codfish, great steaks, and the freshest daily caught fish are what keep people coming back to Castelinho. That and the stunning harbor views.

## FAJÃ DA CALDEIRA DE SANTO CRISTO
### Azorean
### ★ O BORGES

*Rua Ribeira; tel. 918 650 613; daily 7am-midnight; €20*

O Borges is a traditional eatery serving home-cooked typical island cuisines, including a local specialty, clams from the Santo Cristo Caldera, for which the restaurant is famed. O Borges has become something of a compulsory stop for those wanting to experience genuine island cuisine.

# Accommodations

There's a wide range of quality hotels on São Jorge, from polished hotel units conveniently located in the main town Velas, to rustic farmhouses on the *fajãs* where you can really enjoy peace and quiet.

## VELAS
### €100-150
### HOTEL SÃO JORGE GARDEN

*Avenida dos Baleeiros; tel. 295 430 100; https:// oceanohoteis.com; €100 d*

Hotel São Jorge Garden is a sprawling low-rise hotel set in lush, manicured gardens, with privileged views of Pico island. Conveniently located close to the heart of Velas, it is family-friendly, with well-proportioned rooms. All balconies have sea views, and facilities include a salt-water pool and an on-site bar and café. A large supermarket is a stone's throw away.

### HOTEL OS MOINHOS

*Travessa de S. Tiago, Santo Amaro; tel. 295 432 415; www.osmoinhos.com; €100 d*

Home to the renowned Fornos de Lava restaurant, with its panoramic rounded glass front and stunning views, family-run Hotel Os Moinhos, on the outskirts of Velas, is a small but perfectly formed hotel made up of traditional stone cottages, with big, clean rooms and a rustic-chic décor.

## URZELINA
Over €200
### QUINTA DA MAGNOLIA
*São Mateus Urzelina; tel. 295 414 211; www.*
*quintadamagnolia.com; €304 (minimum 2-night stay)*
A beautiful old stone house on the outside, fully refurbished, modern, and elegant on this inside, this small, cozy accommodation provides a personalized service and a great place to stay on the island. It has a lovely pool and breathtaking sea views.

## FAJÃ DA CALDEIRA DE SANTO CRISTO
Under €100
### CALDEIRA GUESTHOUSE & SURF CAMP
*Fajã da Caldeira de Santo Cristo; tel. 912 517 001;*
*https://caldeirasurfcamp.com/en; from €70*
Soak up the tranquility of the Fajã da Caldeira de Santo Cristo at this restored rural house on the *fajã*. It comprises three bedrooms (option of double or single beds) with private bathrooms, two mezzanines, and one open space with excellent conditions. Breakfast can be provided on request.

# Information and Services

**Velas,** São Jorge's main town, has all facilities visitors need for a stay on the island, including a tourist office, health center, and police station. There are also other key amenities in Velas like banks, a post office, and a pharmacy, all within walking distance of the quay. However, the nearest hospitals are on Faial, Terceira, and, the biggest, on São Miguel. Emergency cases will be transferred to one of these units. There's also a small shopping mall, **Eurovelas - Compre Bem** (Avenida do Livramento; tel. 295 430 060; http://hipercomprebem.almeidaeazevedo.com; Mon.-Sat. 8:30am-8pm, Sun. 9am-6pm), a short walk north of the quay.

- **Tourist Office:** Rua Conselheiro Dr. José Pereira no. 1 r/c; tel. 295 412 440; www.visitportugal.com/pt; daily 9am-1pm and 3pm-7pm

- **PSP Police:** Largo Conselheiro Doutor João Pereira 1; tel. 295 412 339; www.psp.pt; open 24/7

- **Velas Health Center:** Rua Corpo Santo; tel. 295 412 122/240/290; https://postodesaude.pt/unidade/centro-de-saude/centro-de-saude-de-velas; open 24/7

- **Velas pharmacy:** Farmácia da Misericórdia, Rua do Corpo Santo; tel. 295 412 071; Mon.-Fri. 8:30am-7pm, Sat. 9am-1pm

- **Velas Post Office:** Rua Doutor Miguel Teixeira; tel. 295 430 000; www.ctt.pt; Mon.-Fri. 9am-1:30pm

# Pico

## Home to one of Europe's most epic hikes and

iconic scenery, Pico is as famous for its majestic eponymous volcano, the highest point in Portugal, as it is for the volcanic wines that come from its unique vineyards. Also known for being one of the best islands in the Azores for whale-watching, Pico is nicknamed the Gray Island due to the amount of exposed lava rock that makes the scenery so unmistakably volcanic. Scarcely populated and peaceful, Pico is a realm of mystique and unique experiences, from sleeping overnight on dormant Mount Pico to watch a magical sunrise, to trying volcanic wines made according to time-honored traditions. Pico's characteristic basalt drywall vineyards are designated a UNESCO World Heritage Site and produce the most famous wines to come from the Azores.

# Highlights

Look for ★ to find recommended sights, activities, dining, and lodging.

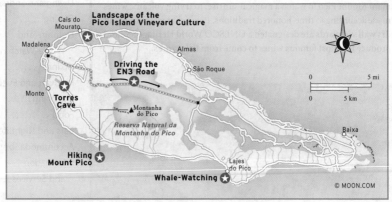

Cais do Mourato

Landscape of the
Pico Island Vineyard Culture

Madalena

Almas

Driving the
EN3 Road

São Roque

Monte

Torres
Cave

Montanha
do Pico

Reserva Natural da
Montanha do Pico

Baixa

Hiking
Mount Pico

Lajes
do Pico

Whale-Watching

0          5 mi

0      5 km

© MOON.COM

★ **Landscape of the Pico Island Vineyard Culture:** Admire this unique latticework of stone vine pens, a defining feature of Pico's landscape and a UNESCO World Heritage Site (page 214).

★ **Torres Cave:** Admire the earth's ancient innards as you descend into this cavernous cave (page 218).

★ **Driving the EN3 Road:** This road from Madalena in the west to the middle of the island,

past Mount Pico, is often cited as one of the most scenic drives in Portugal (page 219).

★ **Whale-Watching:** Pico's pristine waters make whale-watching off the island stand out in an archipelago with some of the best whale-watching in the world (page 227).

★ **Hiking Mount Pico:** Take on the Azores' ultimate challenge and hike to the highest point in Portugal (page 228).

Far less developed than many of its peers despite being the Azores' second-largest island (after São Miguel), Pico is a destination that begs to be experienced, not just looked at. The scenery is stunning, but it is the activities that Pico affords that make it special. There are hikes, biking, whale-watching, tidal pools and sandy beaches, horse and donkey rides, incredible sunrises, and breathtaking vistas around every bend. A bubble of calm, Pico combines lush vegetation, ancient volcanic landscapes, and, in its two biggest towns of Madalena and São Roque do Pico, cool architecture and surprisingly creative cuisine.

Pico is part of the central group of five islands, and is part of the Azores' "triangle" along with São Jorge and Faial. Madalena faces the island of Faial; São Roque do Pico faces São Jorge. Ferry trips between the three are short, cheap, and run year-round.

## GETTING THERE

Like all of the Azores islands, there are just two ways to get to Pico: by air or by sea. The island is located in the deep mid-Atlantic, in the Azores central group, roughly 248 kilometers (154 mi) northwest of **São Miguel,** 8 kilometers (5 mi) west of **Faial,** and 20 kilometers (12 mi) south of **São Jorge.** Pico can be reached via interisland **flight** from São Miguel or nearer-by **Terceira** island; by **ferry,** year-round from São Jorge and Faial (the closest islands, part of the Azores "triangle" with Pico); or by seasonal ferry from São Miguel (May-Sept.), although the journey takes close to 14 hours and stops at other islands too.

### Air
**PICO AIRPORT**
*Bandeiras; tel. 292 628 380*
There are no direct flights from outside Portugal to Pico Airport (PIX); an interisland flight from **São Miguel** (50 minutes) or **Terceira** (35 minutes) is usually

necessary, though **Azores Airlines** (www. azoresairlines.pt) runs a seasonal direct flight (Jun-Sept.) between **Lisbon** and Pico three times a week (2 hours and 45 minutes). There are at least two daily flights from São Miguel to Pico, and at least one direct flight a day between Terceira and Pico.

Pico's little airport is located on the north coast, 15 minutes (8 km/5 mi) east of the island's main city, **Madalena,** on the ER1 road, which circumscribes the entire island. You can **rent a car** from the airport, catch the local **Carreira do Norte** (North Line; https://cristianolimitada.pt/horarios_cristiano_limitada.html) bus, which takes around 20 minutes and costs €2, or catch a **taxi** for around €13. There is a taxi rank outside arrivals.

### Ferry
It's pretty easy and cheap to reach Pico from both São Jorge and Faial, its closest neighbors, by ferry. These three islands form the Azores' so-called "triangle," with ferries running year-round between them due to their proximity. Ferries from São Jorge and Faial sail to **João Quaresma Maritime Ferry Terminal** (Rua dona Maria da Glória Duarte; tel. 292 623 340; www.atlanticoline.pt) in Madalena, Pico's main town, on the island's northwestern tip, or to **São Roque do Pico Terminal** (Gare Marítima de São Roque; tel. 292 642 482; www.atlanticoline.pt), on its northwestern flank.

#### FROM SÃO JORGE
There are around half a dozen weekly ferry links between the **Velas ferry terminal** (Cais Velas; tel. 295 412 047) on São Jorge and Pico (to both Madalena and São Roque). Sail time from Velas to **Madalena** is 1 hour and 40 minutes, and 1 hour to **São Roque.** Tickets prices range €10-16 one-way. The daily ferry, the **Green Line,** is operated by **Atlanticoline** (tel. 707 201 572; www.atlanticoline.pt).

---

**Previous:** view of Madalena village and Mount Pico; Landscape of the Pico Island Vineyard Culture; cows standing on the EN3 road.

# Pico

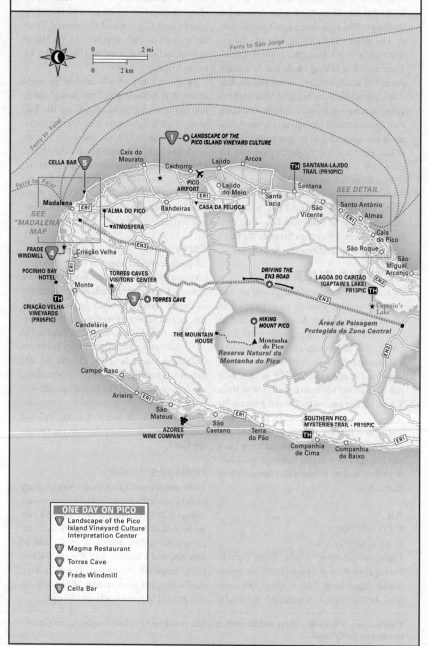

Ferry to São Jorge

Ferry to Faial

Ferry to Faial

**CELLA BAR** 5

Cais do Mourato

Cachorro

**1** ★ LANDSCAPE OF THE PICO ISLAND VINEYARD CULTURE

Lajido          Arcos

**TH** **SANTANA-LAJIDO TRAIL (PR10PIC)**

SEE DETAIL

**Madalena**

PICO AIRPORT

Lajido do Meio

Santa Luzia

Santana

Santo António

Almas

**ALMA DO PICO**

Bandeiras

**CASA DA FEIJOCA**

São Vicente

ER1

Cais do Pico

SEE "MADALENA" MAP

▼**ATMOSFERA**

ER1

EN3

São Roque

São Miguel Arcanjo

**FRADE WINDMILL** **4**

Criação Velha

EN2

**POCINHO BAY HOTEL**

Monte

**TORRES CAVES VISITORS' CENTER**

**DRIVING THE EN3 ROAD**

**LAGOA DO CAPITÃO (CAPTAIN'S LAKE) PR13PIC** **TH**

EN3

**CRIAÇÃO VELHA VINEYARDS (PR05PIC)** **TH**

**3** ✪ **TORRES CAVE**

★ Captain's Lake

Candelária

*Área de Paisagem Protegida da Zona Central*

✪ **HIKING MOUNT PICO**

EN2

**THE MOUNTAIN HOUSE**

▲ Montanha do Pico

*Reserva Natural da Montanha do Pico*

Campo Raso

Arieiro

ER1

São Mateus

ER1

**AZORES WINE COMPANY**

São Caetano

Terra do Pão

**SOUTHERN PICO MYSTERIES TRAIL - PR15PIC**

ER1

**TH**

Companhia de Cima

Companhia de Baixo

## ONE DAY ON PICO

**1** Landscape of the Pico Island Vineyard Culture Interpretation Center

**2** Magma Restaurant

**3** Torres Cave

**4** Frade Windmill

**5** Cella Bar

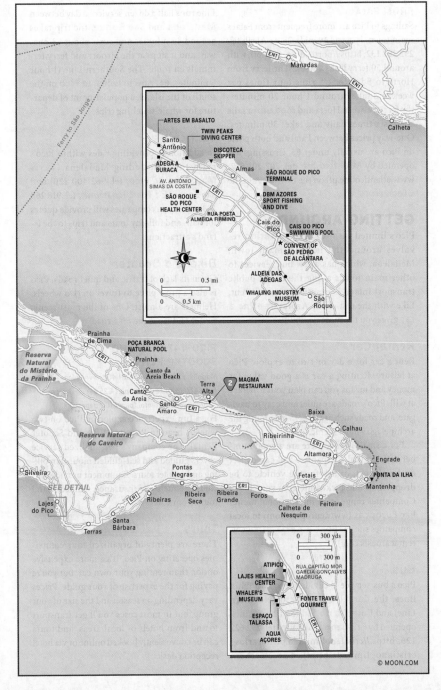

© MOON.COM

### FROM FAIAL

Sailings to Pico are more frequent from Faial's main town, Horta (Avenida 25 de Abril; tel. 292 292 132; https://portosdosacores.pt), with around 50 ferry links a week. The ferry from Horta to São Roque runs four times per week and takes around 1 hour 20 minutes; the ferry between Horta and Madalena sails about six times daily and takes 30 minutes. One-way prices between Faial and both ports on Pico are usually under €5. Crossings are operated by Atlanticoline (tel. 707 201 572; www.atlanticoline.pt) on the Blue Line or the Green Line.

## GETTING AROUND

Pico's limited public transportation revolves around the island's main town, Madalena, which has a few bus services to other main towns along the coast; public transport inland is practically nonexistent. Like with the rest of the Azores, renting a car gives you the most flexibility.

### Rental Car

Rent a car for a day or two to explore Pico at leisure. Renting a car is a good value for money and means you can plan your itinerary at will. Pico's roads are quiet and easy to navigate, and roads such as the EN3 are among the archipelago's most scenic.

For a small island, there are a good number of car rental companies. You can collect at the airport, or ask for the vehicle to be dropped off and picked up from your hotel. Companies range from international names like Europcar (www.europcar.com) to local companies such as Rent-a-Car Oásis (www. rentacaroasis.com).

### Bus

Pico's bus service is divided into two main lines: the Carreira do Norte (Northern Line) and Carreira do Sul (Southern Line), operated by Cristiano Limitada (tel. 292 622 126; https://cristianolimitada.pt/horarios_cristiano_limitada.html). The Northern Line runs half a dozen services a day between Madalena and São Roque; the trip takes around 45 minutes and costs about €3 one-way, and it stops at the airport and ferry terminals en route. The Southern Line (1 hour 5 minutes; €4) runs to Lajes do Pico on the south of the island, a popular point of departure for whale-watching trips.

### Taxi

In addition to providing rides within Pico's main towns including Madalena (Taxis Madalena do Pico; tel. 962 400 120) and São Roque (E'z Taxi Pico Island; tel. 918 268 183), most taxi companies will provide quotes for half- and full-day tours and trips to the island's attractions.

### Bike and Scooter

Given its lack of traffic and quiet roads, Pico is also a great place to travel on two wheels. Helmets are a must. One of the most scenic routes on Pico is the EN3 road.

### PICO 447 BIKE AND SCOOTER RENTAL

*Madalena Docks; tel. 961 101 404; www.pico447.com; from €17/day bike rental (plus €25 deposit), from €25/day scooter rental (plus €100 deposit)*

For a fun experience exploring Pico on two wheels, head to Pico 447 Bike and Scooter Rental. The company's personalized service covers guided and self-guided mountain biking and scooter tours. Equipment provided includes helmets and insurance. Guided island tours from €30.

### Tours

There are plenty of organized tour companies operating on Pico. It's a more expensive option than renting your own car, but you're paying for the expertise of your guide. Prices vary depending on season and the size of your group, but in most cases you'll get transport to and from hotels or local areas, and tours can be conveniently booked online or via hotel reception desks.

### ÉPICO URACTIVE
*tel. 962 956 196; http://epico.uractive.com*
In addition to leading groups to the summit of Mount Pico, Épico also offers other excursions, such as wine tours and picnics.

### TERRALTA NATURE TOURS
*tel. 938 972 678 or 960 322 195; www.*
*terraltanaturetours.com*
Madalena-based Terralta Nature Tours aims to showcase Pico's natural magnificence with fun jeep safaris, combining nature with adventure off the beaten track.

### FUTURISMO PICO AZORES ADVENTURES
*tel. 968 473 981; www.futurismo.pt/en*
Futurismo, based in Lajes do Pico, is one of Pico's foremost companies for whale-watching trips and has a huge selection of exciting land and sea adventure tours.

## ORIENTATION
Shaped a bit like a whale, Pico island covers some 447 square kilometers (173 sq mi). It is the second biggest island in the Azores archipelago after São Miguel, and it is around 50 kilometers (30 mi) long, east to west. Both of Pico's two biggest towns, Madalena and São Roque do Pico (often called just São Roque) are located on the northern half of the island, along with the Landscape of the Pico Island Vineyard Culture. The best places to see Pico's distinctive basalt-lined vineyards are in the parishes of Criação Velha and Santa Luzia. Otherwise, most of Pico's sights are in the western half of the island, including Mount Pico. One exception is Lajes do Pico, which is on the south coast, the main point of departure for whale-watching trips and home to Pico's fascinating Whaling Industry Museum.

Fishing port Madalena, considered Pico's main town, is located on its westernmost point, while São Roque, a popular rural tourism destination, is kitty-corner across, on the northeastern flank of the island. Most of the island's best beaches stretch in between, on Pico's north coast.

The ER1 road traces the island's coast; driving around the entire island would take around 3 hours. The EN2 winds through the middle of the island, north-south, dividing the island more or less and half. Make sure to drive the EN3 road, also known as the Longitudinal, which links Madalena to São Roque or Lajes.

## PLANNING YOUR TIME
Plan to spend at least two full days on Pico, three if possible. You'll need at least one full day to climb Mount Pico, if that's your reason for visiting, and an extra day would be ideal to see the rest of Pico's unique sights, including the Landscape of the Pico Island Vineyard Culture and a possible whale-watching trip.

Since July and August are peak tourist season and much hotter than the rest of the year, and main attractions might be busier, it might be advisable to scale Mount Pico outside the heat of summer, say in April or October. Whales can be spotted year-round, thanks to the many different specifies that inhabit the waters around Pico, but the best time, especially to sight blue whales, is spring.

Close to the airport and João Quaresma Maritime Ferry Terminal, Pico's main town, Madalena, is a convenient base for staying on and exploring the island. São Roque do Pico is another alternative, with the more laid-back feel of a seaside resort, but it's also not too far away from any of the island's main attractions.

# Itinerary Idea

Before or after a whole day spent climbing **Mount Pico,** spend a day exploring the wineries and Europe's largest lava tube. Be sure to reserve in advance at the popular Madalena restaurant **Cella Bar** for dinner.

## ONE DAY ON PICO

**1** From your base in Madalena, after breakfast, jump in the car and drive 10 minutes northeast along the island's main ER1 road to the Landscape of the Pico Island Vineyard Culture. Start with a visit to the **Landscape of the Pico Island Vineyard Culture Interpretation Center,** where you can learn all about Pico's long and distinctive winemaking history and try some wines.

**2** After spending the morning absorbing this unique landscape, keep following the ER1 east for another 40 minutes. You'll enjoy lunch at the fabulous seaside **Magma Restaurant.**

**3** After lunch, take the ER1 to the EN3 to cut through the middle of the island and stop to explore the **Torres Cave,** the largest lava tube in Europe.

**4** Not far from here, about an 8-minute drive west, is the bright-red-capped **Frade Windmill,** surrounded by more of the black basalt-walled vineyards so distinctive to the island.

**5** Back in Madalena, about a 10-minute drive north, have dinner at the extraordinary **Cella Bar,** whose rooftop terrace is the perfect place for a memorable sundowner.

# Sights

## ★ LANDSCAPE OF THE PICO ISLAND VINEYARD CULTURE

(Paisagem da Cultura da Vinha da Ilha do Pico)

*Northern coast of Pico island; open 24/7; free*

With a viticulture dating back to the 15th century, Pico island is famed for its winemaking. Vast swathes of the island are covered with woven grids of basalt rock walls that stretch for miles, forming pens called *currais* within which the island vines grow. The *currais* are designed to protect the vines from harsh sea air as well as release heat overnight to regulate the grapes' temperatures—and they create a distinct visual effect that has become synonymous with Azorean winemaking. So unique

and characteristic is this lattice-like landscape that it has been classified a UNESCO World Heritage Site since 2004. The designated Landscape of the Pico Island Vineyard Culture covers over 3 hectares (7 acres) of the northwestern flank of the island, an excellent example of historic farming practices being preserved and continued today.

Drive around or park and get out to wander among the *currais,* feeling and breathing one of the most unique and exquisitely preserved winemaking traditions on the planet. Visit the Vineyard Culture Interpretation Center, enjoy a tasting of local wines, and see other historic artifacts linked to the island's winemaking, such as the old stone-built manor houses, wine cellars, warehouses, churches, and wells.

# The Basalt Wines of Pico

The Azores' wine production is believed to date back to the 15th century; the first vines on Pico were reputedly planted by Franciscan friars, who were among the first settlers on the island. Battling extreme elements like blasts of salty winds from the open Atlantic, mineral-rich volcanic soil, humidity, and proximity to the sea, the vines thrive in the most remarkable conditions, grown in ancient basalt-walled pens known as *currais,* producing equally distinct flavors.

## WINES TO TRY

Pico's wines are mostly produced from three varietals of grape: **Verdelho, Arinto dos Açores,** and **Terrantez do Pico.** Once most famous for the production of its *licoroso* fortified wine, still sometimes available from Pico's wineries, the island's forte today is without doubt its **white wines:** crisp, citrusy, and some with an oddly salty, minerally note.

**Frei Gigante, Terras de Lava,** and **Basalto** brands, produced by the Pico Island Wine Cooperative, are among the top wines to look out for, as well as **Curral Atlantis, Arinto dos Açores,** and **Cancela do Porco.** You may also encounter *vinho de cheiro,* a light red wine with a perfume-like fragrance. And make sure to try the **Lajido** or **Czar** *licoroso* fortified wines.

## Landscape of the Pico Island Vineyard Culture Interpretation Center

### (Centro de Interpretação da Paisagem da Cultura da Vinha da Ilha do Pico)

*Rua do Lajido Santa Luzia; tel. 965 896 313; http:// parquesnaturais.azores.gov.pt/pt/pico/o-que-visitar/ centros-de-interpretacao/centro-de-interpretacao- da-paisagem-da-cultura-da-vinha; Tues.-Sat. 10am-1pm and 1:30pm-5pm Nov. 1-Mar. 31, daily 10am-1pm and 2pm-6pm Apr. 1-Oct. 31; €3*

Start your visit to the Landscape of the Pico Island Vineyard Culture by learning more about the fascinating history of Pico's wine-making at the Interpretation Center, located in the parish of Santa Luzia. Enjoy a **wine-tasting and guided tour** of the beautiful vineyards and volcanic *currais* (€5 pp by appointment, request 48 hours in advance).

Next door to the center is a traditional building built from basalt rock with the typical red and green doors and windows, known as the **Volcanoes' House** (Rua do Lajido, Santa Luzia; tel. 292 644 328; http:// parquesnaturais.azores.gov.pt/pt/pico/o-que-visitar/centros-de-interpretacao/110-pni-pico/3289-casa-dos-vulcoes; Tues.-Sat. 10am-1pm and 1:30pm-5pm Nov.-Mar., daily 10am-1pm and 2pm-6pm Apr.-Oct.; €7); a combined ticket to see both attractions costs €8. In this quirky little interactive center dedicated to volcanoes and volcanic activity, visitors can experience the sensation of an earthquake in a seismic simulator and see what it would look like to travel to the earth's core.

## MADALENA AND AROUND

Madalena do Pico, more often referred to as simply Madalena, is a pretty and traditional little Azorean town. Facing Horta on neighboring Faial, Madalena is at the northwestern tip of the island. Its quaint town center is dominated by a 17th-century church, the **Church of Holy Mary Magdalene** (Igreja de Santa Maria Madalena), with a picturesque harbor and charming streets.

## Pico Wine Museum

*Rua dos Baleiros 13, Madalena; tel. 292 672 276; www.museu-pico.azores.gov.pt/museu/ museu-do-vinho; Tues.-Fri. 9am-12:30pm and 2pm-5:30pm, Sat.-Sun. 9am-12:30pm; €2*

This lovely little museum dedicated to island winemaking is housed in an old Carmelite convent and former winery. Simple, well-curated exhibits offer visitors a comprehensive overview of Pico's wine heritage and general culture. Highlights include a centuries-old

# Madelena

PICO 447 BIKE AND
SCOOTER RENTAL

JOÃO QUARESMA
MARITIME
FERRY TERMINAL

TRIPIX
AZORES

PICO
SPORT

HOTEL
CARVELAS

CW
AZORES

PICO ISLAND
ADVENTURES

0     100 yds
0     100 m

SEE DETAIL

AVENIDA MACHADO SERPA

CELLA BAR

VILA BARCA

BARCA
NATURAL
POOL

PICO
WINE
MUSEUM ★

RUA CARLOS DABNEY

MERCADO
BIO

PICO ISLAND
WINE COOPERATIVE

TASCA O PETISCA

TABERNA
DO CANAL

ANCORADOURO

MADALENA
HEALTH CENTER

DRIVING THE
EN3 ROAD

ESTRADA LONGITUDINAL

EN3

0     0.25 mi
0     0.25 km

CAFÉ
CONCERTO

To Frade
Windmill ▼

© MOON.COM

dragon tree, a building dedicated to alembic stills, and interesting explanations of Pico's unique wine-growing system.

## Frade Windmill
### (Moinho de Frade)

*4 kilometers (2 mi) south from Madalena center, Natural Park of Pico, Lajido de Santa Luzia; tel. 292 207 375; open 24/7; free*

Just south of Madalena is Pico's most famous

windmill, the Frade Windmill. Showing a distinctive Flemish influence from the island's earliest settlers, its distinctive red cap sits in stark contrast with the black volcanic landscape. This cute little windmill, originally used to grind cereals, was carefully restored in 2003-2004. It is today classified as a Property of Public Interest, and the views from here over the ancestral *currais* are superb.

---

1: Pico Wine Museum 2: Frade Windmill 3: Torres Cave 4: Captain's Lake

## ★ Torres Cave
### (Gruta das Torres)

*Caminho da Gruta das Torres; daily 10am-6pm Apr. 1-Oct. 31; daily 10am-1:30pm and 2pm-5pm Nov. 1-Mar. 31; €8*

Stretching over 5,150 meters (3.2 mi), the Torres Cave is the longest lava tube in Portugal. It is believed to have been formed when underground magma flows cooled following an eruption some 1,500 years ago. Located in the parish of Criação Velha, around 8 kilometers (5 mi) southeast of Madalena (about 10 minutes by car), this historic lava formation's main cavity, the gaping Torres Cave, measures around 450 meters (1,500 ft). With intriguing geological formations exposing different types of lava, the Torres Cave is one of Pico's top attractions.

Expect to spend 1-1.5 hours in this fascinating, dark, and dripping place. The ground is uneven underfoot, so sensible footwear is necessary, and this experience is not recommended for anyone uncomfortable in the dark. Safety equipment such as flashlights and helmets are included in the entry fee via the Visitors Center; guided tours are available.

### TORRES CAVE VISITORS CENTER

*Caminho da Gruta das Torres, Criação Velha; tel. 924 403 921; http://parquesnaturais.azores.gov. pt/pt/pico/o-que-visitar/centros-de-interpretacao/ centro-de-visitantes-da-gruta-das-torres; Tues.-Fri. 10am-5pm, Sat. 2pm-5:30pm; €8*

To get an in-depth understanding of the Torres Cave, spend some time in the Visitors Center, where interesting facts and cool trivia about the tube, the island, and the Azores' volcanic history can be enjoyed. Visitors will pass through this compelling little museum to access the stairs that lead down to the cave.

## MOUNT PICO
### (Montanha Pico)

*middle of Pico island; http://parquesnaturais.azores. gov.pt/pt/pico/o-que-visitar/areas-protegidas/ reserva-natural/montanha-do-pico; mountain house admission center open 24/7 May 1-Sept. 30, Mon.-Thurs. 8am-8pm, Fri. 8am-Sun. 8pm uninterrupted Apr. and Oct., daily 8am-6pm Nov. 1-Mar. 31; €15*

Its soaring, conical outline rising voluptuously from its base is unmistakable. The highest point in Portugal, the stratovolcano's summit stands at 2,351 meters (7,713 ft) above sea level, double the height of any other peak in the Azores. On a cloudy day, the peak photogenically perforates the clouds, peering triumphantly over the island. Pico actually has a double peak: The top of the mountain is capped by a huge crater, Pico Grande, on which sits another little cone, Pico Pequeno.

The Azores are renowned for their hikes, but maybe none as epic as ascending Pico. Mount Pico calls to hikers worldwide, but it's not for the fainthearted. However, the breathtaking 360-degree views at the top, even on the way up, are the ultimate reward. The climb is Pico's number one activity, so the number of people allowed on the dormant volcano at any one time is limited, and climbing with an experienced guide is highly recommended.

## CAPTAIN'S LAKE
### (Lagoa do Capitão)

*Estrada Longitudinal ER 3-2*

Stretching out in front of Mount Pico like a pewter mirror, Captain's Lake is perhaps the most photographed lake on the island thanks to its sharp reflection of the towering dormant volcano. Though small by comparison to some other lakes in the Azores, Captain's Lake is a pleasant spot for a walk, to admire grazing cows and tame bobbing ducks. Walk around the magical lake, and behind a small hill on the right side you can enjoy stunning views over the island's north coast and neighboring São Jorge island. Captain's Lake is situated in the middle of Pico island, along a secondary road, just off the R3-2.

## SÃO ROQUE DO PICO

Pico's "second city" on the north coast, São Roque do Pico has a bustling port town feel about it. It is divided into two main areas: São Roque do Pico town, and Cais do Pico, the

# ☆ Driving the EN3 Road

the EN3 road

Widely considered one of the most beautiful roads in Portugal, the EN3, or Longitudinal, stretches from Madalena in the west, through the heart of Pico, past Mount Pico, to join the EN2 that connects São Roque on the north coast to Lajes do Pico in the south. This is without a doubt the most scenic drive on the island, a long, straight road with omnipresent views of Mount Pico and various lakes, including Captain's Lake. It takes only 20 minutes to drive the 22.4-kilometer (13.9-mi) road start to finish, but you'll want to allow more time to stop for the beautiful views.

The road starts off quite straight from **Madalena,** before curving to the right and gaining altitude, about 6 minutes (5.5 km/3.4 mi) in. Just over 20 minutes (10.9 km/6.8 mi) from Madalena, if you'd like to stop for a snack and more breathtaking views, turn right on an unnamed road to the **Mountain House.** Here you'll find a bar as well as useful information about the geology and history of **Mount Pico.**

Return back to the EN3. After another 8.6 kilometers (5.3 mi), you'll see the beautiful **Captain's Lake** on your left. Get out of your car for a walk around this small body of water, which reflects Mount Pico perfectly on clear days.

You're now almost to the end of the EN3 road; another 2 minutes (2 km/1.2 mi) will bring you to the **EN2,** which bisects Pico north to south. From here, you could head 10 minutes (9.6 km/6 mi) north to **São Roque do Pico,** around which you'll find some of the island's best places to swim; or 14 minutes (13 km/8 mi) south to **Lajes do Pico,** the island's whale-watching hub. But you may just want to turn around and drive the EN3 again, to see the beauty from the opposite direction.

busy port area just north of the main town where most of the town's daily activity unfurls. Cais do Pico receives the daily ferry from neighboring São Jorge.

A pleasant-looking town centered on the harbor, São Roque has a strong whaling history, evident in local statues, monuments, and museums. A row of quaint whitewashed buildings lines the waterfront, with soaring green hills behind them, and the harbor being overshadowed by the handsome **Convent of São Pedro de Alcântara.** Most of the town's shops, restaurants, cafés, and hotels are located around the waterfront. The main **ER1** coastal road runs through São Roque, and there is also a pretty waterfront walkway, the

Avenida do Mar, which runs along the São Roque town coastline.

## Whaling Industry Museum
### (Museu da Industria Baleeria)

*Rua do Poço; tel. 292 642 096; www.museu-pico.azores.gov.pt/museu/museu-da-industria-baleeira; Tues.-Sun. 10am-5:30pm Apr. 1-Sept. 30, Tues.-Sun. 9:30am-5pm Oct. 1-Mar. 31; free*

Housed in an old whaling byproducts factory in the town of São Roque do Pico, the Whaling Industry Museum showcases the manufacturing side of the Azores' now-extinct whaling industry, demonstrating the importance the activity had for the island. Vestiges of the ancient whaling tradition can be spotted across the island, in old look-out stations (*vigias*) and monuments, but this museum focuses on the industry itself. Operational from 1946 to 1984, the former factory became a museum in 2007. Exhibits include a wealth of machinery, like boilers, furnaces, and other equipment once used to transform whales into oil and flours. This museum has garnered international acclaim as one of the best in the world of its kind.

## Convent of São Pedro de Alcântara

*Rua João Bento de Lima*

Tucked away just a stone's throw from the São Roque harbor in the center of town, this beautiful 18th-century Baroque convent and three-story church complex pay testament to Pico's religious heritage and volcanic past. Its exterior is typically Azorean, whitewashed with basalt-gray stonework.

The decision to build a Franciscan convent in São Roque do Pico goes hand in hand with Mount Pico's 1720 eruption, when lava destroyed part of the parish of Santa Luzia in São Roque do Pico, making room for this new construction. This handsome monastic building is the subject of fables and folklore, as local legend has it that at one time there was an underground tunnel running between the convent and Portinho de São Roque Bay. Within the grounds, passersby can still see the original courtyard and twin bell tower. This old convent is no longer open to the public but is still worth seeing from the outside.

# LAJES DO PICO

Having grown around an old port on Pico's south coast, Lajes do Pico's strong ties to the sea are evident. Known for being a hub for whale-watching excursions, its port has historic links to the island's whaling heritage and is home to one of the best little museums on Pico. Old whaling warehouses and factories can also be seen around the port area.

Fashioned into a bay at the foot of a rolling hill, Pico Town is charmingly traditional and quaint. Three or four little parallel streets extend between the portside and the main ER1 island ring road; in this area visitors will find cafés, restaurants, and services like shops, banks, and the post office.

## Whaler's Museum
### (Museu dos Baleeiros)

*Rua dos Baleeiros 13; tel. 292 679 340; www.museu-pico.azores.gov.pt; Tues.-Sun. 9am-5pm; €2*

This comprehensive little museum houses relics and paraphernalia from the Azores' whaling days. It might not be to everyone's liking, but it depicts in detail a significant chapter of the Azores' history, warts and all. The well-organized little museum with curated exhibitions provides an interesting insight into local heritage and culture, while at the same time explaining how the Azoreans went from being whale hunters to proud guardians of the extraordinary mammals and their habitat.

---

1: São Roque do Pico 2: Lajes do Pico

# From Whaling to Whale-Watching

The Azores archipelago is today one of few places on the planet that unreservedly showcases its whaling tradition, warts and all. While the activity has long been eradicated in this part of the world, its heritage remains ingrained in the region, clear for all to see. Most islands have statues or monuments alluding to the islands' former lifeblood; former whaling factories have been converted into modern museums; old wooden whale boats are proudly restored and used as showpieces in museums or regattas; and festivals, such as Pico's **Whalers Week** and Faial's **Sea Week,** celebrate time-honored whaling traditions and the Azores' long-standing links to the sea.

Whaling arrived in the Azores from the Americas in the late 18th century, when large American ships began to explore the untapped bounty of whales in the cool blue waters off the islands. Azoreans learned their whaling techniques from the visiting Americans, later building their own vessels and taking up the profitable activity as the American whaling industry began to decline. Whaling rapidly became a key pillar for the local economy and an intrinsic part of the archipelago's culture.

## A DANGEROUS OCCUPATION

Whales swam so close to the shores of the Azores that rudimentary techniques and equipment could be used to spot and kill the whales. Watchmen spent long hours sighting them with binoculars from *vigias* on land, sending signals to whalers to chase the huge mammals down on wide, open wooden row-boats, from which the whalers slaughtered the whales with hand-thrown harpoons. These old-fashioned, 18th-century, hand-powered techniques were still being employed well into the early 20th century, an unsophisticated form of hunting that made whaling a dangerous occupation, earning Azorean whalers a reputation as fearless fishermen. Whales were then towed back to land, tied to the boats with ropes, to be transformed into lucrative byproducts. Fat was transformed into oil and exported to be used as fuel, lubricant, and in cosmetics; bones were ground and used as fertility treatments.

## TRANSITION TO CONSERVATION

Whaling in the Azores came to a staggered end in the 1980s after being officially banned in 1982. The ban was only fully implemented in 1986, and, famously, the last whale in the Azores was killed in 1987 as a protest from a few staunch whalers from Pico. Thus, hundreds of years of whaling tradition were brought to a somewhat reluctant end.

As tourism crept into the Azores, the region gradually established itself as one of the foremost whale-spotting sites on the globe. Tourism has thrived hand in hand with marine conservation, with preservation replacing profitability. Today, the Azores' waters provide a safe haven for over 20 species of whales that can be spotted year-round, one of the most magical experiences on offer in the Azores.

## LEARNING ABOUT AZOREAN WHALING HERITAGE TODAY

Remnants of the whaling industry can be seen all over Pico, especially in the *vigias* (lookouts) dotting the island's coasts that were once used by whalers to spot their prey. But a visit to the excellent museums dedicated to the history of whaling, followed by seeing the majestic animals up close on a whale-watching tour, will provide the best education.

- **Whaling Industry Museum:** This former factory in São Roque do Pico teaches visitors all about how whales were processed into the products that made them so valuable (page 221).

- **Whaler's Museum:** This museum in Lajes do Pico focuses on the heritage and culture of the former Azorean whaling industry (page 221).

- **Whale-Watching:** Pico's relative lack of development, even by Azorean standards, means it is perhaps the best island in the archipelago for whale-watching. Set off on your expedition from Lajes do Pico, the island's whale-watching center (page 227).

# The 1720 Eruption

Mount Pico may be dormant now, but it was once a formidable mid-Atlantic volcano. Its last major eruption was in 1720, a cataclysm that changed the island's landscape forever. After simmering for much of 1718, the 1720 eruption began on July 10, preceded by numerous earthquakes, before flooding swathes of Pico with fiery lava, destroying land, vineyards, and 30 houses, whose residents survived by running for their lives. The eruption went on until December of that year.

## EVIDENCE OF THE ERUPTION

Although it has shown signs of activity as recently as 2009, Mount Pico nowadays is a gentle sleeping giant. But remnants of the 1720 natural disaster can still be seen across Pico:

- The terrain is soilless, covered instead with a crust of pumice, visible in the São João Forest Park, on the **Southern Pico Mysteries Trail** (page 232).

- Lava boulders have been used widely in construction, such as in the *currais* vineyards. See the *currais* up close at the **Landscape of the Pico Island Vineyard Culture** (page 214).

- The **Convent of São Pedro de Alcântara** in São Roque was built after much of the parish had been destroyed by the eruption (page 221).

# Wineries and Wine-Tasting

Perhaps the best-known island for Azorean winemaking—and the most productive—is Pico. So unique and distinctive is its viticulture that UNESCO has classified a 987-hectare (2,440-acre) swathe of Pico, with its trademark sprawling network of rock-wall vine pens, as a World Heritage Site. The two main areas on Pico to see these landscapes is the **Landscape of the Pico Island Vineyard Culture site,** a short drive northeast from the airport and Madalena, and the area around the town of **São Mateus,** on the island's southwest coast, a 20-minute drive southeast from Madalena on the main ER1 ring road.

## PICO ISLAND WINE COOPERATIVE (Cooperativa Vitivinícola da Ilha do Pico)

*Av. Padre Nunes Rosa 29, Madalena; tel. 292 622 262 or 912 533 243; www.picowines.com; Mon.-Fri. 8am-8pm, Sat. 3pm-8pm*

One of the best places to enjoy an introduction to Pico's wines is at the Pico Island Wine Cooperative in Madalena, a working cooperative where local wines and liquors

are produced and sold. The largest and oldest wine-producing cooperative on Pico, the Pico Island Wine Cooperative is responsible for some of the island's most famous brands. The Cooperative offers several **tour** options: the Traditional Tour (€6/person) includes a tasting of three wines, while the Wine and Tapas Tour (€25/person) includes a tasting of six wines paired with local specialties. Check the website for tour times and to book ahead. Afterward, pop into the **gift shop** on your way out to stock up on Pico wines, or maybe a T-shirt!

## AZORES WINE COMPANY

*Rua dos Biscoitos, 3, São Mateus; tel. 912 530 237; http://azoreswinecompany.com; Mon.-Fri. 11am-12:30pm and 4pm-5:30pm*

Founded in 2014 to produce and promote Pico's unique wines and singular wine heritage, the privately run Azores Wine Company has recovered about 40 hectares (100 acres) of vineyard on the island of Pico for its own production, and is on track to become the largest private producer in the Azores. They're based

out of São Mateus on Pico's southeast coast, a 20-minute drive southeast of Madalena. **Themed tastings** with catchy names like Volcanic Wines, Salt & Spices, and Crazy About Whites, are available four times a day, every day of the week (prices upon request; call or email to inquire or make a reservation).

# Beaches and Pools

Most of Pico's popular beaches and are found on the island's northern coast. Pico island has one single, tiny sandy beach, Canto da Areia Beach, and the rest are lovely rocky tidal pools dotted around the coast.

## MADALENA
### BARCA NATURAL POOL
### (Piscina Natural da Barca)
*Zona Balnear da Barca; open 24/7; free*
Just 50 meters (160 ft) from the Vila Barca hotel and a short stroll to the acclaimed Cella Bar, the Barca natural pool on the northern outskirts of Madalena is a lovely spot for a refreshing dip. There is a roomy cement deck and a little seawater pool encircled by jagged black volcanic rock where you can swim while looking out to sea and Faial island.

## SÃO ROQUE DO PICO
### CAIS DO PICO SWIMMING POOL
### (Piscina Cais do Pico)
*Cais do Pico; www.visitportugal.com/en/content/piscina-do-cais-do-pico; open 24/7; free*
Just north of São Roque do Pico in tiny Cais do Pico, this natural tidal pool with concrete walkways and sundeck is a lovely place for a refreshing dip. It also offers access to the open sea, along with other amenities including a children's play area, showers, parking, and a popular nearby bar, **Snack-bar Aço** (ER1 9940-334, Cais do Pico; Mon.-Wed. and Fri.-Sat. 7am-2am, Thurs. and Sun. 7am-midnight).

### CANTO DA AREIA BEACH
### (Praia do Canto da Areia)
*Canto da Areia; open 24/7; free*
The only sandy beach on Pico and one of few in the Azores, Canto da Areia, on Pico's north coast, is one of the island's most popular beaches. It's located a 15-minute drive southeast on the ER1 road from São Roque. Clean and family-friendly, this bijou black sand beach, at about 80 meters (260 ft) long, is the closest point on Pico island to neighboring São Jorge island; interestingly, because of this proximity, underwater cables have long ensured communication between the two. Freshwater showers and toilets are available at the access to the beach, and there's a cute little **beach bar** too. As this beach forms a little basin facing neighboring São Jorge, the waters are generally calm and ideal for swimming and snorkeling.

### POÇA BRANCA NATURAL POOL
### (Zona Balnear Poça Branca)
*Prainha; open 24/7; free*
A 20-minute drive southeast on the ER1 road from São Roque, this natural swimming pool on the northern coast has a sundeck, washrooms, a picnic area, and a seasonal kiosk for beverages and snacks. It's also a popular snorkeling spot and is on the PRC9PIC hiking trail.

---

1: Pico vineyards 2: Cais do Pico swimming pool

# Kayaking and Stand-Up Paddle Boarding

Pico's magnificent coastline is an awesome setting for kayaking and SUP. A striking contrast of black volcanic rock topped with vibrant green set against the deep blue of the ocean, the nooks, bays, and crevices beckon to be explored. Anywhere along Pico's coastline is a good place to kayak or SUP, with the magnificent, sometimes snow-capped Mount Pico in the background. **Canto da Areia Beach** provides access into the ocean for SUP boards, and **Areia Larga Port** in Madalena is a popular and scenic spot for kayaking.

Both of the rental providers mentioned below are based in **Madalena;** inquire about bringing kayaks to other parts of the island.

### TRIPIX AZORES

*Madalena Docks; tel. 912 087 199; www.tripixazores.com; open 24/7; from €45 pp (2 people/half day)*

See Pico's magnificent cliffs from a different angle as you paddle and glide along the pristine water of the Atlantic Ocean. Dip in and out of secret alcoves and explore this unspoiled island's coastal features on a guided tour. Alternatively, take a SUP class or enjoy some SUP yoga.

### PICO ISLAND ADVENTURES

*Rua Doutor Freitas Pimentel r/c; tel. 292 622 980; http://pico-island-adventures.com; daily 8am-9pm; tours from €45, rentals from €5/hour*

Explore the island's impressive coastline and enjoy the sunshine and sea breeze in the comfort of a kayak. From hourly and full-day rentals, to three-hour kayak tours or combined kayak and snorkel tours, Pico Island Adventures is the leading company for all things kayak.

# Diving and Snorkeling

The untainted waters around Pico island and the abundance of marine life living there make them a magnet for divers of all levels. With a range of compelling and exciting dive sites, amid sea mounts, reefs, and wrecks, Pico is a strong option for underwater enthusiasts. If you don't have time for a more extensive scuba dive but still want a peek underwater, **Poça Branca Natural Pool** on the island's northern coast and **Canto da Areia Beach** are great spots for snorkeling.

## DIVE SPOTS

### PRINCESS ALICE SEAMOUNT

*Roughly 50 miles southwest off the coast of Pico*
Remote, deep, and challenging, the legendary Princess Alice Seamount is reputedly one of best dives sites in Atlantic Ocean and one

of the most famous in the Azores. Located southwest of the islands of Pico and Faial, it takes approximately 3 hours to get there by boat. Once arrived, visitors are greeted with crystal-clear water teeming with hammerhead sharks, blue sharks, schools of barracuda, dolphins, mobulas, tuna, and black marlin. The tip of this incredible seamount is around 30-40 meters (100-130 ft) deep, with the base of the mountain plunging to depths of over 500 meters (1,300 ft). Depending on the currents and conditions, there's not always a lot to see, but some of the best experiences are enjoyed as you follow the descent line down and back up again; if you're lucky, majestic rays and other large sea creatures glide up to meet their guests. Due to its remoteness, depth, and strong open ocean currents, this dive is suited to experienced, disciplined divers, and excursions generally take place in good-weather windows only. Both of the dive centers listed below run trips to the Princess Alice Seamount.

## DIVE CENTERS AND SCHOOLS

### PICO SPORT

*Madalena Docks; tel. 292 622 980; http://pico-sport.com; daily 8am-9pm; from €45*

One of Pico's foremost dive centers, Pico Sport excels in underwater experiences. In addition to popular tourist excursions like diving around Pico island and out at sea, swimming with dolphins, shark dives, and dive cruises, the company also applies their experience

to assisting with professional projects like TV and movie productions and underwater photography.

### TWIN PEAKS DIVING CENTER

*São Roque do Pico; tel. 910 634 403; www.twinpeaksdivingcentre.com; Mon.-Tues. and Thurs.-Sat. 8am-7pm, Wed. 8am-10pm, Sun. 10am-7pm; from €45*

Located on Pico's north coast, the Twin Peaks Diving Center pledges to lift the lid on what is one of Europe's best-kept secret dive destinations. With over a decade of experience diving in the Azores, the company provides a high-quality, certified, professional, and friendly experience to make exploring Pico's underwater attractions memorable.

# Fishing

The abundance of fish off and around Pico makes it a fishing paradise. The waters teem with all sorts of species, from small sardines to large barracudas, even sharks, and especially the desirable blue and white marlins. Great for all different types of fishing—big game, trolling, bottom, jigging, and spear-fishing—the waters around this island afford a fulfilling and enjoyable fishing experience, enhanced by the experienced companies who provide quality tours to the best spots.

### DBM AZORES SPORT FISHING AND DIVE

*Rua do Baleeiro; tel. 960 018 362 or 916 635 932; www.dbmazores.com*

Based in São Roque do Pico, DBM Azores has over two decades of experience conducting fishing and diving trips. It's run by a team of avid fishermen and sea lovers, and activities include fishing, diving, spear-fishing, and whale- and dolphin-watching tours.

# ★ Dolphin- and Whale-Watching

Pico island is famous for having some of the best conditions for whale-watching in the Azores. Being far less developed than many other main islands means whales come within close proximity of Pico, and the pristine waters around the island are a natural haven for many species of both whales and dolphins.

Various companies run trips offering the magical experience of seeing these majestic

beasts up close, mostly during peak season (Apr.-Oct.), although whales can be seen year-round. The species spotted vary from season to season, but may include sperm whales, bottlenose and Risso's dolphins, and more rarely blue whales, fin whales, sei whales, and humpback whales, among others. Your best bet to see blue whales is in the spring.

Most whale-watching trips depart from **Lajes do Pico,** on the south coast of the island, and last 3-4 hours (half-day trips). Some companies also run full-day trips (7-8 hours).

## MADALENA
### CW AZORES

*Madalena Docks; tel. 292 622 622; www.cwazores. com; daily 8am-7:30pm; from €65*

Conducting small and personalized dolphin- and whale-watching tours, CW Azores also offers shark-diving trips and snorkeling with dolphins. Experienced skippers and divers lead the excursions, taking guests on an experience of a lifetime.

## LAJES DO PICO
### AQUA AÇORES

*Rua Manuel Paulino de Azevedo e Castro 9; tel. 917 569 453; www.aquaacores.com.pt; daily 8am-8pm; from €50pp*

A family-run business, Aqua Açores endeavors to offer fulfilling whale- and dolphin-watching experiences while at the same time safeguarding the mammals' well-being and protecting their environment. The experienced team provides a privileged window into some of the most mysterious and charismatic inhabitants of the seas.

### ESPAÇO TALASSA

*Lajes do Pico; tel. 292 672 010; www.espacotalassa. com/en; from €39*

One of the first whale-sighting tour companies on the island, Espaço Talassa has been taking visitors out to sea to spot the gentle giants since 1989, still using the traditional whale-spotting skills of the founders. The company also has weeklong whale-watching packages, comprising walks, talks, boat trips, and more.

# Hiking

Pico island's ultimate attraction for hikers is undeniably Mount Pico, one of the most epic hikes in the Azores and in Europe. Commanding the skyline, Mount Pico's summit dominates the island landscape, defining the outline of Pico from afar. The scenery on the mountain is ever-changing, as is the weather, making each climb individually magical. And don't be fooled: While it might not be on the same scale as Everest, a gentle slope Pico's climb is not; it can be steep and challenging in parts. But for walking enthusiasts who don't feel up to conquering a dormant volcano, there are plenty of other scenic trails on Pico to enjoy.

TOP EXPERIENCE

## ★ HIKING MOUNT PICO

It might not quite be in the same category as climbing Everest or Kilimanjaro, but Pico is by no means a walk in the park. At 2,351 meters (7,713 ft), it is the highest point not only

in the Azores, but the whole of Portugal. It requires some degree of fitness to reach the top, which is roughly 3-4 hours up at a relaxed pace, and the same again back down. Just when you think you've reached the top, there's another little summit—**Piquinho,** or Pico Pequenho—to scale, if you still have the energy. It's a full day's effort and is very steep in parts, meaning appropriate footwear and gloves are essential. Also, plan ahead for the Azores' notorious ever-changing weather, which reduces visibility and swings from pleasant to cool in the blink of an eye, and try to avoid hiking in the hottest hours in summer by starting early. For safety reasons all climbers are required to check in and out at **the Mountain House information center.** If you want an extra-special experience, sign up for the **overnight climb,** so you can witness the most magical of sunrises from the

---

1: whale-watching off the Pico coast 2: Criação Velha Vinyards hiking trail

summit. This is best booked through a tour company who will provide the tents and sleeping bags (which climbers have to carry themselves) and will also find the best spot in the crater to set up camp.

Set aside a whole day to climb Mount Pico. You don't need to be an experienced mountaineer for this challenge, but a certain degree of physical aptitude is required, as the route is demanding. The number of climbers allowed on Pico at any given time is limited to 160, or a daily load of 320, to protect the mountain from being overrun. Only 32 people are allowed to spend the night on the mountain, which is why booking ahead via a tour company is recommended. Overnight stays are permitted for climbs starting after 4pm. Since this is what most people visit Pico for, **book in advance** with the Mountain House. For those climbing independently, at the time of writing it cost €15/person to climb to the crater and €25/person to climb to Piquinho. It's highly recommended to go with an experienced **guide.**

Pack some **snacks** and **water,** and **layer** up, as the Azorean weather can infamously change rapidly. If hiking during summer, don't forget the sunscreen, a hat, and more water! Geological formations en route provide some natural shelter to rest and escape inclement weather, but there are no toilets.

To reach the mountain, head southwest from **Madalena** following the signs that, appropriately, say "Mountain." The official trail starts at the Mountain House, a 25-minute drive from Madalena. A one-way **taxi** trip from Madalena to the Mountain House should cost in the region of €25.

### THE MOUNTAIN HOUSE

*Caminho Florestal 9, Candelária; tel. 967 303 519; http://parquesnaturais.azores.gov.pt/pt/pico/o-que-visitar/centros-de-interpretacao/casa-da-montanha; open 24/7 May 1-Sept. 30, Mon.-Thurs. 8am-8pm, Fri. 8am-Sun. 8pm uninterrupted Apr. and Oct., daily 8am-6pm Nov. 1-Mar. 31*

Anyone who wants to climb Mount Pico must first check in at the Mountain House. It is an obligatory stop for climbers, to check in and register for safety and security reasons Hikers wanting to climb autonoumosly can reserve their place on the mountain via www.montanhapico.azores.gov.pt. Bookings via a tour guide take care of all reservations and logistics. As well as providing this essential tracking service, the Mountain House offers a wealth of information on the Pico Mountain Nature Reserve's specific geology, biology,

hiking Mount Pico

history, and climate, as well as its rules and regulations. It also houses a **bar** with stunning views over the mountain's west coast and neighboring Faial. The Mountain House does not provide tours or guide services.

## Guides

An experienced guide is highly recommended for anyone thinking of attempting to scale Pico. There are several companies on Pico that specialize in the scaling the mountain.

### TRIPIX AZORES

*Madalena Docks; tel. 912 087 199; www.tripixazores.*

*com; open 24/7; from €65 pp (day climb)*

Highly recommended Pico guides Tripix offer three different types of climb: a day climb, a night climb to see the sunrise, and an overnight stay in the volcano's crater, complete with camping gear, where you'll get to enjoy sunset and sunrise as well as sleeping under the stars. All climbs include a certified guide, access to the mountain, transfers to and from Madalena, walking poles, obligatory locator, personal accident insurance, and a climb certificate.

### ATIPICO

*Rua Eng. Falcão s/n, Lajes do Pico; tel. 915 340 487*

*or 919 991 776; http://atipicoazores.com; from €50*

*pp*

Whether you want to do a day climb or a night climb to see the sunrise, Atipico's team of certified guides take guided tours to a new level. Inject fun and fascinating facts into your climb and make it an unforgettable experience. Atipico's overnight climbs start during the night to reach the peak for sunrise, so no sleeping on the mountain. If you would like to book a private guide, a minimum of two people is required and double fee in the case of a single person.

## OTHER HIKES

### SANTANA-LAJIDO TRAIL (PR10PIC)

**Hiking Distance:** *8.7 kilometers (5.4 mi)*

*one-way*

**Hiking Time:** *2.5 hours one-way*

**Trailhead:** *Regional road on the border between the villages of Santana and São Vicente Ferreira*

**Information and Maps:** *http://trails.*

*visitazores.com/en/trails-azores/pico/santana-lajido*

Enjoy stunning scenery on this lovely linear route that travels through orchards and vineyards and passes tidal pools and beautiful bays as it hugs the coast. The ever-changing scenery sees forests and fields of Azorean heather give way to volcanic rocks and the royal blue ocean. This route terminates in the center of Lajido village, one of the island's northernmost points, near the Interpretation Center for the UNESCO vineyards of Pico. From here you can hail a cab back to your base, or to the start of the hike where your car is parked.

### CRIAÇÃO VELHA VINEYARDS (PR05PIC)

**Hiking Distance:** *6.9 kilometers (4.3 mi)*

*one-way*

**Hiking Time:** *2 hours one-way*

**Trailhead:** *Calhau Port, Calhau, 15 minutes south of Madalena*

**Information and Maps:** *http://trails.*

*visitazores.com/en/trails-azores/pico/vinhas-da-criacao-velha*

This is an easy linear trek through the stunning protected landscapes and UNESCO World Heritage basalt vineyards of Criação Velha parish. This historically intriguing hike is one of the Azores' most outstanding. En route, walkers will see a wealth of elements associated with Pico's traditional viticulture: from carvings in the slopes from where barrels were rolled and carvings in the ground from old ox carts, to cellars, wells, and also the famous Frade Windmill. The trailhead starts at the picturesque Calhau Port in the parish of Calhau, and ends at an old manor house near the restaurant Ancoradouro in Madalena.

### CAPTAIN'S LAKE (PR13PIC)

**Hiking Distance:** *9.2 kilometers (5.7 mi)*

*one-way*

**Hiking Time:** *3 hours one-way*

**Trailhead:** *Estrada Transversal road*

**Information and Maps:** *http:// trails.visitazores.com/en/trails-azores/pico/ lagoa-do-capitao*

This is a medium-intensity linear hike along the bank of the mirror-like Captain's Lake, which reflects Mount Pico in the background. The trailhead begins in the central highlands of the island, next to the Estrada Transversal road, and ends at the Convent of São Pedro de Alcântara in São Roque. This route of charming landscapes traverses pastures and picnic spots, with Mount Pico as a backdrop.

### SOUTHERN PICO MYSTERIES TRAIL (PR15PIC)

**Hiking Distance:** *8.5 kilometers (5.3 mi) one-way*

**Hiking Time:** *3 hours one-way*

**Trailhead:** *São João Forest Park*

**Information and Maps:** *http://trails. visitazores.com/pt-pt/trilhos-dos-acores/pico/ misterios-do-sul-do-pico*

This easy, linear trek begins in the **São João Forest Park** (Estrada Regional no. 1; http://drrf-sraa.azores.gov.pt/areas/reservas-recreio/Paginas/RFR_Misterios_SJ_pt.aspx; open 24/7; free) and passes through two lava fields. The highly scenic route takes in tidal pools, barbecue areas, churches, and water mills. This is a greatly enjoyable and culturally enhancing coastal walk.

# Festivals and Events

### MONTANHA PICO FESTIVAL

*Estrada Regional 29; tel. 963 639 996; www.facebook. com/pg/MontanhaPicoFestival; throughout Jan.*

Staged at venues in main towns across the island, this festival aims to celebrate the spirit of adventure that Pico island's main centerpiece—Mount Pico—presents, as well as promote the island and mountain culture. The Montanha Pico Festival features a full, monthlong program of arty events, including art exhibitions, book launches, presentation of films and performances, photography and walking on Mount Pico, ballet, musical compositions, and mural paintings.

### WHALERS WEEK (Semana dos Baleeiros)

*Lajes do Pico; tel. 292 679 700; www.facebook.com/ pg/semanadosbaleeiros; last week of Aug.*

Dating back to the 19th century, when a statue of Nossa Senhora de Lourdes, the patron saint of whalers, arrived on the island, whalers gradually took more and more of a role in the religious procession, now one of the island's largest festivals. There's a fair where local handicrafts are sold, concerts and folk group performances, parades, and regattas in traditionally, carefully restored whalers' boats.

# Shopping

Pico is a lovely little island for authentic souvenirs and locally manufactured and handmade goods. Don't expect large malls or flashy tourist shops; down-to-earth boutiques and traditional stores can be found in town centers. Typical goods to look out for include goods made from basalt, Vaquinha cheese, and Pico wines.

## SÃO ROQUE DO PICO
### ARTES EM BASALTO
*Rua da Igreja 9; tel. 914 213 047; daily 10am-8pm*
Before leaving Pico, make sure to visit this cute little specialty shop not far from São Roque do Pico (a 5-minute drive northwest) that sells products made from island basalt rock, for the ultimate unique Pico souvenir. A vast range of individual handcrafted goods, ranging from jewelry to crockery, all made from Pico's signature beautiful black porous volcanic rock, make for stunning keepsakes from your visit.

### ADEGA A BURACA
*Estrada Regional 1; tel. 292 642 119; www. adegaaburaca.com; Mon.-Sat. 9am-1pm and 2pm-6pm*
Stock up on typical local island produce at Adega A Buraca, a 5-minute drive northwest of São Roque on the ER1 road. The shop is a veritable voyage through the genuine flavors of Pico, where you can try and buy gourmet produce such as wines, liquors, and cheeses.

## LAJES DO PICO
### FONTE TRAVEL GOURMET
*Rua Captião-Mor Garcia Goncalves Madruga 26-B; www.fontetravel.com/fonte-gourmet; Mon.-Fri. 10am-5pm, Sat. 10am-1pm*
Located in the heart of Lajes do Pico, this shop houses a wide variety of authentic national brands, with the onus on regional Azorean products, ranging from canned fish preserves to jams, teas, wines, textiles, and handicrafts, among others.

# Food

Pico's food scene is quite accomplished for a small island. The island boasts all sorts of enjoyable gastronomic offerings, from tapas made from typical island produce to contemporary cuisine, and restaurants that range from cool seaside seafood joints to award-winning architectural delights.

## MADALENA
### Traditional Portuguese
#### MERCADO BIO
*Rua Carlos Dabney no. 6 r/c; tel. 292 623 778; Mon.-Fri. 8am-10pm, Sat. 9am-10pm, Sun. 10am-10pm; €15*
Packed with fresh, quality produce made into tasty dishes, Mercado Bio (Bio Market) is a warm and surprisingly chic eatery where healthy eating meets local cuisine. Make the most of your visit by stocking up on produce to take home.

### CASA DA FEIJOCA
*Rua do Farrobo 24; tel. 292 098 330; www.facebook. com/casadafeijoca; Wed.-Mon. noon-3pm and 7pm-9:30pm; €20*
A hidden gem, this homey little restaurant in a traditional stone house serves authentic island produce to traditional recipes. Meat, especially the prime rib, is a specialty. It's a 10-minute drive outside Madalena on the ER1, part of the hotel O Farrobo.

# Figs, Fish, and Fresh Cheese

Pico is a veritable picnic basket overflowing with delicious, locally sourced treats. While many of the foods for which Pico is famed are delicate, like figs and seafood, mains center largely on hearty stews. Be sure to wash all these solid culinary offerings down with a glass of crisp island wine made from the famous Verdelho grape.

- **Figs:** Pico is perhaps best known for its juicy, ruby-red figs, which are enjoyed as a fresh treat, sun-dried, or used to make the local aguardente de figo liqueur in old copper alembic stills. The fruits are grown across the island; to buy these juicy beauties head to a local *praça* (market) such as the **Madalena Municipal Market** (Rua Maria Cecília Amaral; Tues.-Sun. 9am-4pm).

- **Seafood:** Like other Azorean islands, fresh seafood is also found in abundance on Pico, with regional delicacies being *lapas* (limpets) and the spindly, lobster-like *cavacos*. For excellent seafood with a sea view, head to the **Ponta da Ilha** restaurant near Lajes do Pico, which is run by a fishermens association and is known for being one of the best seafood restaurants on the island (page 235).

- **Fresh Cheese:** A popular start to meals on Pico is the local Queijo do Pico cheese, enjoyed on traditional Bolo de Milho cornbread. Queijo do Pico is specific to Pico island; its origins are said to date back as far as the 18th century. It is a semi-soft cured cows-milk cheese, with a distinct salty taste and intense smell. Most restaurants will serve the cheese as a starter, or head to a delicatessen selling island products, such as **Adega A Buraca,** just north of São Roque, to stock up on it (page 233).

- **Specialty Meats:** Meaty specialties like *torresmos de porco* (pork rind), *morcela* (blood sausage), and *linguiça com inhames* (Portuguese sausage with yams) are widely enjoyed and found on most menus. **Tasca O Petisca** in Madalena is a sure bet to try them (page 234).

- **Soups and Stews:** Star mains include *molha de carne à moda do Pico* (a traditional rich meat stew), *caldo de peixe* (fish broth), and octopus and squid stewed in wine. To sample these traditional dishes, head to upmarket **Magma Restaurant** in São Roque do Pico (page 235).

## Tapas

### ★ TASCA O PETISCA

*Avenida Padre Nunes da Rosa; tel. 292 622 357; www. facebook.com/tascapetisca; Mon.-Sat. 10am-3pm and 6:30pm-midnight; €15*

Specializing in traditional regional tapas, or snack dishes (*petiscos*), O Petisca was the first restaurant of its kind on the island. Seafood, island beef, local breads, and homemade desserts are among the specialties at this busy and popular eatery.

### TABERNA DO CANAL

*Avenida Padre Nunes Da Rosa; tel. 918 409 397; www.facebook.com/Taberna-do-Canal; Mon.-Sat. noon-3pm and 7pm-9pm; €15*

This is a beautiful tapas bar and restaurant, whose cozy, authentic interior has wooden benches, exposed stone walls, and traditional clay crockery. Specialties include local beef, tuna steaks, limpets, and island honey cake.

### ★ CELLA BAR

*Rua Da Barca; tel. 292 623 654; www.cellabar.pt; Mon.-Fri. 4pm-midnight, Sat.-Sun. noon-late; €20*

Housed within a futuristic-looking, award-winning wooden building attached to a traditional stone house, this bar is unique not only for its striking architecture, but also for its magnificent beachside setting and views. Seafood soup, pork ribs, and tuna steaks all feature on the menu. It's also a great place for some delectable tapas and a sunset cocktail.

## International

### ATMOSFERA

*Rua dos Biscoitos 34; tel. 914 232 760; www. almadopico.com; Wed.-Mon. 7:30pm-9pm; €25*

Atmosfera is an upscale Italian-Mediterranean fusion restaurant. It is a little way out of town (a 4-minute drive east), but it is a perfect place for a romantic meal, as the views of the island's sunsets are something else. It's located within the Alma do Pico nature residence resort.

## Fine Dining
### ANCORADOURO
*Rua João Lima Whitton da Terra, Areia Larga; tel. 292 623 490; Tues.-Sun. noon-3pm and 7pm-10pm; €15*

Smart and polished Ancoradouro is one of Madalena's more upmarket restaurants. It's the place to go for a special occasion, especially if you love fresh fish and seafood. Specialties include cataplana, seafood rice, crab claws, and grilled octopus. For an extra-romantic experience, ask for a table outside on the terrace to enjoy those sunset sea views.

# SÃO ROQUE DO PICO
## Seafood
### ★ MAGMA RESTAURANT
*Travessa do Outeiro das Eiras 2A; tel. 292 241 200; www.facebook.com/Magma.Restaurant.Bar; daily 12:30pm-10pm; €20*

Excellent seafood cuisine with European and regional influences is served at this smart little seaside restaurant. Slightly pricier than the island average, this is the place to go for a special fine-dining experience.

# LAJES DO PICO
## Traditional Portuguese
### PONTA DA ILHA
*Caminho de Baixo; tel. 292 666 708; www.facebook.com/restaurantepontailha; Thurs.-Tues. noon-2:30pm and 6:30pm-9:30pm; €15*

An elegant restaurant located in a traditional stone house on the tip of the island, this is the place to go to try typical dishes like limpets and caramel fig cake. It's known for being among the best seafood eateries on the island.

# Bars and Nightlife

# MADALENA
## CAFÉ CONCERTO
*Caminho do Rosario, 46; tel. 292 623 842; www.facebook.com/BarCafeConcerto; Tues.-Fri. 3pm-2am; Sat. noon-2am; Sun. noon-midnight*

If you fancy a spot of live music while in the middle of the Atlantic, then pop into cool Café Concerto in Madalena. Featuring regular live music sessions and themed events, it's a trendy, arty bar with friendly service—a reflection of Pico's younger side.

# SÃO ROQUE DO PICO
## DISCOTECA SKIPPER
*Zona Industrial de São Roque Nariz de Ferro; tel. 924 195 384; www.facebook.com/discotecaskipper; Sun. 1am-6am*

One of Pico's livelier nightspots, Skipper Disco features live events on weekends. Pico's oldest and most emblematic nightclub, every Saturday night (well, early hours of Sunday morning) usually welcomes a guest DJ, with sporadic seasonal events staged throughout the year.

# Accommodations

Pico has a varied range of quality accommodation, including nice sea-view hotels, quaint B&Bs, woodland cabins, and traditional stone cottages. **Madalena** is probably the best base to stay on the island due to its proximity to the airport and ferry to Horta on neighboring Faial, and it's also Pico's main town.

## MADALENA
### Under €100
### ★ VILA BARCA

*Caminho da Barca; tel. 915 457 152; https://vilabarca. com; €85*

Resembling an elegant boathouse, Vila Barca stylishly blends the old with the new. Comprising five apartments and four rooms, the aparthotel is a 15-minute walk to the center of Madalena. With mountain or sea views from all rooms, which are equipped with mod cons, there is also a natural swimming pool a short stroll away.

### HOTEL CARAVELAS

*Rua Conselheiro Terra Pinheiro 3; tel. 292 628 550; www.hotelcaravelas.com.pt; €90 d*

Though it may be a bit plain, Hotel Caravelas makes up for this in vistas. Surrounded by the ocean and boasting stunning views over Faial island, pleasant and simple Hotel Caravelas has big, air-conditioned rooms with beachy décor and either sea or mountain views. There's also an outdoor pool and free parking, and the hotel is conveniently located near Madalena harbor.

### ★ ALMA DO PICO

*Rua dos Biscoitos 34; tel. 914 232 760; www. almadopico.com; two-person bungalow €95*

Alma do Pico is an enchanting and serene place to stay while visiting Pico. Set in a hectare (2 acres) of stunning woodland, it is a 5-minute drive (€5 taxi ride) from Madalena harbor. Alma do Pico's décor takes inspiration from nature, with cozy accommodation in refined wooden houses.

### €100-200
### ★ POCINHO BAY HOTEL

*Pocinho; tel. 292 629 135; www.pocinhobay.com; €215*

Situated in the heart of the UNESCO-classified Landscape of the Pico Island Vineyard Culture, Pocinho Bay is a relaxing refuge, a peaceful, unassumingly elegant accommodation where old meets new. The traditional stone structure and wood beam ceilings lend a rustic-chic air, while luxurious little touches like down comforters and pillows and satellite television make your stay cozy and comfortable.

## SÃO ROQUE DO PICO
### €100-200
### ALDEIA DAS ADEGAS

*Rua das Adegas, s/n; tel. 292 642 000; www. aldeiadasadegas.com; €120*

Why not make your stay on Pico extra memorable by overnighting in one of the traditional little stone cottages that make up the Aldeia das Adegas village? Comprising 10 cottages, this rural resort blends authentic Pico architecture with modern interior design. It's located between the coast and the mountain, 1.5 kilometers (1 mi) from the center of São Roque.

# Information and Services

Pico has good facilities and amenities. It has a decent primary health care network with well-equipped public health units in larger towns (including Madalena and São Roque), pharmacies in most towns and villages, and an acute medical emergency response service (INEM; tel. 112) that covers the island. As on all smaller islands, emergency and critical health cases will be transferred to hospitals on bigger islands, namely São Miguel, which has the archipelago's main hospital, or back to the mainland if necessary for specialist treatment.

There are **ATMs** available across the island (you'll always find one on main streets in towns, or at the likes of port or airport terminals).

## MADALENA

- **Tourist Office:** Rua Dona Maria da Glória Duarte - Gare Marítimo da Madalena; tel. 292 623 524; www.visitazores.travel; Mon.-Fri. 10am-6pm, or by appointment

- **PSP Police:** Engenheiro Álvaro de Freitas, s/n; tel. 292 622 860; www.psp.pt
- **Madalena Health Center:** Praça Dr. Caetano Mendonça, Alto da Cruz; tel. 292 628 800
- **Pharmacy:** Avenida Machado Serpa, 1; tel. 292 622 159

## SÃO ROQUE DO PICO

- **São Roque do Pico Health Center:** Avenida António Simas Costa; tel. 292 648 070
- **Pharmacy:** Cais do Pico (Docks); tel. 292 642 3644

## LAJES DO PICO

- **Lajes Health Center:** Largo Vigário Gonçalo De Lemos; tel. 292 679 400
- **Pharmacy:** Estrada Regional, 1/2 Piedade; tel. 292 666 733

# Faial and the Western Islands

## Unspoiled and unique, Faial is a natural gem

bursting with character and charm. The lively little island has a bit of a reputation for being *the* meeting place for Atlantic-crossing sailors and is home to renowned volcanic attractions such as Faial Caldera, its gaping centerpiece, and the extraordinary Capelinhos Volcano.

Known as the Blue Island due to the sheer quantity of bright blue hydrangeas that literally cover the island in summer along endless hedgerows, Faial forms one third of the Azores "triangle," along with São Jorge and Pico. It is closest to Pico, separated by an 8-kilometer (5-mi) strait, with stunning views over its neighbor from almost every angle. It's a local joke that you'll find Mount Pico peeping over your shoulder in every photo you take on Faial.

# Highlights

Look for ★ to find recommended sights, activities, dining, and lodging.

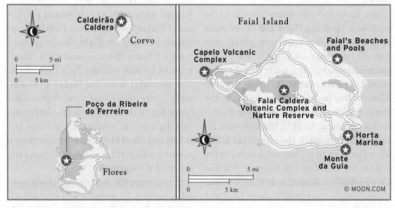

★ **Horta Marina:** This colorful marina, world-famous among sailors, is a great place to absorb the seafaring nature of the town, with the Jetty Murals and legendary Peter Café Sport bar right on the water (page 248).

★ **Monte da Guia:** This action-packed peninsula off Horta, formed by an undersea volcano, boasts some of the best views on the island, as well as a museum and aquarium (page 250).

★ **Faial Caldera Volcanic Complex and Nature Reserve:** The giant, green bowl of this monumental caldera and the gorgeous, untouched scenery around it will keep your gaze occupied for hours (page 254).

★ **Capelo Volcanic Complex:** Discover a lunar desert-like landscape molded from a not-so-long-ago volcanic eruption (page 255).

★ **Faial's Beaches and Pools:** From the many soft black-sand beaches that border the edges of the island to the Porto do Comprido Natural Pool—one of the most attractive tidal pools in the archipelago—Faial is a swimmer's paradise (page 257).

★ **Poço da Ribeira do Ferreiro:** Surround yourself with uncountable shades of green at this enchanted beauty spot on Flores, a secluded lagoon fed by myriad waterfalls (page 274).

★ **Caldeirão Caldera:** This massive crater, filled with two lakes and green pastures, dominates the tiny island of Corvo (page 280).

An obligatory port of call for transatlantic yachters, the island's picturesque main town, Horta, is a jumble of colorful buildings piled on hills that encase the waterfront, where every year thousands of bobbing yachts enjoy a well-earned rest in the local marina. It played an important role in the history of transatlantic sailing and was once the most important port in the archipelago. The ultimate sailors' haven, cosmopolitan Faial has a natural cheer about it. From Cabeço Gordo, the island's highest point, to the sandy beaches and attractive tidal pools that skirt it, Faial's slopes are a symphony of contrasting landscapes, recreation, and tranquility. Perhaps one of the prettiest islands in the Azores, Faial has, until recently, been something of a well-kept secret among savvy sailors.

Just under 250 kilometers (150 mi) to the northwest, far-flung Flores and Corvo make up the archipelago's western group—the Azores' two remotest, and Europe's westernmost, islands. Until fairly recently, they existed in relative isolation, out in the deep Atlantic, like lands that time forgot. Petite Flores and even smaller Corvo were discovered sometime circa 1452, through were inhabited decades apart: Flores from the 1480s, while Corvo's first settlers only arrived in the mid- to late 16th century. History has it that Corvo's first inhabitants were Cape Verdean slaves, sent to the island to farm land and cattle.

Both Flores and Corvo boast riveting, unspoiled beauty and a simplicity that few reachable European destinations can offer today. Flores, known as the Pink Island due to its flower-laden scenery, is a mystical island of tumbling waterfalls, languid lakes, and soaring green-coated cliffs. Corvo, contrarily, is known as the Black Island. Despite being the Azores' smallest island, it boasts remarkable volcanic landmarks, the centerpiece being its curvaceous Caldeirão Caldera, an amphitheater designed by Mother Nature herself. Both islands have small airfields and ports, vital transport links to the rest of the archipelago for these isolated destinations.

## GETTING TO FAIAL

Fly direct to Faial from Lisbon, or take an interisland flight from São Miguel or Terceira. Faial is also well connected by ferry to the other two "triangle" islands, Pico and São Jorge. It's possible to take the ferry to Faial from São Miguel in the summer, but the rough Atlantic makes this crossing long and unreliable.

### Air
#### HORTA AIRPORT
*Castelo Branco, Horta; tel. 292 943 511; www.aeroportohorta.pt*

**Azores Airlines** (SATA; www.sata.pt) runs direct flights from **Lisbon** to Horta Airport (HOR) in Faial; the flight time is approximately 2 hours (from around €200 roundtrip). SATA also operates daily flights from **São Miguel** (1 hour) and **Terceira** (40 minutes). There are around three flights a day (some direct) from São Miguel to Horta; nonstop flight time is 50 minutes, and round-trip tickets cost about €150. From Terceira there is at least one direct flight a day, with round-trip tickets in the region of €135.

A taxi from the airport into Horta town takes around 10 minutes will cost €10-15. Taxis can be found outside the arrivals terminal, or contact Taxi – Horta Açores (tel. 925 863 592). Buses run past the airport four times a day (7:40am, 8:30am, 1:15pm, and 4pm) and take 15 minutes to get into Horta. One-way fares are around €1.50. There is just one bus on Saturdays (8.30am), and none on Sundays or bank holidays. The buses stop on the main ER regional road, 150 meters (500 ft) from the terminal. By rental car, from the airport to Horta it's about 9 kilometers (6 mi), heading east along the EN1-1A and EN2-2A roads.

---

**Previous:** Faial landscape; Horta Marina; Monte da Guia.

## Ferry

### HORTA PORT TERMINAL
### PASSENGER FERRY

*Avenida 25 de Abril; tel. 292 292 132; https://portosdosacores.pt*

Faial, part of the central group's "triangle" of islands—which also including São Jorge and Pico—benefits from year-round ferries between the three, especially from Pico, its closest neighbor. All connections are operated by Azores ferry company **Atlanticoline** (tel. 707 201 572; www.atlanticoline.pt/en). Horta's ferry terminal is a pleasant 15-minute walk along the waterfront from the town center.

From **Pico,** ferries leave from both **São Roque do Pico** (Gare Marítima de São Roque; tel. 292 642 482; www.atlanticoline. pt) and **Madalena** (Rua dona Maria da Glória Duarte; tel. 292 623 340; www.atlanticoline. pt), arriving in Horta, a total of about 46 times a week. The São Roque do Pico ferry sails twice a week; the journey takes about 1 hour 20 minutes, and tickets cost €10-15. The Madalena to Horta ferry is much more frequent, sailing daily and around every four hours. The journey takes 30 minutes and one-way fares are around €5.

There is currently only one route between **São Jorge** and Faial, between **Velas** (Cais Velas; tel. 295 412 047) and Horta, a journey of about 1 hour 40 minutes, about €20 one-way.

There are also seasonal (May-Sept.) ferry routes to Horta on Faial from **Ponta Delgada** on **São Miguel** (Portas do Mar; tel. 296 629 424; open 24/7), stopping at all the other central islands (Terceira, Graciosa, Pico, and São Miguel) en route. The ferry from São Miguel to Faial takes in the region of 14-16 hours and costs around €150 one-way

## GETTING AROUND FAIAL

As with all the Azores, a **rental car** is the best way to explore here, although on smaller islands like Faial, **rented scooters** are also a good option. One of the best routes on the island to see the dazzling blue hydrangeas that give Faial its nickname, the Blue Island, is the road from **Ribeirinha** parish (north of Horta) west, toward the Caldera, to **Cabouco** parish.

## Rental Car

Faial is easily covered by car. Renting a car is a good value for your money, and gives visitors the ability to explore the island at leisure and to reach inland areas not served by public transport. You can drive the full circle around the island in approximately 2 hours via the 54-kilometer (34-mi) ring road, the **EN1-1A,** that encircles the island. Faial's roads are light in traffic and well-surfaced, and the scenery as you drive around the island is as inspiring as the sights themselves, with breathtaking views around every bend, though some of the roads are steep.

There are a number of car rental companies operating on Faial, either from the airport, or in Horta harbor or town center. Companies including **Ilha Verde Rent a Car** (tel. 292 392 786; www.ilhaverde.com/pt) and **Europcar** (tel. 918 611 766; www.europcar.pt) can be found on Horta waterfront and at the airport, or try a local company, like **Auto Turística Faialense** (Rua Conselheiro Medeiros 12; tel. 292 292 308; www.autoturisticafaialense. com).

## Bus

Public transport is limited on Faial. **Farias** (tel. 292 292 482; www.farias.pt) operates services mostly covering the area in and around **Horta,** as well as to main towns along the coast such as **Capelo** and **Almoxarife Beach,** but only two or three services a day. There's a regular-ish bus service between the airport and the Avenida. Buses run past the airport four times a day (7:40am, 8:30am, 1:15pm, and 4pm) and take 15 minutes to get into Horta. One-way fares are around €1.50. There is just one bus on Saturdays (8:30am), and none on Sundays or bank holidays. The buses stop on the main ER regional road, 150 meters (500 ft) from the terminal There are no bus services inland.

In Horta, buses leave from along the main

# Faial

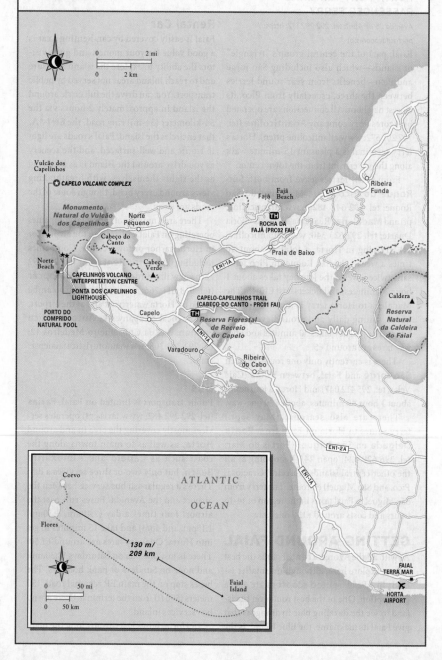

Vulcão dos Capelinhos

CAPELO VOLCANIC COMPLEX

Monumento Natural do Vulcão dos Capelinhos

Norte Pequeno

Fajã

Fajã Beach

ROCHA DA FAJÃ (PRC02 FAI)

Cabeço do Canto

Praia de Baixo

Norte Beach

CAPELINHOS VOLCANO INTERPRETATION CENTRE

Cabeço Verde

PONTA DOS CAPELINHOS LIGHTHOUSE

PORTO DO COMPRIDO NATURAL POOL

Capelo

CAPELO-CAPELINHOS TRAIL (CABEÇO DO CANTO - PRC01 FAI)

Reserva Florestal de Recreio do Capelo

Ribeira Funda

EN1-1A

EN1-1A

Caldera

Reserva Natural da Caldeira do Faial

Varadouro

Ribeira do Cabo

EN1-2A

EN1-1A

FAIAL TERRA MAR

HORTA AIRPORT

Corvo

Flores

ATLANTIC OCEAN

130 m / 209 km

Faial Island

0     50 mi

0     50 km

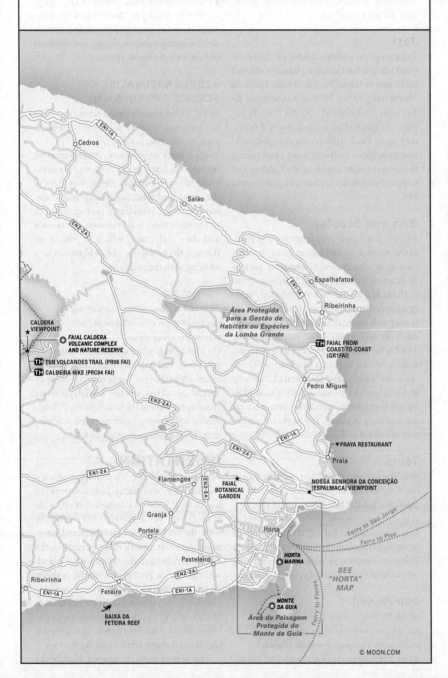

© MOON.COM

waterfront avenue, **Avenida 25 de Abril,** near the ferry terminal.

## Taxi

Taxis are not as widely available on Faial as on other islands, but there are a handful of small taxi firms in Horta, such as **Rádio Táxis da Horta** (tel. 292 391 500) or **Associação de Taxistas do Faial** (tel. 292 391 300). In addition to quick trips around Horta if necessary, given Faial's diminutive size, you could also consider a half-day **taxi tour** taking in the main sights, such as the Caldera and Capelinhos Volcano. This will cost around €55.

## Bike and Scooter

Scooters are a great way to get around Faial, as the roads are quiet and in good shape. A number of scooter rental companies, such as **JP Scooter Rental** (Yellow Scooter, in front of Horta Marina; tel. 965 516 252; daily 9am-7pm) operate in Horta, and renting a scooter is easy and affordable, from €25 a day. The roads are decent, quiet, and easy to navigate. The higher elevation areas can be blustery, misty, and cool, so pack a windbreaker. Given the size of Faial island (21.2 km/13.2 mi long and 16.2 km/10.1 mi wide), getting around by bicycle is an option, even if the terrain is rugged and steep in places. The roads are of a decent condition and quiet.

## Tours

Skip the car rental and fast track to Faial's main sights with an organized tour to its attractions. See the best of the island comfortably and conveniently. There are a number of tour companies on Faial that run excursions to top sights such as the Caldeira and Capelo Volcanic Complex, picking and dropping off guests at their places of accommodation..

### OUR ISLAND

*tel. 967 172 754; https://ourisland-azores.com; half-day van tour from €65 per person (based on 2 people; prices vary according to size of group )*

Enjoy a private tour of Faial with Our Island,

a local company with extensive knowledge on all of Faial's sights. Day and half-day tours range from city tours and descending the caldera, to cooking classes, hiking, and van tours of Faial's most icnonic spots.

### AZORES NATURALIST - SCIENCE AND TOURISM

*tel. 967 172 754; https://ourisland-azores.com; half-day van tour from €50 per person (1-5 people; prices vary according to size of group)*

Horta-based tour company Azores Naturalist operates land and sea excursions. These include full- and half-day jeep or van tours of the island, bird-watching, hiking, and whale-watching trips. Working in partnership with universities, there is also an onus on research and data collection, which is passed on through the biologists and field researchers working with the company.

### TRILHOS R

*tel. 961 617 201; www.trilhosr.com; half-day van tour from €50 per person (2-5 people; prices vary according to size of group)*

On foot or four wheels, Trilhos R have some great full- and half-day excursions of Faial island. Whether you want to walk down or around the caldera, or enjoy a full day of being chauffeured around the island, seeing its landmarks, and enjoying lunch in a typical restaurant, Trilhos R has an option to suit.

## ORIENTATION

Faial sort of resembles a pentagon, albeit a crooked one, measuring 21 kilometers (13 mi) in length and 14 kilometers (9 mi) wide at its fattest. A 54-kilometer (34-mi) ring road, the **EN1-1A,** encircles the island, hemming the coast. Faial's main attraction, the **Caldera,** is bang in the middle of the island, while the main port town, **Horta,** is down on the southeast end, facing Pico. Some 8 kilometers (5 mi) of water separate Horta from Madalena on Pico, the shortest distance between any two Azores islands, and there are regular and cheap ferries linking the two.

The almost crescent-shaped **Monte da**

Guia protrudes south from Horta, with **Porto Pim Bay** to the west and **Horta Marina** to the east. The island's other main attraction, the **Capelinhos Volcano,** in the **Capelo Volcanic Complex,** is on the opposite side of the island from Horta.

Far (250 km/150 mi) to the northwest of Faial, **Flores** and **Corvo** form the Azores' western group of islands. They're about a 45-minute flight from Faial, also accessible by plane from São Miguel (1 hour 20 minutes) and Terceira (1 hour).

## PLANNING YOUR TIME

You can see most of Faial's main attractions in a day, so you could technically visit it as a **day trip** from **Pico** or **São Jorge** (more practicable from Pico, which is only 30 minutes away by ferry with several departures a day). But it's worth staying a night or two to spread the sights out, relax on Faial's unusual number of soft, sandy **beaches** or in one of its many **tidal pools,** and enjoy a sundowner in the legendary **Peter Café Sport Bar,** soaking up the atmosphere of a genuine sailors' town.

Make lively **Horta,** the island's main point of entry, your base, and enjoy a night in the vibrant town, with Mount Pico on neighboring Pico island as a backdrop. Most of Horta's sights are centered on the waterfront; drawing a line diagonally northwest from Horta (which is on the southeast tip of the island), the **Caldera** is in the middle, and the **Capelinhos Volcano** is on the island's westernmost tip. If nothing else, the **Caldera** and **Capelinhos** should be must-sees for any trip to Faial.

Navigating the island is easy. Like many of the other islands, Faial has one main coastal ring road running around its edge—the **EN1-1A**—and a road running horizontally across the lower flank, the **EN1-2A,** connecting the east coast to the west.

If you make the trip out to the western islands, plan to spend one or two nights, as each of them can be seen in a day. On Flores, spend one day taking in the island's main **Santa Cruz das Flores** town and the **Poço da Ribeira do Ferreiro** pool, surrounded by waterfalls; spend the night here, as accommodations on Corvo are limited. Early the next morning, take the **ferry** or **RIB boat** to **Vila do Corvo,** Corvo's main town, and spend the day there. Make sure to visit the massive **Caldeirão Caldera;** for around €5 one-way, you can take a **shuttle bus** there from the Vila do Corvo jetty. Be aware that **June** is a foggy month on these islands, which could hamper travel and sightseeing plans. **July and August** are the best times to visit Flores and Corvo, when the weather is sunniest; in **April, May, or September,** the weather is still fine, but cooler than summer.

You don't really need to worry about renting a car on Corvo as the island is tiny enough to explore **on foot** and there is regular transport to its main attraction, the Caldeirão, if you don't want to walk. A **rental car** is recommended to freely explore Flores, which has just one main coastal road, the **ER1-2,** and a handful of secondary roads, and the scenery is breathtaking.

# Itinerary Ideas

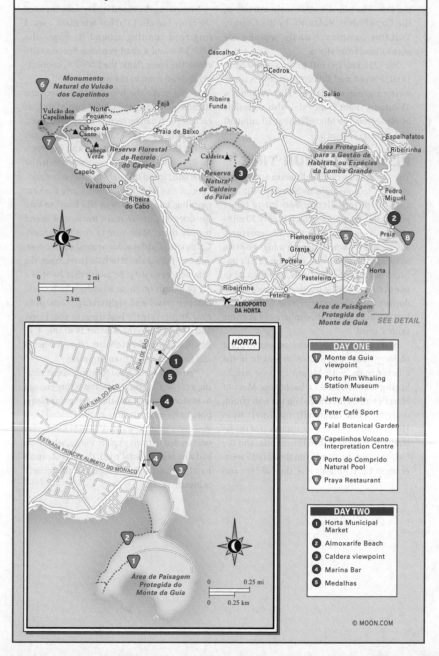

**HORTA**

## DAY ONE

1. Monte da Guia viewpoint
2. Porto Pim Whaling Station Museum
3. Jetty Murals
4. Peter Café Sport
5. Faial Botanical Garden
6. Capelinhos Volcano Interpretation Centre
7. Porto do Comprido Natural Pool
8. Praya Restaurant

## DAY TWO

1. Horta Municipal Market
2. Almoxarife Beach
3. Caldera viewpoint
4. Marina Bar
5. Medalhas

© MOON.COM

# Itinerary Ideas

## TWO DAYS ON FAIAL

Make sure to pack your swimsuit and some comfortable hiking shoes for these two active days.

### Day One

**1** From central Horta, take a pleasant 45-minute walk to Monte da Guia, the volcanic outcrop overlooking the town. Spend the first part of the morning here exploring its sights, making sure to get a picture from the **Monte da Guia viewpoint.**

**2** Make your way back down Monte da Guia to visit the **Porto Pim Whaling Station Museum** at the foot of the hill.

**3** With a newfound understanding of the whaling industry on Faial, walk back to Horta town center along the beautiful crescent moon beach of Porto Pim Bay. Make your way to the marina to see the colorful **Jetty Murals.**

**4** Stop here for lunch, taking in the swashbuckling stories of transatlantic sailors at the famous **Peter Café Sport.**

**5** After lunch, jump in your rental car (or on your scooter) and make the short 7-minute drive north to the beautiful **Faial Botanical Garden.**

**6** Head west along the EN1-2A road, which will eventually join the EN1-1A, taking you to the **Capelinhos Volcano Interpretation Centre** after about 40 minutes. Spend a couple of hours exploring the eerily desolate volcanic complex surrounding the center.

**7** Follow this with a dip in the nearby **Porto do Comprido Natural Pool,** just a minute farther down the road toward the coast in your car.

**8** Head back to the island's southeast coast for dinner at the stunning **Praya Restaurant.**

### Day Two

**1** Start your morning with a trip to the **Horta Municipal Market** to grab some fresh produce for a picnic lunch.

**2** Head 10 minutes north on the EN1-1A road in your rental car to **Almoxarife Beach** to spend an hour or so having a leisurely walk or swim.

**3** Jump back in the car, driving 25 minutes inland via the EN1-2A and the EN2-2A toward the Faial Caldera crater. From the **Caldera viewpoint,** enjoy the Caldeira hike (PRC04 FAI) around the crater's rim, taking in the astounding scenery, like a big open bowl. The hike should take about 2.5 hours; find the best spot to enjoy your alfresco lunch.

**4** Take a detour on your way back to Horta, via a scenic drive along the island's north coast, following the EN1-1A ring road. Once back in town, make your way to the marina for a sundowner at the **Marina Bar.**

**5** Round off your stay with the traditional flavors of the island with a hearty dinner at the tavern-esque **Medalhas** restaurant.

# Sights

## HORTA

Set out over a vast sweeping bay, Horta is the Azores' seafaring capital, and has been a regular meeting point for transatlantic sailors and a legendary port of call for vessels over many centuries. The charming town is dominated by two imposing churches that tower over the whitewashed townhouses and red roofs flanking them, which step up the hillside from the lovely marina—the first in the Azores. The colorful marina area is an attractive and friendly place to walk around. South of the main town is the claw-like **Monte da Guia promontory,** whose western flank forms the pretty **Porto Pim Bay,** an area steeped in whaling heritage. Horta has a genteel and cosmopolitan vibe, which enhances its reputation as an eclectic and obligatory port of call. Its rich architecture with hints of colonial and art deco styles nods to the island's heyday days as a prosperous and international island, particularly as it developed in the 19th and 20th centuries.

TOP EXPERIENCE

### ★ Horta Marina

*Cais de Santa Cruz; tel. 292 391 693; http://turismo.cmhorta.pt/index.php/pt/oquevisitar/marina-da-horta; open 24/7*

For centuries, the colorful little town has been a mid-ocean meeting point for transatlantic sailors, a hub of enthralling seafaring tales recounted over a beer by the hundreds of yachters who pass through every year. The modern marina is an extension of Horta harbor and Horta Bay, which protects it and makes it one of the safest in the archipelago. Overlooked by a colorful town of charming buildings piled haphazardly above the waterfront, Horta Marina is among the top five most-visited ports in the world and is also one of the most charismatic, a legendary Atlantic port of call.

Horta port really boomed in the 17th century, when Faial's reputation as a secure and strategic harbor saw international trade bloom, especially for produce being exported from neighboring islands. Consequently, the island prospered. In the 19th century it also harbored whaling ships crossing the Atlantic. Horta was the chosen landing point for the first transatlantic crossing by seaplane, and soon after 1933 it became a regular stopover for the Pan Am clipper flights traveling between America and Europe, swiftly followed by a series of European airlines. The area further provided prime conditions for intercontinental submarine cable stations, which saw Horta become one of the most important cable centers in the world. It also played a key role as a naval base throughout the two world wars.

Its **Jetty Murals,** colorful pictures that visiting sailors leave along the marina walls and pavement, are famous. Horta Marina is also where keen sailors will find the iconic **Peter Café Sport Bar,** the ultimate mariners haunt in the historic heart of Horta. It hosts several international sailing regattas every year. With stunning views of Mount Pico, which proudly stands guard over its eponymous island across the way, Horta Marina has a unique charm and a great atmosphere.

### JETTY MURALS

*Horta Marina; open 24/7*

The colorful Horta Marina Jetty Murals are fascinating to observe, each telling a story or conveying a message from the hundreds of international sailors who pass through every year. It has become something of a tradition for visiting sailors to paint a mural before departing, and paints are sold in local stores for the purpose. You could spend ages just musing the lively images from crews from all over the globe, which brings home how remote—but at the same time how central—Horta is to the

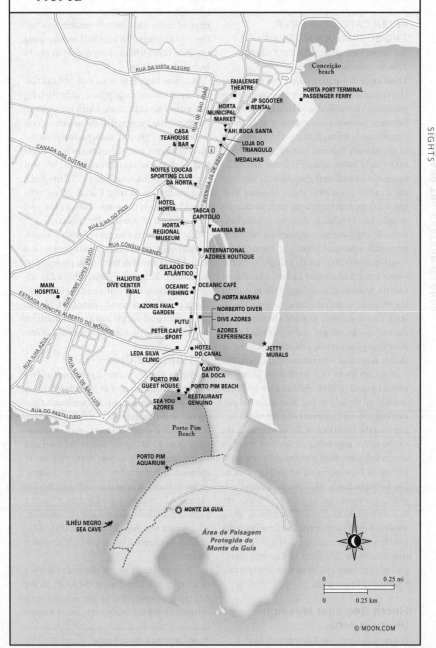

# Horta

RUA DA VISTA ALEGRE

Conceição beach

FAIALENSE THEATRE

JP SCOOTER RENTAL

HORTA PORT TERMINAL PASSENGER FERRY

HORTA MUNICIPAL MARKET

RUA DE SÃO JOÃO

CASA TEAHOUSE & BAR

AH! BOCA SANTA

CANADA DAS DUTRAS

LOJA DO TRIANGULO

MEDALHAS

NOITES LOUCAS SPORTING CLUB DA HORTA

AVENIDA 26 DE ABRIL

HOTEL HORTA

TASCA O CAPITOLIO

RUA ILHA DO PICO

HORTA REGIONAL MUSEUM

MARINA BAR

RUA CÔNSUL DABNEY

INTERNATIONAL AZORES BOUTIQUE

GELADOS DO ATLÂNTICO

HALIOTIS DIVE CENTER FAIAL

OCEANIC CAFÉ

MAIN HOSPITAL

OCEANIC FISHING

RUA JAIME LOPES (EEIJO)

ESTRADA PRÍNCIPE ALBERTO DO MÓNACO

HORTA MARINA

AZORIS FAIAL GARDEN

NORBERTO DIVER

PUTU

DIVE AZORES

PETER CAFÉ SPORT

AZORES EXPERIENCES

RUA ILHA AZUL

LEDA SILVA CLINIC

HOTEL DO CANAL

JETTY MURALS

RUA ILHA DE SÃO LUIS

CANTO DA DOCA

PORTO PIM GUEST HOUSE

PORTO PIM BEACH

RUA DO PASTELEIRO

SEA YOU AZORES

RESTAURANT GENUÍNO

Porto Pim Beach

PORTO PIM AQUARIUM

MONTE DA GUIA

ILHÉU NEGRO SEA CAVE

Área de Paisagem Protegida do Monte da Guia

0        0.25 mi

0        0.25 km

© MOON.COM

world. It's a fun and enjoyable way to spend a half hour, admiring fellow travelers' creativity.

## PETER CAFÉ SPORT BAR AND SCRIMSHAW MUSEUM

*Rua Tenente Valadim; tel. 292 292 327; Mon.-Sat. 10am-noon and 2pm-4pm; €2.50*

There's a saying among sailors that if you visit Horta and don't visit Peter Café Sport then you haven't actually visited Horta. This establishment has become something of an institution among transatlantic yachters and part of the island's cultural history. It dates back to the early 1900s, when the venue originally opened as a handicraft shop, later incorporating a bar to quench the thirst of weary sailors. Its fame and popularity grew decade on decade, and eventually three more establishments by the same name opened on mainland Portugal in Oeiras, Lisbon, and Porto. At the flagship Horta bar, locals mingle with the steady stream of visiting sailors, a beacon of a warm, friendly atmosphere in the middle of the Atlantic, and a mandatory stop on the island. It's a lively place to enjoy a beer or one of the bar's renowned gin and tonics and banter after many days at sea, and every inch inside the bar is covered with nautical paraphernalia.

It is also home to a Scrimshaw Museum, which opened in 1986 and has what is widely considered the largest and most beautiful private collection of scrimshaw in the world, occupying the first floor of the bar. Scrimshaw, or the art of engraving on bone or ivory, is commonly associated with the elaborate carvings done by whalers on whale byproducts, like bones or teeth. This unique form of artwork, also known as "whaling art," is thought to date back to the late 18th century, when whalers would carve intricate pictures on the readily available carcass castoffs to fill their free time at sea. Excellent and unique examples of scrimshaw can be seen on Horta at this fantastic little museum.

## Horta Regional Museum (Museu da Horta)

*Palacio do Colegio, Largo Duque de Avila Bolama;*

*tel. 292 392 784; www.museu-horta.azores.gov.pt; Tues.-Sun. 10am-5:30pm Apr. 1-Sept. 30, Tues.-Sun. 9:30am-5pm Oct. 1-Mar. 31; €2*

Housed in the 18th-century building of a former Jesuit college, this cute little archeological museum offers a fascinating insight to Faial's history and culture.

A major highlight is an exceptional collection of intricate sculptures made from fig tree pith. This collection, which is unique in the world, has been part of the museum's collection since 1980 and mainly features exquisitely elaborate miniature houses and vessels that portray the evolution of local life and navigation throughout history. All the items were made by local artist Euclides Rosa, who started work on the models circa 1936 and took a decade to complete the collection.

The museum is also packed with a wealth of other collections spanning a chronological period from the 16th century to present day, including ethnography (objects linked to ancient and traditional crafts and the history of Horta port), religious art, visual art, photographic documents, printed and handwritten documents, and specimens of natural history.

## ★ Monte da Guia

Monte da Guia is an amalgamation of two volcanoes (one formed at sea, the other on land), which form a sort of peninsula connected to the mainland by a sandy isthmus. A short stroll south of Horta center, the outcrop forms a claw on the foot of the town and affords amazing views over Porto Pim Bay to the west, and Horta Bay and Horta's historic center to the east, as well as over neighboring islands. A little chapel, the **Chapel of Nossa Senhora da Guia,** patron saint of fishermen, after whom the mount takes its name, is located on the summit of the hill and dominates the landscape.

The town-facing side of Monte da Guia is a relatively gentle slope, while the south-facing side is bay-shaped. Part of this side has been battered by the ocean, forming inlets known

---

**1:** view of Horta **2:** Horta Marina

1

2

as the Caldeira do Inferno (Caldera of Hell) or Baía das Caldeirinhas (Bay of Little Calderas). A number of little buildings linked to whaling, such as *vigias* (lookouts) and old processing factories, can still be seen flanking the mount. To reach the top of the hills, just follow a **path** that leads from the mouth of Horta port.

Learn more about Horta and Faial's whaling industry and see its heritage by following a themed guided walk, the **Monte da Guia Whaling Route** (tel. 292 292 140; geral@ oma.pt, http://oma.centrosciencia.azores. gov.pt/actividade/percurso-tem%C3%A1tico- roteiro-baleeiro-do-monte-da-guia). The pedestrian trail tours attractions including Porto Pim Bay and its aquarium, and the Porto Pim Whaling Station Museum. It starts at the Monte da Guia *vigia* lookout. Organized by the **Azores Sea Observatory** (http://oma. centrosciencia.azores.gov.pt), the walks take place on Monday and Thursday; the number of participants is limited, and registrations must be made by phone or email up to the day before the walk.

## MONTE DA GUIA VIEWPOINT
*Monte da Guia; open 24/7; free*

It's approximately a 45-minute walk south from Horta town center, past scenic Porto Pim Bay, up to the top of Monte da Guia. It involves a gentle climb, but the views once up at the top are fabulous. You can gaze over Horta, as well as enjoy excellent views to the islands of Pico, São Jorge, and Graciosa, surrounded by infinite sea. On the crest of the hill, next to the Chapel of Nossa Senhora da Guia, are the remnants of a military battery and bunker, as well as support facilities for Horta Airport.

## PORTO PIM WHALING STATION MUSEUM
## (Museu da Baleia)
*Monte da Guia; tel. 292 292 140; www.oma.pt; Mon.-Fri. 10am-5pm Nov. 1-Mar. 31, daily 10am-6pm Apr. 1-Oct. 31; €4*

Located in the southwest part of Porto Pim Bay, on the slope of Monte da Guia, the Porto Pim Whaling Station Museum takes visitors on a tour of the former sperm-whale-processing factory. The museum features several well-staged rooms showcasing old machinery that was used in the oil- and grease-extraction processes, as well as for meat, bones, and blood milling. In another of the rooms is a full 10-meter (30-ft) skeleton of a female sperm whale. Attracting several thousand visitors every year, the Whaling Station Museum is one of the best examples of the extinct Azorean whaling industry and pays testament to the historical, economic, and social importance of this activity in the region, until its complete prohibition in the late 1980s. Following a thorough renovation in 2018, the museum is modern and provides thought-provoking, if at times challenging insights to the different aspects of the whaling tradition.

## PORTO PIM AQUARIUM
## (Aquario do Porto Pim)
*Monte da Guia; tel. 964 971 484; http:// parquesnaturais.azores.gov.pt/pt/faial/oquevisitar/ centros-ambientais/aquario-do-porto-pim- estacao-de-peixes-vivos; Tues.-Sat. 10am-1pm and 1:30pm-5pm; €4*

Dive beneath the surface of the sea at the Porto Pim Aquarium, which, along with the nearby Whaling Station Museum, is a great way to spend a few hours if the weather is inclement. Seize the opportunity to see turtles and other common coastal species of the Azores in the live tanks. An interesting exhibition on the Azores Marine Park and a film about the deep sea surrounding the archipelago can also be enjoyed. This little aquarium is small, more of a conservation/rescue project than a tourist attraction, but staff are delighted to welcome visitors and share their knowledge about the local sea life.

**1:** Jetty Murals **2:** Horta Regional Museum

# The Blue Island: Faial's Hydrangeas

Faial is beautiful any time of year, but it really comes into its own in summer. In **July and August,** the beautiful powder-blue hydrangeas are in full bloom all over the island, creating a visual spectacle from which Faial takes its nickname, the Blue Island. These vibrant blue flowers can be seen along pretty much **every road and pathway** you travel, covering the island in a deep blue hue rivaled only by the Atlantic.

Most if not all of the Azores islands are blanketed with gorgeous hydrangeas in summer, which vary in tonality, from baby blue to vibrant pink and purple. This difference in color is said to arise from the varying levels of minerals and pH acidity in the islands' volcanic terrain. Generally speaking, **acidic soil** results in blue or lavender hydrangeas, while **alkaline soil** yields pinks and reds.

## WHERE TO SEE THEM

Faial's hydrangeas

One of the best spots on the island to see these stunning flowers is along the secondary roads that run inland from the parish of **Ribeirinha** on the east coast to **Cabouco** in the middle of the island. To get to Ribeirinha parish, take the EN1-1A north from Horta, then turn west, inland, before or after the hamlets of Relvinha or Espalhafatos. Most of the smaller roads around the center of the island will offer up a good opportunity to see these stunning explosions of color in full bloom.

Considered a symbol of regional heritage, it is **forbidden to pick the flowers.** They thrive in the island's unique volcanic soil, which is extremely fertile and acidic, making it ideal for the hydrangea. Botanical gardens are also good places to see the hydrangeas.

## Faial Botanical Garden

*Rua de São Lourenço, no. 23; tel. 292 207 360; http://parquesnaturais.azores.gov.pt/en/faial-eng; Tues.-Fri. 10am-5pm Nov. 1-Mar. 31, daily 10am-6pm Apr. 1-Oct. 31; €7.50*

Inaugurated in 1986, Faial Botanical Garden is a bubble of natural beauty on the outskirts of Horta, created to promote the conservation and study of the Azores natural flora. Its main attractions include the Azores Seed Bank, an orchidarium that houses a magnificent orchid collection, and rare, unique, and endemic plant species. About 2.5 kilometers (1.5 mi) from Horta center (mostly an uphill walk, if you want to attempt it by foot), the well-kept gardens are a wonderful place to while away and hour or two.

## ★ FAIAL CALDERA VOLCANIC COMPLEX AND NATURE RESERVE

(Reserva Natural da Caldeira do Faial)

*http://parquesnaturais.azores.gov.pt/pt/faial/oquevisitar/areasprotegidas/reservanatural1/caldeirafaial; open 24/7; free*

Covering 313 hectares (749 acres) in the very middle of Faial island, the Faial Caldera Volcanic Complex and Nature Reserve is a unique and rather special place. One of the last remaining havens for the Azores' natural laurissilva forest, home to many species of rare and endemic flora, the area is practically untouched by human hands. The real showstopper is a monumental caldera whose landscape is truly staggering, like a Hawaiian Grand Canyon. It's an immense geological formation carpeted in varying shades of green fuzz, with soaring sides that encircle the flat crater bottom, creating dramatic and breathtaking—almost prehistoric—scenery.

## Faial Caldera
### (Caldeira do Faial)

*middle of Faial island; open 24/7; free*

The Faial volcanic cone houses a gargantuan 2-kilometer-wide (1-mi-wide), 400-meter-deep (1,300-ft-deep) crater known as the Caldera. Visitors are free to walk the crest of the caldera (around 8 km/5 mi; 3 hours), but descending the steep slopes to the flat bottom, one of the island's top activities, is controlled and permitted only with an official guide. Various outdoor activity companies, such as Our Island (tel. 967 172 754; https://ourisland-azores.com; from €115 pp), organize the popular descents, which usually take around 1.5 hours. Admiring the crater will keep you occupied for ages; the scenery on the outside is ever-changing, while inside the bowl is a kaleidoscope of green, the verdant shades rippling from darker to lighter as the sun plays through the clouds. If you don't have a car, a taxi to the Caldera will cost around €20 each way from Horta. Walking trails start from the parking lot.

## Caldera Viewpoint

*Caldera Volcanic Complex and Nature Reserve*

To enjoy the best views of the Caldera—and one of the finest viewpoints on the entire island—head to the Caldera viewpoint. It's accessed via a short tunnel at the top of the Caldera, which is also the start and finish point of the circular Caldeira Hike around the rim. The experience of seeing the monumental green crater with its towering, craggy sides open up before you as you exit the tunnel is awe-inspiring.

## ★ CAPELO VOLCANIC COMPLEX

*Ponta dos Capelinhos, west coast; open 24/7; free*

The Capelo Volcanic Complex, part of which is formed by the Capelinhos Volcano, is a geographical wonder, given that the complex, a sort of peninsula, is the "newest" piece of land in Portugal. Capelinhos is also the name associated with the cape that extends from Capelo parish, in which it is situated. It was formed relatively recently, in the late 1950s, following a violent underwater eruption.

The submerged Capelinhos Volcano exploded in 1957 and rumbled on for 13 months before going dormant. Spewing white-hot sand, rock, and ashes, along with molten lava, destroyed swathes of the surrounding area, triggering mass evacuations. After streaming into the sea and cooling, the disgorged lava formed a stark, dark volcanic landscape: an isthmus, rugged in some places, smooth-flowing in others, connecting to Faial island. The Capelo Volcanic Complex has an almost Martian feel, which is what makes it such unique attraction. It is also unique because it is the only underwater eruption in history to have been documented from start to finish, projecting the Azores via news reports and scientific magazines around the globe. An adverse effect of the terrifying activity was that up to 2,000 islanders decided to move away, many to the United States, reducing the local Capelo population by half.

This barren moonscape is also home to the old Capelinhos Lighthouse, which was destroyed and partially buried by the eruption, and a modern Interpretation Centre. A purpose-built causeway links the Interpretation Centre and lighthouse to the caldera summit. A number of the island's official hikes, such as the Faial from Coast to Coast (GR1FAI) and Ten Volcanoes Trail (PR06 FAI) pass through or culminate in the Capelo Volcanic Complex, and the popular Porto do Comprido Natural Pool and Norte Beach are also nearby.

## Capelinhos Volcano Interpretation Centre
### (Centro de Interpretaçao do Vulcão dos Capelinhos)

*Farol dos Capelinhos; tel. 292 200 470; http:// parquesnaturais.azores.gov.pt/pt/faial/oquevisitar/*

centros-ambientais/centro-de-interpretacao-
do-vulcao-dos-capelinhos; Tues.-Fri. 10am-5pm,
Sat.-Sun. 2pm-5:30pm; €9

With world-class exhibits and compelling information on the terrifying Capelinhos eruption, the Capelinhos Volcano Interpretation Centre is a fascinating little museum. Videos, photographs, and locally sourced relics pay testament to the astounding phenomenon, whose new lava formations literally changed the shape of Faial and the size of Portugal. The center has been sympathetically created underground so as to not distract or detract from the unique landscape. It provides a richly descriptive insight into the history of the volcanic event and how it affected the local populations. Much of the scientific research that was conducted over the 13-month eruption can also be been here.

## Ponta dos Capelinhos Lighthouse
### (Farol dos Capelinhos)

Having unwillingly become a symbol of the 1957-1958 eruption that shaped a new Faial, the Capelinhos Lighthouse stands waist-deep in what would have been ash and lava. Left to fend for itself as the earth began to shake, the building's lower floor was completely engulfed by the eruption, meaning only its first floor and tower can still be seen. Inaugurated in 1894, the lighthouse was blackened and battered by the yearlong volcanic torment, but despite being half-buried, the surviving structure is surprisingly intact. Visitors can walk to the lighthouse along a futuristic-looking walkway from the Interpretation Centre and climb the 20-meter-high (70-ft-high) tower to get the best views of the movie-like scenery.

## ★ Beaches and Pools

Faial, unusually for Azorean islands, has a number of soft, sandy beaches that range from light beige to the unique black volcanic hue, as well as picturesque tidal pools. This is in part due to the island's most recent volcanic activity, the 1957-1958 eruption at Capelinhos, which saw Faial's coast drenched in ash, adding layers of fine sand to the beaches. The island's most popular beaches are the long blond bay of Porto Pim, the dark Almoxarife Beach, which also has soft sand.

## HORTA
### PORTO PIM BEACH
### (Praia do Porto Pim)

*Porto Pim Bay; open 24/4; free*

A lovely shell-like sweep of a bay with soft, fine sand and calm waters, Porto Pim Bay connects Horta town and the Monte da Guia outcrop. It is a popular bathing site, directly accessed through Horta town, protected by high cliffs and Monte da Guia. A pool of tranquil turquoise sea laps the thin slither of sand, which, despite being skinny, is long and offers plenty of towel space in summer. There are a number of **bars** and **restaurants** in the vicinity to enjoy a sundowner overlooking the beach. It also has excellent public facilities such as restrooms, showers, lifeguards during beach season, and accessibility for disabled people.

### CONCEIÇÃO BEACH
### (Praia da Conceição)

*after the ferry terminal; open 24/7; free*

Just beyond the ferry terminal jetty, on the outskirts of town on the north side of Horta Bay, Conceição Beach is a short-ish but quite thick strip of soft, black sand. It's also sometimes called **Praia da Alagoa.** The waves here on Faial's eastern coast can sometimes be rough. There are free sun loungers and parasols available on the beach, located next to a large park **(Alagoa Park),** where visitors will also find an indoor pool, a picnic area,

1: Capelo Volcanic Complex 2: Ponta dos Capelinhos Lighthouse

1

2

and tennis courts (park free to visit, fees apply to facilities).

## ALMOXARIFE BEACH
## (Praia do Almoxarife)

*Conceição parish, east coast; open 24/7; free*

About 3 kilometers (2 mi) north of Horta on the island's east coast, this stretch of soft, black sand is one of the largest beaches on the island, and very clean. Surrounded by strikingly beautiful, lush landscape, it is also supported by good nearby facilities, including a campsite, a few **beach bars and restaurants** just off the beach, showers and toilets, parking, and lifeguards in summer months. It also has incredible views to Pico island.

## CAPELO VOLCANIC COMPLEX
## NORTE BEACH
## (Praia do Norte)

*north coast, near Capelo; open 24/7; free*

The parish of Praia do Norte, near Capelo, on Faial's north coast, was one of the locales affected by the 1957-1958 eruption. It is home to the only *fajã* (small flat areas at the foot of cliffs, at sea level, formed by lava flows) on the island. Nearby this *fajã* is a large black sand beach at the foot of soaring cliffs. Widely considered one of the most beautiful on the island, Norte Beach and the *fajã* are the main draws to this corner of the island. There are no public facilities.

## FAJÃ BEACH
## (Praia da Fajã)

*just before Norte Beach; open 24/7; free*

This dark black sand beach on the north of the island sits in sharp contrast with the lush greenery that surrounds it. It has a short section of soft sand in the middle, bookended by rocky sections. There are no public facilities on this beach.

## PORTO DO COMPRIDO NATURAL POOL

*near Capelo; open 24/7; free*

Close to the Capelo Volcanic Complex and the charming little village of Capelo, the Porto do Comprido Natural Pool is a large public tidal pool that perfectly encapsulates the natural volcanic beauty of Faial. For a number of years one of the island's most important whaling stations was located nearby, and it was from here that many of the intrepid whale boats set off. The water here is crystal clear and warm and fills the jagged basalt rocks that create the pools. No public facilities are available at the site.

# Kayaking and Stand-Up Paddle Boarding

Some of the best kayaking on the island is possible right off Horta: Seize the opportunity to explore a strait between two Azores islands and take to the **Faial-Pico channel,** gazing at the outstanding natural beauty of Faial on the one side, and majestic Pico and its dominant volcano on the other. Or gracefully paddle around the beautiful **Porto Pim Bay,** exploring rock formations and caves along the bay's coastline.

## SEA YOU AZORES

*Travessa Porto Pim; tel. 913 762 039; https://pt-pt. facebook.com/seayouazores; daily 8am-8pm; from €20*

Join Sea You Azores's qualified instructors and guides for an enjoyable tour of the southern Faial coastline, or rent your own kayak or SUP board to enjoy at leisure. Cave tours, family packs, and lessons are also available.

**1:** Porto Pim Beach **2:** Almoxarife Beach

# Diving and Snorkeling

Immerse yourself in a thrilling submarine sea world with a Faial diving expedition. Faial offers dive sites for all levels of experience. Top spots include the Ilhéu Negro Sea Cave, the Entre-os-Montes Bay, and Baixa da Feiteira Reef.

## DIVE SPOTS

### ILHÉU NEGRO SEA CAVE

*under Monte da Guia, entry point Porto Pim Beach*

At a depth of 19 meters (62 ft), the Ilhéu Negro Sea Cave, under Monte da Guia, is a trove of interesting rock formations that brims with fantastic sea life, like turtles, octopus, shrimp, barracudas, and bream. Dives can be enjoyed here year-round, but the spot is prone to strong currents, making this spot best suited to advanced divers. Visibility can reach up to 25 meters (82 ft), so if you make this dive on a fair-weather day, the sunlight will penetrate the pristine water and illuminate the way down to the cave mouth.

### ENTRE MONTES BAY

*close to Monte da Guia*

One of the best dive spots on the island, the Entre Montes Bay, close to Monte da Guia, is a shallow, sheltered, and relatively uniform dive spot that revolves mainly around three large rocks. Just 5 minutes from Horta harbor, this is a great spot for divers of all levels, including beginners, snorkelers, and night dives. The gentle waters in this protected bay range from an entry depth of 7 meters (23 ft) to a maximum of 20 meters (66 ft). The bay hosts a wealth of sea life, including various species of moray eels, common octopuses, a rainbow of anemones that emerge from the crevices in the rock formations, common stingrays, and the occasional dusky grouper in the deepest parts of the dive.

### BAIXA DA FETEIRA REEF

*Faial south coast*

The Baixa da Feiteira Reef is a treat for accomplished divers. The tip of the reef is at a depth of 12 meters (39 ft), dropping to 32 meters (105 ft) at its deepest. The reef rises and plunges as you glide along, attracting several pelagic species such as Atlantic bonitos and yellow-mouth barracudas, as well as dusky groupers in the deeper spots and common eagle rays on the north side. The south side, the deepest part of the dive, has a particularly interesting feature, as the seabed is carpeted with vast swathes of black coral and European fan worms. Despite being less than a kilometer from the coast, this site is exposed to strong currents, and is therefore best suited to experienced divers.

## DIVE CENTERS AND SCHOOLS

### DIVE AZORES

*Horta Marina, Horta; tel. 967 882 214; https:// diveazores.net; daily 8:30am-6pm; from €45*

Owned and run by Joana and Tiago, who are both marine biologists and diving instructors, Dive Azores is a PADI Dive Resort and a Whale & Dolphin Watching Eco-Operator. Based in Horta Marina, the company operates thrilling dives, like shark-diving expeditions, scuba diving trips, snorkeling with dolphins, and dive courses, among others. Dive Azores provides guided dives to all the sites listed above.

### HALIOTIS DIVE CENTER FAIAL

*Rua Consul Dabney, Faial Resort Hotel, Horta; tel. 913 054 926; www.haliotis.pt; daily 9am-7pm; from €40*

Organizing dives to some of the top spots in and around Faial, regional company Haliotis has extensive international experience in spearheading fulfilling dives. With a complete shop, a top-of-the-range semi-rigid boat, quality equipment, and fully qualified instructors, Haliotis ticks all the boxes for a safe and enjoyable dive. Haliotis runs dives to the Baixa da Feteira Reef and Entre Montes Bay.

# Fishing

Bathed by waters that maintain a pretty constant temperature year-round thanks to the gulf stream, sheltered Faial is a great spot to hunt for big fish, including the prized blue marlin and the more common white marlin, spearfish, bluefin and yellowfin tuna, skipjack, bigeye tuna, and even sharks (predominantly the mako, hammerhead, blue, and six-gill species). The waters a short distance off the coast of Faial are prime territory for these species, some of which can be found in abundance, depending on the season.

True to its close links to the sea, **Horta harbor** is home to a large number of fishing fleets with highly experienced crews and top-notch vessels, ready to take you out for a day of memorable and rewarding fishing.

## OCEANIC FISHING

*Rua Vasco da Gama 46A; tel. 966 783 101; www. oceanic-fishing.com; charter rentals from €1,200/day*

Enjoy some of the world's finest blue marlin fishing with experts Oceanic Fishing. Oceanic's charters take visitors to blue marlin hotspots courtesy of seasoned captain Les Gallagher, who has considerable international experience in big-fish catching. Other types of fishing are also available according to the season. Fishing enthusiasts of all levels are welcome, from amateurs to the experienced.

## FAIAL TERRA MAR

*Ribeira da Lombega (Castelo Branco parish, west of Horta, near the airport); tel. 969 736 181; www. faialterramar.net; half-day charters from €250, maximum 6 people*

Leaders in sustainable coastal fishing charters, Faial Terra Mar runs bottom fishing trips (with organic bait), jigging, spinning, and trolling. Boats operate all year round for 4- and 8-hour trips; complete packages including accommodation can be arranged.

# Dolphin- and Whale-Watching

The ocean off the south of Faial is rich in enigmatic and captivating sea life—a great place for spotting sperm whales, along with more than two dozen other species of cetaceans. Most of Faial's whale- and dolphin-spotting boat trips depart from **Horta Marina.**

## AZORES EXPERIENCES

*Cais de Santa Cruz, Horta Marina; tel. 965 251 322; www.facebook.com/Azores-Experiences-Whale-Watching-Jeep-Tours-206485046056828; daily 8:30am-6pm; €65 pp*

Local adventure company Azores Experiences has crafted a range of sea experiences from their passion for the ocean and the Azores,

to share with visitors. They may be a young and dynamic team, but their knowledge and experience of all things sea-related, especially cetaceans, is second to none.

## NORBERTO DIVER

*Horta Marina; tel. 292 293 891; http://norbertodiver. pt; daily 8:30am-8pm; €65 pp*

Make memories on the waves off Faial with local expert Norberto Diver, who has over two decades' experience working with marine life above and beneath the surface. Tours include whale-watching, swimming with dolphins, scuba diving and snorkeling, and private boat rides.

# Hiking

## FAIAL FROM COAST TO COAST (GR1FAI)

**Hiking Distance:** 36.8 kilometers (22.9 mi) one-way

**Hiking Time:** 12 hours one-way

**Trailhead:** Ribeirinha Parish Council (Rua da Igreja, 227)

**Information and Maps:** http://parquesnaturais.azores.gov.pt/en/faial-eng/what-visit/trails/walking-trails/94-pni-faialeng/3179-faial-from-coast-to-coast-gr1fai

Set an entire day aside, pack snacks and layered clothing for changing weather, and make sure your boots are comfy for this mammoth trek. It traverses the island across the middle from east to west, starting in the parish of Ribeirinha, one of the island's easternmost points. On this route you'll be able to admire the enigmatic volcanic landscape, taking in natural attributes like volcanic cones, craters, caves, and grottos, as well as some of the lesser-known nooks and crannies. It offers a clear understanding of the island's formation, following ancient pathways across its middle to a maximum altitude of 1,000 meters (3,000 ft), through the famed Faial Caldera, ending at the moonscape of the Capelo Volcanic Complex.

A taxi will likely be necessary to either return to the starting point or go back to Horta. A taxi ride back to the starting point will take around 30 minutes and cost in the region of €30; back to Horta the ride is about 25 minutes and €25. There are buses from the Capelo Volcanic Complex both along the north coast back to Ribeirinha (which takes close to 2 hours) and along the south coast to Horta, about five times a day. For timetables and prices, contact **Farias** (tel. 292 292 482; www.farias.pt).

## CALDERA VOLCANIC COMPLEX AND NATURE RESERVE

Covering 313 hectares (749 acres) of prime volcanic terrain, the Caldera Volcanic Complex and Nature Reserve is a hiker's heaven, offering up a multitude of hikes for varying levels of aptitude, from an easy stroll around the rim, to the more challenging Ten Volcanoes Trail.

### CALDEIRA HIKE (PRC04 FAI)

**Hiking Distance:** 8 kilometers (5 mi) round-trip

**Hiking Time:** 2.5 hours round-trip

**Trailhead:** Caldera viewpoint

**Information and Maps:** http://trails.visitazores.com/en/trails-azores/faial/caldeira

Gaze in awe at the ever-changing scenery on both sides as you make the comfortable stroll around the rim of the Caldera's crater. With endless deep-blue ocean on one side and varying shades of lush green carpeting the innards of the crater bowl on the other, this enjoyable circular hike along the Caldera's crest ascends to altitudes of 840-1,040 meters (2,800-3,400 ft), meaning it's best to try this hike in good, clear weather.

### TEN VOLCANOES TRAIL (PR06 FAI)

**Hiking Distance:** 19.3 kilometers (12 mi) one-way

**Hiking Time:** 5 hours one-way

**Trailhead:** Caldera viewpoint

**Information and Maps:** http://trails.visitazores.com/en/trails-azores/faial/dez-vulcoes

One of the toughest but most scenic and diverse treks on the island, the Ten Volcanoes Trail is challenging. It starts at the Caldera viewpoint before heading west to Capelinhos,

# Faial's Best Views

The varied, hilly, volcanic landscape of Faial, and its proximity to the other islands in the Azores "triangle," means it boasts some of the best views in the archipelago. Below are some of the best viewpoints on the island to take your breath away.

- **Caldera Viewpoint:** At the end of a tunnel through the crater, you'll find a platform to one of the greatest views on the island. For many, it's a highlight of a trip to the Faial Caldera (page 255).

- **Capelinhos Lighthouse:** Climb to the top of this tower for the best views over the extraordinary Capelo Volcanic Complex (page 257).

- **Nossa Senhora da Conceição (Espalmaca) Viewpoint:** Protected by a 30-meter-high (100-ft-high) cross and a monument of Nossa Senhora da Conceição (Our Lady of Conception), the eponymous viewpoint affords some of the best views over Horta Bay and neighboring islands Pico, São Jorge, and Graciosa (along the EN1-1A, north of Horta).

climbing and descending a series of mounts en route. It passes along some of the island's most famous volcanoes, taking in the Cabeço Gordo mountain, the highest point on Faial, and Capelinhos. It ends at the Capelinhos Volcano Interpretation Centre, and en route weaves though typical Azorean fields and forests. It's an enchanting, scenic, and challenging hike.

The only way to get back to the Caldeira starting point from Capelo is by taxi, which will cost around €30 and takes 30 minutes. A taxi from Capelo back to Horta is about 25 minutes and €25.

## CAPELO VOLCANIC COMPLEX

Located on the western coast of Faial, in the parish of Capelo, the Capelinhos volcanic cone is part of the larger Capelo Volcanic Complex. Along with the abandoned lighthouse and the quirky interpretation center, it has become a tourist magnet, one of the most popular and unique attractions on Faial. The almost lunar landscape that distinguishes the complex gives hikers the opportunity to enjoy a completely different vista, desolate and otherworldly, devoid of the Azores' usual lush greenery.

### CAPELO-CAPELINHOS TRAIL (CABEÇO DO CANTO - PRC01 FAI)

**Hiking Distance:** 2.6 kilometers (1.6 mi) round-trip

**Hiking Time:** 2 hours round-trip

**Trailhead:** Capelo village (near access road to Cabeço Verde)

**Information and Maps:** http:// trails.visitazores.com/en/trails-azores/faial/ cabeco-do-canto

This slightly challenging circular hike starts and ends near the road to Cabeço Verde parish. This fascinating route weaves through the protected landscape of the central area, passing rich and intriguing landscapes of volcanic importance, such as deep lava caves, volcanic cones, and fresh laurel forests and woods. See how the landscape changes as you near the Capelo Volcanic Complex and Capelinhos Cape, from bright green and scrubby to undulating, bare, and dark.

### ROCHA DA FAJÃ (PRC02 FAI)

**Hiking Distance:** 5 kilometers (3 mi) round-trip

**Hiking Time:** 2 hours round-trip

**Trailhead:** Praia do Norte Parish Council (Largo da Igreja church square, EN1-1A road)

**Information and Maps:** http://trails. visitazores.com/en/trails-azores/faial/rocha-da-faja

This easy loop is in the protected area of Capelinhos. The scenic route takes hikers on a journey through time to explore the effects of a 1672 eruption on this area, and the formation of the island's only *fajã*, in popular Praia do Norte. Enjoy the scenery as you pass by springs and fountains, cross over streams, and hike past pretty coastal picnic areas, until you arrive in the heart of the pretty village of Praia do Norte, and back to where you started.

# Entertainment and Events

## THE ARTS

### FAIALENSE THEATRE

*Alameda Barão de Roches 31, Horta; tel. 292 292 016; www.facebook.com/teatro.faialense; venue opens 2 hours before performances, ticket office Fri. 3pm-6pm and 7:30pm-9:30pm, Sat. 7:30pm-9:30pm, Sun. 2pm-4pm and 7:30pm-9:30pm*

Housed in a handsome building, the Faialense Theatre is a hub of cultural events and performing arts. Its dates back to 1856, when it was the first mainstream theater in the Azores. It has been rebuilt over the years, renovated and modernized again in the 20th century to offer state-of-the-art facilities. It currently houses a movie theater, auditorium, multipurpose room, and a bar. The theater promotes an ever-changing program of predominantly national dance, musical, and theatrical productions.

## FESTIVALS AND EVENTS

### NOSSA SENHORA DAS ANGÚSTIAS FESTIVAL

*across Faial (mainly Horta); sixth Sun. after Easter Sun.*

The biggest religious celebration on Faial, the Nossa Senhora das Angústias Festival sees the streets of main town Horta explode with color and a large procession. The festival also pays homage to the island's earliest settlement, when a statue of Nossa Senhora das Angústias (Our Lady of Anguishes) was brought to the island from Flanders. What started out as a parish pilgrimage turned into an islandwide occasion, and the festival, also one of the oldest on Faial, is now seen as the unofficial launch of the summer festival agenda.

### SÃO JOÃO FESTIVAL

*Largo Jaime Melo; June 24*

Held every year on June 24, the São João festival is a summer highlight. The festivity marks the settlement of the island by nobility from Terceira island. Brass bands from across the island make their way to Largo Jaime Melo (north of Horta, where the EN1-2A road intersects with the EN2-2A) where a chapel, the Ermida de São João, was built by the faithful in honor of São João (Saint John). Concerts, folk dancing, and food stalls touting local specialties keep the merriment going throughout the day.

### SENHORA DA GUIA FESTIVAL + SEA WEEK

*Porto Pim; www.cmhorta.pt; first Sun. in Aug. and following week*

Faial's Sea Week is a veritable celebration of all things sea-related. One of the biggest and highly anticipated summer events in the archipelago, festivities kick off on August 1 with the time-honored Senhora da Guia Festival, when a pageant of ships carries a statue of the Virgin across Horta Bay from sandy Porto Pim to the harbor. This is followed by a weeklong program of sea-inspired events across the island, including concerts, arts, crafts, and culinary fairs, and boat regattas including a display of whaling boats that cross the channel between Faial and Pico. Locals flood the streets for Sea Week, especially at night, to enjoy the jolly atmosphere and lovely temperatures.

# Shopping

Pop into one of the island's specialty shops and take a slice of Faial home with you.

## HORTA
### Gourmet and Food
#### LOJA DO TRIANGULO

*Rua Serpa Pinto 28; tel. 292 292 090; Mon.-Sat. 9am-6pm*

Loje do Triangulo is packed with quality island and regional gourmet products, including jams, cheeses, cured meats, liqueurs, and wines. It focuses on delicacies from the "triangle" islands; Faial, Pico, and São Jorge. Other delights include fresh farm produce, freshly baked treats, and traditional handicrafts, all under one roof.

### Boutiques and Clothing
#### PUTU

*Rua Vasco da Gama no. 20; tel. 966 770 958; www. meuputu.com; Mon.-Thurs. 10am-12:30pm and 1:30pm-5:30pm, Fri. 1:30pm-5:30pm, Sat. 11am-1pm*

Founded on Faial in 2012, Putu sells handcrafted, one-size-fits-all textile accessories. All garments are unique and colorful, a perfect and unusual gift for men, women, and children. Neckpieces and hoodies are among the best-selling items.

## CAPELO VOLCANIC COMPLEX
### Arts and Crafts
#### CAPELO CRAFTS CENTER

*EN1-1A; tel. 292 945 027; www.facebook.com/ centroartesanatocapelo; Mon.-Fri. 10am-5pm, Sat.-Sun. by appointment for large groups*

For an authentic Faial souvenir, visit the Capelo Crafts Center (Centro de Artesenato do Capelo) near the Capelo Volcanic Complex to see the range of regional arts and crafts on offer. Handmade by local artisans to time-honored methods, this popular center is where you can buy typical island embroideries, straw baskets, and other traditional trinkets, as well as homemade jams and preserves, among many other delightful and unique gifts.

# Food

Faial's food scene is based largely in and around Horta and Porto Pim, boasting an eclectic mix of eateries to cater to international palates. Peppered with contemporary and funky new ideas, there is a great representation of traditional island fare with a cool and modern twist.

One of Faial's time-honored dishes, said to be typical of Faial island and also Terceira, is *Sopa do Espirito Santo*, or **Holy Spirit soup,** also known as *Impérios* soup. This peasant-ish dish is usually eaten during the revered Espirito Santo festivities between Pentecost Sunday and the seventh Sunday after Easter. It is based on slices of dry bread and butter covered in the stock from meat stew. Fish stew (*caldeirada*) and squid braised in red wine are other typical island dishes.

## HORTA
### Markets
#### HORTA MUNICIPAL MARKET

*Rua Serpa Pinto; tel. 292 202 074; www.cmhorta.pt/ index.php/servicos-municipais/mercado-municipal; Mon.-Fri. 6:30am-7pm, Sat.-Sun. 6:30am-1pm*

Pack your picnic basket with fresh produce from local farmers at the small but busy Horta Municipal Market. This is a great place for a photo op with locals and their produce, like fish, fruit, and vegetables, and the market has a number of great little bakeries and cafés in the vicinity.

## Azorean

### AH! BOCA SANTA

*Rua Serpa Pinto; tel. 968 305 135; www.facebook. com/ahbocasanta; Tues.-Wed. 11:30am-3pm, Thurs.-Fri. 11:30am-3pm and 6pm-10pm, Sat. 9am-3pm and 6pm-10pm, Sun. 9:30am-12:30pm; €5.50*

Reinventing the wheel on authentic Azorean food, this cool, trendy burger joint serves up excellent artisanal burgers and fries, contemporary comfort food, lighter dishes like salads, breakfasts and brunch, and outstanding homemade sweet treats like brownies. What started off as a cool little food truck has garnered a solid following and a permanent spot at Horta's municipal market.

### CANTO DA DOCA

*Rua Nova; tel. 292 292 444; daily noon-2:30pm and 7pm-11pm; €15*

Head to Canto da Doca for a dinner with a difference. Here the house specialty is food cooked on sizzling lava stones. Quality fresh fish and meats are served in slithers to be cooked at the table on a slab of piping hot stone. Accompanied by salad, fries, and dips, meals are rounded off with an extensive homemade dessert list. Canto da Doca is basic but clean and comfortable; the enjoyable novel experience and good food speaks for itself.

### MEDALHAS

*Rua Serpa Pinto 22 r/c; tel. 292 391 026; www.facebook.com/Restaurante-Medalhas-1382325028753620; Mon.-Sat. noon-10pm; €15*

Medalhas oozes island tradition, with its wooden window shutters and red gingham tablecloths. Authentic local cuisine comes from the kitchen to the table on traditional earthenware crockery, adding to the rustic flavor. Traditional Azorean dishes of the day are varied and are a great value. A fab, centrally located spot for a leisurely lunch.

### TASCA O CAPITÓLIO

*Rua Conselheiro Medeiros 23; tel. 292 701 385; www. facebook.com/oCapitolio; Mon.-Fri. noon-3pm and 6:30pm-11pm; Sat. 6:30pm-11pm; €18*

Located in the heart of Horta, Tasca O Capitólio is a down-to-earth tavern where traditional Portuguese cuisine and fresh fish dishes hog the limelight. All island specialties, including limpets, cheeses, tuna steaks, and regional beef dishes, can be enjoyed at this small and cozy wood-clad *tasca*.

### ★ RESTAURANT GENUÍNO

*Rua Nova; tel. 292 701 542; www.genuino.pt, Thurs.-Tues. noon-3pm and 6:30pm-10pm; €20*

With gorgeous views over Porto Pim Bay, this is a great little restaurant to enjoy the finest flavors of the sea. Meat dishes are also available, but ocean delights straight from the ocean to the table, like simple grilled fish, fish soups, stews, and more unusual feasts like tuna meatballs, burgers, and rice dishes are the specialty here. This authentic gem of a restaurant brings the ocean theme inside—it looks a little like a ship, with warm wooden cladding, sails on the ceiling, and simple wooden bench-tables—and its popularity has attracted the likes of visiting dignitaries. The restaurant's charismatic owner, Genuíno Madruga, is himself an avid sailor and has circumnavigated the globe by boat more than once.

## Contemporary

### PRAYA RESTAURANT

*Largo Coronel Silva Leal; tel. 292 701 037; https:// pt-pt.facebook.com/praya.restaurante; Tues.-Sun. noon-2:30pm and 7pm-10:30pm; €20*

This impressive wood and glass construction lends a touch of architectural jazz to Faial. Located 5 minutes north of Horta on Faial's east coast, Praya is a stunning beachside eatery with amazing views over to Pico island and its majestic mountain. The menu comprises dishes made for sharing while enjoying the views, as well as fresh fish and locally produced meat mains and typical desserts.

## Cafés and Light Bites
### ★ GELADOS DO ATLÂNTICO

*Praça Infante Dom Henrique 2; tel. 925*
*460 688; www.facebook.com/Gelados-do-*
*Atl%C3%A2ntico-996585803693228; Fri.-Sun.*
*2pm-8pm; €5*

Indulge with a scoop or two of unique and re-freshing artisanal ice cream made with local fruity flavors like pineapple, guava, passion fruit, cherry, papaya, and cardamom and green apple, and unusual daily specials like chili chocolate or kefir. Homemade wafer cones perfectly complement the ice cream, and waffles and crepes are also delicious on cooler days, all to be savored slowly while enjoying lovely waterfront views over Pico. Bruch menus are also available.

### CASA TEAHOUSE & BAR

*Rua de Sao Bento; tel. 292 700 053; www.casa38a.*
*com; Mon.-Fri. 11am-9pm, Sun. 4pm-9pm; €5*

Delve into a delicious afternoon tea spread with fresh cakes and home-baked bread at this pleasant teahouse. Sit in the garden to enjoy a genteel, sun-dappled tea at this trendy little oasis in Horta with over 100 teas to choose from. Or if you're feeling a little hungrier, enjoy a dish from the slow-cooked, market kitchen inspired menu.

# Bars and Nightlife

## HORTA
### ★ PETER CAFÉ SPORT

*Rua José Azevedo 9; tel. 292 392 027; www.*
*petercafesport.com; daily 8am-1am*

Soak up the vibe at the most famous sailors' bar in the world. Swap swashbuckling stories with the regulars or simply enjoy the unique atmosphere with a refreshing local beer or a trademark gin and tonic as the sun sets over Horta harbor.

### NOITES LOUCAS - SPORTING CLUB DA HORTA

*Travessa do Monturo; www.facebook.com/*
*NLEventos12; weekends 11pm-6am in summer*

The Noites Loucas events based at the Sporting Club da Horta are organized throughout summer to get Horta dancing. Themed and open-air dance events take place on weekends in summer, featuring guest DJs, from late until sunrise.

### MARINA BAR

*Av. 25 de Abril, Horta Marina; tel. 292 292 695; daily*
*8am-10pm*

Located on the docks, the cool and casual Marina Bar overlooks the lovely Horta bay and its marina. It is a modern bar with indoor and outdoor seating areas as well as a dining area and a terrace and lounge section. A melt-ing pot of international visitors to the island, it aims to provide excellent service in a warm, inviting, and cosmopolitan environment as well as regular live entertainment.

### OCEANIC CAFÉ

*Rua Vasco da Gama 46A; tel. 966 783 101; www.*
*azores-oceanic.com/oceanic-café; Thurs.-Sat.*
*6pm-2am*

Housed in a historic building dating back to the early 1800s, Oceanic Café is a sea-themed bar overlooking Horta Marina with regular live music starting at 11pm most Fridays and Saturdays. It's a lively, warm, and welcoming bar with a great friendly vibe.

# Accommodations

Most of Faial's bigger hotel units and guesthouses are located in Horta, although smaller, private accommodations like apartments and houses can be found in other parts of the island, especially near Almoxarife Beach and along the southwest coast toward the Capelo Volcanic Complex.

## HORTA
### Under €100
### PORTO PIM GUEST HOUSE
*Rua Monsenhor António Silveira Medeiros no. 6; tel. 916 746 917; http://porto-pim-guest-house-horta. visit-azores.info/en; €60*

Porto Pim is a sweet guesthouse located a few streets back from Porto Pim bayside. Peaceful and spotless, it has roomy bedrooms and bathrooms and a communal kitchen. A great base for a few nights in Horta.

### ★ AZORIS FAIAL GARDEN
*Rua Consul Dabney; tel. 292 207 400; www. azorishotels.com; €84 d*

Azoris Faial Garden combines the tranquility of nature with a great location. Offering incredible views over Pico, this four-star hotel is within walking distance of Horta's main attractions, a 5-minute stroll to the marina. Accommodation is in the form of rooms that range from classic singles to deluxe suites.

### €100-200
### INTERNATIONAL AZORES BOUTIQUE
*Rua Conselheiro Medeiros 1; tel. 292 292 216; http:// internacionalazores.com/home; €100*

Take the refinement up a notch at this gorgeous boutique townhouse with its distinctive turquoise facade, eclectic art deco features, and tasteful interior décor. Rooms are clean, bright, elegant, and spacious, ranging from high-quality dorms to VIP sea-view rooms, all equipped with mod cons. Located right on Horta Marina, the building is intrinsically linked to the early hydro-aviation period.

### HOTEL DO CANAL
*Largo Dr. Manuel de Arriaga; tel. 292 202 120; www. bensaude.pt; €115 d*

This elegant white building stretches along Horta waterfront, offering wonderful views over the city, bay, and Pico island. Comfortable and relaxed, Hotel do Canal provides a homey and elegant base for travelers, who are welcomed with typical island hospitality. Rooms are plush and cozy, with idyllic sea and mountain views.

### HOTEL HORTA
*Rua Marcelino Lima; tel. 292 208 200; www. hotelhorta.pt; €120 d*

Located in historic Horta, Hotel Horta is a well-equipped refuge with a large garden and nice outdoor pool. About 1.5 kilometers (1 mi) from the waterfront, it comprises 80 modern rooms spread over five floors, including one luxury suite. There's also a panoramic restaurant offering stunning views over Pico.

# Information and Services

Horta has a good standard of public services including banks, ATMs, pharmacies, dental clinics, and more. Faial also has one of the region's three modern and well-equipped hospitals (the other two being on Terceira island, and the main hospital on São Miguel). Faial Hospital underwent remodeling works in 2019 and the first brick was laid for a new health center, but urgent or more complex cases will likely be transferred to the bigger units on Terceira or São Miguel, or back to the mainland.

- **Tourist Office:** Rua Comendador Ernesto Rebelo 14, Horta; tel. 292 200 500; www.visitazores.com; daily 10am-10pm

- **PSP Police:** Av. Gago Coutinho e Sacadura Cabral s/n, Horta; tel. 292 208 510; www.psp.pt

- **Main hospital:** Rua Comendador Ernesto Rebelo 14, Horta; tel. 292 200 500; www.visitazores.com, daily 10am-10pm

- **Pharmacy Ayres Pinheiro:** Rua Serpa Pinto 26, close to ferry terminal; tel. 292 292 749; Mon.-Fri. 9am-7pm, Sat. 9am-1pm

# Flores

Flores rises dramatically from the sea, delimited by a vertiginous coastline. Those who visit Flores say it is one of the prettiest places on earth. Flores, which literally translates to "flowers," takes its name from the abundance of flora that swamps the island, and it is part of the global network of UNESCO Biosphere Reserves. Green and luscious with cascading waterfalls and crystal-clear lakes, Flores has an untouched, almost prehistoric, Jurassic Park look about it. Jaw-droppingly beautiful any time of year, the island is at its most luxuriant in late spring or early summer, after the winter rains. It takes its nickname, the Pink Island, from the abundance of rosy azaleas and hydrangeas that blossom there.

At just over 16 kilometers (10 mi) long and 12 kilometers (7 mi) wide, or a total land mass of about 143 square kilometers (55 sq mi), it's a small, mid-Atlantic Eden. But it's not just all about the luscious vegetation; Flores is rampant with stunning natural features, from cascading waterfalls and gorgeous lakes and lagoons, to quintessential Azorean villages and soaring cliffs covered in mossy greenery. Flores island has a jungle-like, mythological

feel about it, especially the island's main sight, the otherworldly Poço Ribeira do Ferreiro pool, fed by several waterfalls. It's a rugged haven of immense beauty and tranquility.

## GETTING THERE

The best way to get to Flores is by plane, with flights from Faial, São Miguel, and Terceira; there are no direct flights to Flores from outside the Azores. A seasonal ferry route also runs between Flores and the other island groups, the last stop before Flores being Faial.

### Air
#### SANTA CRUZ DAS FLORES AIRPORT
#### (Aeroporto das Flores)

*Santa Cruz das Flores; tel. 800 201 201; www.aeroportoflores.pt*

**SATA Azores Airlines** (www.azoresairlines.pt) operates flights between Flores Airport (FLW) and **Horta Airport** on Faial (45 minutes; from €100 round-trip) and **Ponta Delgada Airport** on São Miguel (1 hour 20 minutes; €100 round-trip).

Flores Airport is more or less in **Santa**

# Flores

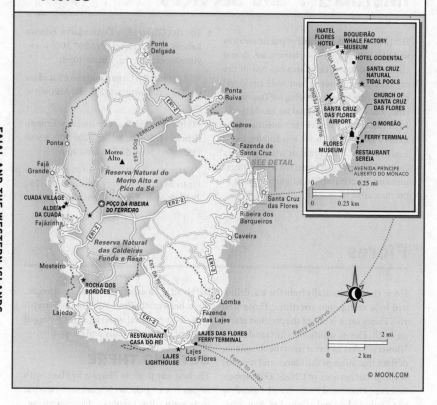

Cruz das Flores town, with its airstrip bordering up against the town. It is less than 1 kilometer (0.6 mi) from the center of Santa Cruz. A number of car rental companies operate from Flores Airport, including **Europcar** (www.europcar.pt), **Ilha Verde Rent a Car** (www.ilhaverde.com), and **Autatlantis** (https://autatlantis.com), but vehicles are limited so book in advance. The easiest way to get from the airport to main town is by taxi—there is a taxi rank outside the terminal—or rental car; the drive to town takes just a couple of minutes. Or, it's a 10-minute walk into the town.

## Ferry

There are two ferry terminals on Flores, one

in **Santa Cruz das Flores** (Porto da Santa Cruz das Flores; tel. 292 592 224) and another farther south, on the southeastern tip of the island, in **Lajes das Flores** (Porto Comercial da Ilha das Flores; tel. 292 593 148). There is one weekly sailing between Lajes and neighboring island Corvo (1 hour 20 minutes; €15), and up to 18 weekly sailings (40 minutes; €10) from Santa Cruz. The seasonal **Yellow Line,** which runs May-September, links to Flores from **Faial** (and the other island groups). It's about a 9-hour trip from Faial, and a one-way ticket costs €95-125.

From the ferry terminal, it is a 500-meter (0.3-mi) walk into the center of Santa Cruz town. There is a taxi rank a short walk west from the ferry terminal, following the main

Rua da Conceição; a taxi to the southern town of Lajes will cost around €20 and take 20 minutes, while a taxi from the taxi rank to main attractions such as the breathtaking Poço da Ribeira do Ferreiro waterfalls on the opposite sideof the island, on the west coast, will also cost around €20.

## GETTING AROUND

There's no public transport on Flores. There are three main ways to get around: renting a car, by taxi, or **hitchhiking**, which is common on the island, pretty safe, and the locals are happy to oblige. Renting a car is highly recommended to explore Flores's incredible natural beauty and vistas at leisure.

### Car

There are a number of car rental companies operating on Flores, although due to the size of the island, the number of vehicles available is limited. These include **Europcar** (www.europcar.pt), **Ilha Verde Rent a Car** (www.ilhaverde.com), and **Autatlantis** (https://autatlantis.com). Driving around Flores is an amazing way to take in the jaw-dropping scenery, meaning you can stop and start at lesirue to get snaps of those awesome and unique landscapes.

### Taxi

A taxi is a handy way of getting around Flores if you don't want to rent a car. A trip to anywhere on the island, from one end to the other, will rarely cost more than €30. Most of Flores's taxis are privately owned—there is no taxi "central"—but the individual drivers offer set tours of the island. A recommended taxi driver who operates full- and half-day tours of the island with fixed prices is **Silvio Medina - Tours of Flores** (tel. 910 401 976; www.toursofflores.com; half-day tours (5 hours) from €100 (1-4 people), full-day tours (7-8 hours) from €150, prices for customized tours vary).

## ORIENTATION

Flores is a small island that takes under three hours to completely circumnavigate by car. It has two main towns, both on the island's eastern coast: To the north, just over halfway up the island, is Santa Cruz das Flores, the larger of the two, pinned to the coast by tiny Flores Airport's single airstrip, and Lajes das Flores is on the south. Most of the island's main attractions, such as the impressive **Rocha dos Bordões** rock formation, the spectacular **Poço da Ribeira do Ferreiro** waterfalls and pool, and the authentic **Aldeia da Cuada** stone village, can be found on the western half of the island, more specifically along the west coast.

There is one main road on Flores island, the **ER1-2**, which starts on the northern tip and runs down the east coast clockwise around the island and halfway up the west coast, where it stops in a nature reserve (the Morro Alto e Pico da Se Natural Forest Reserve) in the center of the island. From here a seconday inland road, the **ER2-2**, links back to Santa Cruz.

## SIGHTS

### Santa Cruz das Flores

Flores's main town of Santa Cruz das Flores, or simply Santa Cruz, is located just over halfway up the island's east coast. It's a sparse, whitewashed town, scattered over a swath of clifftop, wedged between the Atlantic Ocean and Flores Airport's airstrip. Despite being small, there's plenty of attractions to enjoy in town, including its **natural tidal pools** (one of the island's most popular bathing sites in summer), the intriguing Boqueirão Whale Factory Museum, Flores Museum, and the ornate Church of Santa Cruz das Flores.

#### BOQUEIRÃO WHALE FACTORY MUSEUM
#### (Fábrica da Baleia do Boqueirão)
*Rua do Boqueirão no. 2; tel. 292 542 932;*
*https://museudafabricadabaleia.com; Mon.-Fri.*

9am-5:30pm, Sat.-Sun. 2pm-5:30pm June-Sept., Mon.-Sat. 9am-12:30pm and 2pm-5:30pm, Sun. 2pm-5:30pm Oct.-May; €2.50

This former whale factory was abandoned in the 1980s but has been admirably restored into a modern and handsome building that gives an interesting insight into the archipelago's divisive whaling heritage. See an original wooden whaling boat, and try not to be too disturbed by the huge model of a sperm whale sawed in half outside the museum.

## FLORES MUSEUM
## (Museu das Flores)

Largo da Misericórdia; tel. 292 592 159; www. patrimoniocultural.gov.pt/pt/museus-e-monumentos/ rede-portuguesa/m/museu-das-flores; Mon.-Fri. 9am-12:30pm and 2pm-5:30pm; €1 for both nuclei

Divided over two nearby locations in town— the former Convent of São Boaventura on Largo da Misericórdia, and Casa Pimentel de Mesquita on Rua da Conceição—Flores Museum explores the island's history with in-depth exhibitions on its heritage, covering the likes of farming, scrimshaw, carpentry, blacksmithing, and linen and wool textiles. Established in 1977, visitors can also see artifacts from a vessel that was shipwrecked off the island's coast in 1909.

## CHURCH OF SANTA
## CRUZ DAS FLORES
## (Igreja Matriz de Santa
## Cruz das Flores)

Rua da Conceição; tel. 292 593 356

For a small town, this is a big, handsome church, with an ornate facade and twin bell tower. Construction on the present building started in 1859, replacing an earlier church, built in 1781. The building takes pride of place in the center of Santa Cruz and can be seen from pretty much anywhere in town. Square and solid, the church's whitewashed facade is embellished with a decorative basalt stone trim. Five wide steps climb to the front door.

1: Santa Cruz das Flores 2: Church of Santa Cruz das Flores 3: Poço da Ribeira do Ferreiro 4: Rocha dos Bordões rock formation

The main chapel of this church is one of the largest in the entire archipelago. Its central altar features a 2.3-meter-high (7.5-ft-tall) image of Nossa Senhora da Conceição, the building's patron saint.

## Lajes das Flores

Flores's other town, Lajes das Flores, sits on the bottom-right corner of the island some 17 kilometers (11 mi) south of Santa Cruz das Flores, along the ER1-2 road. It's located in a region of deep valleys, sheer cliffs, tumbling waterfalls, and crystal-clear lakes. Besides being home to the island's largest commercial **port** and the nearby Lajes Lighthouse, there is little else of note in the town itself.

## LAJES LIGHTHOUSE
## (Farol das Lajes)

Lajes das Flores; tel. 292 592 369; www.amn.pt/DF/ Paginas/FaroldaPontadasLajes.aspx; Wed. 2pm-5pm; free

In operation since 1910, the Lajes Lighthouse is one of the largest and most powerful lighthouses in the Azores. It sits some 90 meters (300 ft) above sea level on Lajes Point, its 16-meter-tall (52-ft-tall) quadrangular prismatic tower emitting three flashes every 15 seconds. The flashes of light penetrate 26 nautical miles into the inky Atlantic darkness, guiding vessels crossing from the Americas as well as the Faial-Flores channel.

## Western Flores
## ROCHA DOS BORDÕES

Lajes das Flores, near the parish of Mosteiros, between Santa Cruz and Fajã Grande; open 24/7; free

Perhaps Flores's most iconic landscape, the Rocha dos Bordões rock formation is one of the island's distinguishing geological formations. An 18-minute (16 km/10 mi) drive southwest from Santa Cruz along the ER2-2 road (or a 10-minute drive along the same road from Lajes, heading northwest), this landmark looks a bit like someone has chiseled away at the base of the huge rock and left the top half untouched. A band of soaring basalt columns wraps around the massif, creating a church-organ effect around its base. It's one of the Azores' most unusual natural monuments.

You can't miss this landmark when driving around the ER2-2 on this part of the island; see how its color changes throughout the day with the sun. Pull up at the designated **viewpoint** along the road and gaze in awe at Mother Nature's cleverness.

### ★ POÇO DA RIBEIRA DO FERREIRO

*Fajã Grande parish, Lajes das Flores; open 24/7; free*

Also known as the **Poço da Alagoinha,** this almost primordial beauty spot on Flores's west coast, directly across the island opposite Santa Cruz (a 25-minute, 20-km/12-mi drive along the ER2-2 road) is considered by many as the island's most paradisiacal location and an obligatory stop for visitors to Flores. The road to the spot is signposted, and from the designated parking lot it's a well-marked 15-minute hike along a purpose-created pathway to this staggeringly stunning secret Garden of Eden. A curtain of over a dozen waterfalls cascades rhythmically down a towering cliff covered in dense, lush vegetation, pooling into a photogenic green lake. Bird and frog song creates a soundtrack against the noise of whooshing water as it cuts through the mossy coat blanketing the cliffs. An idyllic place to just sit quietly and contemplate the sound of water and nature (swimming in the lake is not advised), this is without doubt one of Flores's must-see and most memorable attractions.

### CUADA VILLAGE (Aldeia da Cuada)

*between the parishes of Fajã Grande and Fajãzinha, Lajes das Flores; open 24/7; free*

This little stone-built hamlet, whose origins stretch back to the 17th century, is a quintessential example of a genuine Azorean village from yesteryear. The village was originally built to house local farmers, who, according to accounts, lived a hard and basic life,

tending the land with few comforts. The village had been inhabited since the 18th century, but was completely abandoned in the 1960s when its last remaining residents emigrated to the United States. Overshadowed by a towering mossy massif, this cluster of 15 little cottages had sat practically abandoned ever since, until private investors painstakingly restored it for tourism purposes. Now, tourists to the island looking for the ultimate rural retreat can stay in one of the little cottages as a base for their stay. The epitome of rural, without television or internet, this delightful little village is like a true time capsule, simple, rustic, and charming. Curious visitors are invited to stroll around the village, admore the historic architecture, soak up its unique atmosphere, see the traditional stone farmhouses, and use their imagination to see how life might have been in a bygone era.

## BEACHES AND POOLS

Flores's rocky coastline hosts a series of natural tidal pools for a refreshing dip around the Santa Cruz das Flores area, and sandier beaches farther south near Lajes das Flores. There is also a pebbly beach in Fajã Grande, or take a dip in one of the island's various ponds and lagoons.

### Santa Cruz das Flores
SANTA CRUZ NATURAL TIDAL POOLS

*town seafront; open 24/7; free*

The Santa Cruz natural tidal pools are located just north of Santa Cruz town center, a short walk along the main seafront boardwalk. In summer, these pretty pools formed by seawater-filled lava crevices attract islanders from far and wide. There is parking on the doorstep, and access to the pools requires walking down a flight of steps. They're a perfect spot to sit, soak, and cool down in warmer months, and they showcase the Azores' volcanic splendor. There are no public facilities like changing rooms or bathrooms on site.

# SAILING AND BOAT TOURS

Flores's scenery is best viewed not on the island itself, but from the water around it. To see some of its most spectacular natural features, take a boat trip around the island's coastline, exploring secret caves and grottos, towering cliffs with rock formations, intriguing islets, and cascading waterfalls that rush off the edge of the island.

## Santa Cruz das Flores
### FLORES BY SEA

*Rua da Fazenda no. 33-A; tel. 292 592 138 or 926 625 878; https://floresbysea.pt/en/home-2; open 24/7; from €25 pp*

Santa Cruz-based boat tourism company Flores by Sea operates boat trips to Corvo island, around Flores island, and in and around the caves of Flores. An added bonus is that you might also spot dolphins on your tour.

# FOOD

Flores boasts a great selection of traditional local restaurants, lots of fabulous seafood, and some rather innovative cuisine. As these westernmost islands survived for centuries without influence or help from the outside world, the gastronomy is purely local and based on home-grown ingredients, and centers on fresh fish and hearty meat dishes that sustained the hardworking farmers. Most restaurants are in the main towns of Santa Cruz or Lajes.

## Santa Cruz das Flores
### RESTAURANT SEREIA

*Rua Dr. Armas da Silveira; tel. 292 592 093; Mon.-Sat. 11:30am-3pm and 7pm-10pm, Sun. noon-2:30pm and 7pm-10pm; €15*

Singled out for its light meals and service, Sereia, plain on the outside and simple on the inside, is nonetheless one of the most popular eateries in Santa Cruz das Flores. Small but welcoming, the eclectic menu caters for a range of palates, from hamburgers and chips to ribs and grilled fish including local delicacies *chicharrinhos* (little fried horse mackerel) and limpets. All fresh and home-cooked.

Sereia is very popular among the locals and can get quite busy; make sure you book in advance to avoid disappointment.

### O MOREÃO

*Rua Dr. Armas da Silveira 21; tel. 964 619 142; www.facebook.com/pg/O-More%C3%A3o-292188604804668/reviews/?ref=page_internal; daily noon-11pm; €15*

O Moreão is fish and seafood heaven. A relative newcomer on Flores's gastronomic scene, here you can enjoy locally caught delicacies like limpets, *cracas* (barnacles), prawns, octopus, tender swordfish steaks, *goraz*, and *bocanegra*. Family-run and down-to-earth, this small restaurant has personable staff and a great busy vibe to it. Round off the meal nicely with homemade desserts.

## Lajes das Flores
### ★ RESTAURANT CASA DO REI

*Rua Peixoto Pimentel 33; tel. 292 593 262; https://restaurantcasadorei.com; Wed.-Mon. 6pm-9:30pm; €15*

Just 1.5 kilometers (1 mi) from the port in Lajes das Flores, this small and cozy restaurant ranks among the best on the island. The menu is a mixed European bag, with German, French, and Azorean inspiration used to create new and inventive dishes from fresh local produce. Mains include pork with honey and nuts, almond-crusted fish, and schnitzel and veal "Caldeirão," while homemade desserts include crepe suzette.

# ACCOMMODATIONS

There are a handful of small but decent hotels on Flores, mainly in the larger towns of Santa Cruz and Lajes, or private rural accommodation elsewhere, such as the Cuada Village on the west coast.

## Santa Cruz das Flores
### HOTEL OCIDENTAL

*Avenida dos Baleeiros; tel. 292 590 100; www.hotelocidental.pt*

Conveniently located in the center of Santa Cruz, the pretty Hotel Ocidental is a basic and simple two-star hotel that claims to be Europe's westernmost hotel. With unobstructed sea views, it has 36 rooms and a pool.

### INATEL FLORES HOTEL

*Rua do Boqueirao; tel. 292 590 420; https://hoteis.inatel.pt*

Overlooking staggering coastal scenery, this small, 26-room modern hotel in Santa Cruz provides clean and comfortable lodgings for a stay on Flores with a fully equipped bar, restaurant, swimming pool, sun terrace, Wi-Fi, and private parking. A quality four-star hotel, it offers a little touch of luxury and is centrally located, with most of the town's attractions within walking distance.

### Western Flores

#### ★ ALDEIA DA CUADA

*Faja Grande; tel. 292 552 127; http://aldeiadacuada.com*

For the ultimate island experience, stay in a traditional Azorean village at the lovingly restored Cuada Village. It comprises a cluster of 15 typical stone-built cottages dating to the 17th century, and there is also a good restaurant on site as well as a village bar/breakfast venue. The fully equipped houses range from one to six bedrooms.

## INFORMATION AND SERVICES

Flores today has a good range of services and amenities, including a health center, police service, fire service, and tourism office. ATMs are available on the island.

- **Tourist Office:** Rua Dr. Armas da Silveira, Santa Cruz; tel. 292 592 369. There is also a tourism bureu at the airport.

- **Police:** Antigo Bairro dos Franceses, Santa Cruz; tel. 292 592 115 and Rua da Autonomia no. 21, Lajes; tel. 292 593 186

- **Health Centers:** Largo 25 de Abril, Santa Cruz; tel. 292 590 270 and Avenida Emigrante, Lajes; tel. 292 593 662

- **Pharmacies:** Rua do Hospital, Santa Cruz; tel. 292 592 294 and Lajes; tel. 292 593 373

# Corvo

Located some 46 kilometers (29 mi) north of Flores, tiny Corvo, the Azores' smallest island, currently has a resident population of around just 450 people, meaning you can bag the bragging rights of having been to one of Europe's remotest places with a visit. A big portion of the island is swallowed up by its main attraction, the Caldeirão, an enormous caldera with lakes and a dozen little peaks in the bottom. At just over 17 square kilometers (7 sq mi) (6 km/4 ft long and 4 km/2 mi wide), Corvo is so small that it is the only island on the archipelago that doesn't have a taxi service, as everywhere on the island is reachable by foot. You might also notice that the island doesn't have traffic lights, fast food outlets, shopping malls, or outdoor advertising. A UNESCO World Biosphere Reserve, farming and fishing remain the lifeblood of unspoiled Corvo, as does cheese production; the number of cows on the island are said to outnumber the inhabitants by more than twofold. On an island where modern conveniences are sparse (although there is Wi-Fi!) and life is simplistic and impervious), visitors will experience the warmest welcome and a unique community spirit.

## GETTING THERE

You can fly to Corvo from Flores in just 5-10 minutes, or take the year-round, daily, 40-minute ferry between Santa Cruz das Flores (Flores) and Vila do Corvo (Corvo).

### Air

#### CORVO AIRPORT

#### (Aeródromo do Corvo)

*Vila do Corvo; tel. 292 590 310; www.sata.pt*

# Corvo

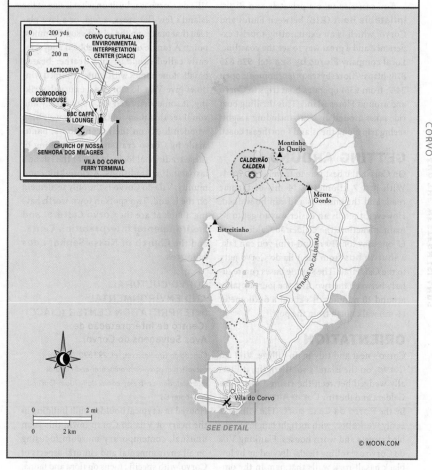

© MOON.COM

The short hop by plane between **Flores Airport** and Corvo Airport (CVU) is just 5-10 minutes, and tickets can be found for around €60 round-trip. There are also flights to Corvo from **Horta Airport** on Faial, with a flight time of around 45 minutes (from about €100 round-trip). Flights are operated by **SATA – Air Açores** (the only airline that flies to Corvo). There are daily flights during summer (July-August) and three times a week (Mon., Wed., and Fri.) the rest of the year. It's a 6-minute walk (530 meters/1,700 ft) from the airdrome to Vila do Corvo town center.

## Ferry
### PORTO DA CASA - CORVO PORT
*www.corvovirtual.pt/porto-da-casa*

Azores ferry company **Atlanticoline** (www. atlanticoline.pt) operates a regular ferry crossing between **Flores** (Santa Cruz das Flores) and Corvo (Vila do Corvo; 40 minutes; twice daily in low season, more regularly in summer; €10), via the **Pink Line.** The last ferry back to Flores is usually around 5pm (6pm mid-July-mid-Aug., 4pm Sept.-Dec.).

You can also take a privately run **Rigid Inflatable Boat** (RIB) between Flores and Corvo, which is an exhilarating tourist experience and a great way to see the coastline. Local company **Flores by Sea** (tel. 926 625 878; https://floresbysea.pt/en/home-2; open 24/7; from €35) operates boat trips to Corvo and around Flores island. This thrilling boat ride takes around an hour, including a sightseeing trip along the island's northeast coast.

## GETTING AROUND

On Corvo, the best way to travel is **on foot.** With just 7 kilometers (4 mi) of tarmac road, and the entire island can be walked. However, there is an easier way to get to its main attraction, the Caldeirão Caldera: For €5 one-way (or €10 round-trip) you can take a **shuttle bus** from the Vila do Corvo jetty to the Caldeirão. The shuttle buses run regularly between the two, and the journey takes around 10 minutes. It's about a 6-kilometer (4-mi) walk north from the port.

## ORIENTATION

Corvo's neat and tidy main village, **Vila do Corvo,** on the island's southern tip, is literally wedged between the rising **Caldeirão** Caldera and the tiny **Corvo Airport,** fronted by the **Porto da Casa port.** The village is easily **walkable,** with its tight tangle of cobbled streets and worn houses. Flanking Vila do Corvo are rolling fields, divvied up by low black basalt rock walls that hem in the omnipresent cows and vegetation. The island has few tarmac roads, its main routes being the road out of Vila Nova do Corvo to the Caldeirão (Estrada do Caldeirão), and the stretch heading north along the east coast to the Caldeirão Caldera (Estrada do Pico do João Moura). The Caldeirão has a viewpoint on its southeastern flank, the **Miradouro do Caldeirão,** next to which is a free parking lot.

## SIGHTS
### Vila do Corvo

Vila do Corvo was built on what is one of the island's few flat areas, a *fajã*, or a lava plateau that makes up the island's southernmost point. A tangle of narrow pebbled alleys, locally called *canadas,* and weather-beaten basalt-stone homes with white-trimmed windows give Vila do Corvo an unusual, striking, if somewhat tired air. Look closely and you'll see that many of the little houses have wooden locks on their front doors, handmade by Corvo craftsmen; the making of these traditional locks is one of the island's last-standing traditions. A close-knit community, Vila do Corvo is the only settlement on the island. Two spots in town worth having a look at are the **Corvo Cultural and Environmental Interpretation Center** and the **Church of Nossa Senhora dos Milagres.**

### CORVO CULTURAL AND ENVIRONMENTAL INTERPRETATION CENTER (CIACC)
(Centro de Interpretação de Aves Selvagens do Corvo)

*Canada do Graciosa s/n; tel. 292 590 200; www. corvovirtual.pt/en/environmental-and-cultural-interpretation-centre-of-corvo; daily 10am-1pm and 2pm-6pm; €3*

Housed in a typical boulder-built building in the heart of Vila do Corvo town, this is an unusual, contemporary museum focusing on all environmental and cultural aspects of Corvo, with specific focus on flora and fauna. The building was purposely restored by the regional government to house the center, which is part of a wider project to regenerate the island. New arrivals on Corvo should make a beeline here to learn about the island's main attractions, natural heritage, and traditions. This little gem provides a window into Corvo's makeup.

1: Vila do Corvo 2: Caldeirão Caldera

## CHURCH OF NOSSA SENHORA DOS MILAGRES
### (Igreja de Nossa Senhora dos Milagres)

*Largo do Outeiro; daily 9am-6pm; free*

Overlooking the waterfront, taking center stage in the town's main square, the Church of Nossa Senhora dos Milagres is a 16th-century church that, from the outside, is nothing really to write home about. But the inside is fascinating. This little church has been destroyed and rebuilt twice; first by pirates in 1632, and then after being completely devastated by a fire in 1932. Following the pirate attack, an exquisite statue of Our Lady of the Rosary, believed to be of Flemish origin, appeared in the sea; local folklore claims that the image saved the people of Corvo from the bullets of the pirates' attacks. That image survived the 1932 blaze, and is now referred to as Our Lady of Miracles. This precious statue of the island's patron saint is kept at the church and is one of Corvo's most prized possessions. It is on display and can been seen by visitors, along with an Indo-Portuguese ivory crucifix.

## ★ Caldeirão Caldera

*6 kilometers (4 mi) north of Vila do Corvo; open 24/7; free*

You can't visit Corvo and not see the Caldeirão volcanic crater. Located on the northern half of the island, the Caldeirão is huge. At 300 meters (1,000 ft) deep and 3.5 kilometers (2.2 mi) in circumference, it is a mesmerizing bowl of rolling walls lined with innumerable shades of green and a mossy basin, scattered with little peaks and lagoons forming islets in the bottom. The contrast of the patchwork of green against the deep blue of the ocean is simply stunning. Most people enjoy a 4.8-kilometer (3-mi) walk around the rim of the crater, starting at the Miradouro do Caldeirão viewpoint, which takes about 2.5 hours. Descending to the lakes is also possible, though care is required as the grassy sides can be steep and slippery, especially if wet. There are marked pathways down to the bottom; it's about a 2-kilometer (1 mi; 45 minute) hike down and back up again.

You can walk to the Caldeirão Caldera and back from Vila do Corvo; it's a 6.1-kilometer (4-mi) trek (1 hour 35 minutes) from the harbor along two of the island's few asphalt roads, Estada do Caldeirão and Estudante do Pico do João Moura, which terminate at the caldera's northeastern rim. It's a constant gradual climb going, and a constant downward slope down on the way back, so it's probably best to take the shuttle there and walk back, if you want to enjoy a walk. En route you can enjoy lovely scenery, including endless rows of hydrangeas, rolling fields divvied up by low basalt rock walls, typical basalt-built cottages, and peacefully grazing cows and wild horses.

# FOOD

There are a number of small eateries in Vila do Corvo, mostly cafés, snack bars, and down-to-earth little local restaurants. The food on Corvo is extra fresh, plucked either straight from the sea or the fields. Cornbread is a freshly baked local specialty, served as a starter to most meals. Another typical dish to look out for, especially for the more adventurous palate, is Torta de Erva do Calhau (rock grass tart); a tart made from seaweed picked from the rocks, added to beaten eggs, and fried in lard.

## BBC CAFFÉ & LOUNGE

*Avenida Nova; tel. 292 596 030; www.facebook.com/ bbccorvo; Mon.-Fri. 8am-11pm, Sat. 7pm-midnight; Sun. 11am-10pm; €5*

This is an almost compulsory stop for anyone visiting Corvo. Located in Vila do Corvo town center, it's a great place to refuel after walking to or from the Caldeirão. It's where everyone from the village goes: a lofty eatery that's great for quick, filling snacks. The menu comprises the likes of hamburgers, toasties, sandwiches, cakes, and fresh soup. At night the upper floor becomes a social club, and, with beers for just over €1 and cocktails around €3, it's a great place to unwind and meet the locals. And probably the only place on the island for a late-night bite and drink.

# Corvo's Artisanal Cured Cheese

When visiting Corvo, you must try its artisanal cured cheese, a delicacy on the island. Cured for 60 days, it is yellow in color and has a strong, almost spicy taste. Queijo do Corvo can be tried at most restaurants and bought from greengrocers on the island. There are two or three little supermarkets and grocery stores in the village. But where better to sample it than at its real home, the **Lacticorvo** factory and specialty store (Caminho da Horta funda; tel. 292 596 163; www.facebook.com/lacticorvo; Mon.-Fri. 9am-5pm), a 5-minute walk north of Corvo town center.

## ACCOMMODATIONS

Accommodation on Corvo is limited; there's one main guesthouse on the island and a smattering of privately run apartments and townhouses. If you're planning to stay the night, in summer particularly, make sure you book well ahead.

### COMODORO GUESTHOUSE

*Caminho do Areeiro s/n; tel. 292 596 128; www. comodoroazores.com; €50 d*

Located in Vila do Corvo town center, Comodoro Guesthouse is one of few lodging options on Corvo island. With 14 clean and comfortable double rooms and walking distance to pretty much everywhere on the island, the hotel boasts magnificent views over Corvo as well as free high-speed internet. The guesthouse also provides free transportation to and from the airport and port.

## INFORMATION AND SERVICES

There is a basic health unit in Corvo village, a post office, a pharmacy, and a tourist information bureau located about halfway between the port and the village center. There's also a GNR police station, and **ATMs** are available on the island.

- **Tourist bureau:** Caminho dos Moinhos; tel. 292 596 227
- **GNR police:** Rua da Cruz; tel. 292 596 261
- **Vila Nova do Corvo health unit:** Avenida do Corvo; tel. 292 596 153 or 292 596 154
- **Pharmacy:** Rua do Jogo da Bola; tel. 292 596 085
- **CTT post office:** Road to the Caldeirão; tel. 292 596 053

# Stopover in Lisbon

**Portugal's magnificent capital is currently one** of Europe's most up-and-coming cities—vibrant and culturally rich, where the historic blends seamlessly with the cool and contemporary. At the mouth of the Tagus River (Rio Tejo), the "City of Seven Hills" is buzzing and cosmopolitan, home to melodic fado music and a vivid nightlife scene. Traditional tile-clad facades and redbrick roofs conceal a tangle of charming cobbled streets and elegant avenues that beckon to be explored.

Lisbon's impressive monuments, historic neighborhoods, and edgy vibe welcome visitors to drink in stunning bird's-eye views from many panoramic *miradouro* viewpoints or hip hotel rooftop bars. Stroll the chic boulevards with their many boutiques, admire striking riverfront

# Highlights

Look for ★ to find recommended sights, activities, dining, and lodging.

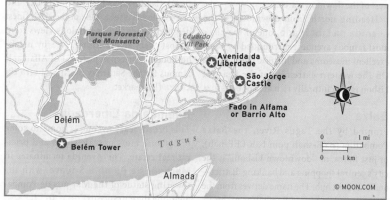

© MOON.COM

★ **São Jorge Castle:** On a hilltop in the heart of Lisbon, this imposing Moorish monument commands spectacular views of the historic city center and the Tagus River (page 290).

★ **Avenida da Liberdade:** An appealing mix of historic and contemporary buildings, high-end boutiques, and tree-shaded cafés lines the country's most famous avenue (page 291).

★ **Belém Tower:** At the mouth of the Tagus River, this fortified tower was the last and first sight the country's intrepid sailors had of their homeland when setting off and returning from their voyages (page 297).

★ **Fado in Alfama or Bairro Alto:** A night of soulful fado in its reputed birthplace is a can't-miss, unforgettable experience (page 310).

monuments, explore the many museums, or for the classic Lisbon experience, take the famous tram 28 around the city's historic nooks and crannies before enjoying mesmerizing fado in one of the many original haunts in Alfama or Bairro Alto.

# ORIENTATION

Hilly Lisbon is divided into many neighborhoods and parishes, or *bairros*. The heart of Lisbon's historic area is the **Baixa Pombalina**, often simply referred to as the Baixa; it's the main downtown commercial and banking area along the river. Baixa is immediately fringed by several of the city's other most famous neighborhoods: labyrinth-like **Alfama**, cultural and hip nighttime hangout **Chiado** and **Bairro Alto**, and cool and arty **Cais do Sodré**. **Alcântara**, a former docks area currently enjoying a hipster revival, is west of the downtown area.

Heading north from downtown is the **Avenida da Liberdade**, one of the city's most famous avenues, surrounded by some excellent museums and historic monuments. On the western extremity of the heart of Lisbon is the culturally rich area of **Belém**.

## Baixa

Fronted by the Tagus River, the Baixa Pombalina (BYE-shah pom-bah-LEE-nah), or just Baixa, or "downtown Lisbon," is the city's central shopping and banking district—and its tourist hub. The name derives from the distinctive Portuguese Pombaline architectural style employed to rebuild the city after the 1755 earthquake, under the guidance of Sebastião José de Carvalho e Melo, the 1st Marquis of Pombal. Elegant neoclassical facades and patterned cobbled streets give the neighborhood an air of graceful uniformity. Two main streets, **Rua Augusta** and **Rua da Prata**, are laden with buzzing shops and restaurants. The main Metro stops in the Baixa area are Avenida, Restauradores, Rossio,

Baixa-Chiado, and Terreiro do Paço, on the Green and Blue Lines.

## Alfama

Alfama (al-FAH-mah), just east of Baixa, is Lisbon's oldest and most soulful neighborhood and claims to be the birthplace of fado, although Bairro Alto also makes this claim. Inhabited from the 5th century by the Visigoths, the narrow cobbled streets of this unpolished neighborhood create a stepped labyrinth of historic houses and quirky shops. It was once rough and home to dockworkers and seafarers. As the city's port prospered, so did Alfama, although its rugged charisma remains. Alfama boasts monuments, traditional **fado houses**, and many fabulous **viewpoints** along its slopes.

In the northern part of Alfama, the stately and traditional area around **São Jorge Castle** is known as Lisbon's birthplace and often called **Castelo.** One of the city's finest neighborhoods, it has fabulous views from almost every street corner. Nearby neighborhood São Vicente, just west of Alfama, is famous for the Saturday morning **Feira da Ladra** flea market.

## Avenida da Liberdade

This broad, leafy avenue is home to some of Lisbon's most upscale shops and priciest real estate. The Avenida terminates in **Marquês de Pombal Square,** with the towering statue of the Marquis de Pombal guarding the entrance to **Eduardo VII Park,** and is surrounded by some of the city's best museums.

## Chiado and Bairro Alto

Just northwest of Baixa, centered on the **Chiado Square**, Chiado (SHEE-aah-doo) neighborhood is the core of Lisbon's cultural scene—a district packed with theaters, museums, and galleries. Sandwiched between the Baixa and Bairro Alto, the emblematic

---

**Previous:** Comércio Square; São Jorge Castle; fado venue in Alfama.

square is lined with traditional commerce, fashionable boutiques, and cultural venues galore.

A bit farther northwest, Bairro Alto (BYE-rroo AL-too) has long been Lisbon's bohemian hangout, a favorite haunt for artists and writers. In the evenings, its grid of steep streets echoes with melancholic fado. Visit after 11pm, when the innumerable **small bars** and **colorful nightspots** really start to hit their stride. The neighborhood's historical significance dates to its expansion in the 16th century to accommodate the city's booming economic and social transformation.

## Cais do Sodré

Fronting Lisbon's downtown to the west is Cais do Sodré—or the Sodré Docks—a trendy, underrated part of Lisbon on the riverside. Historically important and one of the city's busiest areas for nightlife, Cais do Sodré is also the location of one of the main **ferry terminals** for crossing the Tagus as well as the train terminus for the **Lisbon-Cascais train line.** Because of this, the area sees heavy traffic of students and commuters passing through daily.

## Alcântara

Wedged halfway between downtown Lisbon (Baixa) and Belém, directly beneath the **25 de Abril Bridge,** is Alcântara (al-KHAAN-ta-ra), a riverside area of significant urban revival, popular among locals. Said to take its name from the Arabic word for "bridge," the former port and industrial area is today one of the city's busiest **nightlife** spots, its old warehouses having given way to hip bars and restaurants. With a growing art scene, it is one of Lisbon's liveliest areas.

Across the 25 de Abril Bridge, in the town of Almada, is the the *Christ the King* statue, whose outstretched arms dominate the skyline of the Tagus's west bank.

## Belém

Just west of downtown in bright and breezy Belém (beh-LAYN), iconic landmarks such as the **Jerónimos Monastery** and **Belém Tower** pay tribute to key chapters in Portugal's history, sharing a riverside location with modern museums, cafés, and gardens. During the Age of Discoveries, this is where ships set off to explore the globe. Belém, home of the famous *pastel de Belém* tart, can be uncomfortably busy, particularly in the heat of summer; expect long queues.

To get to Belém from downtown Lisbon, take tram 15 or 127 from the main Comércio Square, or the Cascais train from Cais do Sodré to Cascais. Jump off when you see the Jerónimos Monastery, and walk to the sights. A taxi from downtown Lisbon costs around €14 one-way.

## SAFETY

As with many tourist destinations, Lisbon is afflicted by petty and opportunistic crime. Take basic precautions such as not walking along dark streets alone at night, not leaving valuables in rental vehicles, and not carrying large amounts of cash. Pickpockets are an issue, so make sure backpacks are worn in front in crowded areas and on public transport. Better still, use concealed pouches, and never keep cash and documents in the same pouch. Call the **PSP tourist police** (tel. 213 421 623) or visit the nearest police station. In an **emergency,** call **112.**

## PLANNING YOUR TIME

With just a day or so to spend in Lisbon before or after your trip to the Azores, a great way to cover the must-sees is either a **hop-on hop-off bus** that stops at all main attractions and landmarks, or **tram 28,** which circumnavigates Lisbon's main neighborhoods. Other good options to explore include a neatly organized **subway,** nifty *tuk-tuk* **carts,** and a **hop-on hop-off ferryboat.** While in Lisbon, an absolute must is dinner at a **fado restaurant** in Bairro Alto. Make reservations well in advance, as these are popular attractions.

In mid-June, the traditional **Santo António festivities,** dedicated to the city's

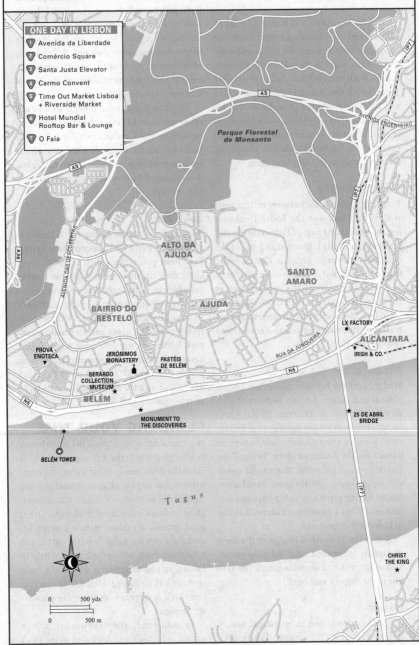

# Lisbon

**ONE DAY IN LISBON**

1. Avenida da Liberdade
2. Comércio Square
3. Santa Justa Elevator
4. Carmo Convent
5. Time Out Market Lisboa + Riverside Market
6. Hotel Mundial Rooftop Bar & Lounge
7. O Faia

Parque Florestal de Monsanto

ALTO DA AJUDA

SANTO AMARO

AJUDA

BAIRRO DO RESTELO

LX FACTORY

ALCÂNTARA

IRISH & CO.

RUA DA JUNQUEIRA

PROVA ENOTECA

JERÓNIMOS MONASTERY

PASTÉIS DE BELÉM

BERARDO COLLECTION MUSEUM

BELÉM

MONUMENT TO THE DISCOVERIES

25 DE ABRIL BRIDGE

BELÉM TOWER

Tagus

CHRIST THE KING

0        500 yds

0        500 m

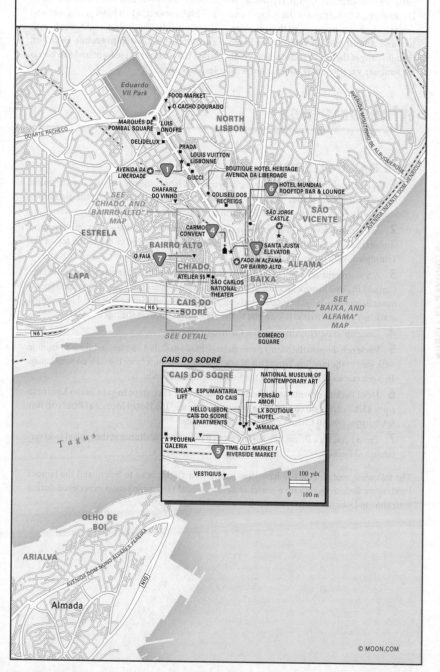

patron saint, explode into party mode. In December, **Christmas** trimmings and roasted chestnuts bring warmth to the city. July and August can get very hot, and even though many of the city's residents head south for summer vacation, it is still packed with tourists. **Summer** and **New Year** are tourism high seasons, when hotel prices soar and the city is full of visitors. Good times to visit are **March-May** and **September-October,** when the weather is pleasant and the hotels less expensive.

# Itinerary Idea

## ONE DAY IN LISBON

**1** Spend the morning discovering downtown Lisbon. Begin by walking the main **Avenida da Liberdade,** heading south toward the Tagus River. Peruse the glamorous window displays and stop for a mid-morning coffee at one of the picturesque cafés.

**2** In the main downtown area, explore famous **Comércio Square** and its museums and landmarks—they're all within walking distance. Make sure you climb to the top of the Triumphal Arch on Rua Augusta.

**3** A few streets back from the main square is the **Santa Justa Elevator,** also called the Carmo Lift. This historical contraption transports passengers from downtown up to the famous Bairro Alto neighborhood. Hop onto the elevator and admire how the old-fashioned machinery comes to life, taking you to the viewing platform at the top.

**4** Once up in Bairro Alto, visit the **Carmo Convent.**

**5** For lunch, hop on the Metro (from Baixa-Chiado to Cais do Sodré) or take a 20-minute walk west to the bustling **Time Out Market Lisboa,** set back from the Cais do Sodré quay. This eclectic food hall showcases the finest Portuguese products.

**6** Head back to downtown Lisbon via tram, bus, or taxi, stopping at Chiado Square to enjoy a late-afternoon cocktail on a panoramic terrace. The **Hotel Mundial Rooftop Bar & Lounge,** just off Chiado Square, is a good choice.

**7** From here, it's a 20-minute stroll west to Bairro Alto for dinner at the typical fado restaurant **O Faia.**

The following morning, if you have time before your flight, head to Belém and the famous **Pastéis de Belém** bakery for a *pastel de Belém* custard tart, a can't-miss experience during your time in Lisbon.

# Sights

## BAIXA

### Comércio Square
(Praça do Comércio)

This vast square, with views of the Tagus River, bustles with visitors and features a statue of King José I on his horse. The impressive colonnades that frame it on three sides house several ministries, museums, shops, and restaurants. It's one of the city's main transport hubs, with many trams and buses running from here; it's also directly across from the Cais do Sodré ferry terminal.

### Augusta Triumphal Arch
(Arco da Rua Augusta)

*Rua Augusta 2; tel. 210 998 599; www.visitlisboa. com; daily 9am-8pm; viewing terrace €3; Metro Terreiro do Paço, Blue Line*

The formal entrance to the Baixa neighborhood, the decorative Augusta Triumphal Arch was built to mark the city's resilience and glorious rebirth following the 1755 earthquake. Historical Portuguese figures such as explorer Vasco da Gama and the Marquis of Pombal adorn the gateway's six columns, gazing over Comércio Square and out to the river. Inside the arch, a narrow spiral staircase made from solid stone climbs to a viewing terrace that offers sweeping views of the plaza.

### Santa Justa Elevator
(Elevador de Santa Justa)

*www.carris.pt; daily 7am-11pm Mar.-Oct., daily 7am-9pm Nov.-Feb.; round-trip €5.30; Metro Baixa-Chiado, Green/Blue Lines*

Also called the **Carmo Lift,** the 19th-century neo-Gothic, wrought-iron Santa Justa Elevator is the only vertical lift in Lisbon, connecting the Baixa area to the Bairro Alto neighborhood, saving a steep climb. Inaugurated in 1902, it is classified as a national monument. Standing at 45 meters (148 ft) tall, it was designed by engineer Raoul Mesnier de Ponsard in a style similar to that of the Eiffel Tower. The lift is stunning at night when lit up and has a fabulous viewing platform at the top. Intriguingly, it can transport more people going up than coming down. It is accessed via Rua do Ouro at the bottom or **Carmo Square** at the top. The viewing platform (access to platform €1.50) is also accessible directly from Carmo Square, up the hill behind the lift.

### Rossio Square
(Praça Dom Pedro IV)

*Metro Rossio, Green Line*

The beating heart of Lisbon, located downtown, Rossio Square has long been one of the city's main meeting places, a lively, genteel square of Pombaline architecture lined with cafés, trees, and two grand Baroque fountains at either end. Housed in the impressive buildings framing the square are the stately **Dona Maria II National Theater (Teatro Nacional de Dona Maria II)** and the historic **Café Nicola,** which dates to the 18th century and was one of the first cafés to emerge in Lisbon. Also nearby is the ornate **Rossio train station,** which is typically Manueline in its architecture. One of the square's distinguishing features is the wavy black-and-white cobblestone paving.

### Glória Funicular
(Elevador da Glória)

*www.carris.pt; Mon.-Thurs. 7:15am-11:55pm, Fri. 7:15am-12:25am, Sat. 8:45am-12:25pm, Sun. and holidays 9:15am-11:55pm; round-trip €3.80*

The quirky Glória Funicular puts the "fun" in funicular. It has become an emblem of Lisbon, its graffiti scrawl only adding to its charm, mirroring its urban surroundings. Inaugurated in 1885, it connects the Baixa (Restauradores Square) to the **São Pedro de Alcântara viewpoint** in Bairro Alto via a steep track that cuts straight through a dense residential area packed with 19th-century

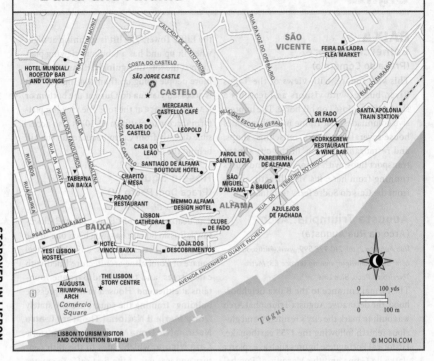

# Baixa and Alfama

HOTEL MUNDIAL/
ROOFTOP BAR
AND LOUNGE

CALÇADA DE SANTO ANDRÉ

COSTA DO CASTELO

SÃO JORGE CASTLE

★ CASTELO

RUA DA VOZ DO OPERÁRIO

SÃO
VICENTE

FEIRA DA LADRA
FLEA MARKET

RUA DO PARAÍSO

PRAÇA MARTIM MONIZ

RUA DOS FANQUEIROS

RUA DA
MADALENA

RUA DA
PRATA

RUA DOS

RUA AUREA

COSTA DO CASTELO

MERCEARIA
CASTELLO CAFÉ

RUA DAS ESCOLAS GERAIS

SOLAR DO
CASTELO

LEOPOLD

SR FADO
DE ALFAMA

SANTA APOLÓNIA
TRAIN STATION

CASA DO
LEÃO

FAROL DE
SANTA LUZIA

PARREIRINHA
DE ALFAMA

CORKSCREW
RESTAURANT
& WINE BAR

SANTIAGO DE ALFAMA
BOUTIQUE HOTEL

SÃO
MIGUEL
D'ALFAMA

Á BAIUCA

TABERNA
DA BAIXA

CHAPITÔ
Á MESA

PRADO
RESTAURANT

MEMMO ALFAMA
DESIGN HOTEL

ALFAMA

RUA DO TERREIRO DO TRIGO

AZULEJOS
DE FACHADA

BAIXA

RUA DA CONCEIÇÃO

LISBON
CATHEDRAL

CLUBE
DE FADO

YESI LISBON
HOSTEL

HOTEL
VINCCI BAIXA

LOJA DOS
DESCOBRIMENTOS

AVENIDA ENGENHEIRO DUARTE PACHECO

AUGUSTA
TRIUMPHAL
ARCH

THE LISBON
STORY CENTRE

Comércio
Square

Tagus

0      100 yds

0      100 m

LISBON TOURISM VISITOR
AND CONVENTION BUREAU

© MOON.COM

buildings. Practical for locals, it's a treat for visitors.

# ALFAMA
## ★ São Jorge Castle
### (Castelo de São Jorge)

*Rua de Santa Cruz do Castelo; tel. 218 800 620; www.castelodesaojorge.pt; daily 9am-9pm Mar.-Oct., daily 9am-6pm Nov.-Feb.; €10*

The São Jorge Castle sits on a summit high above historic Baixa. The original fortress was built by the Visigoths in the 5th century and expanded by the Moors in the mid-11th century due to its prime defensive location. It contains the medieval castle, ruins of the former royal palace, stunning gardens, and part of an 11th-century citadel.

A permanent exhibition of relics uncovered here includes objects from the 7th century BC to the 18th century. The Black Chamber,

a camera obscura, provides 360-degree views of the city through an optical system of mirrors and lenses, while an open-air viewpoint looks over the city center and the Tagus River. Renowned restaurant Casa do Leão and a casual café are also within the castle walls. To get there from downtown Lisbon, take tram 28 or the Castelo Bus, line 737.

## Lisbon Cathedral
### (Sé de Lisboa)

*Largo da Sé; tel. 218 866 752; www.patriarcado-lisboa.pt; daily 9am-7pm; main cathedral free; tram 28 or 12*

Between the Alfama neighborhood and Castelo, Lisbon Cathedral is the oldest and most famous church in the city. Its official name is the Church of Santa Maria Maior, but it is often simply called the Sé. Construction began in 1147, and successive modifications

# Lisbon's Best Views

Because Lisbon is laid out over seven hills, gorgeous views can be found throughout the city. Public viewing points (*miradouros*) offer views of the cityscape. Some are enhanced with cafés and restaurants, landscaped gardens, and even chic lounges. Best of all, they're free. Visit at sunset for a truly special experience.

- The famous **Miradouro São Pedro de Alcântara** (Rua São Pedro de Alcântara) provides panoramic views over São Jorge Castle and Alfama, as well as Lisbon Cathedral and the Tagus.

- The romantic **Miradouro da Nossa Senhora do Monte** (Largo Monte) is the highest viewpoint, offering bird's-eye views over the old quarters and castle all the way to the Tagus River.

- The **Miradouro Portas do Sol** (Largo Portas do Sol) overlooks the charismatic Alfama neighborhood.

- The **Miradouro da Graça** (Calçada da Graça) peers over São Jorge Castle.

Along with the *miradouros,* the **São Jorge Castle** has possibly the best views in the city. Panoramas can also be enjoyed from hotel rooftop bars, such as the **Hotel Mundial** (Praça Martim Moniz 2), where the Sunset Parties have a cult following.

and renovations span the centuries. Its exterior is austere, with two robust towers. Inside, a wealth of decorative features reflect different eras. The neoclassical and rococo main chapel contains the tombs of King Afonso IV and his family. You'll also see lofty Gothic vaults, sculptured Romanesque motifs, stained-glass rose windows, and a Baroque sacristy. The **Cloister** (Mon.-Sat. 10am-5pm, Sun. 2pm-5pm, extended hours until 7pm May-Sept.; €2.50) houses Roman, Arab, and medieval relics excavated during archaeological digs. The **Treasury** (Mon.-Sat. 10am-5pm; €2.50) on the second floor contains jewels from various periods. Tram 28 stops right outside the cathedral's door.

## ★ AVENIDA DA LIBERDADE

Stretching 1.5 kilometers (0.9 mi) between the Baixa downtown area and the Eduardo VII Park, the Avenida da Liberdade is Lisbon's main boulevard, an elegant, almost regal main avenue running through the heart of the city. It's dotted with distinguished statues and monuments, high-end designer boutiques, lovely little coffee kiosks, arts and crafts stalls, chic hotels, and trendy bars and restaurants, and lined with leafy trees. It was almost completely rebuilt after the devastating 1755 earthquake, styled on the chic boulevards of Paris, and originally intended for Lisbon's wealthy. Its main terminuses are the Restauradores Square in the Baixa and the noble Marquês de Pombal Square in front of the Eduardo VII garden.

This bustling artery adopts the spirit of each season, with cute Christmas markets in winter, spring sales for shoppers, an alfresco atmosphere in summer when it plays host to the popular saints festivities, and falling golden brown leaves in autumn. Along this lavish avenue there are lovely water features, and it boasts the typical grandiose classical architecture of 19th-century Portugal.

A fantastic place for window-shopping and people-watching, everything about the Avenida da Liberdade is distinguished and grand; the walk downhill from the Praça dos Restauradores to the Baixa is a lovely introduction to Lisbon.

### Marquês de Pombal Square
#### (Praça Marquês de Pombal)

The massive statue of the Marquis of Pombal towering in the middle of this busy

# Chiado and Bairro Alto

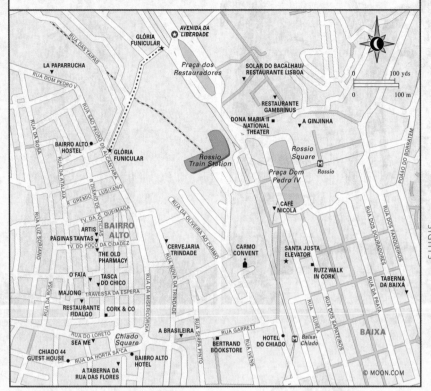

roundabout is one of Lisbon's most recognizable landmarks. Sebastião José de Carvalho e Melo, the 1st Marquis of Pombal, was prime minister in the 18th century. His soaring statue faces the Tagus River, strategically between Eduardo VII Park and the cosmopolitan Avenida da Liberdade, the start of several main thoroughfares. Get here by taking the Metro to Marquês de Pombal station (Blue/Yellow Lines).

## CHIADO AND BAIRRO ALTO

Named after acclaimed Portuguese poet Almeida Garrett, **Garrett Street** (Rua

1: Avenida da Liberdade 2: Marquês de Pombal Square

Garrett) is the main vein traversing Chiado, a pulsing shopping street flanked by handsome cultural venues, such as the **São Carlos National Theatre, Livraria Bertrand**, believed to be one of the oldest bookstores in the world, and the century-old **A Brasileira** café, once the meeting point of Lisbon's intellectuals and luminaries.

## Carmo Convent
### (Convento do Carmo)

*Largo do Carmo; tel. 213 478 629; www. museuarqueologicodocarmo.pt; Mon.-Sat. 10am-7pm May-Sept., Mon.-Sat. 10am-6pm Oct.-Apr.; €5; Metro Baixa-Chiado or Rossio, Green/Blue Lines*

Once Lisbon's largest church, the Carmo Convent is a stark reminder of the vast devastation caused by the 1755 earthquake, which

razed the city and large swaths of Portugal. Originally built in 1389 by order of Nuno Álvares Pereira, an influential knight who led the Portuguese army, the church and convent sit on a hill directly opposite the São Jorge Castle. Today only its naked Gothic ruins still stand. The site is also home to the Museu Arqueológico do Carmo, a museum with a collection of relics from dissolved monasteries, including sarcophagi and grisly but well-preserved Peruvian sacrificial mummies.

## CAIS DO SODRÉ

Cais do Sodré has recently undergone a much-needed facelift that elevated the neighborhood from seedy to swanky. Gone are the days when swashbuckling sailors sought their thrills during layovers in Lisbon and fishermen told their colorful tales in the many tackle shops that dotted the area; nowadays the tackle shops have been converted into cool hangouts, brothels into trendy bars, and the hip **Time Out Market Lisboa** is where new gastro trends are set.

### Bica Lift
#### (Ascensor da Bica)

*Calçada da Bica Pequena 1; tel. 213 613 000; Mon.-Sat. 7am-9pm, Sun. and public holidays 9am-9pm; €3.80 (round-trip, purchased on-board)*

Inaugurated in 1892, this funicular connects Lisbon's downtown to the Bica and Bairro Alto neighborhoods, running every 15 minutes between Rua de São Paulo, near Cais do Sodré's Time Out Market Lisboa, and Largo do Calhariz (Calhariz Square). Its route takes passengers up one of Lisbon's steepest hills, Bica de Duarte Belo Street, on what is arguably one of the city's most picturesque funicular routes, passing quaint houses and traditional commerce. The funicular's traction system was originally powered by steam engines before being electrified in 1914. It was declared a National Monument in 2002 and is one of the city's most popular tourist

1: Carmo Convent 2: *Christ the King* statue 3: Belém Tower

activities. Once up at the top, make sure to visit the Santa Catarina viewpoint, which offers stunning bird's-eye views of the city.

## ALCÂNTARA
### 25 de Abril Bridge
#### (Ponte 25 de Abril)

*tel. 212 947 920; www.lusoponte.pt; tolls €1.75-7 (northbound only)*

Lisbon's iconic 25 de Abril Bridge dominates the skyline from most directions. Stand underneath it and the buzz of the vehicles whooshing above is hypnotic. It was inaugurated in 1966, and prior to the Carnation Revolution it was named the Salazar Bridge, after statesman António de Oliveira Salazar. Post-independence it was renamed the 25 de Abril Bridge, in tribute to the bloodless uprising that overthrew Salazar's dictatorial regime and gave Portugal independence and democracy, on April 25, 1974. Spanning 2,277 meters (1.4 mi) the bright red suspension bridge connects Lisbon to Almada, on the south bank of the Tagus River. The upper deck carries six vehicle lanes, and the bottom deck is a double electrified rail track, added in 1999. Crossed by some 150,000 cars every day, it offers the most incredible views of the Lisbon for those who come into the city over the bridge.

The bridge is also home to one of Lisbon's newest tourist attractions, the **Pillar 7 Experience** (Avenida da Índia (N6 34); tel. 211 117 880; www.visitlisboa.com/en/places/pilar-7-bridge-experience; daily 10am-8pm May-Sept., daily 10am-6pm Oct.-Apr.; €6), an interactive museum that allows visitors to explore inside one of the famous bridge's pillars. Those with a head for heights can take an elevator to a 72-meter-high (236-ft-high) panoramic glass viewing platform adjacent to the pillar. Vertigo-sufferers be warned—the floor is glass, too (but the views are worth the shaky legs)!

### Christ the King
#### (Cristo Rei)

*Alto do Pragal, Av. Cristo Rei; tel. 212 751 000 or 212 721 270; www.cristorei.pt; daily 9:30am-6:30pm; €4*

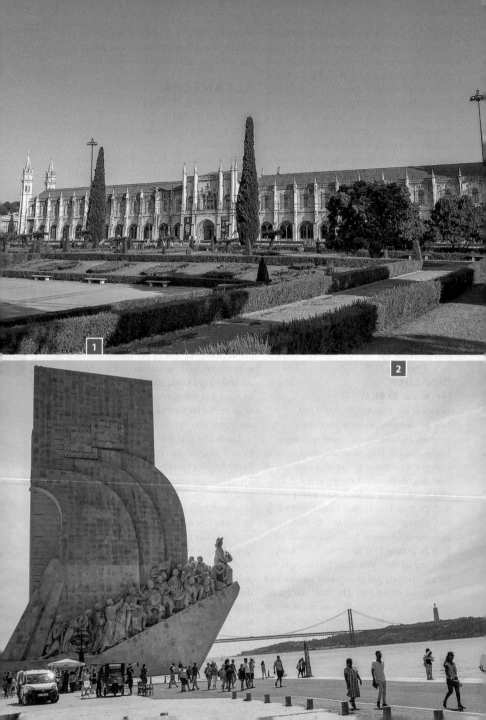

Dominating the skyline of the Tagus's south bank just across from the 25 de Abril Bridge is the *Christ the King* statue, standing with arms outstretched and epitomizing Portugal's Catholic faith. The idea to build the monument came after the Cardinal Patriarch of Lisbon visited Rio de Janeiro in 1934 and was impressed by its imposing *Christ the Redeemer* statue. Built on an isolated cliff top in the town of Almada, the statue stands 192 meters (630 ft) above the Tagus River. An express elevator whizzes visitors to a viewing platform at 82 meters (269 ft), which affords dazzling views over the city. At the statue's base is a chapel. The statue's interior contains a library, a large café, two halls, and another chapel.

# BELÉM

## ★ Belém Tower
### (Torre de Belém)

*Av. Brasília; tel. 213 620 034; www.torrebelem.gov. pt; daily 10am-5:30pm Oct.-Apr., daily 10am-6:30pm May-Sept.; €6*

Jutting into the Tagus River, Belém Tower is Portugal's most famous monument and a UNESCO World Heritage Site due to its significance as a launchpad during the Age of Discoveries. Built in the early 16th century at the river mouth, the fortified tower was both functional and ornamental, defending Lisbon from sea raiders and also providing a ceremonial entrance to the city. The ornate white Manueline tower was the last and first sight sailors had of their homeland. The elaborate detail of the exterior belies the starkness of the interior.

Entering the tower over an ancient drawbridge, visitors access a bulwark housing artillery, in the middle of which is a small courtyard flanked by Gothic arches. Inside the tower are the Governor's Room, the King's Room, the Audience Room, and a chapel, all devoid of furnishings, showcasing only the bare stonework. The tower is built over five floors, connected by a narrow spiral staircase, each floor having lovely balconies, and topped

1: Jerónimos Monastery 2: Monument to the Discoveries

by a viewing terrace. It's worth the climb to the top for views over the Tagus estuary and the Belém neighborhood's monuments.

## Jerónimos Monastery
### (Mosteiro dos Jerónimos)

*Praça do Império; tel. 213 620 034; www. mosteirojeronimos.gov.pt; Tues.-Sun. 10am-5:30pm Oct.-Apr., Tues.-Sun. 10am-6:30pm May-Sept.; €10; ticket including the Maritime Museum and the Archaeology Museum €12; bus 727, 728, 729, 714, 751, tram 15, suburban train to Belém*

Parallel to the Tagus River, with the stately Imperial Square Gardens sprawling in front of it, the exuberant Jerónimos Monastery is Belém's breathtaking centerpiece. A prime example of ornate Manueline architecture, it is also a UNESCO World Heritage Site. Construction on the impressive landmark began in 1501 on the order of King Manuel I, who wanted to honor the memory of explorer Henry the Navigator, as well as demonstrate his own devotion to Saint Jerome. The vast building took 100 years to complete. Its several architectural styles include Renaissance and the lavishly ornate Spanish plateresque style. The magnificent riverside facade has a figure of Our Lady of Belém, while inside is the Latin-cross-shaped Church of Santa Maria, the final resting place of explorer Vasco da Gama and one of Portugal's greatest poets, Luís Vaz de Camões. Today the monastery's long, regal wings house the naval museum.

Also located in the expansive wings of the Jerónimos Monastery is the **National Archaeology Museum** (Museu Nacional de Arqueologia; €5, ticket including Jerónimos Monastery and the Maritime Museum €12), devoted to ancient Iberian art. Among its collections are ancient jewelry, busts, mosaics, and epigraphs, as well as metal artifacts, medals, and coins.

## Monument to the Discoveries
### (Padrão dos Descobrimentos)

*Av. Brasília; tel. 213 031 950; www. padraodosdescobrimentos.pt; daily 10am-7pm Mar.-Sept., Tues.-Sun. 10am-6pm Oct.-Feb.; €3*

A short stroll from Belém Tower along the Tagus riverside is the Monument to the Discoveries. First erected in 1940 and made permanent in 1960 to mark 500 years since Henry the Navigator's death, the monument celebrates the Age of Discoveries in the 15th and 16th centuries with statues of Henry the Navigator, Pedro Álvares Cabral, and Vasco da Gama. Shaped like a caravel—a small Portuguese sailing ship—it also houses an auditorium and a museum with changing exhibitions and has a viewing platform on top. In the square out front is the stunning **Compass Rose,** an elaborate decorative work of paving art shaped like a compass, 50 meters (164 ft) across, in black and red *lioz* limestone. In the center is a map of the world during the Age of Discoveries, surrounded by decorative figures like mermaids, stars, and leaves.

## Berardo Collection Museum (Museu Colecção Berardo)

*Praça do Império; tel. 213 612 878; www. museuberardo.pt; daily 10am-7pm; €5 (free entry on Saturdays); tram 15, bus 714, 728*

Lisbon's most-visited museum is indeed a must-see for modern art lovers. Comprising a vast selection of carefully curated modern and contemporary art, spanning all genres from Cubism to Pop Art, the outstanding Berardo Collection Museum is a private collection that features iconic pieces by the greats—works by Mondrian, Picasso, Duchamp, Andy Warhol, Jackson Pollock, Salvador Dalí, and Francis Bacon can all be found here—as well as emerging artists. The permanent collection occupies the entire second floor, with rotating exhibitions on the lower floor.

# Sports and Recreation

## TAGUS RIVER BOAT TOURS

A nice view of Lisbon is on approach from the opposite side of the Tagus River, and, given the nation's seafaring history, a boat trip offers a uniquely appropriate vantage point to see the city.

### LISBON BY BOAT

*tel. 933 914 740; www.lisbonbyboat.com*

Lisbon by Boat offers a variety of tours, from guided sightseeing trips to romantic sunset cruises, but all promise unforgettable views of the Portuguese capital. By motorboat or by yacht, trips range 1-6 hours, starting from around €35 pp for an hour-long historic Lisbon sightseeing cruise.

### YELLOW BOAT TOUR

*www.yellowbustours.com; from €20*

An alternative way to explore Lisbon is on the hop-on hop-off Yellow Boat Tour. Purchase a 24-hour ticket that allows access at points of interest on both sides of the Tagus. A nonstop circuit takes 1.5 hours, with a running commentary on sights in a number of languages, including English.

## SEGWAY TOURS

### LISBON SEGWAY TOURS

*www.lisbonsegwaytours.pt; from €35*

Lisbon Segway Tours are a fun way to zip around the city and really get into its nooks and crannies. Tours visit different areas, including a riverside tour, a tour of Alfama, a city center tour, and a Belém tour. More unusual itineraries are a Lisbon by Night tour, a gastronomic tour to discover the city's foodie delights, and a three-hour super tour that covers most of the city's main spots.

## WALKING TOURS

Personalized walking tours by locals have become popular in Lisbon, allowing you to explore the city at a leisurely pace. Guided tours are available in English, and many are free. From private tours to foodie tours, pub crawls, and even sunset tours, follow a local guide who knows the city and its secrets as only a native could. Tours take place rain or shine, and can range from just over 1.5 hours to the full day. On free tours, payment is in the form of tips—a suggested tip is €5-12 pp. Specialist walking-tour companies include **Discover Walks Lisbon** (www.discoverwalks. com) and **Discover Lisbon** (tel. 932 060 800; www.discoverlisbon.org).

## CYCLING
### GIRA
*tel. 211 163 060; www.gira-bicicletasdelisboa.pt*
Lisbon City Hall has created an extensive shared-bicycle network and a web of cycle paths. The shared-bicycle scheme Gira comprises about 50 stations around the city, with 500 electric and standard bicycles. Download the app, buy a day pass for €2, and pedal away. Lisbon has more than 60 kilometers (37 miles) of bicycle lanes to explore.

## LISBON BIKE TOUR AND OUTDOORS
*112; tel. 912 272 300; www.lisbonbiketour.com*
Tour companies such as Lisbon Bike Tour and Outdoors have designed exciting tours—all downhill—that cover key historic areas. The company has several bike ranks throughout Lisbon and the surrounding area.

## RENT-A-FUN
*www.rent-a-fun.com*
Rent-a-Fun includes some uphill climbs on its tours, but its bicycles are electric. Standard bike tours such as the Go Tejo - Electric Bike Tour take around 3 hours and cost €32  Rent-a-Fun also rents out electric, regular, and folding bicycles (from €9 per day 9am-6pm for a regular bike), including delivery, a helmet, and a lock. Kids prices are available on some of the activities (usually €10 less).

# Entertainment and Events

## THE ARTS
### SÃO CARLOS NATIONAL THEATER
**(Teatro Nacional de São Carlos)**
*Rua Serpa Pinto, 9; tel. 213 253 000; see https:// tnsc.bol.pt for program; Metro Baixa-Chiado, Green/ Blue Lines*
Portugal's national opera house, the São Carlos National Theater, was inaugurated on June 30, 1793, built by order of Queen Maria I to replace the Tejo Opera House in Comércio Square, which was destroyed by the 1755 earthquake. Inspired by Italy's grandiose La Scala theater in Milan and the San Carlo Theater in Naples, it is still today the only Portuguese theater that produces and showcases opera and choral and symphonic music. Classified a National Monument, the beautiful neoclassical building with ornate rococo touches has long been a centerpiece of the country's cultural scene.

## COLISEU DOS RECREIOS
*Rua Portas de Santo Antão 96; tel. 213 240 580; www.coliseulisboa.com*
Inaugurated in 1890, the famed Coliseu dos Recreios regularly welcomes international productions, traditionally from the realm of ballet, theater, and opera, as well as pop stars, circus troupes, and comedians. Architecturally, the Coliseu was ahead of its time with cutting-edge ironwork, seen in its spectacular German-made iron dome and iron roof.

## DONA MARIA II NATIONAL THEATER
**(Teatro Nacional Dona Maria II)**
*Praça Dom Pedro IV; tel. 213 250 800; www.tndm.pt*
Prestigious Dona Maria II National Theater is a national jewel and cultural heavyweight on noble Rossio Square. Built between 1842 and 1846 in neoclassical style, it celebrates the performing arts with a full agenda of plays, shows, and concerts.

# Santo António and June Festivities

Dedicated to Saint Anthony, the city's patron, Santo António is Portugal's biggest traditional religious festival. Celebrations are staged throughout the capital for the whole month of June, reaching their peak on **June 12**, with jubilant parades and processions into the night. On June 13, the time-honored **Casamentos de Santo António** (Santo António weddings) are held. Established in 1958, this is a mass wedding of a dozen of the city's most impoverished couples, selected from hundreds of applicants. The entire ceremony, from the bridal outfits to the honeymoon, is funded by City Hall and other sponsors. Over these two days, the city parties to pay homage to "matchmaker" Saint Anthony, from the afternoon through the early morning.

During Santo António, Lisbon is at its prettiest. Every garden and square is decked out with colorful trimmings and lights. Food and drink stalls, tables, and chairs are set up with small stages for local artists to perform traditional folk songs. Grilled sardines, sangria, and traditional *caldo verde* (potato and kale) soup are served from stalls to fuel the merriment. The neighborhoods of **Alfama** and Bica are the most popular for Santo António. Each neighborhood also designs a float and takes part in a grand procession along the city's main avenues in the pinnacle of the celebrations to decide which neighborhood wins.

Santo António shouldn't be missed if you're in Portugal in June, but be sure to book accommodations far in advance if you decide to visit during this time.

# Shopping

Lisbon has a sophisticated shopping scene, from upscale stores along stylish Avenida da Liberdade to smaller boutiques and craft shops in the neighborhoods surrounding Baixa. It also has shopping centers galore and plenty of open-air markets.

**Baixa** itself, between Rossio Square and the riverside plazas and smaller boulevards, is the heart of commerce in Lisbon, where mainstream chain stores adjoin traditional grocery stores, boutiques, and souvenir shops. The two main shopping streets in the Baixa are **Rua da Prata** and **Rua Augusta,** parallel to each other from the main Comércio Square up to Rossio. However, for more unique souvenirs, you may want to venture farther afield to neighborhoods like Alfama, Chiado, and Bairro Alto.

## ALFAMA
### Tiles and Ceramics
#### LOJA DOS DESCOBRIMENTOS

*Rua dos Bacalhoeiros 12; tel. 218 865 563; www.loja-descobrimentos.com; daily 9am-7pm*

Loja dos Descobrimentos is a shop and workshop selling brightly colored hand-painted tiles and ceramics in styles from all over Portugal. Meet the artisans in the atelier and watch as they work on tiles, or paint your own.

#### AZULEJOS DE FACHADA

*Beco do Mexias 1; tel. 966 176 953; www. azulejosdefachada.com; Mon.-Fri. 10:30am-12:30pm and 2pm-5:30pm*

Another top place for authentic hand-painted tiles and ceramics with a bright modern twist, Azulejos de Fachada will also take custom orders and ship overseas.

## AVENIDA DA LIBERDADE

Lisbon's most famous avenue, and priciest real estate, Avenida da Liberdade has serious shopping. At 90 meters (295 ft) wide and more than 1 kilometer (0.6 mi) long, this fancy street—the busiest in Portugal—has fashion's biggest players, including **Louis Vuitton Lisbonne** (Av. da Liberdade 190; tel. 213 584 320; www. eu.louisvuitton.com; Mon.-Fri. 10am-8pm, Sat. noon-7pm), **Prada** (Av. da Liberdade 206;

tel. 213 199 490; Mon.-Sat. 10am-8pm, Sun. 11am-7pm), and **Gucci** (Av. da Liberdade 180; tel. 213 145 397; www.gucci.com; Mon.-Sat. 10am-8pm, Sun. 10am-6pm).

With exquisitely patterned cobblestone walkways and magnificent period architecture lining the stately boulevard, enhanced by cool, leafy gardens, it's often compared to Paris's Champs-Élysées. Most buildings along the avenue date from the 19th century, built after the devastating 1755 earthquake that razed most of Lisbon.

## Food and Wine
### DELIDELUX
*Rua Alexandre Herculano 15A; tel. 213 141 474; www. delidelux.pt; daily 9am-11pm*

Just off the Avenida da Liberdade at Rua Alexandre Herculano is the stylish DeliDelux, stocked with beautifully packaged gourmet products like wine, olive oil, and canned fish, which make great gifts.

## Clothing and Accessories
### LUÍS ONOFRE
*Av. da Liberdade 247; tel. 211 313 629; www. luisonofre.com; Mon.-Sat. 10am-7:30pm*

Women's shoe designer Luís Onofre built his brand on generations of family shoemaking history; the shoes are manufactured at a state-of-the art workshop in northern Portugal.

# CHIADO AND BAIRRO ALTO
## Arts and Crafts
### ATELIER 55
*Rua António Maria Cardoso, 70-74; tel. 213 474 192; www.atelier55.blogspot.com; Mon.-Sat. 11am-7pm*

A trove of authentic Portuguese arts and crafts, Atelier 55 brims with handmade ceramics, embroidery, and paintings from local artists.

## Books
### BERTRAND BOOKSTORE
### (Livraria Bertrand)
*Rua Garrett 73-75; tel. 213 476 122; www.bertrand.*

*pt; daily 9am-10pm; Metro Baixa-Chiado, Green/ Blue Lines*

Distinguished by Guinness World Records as the oldest working bookshop in the world, the Bertrand Bookstore in Chiado is housed in a beautiful old building clad in traditional blue and white Portuguese *azulejo* tiles. Open since the mid-1730s, this wonderful bookshop has several rooms packed with literature from some of Portugal's greatest authors—including José Saramago, Eça de Queiroz, Almada Negreiros, Alexandre Herculano, and Sophia de Mello Breyner—as well as a cozy café where visitors are encouraged to "try before you buy" (the books, not the cakes or coffee!).

## Cork
### CORK & CO
*Rua das Salgadeiras 10; tel. 216 090 231; www. corkandcompany.pt; Mon.-Sat. 11am-7pm, Sun. 3pm-7pm*

Everything at Cork & Co, from hats to shoes and all accessories, is made from natural cork.

### RUTZ WALK IN CORK
*Rua Rodrigues Faria 103; tel. 212 477 039; www.rutz. pt; daily 11am-7pm*

Rutz Walk in Cork is a Portuguese brand specializing in shoes, bags, accessories, and gifts made from cork.

# CAIS DO SODRÉ
## Arts and Crafts
### A PEQUENA GALERIA
### (The Little Art Gallery)
*Avenida 24 de Julho, 4C; tel. 213 950 356; www. apequenagaleria.com; Wed.-Sat. 5pm-7:30pm; free; Metro Cais do Sodré, Blue Line*

The Little Art Gallery is a collective project that occupies a snug space right on the riverside, aimed at exhibiting, informing about, and selling art. In the same vein as The Little Galleries of the Photo-Secession—later known as the 291 Art Gallery—in New York, this funky gathering place mainly focuses on photography.

# Feira da Ladra Flea Market

Dating to the 12th century, the São Vicente Feira da Ladra Flea Market, which literally translates as "Thieves' Fair," is a chance to experience the sights and sounds of old-time Lisbon. With an eclectic mix of antiques and secondhand family heirlooms, vendors tout everything from jewels to junk. The vast market starts by the **São Vicente Archway,** near a stop for tram 28, and fills the streets around the **Campo de Santa Clara square** every **Tuesday** and **Saturday** from **9am-6pm.** While some of the traders have properly laid-out stalls, others simply pile their wares onto blankets on the ground.

## ALCÂNTARA
### Arts and Crafts
#### LX FACTORY
*Rua Rodrigues de Faria 103; tel. 213 143 399; www.lxfactory.com; daily 9am-2am; free; tram 15*

Less factory, more arty-hive, this historical industrial complex comprises more than 200 restaurants, shops, businesses, and offices under one roof. Converted from an old fabric-production plant spanning 23,000 square meters (248,000 sq ft), today LX Factory is a hive of cool creativity and a rising tourist attraction. The LX Factory's first floor is entirely dedicated to an ethical market. There is also a food court, and open-plan workspaces allow visitors to see artisans in action. Enjoy the laid-back hipster vibe and grab a drink on one of the terraces overlooking the iconic 25 de Abril Bridge. Live music performances and other events are also staged on occasion—check the website.

# Food

Lisbon's food scene is a crossroads of traditional and contemporary, offering everything from street food and vegan restaurants to gourmet market stalls. One thing that sets Lisbon apart from other European capitals is value for money.

## BAIXA
Bustling Baixa is a hub of restaurants, cafés, and bars, plenty of them arranged around the main Comércio Square, promising people-watching and alfresco dining.

### Portuguese
#### TABERNA DA BAIXA
*Rua dos Fanqueiros, 161-163; tel. 919 847 419; www.tabernadabaixa.pt; daily noon-3pm and 7pm-10:30pm; €15*

This little gem is the perfect place to sample Lisbon's flavors. With a cozy, rustic-chic feel, the small restaurant showcases regional produce in the likes of shared cold platters paired with handpicked wines, and its signature dish, slow-cooked black pig cheeks in red wine. Live shows can also be enjoyed at the venue (check the website for dates).

#### RESTAURANTE GAMBRINUS
*Rua das Portas de Santo Antão 23; tel. 213 421 466; www.restaurante-gambrinus.business.site; daily noon-1:30am; €20-40*

Established in 1936, acclaimed Restaurante Gambrinus has a dedicated following for its tapas and seafood, served in a classic setting with polished dark wood and crisp white tablecloths.

---

**1:** Dona Maria II National Theater **2:** LX Factory
**3:** Café Nicola **4:** Time Out Market Lisboa

## Lisbon's Best Souvenirs: Cork and *Azulejos*

cork souvenirs

Two of Portugal's most distinctive products are cork goods and beautiful *azulejo* tiles and ceramics. Once used to create only bottle stoppers for prestigious champagnes, today Portuguese cork has become fashionable for shoes, handbags, jewelry, and even clothing. **Bairro Alto** is the place to go cork-hunting, and **downtown Baixa-Chiado** brims with local arts and crafts.

Azulejo hand-painted tile plaques adorn walls throughout the city. Many smaller-size replicas of plaques and tiles are now produced as souvenirs. **Alfama** is the place to head for *azulejos*, with shops offering miniature versions of these ceramic squares.

### PRADO RESTAURANT

*Travessa das Pedras Negras 2; tel. 210 534 649; www. pradorestaurante.com; Wed. 7pm-11pm, Thurs.-Sun. noon-3:30pm and 7pm-11pm; €30*

Spearheaded by rising young chef António Galapito, Prado takes clean, fresh flavors of the farm and the sea and magics them into contemporary dishes for the table. The restaurant is housed in a lofty, bright former factory, and the menu is a celebration of seasonal Portuguese produce, concocted into dishes such as black pork tenderloin with quinces and chocolate peppers and Barrosã beef sirloin steak and lettuce salad. Reservations are compulsory for groups of more than six.

### Seafood
### ★ SOLAR DO BACALHAU

*Rua do Jardim do Regedor 30; tel. 213 460 069; www.solardobacalhau.com; daily 10am-midnight; €20*

Cod is king at charming Solar do Bacalhau, one of the best spots to enjoy the Portuguese specialty *bacalhau*. It also serves other meat and fish dishes in a setting with natural stone walls and elegantly laid tables.

### Cafés and Light Bites
### ★ CAFÉ NICOLA

*Praça Dom Pedro IV 24-25; tel. 213 460 579; daily 8am-1am; €8*

With a prime position on posh Rossio

# Appetizers Aren't Free

As soon as you sit down at any table in Lisbon, waiters will almost immediately bring you an array of mouthwatering appetizers, such as a fresh bread basket, butter and pâtés, fritters, and olives and cheeses. Beware—these are not a complimentary welcome gift; the tab is totting up from the moment you butter that bread. Anything you don't want, don't be afraid to politely decline or send back. Always be clear on prices beforehand, as some cheeses and sausages can be pricy, and make sure you pay only for what you eat.

Square, the landmark Café Nicola epitomizes European coffee culture with its art deco interior, excellent coffees, and top-notch breakfasts. It was a favorite of poet Manuel du Bocage, who is memorialized in a statue out front. The celebrated café is excellent for people-watching, but prices are high.

## ALFAMA
### Portuguese
### CORKSCREW RESTAURANT & WINE BAR
*Rua dos Remédios 95; tel. 215 951 774; www.thecorkscrew.pt; Mon.-Fri. 5pm-11pm, Sat.-Sun. 3pm-11pm; €10*
CorkScrew Restaurant & Wine Bar serves great Portuguese tapas of cheeses, cured meats, and fish preserves, accompanied by fantastic Portuguese wines.

### ★ CHAPITÔ À MESA
*Costa do Castelo 7; tel. 218 875 077; www.chapito.org; Sun.-Thurs. noon-6pm and 7pm-midnight, Fri.-Sat. noon-6pm and 7pm-12:30am; €25*
Part of a famous circus arts school, Chapitô à Mesa offers fun, flamboyant cuisine alongside gorgeous views of Lisbon. Choose the snack bar, an alfresco grill terrace, or the elegant restaurant. Menu favorites include grilled shrimp with tropical fruit and pork cheeks with clams and sautéed potatoes.

### ★ CASA DO LEÃO
*Castelo de São Jorge; tel. 218 880 154; www.pousadas.pt; daily 12:30pm-9pm; €28*
Located inside the São Jorge Castle, Casa do Leão takes advantage of its architectural features, including a vaulted brick ceiling, to create an elegant atmosphere. Its culinary masterpieces are concocted from fresh seasonal ingredients. Seafood *cataplana* and Portuguese-style steak are highlights. Even more remarkable are the views from the terrace outside, overlooking the city.

## Seafood
### FAROL DE SANTA LUZIA
*Largo de Santa Luzia 5; tel. 218 863 884; Mon.-Sat. 5:30pm-11pm; €18*
Rustic Farol de Santa Luzia is set in an 18th-century building directly opposite the Santa Luzia viewpoint, near São Jorge Castle. Menu favorites include octopus salad, shellfish *açorda* (a soupy bread dish), and pork *cataplana* with shrimp, clams, and *chouriça* sausage.

## Cafés and Light Bites
### MERCEARIA CASTELLO CAFÉ
*Rua das Flores de Santa Cruz 2; tel. 218 876 111; daily 10am-8pm; €8*
Tradition meets cool at Mercearia Castello Café, a funky little eatery and grocery store. Its wood-clad interior harks back to the old days, and its location at the top of the hill near the castle is second to none. The fresh homemade fare includes quiches, crêpes, and sandwiches made from quality regional products—it hits the spot after climbing to the castle.

## AVENIDA DA LIBERDADE
### Markets
### FOOD MARKET
*Av. Fontes Pereira de Melo 8A; tel. 210 199 258; daily 8am-10pm; from €5*

Just off the Marquês de Pombal roundabout (northeast), Food Market covers breakfast, brunch, lunch, and dinner. The eclectic food hall's stalls tout everything from oysters to éclairs, grilled chicken to smoked fish, to eat in or take out.

## Portuguese
### CHAFARIZ DO VINHO
*Rua da Mãe d'Água; tel. 213 422 079; www. chafarizdovinho.com; Tues.-Sat. 3pm-11pm; €25*

Located in the Príncipe Real neighborhood just north of Baixa, between Rossio and Marquês de Pombal (near the Lisbon University Botanical Gardens), Chafariz do Vinho is a unique gem of a find. It is a fascinating wine and tapas bar housed in an ancient aqueduct with a vast wine cellar and tasty nibbles to accompany the drink.

## Seafood
### O CACHO DOURADO
*Rua Eça de Queiroz 5; tel. 213 543 671; www. ocachodourado.com; Sun.-Fri. 7:30am-11:30pm; €15*

Specializing in authentic Portuguese fish and seafood dishes, O Cacho Dourado is off the tourist track but always busy with regulars. If you visit on a Friday, try the famous codfish dish that has been served on Fridays only for nearly half a century.

# CHIADO AND BAIRRO ALTO

Bohemian Bairro Alto might be better known for its nightlife, but it doesn't disappoint when it comes to restaurants, with a rainbow of international flavors.

## Portuguese
### A TABERNA DA RUA DAS FLORES
*Rua das Flores 103; tel. 213 479 418; Mon.-Sat. noon-4pm and 5pm-11:30pm; €15*

This long, narrow, typically Portuguese eatery, located in an old greengrocer's store, retains original vintage features such as its door and floor tiles. The cozy tavern is popular among locals and tourists alike, serving traditional tapas of yesteryear with a contemporary twist.

### RESTAURANTE FIDALGO
*Rua da Barroca 27; tel. 213 422 900; www. restaurantefidalgo.com; Mon.-Sat. noon-3pm and 7pm-11pm; €20*

A traditional, family-run Portuguese restaurant founded in 1972, Fidalgo serves good old-fashioned Portuguese food at reasonable prices. All the classics—rabbit stew, fresh fish, octopus, and codfish dishes—are on the menu, along with homemade desserts and an excellent selection of national wines that line the walls of the cozy eatery.

## Seafood
### SEA ME
*Rua do Loreto 21; tel. 213 461 564; www. peixariamoderna.com; Mon.-Thurs. 12:30pm-3:30pm and 7pm-midnight, Fri. 12:30pm-3:30pm and 7:30pm-1am, Sat.-Sun. 12:30pm-1am; €28*

Modern, informal Sea Me pays homage to Lisbon's fishmongers with seafood purchased from the counter to be cooked in the kitchen, in a fusion of Japanese and Portuguese cuisines.

## International
### LA PAPARRUCHA
*Rua Dom Pedro V 18-20; tel. 213 425 333; www. lapaparrucha.com; Mon.-Fri. noon-11:30pm, Sat.-Sun. 12:30pm-11:30pm; €25*

Modern meets rustic and meat rules at La Paparrucha, a firm favorite among locals. Almost everything is cooked on an authentic Argentinean grill.

## Cafés and Light Bites
### A BRASILEIRA
*Rua Garrett 122; tel. 213 469 541; www.abrasileira.pt; daily 8am-2am; €5*

The century-old A Brasileira café is one of the oldest and most famous cafés in Lisbon. The emblematic venue has an air of antique grandeur, with its art deco chandeliers, wooden booths, mirrored walls, and checkerboard

# Local Specialties

Ask anyone what Lisbon's most typical dishes are, and here's some of what you will hear:

- **Salted codfish (*bacalhau*),** for which the Portuguese claim to have a different recipe for each day of the year.

- The ubiquitous *pastel de nata* **custard tart,** the national pastry; Pastéis de Belém bakery has its own recipe, which it calls *pastel de Belém*.

- **Seafood** features heavily on menus throughout the city, with other popular dishes including *caldeirada* (fish stew), shellfish, and octopus creations.

- **Bite-size snacks** like codfish pasty *(pastéis de bacalhau)*, green bean fritters *(peixinhos da horta)*, and codfish fritters *(pataniscas de bacalhau)* are also popular, available at most restaurants and snack bars, to be washed down with a cold beer.

- Try a *ginjinha* **cherry liqueur** at its home, the historic A Ginjinha bar in the Baixa's São Domingos Square.

*ginjinha* cherry liqueur

floors. It is a time-honored meeting place for Lisbon's coffee-lovers and has a fascinating history, having once been frequented by the city's intellectuals, artists, writers, and free thinkers. A regular, allegedly, was famous Portuguese poet Fernando Pessoa, and a bronze statue of him sits permanently outside the busy café in tribute. Today it is a must-see tourist attraction, but the coffee is still as popular as it was when A Brazileira opened in the 19th century.

## Brewery
### ★ CERVEJARIA TRINDADE

*Rua Nova da Trindade 20C; tel. 213 423 506; www. cervejariatrindade.pt; Sun.-Thurs. noon-midnight, Fri.-Sat. noon-1am; €28*

One of Portugal's oldest and most beautiful breweries, bright and bold Cervejaria Trindade dates from the mid-1800s, when it was the choice for writers, poets, and politicians. Its huge medieval banquet rooms can accommodate groups of up to 200. National and international beers are accompanied by a different dish of the day, as well as typical Portuguese fish and meat dishes like steak in beer sauce.

## CAIS DO SODRÉ

This waterfront wharf has shed its former seedy image and is now a cool place to eat, drink, and be merry. It's also the location of hip **Pink Street,** which makes it a convenient spot to spend an evening.

## Markets
### ★ TIME OUT MARKET LISBOA + RIVERSIDE MARKET
### (Mercado TimeOut + Mercado da Ribeira)

*Avenida 24 de Julho 49; tel. 213 951 274; Sun.-Thurs. 10am-midnight, Sat.-Sun. 10am-2am; Metro Cais do Sodré, Blue Line*

After its concession was taken over by the team behind the Lisbon edition of *Time Out* magazine, this landmark market hall—the historic Mercado da Ribeira, or Riverside Market, formerly one of Europe's most renowned markets—is today among the city's coolest hangouts. Despite being more than 100 years old (it first opened in the 1890s), this market is livelier than ever, with a huge, often chaotic food court that boasts a vast variety of gourmet stalls showcasing innovative and traditional Portuguese fare. The two-dozen-plus stands are allocated to chefs and restaurants handpicked by *Time Out*'s food writers. The eastern portion of the building still houses the traditional fruit and veg market, which also sells fresh fish, flowers, bread, and souvenirs. It operates 6am-2pm and offers early risers a glimpse of genuine Lisbon market trading. Live music adds to the ambience.

### Portuguese
### ESPUMANTARIA DO CAIS

*Rua Nova do Carvalho 39; tel. 213 470 466; daily 7pm-4am; €15*

Located on Cais do Sodré's famous Pink Street, swanky and minimalistic Espumantaria do Cais is a marble-clad quayside tapas and Champagne bar. Pop open a bottle of bubbly, order a sharing platter like the popular cheeseboard or salmon tacos, and have a wonderful evening with some fizz.

### VESTIGIUS WINE & GIN BAR

*Cais do Sodré 8; tel. 218 203 320; www.vestigius.pt; daily 11am-7pm; €22*

Set in a lofty quayside warehouse, shabby-chic Vestigius Wine & Gin Bar has huge windows and a terrace overlooking the water. A team of young chefs shape innovative flavors into bite-size tapas with Portuguese and Angolan influences. Dishes include calamari with aioli sauce, beef carpaccio, and beef osso buco.

## BELÉM
### Portuguese
### PROVA - ENOTECA

*Rua Duarte Pacheco Pereira 9E; tel. 215 819 080; www.facebook.com/ProvaEnoteca; Tues.-Sun. noon-3:30pm and 6pm-10pm; €10*

As the name of this trendy deli and wine bar indicates (it loosely translates as "try"), the aim here is to sample excellent local produce with a good wine. Plates of cured cold meats and cheeses, salads, veg platters, and fish tapas are all there for the taking, to be paired with a careful selection of great Portuguese wines.

### Bakery
### ★ PASTÉIS DE BELÉM

*Rua Belém 84-92; tel. 213 637 423; www.pasteisdebelem.pt; daily 8am-11pm; €5*

No visit to Lisbon is complete without a taste of the humble, iconic *pastel de nata* custard tart. It can be found throughout Portugal, but Belém is its birthplace. Pastéis de Belém started making the delectable tarts in 1837, following a secret recipe from the Jerónimos Monastery. The buttery pastry contains a creamy, eggy filling, slightly caramelized top, and a sprinkling of cinnamon. Other fresh-baked sweet and savory treats can be enjoyed in the large seating area, which is always packed full.

# Bars and Nightlife

Bohemian and cosmopolitan in equal measures, Lisbon's nightlife has a different vibe in each different part of the city, from giddy Bairro Alto and atmospheric Alfama to the funky Pink Street in Cais do Sodré.

## BAIXA

In comparison to other parts of Lisbon, and with the exception of peak seasons like summer and Christmas, nightlife in the Baixa is rather tame. It's more about having a quiet drink at the end of the day than a big night out.

### Bars
### A GINJINHA

*Largo São Domingos 8; tel. 218 145 374; daily 9am-10pm*

## Pastel de Belém vs. Pastel de Nata

It might look like Portugal's omnipresent *pastel de nata* (custard tart), it might even taste like the ubiquitous *pastel de nata*, but the *pastel de Belém* is a tart in its own right.

### HISTORY
While the *pastel de nata* is found throughout Portugal, the *pastel de Belém* is found only in Belém. History has it that the *pastel de Belém's* secret recipe emerged in the 19th century from the Jerónimos Monastery.

In 1834, when all the monasteries and convents of Portugal were forced to close, the workers decided to start selling the sweet treats to make a living, in the same spot where the **Pastéis de Belém** bakery is today. The bakery was officially inaugurated in 1837.

### TRYING *PASTEL DE BELÉM* TODAY
To this day the tarts are handmade following the same ancient original recipe that came from the Jerónimos Monastery. This recipe is a closely guarded secret, known only by a handful of master bakers at the Belém bakery, which has become one of the area's top tourist attractions.

*pastel de Belém*

There's an old saying that states going to Belém without trying a *pastel de Belém* is like going to Rome without seeing the Pope, and judging by the queues that form outside the bakery every day, there might be some truth in it.

STOPOVER IN LISBON
BARS AND NIGHTLIFE

---

Home to Portugal's award-winning *ginjinha* cherry liqueur, A Ginjinha is a historic hole in the wall serving tiny glasses of the sweet drink over its sticky slab of marble bar-top. *Ginjinha* is served as a shot, with a cherry in the glass if you ask. Soft drinks and beer are also available. This place is standing room only and crowded.

### HOTEL MUNDIAL ROOFTOP BAR & LOUNGE
*Praça Martim Moniz 2; tel. 218 842 000; www. hotel-mundial.pt; daily 5pm-11:30pm*
The swanky terrace of Hotel Mundial Rooftop Bar & Lounge has stunning views. During the warmer months, it is a fashionable in-crowd hangout, popular for sunset parties. The views over Lisbon's downtown are worth a visit, but drinks are pricy, and the terrace can get crowded.

## CHIADO AND BAIRRO ALTO

A quaint and traditional part of Lisbon that is sleepy during the day, bohemian Bairro Alto comes to life at night. The cobbled streets are packed with people and cool nightspots ranging from chic wine bars to historic fado houses and renowned jazz clubs.

### Wine Bars
#### THE OLD PHARMACY
*Rua do Diário de Notícias 73; tel. 920 230 989; daily 5:30pm-midnight*
The Old Pharmacy is a quirky bar that offers a wide selection of wines by the glass or bottle. Wine bottles now fill the cabinets that were once stocked with medicines. Dim lighting and wine-barrel tables add to the allure.

# ☆ A Night of Fado

Enjoy dinner and a show with spellbinding fado. This moving, soulful genre of music can be traced back to Lisbon in the early 19th century, often associated with darkened backstreet taverns where singers, the *fadistas*, accompanied by musicians of traditional Portuguese instruments like guitars and violas, would entertain crowds with melodic tales of longing and daily hardships of the era, with songs ranging from mournful and melancholic to upbeat and jovial. Some of Portugal's biggest musical stars were Fado singers, who, like the great Amália Rodrigues, the Queen of Fado, became revered personalities.

As fado gained popularity as a tourist attraction, it became mainstream for shows to be preceded by a set-priced dinner. Most fado restaurants are cozy and offer traditional Portuguese dining; many fado houses have a minimum fee that covers dinner and the show. It is customary for spectators to be silent while melodic fado is being sung, out of respect for the *fadista* and the accompanying musicians. With livelier songs, however, guests and even the staff join in. Reservations are strongly recommended.

In Lisbon, the best neighborhoods to see fado are Alfama and Bairro Alto; Alfama is widely believed to be the birthplace of fado, but Bairro Alto is popular for its maze of streets with intimate little fado restaurants and characterful bars.

## ALFAMA

- **Sr. Fado de Alfama** (Rua dos Remédios 176; tel. 218 874 298; www.sr-fado.com; Wed.-Thurs and Sat.-Sun. 7:30pm-2am; €35): Family-run Sr. Fado de Alfama belongs to *fadista* Ana Marina and is a cultural mainstay, with good traditional Portuguese food and a healthy dose of fado.

- **São Miguel d'Alfama** (Largo de São Miguel; tel. 968 554 422; www.saomigueldalfama.com; daily 7pm-midnight; €25): Intimate, arabesque-styled São Miguel d'Alfama is famous for its fado and traditional Portuguese food.

- **Clube de Fado** (Rua de São João Praça 86-94; tel. 218 852 704; www.clube-de-fado.com; daily

## ARTIS

*Rua do Diário de Notícias 95; tel. 213 424 795; Sun. and Tues.-Thurs. 5:30pm-2am, Fri.-Sat. 5:30pm-3am*

Iberian-rustic Artis is the ideal place for long conversations over wine, cheese, and tapas.

## Live Music
### PÁGINAS TANTAS

*Rua do Diário de Notícias 85; tel. 966 249 005; Mon.-Thurs. 8:30am-2am, Fri.-Sat. 8:30am-3am, Sun. 8:30am-midnight*

Partake in some foot-tapping at Páginas Tantas, a popular jazz bar with live music. The instrument-themed decor and portraits of jazz greats give the club a colorful, contemporary vibe. Rising and established musicians jam live nightly on a little stage in the corner.

# CAIS DO SODRÉ

Created through a clever urban renewal program, the Pink Street project has taken a part of town that once was a red-light district and turned it into one of the hippest hangouts in Lisbon, with varying ambience along a short, colorful stretch.

## Bars
### PENSÃO AMOR

*Rua do Alecrim 19; tel. 213 143 399; www.pensaoamor.pt; Sun.-Wed. 2pm-3am, Thurs.-Sat. 2pm-4am*

A former inn that once rented rooms to sailors and ladies of the night, Pensão Amor is now a lively and bohemian hangout.

8pm-2am; €40): In the heart of Alfama, behind an unremarkable exterior, famous Clube de Fado serves excellent Portuguese cuisine to the sound of the Portuguese guitar accompanying the *fadista*. It has a warm, romantic, and almost mystic atmosphere.

- **A Baiuca** (Rua São Miguel 20; tel. 218 867 284; Thurs.-Mon. 7:30pm-11:30pm; €25 minimum pp includes dinner, drinks, and dessert): An authentic, classic fado dinner haunt, tiny tavern A Baiuca serves tasty home-cooked Portuguese fare on long tables where patrons sit snugly together. The convivial atmosphere is conducive to a great evening enjoying the magic of fado and new friends.

- **Parreirinha de Alfama** (Beco do Espírito Santo 1; tel. 218 868 209; www. parreirinhadealfama.com; Tues.-Sun. 8pm-1am; minimum consumption per person €40): Small and atmospheric, Parreirinha is one of Lisbon's oldest and most popular fado haunts. A legendary restaurant inextricably intertwined with fado, it was established in 1939 and is owned by acclaimed fado singer Argentina Santos. Some of Portugal's most famous fado singers have graced the stage of Parreirinha over the years, including the great Amália Rodrigues. Its food is equally renowned, based on typical Portuguese flavors. Mains include monkish rice and roast kid. Fado is sung nightly. Cash payments only.

## BAIRRO ALTO

- **O Faia** (Rua da Barroca 54-56; tel. 213 426 742; www.ofaia.com; Mon.-Sat. 8pm-2am; minimum €50): Founded in 1947, O Faia is a famed fado house with a cult following; it hosts nightly shows and has a restaurant that serves traditional Portuguese cuisine with a contemporary twist.

- **Tasca do Chico** (Rua do Diario de Noticias 39; tel. 961 339 696; Sun.-Thurs. 7pm-1:30am, Fri.-Sat. 7pm-3am; €15): Unlike other fado venues, Tasca do Chico is more of a fado bar than a restaurant. Dim lighting in this tiny tavern enhances the atmospheric experience. Drinks and typical Portuguese tapas, such as plates of cured meats, are served. There is no minimum consumption fee, but it's cash only.

### JAMAICA
*Rua Nova do Carvalho 6; tel. 213 421 859; www.*
*facebook.com/jamaicalisboajamaica.com.pt;*
*Tues.-Sat. 11:45pm-6am; door fees may apply*
Jamaica, one of Lisbon's best-known bars, is the place to go to drink and dance. It's not huge, so the dance floor can get crowded, but the DJs play a mix of '70s, '80s, rock, and current hits.

# Accommodations

Lisbon is awash with cool and interesting places to stay, from historic townhouses to converted palaces. The Baixa area is central and convenient. Lodging is generally pricy, but there are quality budget hostels and guesthouses.

## BAIXA
### Under €100
### ★ YES! LISBON HOSTEL

*Rua de São Julião 148; tel. 213 427 171; www. yeshostels.com; €32 dorm, €140 d with shared bath*

Yes! Lisbon Hostel has it all: an excellent location, good service, and budget-friendly prices. Custom-made bunks ensure a good night's sleep, and reception is happy to provide tips on how to get the most out of your stay.

### €100-200
### ★ HOTEL MUNDIAL

*Praça Martim Moniz 2; tel. 218 842 000; www. hotel-mundial.pt; €130-200 d*

Despite its plain exterior, four-star Hotel Mundial is an institution because its rooftop has a great view. Decor is tasteful, beds are comfortable, and the location is second to none. A short walk from Rua do Comércio.

### HOTEL VINCCI BAIXA

*Rua do Comércio 32-38; tel. 218 803 190; www. vinccibaixa.com; €180-250 d*

Square, elegant four-star Hotel Vincci Baixa embodies class and comfort in a prime location.

### Over €200
### BOUTIQUE HOTEL HERITAGE AVENIDA DA LIBERDADE

*Av. da Liberdade 28; tel. 213 404 040; www. heritageavliberdade.com; €200-300 d*

Set back from leafy Avenida da Liberdade, the stately Boutique Hotel Heritage Avenida da Liberdade is in an elegant 18th-century townhouse, a pleasant stroll from the Baixa area.

## ALFAMA
### €100-200
### ★ SOLAR DO CASTELO

*Rua das Cozinhas 2; tel. 218 806 050; www. solardocastelo.com; €160-200 d*

Small, romantic Solar do Castelo is the only hotel within the walls of the São Jorge Castle. Converted from an 18th-century mansion, this eco-retreat with medieval and contemporary style even has specially commissioned furniture to enhance its uniqueness.

### ★ MEMMO ALFAMA DESIGN HOTEL

*Travessa Merceeiras 27; tel. 210 495 660; www. memmoalfama.com; €150-250 d*

Cool and contemporary Memmo Alfama Design Hotel is a 44-room urban retreat fast earning a reputation for its chic, clean design, which blends well with the historic Alfama neighborhood.

### Over €200
### SANTIAGO DE ALFAMA BOUTIQUE HOTEL

*Rua de Santiago 10 a 14; tel. 213 941 616; www. santiagodealfama.com; €200-300 d*

A former 15th-century palace has been reborn as cosmopolitan Santiago de Alfama Boutique Hotel, which oozes authenticity from its tiled floors to its prime location in Alfama. It's one of Europe's most outstanding urban hotels.

## CHIADO AND BAIRRO ALTO
### Under €100
### BAIRRO ALTO HOSTEL

*Travessa da Cara 6; tel. 213 421 079; www. bairroaltohostel.com; from €60 d with shared bath*

Modern and clean Bairro Alto Hostel is in a historic 19th-century building. Private rooms and shared dorms are all equipped with free Wi-Fi; there's a communal lounge and kitchen facilities.

## €100-200

### CHIADO 44 GUEST HOUSE

*Rua Horta Seca 44; tel. 930 544 457; www. chiado44.pt; €120-200 d*

Set in the heart of Chiado in a typical 19th-century building, Chiado 44 is a simple and relaxed three-star hotel with cool, clean décor and river views.

### HOTEL DO CHIADO

*Rua Nova do Almada, 114; tel. 213 256 100; www. hoteldochiado.pt; €170-250 d*

The charming Hotel do Chiado is housed in historic former warehouses that were renovated by leading Portuguese architect Siza Vieira following the catastrophic 1988 neighborhood fire. It's famed for stunning city views from its seventh-floor rooftop terrace and its afternoon tea.

## Over €200

### ★ BAIRRO ALTO HOTEL

*Praça Luis de Camões 2; tel. 213 408 288; www. bairroaltohotel.com; €350-400 d*

Wedged between bohemian Bairro Alto and trendy Chiado, the five-star Bairro Alto Hotel enjoys a dominant position on the main square and has handsome 18th-century architecture. Within walking distance of shops, restaurants, and bars, the 55 rooms are twins, doubles, and suites.

## CAIS DO SODRÉ

### €100-200

### LX BOUTIQUE HOTEL

*Rua do Alecrim 12; tel. 213 474 394; www. lxboutiquehotel.com; €100-200 d*

Overlooking the Tagus River, the decadently decorated LX Boutique Hotel is an atmospheric 19th-century hotel conveniently at the nexus of Chiado, Baixa, and Cais do Sodré.

### ★ HELLO LISBON CAIS DO SODRÉ APARTMENTS

*Rua Nova do Carvalho 43; tel. 937 770 777; www. hello-lisbon.com; €100-200 d*

Clean and comfortable self-catering Hello Lisbon Cais do Sodré Apartments reflect the youth and energy of their location on frenetic Pink Street. Edgy paintings provide a pop of color to the period architecture and smart interiors.

# Information and Services

## VISITOR INFORMATION

**"Ask Me" tourist information desks** can be found throughout Lisbon, at the airport and major bus and train stations and monuments. Most are open daily about 9am-6pm. Also available are the main **Lisbon Tourism Visitors and Convention Bureau** (Rua do Arsenal 21; tel. 210 312 700; www.visitlisboa. com; Mon.-Fri. 9:30am-7pm) and the national tourist board, **Turismo de Portugal** (Rua Ivone Silva, Lote 6; tel. 211 140 200; www. visitportugal.com, www.turismodeportugal. pt; Mon.-Fri. 9am-5:30pm).

## EMBASSIES

- **United States:** Av. das Forças Armadas 133C; tel. 217 273 300; https://pt.usembassy. gov; Mon.-Fri. 8am-5pm
- **Canada:** Av. da Liberdade 196; tel. 213 164 600; www.canadainternational.gc.ca; Mon.-Fri. 9am-noon
- **United Kingdom:** Rua de São Bernardo 33; tel. 213 924 000; www.gov.uk; Mon., Wed., and Fri. 9:30am-2pm
- **Australia:** Av. da Liberdade 200; tel. 213 101 500; www.portugal.embassy.gov.au; Mon.-Fri. 10am-4pm

# MONEY

In Lisbon, most hotels, currency exchanges, travel agencies, some banks, and even some shops have currency exchange facilities. Or you can use your debit card to make a withdrawal from an **ATM** *(multibanco)*, which can be found throughout the city. The currency exchange company **Unicâmbio** (www.unicambio.pt) has more than 80 offices around the country, including the airports at Lisbon, the Rossio train station in central Lisbon, the Cais do Sodré station in Baixa, and El Corte Inglês shopping mall (Av. António Augusto de Aguiar 31).

# HEALTH AND EMERGENCIES

- **European free emergency number:** 112

- **GNR Police Lisbon headquarters:** Largo do Carmo 27; tel. 213 217 000; www. gnr.pt
- **PSP Metropolitan Police Lisbon headquarters:** Av. Moscavide 88; tel. 217 654 242; www.psp.pt
- **PSP Tourist Police Lisbon:** Praça dos Restauradores, Palácio Foz; tel. 213 421 623
- **INEM medical emergency:** Rua Almirante Barroso 36; tel. 213 508 100; www.inem.pt
- **CUF Private Hospital:** Travessa do Castro 3; tel. 213 926 100; www.saudecuf.pt
- **24-Hour pharmacy:** Farmácia Largo do Rato, Av. Alvares Cabral 1; tel. 213 863 044; www.farmaciasdeservico.net

# Getting There and Around

## GETTING THERE

### Air
#### HUMBERTO DELGADO AIRPORT
*Alameda das Comunidades Portuguesas; tel. 218 413 500; www.ana.pt*

Lisbon's Humberto Delgado Airport (LIS,) is Portugal's biggest and busiest international airport. European flights tend to be shorter than four hours and inexpensive. Portugal's national airline, **TAP-Air Portugal** (www. flytap.com), has expanded its operations to the United States and operates several direct daily flights between Portugal and US cities. A number of US airlines also fly to Lisbon.

#### GETTING TO AND FROM THE AIRPORT
Lisbon's airport is 7 kilometers (4.3 mi) north of the city center. The **Metro** runs direct from the airport to Lisbon; the Red Line runs from just outside the airport's main entrance and connects with the Green Line at Alameda station, which runs to the Baixa and Cais do Sodré riverfront, and ends on the Blue Line, at the São Sebastião station. A journey to downtown Lisbon (€1.25) requires one transfer and takes 20 minutes. The **Aerobus** (www.aerobus.pt) shuttle bus runs regularly to the city center and to the financial district from outside the arrivals terminal (daily 7:30am-11pm; €3.15 one-way). Municipal bus company **Carris** (www. carris.pt; €1.85 one-way) runs five bus routes between Lisbon Airport and the city center. **Taxis** can be found outside the arrivals terminal; a trip to Lisbon city center should cost up to €15. Alternately, call an **Uber** (www. uber.com) ride-share.

The cheapest and easiest way to get around Lisbon is to buy a **7 Colinas/Viva Viagem card,** available at the airport from the newsagent on the second floor, or from main bus or Metro stations. The cards are prepaid and can be recharged. The card itself costs €0.50, and they are accepted on all local buses and Metro subways, trams, funiculars, and ferryboats.

Most single trips on any mode cost €2-3. A one-day travel option has a flat rate of €6.

## Bus

**Eurolines** (www.eurolines.com) operates regular international bus service between Lisbon and cities such as London, Madrid, and Paris. National intercity bus company **Rede Expressos** (tel. 707 223 344; www.rede-expressos.pt) operates express bus trips to Lisbon from most of the country's regions, including the Algarve and Porto, each around three hours' journey. Algarve bus company **Eva** (tel. 289 899 760; www.eva-bus.com) also runs daily routes between main bus stations in the Algarve and Lisbon.

The two main bus terminals in Lisbon are **Sete Rios** (Rua Professor Lima Basto 133, opposite Lisbon Zoo; tel. 707 223 344; ticket office daily 7am-11:30pm; Metro Jardim Zoológico, Blue Line), a Rede Expressos' hub, and the modern **Gare do Oriente** (Av. Dom João II, Park of Nations; tel. 218 956 972; Metro Oriente, Red Line), closest to the airport.

## Train

Getting to Portugal from other European countries by train isn't as straightforward as by air, and can sometimes be more expensive, usually involving passing through a hub such as Paris or Madrid, and a few transfers. There are two overnight sleeper trains from Spain: the **Lusitania Hotel Train** (www.cp.pt) from Madrid and the **Sud Expresso** (www.cp.pt) from San Sebastian. Traveling from Europe by train can make sense if you're using a rail pass such as the **Eurail** pass.

The four main railway stations in Lisbon are **Entrecampos** (Rua Dr. Eduardo Neves), **Oriente** (Av. Dom João II), **Sete Rios** (Rua Professor Lima Bastos), and **Santa Apolónia** (Av. Infante Dom Henrique). The Alfa-Pendular runs from Oriente, Santa Apolónia, and Entrecampos.

## Car

Two main motorways connect Lisbon to the country's extremities: the **A1** to the north (Porto) and the **A2** to the south (Algarve). The **A6** is the main motorway from the east. From outside Portugal, you'll cross the entire country from any border point to get to Lisbon. The scenery makes up for any potholes or wrong turns you might endure.

There are two crossings to Lisbon from the south over the Tagus River: the **25 de Abril Bridge,** to the western end of the city, or the newer **Vasco da Gama Bridge**—the longest in Europe—to the Park of Nations area. Both provide stunning views of the city on approach.

## GETTING AROUND

Getting around Lisbon can be cheap and easy on public transport, or expensive if you opt for novelty transport like the city's mushrooming *tuk-tuks*.

### Lisboa Card

The Lisboa Card (www.lisboacard.org), Lisbon's official tourist pass, includes unlimited travel on public buses, trams, the Metro, elevators, and funiculars as well as travel on CP train lines to Sintra and Cascais; free access to 26 museums, monuments, and UNESCO World Heritage Sites; and deals and discounts on tours, shopping, and nightlife. The cost is €20 for a 24-hour card, €34 for a 48-hour card, and €42 for a 72-hour card. Children's cards are half price. These cards can be purchased online, for which a voucher is given that can be exchanged at main tourist points such as the Lisboa Welcome Center, Foz Palace, and Lisbon Airport.

### Public Transit

**Single trips** on buses, trams, ferryboats, and the Metro generally cost under €1.50, and the rechargeable **7 Colinas/Viva Viagem card** can be bought at most newsagents and kiosks, stations, and terminals for €0.50. A **24-hour public transport pass** can be loaded onto the card; it costs €6 and covers all forms of local public transport (buses, trams, and Metro). Some public transport timetables can vary depending on the season, with hours extended later in summer.

## BUS

The capital has an efficient bus service, **Carris** (www.carris.pt), which also manages the city's tram system. It provides good coverage of the city and is inexpensive, with most trips under €2. Most buses run 6am-9pm daily, with the busiest lines running until midnight.

## TRAM

**Carris** (www.carris.pt) operates a network of historic trams and funiculars, a unique way to get into the city's backstreets. Five tram routes carry 60 trams, most of which are vintage vehicles. The star of the show is the famous **tram 28,** which circumnavigates Lisbon's historic neighborhoods Bairro Alto, Alfama, Baixa, and Chiado. A downside is that it is plagued by petty thieves, so stay alert. Trams and funiculars generally operate 6am-11pm daily.

## METRO

Inaugurated in 1959, Lisbon's **Metro** (www.metrolisboa.pt) has consistently grown, including a stop beneath the airport, making travel fast and easy. The Metro has four main lines—Green, Yellow, Red, and Blue—and is simple to navigate, covering the city's important points. Trains run regularly and reliably. A 24-hour pass that also covers funiculars, trams, and buses costs €6. The Metro runs 6:30am-1am daily.

## Taxi and Ride-Share

Taxis in Portugal are plentiful and easy to spot: beige or black with a minty green roof. Each is identified with a number, usually under the driver's side mirror. There are lots of taxi stands throughout the city at train and bus stations, central plazas, and near shopping malls. Hotel reception desks will call a taxi for you, or simply hail one on the street. The main taxi firms in Lisbon are **Taxis Lisboa** (tel. 218 119 000; www.taxislisboa.com), **Cooptaxis** (tel. 217 932 756; www.cooptaxis.pt), and **Teletaxis** (tel. 218 111 100; www.teletaxis.pt).

**Uber** cars are also now popular and widely available in Lisbon, giving taxi drivers a run for their money.

## Tuk-Tuk

A novel way of exploring Lisbon is to jump on a *tuk-tuk*. These nifty little vehicles have taken the city by storm in recent years; it's rare to turn a street corner without hearing or seeing one of the colorful three-wheelers buzzing along. They have the advantage of fitting on streets and lanes where cars can't go, and they're cute and comfortable—but they are more expensive than public transport or taxis. *Tuk-tuk* operators include **Tuk Tuk Lisboa** (www.tuk-tuk-lisboa.pt), **City Tuk** (www.citytuk.pt), **Eco Tuk Tours** (www.ecotuktours.com), and **Tuga Tours Tuk Tuk** (www.tugatours.pt). Expect to pay €55-70 pp for an hour's tour of the sights.

## Rental Car

Getting around Lisbon without a car is easy and convenient thanks to the comprehensive public transport network. Lisbon's historic areas are a web of narrow, steep streets that can be daunting to drive, and finding parking, particularly in the busy city center, can be challenging. A car is only necessary to visit outlying areas. Book one online and pick it up at the airport, or ask your hotel to help. In and around Lisbon Airport, the many vendors include **Europcar** (tel. 218 401 176; www.europcar.com), **Hertz** (tel. 219 426 300; www.hertz.com), and **Budget** (tel. 808 252 627; www.budget.com.pt).

If you do rent a car to drive in Lisbon, check whether your hotel has private parking (which will entail additional cost), or find an underground car park that offers lower-cost "holiday fees," such as the one in Marquês de Pombal Square.

## Hop-On Hop-Off Bus

Lisbon has various companies operating modern hop-on hop-off buses, which are an excellent way to see everything the city has to offer in a relatively short amount of time. An audio guide is available onboard in various languages to provide an explanation of the city's history and main monuments—although the quality and sound of the narrative can be poor. Due to their—and Lisbon's—popularity, there can be long queues for the buses. A good tip is to first stay onboard for the entire circuit, and then get off at what interests you the second time around. There are three main companies operating hop-on hop-off tours; tickets start from around €20 for 24 hour-tickets on basic routes:

- **Yellow Bus – Carristur:** www.yellowbustours.com

- **Cityrama Gray Line:** www.cityrama.pt

- **City Sightseeing:** www.city-sightseeing.com

# Stopover in Porto

**Portugal's second-largest city after Lisbon,** Porto (POR-too) is flanked by vine-laden valleys and historic towns, a hardworking metropolis with newfound fame as a getaway among budget travelers. Significant investment is being made to upgrade Porto's infrastructure and image, but the city's unrefined charm is part of its allure. Shabby in parts, sophisticated in others, as a whole Porto is down-to-earth, relaxed, and endearingly genuine. Northerners are known for using expletives liberally in conversation, but despite the city's lack of airs and graces, beneath the gritty exterior is the warmth of the *tripeiros* (tripe eaters), a nickname derived from the local tradition of tripe-based dishes.

Known among Portuguese as the Cidade Invicta (Unvanquished

# Highlights

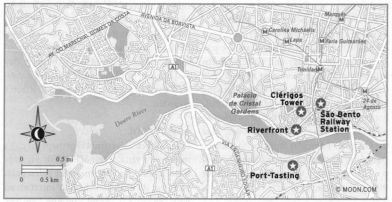

Look for ★ to find recommended sights, activities, dining, and lodging.

© MOON.COM

★ **São Bento Railway Station:** Clad with tile plaques depicting Portugal's history, this early-20th-century transit hub is a work of art (page 324).

★ **Clérigos Tower:** Once the tallest structure in Porto, this spindly landmark is adorned with fantastic Baroque flourishes (page 324).

★ **Porto's Riverfront:** Walk the Ribeira, a hive of activity with distinctive cafés and haphazardly arranged houses (page 327).

★ **Port-Tasting:** Visit the famous Vila Nova de Gaia winemakers to learn more about the history of port wine, and round it off with a tasting or two (page 336).

City), Porto is one of Europe's oldest nuclei, dating to the 1st century BC, when it was known as Portus Cale. Evidence of ancient Celtic and Proto-Celtic citadels has been uncovered here, and under Roman occupation Porto flourished as a commercial port, trading with Lisbon and nearby Braga. In the 14th and 15th centuries, Porto played an important role in shipbuilding and became a seat of power for Portuguese royalty. Porto has historic ties to Great Britain through the marriage of John I (João I) of Portugal to Philippa of Lancaster, celebrated in Porto in 1387, which cemented the oldest alliance in the world that is still in force today. Locals say the weather is more akin to Britain than the balmy Mediterranean—it is noticeably cooler than the rest of the country and one of the wettest major cities in Europe, although occasional gray drizzle does little to dampen the local vivacity.

Porto's best-known export, port wine, is reason enough to visit the city, produced across the river in Vila Nova da Gaia. Despite its centuries of history and culture, Porto still feels young, and like port wine, it only seems to get better with age. Visitors looking for great photos have plenty of opportunities. For breathtaking vistas of the city's jumbled rooftops, climb the Clérigos bell tower. Take the Guindais Funicular from the foot of the Dom Luís I Bridge to Batalha Square. Or if you're brave, climb the Arrábida Bridge for the ultimate view.

## ORIENTATION

Porto is packed with buildings and monuments that range from historically important to quirky and cool. Most can be found in the medieval **downtown** area, a UNESCO World Heritage Site that includes the famous **Ribeira riverside area** and the main **Avenida dos Aliados.** While not without steep streets and climbs, Porto is an easy city to navigate on foot or by public transport.

The **historic electrified trams,** buses, and a modern subway system provide easy access to the fringes.

Northwest of the city's historic hub is the stunning contemporary music hall, the **Casa da Música.** Farther west is the beautiful **Serralves Foundation and Museum,** a major player on the international modern art scene. Farther west on the coast is the clifftop **São Francisco Xavier Fort,** also known as the Castelo do Queijo (Castle of Cheese), which juts into the Atlantic. One long, straight avenue, **Avenida da Boavista,** runs between the Casa da Música and the Castelo do Queijo, connecting the heart of Porto to the coast.

## Downtown

Downtown Porto is where most of the city's key sights, such as the main **Avenida dos Aliados** plaza, **Rua de Santa Catarina** shopping street, **Clérigos Tower, Bolhão Market, Stock Exchange Palace, Porto Cathedral,** and **São Bento Railway Station** are found. This dense jumble of mismatched-size buildings is busy by day and buzzing by night. All of its narrow, cobbled streets flow toward the iconic Ribeira riverside.

## Riverfront

Porto's Ribeira riverfront is perhaps the city's most iconic vista. A row of higgledy-piggledy historic buildings, it is one of the oldest parts of Porto, its illustrious history intertwined with the city's port and shipping industry. Facing the riverside of **Vila Nova da Gaia,** Porto's sister city across the Douro River where **port** is made, Porto's Ribeira is a hotbed of **bars and restaurants,** and a lively area to walk along.

## Northwest Porto

Boavista is a leafy suburb just northwest of Porto city center where the splendid **Casa da Música** concert hall and **Bom Sucesso**

---

**Previous:** Porto and the Douro River; Clérigos Tower; Cálem port cellar.

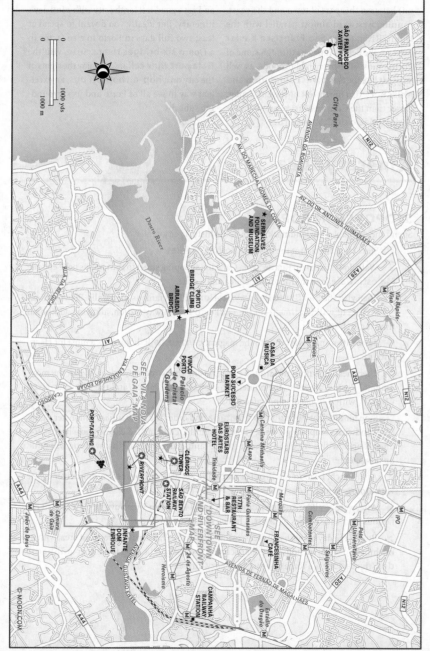

# Porto

0
1000 yds

0
1000 m

SÃO FRANCISCO
XAVIER FORT

City Park

AV. DO MARECHAL GOMES DA COSTA

AVENIDA DA BOAVISTA

AV. DO DR. ANTUNES GUIMARÃES

N12

Douro River

SERRALVES
FOUNDATION
AND MUSEUM

A41

A28

A20

N12

RUA DA VILA NOVA DE GAIA

Via Rápida-
Viso

Framos

M

PORTO
BRIDGE CLIMB

ARRÁBIDA
BRIDGE

CASA DA
MÚSICA

M

VIA NGENHEIRO EDGAR

VINCCI
PORTO Palácio
de Cristal
Gardens

BOM SUCESSO
MARKET

M Carolina Michaelis

Lapa

M

SEE "VILANOVA
DE GAIA" MAP

CARDOSO

PORT TASTING

EUROSTARS
DAS ARTES
HOTEL

A44

M João de deus

M Câmara
de Gaia

RIVERFRONT

CLÉRIGOS
TOWER

SÃO BENTO
RAILWAY
STATION

Trindade

M

17TH
RESTAURANT
& BAR

SEE
"DOWNTOWN
AND RIVERFRONT"
MAP

M Faria Guimarães

M Marquês

FRANCESINHA
CAFÉ

M Combatentes

M IPO

M Salgueiros

M Pólo
Universitário

INFANTE
DOM
HENRIQUE

AVENIDA GUSTAVO EIFFEL

Heroísmo

M 24 de Agosto

AVENIDA DE FERNÃO DE MAGALHÃES

CAMPANHÃ
RAILWAY
STATION

Estádio
do Dragão

A20

N12

© MOON.COM

Market are situated. The elegant **Avenida da Boavista** stretches 5.5 kilometers (3.4 mi) between this part of town and the coast, running westward almost parallel with the Douro River, to the **São Francisco Xavier Fort** on the beach. It passes through some of Porto's most affluent neighborhoods, as well as sights like the **Serralves Foundation and Museum.** Also northwest of the city center, closer than the Casa da Música, are the wonderful **Palácio de Cristal Gardens.**

## PLANNING YOUR TIME

You could see most of Porto's main landmarks and get a good feel for the city with a full day's itinerary. But ideally you'd want to spend at least two full days in Porto to also factor in a Douro **six-bridges river cruise,** visit the **Gaia port wine cellars,** or enjoy the sights of the city on a **hop-on hop-off bus,** an excellent way to see all of Porto and its surrounding suburbs.

# Itinerary Idea

## STOPOVER IN PORTO

Spend the day exploring landmark sights in the historic city center.

**1** Start off at the top, at the bustling **Bolhão Market.**

**2** Walk down the main Rua de Santa Catarina shopping street to the famous belle epoque **Majestic Café** for a mid-morning coffee and a cake.

**3** Then visit the **São Bento Railway Station** with its famous tiled walls. Plan on about 20 minutes of walking time from the market to the railway station, allowing additional time for each stop.

**4** Take a 10-minute walk over to the magical **Livraria Lello** bookshop, a must for Harry Potter fans.

**5** Then, head downhill toward the river, passing the baroque Clérigos Tower, the monumental Porto Cathedral, the opulent Stock Exchange Palace, and the **São Francisco Church,** with its museum and catacombs.

**6** Stop for lunch at **Petisqueira Volataria** and order the *francesinha*, a monster signature sandwich comprising a stack of meats, smothered in melted cheese and a beer sauce, often topped with a fried egg. It's not for the fainthearted, but all that walking will build up an appetite.

**7** After lunch, head to the **Ribeira dock** and set aside an hour for a short river cruise with Douro Acima.

**8** Afterward, walk across the iconic Dom Luís I Bridge to Vila Nova de Gaia to visit the famous port wine cellars of **Croft,** a famed local port producer.

**9** Round the day off with a sunset stroll along Porto's charismatic riverfront area, with its mishmash of colorful houses. It's particularly lovely at night. Stop for dinner at **Taberna dos Mercadores,** a romantic spot for a cozy dinner.

# Itinerary Idea

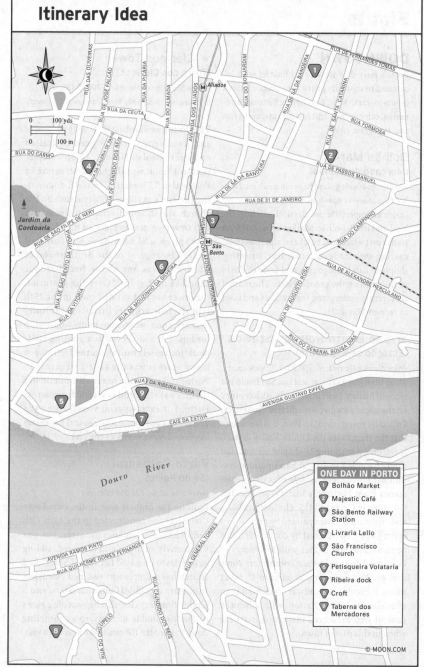

**ONE DAY IN PORTO**

1. Bolhão Market
2. Majestic Café
3. São Bento Railway Station
4. Livraria Lello
5. São Francisco Church
6. Petisqueira Volataria
7. Ribeira dock
8. Croft
9. Taberna dos Mercadores

© MOON.COM

# Sights

## DOWNTOWN

Porto's busy downtown area bustles with locals and tourists. Its gritty appearance hides a down-to-earth soul, fascinating historic landmarks, eclectic bars and restaurants, and a fun and energetic vibe.

### Bolhão Market
### (Mercado do Bolhão)

*Rua Formosa (main ground floor entrance); tel. 223 326 024; Mon.-Fri. 8am-8pm, Sat. 8am-6pm*

Inside an impressive neoclassical building, the loud and lively Bolhão Market is packed with stalls run by farmers, butchers, and fisherfolk, roaring with trade each morning. Browsing shoppers can indulge in a real taste of Porto in the cafés on the ground floor. The market is currently undergoing renovations and is set to reopen May 2021.

### ★ São Bento Railway Station
### (Estação de São Bento)

*Praça Almeida Garrett; tel. 707 210 220; www.cp.pt*

More than just a railway station, São Bento is a piece of history, built in the early 20th century on the site of a former Benedictine monastery. Officially inaugurated in 1916, it is from here that the trains into the Douro Valley depart. It features a stunning U-shaped atrium clad floor-to-ceiling in 20,000 hand-painted traditional Portuguese *azulejo* tiles that depict scenes from Portugal's history, such as the Conquest of Ceuta in 1415. The oversize blue-and-white friezes were painted by preeminent artist Jorge Colaço. Used by commuters, this open-air museum buzzes with the energy of everyday life as suburban commuters come and go. Not huge by comparison to other major European city railway stations, it is an efficient city center station, with a healthy dose of well-preserved history. A must-see when in this part of town.

### ★ Clérigos Tower
### (Torre dos Clérigos)

*Rua de São Filipe de Nery; tel. 220 145 489; www. torredosclerigos.pt; daily 9am-7pm; tower €6, church free*

The baroque landmark Clérigos Tower and its church were designed by Italian architect Nicolau Nasoni. Upon completion in 1763, it was the tallest structure in Portugal at 75 meters (246 feet), dominating the city's skyline. Construction on the church and its spindly, heavily decorative bell tower—a masterpiece of motifs, delicate spires, and carvings—was initiated in 1754 by request of the Brotherhood of Clerics. It was one of the first Baroque churches in Portugal. Over the centuries, the tower has had various uses; in the 19th century, mortars were fired from the tower to mark noon, when merchants would stop for lunch. It also served as a guiding landmark for vessels sailing on the Douro. For many years it was the tallest structure in Porto, and today the tower still dominates the city's skyline and is visible from across Porto. For extra-special views, climb the 225 stone steps of the inner spiral for amazing 360-degree views of the city.

### Porto Cathedral
### (Sé do Porto)

*Terreiro da Sé; tel. 222 059 028; free*

Built on the highest spot in the city, Porto Cathedral was constructed in the 12th-13th centuries in a Romanesque style, but was successively enlarged and extended, adding new styles to its mixed heritage. The fortified church has a simple whitewashed extension. Inside are a gold-leaf altar, cloisters, and a Gothic funerary chapel. The sweeping views of Porto's jumble of rusty roofs rambling down toward the Ribeira make it worth a visit.

# Downtown and Riverfront

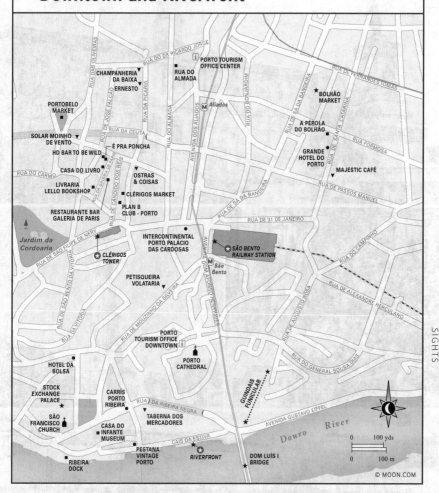

PORTO TOURISM OFFICE CENTER

CHAMPANHERIA DA BAIXA
ERNESTO
RUA DO ALMADA
BOLHÃO MARKET

PORTOBELO MARKET

A PÉROLA DO BOLHÃO

SOLAR MOINHO DE VENTO
HD BAR TO BE WILD

GRANDE HOTEL DO PORTO

É PRA PONCHA

MAJESTIC CAFÉ

CASA DO LIVRO

OSTRAS & COISAS

LIVRARIA LELLO BOOKSHOP

CLÉRIGOS MARKET

PLAN B CLUB - PORTO

RESTAURANTE BAR GALERIA DE PARIS

Jardim da Cordoaria

INTERCONTINENTAL PORTO PALÁCIO DAS CARDOSAS

SÃO BENTO RAILWAY STATION

CLÉRIGOS TOWER

São Bento

PETISQUEIRA VOLATARIA

PORTO TOURISM OFFICE DOWNTOWN

HOTEL DA BOLSA

PORTO CATHEDRAL

STOCK EXCHANGE PALACE

CARRIS PORTO RIBEIRA

GUINDAIS FUNICULAR

SÃO FRANCISCO CHURCH

TABERNA DOS MERCADORES

CASA DO INFANTE MUSEUM

Douro River

RIBEIRA DOCK

PESTANA VINTAGE PORTO

RIVERFRONT

DOM LUÍS I BRIDGE

0    100 yds
0    100 m

© MOON.COM

The church is open Monday-Saturday 9am-7pm, Sunday and holy days 9am-12:30pm and 2:30pm-7pm April-October, Monday-Saturday 9am-6pm, Sunday and holy days 9am-12:30pm and 2:30pm-7pm November-March. The cloisters are open Monday-Saturday 9am-6:30pm, Sunday and holy days 2:30pm-6:30pm April-October, Monday-Saturday 9am-5:30pm, Sunday and holy days 2:30pm-5:30pm November-March.

## Stock Exchange Palace (Palácio da Bolsa)

*Rua de Ferreira Borges; tel. 223 399 090; www.palaciodabolsa.com; daily 9am-6:30pm Apr.-Oct., daily 9am-1pm and 2pm-5:30pm Nov.-Mar.; €11*

The magnificent Palácio da Bolsa is an imposing neoclassical building that once housed Porto's stock exchange. Built between 1842 and 1910 on the ruins of an old convent, it was meant to impress visiting businesspeople, dignitaries, and heads of state with the city's

economic vitality. Beyond its stately facade are the even more impressive glass-domed Hall of Nations and the opulent Arabian Hall, with Moorish nuances and floor-to-ceiling gilding. Guided tours run regularly throughout the day.

## São Francisco Church
### (Igreja de São Francisco)

*Rua do Infante Dom Henrique; tel. 222 062 125; www. ordemsaofrancisco.pt; daily 9am-5:30pm Nov.-Feb., daily 9am-7pm Mar.-Oct., daily 9am-8pm July-Sept.; €7.50*

Facing the riverside, the 14th-century São Francisco Church is a church of surprises. Its austere gray Gothic exterior hides a mindblowing baroque interior. Construction began in 1245 but was disrupted by a huge fire that destroyed the old cloister. Over 300 kilograms (660 pounds) of gold dust clad the lavish new interior, radiating a golden glow and dripping with cherubs and animals, vaulted pillars and marble columns, and soaring ogival (pointed) arches. Distinguished citizens are interred in the catacombs.

## ★ RIVERFRONT
### (Ribeira)

One of Porto's oldest and most typical areas, the Ribeira is most tourists' first port of call, to soak up the genuine atmosphere of the city, enjoy a river cruise, or cross one of its iconic bridges on foot to Gaia.

You can't say you've been to Porto until you've walked the riverside, the lively **Riverside Docks** (Cais da Ribeira), which date to medieval times. Disorderly narrow pastel buildings of mismatched heights, sizes, and colors seem to teeter into each other. Their fronts are adorned with tiny wroughtiron balconies and freshly washed laundry as well as more modern trappings like satellite dishes. Traditional flat-bottomed *rabelo* bob up and down on the Douro, adding to the romantic ambience. Used for centuries to

---

1: the Stock Exchange Palace 2: Bolhão Market
3: Clérigos Tower 4: traditional wooden *rabelo* boats on the Douro River

ferry barrels of port and other cargo on the river, the boats are today mostly decorative. At ground level, a series of busy restaurants and tourist shops run along the river. Have refreshments or a relaxed meal in one of the myriad establishments, most enjoyable during and after sunset.

## Arrábida Bridge
*Douro Rivermouth*

Located downstream from the iconic **Dom Luís I Bridge,** the Arrabida Bridge is closest to the Douro River mouth, where it stands triumphant, sweeping over the outlet into the Atlantic. Built between 1957 and 1963, the symmetrical reinforced concrete structure is remarkably contemporary in its look, At the time of its inauguration, it was considered an extraordinary feat of engineering and architecture: the biggest single concrete arch bridge in the world. It links Porto and Gaia's main through roads, carrying six lanes of traffic over the Douro River. It also plays host to one of Porto's most unique tourist attractions, to Porto Bridge Climb.

Ascend to the tip of the landmark Arrábida Bridge's sweeping inner arch on the **Porto Bridge Climb** (Rua do Ouro 680; tel. 929 207 117; www.portobridgeclimb.com; climbs leave every 45 minutes 2:30pm-8:30pm daily; €15-16.5; the climb itself takes around 30 minutes), in which experienced guides lead you up the 262 steps to the peak of the sleek cement arch. Once the longest single cement arch in the world, it reopened in 2016 for the first time since the 1960s. One of Porto's best-kept secrets, these tours run for groups of five or more people, minimum age 12. Fullmoon and sunrise climbs are also available. Reservations are required.

## Douro River Boat Tours

Each of Porto's bridges has a story to tell, and a cruise along the Douro is the best way to hear them. Enjoy a relaxing hour sailing on modernized *rabelo* boats, learning the history of the Unvanquished City. Cruises depart regularly from the quaysides in both

# Six Bridges

Known as the City of Bridges, Porto has six bridges that unite it with Vila Nova de Gaia across the Douro River. Counting inward from the *foz* (river mouth), the bridges are the Arrábida, Dom Luís I, Infante Dom Henrique, Dona Maria Pia, São João, and Freixo.

The two most famous, standing side by side, are named after a husband and wife, King Luís I and Maria Pia of Savoy. The **Dona Maria Pia Bridge** was designed by Gustave Eiffel, famous for the tower that bears his name in Paris. The 142-meter (466-ft) double-deck **Dom Luís I Bridge,** built between 1881 and 1886 and designed by Eiffel's disciple, Théophile Seyrig, has become emblematic of the city. While both master and disciple initially worked on the design, their relationship soured and Seyrig completed the project alone. Keen eyes will still note the resemblance in their intricate metal frameworks. Both of the Dom Luís I Bridge's decks are open to pedestrians, with the upper platform 60 meters (200 ft) above water level; the views are worth the vertigo. Cars use the lower deck, while the Metro crosses on the upper deck.

The other four Douro bridges are built from concrete with more streamlined silhouettes. Inaugurated in 2003, the modern **Dom Infante Henrique Bridge** was the last of the six to be built and boasts the longest single-platform arch in the world.

Porto riverfront and Vila Nova de Gaia, in all weather, and last around 50 minutes.

### DOURO ACIMA

*Ribeira dock; tel. 222 006 418; www.douroacima.pt; daily every 30 minutes 10am-6pm Apr.-Oct., daily hourly 10am-4pm Nov.-Mar.; from €15*

Douro Acima operates cruises from Porto's Ribeira dock (in front of Cubo Square).

### DOURO AZUL

*Rua de Miragaia 103, departs from Gaia docks; tel. 223 402 500; www.douroazul.com; every 30 minutes 9:30am-5:30pm summer, every 60 minutes 9:30am-4:30pm winter; 50-minute bridge cruises from €14*

Douro Azul operates daylong hop-on hop-off cruises that allow passengers to board either at the Gaia pier or at the Ribeira dock in Porto. Audio guides are available in 16 languages.

## Guindais Funicular

*R. da Ribeira Negra 314; tel. 808 205 060; www.metrodoporto.pt; Sun.-Thurs. 8am-8pm, Fri.-Sat. 8am-10pm Nov.-Mar., Sun.-Thurs. 8am-10pm, Fri.-Sat. 8am-midnight Apr.-Oct.; €2.50*

The Guindais Funicular runs between Batalha Square, near Porto Cathedral, and the riverside far below. Inaugurated in 1891, the original line has been successively upgraded for a short and swift journey, and the views over the river are phenomenal.

# NORTHWEST PORTO

## Palácio de Cristal Gardens
### (Jardim do Palácio de Cristal)

*Rua de D. Manuel II; tel. 225 320 080; www.cm-porto. pt/jardins-e-parques/palacio-de-cristal_33; daily 8am-9pm Apr.-Sept., daily 8am-7pm Oct.-Mar.; free*

Occupying 8 hectares (20 acres) in the center of Porto, the Palácio de Cristal Gardens are a jigsaw of manicured lawns, colorful flowerbeds, and beautiful water features, divided by walkways and inhabited by peacocks. The garden's terraces are called the "verandas of the Douro" for their views of the river and its bridges. Although the gardens were designed by a German landscape architect for a 19th-century exhibition, little remains of the original crystal palace, replaced in the 1950s by a modern pavilion, now slightly run-down. The gardens are about 30 minutes' walk west of the city center.

## Serralves Foundation and Museum
### (Fundação e Museu de Serralves)

*Rua D. João de Castro 210; tel. 226 156 500; www.serralves.pt; Mon.-Fri. 10am-7pm, Sat.-Sun. 10am-8pmApr.-Sept.; Mon.-Fri. 10am-6pm, Sat.-Sun. 10am-7pm Oct.-Mar.; general ticket (access to all* areas) €20, museum only €12, art deco villa only €12, park only €12

The Serralves Foundation and Museum seeks to promote contemporary art, thought, architecture, and landscape. The **Serralves Museum (Museu Serralves)** features contemporary art in a building designed by distinguished architect Álvaro Siza. **Casa de Serralves,** a pink art deco villa built in the 1930s, offers insight into the architectural and decorative details of the era; it also serves as the foundation's office. Both are surrounded by the 18-hectare (45-acre) **Parque de Serralves,** with its sprawling gardens, woodland, and a farm. Serralves is 5.5 kilometers (3.4 mi) west of the city center.

### São Francisco Xavier Fort
### (Forte de São Francisco Xavier)

*Praça de Gonçalves Zarco 20*

Perched on a cliff jutting out between the Douro and Matosinhos river mouths, the São Francisco Xavier Fort offers lovely ocean views. The fort was built in the 17th century to protect the city from attack. It's commonly called the Castelo do Queijo, "Castle of Cheese," because it was built on a rotund granite rock that looks like a cheese round. The trapezoidal walls are built from chunky granite blocks that give the small fortress a robust look, enforced by a dry moat and drawbridge, turreted watchtowers, and cannons. Inside is an exhibition of military paraphernalia. Two of Porto's most popular beaches are on either side of the fort. It's located approximately 8 kilometers (5 mi) west of the city center at the end of Porto's main Avenida da Boavista, which links the city center to the coast.

Nearby is the idyllic **City Park (Parque da Cidade)** (Praça de Gonçalves Zarco; tel. 226 181 067; www.monumentos.gov.pt; Tues.-Sun. 1pm-6pm late Mar.-early Oct., Tues.-Sun. 1pm-5pm late Oct.-early Mar.; €0.50), nice for a relaxing walk.

# Entertainment and Events

## THE ARTS
### CASA DA MÚSICA

*Av. da Boavista 604-610; tel. 220 120 220; www.casadamusica.com; Mon.-Sat. 9:30am-7pm, Sun. 9:30am-6pm*

Northwest of the city's historic hub, the Casa da Música stages year-round concerts and events ranging from classical to contemporary. Its striking modern building, designed by Dutch architect Rem Koolhaas, has a fluid, sleek look, in stark contrast with the rugged city surrounding it. Private tours of the building (€10) are available in English twice daily.

## FESTIVALS AND EVENTS
### SÃO JOÃO FESTIVAL

*throughout Porto city center and riverside; www.visitar-porto.com/en/whats-on/porto-events/festa-de-sao-joao.html; June*

This 600-year-old festival, honoring Saint John, patron saint of lovers, is one of the most raucous street parties in Portugal. Every year, thousands flock to Porto for the 24-hour-long *festa* that starts on the eve of June 23.

Thousands of floating lanterns are launched, creating a dazzling picture in the night sky overhead. One of São João's quirky traditions is to bash and be bashed over the head with leeks, which in recent times have given way to squeaky plastic hammers. Even though this bashing can get quite vigorous, it's all good-natured, a wish for luck in love and fertility. Almost every home in the city is draped in cheery bunting. Stalls selling beer, sangria, grilled sardines, and kale soups spring up all over the city.

The party bubbles feverishly until a gigantic fireworks display over the Douro River at midnight, when the city's main squares and avenues become dance floors as live bands and DJs play until dawn. The day after is a much-needed local holiday.

# Shopping

**Rua de Santa Catarina** is lined with a mixture of international chain stores such as Mango, Zara, and H&M, along with boutiques that give it a cool cosmopolitan feel. Major brands can also be found along the **Avenida da Boavista**, while **Rua do Almada** is a hub of alternative shops. Peruse the chic window displays along **Rua Miguel Bombarda**, interspersed with arty galleries.

## DOWNTOWN
### Markets
### CLERIGOS MARKET
### (Mercadinho dos Clérigos)
*Rua Cândido dos Reis; last Sat. of each month*
*10am-8pm*
On the second and last Saturday of every month, Rua Cândido dos Reis hosts Mercadinho dos Clérigos, a marketplace bursting with crafts, antiques, music, and even gastronomy.

### PORTOBELO MARKET
### (Mercado de Portobelo)
*Praça Carlos Alberto; Sat. noon-7pm*
Vintage clothing, antiques, and decorative objects are found alongside local produce in Mercado Porto Belo.

## Books
### LIVRARIA LELLO
*Rua das Carmelitas 144; tel. 222 002 037; www. livrarialello.pt; daily 9:30am-7pm; entry €5, fully deductible from any book purchase from the store*
A frontrunner for the title of most beautiful bookshop in the world, Livraria Lello inspired author J. K. Rowling, who lived in Porto in the 1990s: The shop served as the basis for the Flourish & Blotts bookshop in her Harry Potter novels. Close to the Clérigos Tower, the bookshop dates to 1881 and is housed in a 1906 building with a magical feel, with a ghostly-white facade of neo-Gothic and art nouveau architecture, a sweeping crimson central staircase, and a spectacular stained-glass skylight. Outside, the front is embellished with two figurines, painted by José Bielman, symbolizing science and art, while inside, the stained-glass ceiling bears detailing of Lello's motto, *Vecus in Labore* (Dignity in Work). Besides books in several languages, the shop has a **café** upstairs that sells coffee, port wine, and cigars. The small shop is so popular, especially with Harry Potter fans, that long queues form at the door. It's worth braving the crowds. Tickets can be bought online or from a shop just around the corner.

**1:** São João Festival **2:** bottles of port wine **3:** the stairs inside the Livraria Lello bookshop **4:** bridges over the Douro River

# Food

**Offal** is a staple in Porto's regional cuisine, as are rice and beans. Classic dishes include chicken *cabidela* (chicken stewed with giblets, blood, and rice) and Porto-style **tripe,** with various meats, sausages, and beans in a rich, seasoned sauce that led to the nickname *tripeiros* (tripe eaters) for the locals. No trip to Porto would be complete without trying a meaty *francesinha* sandwich—covered in thick sauce—at least once, but it's so filling you may never eat again. Rounding off a meal with a glass of **port** is virtually compulsory.

## DOWNTOWN
### Market
#### A PÉROLA DO BOLHÃO
*Rua Formosa 279; tel. 222 004 009; Mon.-Fri. 9:30am-7:30pm, Sat. 9am-1pm*
Opened in 1917, A Pérola do Bolhão is a gorgeous grocery and delicatessen with an eye-catching art nouveau facade. Inside, it's stuffed to the rafters with colorful traditional products, including sweets, nuts, dried fruits, cookies, local cheeses, cured meats, and, of course, port wines. It's near the busy Bolhão Market.

### Local Specialties
#### FRANCESINHA CAFÉ
*Rua da Alegria 946; tel. 912 653 883; Mon.-Sat. 12:30pm-3pm and 7pm-11pm; €8*
A definite contender for the best *francesinha* is found on the edge of downtown at the Francesinha Café. It looks unremarkable, but the huge picture of the namesake sandwich in the window gives its secret away.

#### ★ PETISQUEIRA VOLATARIA
*Rua Afonso Martins Alho 109; tel. 223 256 593 or 913 885 252; Thurs.-Tues. 11am-10pm; €12*
If you can get a table at Petisqueira Volataria, a narrow tapas place near the São Bento Railway Station, thank your lucky stars. Sharing

platters are creatively conjured with local delicacies in sample-size portions, a great way to savor the scope of local gastronomy in one sitting. Also on the menu is the ubiquitous *francesinha.*

#### SOLAR DO MOINHO DE VENTO
*Rua de Sá de Noronha 81; tel. 222 051 158; www. solarmoinhodevento.com; Mon.-Sat. noon-3:30pm and 7pm-10pm, Sun. noon-3pm; €13*
Cozy Solar do Moinho de Vento serves hearty portions of quality home-cooked local dishes, such as octopus with tomato rice, Porto-style tripe, and chicken *cabidela* rice.

#### ★ ERNESTO
*Rua da Picaria 85; tel. 222 002 600; www.oernesto. pt; Mon. 8:30am-3pm, Tues.-Sat. 8:30am-3pm and 6:30pm-midnight; €15*
Ernesto is a local family favorite. Dishes include Alheira sausage with fries and *marmota frita,* fish fried whole with its tail in its mouth. Inside, the exposed stone walls and gleaming crockery provide a fresh, warm feel.

#### TABERNA DOS MERCADORES
*Rua dos Mercadores 36; tel. 222 010 510; Tues.-Fri. and Sun. 12:30pm-11pm, Sat. 12:30pm-3:30pm and 7pm-11pm; €20*
Busy Taberna dos Mercadores is hidden behind heavy wooden doors on a narrow street near the riverside. The rustic and romantic interior is complemented by tasty traditional dishes and local specialties.

### Tapas
#### CHAMPANHERIA DA BAIXA
*Largo Mompilher 1-2; tel. 223 235 254; www. champanheriadabaixa.com; Mon.-Thurs. noon-12:30am, Fri.-Sat. noon-2:30am; €8*
If you like finger food and fancy drinks, you'll love sophisticated Champanheria da Baixa downtown. The décor is bohemian

# All About *Francesinhas*

the *francesinha* sandwich

It might sound elegant, but there's nothing petite about the *francesinha,* which translates literally as "little Frenchie." Porto's ubiquitous monster sandwich with a cult following is less a snack and more a gut-busting meal. This mound of a sandwich comprises cured and cold meats, such as *chouriço* sausage and bacon, piled on top of slices of roast pork or beefsteak and fresh sausage, wedged between two slices of bread, covered first in melted cheese, then in a hot beer and tomato sauce, and served with fries and a fried egg on top for good measure. Variations include hamburger patties instead of pork or beef, and a spicier sauce made with piri piri.

## ORIGINS

The *francesinha* is believed to derive from its daintier French cousin, the *croque monsieur* (a fried or grilled sandwich with cheese and ham). A local tale pinpoints its origins to a man named Daniel David Silva, who, after living in France and Belgium, brought the *croque monsieur* back to Porto and transformed it into today's *francesinha.* He called the sandwich "little Frenchie" because, he said, French women were the sauciest he had ever met. Silva made his name serving his creation at the A Regaleira restaurant, established in 1953 in Porto, arguably the home of the *francesinha* (it closed in 2018). Legend has it that the recipe for Silva's sauce was a fiercely guarded secret until an employee passed it on to a rival restaurant across the river in Vila Nova de Gaia.

Another theory about the *francesinha's* origins dates to the early-19th-century Peninsular War, when Napoleonic troops would eat all sorts of meats and heaps of cheese in bread as sustenance. The sauce was Porto's contribution later on.

Whatever its origins, this classic Porto dish is now served at eateries throughout the country.

## THE BEST *FRANCESINHA*

It's generally agreed that the *francesinha* sandwich, stuffed with meats and covered in rich tomato and beer sauce, should be washed down with an ice-cold beer. However, the best *francesinha* in town remains hotly debated; try one at any of the following restaurants and decide for yourself.

- **Francesinha Café** (page 332)
- **Petisqueira Volataria** (page 332)
- **Majestic Café** (page 334)

and atmospheric, and the tapas are delicious. Wash it all down with cocktails, sangria, or champagne.

## Seafood
### ★ OSTRAS & COISAS

*Rua da Fábrica 73; tel. 918 854 709; www. ostrasecoisas.pt; Tues.-Thurs. 6pm-11pm, Fri.-Sat. noon-midnight, Sun. noon-11pm; €30*

Trendy Ostras & Coisas serves fresh seafood straight from the docks. Indulge in Mozambican-style shrimp, clams Bulhão Pato-style, or, as the restaurant's name suggests, go for the oysters. Mixed platters for two are a specialty.

## Mediterranean
### ★ 17TH

*Rua do Bolhão 223; tel. 223 401 617; www. decimosetimo.pt; Sun.-Thurs. 12:30pm-3pm and 7:30pm-10:30pm, Fri.-Sat. 12:30pm-3pm and 7:30pm-11pm; €30*

On the top two floors of Porto's Dom Henrique Hotel, the elegant 17 Restaurant & Bar offers a fabulous gastronomic experience alongside bird's-eye city views. The menu fuses traditional Portuguese dishes with Mediterranean flavors.

## Cafés and Light Bites
### ★ MAJESTIC CAFÉ

*Rua de Santa Catarina 112; tel. 222 003 887; www. cafemajestic.com; Mon.-Sat. 9am-11:30pm*

Opened in the 1920s to cater to high society, glittering Majestic Café has carried its splendor across the decades. Decked out with distinctive belle epoque furnishings, including elegant chandeliers and oversize mirrors, Majestic is on a busy shopping street, perfect for a refined afternoon tea, a snack, or a light meal. Or to try the famous *fracesinha*. Fame comes at a price; be prepared to pay more (a regular coffee is around €5) and wait in a queue to get in, unless you reserve ahead online.

# NORTHWEST PORTO
## Market
### BOM SUCESSO MARKET

*Praça Bom Sucesso 74-90; tel. 226 056 610; www. mercadobomsucesso.pt; Sun.-Thurs. 10am-11pm, Fri.-Sat. 10am-midnight*

Tantalize your taste buds at Bom Sucesso Market, browsing the 40-plus stalls serving myriad gastronomic treats, from traditional savory snacks to handmade chocolates and Portuguese wines and gin.

Majestic Café

## Seafood
### ★ PESCARIA DO BAIRRO

*Rua da Senhora da Luz 142; tel. 222 437 652;*
*Tues.-Sat. noon-3:30pm and 7pm-11pm, Sun.*
*8am-11pm; €20*

Delicious fresh fish is always the dish of the day at the Pescaria do Bairro, whose name translates as "neighborhood fishmonger," a lively little joint a short walk from the beachfront and Castelo do Queijo. Fish, from meaty tuna steaks and juicy sea bass to salmon, appear on the menu.

# Bars and Nightlife

Porto's colorful nightlife is consistent with the city's work-hard, play-hard ethos. The city's most popular bar street is **Rua Galeria de Paris.** If one full street of bars does not suffice, try the parallel **Rua Cândido dos Reis.** Both are in the historic area, just off the Clérigos Tower. Nightlife doesn't get into full swing until after 11pm, although most bars are open earlier. Be prepared to stay up late.

## DOWNTOWN
### Bars
#### HD BAR TO BE WILD

*Rua Galeria de Paris 113; tel. 222 032 514; daily 6pm-2am*

Decorated with Harley Davidson memorabilia, laid-back biker bar HD Bar to Be Wild has an American jukebox and an energizing road-trip soundtrack.

#### É PRA PONCHA BAR

*Rua Galeria de Paris 99; tel. 969 472 546; Mon.-Sat. 5pm-4am*

É Pra Poncha Bar, a narrow cave-like space with a wavy multicolored ceiling, is the setting for great punch-based cocktails like Madeira Poncha.

### Live Music
#### CASA DO LIVRO

*Rua Galeria de Paris 85; tel. 222 025 101; Tues.-Thurs. 9pm-3am, Fri.-Sat. 9pm-4am*

Once upon a time, Casa do Livro was a bookshop, but now it's a nightlife classic, with diverse music from DJs and live musicians. Its walls are decorated with the bookshelves of its former life, while gleaming polished wood and low-lit lamps provide a warm glow, contributing to the intimate drawing-room atmosphere.

#### GALERIA DE PARIS

*Rua Galeria de Paris 56; tel. 222 016 218; daily 10am-3am*

Housed in a former warehouse, Galeria de Paris is packed with vintage paraphernalia: old toys, musical instruments, and even bicycles hanging from the ceilings. Enjoy eclectic live acts, from jazz bands to trapeze artists and belly dancers. Candlelit tables add a touch of romance. Galeria also serves breakfast, lunch, and dinner.

#### PLAN B CLUB

*Rua de Cândido dos Reis 30; tel. 222 012 500; planobporto.com; Wed.-Sat 10pm-6am*

One of Porto's best dance venues, boho-chic Plano B offers an interesting mashup of music and art, design and culture, and a regular lineup of DJs and live acts playing everything from R&B and techno to hip-hop.

# ☆ Port-Tasting in Vila Nova de Gaia

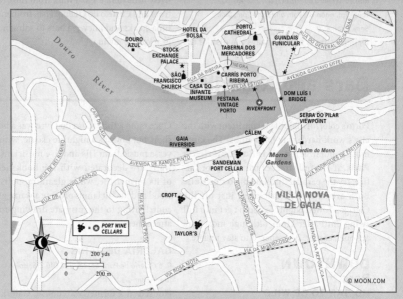

Deep, rich, fortified port wine has become an ambassador not only for its namesake Porto but for Portugal as a whole. Only port wine produced in northern Portugal may be labeled port, and authentic port is produced exclusively in vineyards in the Douro Region, demarcated in 1756, with mostly native grape varieties. It is transported downriver and aged in barrels stored in cellars such as those in **Vila Nova de Gaia,** just over the Douro River from Porto.

Generally enjoyed as a dessert drink, the best-known port is typically ruby red in color. **Ruby** is the younger, lighter, fruitier variety, while **tawny** varieties are older and nuttier. Exceptional **vintage** port is produced only from the finest harvests and aged for long periods in oak casks. **Rosé** and **white** varieties have recently given the wine a trendy makeover as an ingredient of white port and tonic, a popular summer cocktail. The essence of the north in a bottle, port wine is the quintessential Porto souvenir.

# Accommodations

Porto offers a wide range of options, from basic to high-end historic conversions, all with central locations.

## DOWNTOWN
### €100-200
#### HOTEL DA BOLSA
*Rua de Ferreira Borges 101; tel. 222 026 768; www. hoteldabolsa.com; €100*

Just 100 meters (300 ft) from the Palácio da Bolsa, three-star Hotel da Bolsa offers 34 comfortable rooms, a good buffet breakfast, an on-site bar, and a great location.

#### ★ GRANDE HOTEL DO PORTO
*Rua de Santa Catarina 197; tel. 222 076 690; www. grandehotelporto.com; €171*

Just around the corner from the iconic

## PORT LODGES

Some of Portugal's oldest port companies were founded by British mercantile families in the 17th and 18th centuries in Vila Nova da Gaia and are still run by their descendants. Most of the lodges offer **guided tours** in multiple languages, including English, taking visitors through the history of port-making, culminating in a tasting session. Basic tours of the cellars (€10-12, including tasting) last about an hour. All of the lodges listed below are open 10am-6pm daily year-round.

- **Cálem** (Av. Diogo Leite 344; tel. 916 113 451; https://tour.calem.pt; from €13): Founded in 1859, Cálem is one of Portugal's signature ports. Tour options include tastings, food, and even fado performances.

- **Sandeman** (Largo Miguel Bombarda 47; tel. 223 740 534; www.sandeman.com; from €14): Globally renowned since 1790, tours of the magnificent 200-year-old cellars include a 1970 vintage tour and a 100-Year-Old Tawnies tour.

- **Croft** (Rua Barão Forrester 412; tel. 220 109 825; www.croftport.com; from €14): Founded in 1588, Croft is the oldest active port producer. A visit to Croft's cellars includes a guided tour and tasting of three ports.

- **Taylor's** (Rua do Choupelo 250; tel. 223 772 973; www.taylor.pt; €15): Producing port since 1692, Taylor's is among Portugal's oldest port houses. Its extensive audio-guided tours provide a wealth of information in 11 languages.

- **Porto Walkers** (tel. 918 291 519; www.portowalkers.pt; from €27): Porto Walkers takes groups on half-day walking tours that include a trio of different lodges. Knowledgeable guides teach you about the origins of port, and even how to sample the drink properly.

## GETTING THERE

Vila Nova de Gaia is a short walk across the **Dom Luís I Bridge** from Porto's riverside. Take the upper platform for the Monastery of Serra do Pilar and Morro Gardens or the lower deck for the riverside and port cellars. Alternatively, Porto's Metro (tel. 225 081 000; www.metrodoporto.pt; €1.20 one-way) light-rail system runs regularly between the two cities; take the **D Line** to **Santo Ovidio** from the São Bento station, stopping at Jardim do Morro. This line crosses the Dom Luís I Bridge's upper deck. Metro trains run every six minutes weekdays 6am-1am, every 15 minutes on the weekend.

Majestic Café on busy Rua de Santa Catarina, Grand Hotel do Porto is a stately 94-room retreat on the doorstep of the city's best monuments theaters, and shops. Established in 1880, it embodies the grandeur of bygone eras, brought up to date with modern comforts.

### Over €200
### ★ INTERCONTINENTAL PORTO PALÁCIO DAS CARDOSAS

*Praça da Liberdade 25; tel. 220 035 600; www.ihg. com; €256*

Feel like royalty at the opulent five-star

Intercontinental Porto Palácio das Cardosas, a beautiful 18th-century palace reborn. Think grand chandeliers, polished marble floors, and Romanesque columns. It's just a short stroll from the São Bento Railway Station and the Livraria Lello bookshop.

## RIVERFRONT
### €100-200
### CARRIS PORTO RIBEIRA

*Rua do Infante D. Henrique 1; tel. 220 965 786; www. carrisportoribeira.com; €120*

A few streets back from the riverfront in the

old Ribeira, four-star Carris Porto Ribeira occupies a refurbished 17th-century building with chic rooms, a cozy tapas bar, and views across the Douro.

### Over €200
★ **PESTANA VINTAGE PORTO**

*Praça da Ribeira 1; tel. 223 402 300; www. pestanacollection.com; €227*

On the romantic riverfront, five-star Pestana Vintage Porto was created from a set of 18 pastel-color historic buildings emblematic of Porto's cityscape. Some date to the 16th century. Inside, it's plush and comfortable, and the on-site restaurant, Rib Beef & Wine, is excellent.

## NORTHWEST PORTO
### €100-200
★ **EUROSTARS DAS ARTES HOTEL**

*Rua do Rosário 160-165; tel. 222 071 250; www. eurostarshotels.com.pt; €138*

In central Porto, Eurostars das Artes Hotel is an art lover's dream. In an area surrounded by galleries and museums, it features boutique accommodations, with rotating exhibitions inside the hotel, and a peaceful outdoor deck. It straddles two structures: a palatial older building with a sky-blue tiled facade and its contemporary sibling.

★ **VINCCI PORTO**

*Alameda de Basílio Teles 29; tel. 220 439 620; www. vincciporto.com; from €171 d*

Four-star Vincci Porto is a stylish retreat in a renovation of the landmark Bolsa do Pescado fish market. It has a big, bright, and airy glass-brick atrium, distinctive avant-garde décor, and a terrace with views over the Douro.

# Information and Services

## Tourist Information
- **Porto Tourism Office Downtown:** Calçada Dom Pedro Pitões 15; tel. 223 326 751; www.visitporto.travel; daily 9am-8pm
- **Porto Tourism Office Center:** Rua Clube dos Fenianos 25; tel. 223 326 751; www.visitporto.travel; daily 9am-8pm

## Health and Safety
- **European emergency number:** tel. 112
- **PSP Metropolitan Police:** Largo 1º de Dezembro 3; tel. 222 092 000; www.psp.pt
- **PSP Tourist Police:** Rua Clube dos Fenianos 19; tel. 222 092 006

- **Santo António General State Hospital (Centro Hospitalar do Porto):** Largo do Professor Abel Salazar; tel. 222 077 500; www.chporto.pt
- **Santa Maria Private Hospital:** Rua de Camões 906; tel. 225 082 000; www.hsmporto.pt
- **24-hour pharmacy:** Farmácia Antunes, Rua do Bonjardim 485; tel. 222 007 936

## Post Office
- **Main Downtown Branch:** Allied Post Office, Praça General Humberto Delgado 320; www.ctt.pt; Mon.-Fri. 8:30am-9pm

# Getting There and Around

## GETTING THERE

Porto is northern Portugal's major transport hub and is easily accessed from all over the country. Bus and train connections run from all major towns and cities and are cost-efficient; road routes are straightforward and in good condition; and short domestic flights link the north to Lisbon, the Algarve, and the islands. From the Algarve, it can often be cheaper to fly to Porto than to go by car or public transport.

### Air

#### SÁ CARNEIRO INTERNATIONAL AIRPORT

*tel. 229 432 400; www.aeroportoporto.pt*

Porto's Sá Carneiro International Airport (OPO) has daily flights from dozens of European destinations year-round as well as regular direct flights from Canada, the United States, South America, and Africa. Daily domestic flights operate to the Azores; there's also an hourly express flight between Porto and Lisbon. From Lisbon, the hourly express flight operated by regional **TAP Express** takes 1 hour and costs around €70 one-way; in addition, **Ryanair** offers less frequent flights.

To the Azores (Ponta Delgada), there are at least three daily flights, generally noon-5pm, operated by **Azores Airlines, TAP Air Portugal,** and **Ryanair,** which take around 2.5 hours. Round-trip flights can be found for under €100, depending on the season.

Porto's airport is in Maia, 10 kilometers (6 mi) north of Porto city center and served by the **Metro** (tel. 225 081 000 or 808 205 060; www.metrodoporto.pt) light rail and tram system to central Porto, every 20 minutes Monday-Friday, less frequently on weekends and holidays. It takes around 30 minutes to reach Porto by Metro, and a one-way ticket costs €2.55. Tickets can be purchased from ticket machines or the airport's tourist information office.

There is little to no public transport midnight-6am (a late-night bus service runs hourly between the airport and the downtown Aliados area), so a taxi might be necessary. Both conventional taxis and Uber operate in Porto. From the airport, the trip costs €20-30.

### Train

The **Celta high-speed train** (www.cp.pt) operates twice daily between Porto's **Campanhã station** (Rua Pinheiro de Campanhã, Largo da Estação) and **Vigo, Spain.** The journey takes around 3 hours, €14.95 one-way). Other international trains from London, Paris, and Madrid require a change in Lisbon.

**CP** (tel. 707 210 220; www.cp.pt) operates high-speed Alfa-Pendular trains and the slightly slower Intercidades (Intercity) train service that connect Lisbon and the Algarve to Porto's Campanhã station (Rua Pinheiro de Campanhã, Largo da Estação) at various times daily. Campanhã station is 5 kilometers (3 mi) east of Porto's downtown.

From **Lisbon,** the Alfa-Pendular runs almost hourly from the Santa Apolónia and Oriente stations and takes 3 hours to reach Porto. Tickets cost €31.60 one-way for second class, €43.70 first class.

Tickets can be booked online (www.cp.pt) and can be cheaper if bought in advance.

### Bus

Porto doesn't have a main bus terminal but instead has several hubs for long-distance buses located around the city. The main intercity bus company between Lisbon and Porto is **Rede Expressos** (tel. 707 223 344; www.rede-expressos.pt; 8am-9pm daily), whose buses are modern, comfortable, and air-conditioned. Bus travel is cheaper than rail but takes longer. Dozens of buses depart daily between **Lisbon** and Porto, and the journey takes 3.5-4 hours. Rede Expressos buses depart Lisbon's Oriente station (in the Park of Nations area) every few hours, and hourly from the Sete Rios hub (near the zoo). Buses arrive at Porto's main bus hub, **Campo 24 Agosto** (Campo 24 de Agosto 125), about 1 kilometer (0.6 mi) east of Porto's Bolhão Market; it has a nearby Metro station with the same name. Journeys take approximately 3.5 hours, and one-way tickets cost €19.

International buses from **Vigo** in Spain tend to stop in Porto's downtown Aliados area, although some go to the Campo 24 Agosto terminal if passengers are connecting southward. Other international bus lines, such as **AVIC, Internorte, Eurolines,** and **Resende,** stop at the **Casa da Música,** while many urban buses drop off and depart from the **São João Hospital** (Alameda Professor Hernâni Monteiro), north of the city center, and the **Camelias Park** (Rua de Augusto Rosa) in downtown Porto, just before Batalha Square.

**Eurolines** (www.eurolines.com) operates regular international bus services between Porto and London, Madrid, and Paris. **Internorte** (tel. 707 200 512; www.internorte. pt) is another option. Most international buses use Porto's Casa da Música or Campo 24 Agosto stops.

## Car

Porto is 300 kilometers (185 mi) north of Lisbon. It's served by an excellent network of motorways, although it can be costly as tolls apply to most A-roads. The main A1 motorway links Lisbon to Porto in under three hours.

# GETTING AROUND

Getting around Porto is easy, with several efficient forms of transport. The historic center is compact and easy to cover on foot, but the cobbled streets can be very steep. Bus, car, or Metro travel is required to see sights on the outskirts, such as the São Francisco Xavier Fort and the Serralves Foundation and Museum.

An all-encompassing multimodal travel card called the **Andante Tour Card** (tel. 225 071 000; www.stcp.pt) covers bus, tram, Metro, and urban train lines between Espinho, Valongo, and Travagem stations. It is great for getting around stress-free and comes in two versions: Andante Tour 1 (€7) is valid for 24 hours after first validation. Andante Tour 3 (€15) is valid for 72 hours. Andante tickets can be purchased from all bus and Metro ticket machines and booths, or from tourism offices. The rechargeable card costs €0.60.

If passengers are caught traveling without a valid ticket on any form of Porto's public transport, the fines can be hefty, ranging from €120 to €350. Be sure to hold on to your ticket to avoid getting fined, whichever type of public transit you're using.

## Bus

Porto's transport company **STCP** (tel. 225 071 000; www.stcp.pt) runs wide-ranging bus service, including less extensive late-night bus service in the main Aliados and airport areas 12:30am-5:30am. Late-night service operates hourly. Most single-journey tickets cost €1.95.

## Tram

Porto has gorgeous vintage 1920s wooden trams (tel. 225 071 000; www.stcp.pt) that rattle around the city. The three main tram lines are **line 1,** along the riverfront area between Porto's historic area and the Passeio Alegre garden; **line 18,** between Massarelos and Carmos; and **line 22,** a circular route through downtown. Tickets (€3) can be bought on board. A 48-hour tram pass (adults €10, children €5) can also be bought on board as well as from most hotels and tour agencies. Trams come along every 20 minutes daily 8am-8pm.

## Metro

Porto's Metro (tel. 225 081 000; www. metrodoporto.pt) is a light-rail network that runs above ground in the suburbs and underground in the city center. Trains run every 10-20 minutes daily 6am-midnight. Scenic

Line D runs across the Douro River over a bridge to Gaia. Metro also runs to the **airport** in Maia. Trips are priced by zones and cost just over €1 for a two-zone single trip; cards are rechargeable.

## Taxi

Local taxi companies include **Taxis Invicta** (Rua de Cunha Júnior 41B; tel. 225 076 400; www.taxisinvicta.com), **Taxis Porto** (Rua da Constituição 823; tel. 220 997 336; www.taxisporto.pt), and **Taxis do Porto** (Av. da Boavista 1002; tel. 223 206 059; www.taxisporto.pt). Getting a taxi is easy; taxi ranks can be found at the airport and bus and train stations, outside shopping centers and hospitals, near the riverside, and along the main Avenida dos Aliados. Taxis can also be hailed in the street.

## Car

There's no need for a car in Porto, but a car can be useful to explore neighboring cities and the northern region. Rental companies operating at the airport include **Sixt** (Francisco Sá Carneiro Airport; tel. 255 788 199; www.sixt.pt) and **Europcar** (Av. do Aeroporto 322; tel. 229 482 452; www.europcar.pt). Most rental car depots are near the airport. A free **shuttle** takes passengers from arrivals to the depot, and most are open 7am-midnight daily. There are also a few car-rental offices (Mon.-Fri. 9am-1pm and 3pm-6:30pm, Sat. 10am-noon) at Porto's **Campanhã train station.**

The traffic in Porto can be dense and chaotic, especially on weekdays during rush hours, and parking can be hard to find, particularly in summer and during major festivities such as São João.

**STOPOVER IN PORTO**
GETTING THERE AND AROUND

# Background

## The Landscape

Scattered over a swathe of deep the north Atlantic Ocean, located about 1,500 kilometers (930 mi) west of mainland Portugal and 2,500 kilometers (1,600 mi) southeast of Newfoundland, Canada, the Azores archipelago is a chain of nine volcanic islands that span a belt of water around 600 kilometers (400 mi) wide. The islands can be divided into three groups: the eastern group (São Miguel and Santa Maria), the central group (Terceira, Graciosa, São Jorge, Pico, and Faial), and the western group (Flores and Corvo). The central group is often broken

down further into the Azores "triangle" (São Jorge, Pico, and Faial) due to these islands' close proximity.

Each island has its own distinct personality and character, but all are richly volcanic, blessed with magical waterfalls cascading down jagged lava curtains, jungle-like flora, gaping mossy calderas, mirror-like lakes, hot springs, and stunning tidal pools. Few islands have any significant urban sprawl, not even São Miguel, the archipelago's biggest island and main gateway. In São Miguel's principal city, Ponta Delgada, the autonomous region's economic capital, high-rises are few and far between. The other islands are pastoral by comparison, with larger towns showcasing traditional island architecture ensconced amid rolling massifs, lush pastures, and glinting sea views from almost every street.

## GEOGRAPHY

The Azores were formed tens of millions of years ago sometime between the Cretaceous and Cenozoic periods, through volcanic and seismic activity due to their location on the junction of the North American, Eurasian, and African tectonic plates. The archipelago's volcanic heritage is omnipresent, evident in spiky conical peaks, huge bowl-like calderas, steaming hot springs and bubbling fumaroles, underground caves, grottoes, and lava tubes and formations. Most of the islands boast yawning calderas, like huge pock marks on the ragged landscapes, and volcanic chain massifs. They also experience frequent quakes and tremors, mostly of low-to-moderate intensity that usually go unnoticed.

The islands are mostly basalt stone, with gritty, black, volcanic sand beaches. Santa Maria is an exception, with blond sand beaches and limestone—the island remained submerged until just a few thousand years ago, leading to the unique sedimentary composition. *Fajãs* are a unique feature of the islands, and they are found in greatest numbers on

São Jorge. These tongues of lava and debris splayed at the foot of the islands' sheer cliffs, which cooled as they hit the sea, form fertile flatlands peppered with unique lagoons and plant life. São Miguel island is famed for its hot springs and geothermal activity. Faial is home to the "newest" piece of land in Portugal, the Capelinhos Volcano site, formed by the islands' most recent volcanic eruption in 1958. Pico, the archipelago's youngest island, boasts Mount Pico, a stratovolcano that is the highest point in Portugal.

## CLIMATE

With a subtropical climate, the Azores' weather is generally mild year-round and less prone to the extreme temperatures and meteorological phenomena that mainland Europe has increasingly suffered in recent years. The most common inconvenience is stormy weather: High winds and heavy rain can play havoc with flights and ferry travel, especially in winter. The unpredictability of the Azores' climate, where four seasons can famously be experienced in a day, is something the locals just take in stride. Temperatures are relatively stable, fluctuating by an average of 10-15°C (50-59°F) from winter to summer, rarely dipping below 12°C (54°F) or climbing above 26°C (79°F). May-October sees the warmest and driest of the weather, August the hottest, and November-December the rainiest.

## ENVIRONMENTAL ISSUES

The Azores suffers from few serious environmental issues, due to their remoteness and relative lack of development. One of their biggest battles today is microplastics, as their unique and fragile ecosystem is being slowly threatened by ocean pollution. Sustainable development and environmental preservation are a big deal on the islands, where there is huge scope and potential for renewable energies due to the great potential for high-temperature

Previous: the town of Velas, São Jorge.

geothermal resources, hydropower, and wind power, thanks to the archipelago's volcanic nature and exposed mid-Atlantic location. Tour operators make concerted efforts to preserve the Azores' environmental heritage, especially their label as a sea life sanctuary. Important research on ocean biodiversity is carried out by island-based scientists, much of which is passed on to visitors via the likes of marine biologists who collaborate with dolphin- and whale-watching trips. Waste prevention and management is touted as key to achieving the Azores' sustainability goals, and are government priorities.

# Plants and Animals

Due to their subtropical climate and widely diverse landscapes, ranging from boggy marshes to barren lava plains, the Azores are home to a vast array of endemic and nonnative species of flora and fauna. Of the close to 5,000 species and subspecies of terrestrial plants and animals known to inhabit the archipelago, just over 400 are found nowhere else on the planet. Upon the islands' discovery, they were devoid of land mammals; most of the animals found in the Azores today, and many of the plants, were introduced by humans. The islands' unique position in the mid-Atlantic also means they welcome many exciting migratory animals.

## VEGETATION ZONES

Though small, the Azores boast a wide variety of vegetation, from the hardy shrubs and grasses that can survive on rocky, exposed lava coasts, to wetlands surrounding caldera lakes, to forests populated by endemic Azorean laurel. In general terms the islands are green and luxuriant, largely blanketed by patchworks of fields, meadows, and woodlands in a kaleidoscope of greens. The soils range from deep, mineralrich, and fertile, to thin crusts of arid lava where little grows. Among the best places to find a wealth of endemic species are the peat bogs found on Flores and Terceira, while Pico is one of the few islands with enough altitude to have timberline and alpine vegetation. Many of the endemic belts of vegetation are protected to preserve the flora's heritage.

## TREES

The Azores are blessed with a vast range of trees. Trees unique to the Azores include the evergreen Azorean juniperus tree and laurel tree, buckthorn, and pau-branco. Isolated swathes of laurissilva forests can be found on all islands, but most prominently on Pico, Terceira, and São Miguel.

Many species were introduced to the archipelago from around the world for ornamental purposes, with some of these adopting the archipelago as their own and growing their own forests. Among the most commonly found introduced species of tree are the huge New Zealand Christmas trees, Norfolk Island pines, Victorian box trees, Brazilian mahogany, dogwood, Japanese cryptomeria, and acacia.

## FLOWERS AND OTHER PLANT LIFE

Thanks to its mineral-rich soil, lashings of rain, and bursts of sunshine, pretty much anything will flourish in the Azores, making their plant life among the most interesting and diverse in Europe. The islands are of course most famous for their pillowy bursts of powder-blue, pink, and purply hydrangeas, which literally coat the landscape in summer, allegedly brought to the archipelago from the United States circa the 17th century. Terceira and Faial are nicknamed the Lilac and Blue Islands, respectively, for their particular abundance of these flowers. The differing levels of pH in the islands' soils are said to influence the varying colors of the hydrangeas.

Several hundred species of flowers and

other plant life were introduced to the Azores for commercial purposes, like azalea and camellia. The archipelago's main endemic plant species are Azores heather, colicwood, and the vidalia flower.

## LAND MAMMALS

The Azores can claim the peculiarity of having only small wild mammals, such as rabbits, hedgehogs, weasels, ferrets, rats, mice, and bats. The Azores' "happy cows" are, of course, famous, and cows and other livestock often outnumber humans on the islands. Only one mammal is native to the archipelago: two species of bat, the Azores noctule (Nyctalus azoreum), a diurnal insectivorous bat, and the greater mouse-eared bat (Myotis myotis). They tend to roost in empty buildings, caves, and hollow trees.

## SEA LIFE

The waters around the Azores islands are a trove of enchanting and exciting sea life. Whale- and dolphin-watching can be enjoyed in the Azores year-round, although the prime season is April-October. Some of the main species of whale that can be sighted in the islands' waters are humpback whales, sperm whales, and fin and sei whales, along with numerous pods of playful common and bottlenose dolphins. A rarer sight is the whale shark, which is sometimes spotted off the island of Santa Maria.

Other interesting sea life found in the Azores' pristine waters include graceful leatherback and loggerhead turtles, rays, hammerhead sharks, and flying fish. Fish species found in the waters around the islands include swordfish, marlin, and yellowfin tuna, which makes fishing in the Azores a rewarding sport. Devil rays, and the potently poisonous Portuguese man o' war, can also be found on the islands.

## BIRDS

Due to their unique geographical location halfway between the US and Europe and variety of habitats, the Azores are particularly interesting for bird-watchers. The archipelago is renowned as a breeding ground for some 30 species of birds and is home to the biggest and most important Cory's shearwater and roseate tern colonies on the planet. The islands also provide sanctuary to North American species rarely found elsewhere in Europe, and the even rarer Monteiro's storm petrel.

The Azores bullfinch, one of the rarest birds in Europe, is endemic to a small area of the island of São Miguel. Many consider spotting the Azores bullfinch the ultimate goal of an Azores bird-watching trip; the bird is emblematic of the island's laurissilva forests. Other highlights include the Atlantic canary and several subspecies such as the chaffinch, São Miguel goldcrest, Azores wood pigeon, and the common buzzard.

## REPTILES AND AMPHIBIANS

With the exception of common lizards, the Azores have few retiles on the islands, and no snakes. The Madeiran wall lizard, endemic to Madeira, was introduced to the Azores due to the shipping trade between the two archipelagos. The Iberian frog and northern or great crested newt, currently one of the most endangered amphibians in Europe, call the Azores home. The great crested newt, accidentally introduced to the Azores, settled in the ponds and lakes in central São Miguel.

## INSECTS AND ARACHNIDS

The Azores' woodlands and laurel forests are especially rich in insects and arachnids. Around 250 endemic species of arthropods are known to inhabit the Azores, and scientists expect that this number will grow to 400 species. There are no poisonous insects in the Azores; when it comes to itchy bites, mosquitoes are usually the culprit.

# History

Enshrouded in mystique since the earliest times, the Azores were officially discovered and settled by the Portuguese in the early 15th century, but exactly who discovered the archipelago and when remains one of the most controversial debates in Portuguese navigation history. What is known is that Portuguese navigator Gonçalo Velho, a close aide of Prince Henry the Navigator, landed on Santa Maria, the first island to be populated, in 1431, although there are also suggestions that Santa Maria and São Miguel were discovered by fellow Portuguese navigator Diogo de Silves circa 1427. History has it that Henry and his men struggled to rally much interest among the Portuguese in settling in the Azores, so some of the islands, particularly in the central group, were colonized first with the help of the Flemish from the Flanders region of Belgium, then by British, French, Italians, Jewish farmers, and enslaved Africans, who joined the earliest settlers to help with the hard task of making the remote islands habitable. Over the centuries, the islands have been subjected to earthquakes and eruptions, pirate pillages, invasions, and occupation, and now are an increasingly popular tourist destination.

## ANCIENT TIMES

Tales of islands in the middle of the Atlantic can be found in seafaring folklore as far back as the classical era. Some people associate the Azores with the mythical kingdom of Atlantis mentioned by Plato.

The archipelago does appear on maps well before its official discovery date. The Catalan Atlas of 1375 is the first map to depict the Azores, identifying three islands with the names of Corvo, Flores, and São Jorge, hinting that possibly the Genovese discovered the Azores, although it is widely presumed that these were likely merely sightings rather than actual landings. Other historians claim the islands were already chartered on the Medici Atlas in the early 14th century, or that they were happened upon during 14th-century expeditions to the Canary Islands sponsored by King Afonso IV of Portugal.

## PORTUGUSE EXPLORATION

Roughly spanning from the 15th to the 18th century, the Age of Discoveries saw intrepid Portuguese seafarers led by Portugal's most famous captain, Prince Henry the Navigator, sail around the world, the Azores being no exception. The Portuguese explored the Atlantic archipelagos and African coast, before rounding the Cape of Good Hope in 1488, under the leadership of Bartolomeu Dias, and finally reaching India a decade later in 1498, guided by Vasco da Gama.

According to the history books, the official date of the discovery of the Azores is 1427, by the Portuguese explorer Diogo de Silves. He landed first on the islands of Santa Maria and São Miguel before quickly progressing westward. However, this is a point of contention as many claim it was merely a "re-discovery," as the islands appeared on earlier maps, meaning they were not unknown to sailors—though they may have simply been sighted and recorded.

Prince Henry the Navigator was the driving force behind the Portuguese claiming the Azores; he set his sights on the islands and their settlement as part of his program of exploration and discovery toward India. As far as Azoreans are concerned, Prince Henry is one of the archipelago's founding fathers. After the initial "re-discovery," a series of explorative trips to the Azores were made in swift succession, to map the outline of the coasts and disembark farm animals to provide future settlers with sustenance.

Various suggestion have been put forward regarding the naming of the Azores, with the main theories being the archipelago was given its name after Portuguese explorers believed the many buzzards sighted circling above the islands were hawks, called "açores" in Portuguese. Or, it's a Portuguese variant of the Genovese or Florentine word *azzurre* or *azzorre*, meaning "blue."

## SETTLEMENT

The first settlers of the Azores arrived on the island of Santa Maria, in the Angels' Bay area on the north of the island, in the early 1430s. The settlers were primarily Portuguese, from the southern Algarve and Alentejo regions, attracted by advertisements and promotions by João Soares de Albergaria, nephew and heir of Portuguese monk and Commander in the Order of Christ Gonçalo Velho Cabral, hereditary landowner responsible for administering Crown lands on the Azores during the Portuguese Age of Discovery. The bigger nearby island of São Miguel was settled in quick succession, and colonization moved progressively westward over the decades, to the central group in the mid-1400s, reaching Flores in 1480 (although Flores was first populated by sheep only, in 1475). There was a whole century between the colonization of Flores in 1480 and its neighbor, tiny Corvo, circa 1580. The early settlements were largely small and agricultural; farming produce such as woad and wheat.

While Prince Henry the Navigator initially struggled to attract Portuguese settlers to the isolated archipelago, the central islands were settled by the Flemish, who were desperate to flee the Hundred Years' War, which had devastated Flanders. They brought with them modern farming techniques different than those of the Portuguese, still evident today in São Jorge's cheese-making methods and Pico's windmills and dry-stone vine pens.

## GROWING IMPORTANCE IN MIDATLANTIC TRADE

The Azores' position in the middle of the Atlantic made the islands a stopover on trade routes. Ships stopped there on their transatlantic voyages to refuel and resupply, or for repairs when seeking refuge from formidable storms. Predominantly agricultural, thanks to trade, the archipelago has enjoyed repeated dalliances with wealth. Horta, on the island of Faial, was establishing a reputation as the mid-Atlantic's main refueling station, for vessels returning from the New World, and, later, a key service station for cod and sugar fleets. Exotic fruits like oranges and pineapples became well established in the Azores over this period, and bustling transatlantic trade meant they could be profitably exported. Turning its hand to producing wine, the Azores also supplied the fleets' crews with tipple, to drink onboard and to resell elsewhere.

## SPANISH ANNEXATION AND INDEPENDENCE

Crippled by a dynastic crisis that saw the Portuguese throne left without a successor in the late 16th century, King Philip II of Spain gained control over the Portuguese crown, which brought the entire Iberian Peninsula and Portugal's overseas territories under Spanish rule. This era spanned 1580-1640, until the Portuguese Restoration War saw the House of Braganza established as Portugal's new ruling dynasty.

King Philip II of Spain made two attempts to take control of the Azores. The first, in 1581, culminated in the Battle of Salga. Loyal to António, Prior of Crato, who Azoreans believed was the rightful successor to the Portuguese throne, the islands defeated the Spanish in the Bay of Salga on Terceira. Two years later, in 1583, with the help of French and English troops, Azoreans again opposed the Spanish, but fighters were this time taken prisoners of war and even hanged. Spain fortified Terceira with a huge fortress, designed to protect fleets crossing from Mexico, and during this time of occupation the Azores served as a port of call for Spanish galleons. The region was handed back to Portuguese control with the end of the Iberian Union in December 1640.

# 20TH CENTURY

Due to their strategic location, the Azores have historically had an essential role in transatlantic sea and air travel. In the early 20th century, the Azores became a stepping-stone for seaplane and commercial transatlantic flights, with planes crossing between the US and Europe stopping there to refuel. In the 1930s, the archipelago was a haven for American whaling ships, which frequently trawled the archipelago's waters and used the islands for boat repairs and to stock up. Technical progress from the 1960s meant both ships and planes could travel longer distances without the need to stop and refuel, ending a prosperous time for the archipelago.

# CONTEMPORARY TIMES

Following Portugal's Carnation Revolution in April 1974, which saw ruler António de Oliveira Salazar's dictatorship overturned and democracy introduced in a peaceful, almost bloodless uprising, the Azores were given political autonomy in the 1976 Portuguese Constitution. Isolated and to some degree autonomous, the Azores have remained relatively undeveloped through the 21st century until recently, when tourism to the islands has begun to increase.

# Government and Economy

## GOVERNMENT

The Republic of Portugal is a sovereign democracy. The Azores, while part of the Portuguese Republic, have, since 1976, been an autonomously governed region.

### Organization

The Azores' organs of self-government are the Legislative Assembly (Parliament) and the Regional Government, both elected via the democratically expressed will of the Azorean people.

The Legislative Assembly is a unicameral parliament, a representative and legislative body that is also responsible for supervising government action. At the time of writing, it comprised 57 Members of Parliament (MPs) from six different political parties, elected every four years via regional election. The executive branch of the Azores' regional authority is located in Ponta Delgada (São Miguel island), the legislative branch in Horta (Faial), and the judicial branch in Angra do Heroísmo (Terceira).

The Regional Government of the Azores is the region's highest executive power. It is headed by a president and by regional secretaries, can include vice presidents and regional undersecretaries, and takes office before the Legislative Assembly. The Regional Government is politically accountable to the Legislative Assembly. The president at the time of writing was Vasco Cordeiro (Socialist Party). Presidents are appointed based on electoral results, taking into account the partisan composition of parliament. The members of the Regional Government are appointed and dismissed by the representative of the republic (at the time of writing, Pedro Catarino), at the proposal of the president. The government only assumes the full extent of its powers after parliamentary investiture, which happens with the Legislative Assembly's approval of its government program.

Law enforcement in the Azores remains the responsibility of Portugal's Central Government, exercised by the country's main police forces, the PSP, PJ, and GNR police. Nationally, at the time of writing, Portugal's prime minister is António Costa, of the Socialist Party, and its president is Marcelo Rebelo de Sousa of the Social Democratic Party.

### Political Parties

Since the 1974 Carnation Revolution, like

the mainland, the islands' political scene is dominated by two key parties: the center-left PS Socialist Party, and the center-right PSD Social Democratic Party. Other parties included the conservative Christian-democratic CDS-PP People's Party, the BE Left Bloc, the Unitarian Democratic Coalition (CDU), and the People's Monarchist Party (PPM).

## Elections
Regional elections are held every four years. The Azores regional parliament elects 57 members through a proportional system in which the nine islands elect a number of MPs proportional to the number of registered voters. A regional election is due to be held in the Azores no later than October 2020, with exact timing made uncertain by the impact of the 2020 coronavirus crisis.

# ECONOMY
Still predominantly agricultural, today the Azores enjoy a limited but steady economy. The main industries are agriculture, livestock breeding and dairy farming, and fishing, but tourism is fast establishing itself as the most important industry in the region.

## Agriculture
Agriculture is a vital pillar in the Azores' economy. Farming has been the Azores' main lifeblood for over five centuries, and today is still the region's main economic driver. Recent investment has greatly modernized the sector, making it a stable earner.

Central to the Azores' agriculture sector is cattle farming, essential to the high-quality dairy and meat products for which the region is famed. Livestock are raised in vast numbers on the excellent pastures found on all islands, to the extent that on some of the islands the cows are said to outnumber the people. The Azores' renowned dairy products—cheeses, butters, and milks—are its top exports, while Azorean beef enjoys demand from swanky restaurants nationally and internationally.

The Azores were a top wheat and orange producer in the 18th century before the crops were wiped out by an imported pest, which attacked orange leaves and decimated production. Decades later, orange production was replaced with exotic fruits, like pineapple and passion fruit, as well as tobacco, beetroot, sweet potato, grapes, and tea.

## Fishing
The marine surface area of the Azores islands is close to 1,000,000 square kilometers (400,000 sq mi), making it one of the largest exclusive economic zones (EEZ) in the entire Eurozone. The Azorean Exclusive Economic Zone currently represents 55 percent of the Portuguese EEZ and approximately six percent of the European EEZ. The sheer size and abundance of fish species in this zone offers up huge potential and resources. Aquaculture is seen to have particular promise.

The Azores fishing industry is another of its key economic drivers; it is supported by four key pillars: a small-net fishery for small pelagic species like mackerel, a pole-and-line tuna fishery, bottom longline and handline targeting demersal fishes, and pelagic longline targeting swordfish. In terms of revenue, tuna is the most important species and the Azores' commercial fishing fleet's main catch. The region is renowned for its tuna processing and canning industry, with such products being another of the archipelago's top exports. The award-winning Azorean Santa Catarina brand is celebrated for its tuna products and is one of the region's most recognizable brands. The principal nonindustrial or artisan catches include herring, sea bream, conger eel, fork beard, and mackerel. Around 500 people are directly employed in fishing in the Azores, and a further 1,000 in the fish-processing industry.

## Tourism
Tourism has grown steadily in the Azores since flights to the archipelago became more available in 2015, and is seen as one of the sectors with the greatest potential for growth. This is reflected in the ever-growing number of tourists and flights that shuttle to the islands, the number of tourism-oriented

companies setting up there, and the number of properties being registered as local accommodation units for tourists. Azores' tourism companies place a huge emphasis on sustainability and environmental awareness to protect the region's unique natural attributes and avoid mass tourism.

## Distribution of Wealth

The Azores are among the poorest regions in Portugal, with one of the highest numbers of people receiving benefits in proportion to the resident population. While you will see buildings that have fallen into disrepair, key infrastructures like roads and hospitals are of good condition. However, around one in every three residents can be considered poor. Recent statistics place the Azores as the second region in Portugal with the greatest inequality of income distribution, after Lisbon.

# People and Culture

## DEMOGRAPHY AND DIVERSITY

The Azores archipelago currently has a resident population of around 450,000 inhabitants, the vast majority of whom live on São Miguel. Island populations range from 140,000 inhabitants on São Miguel, the archipelago's biggest island, to around 400 on Corvo, the smallest. Having been populated by Portuguese from various mainland regions and later from Flanders and other parts of Europe, each of the Azores' islands are unique, with local accents, gastronomy, and architecture.

## RELIGION

As on the mainland, in the Azores the predominant religion is Roman Catholicism. The Portuguese are by and large devoutly religious, and many of the local populations attend Mass on Sunday. Religious festivals and celebrations play a prominent role in local culture.

## LANGUAGE

European Portuguese is the language spoken in the Azores. A West Romance language, Portuguese is the seventh-most widely spoken language in the world and the sole official language of Portugal. The Portuguese spoken in the Azores has a unique accent believed to originate from an archaic form of European Portuguese with a strong French influence, and which varies from island to island. Curiously, the island of Corvo, the most remote of the Azores' islands, has maintained its own dialect, while the Portuguese spoken on the island of São Miguel is said to have the heaviest accent in the Azores.

English is the most widely spoken second language, followed by French and Spanish. Most tours will have a guide who speaks very good English, and signage will usually have an English translation, especially at main monuments and attractions. Generally, the less prominent the attraction, the poorer the level of English. In the Azores, English is not as widely spoken as on the mainland, particularly among older communities, but among the growing number of students, young professionals, and companies run by young entrepreneurs, you will find a good level of conversational English.

## THE ARTS
### Literature

The Azores has a handful of prolific writers and poets who are widely read in Portugal and internationally in translation. Among the most famous are São Miguel-born poet and philosopher Antero de Quental (1842-1891), renowned for his *Odes Modernas,* published in 1865; writer, playwright, and politician Teófilo Braga, also born in Ponta Delgada, who went on to become president of Portugal in 1910 and 1915; Terceiran poet, author, and intellectual Vitorino Nemésio, best known for his novel *Mau Tempo No Canal;* and Natália Correia, born on São Miguel island in 1923, an intellectual, poet, and social activist, as well as the author of the official lyrics of the "Hino dos Açores," the regional anthem of the Autonomous Region of the Azores.

## Visual Arts

The Azores makes concerted efforts to promote its visual arts scene; a century-old former alcohol factory in Ribeira Grande, São Miguel island, has been converted into an outstanding center for modern arts, the Arquipélago Contemporary Arts Center, while the renowned Walk & Talk Festival on São Miguel and Terceira promotes visual and performing arts.

## Music and Dance

The Azores' music and dance, originating from its blended heritage, and are both hugely enjoyed, taking on a starring role in festivities and celebrations. The archipelago has an appetite for traditional festivities, and folk music and dance underpin regional celebrations.

Most islands will have the same basis of dances, but with their own local flair. Folk customs of the Azores include the *chimarrita* dance, popular on all islands but chiefly on Pico and Faial, often performed at weddings and Holy Ghost Festival celebrations. *Pezinho* and *sapateira* are two other forms of dance, accompanied by traditional folk music. The São Macaio is a traditional song-dance enjoyed most prevalently on Terceira island, although its tradition became widespread.

Most traditional folk dances are usually accompanied by the quintessential Azorean instrument the Azorean viola, or *viola açoreana,* first brought to the Azores in the 15th century. It was developed on Terceira island and uses 15 strings. Over time the viola was adapted to make it larger with more notes. The other islands mainly use a smaller version of the viola called *viola dos dois coracoes* (the Viola of Two Hearts). These guitars are regarded as objects of true beauty and are handcrafted from pine, cedar, jacaranda, and other imported woods. This instrument is highly esteemed in the Azores, as are the musicians who play it, and is a key element to festivities.

# Essentials

## Transportation

### GETTING THERE

The best way to get to the Azores is by plane, most likely via Lisbon on the Portuguese mainland, though not necessarily. The only other options are a transatlantic cruise or chartering your own sailboat. An increasing number of **international flights** fly directly to the Azores from North America and mainland Europe, most frequently to São Miguel's **Ponta Delgada Airport** (Aeroporto de Ponta Delgada, PDL; tel. 296 205 400; www.aeroportopontadelgada.pt), though Terceira's **Lajes Airport** (Aeroporto das Lajes, TER; tel. 295 545 454; www.

aerogarelajes.azores.gov.pt) receives some international flights as well.

## From Mainland Portugal

From Portugal, you can fly between **Lisbon Airport** (Aeroporto de Lisboa, also known as Humberto Delgado Airport or Lisbon Portela Airport, LIS; tel. 218 413 500; www. aeroportolisboa.pt/pt) to the islands of São Miguel, Terceira, Pico, and Faial; **Porto Airport** (Aeroporto do Porto, also known as Francisco Sá Carneiro Airport, OPO; tel. 229 432 400; www.aeroportoporto.pt) also has frequent flights to São Miguel and Terceira. Flights from the mainland are 2-3 hours and can be as cheap as €100 round-trip depending on when you buy.

The main airlines flying between mainland Portugal and the Azores are national flag-carrier **TAP Air Portugal** (tel. 707 205 700; www.flytap.com), Azores regional carrier **SATA Azores Airlines** (tel. 707 227 282; www.sata.pt), and Irish low-cost airline **Ryanair** (Tel. + 44 871 246 0002; www. ryanair.com). TAP has regular direct flights from Lisbon and Porto to São Miguel and Pico. Ryanair flies regularly between Lisbon, Porto, and São Miguel, and also (less regularly) to Terceira. SATA Azores Airlines flies regularly between airports on mainland Portugal to São Miguel, Faial, Pico, and Terceira.

Once in the Azores, **flights between the islands** are quick, frequent, and can usually be found for under €100 round-trip; the longest interisland flight, from São Miguel to tiny **Flores Airport** (Aeroporto das Flores, FLW; tel. 800 201 201; www.aeroportoflores.pt), is 1 hour 15 minutes.

## From Elsewhere in Europe
### AIR

There are an increasing number of direct flights to the Azores (again, mostly to São Miguel, though there are some flights to Terceira as well) from several destinations in Europe, including **Belgium, Denmark, Germany,** the **Netherlands, Spain,** and the **United Kingdom.** These flights are generally short (around 4 hours), and fairly cheap (from €100-200 round-trip).

To Lisbon and Porto on mainland Portugal, the vast majority of flights are from the United Kingdom, Ireland, France, Germany, the Netherlands, and Belgium, all 2.5-3 hours away.

The ever-expanding availability of European flights includes a number of low-cost airlines such as **Ryanair** (Ireland, www. ryanair.com), **easyJet** (UK, www.easyjet. com), **Vueling** (Spain, www.vueling.com), **Eurowings** (Germany, www.eurowings. com), and **Transavia** (France, www.transavia. com), meaning travel between European destinations and Lisbon or Porto can cost less than €100 round-trip. Prices within Europe can vary widely, heavily influenced by school holidays at Easter, summer, and Christmas-New Year's, as well as peak tourist seasons in Portugal, especially July-August.

It's also possible to arrive in Lisbon or Porto from other parts of Europe by train, bus, or car, but these options are time-consuming for Azores-focused trips.

## From North America

Direct flights from North America to São Miguel in the Azores depart year-round from **Boston** and **Toronto,** and seasonally from **Montreal** and **Oakland,** California. Flights to and from Boston range from 4-6 hours and start at around €500 round-trip; from Toronto, flights are 5-7 hours and start at around €600. All flights are operated by **SATA Azores Airlines** (www.azoresairlines.pt).

Otherwise, you'll want to fly into Lisbon or Porto, or another city in Europe, for your connecting flight to one of the Azores islands. Direct flights between northeastern North America and mainland Portugal

---

**Previous:** Praia da Vitória's main shopping street, Terceira.

are about 7 hours eastbound, 9 hours westbound, and can be found for as cheap as €600 round-trip. Portugal's national carrier, **TAP Air Portugal** (www.flytap.pt), has regular direct flights between mainland Portugal and New York (JFK and Newark), Boston, Miami, and Philadelphia. US airline **United** (www.united.com) also has direct flights to Portugal. **Azores Airlines** and **Air Canada** (www.aircanada.com) operate direct flights between Portugal and Canada.

When flying with SATA on one of the airline's transatlantic routes (from Boston and Toronto to Lisbon, Porto, or Madeira), you can opt for a **stopover** on the Azores islands of São Miguel or Terceira, for anything from a few hours up to seven days, in either direction, at no extra cost. For more information, go to https://stopover.azoresairlines.pt. This is also an option on the way to Gran Canaria, Cape Verde, or Frankfurt (Germany).

## From Australia and New Zealand

There are no direct flights between mainland Portugal and Australia or New Zealand, let alone to the Azores. Travel between Australia and the Azores will require at least two or three flights and take up to 30 hours of travel; total flight costs range approximately €900-€1,600 one-way. From New Zealand the flight time is slightly longer, taking over 30 hours, and more expensive (flights can cost up to €2,000 one-way).

Getting to Europe generally requires connecting via somewhere in Asia; there's a daily direct flight between Lisbon and **Dubai** on **Emirates** (www.emirates.com). There is also a direct nonstop flight between Australia and **London,** from where there are many onward flights to Portugal.

## From South Africa

There are no direct flights from South Africa to the Azores, or even Portugal. **TAP** flies direct to **Maputo** in Mozambique and **Luanda** in Angola, also served by Angolan airline TAAG, and connecting flights can

be arranged from there. Major European carriers such as **British Airways** (www.britishairways.com), Germany's **Lufthansa** (www.lufthansa.com), **Swissair** (www.swissair.com), Spain's **Iberia** (www.iberia.com), and **Air France** (www.airfrance.com) fly direct to South Africa with connecting flights to Lisbon. Flying between South Africa to the Azores via Europe takes anywhere between 19 and 28 hours, with prices ranging between €600-1,800.

## On a Cruise

The Azores' mid-Atlantic location makes them a natural port-of-call for all vessels and sailors crossing the Atlantic to break up the long sailing times. But these little-known exotic gems are also attracting a number of large US and European cruise ships whose operators want to introduce a destination that is a little different. Most cruise itineraries, primarily transatlantic, that stop in the Azores visit the archipelago's biggest and most tourism-oriented island, **São Miguel.** The following companies offer cruises that stop in the Azores.

- **Royal Caribbean** (www.royalcaribbean.com) has 12-night transatlantic cruises departing from **New York** (US) to **Southampton** (UK) and vice-versa, starting from around $870.

- **Celebrity Cruises** (www.celebritycruises.com) operates a 14-night Spain and Azores transatlantic cruise (from **Barcelona** to **Tampa**), starting from $1,249.

- **Norwegian Cruise Line** (www.ncl.com) operates a number of transatlantic cruises, from, for example, **Miami** to **Rome,** Rome to **New York,** New York to **Barcelona,** and Barcelona to **Tampa,** ranging from 14- to 18-day itineraries.

- **Princess Cruises'** (www.princess.com) transatlantic Grand Adventure tours range from 18- to 34-day itineraries, and prices from €1,485.

The coronavirus pandemic has greatly

affected the cruise industry, and most cruises were canceled for the duration of 2020. Many cruise companies are taking reservations for sailings in 2021 and beyond, but whether or not those are able to go forward remains to be seen.

## GETTING AROUND

Once in the Azores, you have more transportation options to consider. For travel between the islands, **interisland flights** are generally the quicker and more reliable option, with the exception of the Azores "triangle" islands of Pico, Faial, and São Jorge, which are connected by frequent **ferries.** On the islands themselves, **renting a car** usually provides the most convenience and flexibility, though guided tours, taxis, motorbikes, scooters, bicycles, and even sometimes traveling on foot can be good options depending on the situation. Public bus services, when present, are usually geared more toward island residents than tourists.

### Between the Islands

To travel from island to island, the general rule is to fly between island groups, and ferry between islands in the same group, though there are some exceptions to this rule.

The islands are generally split into three groups: the **western group,** Flores and Corvo; the **central group** of Terceira, Graciosa, São Jorge, Pico, and Faial; and the **eastern group** of São Miguel and Santa Maria. The central group is often broken down further into the **Azores "triangle,"** which is made up of the closely connected islands of Pico, Faial, and São Jorge. These are the only islands to which the interisland ferry runs year-round; otherwise, the ferry is seasonal, running May-September, with exact start and end dates depending on the weather.

Except for the quick, frequent, year-round, and relatively cheap ferries between the Azores "triangle" islands, interisland flights are usually the best way to travel between the Azores, even if they are more expensive. Other ferries could make sense for those with

a sense of adventure, or with more time, but they can be slow and unreliable due to rough conditions on the Atlantic, and often run infrequently (or not at all in the winter months).

### AIR

It's generally advisable to fly between all of the islands of the Azores, except the three islands of the Azores "triangle." Interisland flights are generally frequent (more so in summer than in winter) and quite quick, with the longest (from São Miguel to Flores) clocking in at a mere 1 hour 15 minutes. Round-trip tickets can usually be found for around €100. Even if flights are more expensive than the ferry, fights will generally save you time. That said, they are not immune to the archipelago's famously changeable weather, especially since the flights are operated on small prop planes. All flights between the islands of the Azores are run by **SATA Azores Airlines.**

The largest airports in the Azores are **Ponta Delgada Airport** on São Miguel and **Lajes Airport** on Terceira. It's possible to fly to most of the other islands in the Azores from either of these two airports, with a few exceptions: **Santa Maria Airport** (Aeroporto de Santa Maria, SMA; tel. 296 820 020; www. aereoportosantamaria.pt), part of the eastern group of islands, is only accessible from Ponta Delgada Airport on São Miguel; and **Graciosa Airport** (Aeroporto da Graciosa, GRW) is only accessible from Lajes Airport on Terceira with some seasonal direct flights from São Miguel.

### FERRY

**Atlanticoline** (tel. 707 201 572 or 965 995 002; www.atlanticoline.pt) operates all the Azores' ferry routes, which all carry vehicles as well as individuals and their luggage. There are four lines: the **Yellow Line,** a seasonal route (May-Sept.) between the three island groups that stops at all of the Azores' islands except Corvo; the **Blue Line,** a quick 30-minute journey between Horta (Faial) and Madalena (Pico); the **Green Line** between Horta (Faial), São Roque (Pico), and Velas

# Come Sail Away: Chartering a Boat in the Azores

Seasoned Azores sailors say the ragged beauty of the archipelago is even more captivating from the deck of a boat. Sailing around the nine islands of the Azores, each with their own unique personality, never gets old; there's always something new to discover, and the amazing marine life is the icing on the cake. For centuries, sailors crossing the Atlantic have sought refuge in the mid-Atlantic archipelago, and even today, yachtsmen still stop there to break up long ocean crossings.

Investment in recent years has reinvented the archipelago as a quality cruising playground. Most of the Azores' little marinas are modern with good facilities, and they harbor hundreds of yachts and their crews every year. The main ports for sailors are **Ponta Delgada** (São Miguel), **Angra do Heroísmo** and **Praia da Vitoria** (Terceira), and perennial favorite **Horta** (Faial), *the* meeting place for Atlantic crossers. For those who would like to sail around the Azores instead of island-hopping by plane or ferry, there are a number of options available, from enjoying a sailing holiday, to chartering a manned boat, or hiring one and sailing yourself.

## KNOW BEFORE YOU GO

It requires solid yachting experience to make the open-ocean crossing to the sub-tropical Azores, a 1,450-kilometer (900-mi) trip from mainland Portugal. Sailing around the paradisiacal Azores is also something for the more experienced sailor, as its rocky topography, shallow bays, temperamental weather, and serrated coastlines can be challenging, as can the open-water passages between island groups.

- **Seasons:** You can sail around the Azores year-round, though the best time is **spring** and **summer,** when the weather is fine and the sea is calmer and generally clear of fog. The main sailing window in the Azores runs April-October; prime season is May-September.

- **Where to Sail:** Due to the proximity of the five different islands, the **central group** (Terceira, Graciosa, and the "triangle" of Pico, São Jorge, and Faial) is especially popular among sailors, but this also brings the potential hazards of shallow waters and tidal currents.

- **Regulations:** Arrivals and departures must be cleared for all ports in the Azores; report to authorities at every port.

(São Jorge); and the **Pink Line,** between Flores and Corvo.

Even ferries that sail daily between the closest islands could run less frequently in winter than summer, and the ever-changing weather can also affect sail times and even cause cancellations. **Tickets** can be purchased directly from ticket desks at the ferry terminals or via the Atlanticoline website. The **Azores 4 You Sea Pass** comprises four trips on all ferries between the same island group (€80 pp) or between groups (€130) with a 50 percent discount on vehicles. Children up to the age of 2 travel free.

## Individual Islands

As a rule of thumb, **renting a car** is the best way to get around all of the islands of the Azores.

## DRIVING

Driving in the Azores is, for the most part, a thoroughly enjoyable and pretty relaxed experience. The vistas are incredibly scenic, the surfacing generally good, and the roads quiet. There's little room to get lost, as, if you just keep heading in the same direction, eventually you'll come back to where you started. Some of the island's roads are rather steep or sloped, and there may be a few dirt roads to negotiate, especially inland, where you might have to have a little patience with the likes of tractors and herds of cows being moved from one field to the next. Fog is another thing to beware of, as it can close in fast.

The same rules apply in the Azores as on the mainland. Cars drive on the **right side** of the road. **Seat belts** are compulsory for all

## PLANNING YOUR TRIP

If you're planning to sail around the Azores, put some thought into packing. The Azores' weather is famously unpredictable, never more so than at sea. **Waterproof, warm clothing** is a must, and pack layers that you can remove or put on as needed. And don't forget a bathing suit. Essential **navigation equipment** like binoculars and a compass are also good things to have on hand. A reliable **weather source** is also a necessity, to stay on top of the weather.

The most straightforward way to sail around the Azores—if you're not sailing across the ocean—is to fly to Ponta Delgada (São Miguel) direct from Europe, Canada, or the United States, and from there take an interisland flight to Faial or Pico, from where you can **charter a boat.** One week is the minimum time frame you should allow for sailing around the Azores; two is ideal.

## TOP BOAT CHARTER COMPANIES

A number of boat charter companies operate in the Azores, a great way to see all or as many of the islands as you would like, without having to worry about booking island-hopping flights or accommodation.

- **SailAzores Yacht Charter** (Rua Maestro F. Lacerda, 13, Velas (São Jorge); tel. 924 128 888 or 916 231 111; www.sailazores.pt): With bases in Horta (Faial island) and Ponta Delgada (São Miguel), this family-run yacht charter company specializes in skippered and bareboat charters. The company has a fleet of 100 percent self-owned, fully licensed, immaculate sail vessels, and runs organized island-hopping trips and can also suggest itineraries. Professional, experienced, and friendly, SailAzores's prices start from €2,900/week in high season.

- **Azores Sailing Adventure Trips & Yacht Charters** (Travessa da Igreja no.3, Água d'Alto, Vila Franca do Campo (São Miguel); tel. 911 938 308; https://sailzen.net): Let someone else take the stern (and do the cooking) with Azores Sailing Adventure Trips & Yacht Charters. With 6- and 10-day itineraries as well as customized tours, the crew is dedicated to making your time on the Azores' waters the time of your life. Shared cabins for solo sailors are also possible. Prices start from €5,000 for a private, six-day sailing trip.

occupants. National **speed limits** are easy to remember, although many drivers seem to struggle to abide by them: 50 km/h (31 mph) in residential areas, 90 km/h (56 mph) on rural roads, and 120 km/h (74 mph) on motorways. You must park facing the same direction as the traffic flow. It's also illegal to use a mobile phone while driving; that applies to talking and texting. Punishment for drunk driving is harsh, ranging from hefty fines to driving bans. The legal limit is 0.5 gram (0.02 ounce) of alcohol per liter (34 ounces) of blood.

EU citizens require a **valid driver's license** with a photo on it, issued by the bearer's home country, to drive in Portugal. Drivers from outside the EU require a license and an **international driving permit,** which must be shown both to rental agencies for hiring a car and to the authorities if asked. Drivers must be over 18. When you are driving, the vehicle's documents must be in the vehicle at all times, and drivers need a valid ID, such as a passport. It is compulsory to have certain items in a vehicle: a reflective danger jacket, a reflective warning triangle, spare bulbs, a spare tire, and an approved child seat for children under age 12 or 150 centimeters (5 feet). Check that you have these before driving off, as failure to produce them could result in a fine.

Most of the islands' airports and main towns host several **car rental companies,** or ask at your accommodation: Vehicles can be dropped off at most holiday lodgings. Booking well in advance will mean better prices.

Beware of unexpected surprises by double-checking the opening and closing times of the car rental desk at the airport, fuel fees and excess insurance, and electronic toll payments. Even though the minimum legal age to drive is 18, most rental companies require drivers to be 21 or to have held a license for at least 5 years. Costs can vary greatly, from as little as €10 per day in low season but rising exponentially in high season. If you're just visiting one or two areas, a small car is useful as most town centers, including historic hamlets and large cities, have areas that are a tangle of narrow cobbled streets.

**Diesel** (*gasóleo*) is cheaper than **unleaded gasoline** (*gasolina sem chumbo*) in Portugal, and gas stations can be found in abundance in the larger towns. Most large supermarkets and shopping centers have gas stations that offer low-cost fuel options, and there is almost always a gas station near an airport. The main gas stations in Portugal belong to BP, Galp, and Repsol. All these can be found in the Azores, along with lesser-known brands. Most gas stations are open daily 7am-10pm, but stations at service areas on motorways or on main roads should be open 24/7. All petrol stations accept debit and credit cards as well as cash.

**Parking** can be hard to find in town centers given the narrow cobbled streets and tourist demand. Bigger towns and cities have designated parking lots and areas, which charge fees, especially in key touristy places like Ponta Delgada. The closer to the town center, the more expensive the parking will be.

### BUS

Public bus services in the Azores are designed for islanders, and tourists might find them limited. Ponta Delgada on São Miguel has its own inner-city service, but other islands, especially the smaller ones, generally have privately owned services, whose management varies from island to island, which link coastal and larger inland villages to the main towns where inhabitants work or study. Some of the more touristy islands will have limited services to major attractions, and there will generally be a route between the main settlements and main ports and airports. The good news is—if you can find a route that suits your needs—tickets are generally **cheap,** and will usually not set you back more than a few euros, one-way. The best places to ask for detailed info on schedules and routes is at a **tourist bureau** (www.azores.gov.pt), and some hotel receptions might be able to provide a local timetable.

### TAXI

Taxi travel in the Azores is competitively priced (in comparison to guided tours, for example); many taxi firms will offer organized **island tours** and **hike drop-offs/pickups** at set prices, as well as regular door-to-door services. All the islands except Corvo have taxi services. Taxis are usually widespread in bigger towns; you'll find **taxi ranks** in key locations, alongside main squares, harbors, and at airports. Companies vary from island to island, but check at **tourist information offices** or hotel reception desks for the most commonly used and reliable companies.

### SCOOTER AND MOTORBIKE

Scooters and motorbikes are a cheap and cheerful way to explore the Azores islands, especially on the smaller and quieter islands. Many **car rental companies** will have two-wheel vehicles on their portfolios; some islands have scooter **rental kiosks** near their ports. The process is easier and quicker than renting a car, but a **valid driver's license** and other relevant documentation (like ID) is still required. Most scooter rental companies hire them out for around €25/day. It's always best to check the weather ahead: Riding a scooter in the rain and on wet roads is not advisable.

### BICYCLE

Bicycles can be hired on most of the Azores' islands from specialist **cycling shops** or **bicycle tour operators,** often from as little as €10-15/day. The Azores are small and roads are generally quiet and cyclist-friendly, making it seem like an ideal destination to get around by bike, but the mountainous nature of these volcanic islands means cycling in the Azores requires a good degree of physical aptitude.

# Visas and Officialdom

To enter the Azores, and Portugal in general, all travelers are required to have a valid ID. Most European citizens need only a valid ID or a passport and can circulate freely within the EU by land, air, or sea. People from other countries must have a passport and may require a visa. Always check with the relevant authorities before traveling or with your travel provider. Here are some basic guidelines.

## PASSPORTS AND TOURIST VISAS

EU nationals traveling within EU or Schengen states do not require a visa for entering Portugal for any length of stay. They do require a valid passport or official ID card (national citizen's card, driver's license, or residency permit, for example).

**European citizens** traveling between Schengen countries are not required to present an identity document or passport at border crossings, as an open-borders policy is in effect. However, it is recommended that travelers have ID documents with them at all times, as they may be requested at any time by the authorities. In Portugal the law requires everyone to carry a personal ID at all times.

Citizens of the **United Kingdom and Ireland** must produce a passport to enter Portugal, valid for the duration of the proposed stay, and can stay for up to three months. After that, they must register with the local authorities. At the time of writing, the UK was in the transition period of divorcing the EU (Brexit), and trade and travel continued as before. Ireland remains part of the EU, but neither are part of the Schengen area, the 26 countries that abolished passport and other border controls at their shared borders. Expectations are that after the official Brexit transition period, from January 1, 2021, UK travelers will still be allowed to visit the EU for short trips (up to 90 days within any 180-day period) without a visa on the condition that the same rights are granted to EU citizens reciprocally.

People from non-EU countries always require a passport, valid for at least six months, and some may require a visa. **Australian, Canadian,** and **US** travelers require a valid passport but do not need a visa for stays of up to 90 days in any six-month period. While it is not obligatory to have an onward or return ticket, it is advisable to have one.

**South African** nationals need to apply for a Portugal-Schengen visa. This should be done three months before travel. Applicants must have a South African passport valid for six months beyond the date of return with at least three blank pages. They also need a recent passport photo (specify to photographer that it has to meet the Schengen visa requirements), a completed original application form, round-trip tickets from South Africa to Portugal, and proof of prepaid lodging or a letter of invitation if staying with friends or family in Portugal, among other requisites.

### Traveling with Children

All children under the age of 18 must have a valid ID or passport and be accompanied by an adult. Minors traveling alone or with just one parent or guardian should have a formal document of authorization by the absent parent or guardian. Documentation such as custody court rulings in the event of divorce or a death certificate in the event the child is orphaned should also be presented.

Portugal's borders and immigration authority, SEF, advises that children traveling to Portugal alone or without a parent or legal guardian should be met at the airport or point of entry by the parent or guardian or carry a letter of authorization to travel from their parent or guardian, stating the name of the adult in Portugal who will be responsible for them during their stay and including contact details.

## CUSTOMS

Customs is mandatory for all travelers arriving in or leaving Portugal and its autonomous regions (Madeira and the Azores) carrying goods or money, although certain limits apply to what can be brought in or taken out. The rules are the same for the mainland and the islands. Aeroportos de Portugal (ANA) states that all passengers traveling without baggage or transporting cash or monetary assets under the equivalent of €10,000 or carrying personal items not intended for commercial purposes and not prohibited should pass through the "Nothing to Declare" channel. Passengers carrying over €10,000 or whose baggage contains tradable goods in quantities greater than those permitted by law and that are not exempt from value-added tax (VAT) or excise duty must pass through the "Goods to Declare" channel.

Passengers age 17 or older can bring in the following:

From EU member states: 800 cigarettes, 400 cigarillos, 200 cigars, 1 kilogram (2.2 pounds) of smoking tobacco, 10 liters (11 quarts) of alcoholic spirits, 20 liters (21 quarts) of beverages with alcoholic content under 22 percent, 90 liters (95 quarts) of wine, 110 liters (116 quarts) of beer, medications in quantities corresponding to need and accompanied by a prescription.

For travelers from outside the EU: 200 cigarettes, 100 cigarillos, 50 cigars, 250 grams (0.6 pound) of smoking tobacco, 1 liter (1 quart) of alcoholic spirits, 2 liters (2 quarts) of beverages with alcoholic content under 22 percent, 4 liters (4 quarts) of wine, 16 liters (17 quarts) of beer, medications in quantities corresponding to need and accompanied by a prescription.

Quantities exceeding these must be declared, and passengers under age 17 don't get an exemption for alcohol or tobacco.

## EMBASSIES AND CONSULATES

Except for the US Consulate and a few consulates and honorary consulates in Ponta Delgada on São Miguel, the nearest embassy or consulate for your country will likely be in Lisbon on mainland Portugal.

### Azores

- **US Consulate:** Príncipe de Mónaco 6-2F, Ponta Delgada (Azores); tel. 296 308 330; conspontadelgada@state.gov; Mon.-Fri. 8:30am-12:30pm and 1:30pm-5:30pm

- **Consulate of Canada:** Rua D'Água 28, Ponta Delgada; tel. 296 281 488; lsbon. consular@international.gc.ca; Mon.-Fri. 9am-12:30pm and 2pm-4pm

### Mainland Portugal (Lisbon)

- **Australian Embassy:** Av. da Liberdade 200, Lisbon; http://portugal.embassy.gov. au; tel. 213 101 500, Mon.-Fri. 10am-4pm

- **British Embassy:** Rua de São Bernardo 33, Lisbon; tel. 213 924 000, emergency tel. 213 924 000; www.gov.uk/world/organisations/ british-embassy-lisbon; Mon., Wed., and Fri. 9:30am-2pm

- **Canadian Embassy:** Av. da Liberdade 196, Lisbon; tel. 213 164 600; www. canadainternational.gc.ca/portugal; Mon.-Fri. 9am-noon

- **Irish Embassy:** Av. da Liberdade 200, Lisbon; tel. 213 308 200; www.dfa.ie/ irish-embassy/portugal; Mon.-Fri. 9:30am-12:30pm

- **New Zealand Consulate:** Rua da Sociedade Farmacêutica 68, 1st Right, Lisbon; tel. 213 140 780; consulado.nz.pt@

gmail.com, www.mfat.govt.nz; office hours by appointment only

- **South African Embassy:** Av. Luís Bívar 10, Lisbon; tel. 213 192 200; lisbon.consular@dirco.gov.za; Mon.-Thurs. 8am-12:30pm and 1:15pm-5pm, Fri. 8am-1pm, Consular Section (Annex) Mon.-Fri. 8:30am-noon
- **US Embassy:** Av. das Forças Armadas 133C, Lisbon; tel. 217 273 300; https://pt.usembassy.gov/embassy-consulate/lisbon; Mon.-Fri. 8am-5pm

## POLICE
Portugal has three police forces: the **PSP** (Public Safety Police—Polícia de Segurança Pública) (tel. 218 111 000; www.psp.pt) in cities and larger towns; the road traffic police **GNR** (National Republican Guard—Guarda Nacional Republicana) (tel. 213 217 000; www.gnr.pt), also responsible for policing smaller towns and villages and investigating crimes against animals or nature; and the **PJ** (Judiciary Police—Polícia Judiciária) (tel. 211 967 000; www.pj.pt), the criminal investigation bureau, responsible for investigating serious crimes. All three operate in the Azores as well.

The common European **emergency number** is tel. **112,** which redirects to the appropriate services.

# Recreation

## HIKING
With scenery that changes around every bend, contouring mountains, valleys, and idyllic coastline, the Azores islands are a prime destination for outdoor activities, especially hiking. The active traveler will delight in the islands' varying terrains and vistas, which can switch from a frosted volcano peak to a polished marina or hydrangea-drenched village road in the blink of an eye. Being volcanic, the land is seldom flat, and in places it is downright challenging on the legs, but few places reward physical effort so richly.

The Azores are home to some of Europe's most interesting hikes, with the islands of **São Miguel, São Jorge,** and **Pico** taking the top spots on the podium for walkers. Due to the ever-changing weather, routes can close for safety reasons, so check websites such as the **Azores Trails** official tourism website (http://trails.visitazores.com/en) for up-to-date and detailed info on hiking and routes. Five of the nine islands (São Jorge, Santa Maria, Graciosa, Flores, and Faial) have **Grand Routes,** which take in the entire island and are designed to be spread over a number of days, complete with suggestions for accommodations and pit stops along the way.

## BEACHES AND POOLS
There are a few soft sand beaches in the Azores, mostly in the eastern group; **São Miguel** has a number of black volcanic sand beaches, while **Santa Maria** is famed for its golden sands. Lacking of soft, sandy beaches elsewhere, the Azores have had to harness their natural attributes, adapting **tidal pools** formed naturally from jagged volcanic rock around the coastlines with a little cement to create perfectly enjoyable and easily accessible **natural bathing areas.** All of the islands have these delightful natural pools. The most popular bathing sites are usually equipped with toilet and shower facilities as well as cement decks on which to lay out towels. In the height of summer, the tidal pools can become pretty busy, but the good news is that they are free to use.

## SURFING
The Azores are fast earning a reputation for being Europe's best-kept secret surfing destination. Two islands jump out as surfing hot spots: **São Miguel,** particularly Mosteiros Beach, and the *fajãs* on the northern coast of **São Jorge.** The best time to surf in Azores is **November-June,** although there are swells

and decent surf most of the year. The website **Magic Seaweed** (https://magicseaweed.com/Sao-Jorge-Surfing/288) provides detailed information on the Azores' best surf spots.

## KAYAKING AND STAND-UP PADDLE BOARDING

With coastlines that rise breathtakingly from the sea, the Azores islands' edges are fascinating places for kayakers and stand-up paddle-boarders. A growing number of outdoor activity companies are introducing the sports, which also lend themselves perfectly to the islands' exquisite lakes and lagoons, such as Sete Cidades Lake on **São Miguel.** The official Azores **tourism website** (www.visitazores.com) provides lots of information on such activities, outfitters, and suggestions on where to enjoy them on all the islands.

## DIVING AND SNORKELING

Divers and snorkelers will be blown away by the wealth of compelling underwater attractions that can be found off the shores of the Azores. There's a surprise off every island, from grottoes and underwater caves accessed from the shore, to uninhabited offshore islets, eerie shipwrecks, volcanic vents, and reefs inhabited by a rainbow of exquisite sea creatures, from marlins to barracudas, eels, rays, sharks, and turtles.

Some of the best and most original dive sites in the Azores include Entre Montes Bay (Faial), the Princess Alice Seamount (off Pico; a strong contender for the most famous dive site in the Azores), the *SS Dori* shipwreck (off São Miguel), the Underwater Archaeological Park of the Bay of Angra Do Heroísmo (Terceira), and the Formigas Islets and Dollabarat Reef (off Santa Maria).

All islands with the exception of Corvo have dive companies and centers on them. In-depth information on the best dive spots, centers, rules of conduct, and times to dive can be found on the regional **Visit Azores** tourism bureau's webpage (http://dive.visitazores.com/en/topten).

## FISHING

The saying "go big or go home" certainly rings true for fishing in the Azores. The archipelago is a riveting destination for a leisurely few hours' fishing or a full-on fishing holiday, including big-game deep-sea fishing, sports fishing, and spear fishing. Big-game fishers frequently head to the Azores for the huge pelagic fish that thrive in the deep, pristine waters: gigantic blue and white marlins and Atlantic bluefin tuna, among other species of tuna.

The "triangle" of **Faial, Pico,** and **São Jorge** offers some especially great fishing opportunities, but numerous operators specialize in big-game fishing on almost all the islands. See the **Visit Azores** fishing website for more information (www.visitazores.com/en/experience-the-azores/biggamefishing).

## DOLPHIN- AND WHALE-WATCHING

There's no better memory to take from the Azores than the spellbinding experience of seeing whales and dolphins in their natural habitat. Having made the transition from prime whale-hunting ground to one of the largest whale sanctuaries in the world, the waters around the islands are home to species including humpback, sperm, and blue whales and even the mammoth whale shark, which happily put in appearances for the thousands of visitors who set sail to see them.

The graceful mammals can be seen all year round, thanks to the numerous resident and migrating populations found in the waters, so the best time to see them really depends on what species you would like to see. **Spring** (April and May) is generally the more active season, as the migrating species pass through, and **Pico** is one of the best places to whale-watch, though all islands offer a pretty good chance of spotting a whale or dolphin. Some whale- and dolphin-watching companies even offer the chance to swim with dolphins out in the open sea. To learn more about this magical activity in the Azores and the companies and islands that run trips, go to www.visitazores.com/en/experience-the-azores/whale.

# BIRD-WATCHING

An internationally acclaimed bird-watching destination for certain species, this mid-Atlantic cluster of volcanic islands provides a hugely varied range of habitats that attract all types of birds, from endemic species like the Azores bullfinch, migratory birds, seabirds like the Monteiro's storm petrel (one of the rarest seabirds in Europe), and approximately 30 breeding species. The islands also house the most important nesting populations in the world of Cory's shearwaters and Rosy tern.

The archipelago's lakes and lagoons, fields and laurel forests, marshlands and coastline provide fantastic and diverse sites for bird-watching, which can be enjoyed on all the islands, although **São Miguel** and **Graciosa** are known for being the best spots for endemic species, and **Terceira** for gulls and waders from the Nearctic and Palaearctic ecozones. Most of the islands also have specialist companies that run bird-watching excursions; the **Visit Azores** website's dedicated bird-watching page (www.visitazores.com/en/experience-the-azores/birdwatching) has plenty of information on how to get the best bird-watching experience from your trip to the Azores.

# SPAS AND HOT SPRINGS

At the end of a busy day of exploring, what could be nicer than soaking your sore limbs in a steaming-hot, iron-rich spring? A number of islands have thermal springs, but **São Miguel** is number one, specifically the town of **Furnas.** Here you'll find the famed **Poça da Dona Beija hot springs** as well as the huge natural pool in the **Terra Nostra Park,** with its bright orange, piping-hot spring water, which steams aches and pains away. This is an experience to be savored whatever the weather, but don't wear your best bathing suit, as the rusty-colored water can stain.

# Food

It's easy to wax lyrical about Portugal's cuisine: Fresh, flavorful, comforting, and generous, it is the soul of an unassuming seafaring nation. Largely Mediterranean, the staples are fresh fish, meat, fruit, and vegetables prepared with olive oil and washed down with excellent national wines. Dishes vary from light and fresh grilled fish and seafood, to hearty meaty stews and roasts.

Fort the most part, Azorean food is typically Portuguese, with a few twists due to centuries in which the islands developed their own unique takes on classic mainland dishes, as well as a few ingredients widely available in the Azores that can't be found elsewhere. A bounty of the freshest fish and seafood can be found in the cool, pristine waters enveloping the archipelago, which are staples on most restaurant menus, brought from the sea to the table. Meat and dairy from the islands' free-roaming "happy cows" are omnipresent.

## AZOREAN CUISINE

They may be small, but the Azores archipelago abounds with the freshest **seafood** and is blessed with some of the tastiest **beef** and **dairy** on the planet. Some of the more traditional island recipes stem from the archipelago's earliest settlers, brought over in the 15th century from various regions on the mainland, which over the years have fused with the culinary customs of later settlers who arrived from other parts of the world, like the Flemish.

Tuna and swordfish steaks, fresh from the sea, grilled and brought straight to the table, are staples, alongside the succulent island-reared beef steaks. Shellfish is also consumed by the heaped platter-load; *lapas* (limpets) are regional delicacies that visitors must try. Octopus stewed in wine is another indigenous seafood specialty, as are fresh fish soups, which vary from island to island. On the topic of stews, the Azores have two major claims to fame: *alcatra,* a melt-in-the-mouth meat or fish casserole cooked in earthenware, specific to Terceira island; and the *cozido das Furnas,* a traditional Portuguese meat and veg stew cooked underground in the steaming volcanic heat of the shores around Furnas Lake on São Miguel island.

The Azores also grows a bounty of exotic fruits, thanks to their subtropical climate, and are most famous for the small, sweet **pineapples** grown in greenhouses on São Miguel island. And no description of the Azores' cuisine would be complete without mentioning its **cheeses,** especially São Jorge cheese, one of the archipelago's premier exported products.

# DRINKS

It's not just the food where the Azores shines, but drinks too. The islands produce a selection of indigenous **wines,** which, due to the volcanic terrain and mid-Atlantic location, are unique and distinct; **Pico** is perhaps the most famed for its wines. It's a little-known fact that the Azores are also home to the only **coffee** and **tea** plantations in Europe. Tea is grown and produced on the seaside slopes of **São Miguel** island, at the Gorreana Tea Plantation, while **São Jorge** has coffee plantations on its lava plateaus (*fajãs*).

# DINING OUT

The Azores' restaurant scene is a treat for foodies. Most of the islands have a good selection of no-frills, down-to-earth eateries with honest, home-cooked regional fare at great prices, alongside venues that are wonderful for a special occasion. As on mainland Portugal, dining out in the Azores will rarely break the bank; fancier restaurants will be pricier, but there are plenty of good options for diners on a budget. Reservations are strongly recommended for the islands' most popular restaurants; formal dress is only really required for up-market eateries.

# PICNIC SUPPLIES AND GROCERIES

Head to a *mercado municipal* (municipal market) in your island's main town, also sometimes referred to as the *praça,* to buy locally farmed fresh fruits and vegetables, as well as meats, fish, bread, cured meats and cheeses, and baked pastry goods. These are great places to get a real sense of the local community, and pick up picnic supplies to eat on that day's hike or excursion.

# MEALS AND MEALTIMES

Portugal has **three main meals:** a good breakfast in the continental style, with cereals, bread, cold meats and cheese, and jam, generally eaten before work or school; lunch at 1pm-3pm; and dinner starting from 7:30pm-8pm. Main meals tend to be hearty, and lunch and dinner are often preceded by a bowl of soup. The Portuguese also enjoy *lanche,* a light midafternoon snack, as well as a coffee and a pastry midmorning.

# Accommodations

Accommodations in the Azores range from boutique guesthouses to restored rural villages and smart hotels. Types of accommodation can be broken down into five main categories: **traditional hotels, rural accommodation** (predominantly guesthouses and inns), **youth hostels, campsites,** and **AL** (privately owned) local lodgings, like what can be found via platforms such as Airbnb. São Miguel, the archipelago's biggest island, boasts everything from campsites to super-swanky marina-side hotels, whereas Corvo, the smallest island, has just one proper hotel and a few guesthouses. Most islands have a decent selection of two-, three-, and four-star hotels as well as privately run lodgings. There are over two dozen campsites spread across all of the islands, with good facilities, and a number of youth hostels, which, for the most part, provide a cheap and clean bed for the night.

The availability and diversity of accommodation in the Azores has grown steadily in recent times. Most hotel units are small- to medium-size ventures, the onus on local culture and sustainability. National chains such as the **VIP Executive** brand (www.viphotels. com) and **Pestana** group (www.pestana. com) have units in the Azores, but the major regional group is the **Bensaude** hotels chain (www.bensaudehotels.com), which has six attractive hotels on São Miguel, Terceira, and Faial, as well as a unit in Lisbon.

AL-rated (Local Accommodation, or privately owned lodgings such as those available via platforms like Airbnb) accommodations have soared of late. In 2019 the archipelago also became the first in the world to be certified by the **Global Sustainable Tourism Council.**

## MAKING RESERVATIONS

Most people nowadays make bookings online via price-comparison websites or directly with hotels. It's always wise to follow up with a phone call to ensure everything is confirmed and any special requests are clear. If planning to travel to the Azores in summer, **book well ahead,** as hotels sell out fast in peak season. Prices can also be much higher in peak season than in low season.

# Conduct and Customs

The Portuguese are characteristically warm and welcoming and proud to show off their heritage, although they are also modest and conservative. Striking up a conversation about food or soccer, two of Portugal's best-loved pastimes (or sailing or whaling on the islands), is a surefire way of opening communication. Conscious that tourism is a main source of income, the Portuguese are generally friendly and helpful toward visitors, although in rural pockets of the country foreigners are still eyed with curiosity. Staunchly traditional and understated, Portugal is a country where recent acquaintances may be greeted like long-lost friends, but raucous behavior, such as drunken rowdiness, is eschewed. Decorum is much appreciated, which is not to say you can't let your hair down and let loose in the appropriate places. As long as you show courtesy and respect to the locals, you can expect the same back.

## GENERAL ETIQUETTE

Typically friendly and humble, the Portuguese love to show off their language skills and impress visitors, and few are the people who don't know at least a few key phrases in English. Likewise, the Portuguese very much appreciate efforts by visitors in learning even just a few words of the national language. Modest and somewhat reserved, the Portuguese tend to be quite formal in greetings among those less well acquainted. Men usually shake hands while women give air kisses on each cheek; women hardly ever shake hands in Portugal. Children are greeted in the same way as adults. Family is the foundation of Portuguese households and takes precedence over most other social and professional affairs.

## COMMUNICATION STYLES

The Portuguese appreciate polite directness. Eye contact, a smile, and a firm handshake are the cornerstones of communication. Saying *"Bom dia"* (Good day or Hello), *"Por favor"* (Please), and *"Obrigado/a"* (Thank you) go a long way. Overtly exuberant or loud behavior is not appreciated. The Portuguese tend to socialize on the weekends rather than after work during the week.

## BODY LANGUAGE

A big no-no in Portugal generally is pointing—especially pointing at someone. While conversations can sound heated and loud, the Portuguese are not overly demonstrative with hand gestures or body language. Finger-snapping to get someone's attention is also frowned upon.

## TERMS OF ADDRESS

An overtone of formality is required when addressing people, especially strangers. Men should be addressed as *senhor* (abbreviation Sr.) and women *senhora (Sra.)* at all times. A young girl would be *menina* (miss), and a boy, *menino*.

## TABLE MANNERS

Table manners are relaxed but courteous. Sharing from a bowl while talking animatedly is a mainstay around a family table, although politeness, such as wishing everyone *"Bom apetite"* (Bon appétit) before a meal and saying "Thank you" afterward, is expected. Domestic dining begins at the say-so of the head of the table or the cook, and feel free to raise a glass to toast *(saúde)* everyone. Dining out depends on the type of establishment; laid-back eateries are a family-style affair, while upmarket venues require upmarket manners and dress. Arriving late to a meal with friends is acceptable; arriving late to a dinner reservation is not. If invited to dine at someone's home, take a small gift, such as a bottle of wine or flowers.

## PHOTO ETIQUETTE

Places where photos are banned will be signed. Taking photos inside churches during mass is considered disrespectful. If you want to take a picture of a local, Portuguese people are generally happy to collaborate, but always politely seek permission beforehand.

# Health and Safety

Overall, travel and health risks in the Azores are relatively low, with food- and water-borne illnesses like traveler's diarrhea, typhoid, and giardia not a concern in Western Europe. Insect-transmitted diseases, such as Lyme disease and tick fever, however, are found in Portugal. A number of precautionary steps can reduce the risk: Prevent insect bites with repellents, apply sunscreen, drink plenty of water, avoid overindulging in alcohol, don't approach wild or stray animals, wash your hands regularly, carry hand sanitizer, and avoid sharing bodily fluids.

Basic medications such as ibuprofen and antidiarrheal medication can be bought over-the-counter at any pharmacy in Portugal. For emergency medical assistance, call 112 and ask for an ambulance. If you are taken to a hospital, contact your insurance provider immediately. Portugal also has a 24-hour free health help line (tel. 808 242 424) in Portuguese only. For detailed advice before traveling, consult your country's travel health website: www.fitfortravel.nhs.uk (United Kingdom), wwwnc.cdc.gov/travel (United States), www.travel.gc.ca (Canada), or www.smarttraveller.gov.au (Australia).

# VACCINATIONS

There are no compulsory immunization requirements to enter Portugal (including the Azores). The World Health Organization (WHO) recommends all travelers, regardless of destination, are covered for diphtheria, tetanus, measles, mumps, rubella, and polio. See your doctor at least six weeks before departure to ensure your routine vaccinations are up-to-date.

## Rabies

Rabies has been detected in bats in Portugal, but there is a low risk of infection. The US Centers for Disease Control and Prevention (CDC) recommends the rabies vaccine for travelers involved in activities in remote areas that put them at risk for bat bites, such as adventure travel and caving.

## Hepatitis A

A vaccine is recommended for all travelers over age one and not previously vaccinated against hepatitis A. In 2017, a number of European countries, Portugal included, recorded an outbreak of hepatitis A. It is transmitted through contaminated food and water, as well direct contact with infected individuals via the fecal-oral route.

## Hepatitis B

The hepatitis B vaccination is suggested for all nonimmune travelers who may be at risk of acquiring the disease, which is transmitted via infected blood or bodily fluids, such as by sharing needles or unprotected sex.

## Yellow Fever

Yellow fever vaccinations are only required for travelers heading to the Azores if they are arriving from a yellow-fever-infected country in Africa or the Americas.

# HEALTH CONSIDERATIONS
## Sunstroke and Dehydration

The sun and heat in the Azores can be fierce, especially June-September and particularly July-August, although not quite as fierce as on the mainland as it is tempered by the mid-Atlantic breeze. Apply a strong sunblock and use a hat and sunglasses. Avoid physical exertion when the heat is at its peak (noon-3pm) and keep well hydrated by drinking plenty of water or electrolyte-replenishing fluids.

## Undertow

The Azores' few proper sand beaches are generally safe to enjoy, although the surf can get quite rough. Occasionally there can be strong undertow on open beaches. During summer, generally May-September, the sea is calmer and beaches are staffed by lifeguards; off-season they are not. Always obey flags.

## Tap Water

Tap water is consumable throughout the Azores and is safe to use for brushing teeth, washing fruit, or making ice, although many people drink bottled water, as opposed to tap water, even at home.

## Insects

With a subtropical climate, the Azores islands have fewer bugs than on the mainland, but they do still have mosquitoes, bees, spiders, and cockroaches. There is a risk of tick bites in areas with long grass, or from stray animals.

To avoid mosquito bites, use lightweight, light-colored clothing and avoid places with stagnant water. In the hotter months, particularly in early morning or at dusk, apply a repellent.

## Stray Animals

Portugal still battles errant and abandoned animals; the Azores do too, but to a lesser extent than the mainland. What travelers might notice in the Azores, more specifically in rural areas, are farm or guard dogs kept on chains. Travelers are advised to not approach, pet, or feed strays. If you are bitten by a stray animal, wash and disinfect the wound, and seek medical advice promptly.

## Sexually Transmitted Diseases

Travelers are at high risk of acquiring sexually transmitted diseases (STDs) if they engage in unprotected sex. According to research, Portugal has one of the poorest control rates of sexually transmitted infections; gonorrhea and syphilis are common.

# HEALTH CARE
## Medical Services

Portugal's state-funded public health service (SNS, Serviço Nacional de Saúde) provides quality care, particularly in emergency situations and those involving tourists. Overall, the Azorean health service is efficient. There are three main and well-equipped hospitals in the Azores—on São Miguel, Terceira, and Faial—with the biggest and most comprehensive on São Miguel. All other islands, including the smallest, Corvo, will have at least one health center or unit to tend to emergencies. Serous cases are usually transferred by the Air Force to the nearest major hospital or facility best equipped to deal with the incident. There are also private health units such as the Bom Jesus clinic (www.clinicabomjesus.org) in Ponta Delgada.

For minor illnesses and injuries, head to a pharmacy: Most pharmacists speak good English and can suggest treatment. If the problem persists or worsens, seek a doctor. Portugal has two types of pharmacies: traditional pharmacies (farmácia), identified with a big flashing green cross outside, and parapharmacies (parafarmácia), selling only non-prescription medicines.

## Insurance

EU citizens have access to free emergency medical treatment in the Azores through the European Health Insurance Card (EHIC), which replaces the defunct E111 certificate. Non-EU citizens for whom there is no reciprocal agreement for free medical care between Portugal and the traveler's home country should consider fully comprehensive health insurance for serious illness, accident, or emergency. Opt for a policy that covers the worst-case event, like medical evacuation or repatriation. Find out in advance if your insurance will make payments to providers directly or reimburse you later for overseas health expenditures. Travelers to the Azores are advised to acquire wide-ranging travel insurance that provides for medical evacuation in the event of serious illness or injury; serious or complicated problems sometimes require medical evacuation to the mainland.

## Prescriptions

A prescription issued by a doctor in one EU country is valid in all EU countries. However, a medicine prescribed in one country may not be authorized for sale or available in another country, or it might be sold under a different name. EU doctors can issue cross-border prescriptions valid in all EU countries. Opt for paper copies of prescriptions as opposed to electronic copies.

If you're traveling from outside the EU, have enough of your prescription medication to cover the trip. Talk to your doctor beforehand and travel with a doctor's note, a copy of any prescriptions, or a printout for the medication. Medications should be carried in labeled original bottles or packaging, although this is not compulsory. Some prescription medicines may require a medical certificate; always check with your doctor. Ask for an extra written prescription with the generic name of the drug in the event of loss or if your stay is extended. Portuguese pharmacies will accept prescriptions from countries outside the EU, but drugs have to be paid for in full. Even without the state subsidies, drugs are generally cheaper in Portugal than many other EU countries and the United States.

Alternatively, visit a Portuguese doctor and obtain a prescription in Portugal.

Many types of medication—including heart medication, antibiotics, asthma and diabetes medicines, codeine, injectable medicines, and cortisone creams—can only be acquired in Portugal with a prescription. It is illegal to ship medication to Portugal. When traveling, always transport medicines in carry-on luggage.

### Birth Control
Birth control is widely available throughout Portugal and the Azores. Female contraceptive pills, patches, and rings can be bought over the counter in pharmacies, as can the morning-after pill, without a prescription. Condoms are also widely available in pharmacies, supermarkets, petrol stations, and some nightlife venues.

## SAFETY
### Crime
Crime in the Azores as a whole is generally low, and violent crime and crimes against tourists are practically unheard of. However, petty crimes can still occur; popular beaches can be targets for car theft, so keep valuables on your person or at least hidden from view. Don't leave anything of value, such as passports or computers, in vehicles. Take the same precautions you would at home—keep valuables safe and avoid walking alone at night or on backstreets.

### Drugs
Since 2001, Portugal has had a decriminalized drug system, and being caught with a small amount of some recreational drugs, such as marijuana, is no longer a crime but a medical health issue, addressed with rehabilitative action like therapy as opposed to jail. This health-focused legal shift saw drug-related deaths drop dramatically, but that's not to say it's okay to do drugs in Portugal; drug use is prohibited. The law does not differentiate between citizens and visitors, and tourists caught with drugs will be subject to the same process, which could include fines or being brought before a dissuasive committee or a doctor. Producing or dealing drugs in Portugal is a serious criminal offense punishable with lengthy jail terms. Beware when being approached by people selling drugs.

# Practical Details

## WHAT TO PACK
Key items to pack include **mosquito repellent** and **sunblock** (sunblock is expensive in Portugal) plus a **hat** for May-October, a **windbreaker** for all seasons (the Azores region is notoriously unpredictable weather-wise), and warm sweaters, a jacket, and a light raincoat for winter. Temperatures are mild year-round; layering up is probably the smartest way to pack for the Azores' "four-seasons-in-one-day" weather. Comfortable shoes for walking are advised, or proper **hiking shoes** if you're planning to do some serious trekking. And don't forget an **electrical adapter** for chargers. Pack a concealable pouch to carry documents and cash while out and about

exploring, and never carry cash and documents together. If you're planning to hike in the Azores or explore its volcanic attractions, a **backpack** containing **binoculars** and a **flashlight** is a good suggestion, and don't forget a **camera.** If you're factoring a dip in São Miguel's wonderful hot springs into the itinerary, don't forget an **old bathing suit** that you could throw away, as the iron-rich rusty water can stain.

If coronavirus restrictions are still in place, bring enough masks so that you have at least one fresh (or freshly washed) mask for each day. You may want to change masks more often if you plan to engage in activities that will get the mask wet or sweaty.

# BUDGETING

As one of Europe's most affordable countries, Portugal still offers value for money, and the Azores particularly so. As with all the sunshine destinations in Southern Europe and the Mediterranean, hotel rates peak in summer and drop in winter, while spring and autumn can offer the best value in terms of lodging and weather. Car rental rates fluctuate with the tourist seasons, and airfares are influenced by EU school holidays.

Examples of average costs include:

- small espresso coffee: €0.50
- 1.5-liter bottle of water: €0.50
- sandwich: €2
- local bus ticket: €2
- theme park or water park admission: €8
- museums: €2-5
- small glass of wine or beer: €1.50-2
- hotel room: €60-90

# MONEY

## Currency

Since 1999 Portugal's currency has been the euro; before that it was the escudo. There are 100 cents in 1 euro (€1).

## Changing Money

The ability to exchange currency varies greatly by location. In the Azores, few places except airports have exchange bureaus, although their commission rates, along with those in hotels, are more expensive. It's best to bring euros with you, and/or a bank card to make withdrawals from ATMs (*multibancos*), which can be easily found in most towns and parishes, supermarkets, gas stations, etc. Withdrawals are limited to €200 a time, and a maximum of €400 per day. If you do have to change currency, head to a bank or hotel reception.

## Banks

Banks in Portugal are generally open Monday-Friday 8:30am-4pm. In larger towns and cities, they will stay open during lunch, but in smaller locales, banks close 1pm-2pm. Portugal's banks close Saturday-Sunday and national holidays. Banks rarely offer foreign exchange services.

## ATMs

ATM cash withdrawal machines (*multibanco*) can be found widely in most towns and cities. Smaller villages may have just one or two, normally at bank branches, in supermarkets, on main streets and squares, and at major bus and train stations and airports. Charges apply to foreign transactions. There is an option for instructions in English. Maximum withdrawals are €200 a time, but this can be withdrawn several times a day.

## Credit Cards

Credit cards are widely accepted in bigger towns and cities, but not so much in smaller locales. Visa, Mastercard, and American Express cards are widely accepted in hotels, shops, and restaurants. Gas stations usually only take debit cards and cash.

## Sales Tax

The standard sales tax rate in the Azores is 18 percent. Many stores throughout Azores have adopted the Europe Tax Free (ETS) system, which allows non-EU shoppers to recover VAT or sales tax as a refund. Stores adhering to the ETS system have an ETS sign at the entrance. For more information, go to www.globalblue.com/tax-free-shopping/portugal.

## Bargaining

Haggling is increasingly a thing of the past in Portugal, as standardized retail prices are enforced in municipal markets and farmers markets. However, haggling at a flea market is still part of the experience.

## Special Discounts

Students, seniors (65 and over), and children generally benefit from discounts on state-run services such as monuments, museums, municipal swimming pools, and public transport.

## Tipping

Restaurants tend to be the only places in the Azores, and Portugal as a whole, where tipping is exercised, and a tip reflects how much patrons have enjoyed the food and service. As a general rule, 10-15 percent of the overall bill is the standard, but in less formal eateries it's okay just to leave any loose change you have, but at least €1. Gratuities are not included on bills. Waitstaff in Portugal appreciate tips, but they are not compulsory.

# COMMUNICATIONS
## Cell Phones
### MAKING CALLS

Portugal's country code is +351 (00351). To call a phone number in Portugal from abroad, first dial the country code. Within Portugal, there are regional prefixes (area codes), and all start with 2. The Azores prefixes per island are: São Miguel 296; Santa Maria 296; Terceira 295; São Jorge 295; Pico 292; Faial 292; Graciosa 295; Flores 292; and Corvo 292. These are incorporated into phone numbers, which are always nine digits. There is no need to dial 0 or 1 before the area code. Mobile phone numbers start with 9. Toll-free numbers start with 8. Portugal's main landline provider is **Portugal Telecom** (www.telecom.pt).

### MOBILE PHONES

The main mobile providers are **Nós** (www.nos.pt), **Meo** (www.meo.pt), and **Vodafone** (www.vodafone.pt). Mobile phone coverage is decent throughout the country, particularly in major cities and populous areas along the coast, although it can be patchy in rural or high-elevation areas. Foreign handsets that are GSM compatible can be used in Portugal. Using a prepaid SIM card in Portugal is recommended, particularly for non-EU visitors. They are widely available from the stores of the main mobile phone providers, which can be found on retail streets and shopping centers. You will need a copy of your passport or ID to buy one.

In 2017 the EU abolished roaming surcharges for travelers, meaning that people traveling within the EU can call, text, and use data on mobile devices at the same rates they pay at home, but this applies only to EU countries. Surcharges may apply if your consumption exceeds your home usage limits.

## Internet Access

Portugal has an up-to-date communications network, with good phone lines and high-speed internet. Wi-Fi is widely available, and most hotels will either have free Wi-Fi throughout or in designated Wi-Fi areas. Elsewhere, major cities offer Wi-Fi hotspots, as do some public buildings, restaurants, and cafés. Internet cafés can be found throughout Portugal.

## Shipping and Postal Service

Portugal's national postal service is **Correios de Portugal** (tel. 707 262 626; www.ctt.pt), with post offices in all population centers. Postal services range from regular *correio normal* to express *correio azul*. Shipping costs for a 2-kilogram (4.4-pound) package range from €4.50 sent domestically to €15 sent abroad. Postcards and letters up to 20 grams (0.7 ounce) cost €0.86 within Europe, €0.91 to other countries. Express mail letters cost €2.90.

Other shipping services operate in Portugal, including **FedEx** (tel. 229 436 030; www.fedex.com) and **DHL** (tel. 707 505 606; www.dhl.pt).

# OPENING HOURS

In the past, most shops and services in Portugal would close 1pm-3pm for lunch. This is still in practice in many establishments, although a growing number of state and private entities such as banks, post offices, and pharmacies now remain open during lunch.

Major national monuments like castles, churches, and palaces are open every day of the week, and those that aren't tend to close on Monday. Almost all close on bank holidays, such as Christmas Day, New Year's Eve, and

New Year's Day. Smaller museums and monuments also close for lunch.

Attractions stay open longer in summer, opening an hour or so earlier than in winter and closing an hour or so later. Theme parks, especially water parks, and even some hotels and restaurants close for a month or two in winter.

### Public Holidays

There are several bank holidays and commemorative occasions throughout the year where practically all services and amenities close. Should these dates fall on a Thursday or a Tuesday, it is normal for state-run services to be "bridged" to the weekend, for a long bank holiday.

- Christmas Day (Dec. 25)
- New Year's Eve and Day (Dec. 31-Jan. 1)
- Carnival (usually around the last week in Feb.)
- Holy Friday (Friday before Easter Sunday)
- Easter Sunday
- Freedom Day (Apr. 25)
- Labor Day (May 1)
- Portugal Day (June 10)
- Corpus Christi (second Thursday after Pentecost Sunday)
- Republic Day (Oct. 5)
- All Saints Day (Nov. 1)

## WEIGHTS AND MEASURES
### Customary Units

Portugal was the second country after France to adopt the metric system, in 1814. Length is in centimeters, meters, and kilometers, and weight is in grams and kilograms. Temperatures are in degrees Celsius.

In addition, shoes and clothing sizes differ from the British and US systems. For example:

- shoe sizes: US men's 7.5, women's 9 = UK men's 7, women's 6.5 = Portugal 40

- women's dresses and suits: US 6, 8, 10 = UK 8, 10, 12 = Portugal 36, 38, 40
- men's suits and overcoats: US and UK 36, 38, 40 = Portugal 46, 48, 50

### Time Zone

The Azores are one hour earlier than mainland Portugal, which is in the Western European time zone (WET), the same as the United Kingdom and Ireland. Complying with European daylight saving time (DST), clocks advance one hour on the last Sunday in March and lose one hour on the last Sunday in October. In relation to the United States, the Azores are three or four hours ahead of New York.

### Electricity

Portugal has 230-volt, 50-hertz electricity and type C or F sockets. Type C plugs have two round pins; type F have two round pins with two earthing clips on the side. Travelers from the United Kingdom, the rest of Europe, Australia, and most of Asia and Africa will only require an adapter to make the plugs fit. Visitors from the United States, Canada, and most South American countries require an adapter and for some devices a voltage converter. These are available in airports, luggage shops, and most electrical shops. Universal adapters are a great investment as they can be used anywhere.

## TOURIST INFORMATION

Portugal is a tourism-oriented destination with widely available visitor information. All of the Azores islands have at least one tourism bureau on them; the bigger the island the more tourism bureaus. These can usually be found in larger towns, in key spots such as main squares and harbors. For more Azores general tourism information, go to regional tourism site www.visitazores.com. For a list of tourist bureaus, go to www.azores.gov.pt. Most hotels provide good information on what to do and see locally. Portugal's official tourism website, www.visitportugal.com, provides a wealth of information on history, culture, and heritage, as well as useful contacts.

## Tourist Offices

Tourist offices can be found in every city, town, and village that has a tourist attraction or monument. Major cities and destinations like Lisbon and Porto have numerous tourist offices where visitors can drop in with questions and get maps, public transport timetables, and excursion information. Tourist office staffers speak good English.

## Maps

Download maps of the Azores and its various islands free from www.visitazores.com. Most hotel reception desks have maps of the vicinity, or ask at tourist offices.

# Traveler Advice

## OPPORTUNITIES FOR STUDY AND EMPLOYMENT

With a recovering economy firmly on the way up, job opportunities in Portugal are improving. In the Azores, casual work for traveling visitors is less common than on the mainland, and will probably be mostly available within the tourism or hospitality sector, and seasonally (in summer).

Portugal as a whole has many international students and is popular for studying abroad, and the Azores is no exception. The University of the Azores has a variety of courses, internships, and programs for international students (https://international.uac.pt). Portugal is one of the top countries for the EU Erasmus student-exchange program (European Community Action Scheme for the Mobility of University Students). For more information in English on studying in Portugal, see www.studyinportugal.edu.pt.

## ACCESS FOR TRAVELERS WITH DISABILITIES

Portugal prides itself on being an accessible destination for travelers with disabilities, and massive efforts have been made to become inclusive for all. The main airports have services and facilities for wheelchair users, and infrastructure is gradually being modernized to facilitate mobility. Most of the Azores beaches and even the tidal pools are wheelchair-friendly. Some monuments, however, are not wheelchair-friendly, and people with mobility issues might struggle with everyday infrastructure such as cobbled streets and high sidewalks. Companies like **Disabled Access Holidays** (www.disabledaccessholidays.com) can put together bespoke accessible packages to the Azores for disabled travelers.

## TRAVELING WITH CHILDREN

Youngsters in family-friendly Portugal are fawned over and welcomed practically everywhere. It's not unusual to see children dozing on their parents' laps in a café late on a summer night. Restaurants are very accommodating of younger diners, although kids' menus can be limited to the staple chicken nuggets or fish fingers.

Though the Azores lack the water parks, theme parks, and zoos of the mainland, there's plenty of fresh air and open space. When the weather is warm, tourist trains and ice cream shops are found throughout towns and villages, while most resorts and hotels have kids' clubs or at least activities and facilities for children. For some grown-up time, ask your hotel to arrange a babysitter.

To enter and leave Portugal, all minors must have their own passport and be with both parents. If children are not traveling with both parents, legal documentation with formalized permission from the other parent is required. Portugal's border and immigration officials will ask for such papers.

Breastfeeding is applauded in Portugal, although it's rarely done in public, and if it is, it's done discreetly.

## WOMEN TRAVELERS

The Azores is a great destination for women traveling alone, given that it is one of Europe's safest and most peaceful regions, and people as a whole are respectful and obliging. Most people speak decent English and are happy to assist. Besides petty crime in major towns and cities, the serious crime rate is low, and lone women travelers should have no problems. As with any place, common sense should prevail, and taking dark backstreets or walking along deserted streets at night should be avoided.

## SENIOR TRAVELERS

With a year-round pleasant climate and placid, laid-back lifestyle, the Azores are a magnet for the more active senior travelers. Compact, peaceful, and well equipped, with medical facilities (providing you have the right insurance coverage), it meets the needs of travelers of all ages. Geographically, most of the islands can be hilly and challenging on foot. Portugal has discounts for senior travelers (65 and over) with ID on public transport and in museums, and plenty of attractions, like wine-tasting and spa visits, to appeal to the mature tourist.

## LGBTQ TRAVELERS

LGBTQ travelers will find Portugal as a whole mostly welcoming; it legalized same-sex marriage in 2010, the eighth country in Europe to do so. Portugal is currently a popular destination for same-sex weddings. Most Portuguese have a laid-back attitude toward LGBTQ visitors, although attitudes toward same-sex couples can vary by region. Despite being progressive, Portugal is traditionally a Roman Catholic society, and inhabitants of remote and small towns, especially some of the Azores' smaller islands, might raise an eyebrow or scowl at same-sex displays of affection, but rarely will verbal or physical hostility be directed at you. There isn't really much of an LGBTQ scene to speak of in the Azores, but it is overall gay-friendly. There are no official gay bars, but hip and stylish places are forward-thinking and receptive of all genders and sexualities. The **International Gay & Lesbian Travel Association** (IGLTA; www.iglta.org) provides a wealth of information on LGBTQ travel in Portugal, including organized trips, tours, tips, and travel advice.

## TRAVELERS OF COLOR

Portugal is widely regarded as one of Europe's safest, most peaceful, and most tolerant countries, and allegations of color-motivated discrimination and attacks are rare. For the most part, travelers and immigrants of all colors are welcomed and accepted in Portugal, which has one of the most integrated immigrant communities in Europe. That said, the Azores are less diverse than mainland Portugal, perhaps due to their remoteness or lack of mass tourism, but nonetheless have welcome inhabitants and visitors of many different ethnicities. The Azores are as welcoming, friendly, and accepting as the rest of Portugal.

# Resources

## Glossary

*adega:* wine cellar

*arco:* arch

*autoestrada:* motorway (abbreviated A)

*avenida:* avenue

*azulejo:* hand-painted ceramic tile, usually blue and white

*bacalhau:* salted codfish

*bairro:* neighborhood or district

*capela:* chapel

*castelo:* castle

*cataplana:* seafood stew cooked in a copper pan

*cidade:* city or town

*curral:* traditional, fenced wine-making plot (plural *currais*)

*espetada:* skewered meat

*estação:* station

*estalagem:* inn

*estrada municipal:* local municipal road (abbreviated M or EM)

*estrada nacional:* national road (abbreviated N or EN)

*fadista:* fado singer

*fado:* a genre of traditional Portuguese music that is soulful and often mournful

*farmácia:* pharmacy

*feira:* fair or open-air market

*ferroviária:* railway

*festa:* festival

*fortaleza:* fortress

*forte:* fort

*foz:* river mouth

*ginja:* cherry liqueur; also known as *ginjinha*

*gruta:* cave

*igreja:* church

*ilha:* island

*itinerário complementar:* secondary highway (abbreviated IC)

*itinerário principal:* main highway (abbreviated IP)

*jardim:* garden

*lago:* lake

*lagoa:* lagoon or pond

*largo:* small square or plaza

*levada:* irrigation channel

*litoral:* coastal

*livraria:* bookshop

*loja:* shop

*lote:* lot or unit

**Manueline:** lavishly ornate Portuguese architectural style, widely employed in the early 16th century; owes its name to the reign of King Manuel I

*mercado:* market

*miradouro:* viewpoint

*monte:* hill or mountain

*multibanco:* ATM

*museu:* museum

*paço:* palace

*palácio:* palace

*parafarmácia:* pharmacy with only nonprescription medications

*parque:* park

*pastel:* pastry

*pensão residencial:* boardinghouse or bed-and-breakfast

*ponte:* bridge

*pousada:* monument (such as a castle, palace, monastery, or convent) converted into luxurious accommodations

*praça:* square or plaza

*praia:* beach

*quinta:* winery or estate
*rabelo:* traditional flat-bottomed boat
*reconquista:* Christian reconquest of Portugal
*retornado:* Portuguese citizen returned from former colonies
*ria:* lagoon or estuary
*rio:* river
*rua:* street

*santuário:* sanctuary or shrine
*sé:* cathedral
*serra:* mountain range
*tasca:* simple, small eatery
*vila:* village or town
*vinho:* wine
*zona balnear:* swimming area, usually created by naturally occurring rock features

# Portuguese Phrasebook

## PRONUNCIATION
### Vowels

The pronunciation of **nonnasal vowels** is fairly straightforward:

a   pronounced "a" as in "apple," "ah" as in "father," or "uh" as in "addition."

e   pronounced "eh" as in "pet." At the end of a word, it is often silent or barely pronounced.

i   pronounced "ee" as in "tree."

o   pronounced "aw" as in "got." At the end of a word or when it stands alone, it is generally pronounced "oo" as in "zoo."

u   pronounced "oo" as in "zoo."

The **nasal vowels** are much more complicated. Nasal vowels are signaled by a tilde accent (~) as in *não* (no), or by the presence of the letters **m** or **n** following the vowel, such as *sim* (yes) or *fonte* (fountain). When pronouncing them, it helps to exaggerate the sound, focus on your nose and not your mouth, and pretend there is a hidden "n" (or even "ng") on the end. Note that the **ão** combination is pronounced like "own" as in "town."

### Consonants

Portuguese consonant sounds are easy compared with the nasal vowels. There are, however, a few exceptions to be aware of.

c   pronounced "k" as in "kayak." However, when followed by the vowels **e** or **i**, it is pronounced "s" as in "set." When sporting a cedilla accent (ç), it is pronounced with a longer "ss" sound as in "passing."

ch  pronounced "sh" as in "ship."

g   pronounced "g" as in "go." However, when followed by the vowels **e** or **i**, it is pronounced "zh" like the "s" in "measure."

h   always silent.

j   pronounced "zh" like the "s" in "measure."

l   usually pronounced as in English. The exception is when it is followed by **h**, when it acquires a "li" sound similar to "billion."

n   usually pronounced as in English. The exception is when it is followed by **h**, when it acquires a "ni" sound similar to "minion."

r   pronounced with a trill. When doubled (**rr**), it should be pronounced with a longer roll.

s   pronounced "s" as in "set" when found at the beginning of a word. Between vowels, it's pronounced like "z" as in "zap." At the end of a word, it's pronounced like "sh" as in "ship."

x   pronounced "sh" as in "ship" when found at the beginning of a word. Between vowels, the pronunciation varies between "sh" as in "ship," "s" as in "set," "z" as in "zap," and "ks" as in "taxi."

z   pronounced "z" in "zap" when found at the beginning of a word. In the middle or at the end of a word, it is pronounced "zh" like the "s" in "measure."

### Stress

Most Portuguese words carry stress on the second-to-last syllable. There are, however, some exceptions. The stress falls on the last syllable with words that end in **r** as well as words ending in nasal vowels. Vowels with accents over them (~, ´, ` , ^) generally indicate that the stress falls on the syllable containing the vowel.

# PLURAL NOUNS AND ADJECTIVES

In Portuguese, the general rule for making a noun or adjective plural is to simply add an **s**. But there are various exceptions. For instance, words that end in nasal consonants such as **m** or **l** change to **ns** and **is,** respectively. The plural of *estalagem* (inn) is *estalagens,* while the plural of *pastel* (pastry) is *pastéis.* Words that end in nasal vowels also undergo changes: **ão** becomes **ãos, ães,** or **ões,** as in the case of *irmão* (brother), which becomes *irmãos,* and *pão* (bread), which becomes *pães.*

# GENDER

Like French and Spanish, all Portuguese words have masculine and feminine forms of nouns and adjectives. In general, nouns ending in **o** or consonants are masculine, while those ending in **a** are feminine. Many words have both masculine and feminine versions determined by their **o** or **a** ending, such as *menino* (boy) and *menina* (girl). Nouns are always preceded by articles—*o* and *a* (definite) and *um* and *uma* (indefinite)—that announce their gender. For example, *o menino* means "the boy" while *a menina* means "the girl." *Um menino* is "a boy" while *uma menina* is "a girl."

# BASIC EXPRESSIONS

**Hello**  *Olá*
**Good morning**  *Bom dia*
**Good afternoon**  *Boa tarde*
**Good evening/night**  *Boa noite*
**Goodbye**  *Tchau, Adeus*
**How are you?**  *Como está?*
**Fine, and you?**  *Tudo bem, e você?*
**Nice to meet you.**  *Um prazer.*
**Yes**  *Sim*
**No**  *Não*
**I don't know.**  *Não sei.*
**and**  *e*
**or**  *ou*
**Please**  *Por favor*

**Thank you**  *Obrigado* (if you're male), *Obrigada* (if you're female)
**You're welcome.**  *De nada.*
**Excuse me (to pass)**  *Com licença*
**Sorry/Excuse me (to get attention)**  *Desculpe* (if you're male), *Desculpa* (if you're female)
**Can you help me?**  *Pode me ajudar?*
**Where is the bathroom?**  *Onde é o banheiro?*
**What's your name?**  *Como se chama?*
**My name is . . .**  *Meu nome é . . .*
**Where are you from?**  *De onde é que vem?*
**I'm from . . .**  *Sou de . . .*
**Do you speak English?**  *Fala inglês?*
**I don't speak Portuguese.**  *Não falo português.*
**I only speak a little Portuguese.**  *Só falo um pouquinho português.*
**I don't understand.**  *Não entendo.*
**Can you please repeat that?**  *Pode repetir, por favor?*

# TERMS OF ADDRESS

**I**  *eu*
**you**  *você* (formal), *tu* (informal)
**he**  *ele*
**she**  *ela*
**we**  *nós*
**you (plural)**  *vocês*
**they**  *eles* (male or mixed gender), *elas* (female)
**Mr./Sir**  *Senhor*
**Mrs./Madam**  *Senhora*
**boy/girl**  *menino/menina*
**child**  *criança*
**brother/sister**  *irmão/irmã*
**father/mother**  *pai/mãe*
**son/daughter**  *filho/filha*
**husband/wife**  *marido/mulher*
**uncle/aunt**  *tio/tia*
**friend**  *amigo* (male), *amiga* (female)
**boyfriend/girlfriend**  *namorado/namorada*
**single**  *solteiro* (male), *solteira* (female)
**divorced**  *divorciado* (male), *divorciada* (female)

## TRANSPORTATION

**north** *norte*
**south** *sul*
**east** *este*
**west** *oeste*
**left/right** *esquerda/direita*
**Where is . . . ?** *Onde é . . . ?*
**How far away is . . . ?** *Qual é a distância até . . . ?*
**far/close** *longe/perto*
**car** *carro*
**bus** *autocarro, camioneta*
**bus terminal** *terminal das camionetas*
**subway** *metro*
**subway station** *estação do metro*
**train** *comboio*
**train station** *estação de comboio*
**plane** *avião*
**airport** *aeroporto*
**boat** *barco*
**ship** *navio*
**ferryboat** *ferry, balsa*
**port** *porto*
**first** *primeiro*
**last** *último*
**next** *próximo*
**arrival** *chegada*
**departure** *partida*
**How much does a ticket cost?** *Quanto custa uma passagem?*
**one-way** *uma ida*
**round-trip** *ida e volta*
**I'd like a round-trip ticket.** *Quero uma passagem ida e volta.*
**gas station** *bomba de gasolina*
**parking lot** *estacionamento*
**toll** *portagem*
**at the corner** *na esquina*
**one-way street** *sentido único*
**Where can I get a taxi?** *Onde posso apanhar um táxi?*
**Can you take me to this address?** *Pode me levar para este endereço?*
**Can you stop here, please?** *Pode parar aqui, por favor?*

## ACCOMMODATIONS

**Are there any rooms available?** *Tem quartos disponívéis?*
**I want to make a reservation.** *Quero fazer uma reserva.*
**single room** *quarto de solteiro*
**double room** *quarto duplo*
**Is there a view?** *Tem vista?*
**How much does it cost?** *Quanto custa?*
**Can you give me a discount?** *É possível ter um desconto?*
**It's too expensive.** *É muito caro.*
**Is there something cheaper?** *Tem algo mais barato?*
**for just one night** *para uma noite só*
**for three days** *para três dias*
**Can I see it first?** *Posso ver primeiro?*
**comfortable** *confortável*
**change the sheets/towels** *trocar os lençóis/as toalhas*
**private bathroom** *banheiro privado*
**shower** *chuveiro*
**soap** *sabão*
**toilet paper** *papel higiênico*
**key** *chave*

## FOOD

**to eat** *comer*
**to drink** *beber*
**breakfast** *pequeno almoço*
**lunch** *almoço*
**dinner** *jantar*
**snack** *petisco*
**dessert** *sobremesa*
**menu** *ementa*
**plate** *prato*
**glass** *copo*
**cup** *chávena*
**utensils** *talheres*
**fork** *garfo*
**knife** *faca*
**spoon** *colher*
**napkin** *guardanapo*
**hot** *quente*
**cold** *frio*
**sweet** *doce*
**salty** *salgado*
**sour** *azedo, amargo*

spicy *picante*
**I'm a vegetarian.** *Sou vegetariano* (if you're male), *Sou vegetariana* (if you're female).
**I'm ready to order.** *Estou pronto para pedir* (if you're male), *Estou pronta para pedir* (if you're female).
**Can you bring the bill please?** *Pode trazer a conta, por favor?*

## Meat
meat *carne*
beef *carne, bife*
chicken *frango, galinha*
pork *porco, leitão*
ham *fiambre*
cured ham *presunto*
sausage *salsicha*

## Fish and Seafood
fish *peixe*
seafood *frutas do mar, mariscos*
shellfish *marisco*
codfish *bacalhau*
sardines *sardinhas*
tuna *atum*
shrimp *camarão*
crab *caranguejo*
squid *lula*
octopus *polvo*
lobster *lagosta*

## Eggs and Dairy
eggs *ovos*
hard-boiled egg *ovo cozido*
scrambled eggs *ovos mexidos*
whole milk *leite gordo*
skim milk *leite desnatado*
cream *creme de leite*
butter *manteiga*
cheese *queijo*
yogurt *iogurte*
ice cream *gelado*
sorbet *sorvete*

## Vegetables and Legumes
vegetables *verduras, legumes*
salad *salada*

lettuce *alface*
spinach *espinafre*
carrot *cenoura*
tomato *tomate*
potato *batata*
cucumber *pepino*
zucchini *courgette*
eggplant *berinjela*
mushrooms *cogumelos*
olives *azeitonas*
onions *cebolas*
beans *feijões*

## Fruits
fruit *fruta*
apple *maçã*
pear *pêra*
grape *uva*
fig *figo*
orange *laranja*
lemon *limão*
pineapple *ananás*
banana *banana*
apricot *damasco, abricó*
cherry *cereja*
peach *pêssego*
raspberry *framboesa*
strawberry *morango*
melon *melão*

## Seasoning and Condiments
salt *sal*
black pepper *pimenta*
hot pepper *pimenta picante*
garlic *alho*
oil *óleo*
olive oil *azeite*
mustard *mostarda*
mayonnaise *maionese*
vinegar *vinagre*

## Baked Goods and Grains
bread *pão*
pastry *pastel*
cookies *biscoitos*
cake *bolo, torta*
rice *arroz*

## Cooking

roasted, baked *assado*
boiled *cozido*
steamed *cozido no vapor*
grilled *grelhado*
fried *frito*
well done *bem passado*
medium *médio*
rare *mal passado*

## Drinks

beverage *bebida*
water *água*
sparkling water *água com gás*
still water *água sem gás*
soda *refrigerante*
juice *sumo*
milk *leite*
coffee *café*
tea *chá*
with/without sugar *com/sem açúcar*
ice *gelo*
beer *cerveja*
wine *vinho*
Do you have wine? *Tem vinho?*
Red or white? *Tinto ou branco?*
Another, please. *Mais uma, por favor.*

# MONEY AND SHOPPING

money *dinheiro*
ATM *multibanco*
credit card *cartão de crédito*
Do you accept credit cards? *Aceita cartões de crédito?*
Can I exchange money? *Posso trocar dinheiro?*
money exchange *câmbio, troca de dinheiro*
It's too expensive. *É muito caro.*
Is there something cheaper? *Tem algo mais barato?*
more *mais*
less *menos*
a good price *Um preço bom.*

# HEALTH AND SAFETY

I'm sick. *Estou doente.*
I have nausea. *Tenho nausea.*

I have a headache. *Tenho uma dor de cabeça.*
I have a stomachache. *Tenho uma dor de estômago.*
Call a doctor! *Chame um doutor!, Chame um médico!*
Call the police! *Chame a polícia!*
Help! *Socorro!*
pain *dor*
fever *febre*
infection *infecção*
cut *corte*
burn *queimadura*
vomit *vômito*
pill *comprimido*
medicine *remédio, medicamento*
antibiotic *antibiótico*
cotton *algodão*
condom *preservativo*
contraceptive pill *pílula*
toothpaste *pasta de dentes*
toothbrush *escova de dentes*

# NUMBERS

0 *zero*
1 *um* (male), *uma* (female)
2 *dois* (male), *duas* (female)
3 *três*
4 *quatro*
5 *cinco*
6 *seis*
7 *sete*
8 *oito*
9 *nove*
10 *dez*
11 *onze*
12 *doze*
13 *treze*
14 *catorze, quatorze*
15 *quinze*
16 *dezesseis*
17 *dezessete*
18 *dezoito*
19 *dezenove*
20 *vinte*
21 *vinte e um*
30 *trinta*
40 *quarenta*

50 *cinquenta*
60 *sessenta*
70 *setenta*
80 *oitenta*
90 *noventa*
100 *cem*
101 *cento e um*
200 *duzentos*
500 *quinhentos*
1,000 *mil*
2,000 *dois mil*
first *primeiro*
second *segundo*
third *terceiro*
once *uma vez*
twice *duas vezes*
half *metade*

## TIME

What time is it? *Que horas são?*
It's 3 o'clock in the afternoon. *São três horas da tarde.*
It's 3:15. *São três e quinze.*
It's 3:30. *São três e meia.*
It's 3:45. *São três e quarenta-cinco.*
In half an hour. *Daqui a meia hora.*
In an hour. *Daqui a uma hora.*
In two hours. *Daqui a duas horas.*
noon *meio-dia*
midnight *meia-noite*
early *cedo*
late *tarde*
before *antes*
after *depois*

## DAYS AND MONTHS

day *dia*
morning *manhã*
afternoon *tarde*
night *noite*
today *hoje*

yesterday *ontem*
tomorrow *amanhã*
tomorrow morning *amanhã de manhã*
week *semana*
month *mês*
year *ano*
Monday *segunda-feira*
Tuesday *terça-feira*
Wednesday *quarta-feira*
Thursday *quinta-feira*
Friday *sexta-feira*
Saturday *sábado*
Sunday *domingo*
January *janeiro*
February *fevereiro*
March *março*
April *abril*
May *maio*
June *junho*
July *julho*
August *agosto*
September *setembro*
October *outubro*
November *novembro*
December *dezembro*

## SEASONS AND WEATHER

season *estação*
spring *primavera*
summer *verão*
autumn *outuno*
winter *inverno*
weather *o tempo*
sun *sol*
rain *chuva*
cloudy *nublado*
windy *vento*
hot *quente*
cold *frio*

# Index

# List of Maps

# Photo Credits

**ACADIA**
NATIONAL PARK

HILARY NANGLE

**ARCHES &
CANYONLANDS**
NATIONAL PARKS

W.C. MCRAE & JUDY JEWELL

MOON

**BANFF
NATIONAL
PARK**

HIKE·CAMP
SEE WILDLIFE

ANDREW HEMPSTEAD

MOON

**DEATH VALLEY
NATIONAL PARK**

JENNA BLOUGH

MOON

**GLACIER**
NATIONAL PARK

HIKING · CAMPING
LAKES & PEAKS

BECKY LOMAX

MOON

**GRAND
CANYON**

HIKE·CAMP
RAFT THE
COLORADO RIVER

TIM HULL

MOON

**GREAT SMOKY
MOUNTAINS**
NATIONAL PARK

HIKING · CAMPING
SCENIC DRIVES

JASON FRYE

**JOSHUA TREE
& PALM SPRINGS**

JENNA BLOUGH

MOON

**MOUNT RUSHMORE
& THE BLACK HILLS**
INCLUDING THE BADLANDS

LAURAL A. BIDWELL

MOON

**ROCKY
MOUNTAIN**
NATIONAL PARK

HIKE·CAMP
SEE WILDLIFE

ERIN ENGLISH

MOON

**SEQUOIA &
KINGS CANYON**

HIKE·CAMP
SEE REDWOODS

LEIGH BERNACCHI

MOON

**YELLOWSTONE
& GRAND TETON**

HIKE, CAMP,
SEE WILDLIFE

BECKY LOMAX

MOON

**YOSEMITE**
SEQUOIA &
KINGS CANYON

ANN MARIE BROWN

MOON

**ZION &
BRYCE**

Including Arches Canyonlands
Capitol Reef, Grand Staircase-
Escalante & More

W.C. MCRAE & JUDY JEWELL

## In these books:

- Full coverage of gateway cities and towns
- Itineraries from one day to multiple weeks
- Advice on where to stay (or camp) in and around the parks

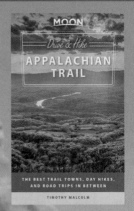
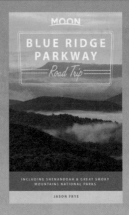

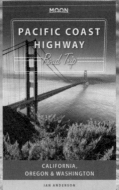
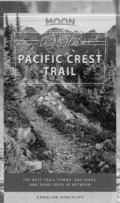

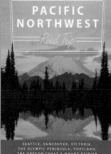

# MOON
## PACIFIC NORTHWEST
*Road Trip*

SEATTLE, VANCOUVER, VICTORIA, THE OLYMPIC PENINSULA, PORTLAND, THE OREGON COAST & MOUNT RAINIER

ALLISON WILLIAMS

# MOON
## ROUTE 66
*Road Trip*

JESSICA DUNHAM

# MOON
## SOUTH FLORIDA & THE KEYS
*Road Trip*

WITH MIAMI, WALT DISNEY WORLD, TAMPA & THE EVERGLADES

JASON FERGUSON

# MOON
## SOUTHERN CALIFORNIA
*Road Trips*

DRIVES ALONG THE BEACHES, MOUNTAINS, AND DESERTS WITH THE BEST STOPS ALONG THE WAY

IAN ANDERSON

# MOON
## SOUTHWEST
*Road Trip*

LAS VEGAS, ZION & BRYCE, MONUMENT VALLEY, SANTA FE & TAOS, AND THE GRAND CANYON

TIM HULL

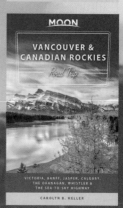

# MOON
## VANCOUVER & CANADIAN ROCKIES
*Road Trip*

VICTORIA, BANFF, JASPER, CALGARY, THE OKANAGAN, WHISTLER & THE SEA-TO-SKY HIGHWAY

CAROLYN B. HELLER

# MOON
## YELLOWSTONE TO GLACIER NATIONAL PARK
*Road Trip*

JACKSON HOLE, CODY, THE GRAND TETONS & THE ROCKY MOUNTAIN FRONT

CARTER G. WALKER

# MOON
## the OPEN ROAD
### 50 BEST ROAD TRIPS in the USA
From Weekend Getaways to Cross-Country Adventures

JESSICA DUNHAM

# MOON
## Road Trip USA
25TH ANNIVERSARY EDITION
CROSS-COUNTRY ADVENTURES ON AMERICA'S TWO-LANE HIGHWAYS

Jamie Jensen

For when your friends want your recommendations.
Keep track of your favorite...

**Restaurants and Meals**

**Neighborhoods and Regions**

**Cultural Experiences**

## Beaches and Recreation

## Day Trips or Scenic Drives

## Travel Memories

# Get inspired for your next adventure

Follow @**moonguides** on Instagram or subscribe to our newsletter at **moon.com**

# MAP SYMBOLS

| | | | |
|---|---|---|---|
| ═══ Expressway | ○ City/Town | ⓘ Information Center | ♣ Park |
| ──── Primary Road | ◉ State Capital | Ⓟ Parking Area | ⛳ Golf Course |
| ━━━━ Secondary Road | ⊛ National Capital | ♦ Church | ✛ Unique Feature |
| ┄┄┄ Unpaved Road | ✪ Highlight | ❦ Winery/Vineyard | ⟲ Waterfall |
| ┄┄┄ Trail | ★ Point of Interest | ⒯ⓗ Trailhead | Λ Camping |
| ┄┄┄ Ferry | • Accommodation | 🚇 Train Station | ▲ Mountain |
| ┅┅┅ Railroad | ▼ Restaurant/Bar | ✈ Airport | ⛷ Ski Area |
| Pedestrian Walkway | ■ Other Location | ✕ Airfield | ⬭ Glacier |
| ▥▥▥ Stairs | | | |

# CONVERSION TABLES

°C = (°F - 32) / 1.8
°F = (°C x 1.8) + 32
1 inch = 2.54 centimeters (cm)
1 foot = 0.304 meters (m)
1 yard = 0.914 meters
1 mile = 1.6093 kilometers (km)
1 km = 0.6214 miles
1 fathom = 1.8288 m
1 chain = 20.1168 m
1 furlong = 201.168 m
1 acre = 0.4047 hectares
1 sq km = 100 hectares
1 sq mile = 2.59 square km
1 ounce = 28.35 grams
1 pound = 0.4536 kilograms
1 short ton = 0.90718 metric ton
1 short ton = 2,000 pounds
1 long ton = 1.016 metric tons
1 long ton = 2,240 pounds
1 metric ton = 1,000 kilograms
1 quart = 0.94635 liters
1 US gallon = 3.7854 liters
1 Imperial gallon = 4.5459 liters
1 nautical mile = 1.852 km

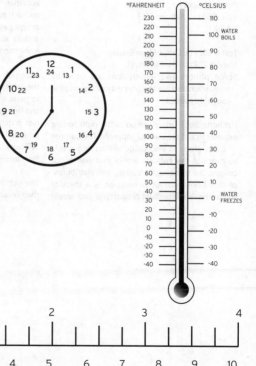

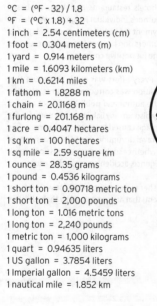

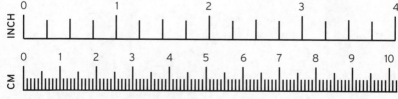

**MOON AZORES**
Avalon Travel
Hachette Book Group
1700 Fourth Street
Berkeley, CA 94710, USA
www.moon.com

Editor: Megan Anderluh
Managing Editor: Hannah Brezack
Production and Graphics Coordinator: Darren Alessi
Cover Design: Faceout Studio, Charles Brock
Interior Design: Domini Dragoone
Moon Logo: Tim McGrath
Map Editor: Kat Bennett
Cartographers: Karin Dahl, Erin Greb, Brian Shotwell, and Alyson Ollivierre
Indexer: Kathryn Roque

ISBN-13: 978-1-64049-403-9

Printing History
1st Edition — January 2021
5 4 3 2 1

Front cover photo: Lagoa do Fogo lake in Sao Miguel Island © Evgeni Fabisuk / Alamy Stock Photo
Back cover photo: viewpoint at Miradouro da Ponta do Sossego, São Miguel © Kristýna Henkeová | Dreamstime.com

Printed in China by RR Donnelley